KB100525

1학기 전과정

적중100plus

영어 기출문제집

중3

미래 | 최연희

Best Collection

구성과 특징

교과서의 주요 학습 내용을 중심으로 학습 영역별 특성에 맞춰 단계별로 다양한 학습 기회를 제공하여
단원별 학습능력 평가는 물론 중간 및 기말고사 시험 등에 완벽하게 대비할 수 있도록 내용을 구성

Words & Expressions

Step1   Key Words 단원별 핵심 단어 설명 및 풀이
         Key Expression 단원별 핵심 숙어 및 관용어 설명
         Word Power 반대 또는 비슷한 뜻 단어 배우기
         English Dictionary 영어로 배우는 영어 단어

Step2   실력평가 단원별 수시평가 대비 주관식, 객관식 문제풀이

Step3   서술형 대비 학업성취도 및 수행능력평가 대비 서술형 문제풀이

Conversation

Step1   핵심 의사소통 소통에 필요한 주요 표현 방법 요약
         핵심 Check 기본적인 표현 방법 및 활용능력 확인

Step2   대화문 익히기 교과서 대화문 심층 분석 및 확인

Step3   교과서 확인학습 빈칸 채우기를 통한 문장 완성 능력 확인

Step4   기본평가 시험대비 기초 학습 능력 평가

Step5   실력평가 단원별 수시평가 대비 주관식, 객관식 문제풀이

Step6   서술형 대비 학업성취도 및 수행능력평가 대비 서술형 문제풀이

Grammar

Step1   주요 문법 단원별 주요 문법 사항과 예문을 알기 쉽게 설명
         핵심 Check 기본 문법사항에 대한 이해 여부 확인

Step2   기본평가 시험대비 기초 학습 능력 평가

Step3   실력평가 단원별 수시평가 대비 주관식, 객관식 문제풀이

Step4   서술형 대비 학업성취도 및 수행능력평가 대비 서술형 문제풀이

Reading

Step1   구문 분석 단원별로 제시된 문장에 대한 구문별 분석과 내용 설명
         확인문제 문장에 대한 기본적인 이해와 인지능력 확인

Step2   확인학습A 빈칸 채우기를 통한 문장 완성 능력 확인

Step3   확인학습B 제시된 우리말을 영어로 완성하여 작문 능력 키우기

Step4   실력평가 단원별 수시평가 대비 주관식, 객관식 문제풀이

Step5   서술형 대비 학업성취도 및 수행능력평가 대비 서술형 문제풀이
         교과서 구석구석 교과서에 나오는 기타 문장까지 완벽 학습

Composition

|영역별 핵심문제|
단어 및 어휘, 대화문, 문법, 독해 등 각 영역별 기출문제의 출제 유형을 분석하여 실전에 대비하고 연습할 수 있도록 문제를 배열

|단원별 예상문제|
기출문제를 분석한 후 새로운 시험 출제 경향을 더하여 새롭게 출제될 수 있는 문제를 포함하여 시험에 완벽하게 대비할 수 있도록 준비

|서술형 실전 및 창의사고력 문제|
학교 시험에서 점차 늘어나는 서술형 시험에 집중 대비하고 고득점을 취득하는데 만전을 기하기 위한 학습 코너

|단원별 모의고사|
영역별, 단계별 학습을 모두 마친 후 실전 연습을 위한 모의고사

교과서 파헤치기

- **단어Test1~3** 영어 단어 우리말 쓰기, 우리말을 영어 단어로 쓰기, 영영풀이에 해당하는 단어와 우리말 쓰기
- **대화문Test1~2** 대화문 빈칸 완성 및 전체 대화문 쓰기
- **본문Test1~5** 빈칸 완성, 우리말 쓰기, 문장 배열연습, 영어 작문하기 복습 등 단계별 반복 학습을 통해 교과서 지문에 대한 완벽한 습득
- **구석구석지문Test1~2** 지문 빈칸 완성 및 전문 영어로 쓰기

Lesson

1

Young Enough to Change the World

 의사소통 기능

- 의향 말하기
  A: What's your plan for this year?
  B: I'm thinking of taking swimming lessons.

- 도움 제안하기
  A: Do you want me to fix it?
  B: Yes, please.

 언어 형식

- 선행사를 포함하는 관계대명사 what
  What you do today can change the world.

- '양보'의 부사절 접속사 although
  Although they are only teenagers, they have actually made a difference in the world.

Words & Expressions

Key Words

- **actually** [ǽktʃuəli] 부 실제로
- **adopt** [ədápt] 동 입양하다
- **although** [ɔːlðóu] 접 ~임에도 불구하고, 비록 ~이지만
- **book review** 서평
- **bring** [briŋ] 동 ~을 가져오다
- **charity** [tʃǽrəti] 명 자선단체, 자선
- **cheetah** [tʃíːtə] 명 치타
- **child-care center** 탁아소, 보육원
- **collect** [kəlékt] 동 모으다, 수집하다
- **deliver** [dilívər] 동 전달하다, 배달하다
- **difficult** [dífikʌlt] 형 어려운
- **donate** [dóuneit] 동 기부하다, 기증하다
- **educate** [édʒukèit] 동 가르치다, 교육하다
- **endangered** [indéindʒərd] 형 멸종 위기의
- **expression** [ikspréʃən] 명 표현
- **fix** [fiks] 동 고치다
- **generation** [dʒènəréiʃən] 명 세대
- **gulf** [gʌlf] 명 만
- **leader** [líːdər] 명 리더, 지도자, 대표
- **marine** [məríːn] 형 해양의
- **mayonnaise** [mèiənéiz] 명 마요네즈
- **neighborhood** [néibərhùd] 명 이웃, 근처
- **non-profit organization** 명 비영리 단체
- **occur** [əkə́ːr] 동 일어나다, 발생하다
- **parking space** 주차 공간
- **probably** [prábəbli] 부 아마도
- **problem** [prábləm] 명 문제
- **raise** [reiz] 동 기르다
- **reduce** [ridʒúːs] 동 줄이다
- **rescue** [réskjuː] 명 구조, 구출
- **rubber** [rʌ́bər] 명 고무
- **signature** [sígnətʃər] 명 서명
- **specialist** [spéʃəlist] 명 전문가
- **spill** [spil] 명 유출
- **supply** [səplái] 명 공급
- **teenager** [tíːnèidʒər] 명 십 대, 청소년
- **throat** [θrout] 명 목구멍, 목
- **translate** [trænsléit] 동 번역하다
- **various** [vɛ́riəs] 형 다양한, 여러 가지의
- **volunteer** [vàləntíər] 명 자원봉사자 동 자원하다
- **waste** [weist] 명 쓰레기

Key Expressions

- **a bit** 조금, 약간
- **a few** 어느 정도, 조금
- **any longer** 더 이상, 이제는
- **ask for help** 도움을 청하다
- **ask+목적어+to 동사원형** …가 ~하는 것을 요청하다
- **be able to 동사원형** ~할 수 있다
- **be covered with** ~으로 뒤덮여 있다
- **break down** 고장나다
- **die from** ~으로 죽다
- **do volunteer work** 자원봉사를 하다
- **for example** 예를 들어
- **in addition to** ~ 이외에, ~에 더하여
- **lend 사물 to 사람** ~에게 ~을 빌려주다
- **name+목적어+목적격보어(명사)** ~를 …라고 이름 짓다
- **read A to B** A를 B에게 읽어주다
- **run into** (곤경, 어려움 등을) 만나다[겪다]
- **send A to B** A를 B에게 보내다
- **share A with B** A를 B와 나누다, 공유하다
- **throw up** 토하다
- **translate ~ into 언어** …를 ~으로 번역하다
- **want+목적어+to부정사** ~가 …하는 것을 원하다

Word Power

※ 명사형 어미 -ion/-tion(행위, 성질, 상태)

- ☐ **act**(행동하다)+**-ion** → **action**(행동)
- ☐ **collect**(모으다, 수집하다)+**-ion** → **collection**(수집)
- ☐ **create**(~을 창조하다, 새로 만들어 내다)+**-ion** → **creation**(창조)
- ☐ **educate**(교육하다, 가르치다)+**-ion** → **education**(교육)
- ☐ **generate**(발생시키다, 일으키다)+**-ion** → **generation**((전기 등의) 발생)
- ☐ **protect**(보호하다)+**-ion** → **protection**(보호)
- ☐ **imagine**(상상하다)+**-tion** → **imagination**(상상)
- ☐ **invite**(초대하다)+**-tion** → **invitation**(초대)

※ **make**와 같이 쓰이는 단어의 짝

- ☐ **make a difference** (차이를 낳다, 변화를 가져오다)
- ☐ **make a discovery** (발견하다)
- ☐ **make a wish** (소원을 빌다)

English Dictionary

☐ **charity** 자선단체
→ an organization which raises money in order to help people who are sick or very poor, or who have a disability
아프거나 가난하거나 장애가 있는 사람들을 돕기 위해 돈을 모으는 단체

☐ **deliver** 전달하다, 배달하다
→ to take goods, letters, packages etc. to a particular place or person
물건, 편지, 소포 등을 특정한 장소나 사람에게 가져다주다

☐ **donate** 기부하다, 기증하다
→ to give something, especially money, to a person or an organization in order to help them
도울 목적으로 사람이나 단체에게 물건, 특히 돈을 주다

☐ **educate** 가르치다, 교육하다
→ to teach a child at a school, college, or university
학교 또는 대학에서 아이들을 가르치다

☐ **endangered** 멸종 위기의
→ in danger of extinction
멸종 위기에 있는

☐ **expression** 표현
→ something you say, write, or do that shows what you think or feel
당신이 생각하거나 느끼는 바를 보여주는 말하거나 쓰거나 또는 행동을 하는 것

☐ **fix** 고치다
→ to repair something that is broken or not working properly
고장나거나 적절하게 작동하지 않는 것을 수리하다

☐ **gulf** 만
→ a large area of sea partly enclosed by land
부분적으로 땅으로 둘러싸인 바다의 큰 지역

☐ **marine** 해양의
→ relating to the sea and the creatures that live there
바다와 거기에 살고 있는 생물과 관련된

☐ **occur** 일어나다, 발생하다
→ to happen
발생하다

☐ **reduce** 줄이다
→ to make something smaller or less in size, amount, or price
어떤 것의 크기, 양 또는 가격을 작게 만들다

☐ **signature** 서명
→ your name written in the way you usually write it, for example at the end of a letter, or on a cheque etc, to show that you have written it
예를 들어 편지의 끝이나 수표에 당신이 썼다는 것을 보여주기 위해 보통 쓰는 방식으로 쓰여진 이름

☐ **specialist** 전문가
→ someone who knows a lot about a particular subject, or is very skilled at it
특정한 주제에 대해 많이 알거나 그것에 대해 매우 숙련된 사람

☐ **translate** 번역하다
→ to change written or spoken words into another language
쓰여지거나 말해진 단어들을 다른 언어로 바꾸다

01 접미사를 붙여 명사로 만들 때 다른 접미사를 사용하는 하나를 고르시오.

① succeed ② imagine
③ act ④ educate
⑤ collect

02 밑줄 친 부분과 바꿔 쓸 수 있는 말을 쓰시오.

> I'm feeling a little tired.

① a lot of ② usually
③ much ④ a bit
⑤ just

03 다음 빈칸 (A)~(C)에 들어갈 말이 바르게 짝지어진 것은?

> • The bank refused to lend the money ___(A)___ us.
> • Don't be afraid to ask ___(B)___ help.
> • The desk was covered ___(C)___ papers.

　(A)　(B)　(C)
① to　– for – with
② to　– to　– by
③ to　– for – for
④ for – for – with
⑤ for – to　– by

서답형

04 다음 영영풀이가 나타내는 말을 주어진 철자로 시작하여 쓰시오.

> to teach a child at a school, college, or university

➡ e_____

05 다음 제시된 단어를 사용하여 자연스러운 문장을 만들 수 없는 것은? (형태 변화 가능)

> bring　educate　fix　occur

① The police said that the accident _____ at about 4:30 p.m.
② The concert organizers say they will _____ all profits to charity.
③ He was _____ at Bristol University.
④ Ellis is able to quickly find and _____ the problem.
⑤ My parents always encouraged us to _____ our friends home.

06 밑줄 친 부분과 바꿔 쓸 수 있는 말을 고르시오.

> We are decreasing costs and investing for more effective ones.

① increasing ② providing
③ requiring ④ reducing
⑤ preventing

서답형

07 다음 우리말에 맞도록 빈칸에 알맞은 말을 쓰시오.

(1) 물병은 많은 플라스틱 쓰레기를 만든다.
➡ Water bottles create too much plastic _____.

(2) 바다에는 많은 해양생물이 있다.
➡ There's a lot of _____ life in the oceans.

01 주어진 우리말과 괄호 안의 단어를 활용하여 빈칸에 알맞은 말을 쓰시오.

(1) 나는 당신의 저녁 초대를 거절해야만 해서 유감입니다.
➡ I'm afraid I have to turn down your _____ to dinner. (invite)

(2) 그 도마뱀들은 멸종 위기종으로 분류되었다.
➡ The lizards are classed as an _____ species. (danger)

02 다음 빈칸에 공통으로 들어갈 말을 쓰시오. (대 · 소문자 무시, 한 단어)

> • _____ it was too cold, kids ran out to play.
> • She didn't eat anything _____ she was too hungry.
> • _____ everyone played well, we lost the game.

03 두 문장이 같은 의미가 되도록 빈칸을 채우시오.

> There are now several different types of cars which are eco-friendly.
> = There are now _____ cars which are eco-friendly.

04 밑줄 친 우리말과 일치하도록 주어진 단어를 이용하여 영작하시오.

(1) 너는 내가 창문을 닫기를 원하니?
➡ _____
(want, close)

(2) 그녀는 자기의 개를 Mary라고 이름 짓기로 결정했다.
➡ _____
(to, name, decide)

(3) 산은 눈으로 뒤덮여 있다.
➡ _____
(cover)

(4) 많은 사람들은 더러운 물을 먹어서 죽는다.
➡ _____
(dirty, from, many)

(5) 나는 방학 동안에 봉사활동을 하려고 계획 중이야.
➡ _____
(during, do, plan)

(6) 그 남자는 담배를 끊으라고 요청받았다.
➡ _____
(smoke, ask, quit, to)

05 다음 빈칸을 〈보기〉에 있는 어휘를 이용하여 채우시오. (단어는 한 번씩만 사용할 것.)

> ┤ 보기 ├
> collect   deliver   raise   translate

(1) The book has been _____ into 27 languages.
(2) One of Tony's hobbies was _____ rare coins.
(3) I have _____ two turtles for one year.
(4) We will _____ your order between noon and 1 p.m.

Conquersation

교과서

① 의향 말하기

> **A** What's your plan for this year? 올해 너의 계획이 뭐니?
> **B** I'm thinking of taking swimming lessons. 나는 수영 강습을 받을까 해.

■ 'I'm thinking of ~.'는 '나는 ~할까 생각 중이다'라는 뜻으로 of 뒤에 동명사를 취해 의도나 계획을 나타낼 때 쓰는 표현이다. 전치사 of 대신 about을 사용하여 'I'm thinking about ~.'으로도 표현한다.

■ 상대방의 의향을 물을 때는 'What do you want to ~?', 'What are you going to ~?', 'What would you like to ~?' 등의 표현을 사용한다.

■ 'I'm thinking of ~.' 대신에 'I'm considering (동)명사 ~.', 'I intend to 동사원형 ~.', 'I'm planning to 동사원형 ~.'을 사용할 수 있다.

의향 말하기

- I'm thinking of (동)명사 ~.
- I'm considering (동)명사 ~.
- I'm planning to 동사원형 ~.
- I intend to 동사원형 ~.

핵심 Check

1. 다음 우리말과 일치하도록 빈칸에 알맞은 말을 쓰시오.

   A: What do you want to eat? (너는 무엇을 먹고 싶니?)

   B: Well, _____ thinking _____ _____ a sandwich.
   (음. 나는 샌드위치를 주문할까 생각 중이야.)

2. 우리말과 일치하도록 주어진 단어를 알맞게 배열하여 문장을 만드시오.

   A: What are you going to buy as a present? (선물로 뭐 살 거예요?)

   B: _____ (a, I'm, buying, of, thinking, scarf)
   (나는 스카프를 살 생각을 하고 있는 걸.)

3. 다음 문장과 같은 의미가 되도록 주어진 단어를 이용하여 쓰시오.

   I'm thinking of buying a car.

   ➡ _____ (consider)

2 도움 제안하기

> **A** Do you want me to fix it? 내가 그것을 고쳐 줄까?
> **B** Yes, please. 응, 부탁해.

■ 'Do you want me to+동사원형 ~?'은 '당신은 내가 ~해 주기를 원하십니까?'라는 뜻으로 상대방에게 도움이 필요한지 묻는 표현이다.

도움 제안하기

- May I help you? (도와드릴까요?)
- Do you need my help? (도움이 필요합니까?)
- Is there anything I can do? (제가 뭐 도와드릴 일이라도 있나요?)
- Let me help you. (제가 도와드릴게요.)
- Can I give you a hand? (제가 도와드릴까요?)

■ 'Let me help you.'를 'Let me+동사원형 ~ (for you).'로 바꿔 쓸 수도 있다.
- A: I don't know how to use it. (나는 그것을 어떻게 사용하는지 몰라.)
  B: Let me help you. (내가 널 도와줄게.) / Let me show you how to use it. (내가 어떻게 사용하는지 보여줄게.)

핵심 Check

4. 대화가 자연스럽게 연결되도록 순서대로 배열하시오.

(A) It is important to check your bike before riding.
(B) What's wrong? Can I give you a hand?
(C) Yes, please. My bike is broken.

➡ _____

5. 우리말과 일치하도록 주어진 단어를 배열하여 영작하시오.

A: _____ (your, you, you, homework, do, to, me, with, help, want) (너는 내가 너의 숙제를 도와주기를 원하니?)
B: Yes, please.

6. 다음 우리말과 일치하도록 빈칸에 알맞은 말을 쓰시오.

A: I need to get up early tomorrow. (나는 내일 일찍 일어나야 해.)
B: Do _____? (너는 내가 너를 깨워주기를 원하니?)
A: Yes, please. (응, 부탁해.)

Listen & Speak 1 A-1

G: ❶What are you doing this weekend?

B: ❷I'm thinking of ❸doing some volunteer work at the child-care center.

G: What would you do there?

B: I would ❹probably read some books to the children.

G: That sounds interesting. ❺Can I join you?

B: Of course.

G: 이번 주말에 뭐 하니?
B: 나는 보육원에서 봉사 활동을 좀 하려고 해.
G: 거기서 뭘 할 것 같아?
B: 아마 아이들에게 책을 좀 읽어 줄 것 같아.
G: 그거 흥미로워 보인다. 나도 함께 가도 될까?
B: 물론이지.

❶ 'What are you doing this weekend?'에서 동사는 'be동사+-ing'로 현재진행형의 형태이지만 this weekend라는 미래를 나타내는 어구와 함께 쓰여 가까운 미래를 나타낸다. 'What are you doing this weekend?'는 이번 주말에 무엇을 할지 물어보는 표현으로 'What are you planning to do this weekend?', 'What are you going to do this weekend?'로 바꿔 말할 수 있다.
❷ 'I'm thinking of ~.'는 '나는 ~할까 생각 중이다'라는 뜻으로 of 뒤에 동명사를 취해 의도나 계획을 나타낼 때 쓰는 표현이다.
❸ do volunteer work: 자원봉사를 하다
❹ probably: 아마도 read A to B: A를 B에게 읽어주다(= read B A)
❺ 어떤 일을 하기 전에 'Can I ~?'를 사용하여 상대방에게 허락을 요청할 수 있다. 바꿔 쓸 수 있는 표현으로 'May I ~?', 'Is it okay if I ~?' 등이 있다.

Check(√) True or False

(1) The boy is considering to read some books at home.   T ☐ F ☐

(2) The girl is interested in reading books to the children at the child-care center.   T ☐ F ☐

 Listen & Speak 2 A-1

G: Dad, I'm ❶a bit hungry. Is there anything ❷to eat?

M: Do you ❸want me to cook tteokbokki for you?

G: ❹That'd be great. I love tteokbokki.

M: O.K. ❺Give me ❻a few minutes.

G: 아빠, 저 배가 좀 고파요. 먹을 게 있나요?
M: 네게 떡볶이를 만들어 줄까?
G: 그거 정말 좋겠어요. 전 떡볶이를 매우 좋아해요.
M: 알겠다. 잠시만 시간을 주렴.

❶ a bit: 조금, 약간
❷ to eat은 to부정사의 형용사적 용법으로 앞의 대명사 anything을 수식하고 있다.
❸ 여기서 want는 5형식 문장으로 사용되어 목적어(me)와 목적격 보어(to cook tteokbokki)를 취하고 있다.
❹ That'd = That would
❺ give는 4형식 동사로 간접목적어(me)와 직접목적어(a few minutes)를 취하고 있다.
❻ a few: 어느 정도, 조금 a few 뒤에는 셀 수 있는 명사가 올 수 있다.

Check(√) True or False

(3) The girl likes tteokbokki.   T ☐ F ☐

(4) The man is going to make tteokbokki for the girl.   T ☐ F ☐

Communicate A

Suho: Anna, do you have any children's books ❶you don't read any longer?

Anna: Sure. Why?

Suho: ❷I'm thinking of sending some books to children in Africa. My aunt ❸told me that they need books ❹to read.

Anna: Good idea, Suho! Wait, aren't your books ❺in Korean?

Suho: Oh, that's a problem.

Anna: Well, ❻how about translating them into English?

Suho: Translating? That's a great idea, Anna.

Anna: Do you ❼want me to help you?

Suho: Sure. If we ❽run into any difficult expressions, ❾let's ask our English teacher for help.

Anna: O.K. ❿It's really great that we can help the children in Africa.

수호: Anna, 너는 더 이상 읽지 않는 아동용 도서들을 가지고 있니?

Anna: 물론이지. 왜?

수호: 나는 아프리카의 아이들에게 책을 좀 보낼 생각을 하고 있어. 우리 이모가 내게 그 아이들이 읽을 책이 필요하다고 말씀하셨어.

Anna: 좋은 생각이야, 수호야! 잠깐만, 네 책들은 한글로 되어 있지 않니?

수호: 오, 그게 문제구나.

Anna: 음, 그것들을 영어로 번역하는 건 어때?

수호: 번역? 그거 좋은 생각이다, Anna.

Anna: 너는 내가 너를 도와주기를 원하니?

수호: 물론이지. 만약 어려운 표현들이 나오면, 영어 선생님께 도움을 요청하자.

Anna: 알겠어. 우리가 아프리카의 아이들을 도울 수 있어서 정말 좋다.

❶ books와 you 사이에 목적격 관계대명사 that[which]이 생략되어 있다. 'you don't read any longer'가 앞의 'any children's books'를 수식하고 있다.

❷ I'm thinking of ~: 나는 ~할까 생각 중이다 send A to B: A를 B에게 보내다

❸ told는 동사 tell의 과거형으로 뒤에 간접목적어 me와 직접목적어 that절을 취하고 있다.

❹ to read는 명사 books를 꾸며주는 to부정사의 형용사적 용법으로 사용되고 있다.

❺ 언어를 나타낼 때 전치사 in을 사용한다.

❻ 'How about 동명사 ~?'는 '~하는 건 어때?'의 의미로 상대방에게 제안할 때 사용한다. translate ~ into 언어: …를 ~로 번역하다, ~를 (~로) 옮기다

❼ want+목적어+to부정사: ~가 …하는 것을 원하다

❽ run into: (곤경, 어려움 등을) 만나다[겪다] expression: 표현

❾ let's+동사원형: ~하자 ask for help: 도움을 청하다

❿ It은 가주어, that절이 진주어로 사용되고 있다.

Check(√) True or False

(5) They have difficult expressions in translating the books in Korean. T ☐ F ☐

(6) Suho wants to help the children in Africa by sending books. T ☐ F ☐

Progress Check 1

B: ❶What are you doing this weekend?

G: ❷I'm thinking of going for a bike ride.

B: Sounds good. Can I join you?

G: Sure. Let's meet ❸in front of the park at ten.

B: O.K.

B: 이번 주말에 뭐 하니?

G: 자전거를 타러 가려고 해.

B: 좋겠구나. 나도 함께 가도 되니?

G: 물론이야. 공원 앞에서 10시에 보자.

B: 그래.

❶ 'be동사+-ing'로 현재진행형의 형태이지만 this weekend라는 미래를 나타내는 어구와 함께 쓰여 가까운 미래를 나타낸다.

❷ I'm thinking of ~: 나는 ~할까 생각 중이다

❸ in front of: ~ 앞에. 시간 앞에는 전치사 at을 사용한다.

Check(√) True or False

(7) They are going to ride a bike this weekend. T ☐ F ☐

(8) The boy doesn't want the girl to ride a bike. T ☐ F ☐

Listen & Speak 1 A-2

B: ❶What are you going to read for the ❷book review homework?
G: ❸I'm thinking of reading a book about young leaders.
B: Good idea. I have the perfect book for you.
G: Oh, could you ❹lend it to me?
B: Sure. I'll bring it tomorrow.

❶ 상대방에게 무엇을 할 계획인지(또는 어떤 계획이 있는지) 물어볼 때 'What are you going[planning] to+동사원형 ~?'을 사용할 수 있다.
❷ book review: 서평
❸ 'I'm thinking of ~.'는 '나는 ~할까 생각 중이다'의 의미로 의도나 의향을 표현할 때 사용한다.
❹ lend 사물 to 사람: …에게 ~을 빌려주다(= lend 사람 사물)

 Listen & Speak 1 B-1

A: ❶What's your plan for this year?
B: I'm thinking of ❷watching a movie every weekend.

❶ plan: 계획 What's your plan for ~?: ~에 무엇을 할 계획이니? (= What are you planning to do for ~? = What are you going to do for ~?)
❷ watch a movie: 영화를 보다

 Listen & Speak 1 B-2

A: What's your plan for this year?
B: I'm thinking of learning ❶how to play baduk.

❶ 'how to 동사원형'은 '~하는 방법'으로 해석하며 learn의 목적어 역할을 하고 있다.

 Listen & Speak 2 A-2

B: Sujin, ❶can you help us?
G: Sure. ❷What can I do for you?
B: ❸We're going to ❹ask the school to make a parking space for bicycles.
G: That's a great idea. ❺Do you want me to help you collect signatures from students?
B: That would help us a lot. Thanks!

❶ 'Can you help us?'는 상대방에게 부탁할 때 사용하는 표현으로, 'Do you mind ~ing?', 'Could you do me a favor?', 'Can I ask you to 동사원형 ~?' 등으로 바꿔 쓸 수 있다.
❷ 'What can I do for you?'는 '무엇을 도와드릴까요?'의 의미로 상대방에게 도움을 제공하고자 할 때 사용한다.
❸ 'be going to 동사원형'은 '~할 것이다, ~할 계획이다'의 의미로 의도나 계획에 대해 말할 때 사용하는 표현이다.

❹ ask+목적어+to 동사원형: …가 ~할 것을 요청하다 parking space: 주차 공간, 주차 구역
❺ 'Do you want me to 동사원형 ~?'은 '당신은 내가 ~해 주기를 원하십니까?'라는 뜻으로 상대방에게 도움이 필요한지 묻는 표현이다. collect: 모으다, 수집하다 signature: 서명

 Listen & Speak 2 B-1

A: My bike ❶broke down.
B: Do you want me to ❷fix it?
A: Yes, please.

❶ break down: 고장 나다
❷ fix: 고치다 it은 앞의 bike를 받는 대명사이다.

 Listen & Speak 2 B-2

A: I didn't ❶bring an umbrella.
B: Do you want me to ❷share my umbrella with you?
A: Yes, please.

❶ bring: ~을 가져오다
❷ share A with B: A를 B와 나누다, 공유하다

 Communication B

A: (춤추는 동작을 한다.)
B: ❶Are you thinking of learning taekwondo?
A: No.
C: Are you thinking of ❷learning to dance?
A: Yes. I'm thinking of learning K-pop dancing.
C: Do you want me to ❸teach you?
A: Sure. That'd be great.

❶ 'Are you thinking of learning taekwondo?'에서 'be thinking of(~을 생각 중이다)'는 현재진행형으로 상대방의 의도를 물어보고 있다.
❷ learn이 to부정사를 목적어로 취하고 있다.
❸ teach+간접목적어(you)+직접목적어(K-pop dancing)인데, 직접목적어가 생략되어 있다.

 Progress Check 2

M: Can we have pancakes ❶for breakfast?
W: Sure. Oh, we don't have any eggs.
M: Do you want me to go to the store and ❷get some?
W: Thanks, Mike. Can you get blueberry syrup, too?
M: Sure.

❶ for breakfast: 아침식사로
❷ get은 앞의 go와 접속사 and로 연결되어 있다. some은 some eggs를 의미한다.

다음 우리말과 일치하도록 빈칸에 알맞은 말을 쓰시오.

Listen & Speak 1 A

1. G: What are you _____ _____ weekend?
   B: I'm _____ _____ doing some _____ work at the child-care center.
   G: _____ would you do there?
   B: I would probably _____ some books _____ the children.
   G: That _____ interesting. Can I _____ you?
   B: Of course.

2. B: What _____ _____ going _____ _____ for the book review homework?
   G: I'm _____ of reading a book about _____ leaders.
   B: Good idea. I _____ the perfect book for you.
   G: Oh, could you _____ it to me?
   B: Sure. I'll _____ it tomorrow.

Listen & Speak 1 B

1. A: _____ your plan for this year?
   B: I'm _____ of watching a movie every weekend.

2. A: _____ your _____ for this year?
   B: I'm _____ learning how to play baduk.

3. A: _____ your _____ _____ this year?
   B: I'm _____ _____ _____ swimming lessons.

Listen & Speak 2 A

1. G: Dad, I'm _____ bit hungry. Is _____ anything _____ eat?
   M: Do you _____ _____ _____ cook tteokbokki for you?
   G: That'd be great. I love tteokbokki.
   M: O.K. Give me a _____ minutes.

2. B: Sujin, can you help us?
   G: Sure. _____ _____ _____ _____ for you?
   B: We're going to _____ the school _____ _____ a parking space for bicycles.
   G: That's a great idea. Do you _____ _____ _____ you _____ signatures from students?
   B: That would help us _____ _____. Thanks!

해석

1. G: 이번 주말에 뭐 하니?
   B: 나는 보육원에서 봉사 활동을 좀 하려고 해.
   G: 거기서 뭘 할 것 같아?
   B: 아마 아이들에게 책을 좀 읽어 줄 것 같아.
   G: 그거 흥미로워 보인다. 나도 함께 가도 될까?
   B: 물론이지.

2. B: 너는 독후감 숙제로 뭘 읽을 거니?
   G: 나는 젊은 지도자들에 관한 책을 읽을까 해.
   B: 좋은 생각이야. 나한테 너에게 딱 맞는 책이 있어.
   G: 오, 내게 빌려줄 수 있어?
   B: 그럼. 내일 그걸 가져올게.

1. A: 올해 너의 계획이 뭐니?
   B: 나는 주말마다 영화를 볼까 해.

2. A: 올해 너의 계획이 뭐니?
   B: 나는 바둑 두는 걸 배울까 해.

3. A: 올해 너의 계획이 뭐니?
   B: 나는 수영 강습을 받을까 해.

1. G: 아빠, 저 배가 좀 고파요. 먹을 게 좀 있나요?
   M: 네게 떡볶이를 만들어 줄까?
   G: 그거 정말 좋겠어요. 전 떡볶이를 매우 좋아해요.
   M: 알겠다. 잠시만 시간을 주렴.

2. B: 수진아, 우리를 좀 도와줄 수 있니?
   G: 물론이야. 무엇을 해 줄까?
   B: 우리는 학교에 자전거 주차 공간을 만들어 달라고 요청하려 해.
   G: 그거 멋진 생각이다. 학생들에게 사인을 받는 것을 도와줄까?
   B: 그건 우리에게 큰 도움이 될 거야. 고마워!

Listen & Speak 2 B

1. **A:** My bike _____ down.

   B: Do you _____ _____ _____ fix it?

   A: Yes, please.

2. **A:** I didn't _____ an umbrella.

   B: Do you want me to _____ my _____ _____ you?

   A: Yes, please.

3. **A:** _____ box is _____ heavy.

   B: Do you _____ _____ _____ _____ you _____ it?

   A: Yes, please.

4. **A:** My _____ is too short.

   B: Do you _____ _____ _____ a picture of you?

   A: Yes, please.

Communicate A

Suho: Anna, do you have any children's books _____ _____ read _____ _____?

Anna: Sure. Why?

Suho: _____ _____ _____ some books to children in Africa. My aunt _____ _____ _____ they need books _____ read.

Anna: Good idea, Suho! Wait, _____ your books in Korean?

Suho: Oh, that's a problem.

Anna: Well, how _____ _____ them _____ English?

Suho: _____? That's a great idea, Anna.

Anna: _____ _____ _____ _____ _____ _____ _____?

Suho: Sure. If we _____ _____ any difficult _____, let's ask our English teacher for help.

Anna: O.K. It's really great _____ _____ can _____ the children in Africa.

해석

1. **A:** 내 자전거가 고장 났어.
   B: 내가 그것을 고쳐 줄까?
   A: 응, 부탁해.

2. **A:** 나 우산을 안 가져왔어.
   B: 내가 우산을 너와 함께 쓸까?
   A: 응, 부탁해.

3. **A:** 이 상자는 너무 무거워.
   B: 내가 그것을 나르는 걸 도와줄까?
   A: 응, 부탁해.

4. **A:** 내 팔이 너무 짧아.
   B: 내가 네 사진을 찍어줄까?
   A: 응, 부탁해.

수호: Anna, 너는 더 이상 읽지 않는 아동용 도서들을 가지고 있니?
Anna: 물론이지. 왜?
수호: 나는 아프리카의 아이들에게 책을 좀 보낼 생각을 하고 있어. 우리 이모가 내게 그 아이들이 읽을 책이 필요하다고 말씀하셨어.
Anna: 좋은 생각이야, 수호야! 잠깐만, 네 책들은 한글로 되어 있지 않니?
수호: 오, 그게 문제구나.
Anna: 음. 그것들을 영어로 번역하는 건 어때?
수호: 번역? 그거 좋은 생각이다, Anna.
Anna: 너는 내가 너를 도와주기를 원하니?
수호: 물론이지. 만약 어려운 표현들이 나오면, 영어 선생님께 도움을 요청하자.
Anna: 알겠어. 우리가 아프리카의 아이들을 도울 수 있어서 정말 좋다.

Communicate B

A: (춤추는 동작을 한다.)

B: Are you _____ _____ _____ taekwondo?

A: No.

C: _____ _____ _____ of learning _____ _____?

A: Yes. _____ _____ of _____ K-pop dancing.

C: Do you _____ _____ _____ teach you?

A: Sure. That'd be great.

해석

A: (춤추는 동작을 한다.)
B: 너 태권도 배우려고 하니?
A: 아니야.
C: 춤추는 걸 배우려고 하니?
A: 그래. K-pop 춤을 배우려고 해.
C: 내가 가르쳐 줄까?
A: 그래. 그거 좋겠다.

Progress Check 1

B: _____ are you _____ this weekend?

G: _____ _____ _____ going for a bike ride.

B: Sounds good. Can I join you?

G: Sure. _____ meet in front of the park at ten.

B: O.K.

B: 이번 주말에 뭐 하니?
G: 자전거를 타러 가려고 해.
B: 좋겠구나. 나도 함께 해도 되니?
G: 물론이야. 공원 앞에서 10시에 보자.
B: 그래.

Progress Check 2

M: _____ _____ have pancakes _____ breakfast?

W: Sure. Oh, we _____ have any eggs.

M: Do you _____ _____ _____ _____ to the store and _____ some?

W: Thanks, Mike. Can you get blueberry syrup, too?

M: Sure.

M: 아침으로 팬케이크를 먹을까요?
W: 좋아요. 오, 달걀이 없네요.
M: 가게에 가서 좀 사올까요?
W: 고마워요, Mike. 블루베리 시럽도 사와 줄래요?
M: 물론이죠.

[01~02] 다음 대화를 읽고 물음에 답하시오.

B: What are you going to read for the book review homework?
G: I'm thinking of reading a book about young leaders.
B: Good idea. I have the perfect book for you.
G: Oh, could you lend it to me?
B: Sure. I'll bring it tomorrow.

01 밑줄 친 부분과 바꿔 쓸 수 있는 것을 고르시오.

① I'll reading a book about young leaders.
② I am planning reading a book about young leaders.
③ I intend to reading a book about young leaders.
④ I'm considering reading a book about young leaders.
⑤ I'm interested in reading a book about young leaders.

02 대화의 내용과 일치하지 않는 것을 고르시오.

① 남자아이는 젊은 지도자들에 대한 책을 가지고 있다.
② 남자아이는 내일 젊은 지도자들에 대한 책을 가지고 올 것이다.
③ 여자아이는 서평 숙제를 할 예정이다.
④ 여자아이는 숙제를 위해 책을 다시 읽어야 한다.
⑤ 남자아이는 여자아이에게 책을 빌려줄 것이다.

03 주어진 문장 이후에 올 대화의 순서를 바르게 배열한 것을 고르시오.

Sujin, can you help us?

(A) That's a great idea. Do you want me to help you collect signatures from students?
(B) Sure. What can I do for you?
(C) We're going to ask the school to make a parking space for bicycles.
(D) That would help us a lot. Thanks!

① (B) – (A) – (C) – (D)   ② (B) – (C) – (A) – (D)
③ (C) – (A) – (B) – (D)   ④ (C) – (B) – (A) – (D)
⑤ (C) – (D) – (B) – (A)

[01~03] 다음 대화를 읽고 물음에 답하시오.

> G: Dad, I'm a bit hungry. (①) Is there anything to eat?
> M: (②) Do you want me ___(A)___ tteokbokki for you? (③)
> G: (④ I love tteokbokki.
> M: O.K. Give me a few minutes. (⑤)

 위 대화의 ①~⑤ 중 주어진 문장이 들어갈 알맞은 곳은?

> That'd be great.

①   ②   ③   ④   ⑤

02 빈칸 (A)에 알맞은 말을 고르시오.

① cook   ② to cook

③ cooking   ④ have cooked

⑤ to be cooked

 대화의 내용과 일치하지 않는 것을 모두 고르시오.

① 아빠는 떡볶이를 좋아한다.

② 여자아이는 자기를 위해 아빠가 떡볶이를 만들어 주는 것을 원한다.

③ 여자아이는 배고파서 먹을 것이 있는지 물었다.

④ 아빠는 떡볶이를 만드는 데 오랜 시간이 걸린다.

⑤ 여자아이는 약간 배고프다.

[04~05] 다음 중 짝지어진 대화가 <u>어색한</u> 것은?

04
① A: What are you planning to do this weekend?
  B: I'm going to visit my grandmother.

② A: What are you going to buy as a present?
  B: I'm thinking of this book.

③ A: What are you planning to bring to the field trip?
  B: I can't wait for the field trip.

④ A: What club are you going to join?
  B: I'm thinking of joining Surprising Magic.

⑤ A: I'm considering buying a car.
  B: That's a good idea.

① A: Do you want me to give you a ride to school?
  B: No, thanks.

② A: Do you need my help?
  B: That would be great.

③ A: Do you want me to help you?
  B: No, thanks. It'll be okay.

④ A: I can't find the train station. I'm so late.
  B: Let me help you.

⑤ A: Do you want me to set the table?
  B: Yes, please. I'll do it.

중요

06 주어진 문장 이후에 올 대화의 순서를 바르게 배열한 것을 고르시오.

> Can we have pancakes for breakfast?

> (A) Sure.
> (B) Thanks, Mike. Can you get blueberry syrup, too?
> (C) Sure. Oh, we don't have any eggs.
> (D) Do you want me to go to the store and get some?

① (B) – (A) – (C) – (D)
② (B) – (C) – (A) – (D)
③ (C) – (A) – (B) – (D)
④ (C) – (B) – (A) – (D)
⑤ (C) – (D) – (B) – (A)

07 대화의 빈칸에 들어갈 말을 고르시오.

> A: I didn't bring an umbrella.
> B: _____
> A: Yes, please.

① Do you want me to share my umbrella with you?
② Do you want me to help you carry it?
③ I'm thinking of eating pizza this weekend.
④ I'm thinking of going for a bike ride.
⑤ Do you want me to take a picture of you?

[08~09] 다음 대화를 읽고 물음에 답하시오.

> G: What are you doing this weekend?
> B: <u>I'm thinking of doing some volunteer work at the child-care center.</u>
> G: What would you do there?

B: I would probably read some books to the children.
G: That sounds interesting. Can I join you?
B: Of course.

08 위 대화의 밑줄 친 문장과 바꿔 쓸 수 <u>없는</u> 것을 <u>모두</u> 고르시오.

① I'd like to do some volunteer work at the child-care center.
② I intend to do some volunteer work at the child-care center.
③ I'm considering doing some volunteer work at the child-care center.
④ I'm planning to do some volunteer work at the child-care center.
⑤ I'm concerned about doing some volunteer work at the child-care center.

중요

09 위 대화를 읽고 답할 수 <u>없는</u> 질문을 고르시오.

① Where is the boy planning to go this weekend?
② How does the boy feel about reading books to the children?
③ Does the boy have a plan this weekend?
④ What will the girl do with the boy this weekend?
⑤ What is the boy going to do at the child-care center?

서답형

10 빈칸을 괄호 안에 주어진 단어를 알맞게 배열하여 채우시오.

> A: What's your plan for this year?
> B: _____ (of, how, I'm, play, to, learning, baduk, thinking)

➡ _____

[01~02] 다음 대화를 읽고 물음에 답하시오.

B: Sujin, can you help us?

G: Sure. What can I do for you?

B: We're going to ask the school ____(A)____ (make) a parking space for bicycles.

G: That's a great idea. (B)학생들에게 사인을 받는 것을 도와줄까?

B: That would help us a lot. Thanks!

01 빈칸 (A)를 괄호 안의 단어를 이용하여 어법에 맞게 채우시오.

➡ _____

02 밑줄 친 우리말과 일치하도록 주어진 단어를 이용하여 쓰시오.

➡ _____

_____ (collect, want, help)

[03~05] 다음 대화를 읽고 물음에 답하시오.

Suho: Anna, (a)너는 더 이상 읽지 않는 아동용 도서들을 가지고 있니?(any, have, don't, children's, longer, do, read, any, you, you, books)

Anna: Sure. Why?

Suho: (b)나는 아프리카의 아이들에게 책을 좀 보낼 생각을 하고 있어. My aunt told me that they need books to read.

Anna: Good idea, Suho! Wait, aren't your books in Korean?

Suho: Oh, that's a problem.

Anna: Well, how about translating them ____(A)____ English?

Suho: Translating? That's a great idea, Anna.

Anna: Do you want me to help you?

Suho: Sure. If we run ____(B)____ any difficult expressions, let's ask our English teacher for help.

Anna: O.K. It's really great that we can help the children in Africa.

03 빈칸 (A)와 (B)에 공통으로 들어갈 말을 쓰시오.

➡ _____

04 밑줄 친 (a)의 우리말과 일치하도록 괄호 안에 주어진 단어를 알맞게 배열하시오.

➡ _____

_____

05 밑줄 친 (b)의 우리말을 주어진 단어를 이용해 영작하시오.

➡ _____

_____ (to, think, in)

06 빈칸을 괄호 안에 주어진 단어를 알맞게 배열하여 채우시오.

G: Dad, I'm a bit hungry. Is there anything to eat?

M: _____
(want, for, tteokbokki, me, do, you, you, cook, to)

G: That'd be great. I love tteokbokki.

M: O.K. Give me a few minutes.

➡ _____

Grammar

교과서

① 관계대명사 what

- This is **what** you can do for the environment. 이것이 환경을 위해 당신이 할 수 있는 것이다.
- **What** I want to eat for dinner is *Bulgogi*. 내가 저녁으로 먹기 원하는 것은 불고기이다.

■ what은 선행사를 포함하는 관계대명사이다.
- She did **what** she could. 그녀는 그녀가 할 수 있는 (모든) 것을 했다.
  = She did **(all) the thing(s) that** she could.
- **What** Betty told me last week was true. Betty가 지난주에 나에게 말했던 것은 사실이었다.
  = **The thing that** Betty told me last week was true.

■ 관계대명사 what은 명사절을 이끈다.
- **What** the boss announced was surprising. 사장님이 발표한 것은 놀라웠다. (주어)
- I can't believe **what** Jane achieved in such a short time. 그렇게 단시간에 Jane이 해낸 것을 나는 믿을 수 없다. (목적어)
- We like the smell of **what** is baked in the oven now. 우리는 지금 오븐 속에서 구워지는 것의 냄새를 좋아한다. (전치사의 목적어)
- This is **what** I mentioned at the meeting. 이것이 회의에서 내가 언급한 것이다. (보어)

■ 의문대명사 what과 문장의 구조는 동일하며, 구분은 해석으로 한다. 관계대명사 what은 '~하는 것'으로, 의문대명사 what은 '무엇(을/이) ~하는지'로 해석한다.
- I wondered **what** my little daughter hid in her hand. 나는 내 어린 딸이 손에 무엇을 감췄는지 궁금했다. (의문대명사)
- **What** she hid there is a ring. 그녀가 그곳에 숨겨둔 것은 반지이다. (관계대명사)

■ 관계대명사 what의 관용적인 표현들
- You should not judge a man by **what he has**. 사람을 그의 재산으로 판단하면 안 된다.
- Abe is **what is called** a poisonous snake. Abe는 말하자면 독사이다.
- **What's better[worse]** is that she became rich. 더욱 좋은[나쁜] 것은 그녀가 부자가 되었다는 것이다.

핵심 Check

1. 다음 우리말에 맞게 괄호 안의 단어를 바르게 배열하시오.
   (1) 그 가게에서 만드는 것은 과자이다. (the shop, what, cookies, are, made, in, are)
   ➡ _____
   (2) Sandra는 그녀가 아는 것을 나에게 말해 주었다. (what, me, told, knew, she, Sandra)
   ➡ _____

2 '양보' 의미의 접속사 although

- **Although** Pam got up late this morning, she didn't miss the train.
  오늘 아침에 비록 Pam이 늦게 일어났지만, 그녀는 기차를 놓치지 않았다.

- **Although** it rained a lot yesterday, the playground is good to play soccer
  now. 비록 어제 비가 많이 왔지만, 지금 운동장은 축구 경기를 하기에 좋다.

■ although는 '비록 ~이지만, ~임에도 불구하고'의 뜻을 가진 접속사로서, 주절의 의미와 상반되는 내용의 종속절을 이끌며, 이를 '양보'의 부사절이라고 부른다.

  - **Although** Mansu made much money, he was not satisfied. 비록 만수는 많은 돈을 벌었지만, 만족하지 않았다.

  - **Although** Baeksu couldn't make much money, he was satisfied. 비록 백수는 많은 돈을 벌 수 없었지만, 그는 만족했다.

■ although 외에 though, even though 등이 있고, 등위 접속사 but도 같은 의미이다.

  - **Although** Alice studied hard, she didn't get good grades. 비록 Alice는 열심히 공부했지만, 좋은 성적을 받지 못했다.
    → **(Even) Though** Alice studied hard, she didn't get good grades.
    → Alice studied hard, **but** she didn't get good grades.

■ despite, in spite of 등은 '~에도 불구하고'라는 '양보' 의미의 전치사(구)로, 접속사 although는 '주어+동사'가 있는 절을, 전치사(구)는 명사나 명사 어구 등이 뒤에 오며, 부사구를 이끈다.

  - **Although** the crowd was noisy, Chad concentrated on the game. 비록 관중들이 시끄러웠지만, Chad는 경기에 집중했다.
    → **Despite** the noisy crowd, Chad concentrated on the game. 시끄러운 관중에도 불구하고, Chad는 경기에 집중했다.
    → **In spite of** the noisy crowd, Chad concentrated on the game.

■ 부사절을 이끄는 접속사에는 다음과 같은 것들도 있다.

  - **Because** his mom caught a cold, Jason made her dinner. Jason의 엄마가 감기에 걸리셔서 그는 엄마께 저녁을 만들어 드렸다. (이유)

  - **If** you know the answer, Dad, please let me know. 아버지, 답을 아신다면 알려주세요. (조건)

  - **While** the guests are eating, you shouldn't speak. 손님들이 식사하는 동안, 너는 말을 해서는 안 된다. (시간)

  - **While** the walls are dark navy, the ceiling is sky blue. 벽이 짙은 네이비색인데 반해, 천장은 하늘빛 파란색이다. (반대)

핵심 Check

2. 다음 괄호 안에서 알맞은 단어를 고르시오.

  (1) (Despite / Although) her hard work, Susan failed the test.

  (2) She didn't make it to the party (because / although) she had much time.

01 다음 문장에서 어법상 어색한 단어를 한 개씩만 찾아 고치시오.

(1) The guards judged the lady by which she held in her hand.

_____ ➡ _____

(2) The children still liked their teacher despite she had hit them.

_____ ➡ _____

(3) Even though Sarah was proud of her son, she did praise him.

_____ ➡ _____

(4) All what Bart Simpson told me at the party was a lie.

_____ ➡ _____

02 다음 중 어법상 바르지 <u>않은</u> 것은?

① Samuel doesn't gain weight even though he eats a lot.
② Despite the sound of the firework, the baby didn't wake up.
③ Although Mary broke the promise, Tom got upset.
④ In spite of his unfriendly reaction, the old lady smiled at him.
⑤ Though many people praise her, she doesn't feel happy.

03 다음 빈칸에 들어갈 말로 알맞은 것은?

> _____ his mother's death, Robert kept smiling.

① Because ② Though ③ Within
④ Despite ⑤ While

04 다음 문장의 밑줄 친 부분을 한 단어로 바꾸시오.

> Barbara donated <u>the things that</u> she bought at the mall to an orphanage.

➡ _____

01 다음 빈칸에 알맞은 것은?

> Is that _____ she wants to buy?

① which
② those
③ where
④ what
⑤ for what

 02 다음 빈칸에 알맞은 말이 순서대로 바르게 짝지어진 것은?

> • _____ Jane drinks coffee, she doesn't like the flavor of roasted coffee beans.
> • _____ I want from my daddy is money.

① Despite – What
② Even though – That
③ Though – What
④ Although – When
⑤ Because – That

03 다음 중 어법상 어색한 문장을 모두 골라 기호를 쓰시오.

> ⓐ The girls are supposed to do which their parents ask them to do.
> ⓑ Taking some light exercise is a good habit what makes you energetic.
> ⓒ The thing cannot be cured must be endured.
> ⓓ That will make them think about what they should or shouldn't do.
> ⓔ I can't believe that I've just seen.
> ⓕ Making a schedule for your vacation, you should consider what you can do.
> ⓖ That you teach can be different from those you know.

➡ _____

04 다음 중 나머지 네 개의 문장들과 뜻이 같지 <u>않은</u> 문장을 찾으시오.

① Although Jessy has reading difficulties, she knows many languages.
② In spite of her reading troubles, Jessy knows many languages.
③ Even though Jessy has trouble reading, she knows a lot of languages.
④ Jessy has reading difficulties, so she knows many languages.
⑤ Though she can't read well, Jessy knows lots of languages.

서답형 **05** 다음 문장에서 어법상 <u>틀린</u> 부분을 찾아 바르게 고쳐 쓰시오.

> Brown's father failed in business, and that was worse, he broke up with his girl friend.

_____ ➡ _____

서답형 **06** 다음 두 문장의 의미가 같도록 빈칸에 알맞은 말을 쓰시오.

> I missed the school bus, but I arrived on time.
> → _____ _____ I missed the school bus, I arrived on time.

07 다음 빈칸에 알맞은 것은?

> I read the boring magazine _____ my teacher warned me not to.

① because of
② with
③ for
④ though
⑤ since

08 다음 밑줄 친 what 중에서 나머지 넷과 같은 용법으로 쓰이지 않은 것은?

① <u>What</u> she said inspired the audience.
② Becky received <u>what</u> her son had sent her.
③ I like <u>what</u> is shown by the magician.
④ She asked me <u>what</u> I was going to do.
⑤ Those are <u>what</u> they suggested.

09 다음 중 밑줄 친 부분의 쓰임이 어색한 것은?

① My mom didn't believe my brother <u>although</u> he was telling the truth.
② <u>Although</u> Jeff caught a cold, he came to school.
③ He was tired <u>although</u> he stayed up all night the day before.
④ <u>Although</u> Henry is quite old enough, he acts like a baby.
⑤ <u>Although</u> it wasn't cold outside, Merrian wore a fur coat.

10 다음 빈칸에 접속사 Although가 들어가기에 어색한 것은?

① _____ Mike has a good job, he always complains about his work.
② _____ Norah caught a bad cold, she had to take the exam.
③ _____ Baker family had very little money, they were happy.
④ _____ Sam was tired, he tried to exercise regularly.
⑤ _____ Susan has much money, she buys expensive goods.

11 다음 빈칸에 들어갈 말로 적절하지 않은 것은?

> A: Was your homework completed?
> B: No, it wasn't. Although my homework wasn't finished, _____.

① my friends kept asking me to go out
② there was plenty of work to do
③ I should do my homework right now
④ my parents made me run an errand
⑤ Betty's asking me to show her mine

12 다음 중 어법상 어색한 문장을 모두 고르면?

① The fans liked what BTS showed them.
② This is not the thing which the president was speaking about.
③ All my friends loved the movie that the director had filmed.
④ This is not the book what Karen wanted to read.
⑤ Which the coach told them at the winning ceremony made them cry.

13 다음 우리말을 바르게 영작한 것은?

> 비록 Taylor는 울고 싶었지만, 그녀는 미소를 짓고 있었다.

① In spite that Taylor felt inclined to cry, she was smiling.
② Even though Taylor felt like crying, but she was smiling.
③ Although Taylor felt like crying, she was smiling.
④ As Taylor felt inclined to cry, she was smiling.
⑤ Taylor felt like crying despite of the situation where she was smiling.

14 다음 중 어법상 옳은 문장은?

① Is this cat what she is looking for?

② Tom bought a new car his daughter to drive.

③ Every student knows what the teacher is giving them a special lesson.

④ The baby boys liked the toy what their aunt bought yesterday.

⑤ What the girl said him was touching.

15 다음 중 어법상 옳은 문장은?

① Even if the fact that I woke up earlier than usual, I was late for work.

② I couldn't get up despite Mom shook me so many times this morning.

③ Despite of the giant storm, my wife's airplane landed safely yesterday.

④ My daughter had nothing but water even though her hunger.

⑤ She felt sick in spite of the fact that she took the prescribed pill.

서답형

16 다음 우리말을, 주어진 단어들을 배열하여 영작할 때, what 은 몇 번째로 오는가?

> 사장님이 하고 있는 말씀에 집중하라. (to, is, pay, the, saying, attention, boss, what)

➡ _____

17 밑줄 친 what의 용법이 나머지 넷과 다른 하나는?

① The beggar got <u>what</u> they threw her.

② That volunteer work at the orphanage was <u>what</u> she wanted to do.

③ Sandra accepted <u>what</u> he offered.

④ I wondered <u>what</u> she would give me.

⑤ That's <u>what</u> I meant to say.

18 다음 중 어법상 <u>어색한</u> 문장은?

① What Miso liked to have is pizza.

② Frank made what his father designed.

③ Sean loved what he was doing.

④ Tony played the game what he was good at.

⑤ He showed her what Dr. Bae had invented.

19 다음 중 어법상 옳은 문장은?

① In spite she has much money, Amy still isn't happy.

② Although his laziness, Marco passed the test with honors.

③ Though Olivia studied hard, she get an F in her monthly report card.

④ Even though worked hard, Andrew couldn't find the solution to his problem.

⑤ They couldn't hear the radio even though they turned it up.

서답형

20 다음 우리말을 영작할 때, 빈칸에 들어갈 알맞은 말을 쓰시오.

> 이제 Smith는 과거의 그가 아니다.
> = Now, Smith is not _____ he _____.

21 다음 중 어법상 옳은 문장은?

① Bill forgot the thing what she had done.

② I know the reason which it's so hot.

③ She realized the way which her husband hid the pocket money.

④ Grandpa took me what my parents had met for the first time.

⑤ The artist did what she could do best.

01 다음 그림을 보고, 빈칸에 들어갈 알맞은 말을 〈보기〉에서 골라 쓰시오.

┤ 보기 ├
fall / playing / their / it / love / read / is / other / soccer / asleep / colors / books / each

(1)

Although he tried not to _____ _____, there still were many _____ to _____.

(2)

Although _____ _____ raining, the boys are _____ _____ on the playground.

(3)

Although _____ _____ are different, they _____ _____ _____.

02 다음 문장에서 어법상 어색한 부분을 찾아 바르게 고쳐 다시 쓰시오.

(1) I don't believe that Eva said to me.

➡ _____

(2) Show me if you put in your pocket.

➡ _____

(3) Though her fear of his attitude, she looked him right in the eye.

➡ _____
_____

(4) What Josh asked me to help her was not natural.

➡ _____

03 주어진 두 문장을 관계대명사 what을 이용하여, 하나의 문장으로 만드시오.

(1) • Sam bought the things.
• They were mystery books.

➡ _____
_____

(2) • Harold couldn't believe the thing.
• The reporters referred to it.

➡ _____
_____

(3) • The thing was discussed.
• It was surprising.

➡ _____
_____

04 다음 우리말과 일치하도록 괄호 안에 주어진 단어들을 바르게 배열하시오. (필요시 동사의 형태를 변형할 것.)

비록 Jackie는 배가 고프지 않았지만, 그녀는 그 요리사가 그녀에게 만들어준 것을 먹었다.
(Jackie, what, for, not, hungry, be, she, Although, the, eat, cook, have, her, make)

➡ _____
_____

05 다음 〈보기〉에 주어진 표현들을 사용하여, 각 문장의 후반부에 접속사 although를 넣어 한 문장으로 완성하시오.

> • Charlie played soccer all day long.
> • He stayed up all night.
> → Charlie stayed up all night although he played soccer all day long.

보기
> • Michael doesn't read the books at all.
> • Kelly was late for the wedding.
> • Mongol is a small country.
> • Walter was a careful driver.

(1) It maintains an old tradition.

➡ _____

(2) She was so easygoing.

➡ _____

(3) He caused a serious car accident.

➡ _____

(4) He regularly buys many books.

➡ _____

06 우리말과 일치하도록 괄호 안에 주어진 어휘를 활용, 글자 수에 맞게 영작하시오.

(1) Mary가 동굴 안에서 발견한 것이 마을 사람들을 놀라게 했다. (find, cave, surprise, villagers, 9 단어)

➡ _____

(2) 미술관의 정책에도 불구하고, 아이들은 조용하지 않았다. (quiet, were, despite, the kids, the museum, the policy, 11 단어)

➡ _____

(3) Candy가 시장에서 산 것들은 모두 비싸지 않은 것이었다. (buy, inexpensive, at, all, 9 단어)

➡ _____

07 다음 문장에서 어법상 어색한 한 단어만을 찾아 바르게 고쳐 다시 쓰시오.

(1) Sue finally accepted that Tom gave.

➡ _____

(2) Though his wealth, he was lonely.

➡ _____

(3) That is far different from which Sunny has been waiting for.

➡ _____

(4) What I met her yesterday is true.

➡ _____

(5) Which people believed in the past is called superstition.

➡ _____

08 다음 우리말과 일치하도록 괄호 안에 주어진 단어들을 빈칸에 바르게 배열하시오.

> 비록 Audrey Hepburn은 25년 전에 세상을 떠났지만, 그녀의 아름다운 정신은 우리와 함께 영원히 남아 있을 것이다.
> (beautiful, ago, Audrey Hepburn, us, remain, away, 25 years, will, although, passed, spirit, with, her)
> → _____ forever.

➡ _____

Teens in Action

Many young people are making the world a better place. For example, Carter and Olivia Ries have become leaders in saving animals. Although they are only teenagers, they have actually made a difference in the world. How were they able to do that? Let's hear from Carter.

When I was five, my little sister Olivia and I each adopted a cheetah. Did we raise cheetahs at home? No, we donated to a charity that protects wild cheetahs in South Africa. Our parents told us that if we did not protect them, we might not be able to see cheetahs in the near future.

We soon became interested in helping other endangered animals. A few years later, with help from our parents, we created a non-profit organization to protect them. We wanted the next generation to be able to see these animals, so we named our organization One More Generation. We also studied endangered animals and educated our friends about them.

for example 예를 들어

leader 리더, 지도자, 대표

although ～임에도 불구하고, 비록 ～이지만

teenager 십 대, 청소년

actually 실제로

be able to ～할 수 있다

adopt 입양하다

cheetah 치타

raise 기르다

donate 기부하다, 기증하다

charity 자선단체, 자선

endangered 멸종 위기의

non-profit organization 비영리 단체

generation 세대

educate 가르치다, 교육하다

 확인문제

● 다음 문장이 본문의 내용과 일치하면 T, 일치하지 않으면 F를 쓰시오.

1 Carter and Olivia Ries are only teenagers, but they have actually made a difference in the world. ☐

2 Carter and Olivia have actually made no difference in the world. ☐

3 Carter and Olivia each adopted a cheetah. ☐

4 Carter and Olivia raised cheetahs at home. ☐

5 Carter and Olivia became interested in helping endangered animals. ☐

6 Carter and Olivia created a profit-making organization to protect endangered animals. ☐

Then one day, a terrible oil spill occurred in the Gulf of Mexico. A lot of sea animals were completely covered with oil, and they were dying. We had to do something. We started collecting animal rescue supplies such as pet carrying cages and rubber gloves from everyone in our neighborhood. Four months later, our family drove to the Gulf of Mexico to deliver what we collected and helped to save the animals. While we were working there, we learned something very useful. When we put mayonnaise into a turtle's throat, the turtle threw up. That way, we were able to get oil out of turtles. I never knew mayonnaise could be used to save animals!

On our last day, we met a marine life specialist. She told us that plastic waste is more dangerous to sea animals than oil spills are. A lot of sea animals and sea birds die from eating plastic waste. After we came home, we created an educational project about how to reduce plastic waste. In addition to this, our organization continues to do various projects to save animals. Although we started small, we are making a big difference. What you do today can change the world, so take that first step!

spill 유출

occur 일어나다, 발생하다

gulf 만

rescue 구조, 구출

supply 공급 (pl. supplies 물품, 보급품)

rubber 고무

neighborhood 이웃, 근처

deliver 전달하다, 배달하다

mayonnaise 마요네즈

throat 목구멍, 목

throw up 토하다

marine 해양의

specialist 전문가

waste 쓰레기

reduce 줄이다

in addition to ~ 이외에, ~에 더하여

various 다양한, 여러 가지의

확인문제

● 다음 문장이 본문의 내용과 일치하면 T, 일치하지 않으면 F를 쓰시오.

1 When a terrible oil spill occurred in the Gulf of Mexico, many sea animals were completely covered with oil. ☐

2 Carter's family drove to the Gulf of Mexico to deliver what they bought. ☐

3 Carter's family helped to save the animals covered with oil. ☐

4 Carter's family were able to get oil out of turtles with their hands. ☐

5 Plastic waste is more dangerous to sea animals than oil spills are. ☐

6 Carter's organization started big, so they are making a big difference. ☐

● 우리말을 참고하여 빈칸에 알맞은 말을 쓰시오.

1 Teens _____ _____

2 Many young people are making the world _____ _____ _____.

3 For example, Carter and Olivia Ries have become leaders _____ _____ _____.

4 _____ they are only teenagers, they _____ _____ _____ _____ _____ in the world.

5 _____ were they _____ _____ do that?

6 Let's _____ _____ Carter.

7 When I was five, my little sister Olivia and I _____ _____ a cheetah.

8 Did we _____ cheetahs _____ _____ ?

9 No, we _____ _____ _____ _____ that protects wild cheetahs in South Africa.

10 Our parents told us that if we did not protect them, we _____ _____ _____ _____ _____ _____ in the near future.

11 We soon _____ _____ _____ helping other _____.

12 A few years later, with help from our parents, we _____ _____ _____ _____ to protect them.

13 We wanted _____ _____ _____ to be able to see these animals, so we named our organization One More Generation.

14 We also studied endangered animals and _____ _____ _____ about them.

15 Then one day, _____ _____ _____ occurred in the Gulf of Mexico.

1 활약하는 십 대들

2 많은 젊은 사람들이 세상을 더 좋은 곳으로 만들고 있다.

3 예를 들어, Carter Ries와 Olivia Ries는 동물을 구하는 일에 리더가 되어 왔다.

4 비록 그들은 십 대일 뿐이지만, 실제로 세상에 변화를 일으켜 왔다.

5 그들은 어떻게 그것을 할 수 있었을까?

6 Carter의 이야기를 들어보자.

7 내가 다섯 살이었을 때, 나의 여동생 Olivia와 나는 각자 치타를 입양했다.

8 우리가 치타를 집에서 길렀을까?

9 아니, 우리는 남아프리카 공화국에 있는 야생 치타를 보호하는 자선단체에 기부했다.

10 부모님께서는 우리에게 우리가 그들을 보호하지 않으면, 가까운 미래에 치타를 볼 수 없을지도 모른다고 말씀하셨다.

11 우리는 곧 다른 멸종 위기의 동물들을 도와주는 것에 관심을 갖게 되었다.

12 몇 년 후에, 부모님의 도움으로, 우리는 그들을 보호하기 위해 비영리 단체를 만들었다.

13 우리는 다음 세대가 이러한 동물들을 볼 수 있기를 원했기에, 우리 단체를 One More Generation이라고 이름 붙였다.

14 우리는 또한 멸종 위기의 동물들을 연구했고 친구들에게 그들에 대해 가르쳐 주었다.

15 그러던 어느 날, 끔찍한 석유 유출 사건이 멕시코만에서 발생했다.

16 A lot of sea animals _____ _____ _____ _____ _____, and they were dying.

17 We _____ _____ _____ something.

18 We started collecting _____ _____ _____ such as pet carrying cages and rubber gloves from everyone _____ _____ _____.

19 Four months later, our family drove to the Gulf of Mexico to deliver _____ _____ _____ and helped _____ _____ _____.

20 While we were working there, we learned _____ _____ _____.

21 When we put mayonnaise into a turtle's throat, the turtle _____ _____.

22 That way, we were able to _____ oil _____ _____ turtles.

23 I never knew mayonnaise _____ _____ _____ to save animals!

24 On our last day, we met a _____ _____ _____.

25 She told us that plastic waste is _____ _____ to sea animals _____ oil spills are.

26 A lot of sea animals and sea birds _____ _____ _____ plastic waste.

27 After we came home, we _____ _____ _____ _____ about how to reduce plastic waste.

28 _____ _____ _____ this, our organization continues to do various projects to save animals.

29 Although we started small, we are _____ _____ _____.

30 _____ you do today can change the world, so _____ _____ _____ _____!

16	많은 해양 동물들이 완전히 기름을 뒤집어썼고, 죽어가고 있었다.
17	우리는 무엇인가를 해야만 했다.
18	우리는 애완동물 수송용 우리와 고무장갑과 같은 동물 구조 물품들을 동네의 모든 사람으로부터 모으기 시작했다.
19	4개월 후에, 우리 가족은 우리가 모았던 것들을 전달하기 위해서 멕시코만으로 운전해 갔으며 동물들을 구하는 일을 도왔다.
20	거기서 일하는 동안에, 우리는 매우 유용한 것을 배웠다.
21	마요네즈를 거북이의 목구멍에 집어넣으면, 거북이가 토했다.
22	그런 식으로, 우리는 거북이들에게서 기름을 빼낼 수 있었다.
23	나는 마요네즈가 동물을 구하는 데 사용될 수 있다는 것을 전혀 알지 못했다!
24	마지막 날에, 우리는 해양 생물 전문가를 만났다.
25	그녀는 우리에게 석유 유출보다 플라스틱 쓰레기가 해양 동물에게 더 위험하다고 말했다.
26	많은 해양 동물과 바다 새들이 플라스틱 쓰레기를 먹어서 죽는다.
27	집으로 돌아온 후, 우리는 플라스틱 쓰레기를 줄일 수 있는 방법에 관한 교육 프로젝트를 만들었다.
28	이것 외에도, 우리 단체는 동물들을 구하기 위한 다양한 프로젝트들을 계속하고 있다.
29	비록 우리는 작은 것부터 시작했지만, 큰 변화를 만들어 내고 있는 중이다.
30	당신이 오늘 하는 일이 세상을 바꿀 수 있기에, 첫발을 내디뎌라!

● 우리말을 참고하여 본문을 영작하시오.

1 활약하는 십 대들

➡ _____

2 많은 젊은 사람들이 세상을 더 좋은 곳으로 만들고 있다.

➡ _____

3 예를 들어, Carter Ries와 Olivia Ries는 동물을 구하는 일에 리더가 되어 왔다.

➡ _____

4 비록 그들은 십 대일 뿐이지만, 실제로 세상에 변화를 일으켜 왔다.

➡ _____

5 그들은 어떻게 그것을 할 수 있었을까?

➡ _____

6 Carter의 이야기를 들어보자.

➡ _____

7 내가 다섯 살이었을 때, 나의 여동생 Olivia와 나는 각자 치타를 입양했다.

➡ _____

8 우리가 치타를 집에서 길렀을까?

➡ _____

9 우리는 남아프리카 공화국에 있는 야생 치타를 보호하는 자선단체에 기부했다.

➡ _____

10 부모님께서는 우리에게 우리가 그들을 보호하지 않으면, 가까운 미래에 치타를 볼 수 없을지도 모른다고 말씀하셨다.

➡ _____

_____

11 우리는 곧 다른 멸종 위기의 동물들을 도와주는 것에 관심을 갖게 되었다.

➡ _____

12 몇 년 후에, 부모님의 도움으로, 우리는 그들을 보호하기 위해 비영리 단체를 만들었다.

➡ _____

13 우리는 다음 세대가 이러한 동물들을 볼 수 있기를 원했기에, 우리 단체를 One More Generation 이라고 이름 붙였다.

➡ _____

_____

14 우리는 또한 멸종 위기의 동물들을 연구했고 친구들에게 그들에 대해 가르쳐 주었다.

➡ _____

15 그러던 어느 날, 끔찍한 석유 유출 사건이 멕시코만에서 발생했다.

➡ _____

16 많은 해양 동물들이 완전히 기름을 뒤집어썼고, 죽어가고 있었다.

➡ _____

17 우리는 무엇인가를 해야만 했다.

➡ _____

18 우리는 애완동물 수송용 우리와 고무장갑과 같은 동물 구조 물품들을 동네의 모든 사람으로부터
모으기 시작했다.

➡ _____

_____

19 4개월 후에, 우리 가족은 우리가 모았던 것들을 전달하기 위해서 멕시코만으로 운전해 갔으며
동물들을 구하는 일을 도왔다.

➡ _____

_____

20 거기서 일하는 동안에, 우리는 매우 유용한 것을 배웠다.

➡ _____

21 마요네즈를 거북이의 목구멍에 집어넣으면, 거북이가 토했다.

➡ _____

22 그런 식으로, 우리는 거북이들에게서 기름을 빼낼 수 있었다.

➡ _____

23 나는 마요네즈가 동물을 구하는 데 사용될 수 있다는 것을 전혀 알지 못했다!

➡ _____

24 마지막 날에, 우리는 해양 생물 전문가를 만났다.

➡ _____

25 그녀는 우리에게 석유 유출보다 플라스틱 쓰레기가 해양 동물에게 더 위험하다고 말했다.

➡ _____

26 많은 해양 동물과 바다 새들이 플라스틱 쓰레기를 먹어서 죽는다.

➡ _____

27 집으로 돌아온 후, 우리는 플라스틱 쓰레기를 줄일 수 있는 방법에 관한 교육 프로젝트를 만들었다.

➡ _____

28 이것 외에도, 우리 단체는 동물들을 구하기 위한 다양한 프로젝트들을 계속하고 있다.

➡ _____

29 비록 우리는 작은 것부터 시작했지만, 큰 변화를 만들어 내고 있는 중이다.

➡ _____

30 당신이 오늘 하는 일이 세상을 바꿀 수 있기에, 첫발을 내디뎌라!

➡ _____

[01~03] 다음 글을 읽고 물음에 답하시오.

Many young people are making the world a better place. ⓐ_____, Carter and Olivia Ries have become leaders in saving animals. Although they are only teenagers, they have ⓑactually made a difference in the world. ⓒHow were they able to do that? Let's hear from Carter.

01 위 글의 빈칸 ⓐ에 들어갈 알맞은 말을 고르시오.

① As a result
② Moreover
③ However
④ For example
⑤ In addition

02 위 글의 밑줄 친 ⓑactually와 뜻이 같은 말을 모두 고르시오.

① in fact
② especially
③ in reality
④ extremely
⑤ probably

서답형
03 위 글의 밑줄 친 ⓒ를 다음과 같이 바꿔 쓸 때 빈칸에 들어갈 알맞은 단어를 쓰시오.

➡ How was it _____ for them to do that?

[04~06] 다음 글을 읽고 물음에 답하시오.

When I was five, my little sister Olivia and I each adopted a cheetah. Did we raise cheetahs at home? No, we donated ⓐ_____ a charity that protects wild cheetahs in South Africa. Our parents told us that if we did not protect ①them, we might not be able to see cheetahs in the near future.

We soon became interested ⓑ_____ helping ②other endangered animals. A few years later, with help from our parents, we created a non-profit organization to protect ③them. We wanted the next generation to be able to see ④these animals, so we named our organization One More Generation. We also studied endangered animals and educated our friends about ⑤them. <I: Carter>

04 위 글의 빈칸 ⓐ와 ⓑ에 들어갈 전치사가 바르게 짝지어진 것은?

　　ⓐ　ⓑ　　　　　　　　　ⓐ　ⓑ
① on – at　　　　　② to – by
③ to – in　　　　　④ for – by
⑤ on – in

05 밑줄 친 ①~⑤ 중에서 가리키는 대상이 나머지 넷과 다른 것은?

①　　　②　　　③　　　④　　　⑤

06 According to the passage, which is NOT true about Carter and Olivia?

① They raised cheetahs at home.
② They became interested in helping other endangered animals.
③ They created a non-profit organization with help from their parents.
④ They named their organization One More Generation.
⑤ They educated their friends about endangered animals.

[07~09] 다음 글을 읽고 물음에 답하시오.

Then one day, a terrible oil spill occurred in the Gulf of Mexico. A lot of sea animals were completely covered with oil, and they were dying. We had to do something. We started collecting animal rescue supplies such as pet carrying cages and rubber gloves from everyone in our neighborhood. Four months later, our family drove to the Gulf of Mexico to deliver what we collected and helped ⓐto save the animals. While we were working there, we learned something very useful. When we put mayonnaise into a turtle's throat, the turtle threw up. That way, we were able to get oil out of turtles. I never knew mayonnaise could be used ⓑto save animals! <I: Carter>

07 다음 보기에서 위 글의 밑줄 친 ⓐto save, ⓑto save와 to 부정사의 용법이 같은 것을 각각 모두 고르시오.

① It is worthwhile to save such animals.
② He was happy to save such animals.
③ It is too late to save such animals.
④ My dream is to save such animals.
⑤ She must be considerate to save such animals.

➡ ⓐ와 같은 것: _____
중요 ⓑ와 같은 것: _____

08 위 글의 주제로 알맞은 것을 고르시오.

① an oil spill and serious water pollution
② the cause of a terrible oil spill in the Gulf of Mexico
③ the activities to save animals dying from an oil spill
④ collecting animal rescue supplies
⑤ the way to use mayonnaise to save animals

09 위 글에서 알 수 있는 Carter의 심경 변화로 가장 알맞은 것을 고르시오.

① delighted → puzzled
② sympathetic → surprised
③ depressed → nervous
④ regretful → confused
⑤ relieved → astonished

[10~12] 다음 글을 읽고 물음에 답하시오.

On our last day, we met a marine life specialist. She told us that plastic waste is more dangerous to sea animals than oil spills are. (A)많은 해양 동물과 바다 새들이 플라스틱 쓰레기를 먹어서 죽는다. After we came home, we created an educational project about how to reduce plastic waste. ___ⓐ___ this, our organization continues to do various projects to save animals. (B)Since we started small, we are making a big difference. What you do today can change the world, so take that first step!

중요
10 위 글의 빈칸 ⓐ에 들어갈 알맞은 말을 모두 고르시오.

① Besides   ② In contrast to
③ Instead of   ④ In addition to
⑤ As a result of

서답형
11 위 글의 밑줄 친 (A)의 우리말에 맞게 주어진 어휘를 이용하여 13 단어로 영작하시오.

a lot of, from

➡ _____
_____

서답형

12 위 글의 밑줄 친 (B)에서 흐름상 어색한 부분을 찾아 고치시오.

_____ ➡ _____

[13~15] 다음 글을 읽고 물음에 답하시오.

Many young people are making the world a better place. For example, Carter and Olivia Ries have become leaders in ⓐsaving animals. Although they are only teenagers, they have actually made a difference in the world. How were they able to ⓑdo that? Let's hear from Carter.

13 아래 〈보기〉에서 위 글의 밑줄 친 ⓐsaving과 문법적 쓰임이 다른 것의 개수를 고르시오.

┌─── 보기 ├───
① Look at the <u>running</u> boys.
② People have fears about <u>barking</u> dogs.
③ He is good at <u>playing</u> tennis.
④ <u>Reading</u> letters from pen pals is pleasant.
⑤ She tried to calm a <u>crying</u> child down.
└────────────┘

① 1개　② 2개　③ 3개　④ 4개　⑤ 5개

서답형

14 밑줄 친 ⓑ를 다음과 같이 바꿔 쓸 때 빈칸에 들어갈 알맞은 말을 한 단어 쓰시오.

➡ make a _____ in the world

15 위 글의 다음에 올 내용으로 가장 알맞은 것을 고르시오.

① the introduction about many leaders in the world
② the story about many interesting animals
③ the process of creating a non-profit organization
④ many challenges to make a difference in the world
⑤ the story of Carter who has made a difference in the world

[16~17] 다음 글을 읽고 물음에 답하시오.

On our last day, we met a marine life specialist. She told us that plastic ⓐwaste is more dangerous to sea animals than oil spills are. A lot of sea animals and sea birds die from eating plastic waste. After we came home, we created an educational project about how to reduce plastic waste. In addition to this, our organization continues to do various projects to save animals. Although we started small, we are making a big difference. What you do today can change the world, so take that first step!

16 위 글의 밑줄 친 ⓐwaste와 같은 의미로 쓰인 것을 고르시오.

① These meetings are a complete <u>waste</u> of time.
② Don't <u>waste</u> a good opportunity.
③ We should reduce household <u>waste</u>.
④ You should utilize your <u>waste</u> talents.
⑤ I have no time to <u>waste</u>.

17 위 글에 어울리는 속담으로 가장 알맞은 것을 고르시오.

① Look before you leap.
② It never rains but it pours.
③ Haste makes waste.
④ A bird in the hand is worth two in the bush.
⑤ Well begun is half done.

[18~20] 다음 글을 읽고 물음에 답하시오.

When I was five, my little sister Olivia and I each ___ⓐ___ a cheetah. Did we raise cheetahs at home? No, we donated to a charity that protects wild cheetahs in South Africa. (①) Our parents told us that if we did not protect them, we might not be able to see cheetahs in the near future. (②)

We soon became interested in helping other endangered animals. (③) We wanted the next generation to be able to see these animals, so we named our organization One More Generation. (④) We also studied endangered animals and educated our friends about them. (⑤)

<I: Carter>

서답형

18 주어진 영영풀이를 참고하여 빈칸 ⓐ에 철자 a로 시작하는 단어를 쓰시오. (시제를 어법에 맞게 쓰시오.)

take into one's family

➡ _____

19 위 글의 흐름으로 보아, 주어진 문장이 들어가기에 가장 적절한 곳은?

A few years later, with help from our parents, we created a non-profit organization to protect them.

①   ②   ③   ④   ⑤

중요

20 위 글의 제목으로 알맞은 것을 고르시오.

① The Easiest Way to Adopt a Cheetah
② The Way to Raise Cheetahs at Home
③ How to See Cheetahs Now and for Ever
④ The Background of the Creation of One More Generation
⑤ How to Create a Non-profit Organization

[21~23] 다음 글을 읽고 물음에 답하시오.

Then one day, a terrible oil spill occurred in the Gulf of Mexico. A lot of sea animals were completely covered with oil, and they were dying. We had to do something. We started collecting animal rescue supplies such as pet carrying cages and rubber gloves from everyone in our neighborhood. Four months later, our family drove to the Gulf of Mexico to deliver ___ⓐ___ we collected and helped to save the animals. While we were working there, we learned something very useful. When we put mayonnaise into a turtle's throat, the turtle ⓑthrew up. That way, we were able to get oil out of turtles. I never knew mayonnaise could be used to save animals!

21 위 글의 빈칸 ⓐ에 들어갈 알맞은 말을 고르시오.

① that   ② when   ③ as
④ what   ⑤ which

서답형

22 위 글의 밑줄 친 ⓑthrew up과 바꿔 쓸 수 있는 한 단어를 쓰시오.

➡ _____

중요

23 According to the passage, which is NOT true?

① One day, there was a terrible oil spill in the Gulf of Mexico.
② A lot of sea animals were dying as they were completely covered with oil.
③ Carter's family collected animal rescue supplies from their neighbors.
④ Carter's family flew to the Gulf of Mexico to deliver what they collected.
⑤ Carter's family learned when they put mayonnaise into a turtle's throat, the turtle threw up.

[01~03] 다음 글을 읽고 물음에 답하시오.

When I was five, my little sister Olivia and I each adopted a cheetah. Did we raise cheetahs at home? No, we donated to a charity that protects wild cheetahs in South Africa. Our parents told us that if we did not protect them, ⓐ we might not be able to see cheetahs in the near future.

We soon became interested in helping other endangered animals. A few years later, ⓑ 부모님의 도움으로, 우리는 그들을 보호하기 위해 비영리 단체를 만들었다. We wanted the next generation to be able to see these animals, so we named our organization One More Generation. We also studied endangered animals and educated our friends about them.

<I: Carter>

01 위 글의 밑줄 친 ⓐ를 참조하여, 다음 빈칸에 알맞은 단어를 넣어 cheetah에 대한 소개를 완성하시오.

> Cheetahs are _____ animals.

02 위 글의 밑줄 친 ⓑ의 우리말에 맞게 주어진 어휘를 이용하여 13 단어로 영작하시오.

> with, to protect

➡ _____

_____ 또는

_____

_____

03 After Carter and Olivia adopted cheetahs, how did they raise them? Answer in English in a full sentence. (12 words)

➡ _____

_____

[04~06] 다음 글을 읽고 물음에 답하시오.

ⓐThen one day, a terrible oil spill was occurred in the Gulf of Mexico. A lot of sea animals were completely covered with oil, and they were dying. We had to do something. We started collecting animal rescue supplies such as pet carrying cages and rubber gloves from everyone in our neighborhood. Four months later, our family drove to the Gulf of Mexico to deliver ⓑ what we collected and helped to save the animals. While we were working there, we learned something very useful. When we put mayonnaise into a turtle's throat, the turtle threw up. That way, we were able to get oil out of turtles. I never knew mayonnaise could be used to save animals!

04 위 글의 밑줄 친 ⓐ에서 어법상 틀린 부분을 찾아 고치시오.

_____ ➡ _____

05 위 글의 밑줄 친 ⓑwhat과 바꿔 쓸 수 있는 말을 세 단어로 쓰시오.

➡ _____

06 What did the writer's family learn while they were working in the Gulf of Mexico? Fill in the blanks (A) and (B) with suitable words.

> They learned that a turtle (A)_____ _____ when they put (B)_____ into the turtle's throat.

[07~09] 다음 글을 읽고 물음에 답하시오.

When I was five, my little sister Olivia and I each adopted a cheetah. Did we raise cheetahs at home? No, we donated to a charity that protects wild cheetahs in South Africa. Our parents told us that if we did not protect them, we might not be able to see cheetahs in the near future.

We soon became interested in helping other endangered animals. A few years later, with help from our parents, we created a non-profit organization to protect them. ⓐWe wanted the next generation to be able to see these animals, so we named our organization One More Generation. We also studied endangered animals and educated our friends about them. <I: Carter>

07 다음 문장에서 위 글의 내용과 <u>다른</u> 부분을 찾아서 고치시오. (두 군데)

> Carter and Olivia adopted a cheetah and donated it to a charity that protects wild cheetahs in South Africa.

_____ ➡ _____, _____ ➡ _____

08 Who helped Carter and Olivia create a non-profit organization to protect the endangered animals? Fill in the blanks with suitable words.

> _____ _____ helped them.

09 위 글의 밑줄 친 ⓐ를 다음과 같이 바꿔 쓸 때 빈칸에 들어갈 알맞은 말을 두 단어로 쓰시오.

➡ _____ we wanted the next generation to be able to see these animals, we named our organization One More Generation.

[10~12] 다음 글을 읽고 물음에 답하시오.

On our last day, we met a marine life specialist. She told us that plastic waste is more dangerous to sea animals than oil spills ⓐare. A lot of sea animals and sea birds die from eating plastic waste. After we came home, we created an educational project about how to reduce plastic waste. In addition to ⓑthis, our organization continues to do various projects to save animals. Although we started small, we are making a big difference. What you do today can change the world, so take that first step! <we: Carter's family>

10 위 글의 밑줄 친 ⓐare 뒤에 생략된 말을 쓰시오.

➡ _____

11 위 글의 밑줄 친 ⓑthis가 가리키는 내용을 우리말로 쓰시오.

➡ _____
_____

12 본문의 내용과 일치하도록 다음 빈칸 (A)와 (B)에 알맞은 단어를 쓰시오.

> Carter's family came to know that plastic waste is more dangerous to sea animals than oil spills are, so they created an educational project about how to _____ _____ _____.

After You Read B

A: Why don't you join One More Generation?
　Why don't you 동사원형 ~? = How[What] about ~ing?: ~하는 게 어때?

B: What is that?

A: It is a non-profit organization that protects endangered animals.
　　　　　　　　　　　　　　　　= which(주격 관계대명사)

B: What does One More Generation mean?

A: The organization wants the next generation to be able to see those animals.
　　　　　　　　　　want+목적어+to부정사　　　　　　　　　= endangered animals

B: That's a great organization. I'll join it.
　　　　　　　　　　　　　　= One More Generation

구문해설 • non-profit organization: 비영리 단체 • endangered: 멸종 위기의 • generation: 세대

해석

A: One More Generation 에 가입하는 것이 어때?

B: 그게 무엇이니?

A: 그것은 멸종 위기의 동물들을 보호하는 비영리 단체야.

B: One More Generation 이 무슨 뜻이니?

A: 그 단체는 다음 세대가 그러한 동물들을 볼 수 있기를 원해.

B: 그것은 멋진 단체구나. 나는 거기에 가입할게.

Link Science – Share

Asian black bears have a white V-shape on their chests. They mostly live

in forests in Asia. They've become endangered because people hunt them
　　　　　　　　　　　　　　　　이유를 나타내는 접속사(= as. since) = Asian black bears

for their body parts and destroy forests. We'll tell you what you can do for
　　　　　　　　　hunt와 접속사 and로 연결　　　　　tell의 간접목적어　　　직접목적어

them. First, use less paper to protect forests. Second, you should not buy any
　　　　　　　　　　　to부정사의 부사적 용법(~하기 위해서)　　　　　~하지 말아야 한다

Asian black bear products.

구문해설 • V-shape: V 모양의, V자 형의 • chest: 가슴 • mostly: 주로 • live in: ~에서 살다
• endangered: 멸종 위기에 처한

아시아흑곰은 가슴에 흰색의 V 모양을 갖고 있습니다. 그들은 주로 아시아의 숲에서 삽니다. 그들은 사람들이 그들의 신체 부분을 얻으려고 사냥을 하고 숲을 파괴하기 때문에 멸종 위기에 처했습니다. 우리는 그들을 위해 여러분이 무엇을 할 수 있는지 말하고자 합니다. 첫째, 숲을 보호하기 위해서 종이를 덜 사용하세요. 둘째, 어떤 아시아의 흑곰 제품도 사지 말아야 합니다.

Write

Air pollution is one of the most serious environmental problems these days.
　　　　　　　　(~들 중) 하나

Although cars make our lives convenient, they produce a lot of smoke that
비록 ~할지라도(접속사)　　　　　　　　　　　= cars　　　= much　　　주격 관계대명사

pollutes the air. That is a big problem. Here is what we can do. We can
　　　　　　　　　　　　　　　　　　　　　관계대명사(선행사 포함)

take the bus or subway more. We can also buy local products because they do
take+교통수단: ~을 타다

not need to be shipped very far. Even simple actions like these can help.
　　　　　　배송되다　　　　심지어(부사)　　　　　~와 같은　　　도움이 되다

구문해설 • air pollution: 공기오염(공해) • serious: 심각한 • these days 요즘
• convenient: 편리한 • local product: 현지 상품

공해는 요즘 가장 심각한 환경 문제들 중의 하나이다. 비록 자동차가 우리의 생활을 편리하게 하지만, 자동차는 공기를 오염시키는 매연을 많이 만들어낸다. 그것은 커다란 문제이다. 우리가 할 수 있는 일이 있다. 우리는 버스나 지하철을 더 많이 이용할 수 있다. 우리는 또한 현지에서 생산된 상품은 매우 멀리 배송될 필요가 없기 때문에 지역의 제품들을 구매할 수 있다. 이런 일들과 같은 간단한 행동들조차 환경에는 도움이 될 수 있다.

Words & Expressions

01 밑줄 친 부분과 바꿔 쓸 수 있는 말을 고르시오.

> Do you think they can <u>repair</u> the damage?

① harm   ② control
③ fix   ④ destroy
⑤ supply

02 빈칸에 들어갈 말이 나머지와 <u>다른</u> 하나를 고르시오.

① In addition _____ discounts, they offer a free gift.
② I share a bedroom _____ my brother.
③ He read the letter aloud _____ us.
④ Can you send it _____ me by fax?
⑤ Can you lend some money _____ me until tomorrow?

03 다음 짝지어진 두 단어의 관계가 같도록 빈칸에 알맞은 말을 쓰시오.

> marry : marriage = protect : _____

04 다음 빈칸에 공통으로 들어갈 말을 쓰시오.

> • I can't tell you how much difference exercise has _____ in my life.
> • They _____ a big discovery of water on the Mars.

Conversation

[05~06] 다음 대화를 읽고 물음에 답하시오.

> B: What are you doing this weekend? (①)
> G: (②) _____ (A) _____
> B: (③) Sounds good. (④) Can I join you?
> G: Sure. (⑤)
> B: O.K.

05 ①~⑤ 중 주어진 문장이 들어갈 곳은?

> Let's meet in front of the park at ten.

①   ②   ③   ④   ⑤

06 빈칸 (A)에 알맞은 말을 고르시오.

① You want me to take a picture.
② I'm reading a book.
③ I am playing soccer with my friends.
④ I'm thinking of watching a movie every weekend.
⑤ I'm thinking of going for a bike ride.

[07~08] 다음 대화를 읽고 물음에 답하시오.

> A: My bike broke ___(A)___ .
> B: Do you want me ___(B)___ (fix) it?
> A: Yes, please.

07 빈칸 (A)에 알맞은 말을 고르시오.

① down   ② with   ③ up
④ on   ⑤ off

08 괄호 안의 단어를 어법에 맞게 빈칸 (B)에 쓰시오

➡ _____

[09~12] 다음 대화를 읽고 물음에 답하시오.

> **Suho:** Anna, do you have any children's books you don't read any longer?
>
> **Anna:** Sure. Why?
>
> **Suho:** I'm thinking of sending some books to children in Africa. My aunt told me that they need books (a)to read.
>
> **Anna:** Good idea, Suho! Wait, aren't your books in Korean?
>
> **Suho:** Oh, that's a problem.
>
> **Anna:** Well, how about translating them into English?
>
> **Suho:** Translating? That's a great idea, Anna.
>
> **Anna:** 너는 내가 너를 도와주기를 원하니?
>
> **Suho:** Sure. ___(A)___ we run into any difficult expressions, let's ask our English teacher for help.
>
> **Anna:** O.K. It's really great that we can help the children in Africa.

09 빈칸 (A)에 알맞은 말을 고르시오.

① Although ② Wherever
③ If ④ Because
⑤ Since

10 밑줄 친 (a)와 같은 용법으로 쓰이지 <u>않은</u> 것을 고르시오.

① Every student wrote down one thing <u>to achieve</u> this year.
② I'd like to open a flea market at school <u>to help</u> poor people.
③ I need a warm jacket <u>to wear</u> at night.
④ I need some books <u>to read</u> on the plane.
⑤ I have many letters <u>to write</u>.

11 대화에서 다음 영영풀이에 해당하는 단어를 찾아 쓰시오.

> to change written or spoken words into another language

➡ _____

12 밑줄 친 우리말을 주어진 단어를 이용하여 영작하시오. (want, help)

➡ _____

Grammar

13 다음 중 어법상 옳은 문장은 <u>모두</u> 몇 개인지 고르시오.

> ⓐ In spite of Brian was a great poet, he wasn't famous at that time.
> ⓑ Despite Jenny is so old, she still leads an active life.
> ⓒ Though the danger sign, my friends and I swam in the river.
> ⓓ The families enjoyed the day at the park even though the bad weather.
> ⓔ Although the heavy snow, the game was not canceled.
> ⓕ The employees drink coffee every day although it makes them anxious.

① 0개 ② 1개 ③ 2개 ④ 3개 ⑤ 4개

14 다음 빈칸에 알맞은 말이 바르게 짝지어진 것은?

> • The photographer showed me _____ were taken in front of the Blue House.
> • Cathy didn't have breakfast _____ she was very hungry.

① what – though ② that – though
③ whose – although ④ what – since
⑤ that – since

15 다음 그림을 보고 빈칸에 맞는 단어를 채우시오.

(1)

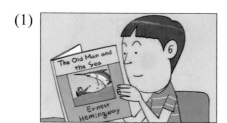

➡ _____ _____ I have been reading *The Old Man and the Sea* for three days, I don't understand it at all.

(2)

➡ The pyramids showed _____ the ancient Egyptians believed 4,000 years ago.

16 다음 중 밑줄 친 부분이 가장 자연스러운 것을 고르시오.

① <u>Although</u> Clara felt uncomfortable with the waist, she came home early.
② <u>Although</u> Tammy was climbing up the mountain, it started to rain.
③ <u>Although</u> my daddy has strong immunity, he caught a bad cold
④ <u>Although</u> Marc was 11 months old, he couldn't understand the situation.
⑤ <u>Although</u> they agree or disagree isn't important.

17 다음 두 문장을 관계대명사를 이용하여, 하나의 문장으로 만드시오.

(1) • This is not the thing.
　　• Hermione has always wanted it.
　➡ _____

(2) • The neighbors know the things.
　　• They happened two months ago.
　➡ _____
　　_____

(3) • Tell Sam's father the things.
　　• The things have bothered him.
　➡ _____

18 다음 두 문장의 의미가 같도록 빈칸에 알맞은 말을 쓰시오.

(1) Helen's family was poor, but they always helped others.
　➡ _____ _____ _____ _____
　　_____, they always helped others.

(2) Figure skating was an unpopular sport, but Yu-na changed people's perception.
　➡ _____ _____ _____ _____
　　_____ _____ _____, Yu-na changed people's perception.

19 다음 그림을 표현하는 문장을 〈보기〉의 단어를 사용하여 쓰시오. (It으로 시작)

┌─ 보기 ┐
I / that / myself / it / sweated / fanned /
so / even / a / hot / was / lot / I / though
└──────┘

➡ _____
　_____

Reading

[20~21] 다음 글을 읽고 물음에 답하시오.

When I was five, my little sister Olivia and I each adopted a cheetah. Did we raise cheetahs at home? No, we donated to a charity ⓐthat protects wild cheetahs in South Africa. Our parents told us ⓑthat if we did not protect them, we might not be able to see cheetahs in the near future.

We soon became interested in helping other endangered animals. A few years later, with help from our parents, we created a non-profit organization to protect them. We wanted the next generation to be able to see these animals, so we named our organization One More Generation. We also studied endangered animals and educated our friends about them.

<I: Carter>

20 다음 〈보기〉에서 위 글의 밑줄 친 ⓐthat, ⓑthat과 문법적 쓰임이 같은 것을 각각 모두 고르시오.

┌─── 보기 ───┐
① There was no hope that she would recover her health.
② This is all that matters.
③ The trouble is that we are short of money.
④ He is so poor that he cannot buy it.
⑤ The people that I spoke to were very helpful.

➡ ⓐthat과 같은 것: _____,
　 ⓑthat과 같은 것: _____

21 다음 중 Carter와 Olivia가 한 일이 <u>아닌</u> 것을 고르시오.

① 각자 치타를 입양했다.
② 남아프리카 공화국에 있는 야생 치타를 보호하는 자선단체에 치타를 기부했다.

③ 멸종 위기의 동물들을 도와주는 것에 관심을 갖게 되었다.
④ 멸종 위기의 동물들을 보호하기 위해 비영리 단체를 만들었다.
⑤ 친구들로부터 멸종 위기의 동물들에 대해 배웠다.

[22~24] 다음 글을 읽고 물음에 답하시오.

Then one day, a terrible oil spill occurred in the Gulf of Mexico. (①) A lot of sea animals were completely covered with oil, and they were dying. (②) We had to do something. (③) Four months later, our family drove to the Gulf of Mexico to deliver what we collected and helped to save the animals. (④) While we were working there, we learned something very useful. (⑤) When we put mayonnaise ⓐ_____ a turtle's throat, the turtle threw up. That way, we were able to get oil ⓑ_____ turtles. I never knew mayonnaise could be used to save animals!

22 위 글의 빈칸 ⓐ와 ⓑ에 들어갈 전치사가 바르게 짝지어진 것은?

| | ⓐ | ⓑ | | ⓐ | ⓑ |
① on – out of　　② into – by
③ for – from　　④ on – from
⑤ into – out of

23 위 글의 흐름으로 보아, 주어진 문장이 들어가기에 가장 적절한 곳은?

We started collecting animal rescue supplies such as pet carrying cages and rubber gloves from everyone in our neighborhood.

①　　②　　③　　④　　⑤

24 다음 중 위 글의 내용에 대한 이해가 옳지 <u>않은</u> 사람을 고르시오.

① 미수: One day, a terrible oil spill occurred in the writer's neighborhood.
② 경혜: Lots of sea animals were dying because they were completely covered with oil.
③ 호영: Four months later, the writer's family delivered what they had collected from their neighbors.
④ 규철: The writer's family learned that the turtle threw up when they put mayonnaise into its throat.
⑤ 성진: The writer never knew mayonnaise could be used to save animals.

[25~27] 다음 글을 읽고 물음에 답하시오.

On our last day, we met a _____ⓐ_____ life specialist. She told us that plastic waste is more dangerous to sea animals than oil spills are. A lot of sea animals and sea birds die from eating plastic waste. After we came home, we created an educational project about how to reduce plastic waste. In addition to this, our organization continues to do various projects to save animals. Although we started small, we are _____ⓑ_____. ⓒ당신이 오늘 하는 일이 세상을 바꿀 수 있다, so take that first step!

<we: Carter's family>

25 주어진 영영풀이를 참고하여 빈칸 ⓐ에는 철자 m으로 시작하는 단어를, 빈칸 ⓑ에는 big을 포함한 4 단어를 쓰시오.

> ⓐ of the sea or relating to the sea
> ⓑ carrying out an action, the result of which is a significant change

➡ ⓐ _____ ⓑ _____

26 위 글의 밑줄 친 ⓒ의 우리말에 맞게 한 단어를 보충하여, 주어진 어휘를 알맞게 배열하시오.

> the world / can / do / change / you / today

➡ _____

27 위 글의 주제로 알맞은 것을 고르시오.

① the effect of dangerous oil spills on marine environment
② the number of sea animals and sea birds eating plastic waste
③ making a big difference by doing various projects to save animals
④ various ways of changing the world
⑤ the difficulty of taking the first step to save animals

[28~29] 다음 대화를 읽고 물음에 답하시오.

A: ⓐ<u>Why don't you join One More Generation?</u>
B: What is ①<u>that</u>?
A: ②<u>It</u> is a non-profit organization that protects endangered animals.
B: What does One More Generation mean?
A: ③<u>The organization</u> wants ④<u>the next generation</u> to be able to see those animals.
B: That's a great organization. I'll join ⑤<u>it</u>.

28 위 글의 밑줄 친 ⓐ를 다음과 같이 바꿔 쓸 때 빈칸에 들어갈 알맞은 말을 두 단어로 쓰시오.

➡ _____ _____ joining One More Generation?

29 밑줄 친 ①~⑤ 중에서 가리키는 대상이 나머지 넷과 <u>다른</u> 것은?

①   ②   ③   ④   ⑤

단원별 예상문제

01 다음 짝지어진 단어의 관계가 같도록 빈칸에 알맞은 말을 쓰시오.

> occur : happen = expert : s_____

02 다음 빈칸에 공통으로 들어갈 말을 쓰시오. (대 · 소문자 무시, 한 단어)

(1)
> • What do you do if children _____ for help with their homework?
> • Is it all right if I _____ you to type this letter?

(2)
> • Here are a couple of tips they shared _____ me.
> • He was covered _____ dust while walking along the road.

03 빈칸 (A)와 (B)에 들어갈 말로 알맞은 것끼리 짝지어진 것을 고르시오.

> • ____(A)____ the people killed, one more was wounded.
> • ____(B)____ she has lots of money, she isn't happy.

	(A)	(B)
①	However	– Although
②	However	– Despite
③	In addition to	– Although
④	In addition to	– Despite
⑤	In addition to	– In spite of

04 다음 주어진 우리말에 맞게 빈칸을 채우시오. (철자가 주어진 경우 주어진 철자로 시작할 것)

(1) 제 고양이를 치료할 수 있겠어요?
➡ Will you be able _____ c_____ my cat?

(2) 그 차는 곧 고장이 날 것 같다.
➡ The car is likely to b_____ _____ soon.

(3) 그들은 재정적인 어려움을 만난 후에 작년에 회사를 팔기로 동의했다.
➡ They agreed to sell the company last year after they r_____ _____ financial problems.

(4) 매년 수많은 사람들이 기아로 죽어간다.
➡ Many thousands of people _____ _____ starvation every year.

[05~06] 다음 대화를 읽고 물음에 답하시오.

> M: Can we have pancakes for breakfast?
> W: (①) Sure. Oh, we don't have any eggs. (②)
> M: 가게에 가서 좀 사올까요? (③)
> W: Thanks, Mike. (④)
> M: Sure. (⑤)

05 ①~⑤ 중 주어진 문장이 들어갈 곳은?

> Can you get blueberry syrup, too?

①   ②   ③   ④   ⑤

출제율 95%

06 밑줄 친 우리말과 일치하도록 주어진 단어를 이용해 문장을 만드시오.

➡ _____

_____ (some, want, store, get)

출제율 95%

07 다음 대화의 빈칸에 들어갈 알맞은 말을 고르시오.

A: My bike broke down.
B: _____
A: Yes, please.

① Do you want me to share my umbrella with you?
② Do you want me to help you carry the box?
③ Do you want me to take a picture of you?
④ Do you want me to go to the store and get some curry?
⑤ Do you want me to fix it?

[08~10] 다음 대화를 읽고 물음에 답하시오.

G: ⓐ[What / How] are you doing this weekend? (①)
B: (②) I'm thinking ___(A)___ doing some volunteer work at the child-care center. (③)
G: What would you do there?
B: I would ⓑ[probable / probably] read some books ___(B)___ the children. (④)
G: That sounds interesting. (⑤)
B: Of course.

출제율 100%

08 ①~⑤ 중 주어진 문장이 들어갈 곳은?

Can I join you?

① ② ③ ④ ⑤

출제율 95%

09 위 대화의 괄호 ⓐ와 ⓑ에서 적절한 것을 골라 쓰시오.

➡ ⓐ _____ ⓑ _____

출제율 90%

10 위 대화의 빈칸 (A)와 (B)에 알맞은 전치사를 쓰시오.

➡ (A) _____ (B) _____

[11~12] 다음 대화를 읽고 물음에 답하시오.

B: What are you going ___ⓐ___ for the book review homework? (①)
G: (②) I'm ___ⓑ___ of ___ⓒ___ a book about young leaders. (③)
B: Good idea. (④)
G: Oh, could you ___ⓓ___ it to me? (⑤)
B: Sure. I'll ___ⓔ___ it tomorrow.

출제율 100%

11 빈칸 ⓐ~ⓔ에 들어가지 않는 말을 고르시오.

① reading   ② to read   ③ lend
④ considering   ⑤ bring

출제율 95%

12 ①~⑤ 중 주어진 문장이 들어갈 곳은?

I have the perfect book for you.

① ② ③ ④ ⑤

13 다음 주어진 문장의 밑줄 친 what과 같은 용법으로 쓰인 것을 모두 고르시오.

> What upset her was his attitude.

① What has she come here for?
② What do you think the speaker meant to deliver?
③ Those are what she has taught for almost 20 years so far.
④ I wonder what you were interested in.
⑤ What was regarded moral in the past is not always seen as such today.

14 다음 문장의 빈칸에 들어가기에 적절한 접속사를 〈보기〉에서 골라 쓰시오.

> ── 보기 ──
> if   although   since

(1) _____ you see a blue sky, let me know it so that I'll dry the laundries.
(2) _____ the problems seemed to be very simple, it took me quite a long time to solve them.
(3) _____ Paul doesn't want to go, I will not go to the meeting, either.
(4) John alone ate pork belly enough for five people _____ he was on a diet.
(5) _____ it rains tomorrow, I will stay home watching TV with my dog.
(6) Sumin often gets lost _____ she is so poor at finding right ways.

15 다음 중 어색한 문장을 모두 고르시오.

① Kelly is the only person which made Karl happy.
② Jane gave him what she had in her purse something valuable.

③ Despite Munch painted *The Scream* in 1893, it still impresses many people.
④ The kids believed what the magician showed them on the stage.
⑤ Though John took care of his sister, his father gave him the cold shoulder.
⑥ It was the books what he bought for Sarah yesterday.
⑦ All the citizens understood what the mayor announced.

16 다음 빈칸에 접속사 since, although 중에서 각각 알맞은 것을 골라 쓰시오.

(1) Alice was late for school _____ she got up early in the morning.
(2) Patrick got an A on the mathematics test _____ he studied very hard.
(3) _____ Daniel always has many friends around, he sometimes looks lonely.

[17~19] 다음 글을 읽고 물음에 답하시오.

Then one day, a (A)[terrible / terrific] oil spill occurred in the Gulf of Mexico. A lot of sea animals were completely covered with oil, and they were dying. We had to do something. We started collecting animal rescue supplies such as pet ⓐcarrying cages and rubber gloves (B)[for / from] everyone in our neighborhood. Four months later, our family drove to the Gulf of Mexico to deliver what we collected and helped to save the animals. While we were working there, we learned (C)[something very useful / very useful something]. When we put mayonnaise into a turtle's throat, the turtle threw up. That way, we were able to get oil out of turtles. I never knew mayonnaise could be used to save animals! <I: Carter>

출제율 90%

17 위 글의 괄호 (A)~(C)에서 문맥이나 어법상 알맞은 낱말을 골라 쓰시오.

➡ (A) _____ (B) _____

(C) _____

출제율 95%

18 위 글의 밑줄 친 @carrying과 문법적 쓰임이 같은 것을 모두 고르시오.

① I don't like a boring story.

② He bought a pair of running shoes.

③ He is a walking dictionary.

④ I need to buy a sleeping bag.

⑤ She is in the waiting room now.

출제율 100%

19 다음 중 글쓴이의 가족이 한 일이 아닌 것을 고르시오.

① 동물 구조 물품들을 동네의 모든 사람으로부터 모으기 시작했다.

② 애완동물 수송용 우리를 만들었다.

③ 그들이 모은 것들을 전달하기 위해서 멕시코만으로 운전해 갔다.

④ 멕시코만에서 동물들을 구하는 일을 도왔다.

⑤ 거북이들에게서 기름을 빼내 주었다.

[20~22] 다음 글을 읽고 물음에 답하시오.

On our (A)[last / latest] day, we met a marine life specialist. (①) She told us that plastic waste is more dangerous to sea animals than oil spills are. (②) A lot of sea animals and sea birds die (B)[for / from] eating plastic waste. (③) (C)[In addition to / In spite of] this, our organization continues to do various projects to save animals. (④) Although we started small, we are making a big difference. (⑤) What you do today can change the world, so take that first step!

출제율 90%

20 위 글의 괄호 (A)~(C)에서 문맥이나 어법상 알맞은 낱말을 골라 쓰시오.

➡ (A) _____ (B) _____

(B) _____

출제율 95%

21 위 글의 흐름으로 보아, 주어진 문장이 들어가기에 가장 적절한 곳은?

After we came home, we created an educational project about how to reduce plastic waste.

① ② ③ ④ ⑤

출제율 100%

22 According to the passage, which is NOT true?

① On their last day, Carter's family met a marine life specialist.

② A marine life specialist said that plastic waste is more dangerous to sea animals than oil spills are.

③ Many sea animals and sea birds die from eating plastic waste.

④ Carter's family created an educational project about how to reduce oil spills.

⑤ Carter's family started small, but they are making a big difference.

[01~02] 다음 대화를 읽고 물음에 답하시오.

> G: Dad, I'm a bit hungry. Is there anything to eat?
> M: _____(A)_____
> G: That'd be great. I love tteokbokki.
> M: O.K. Give me a little minutes.

01 위의 대화에서 어법상 어색한 것을 찾아 바르게 고치시오.

_____ ➡ _____

02 주어진 단어를 이용하여 빈칸 (A)에 도움을 제안하는 문장을 써 넣으시오. (9 단어)

➡ _____

(want, for, cook)

03 밑줄 친 문장과 같은 의미가 되도록 주어진 단어를 이용하여 쓰시오.

> G: What are you doing this weekend?
> B: I'm thinking of doing some volunteer work at the child-care center.
> G: What would you do there?
> B: I would probably read some books to the children.
> G: That sounds interesting. Can I join you?
> B: Of course.

➡ _____
_____ (consider)

➡ _____
_____ (plan)

➡ _____
_____ (intend)

04 다음 문장을 〈보기〉와 같이 접속사 Although를 사용하여 다시 쓰시오.

> ┤ 보기 ├
> Math problems are difficult, but I like to try to solve them.
> →Although math problems are difficult, I like to try to solve them.

(1) James made a few mistakes, but he succeeded in the project.

➡ _____

(2) Mr. Park left for the station earlier than usual, but he missed the train.

➡ _____
_____

(3) Angela caught a bad cold, but she exercised in the morning.

➡ _____

(4) Jinho prepared for the civil service exam for 4 years, but he failed it.

➡ _____
_____

05 다음 우리말과 같은 뜻이 되도록 주어진 단어들을 이용하여, 제시된 글자 수에 맞게 영작하시오.

(1) 여러분이 하는 것이 여러분이 말하는 것보다 훨씬 중요하다. (speak, than, much, important, 11 단어)

➡ _____

(2) Paula는 그녀가 가진 것을 최대한 활용해야 한다. (most, make, must, of, have, 9 단어)

➡ _____
_____

06 다음 두 문장의 의미가 같도록 빈칸에 들어갈 알맞은 말을 쓰시오.

> Lucy didn't notice the thing that Joseph had done.
> = Lucy didn't notice _____ Joseph had done.

[07~09] 다음 글을 읽고 물음에 답하시오.

> On our last day, we met a marine life specialist. She told us that ⓐplastic waste is more dangerous to sea animals than oil spills are. A lot of sea animals and sea birds die from eating plastic waste. After we came home, we created an educational project about ⓑhow to reduce plastic waste. In addition to this, our organization continues to do various projects to save animals. Although we started small, we are making a big difference. What you do today can change the world, so take that first step!
>
> <we: Carter's family>

07 위 글의 밑줄 친 ⓐ와 같은 의미가 되도록 빈칸에 들어갈 알맞은 말을 쓰시오.

➡ oil spills are _____ dangerous to sea animals than plastic waste is

08 위 글의 밑줄 친 ⓑ를 다음과 같이 바꿔 쓸 때 빈칸에 들어갈 알맞은 말을 두 단어로 쓰시오.

➡ how _____ reduce

09 Why does Carter encourage you to take the first step? Fill in the blanks with suitable words.

> It's because what we do today can _____ _____ _____.

[10~12] 다음 글을 읽고 물음에 답하시오.

> When I was five, my little sister Olivia and I each (A)[adapted / adopted] a cheetah. Did we (B)[raise / rise] cheetahs at home? No, we donated to a charity that (C)[prevents / protects] wild cheetahs in South Africa. Our parents told us that if we did not protect them, we might not be able to see cheetahs in the near future.
>
> We soon became interested in helping other endangered animals. A few years later, with help from our parents, we created a non-profit organization to protect them. We wanted the next generation ___ⓐ___ able to see these animals, so we named our organization One More Generation. We also studied endangered animals and educated our friends about them.
>
> <I: Carter>

10 위 글의 빈칸 ⓐ에 be를 알맞은 형태로 쓰시오.

➡ _____

11 위 글의 괄호 (A)~(C)에서 문맥이나 어법상 알맞은 낱말을 골라 쓰시오.

➡ (A) _____ (B) _____ (C) _____

12 Carter와 Olivia가 치타 외의 다른 멸종 위기의 동물들을 도와주는 것에 관심을 갖게 된 이후에 한 활동 세 가지를 우리말로 쓰시오.

➡ (1) _____

_____

(2) _____

(3) _____

01 다음은 Kate의 가족이 이번 주말에 할 계획이다. 이에 대한 정보와 주어진 〈조건〉에 맞게 글을 완성하시오.

> Kate, 언니 – 수영하러 가기
> 엄마 – 미술관 방문하기
> 아빠 – 집에서 책 읽기

조건

1. think of, consider, plan의 어형을 변화시켜 이용할 것
2. 각 문장에 1의 표현을 반드시 차례로 한 번씩만 이용할 것

Kate and her family members have some plans for this weekend. Kate and her sister like to swim. So _____. Kate's mother is not good at swimming but interested in art. _____. Kate's father _____.

02 다음 그림을 보고 〈보기〉에 주어진 어휘를 활용하여, 접속사 although가 들어가는 문장을 쓰시오.

보기

be different / love each other

→ _____
_____

03 다음 내용을 바탕으로 환경 문제와 그 해결 방안을 제시하는 짧은 글을 쓰시오.

> **Problem**
> • A lot of plastic waste goes into the ocean.　• Sea animals eat it.
> **Solution**
> • reuse and recycle　• bring our own bottle and shopping bag

Plastic pollution is one of the most serious environmental problems these days. Although plastic makes our lives convenient, a lot of (A)_____ goes into the ocean and many (B)_____ eat it. That is a big problem. Here is what we can do. We can (C)_____ plastic products. We can also bring our own (D)_____ and (E)_____. Even simple actions like these can help.

단원별 모의고사

01 빈칸 (A)와 (B)에 들어갈 말로 알맞은 것끼리 짝지어진 것을 고르시오.

> • It became an Olympic sport, but ___(A)___ it isn't that new.
> • ___(B)___ he is very young, he can solve this math problem.

	(A)		(B)
①	actually	–	Although
②	actually	–	Since
③	actually	–	Unless
④	though	–	Although
⑤	though	–	Since

[02~03] 빈칸에 들어갈 말로 알맞은 것을 고르시오.

02

> There was an oil _____ and the oil destroyed the nature.

① rescue   ② supply   ③ gulf
④ spill   ⑤ cut

03

> A: How much did you _____?
> B: I sent $100 to charity.

① donate   ② occur   ③ volunteer
④ purchase   ⑤ adopt

04 다음 우리말에 맞도록 빈칸에 알맞은 말을 쓰시오. (철자가 주어진 경우 주어진 철자로 시작할 것.)

(1) 우리는 멸종 위기의 동물들을 보호해야만 한다.
➡ We have to protect e_____ animals.

(2) 당신의 전문 지식을 일주일에 몇 시간씩 비영리 기구에 기부해 봐.
➡ _____ your expertise to a _____ _____ for a few hours a week.

(3) 그 구조 시도는 악천후로 좌절되었다.
➡ The r_____ attempt was frustrated by bad weather.

(4) 그 문제는 아마도 다양한 방법으로 해결될 수 있을 것이다.
➡ The _____ will be p_____ solved in v_____ ways.

05 대화가 자연스럽게 연결되도록 (A)~(D)를 적절하게 배열한 것은?

> (A) O.K. Give me a few minutes.
> (B) That'd be great. I love tteokbokki.
> (C) Dad, I'm a bit hungry. Is there anything to eat?
> (D) Do you want me to cook tteokbokki for you?

① (B) – (A) – (C) – (D)
② (B) – (C) – (A) – (D)
③ (C) – (A) – (B) – (D)
④ (C) – (B) – (A) – (D)
⑤ (C) – (D) – (B) – (A)

[06~07] 다음 대화를 읽고 물음에 답하시오.

A: What are you going to do this year?
B: 나는 주말마다 영화를 볼까 해.

06 밑줄 친 문장과 같은 의미가 되도록 할 때 빈칸에 들어갈 알맞은 말을 주어진 철자로 시작하여 쓰시오.

> What's your _____ for this year?

➡ p_____

07 밑줄 친 우리말과 일치하도록 주어진 단어를 이용하여 영작하시오.

➡ _____

(every, think, watch a movie)

08 빈칸 ⓐ~ⓔ에 들어가지 않는 말을 고르시오.

> A: This box is ⓐ .
> B: Do you _____ me _____ you _____ ⓔ ?
> A: Yes, please.

① want ② carry ③ them
④ to help ⑤ too heavy

[09~12] 다음 대화를 읽고 물음에 답하시오.

Suho: Anna, do you have any children's books you don't read any (A)[better / longer]?
Anna: Sure. ⓐHow?
Suho: ⓑI'm thinking of sending some books to children in Africa. My aunt told me (B)[what / that] they need books to read.
Anna: Good idea, Suho! ⓒWait, aren't your books in Korean?

Suho: ⓓOh, that's a problem.
Anna: Well, how about _____ them into English?
Suho: _____? That's a great idea, Anna.
Anna: ⓔDo you want me to help you?
Suho: Sure. If we run into any difficult (C)[expressions / experiences], let's ask our English teacher for help.
Anna: O.K. It's really great that we can help the children in Africa.

09 위 대화의 빈칸에 공통으로 들어갈 단어를 주어진 철자로 시작하여 쓰시오. (대·소문자 무시)

➡ _____

10 위 대화의 괄호 (A)~(C)에서 적절한 것을 골라 쓰시오.

➡ (A) _____ (B) _____ (C) _____

11 ⓐ~ⓔ 중 문맥상 또는 어법상 어색한 것을 고르시오.

① ⓐ ② ⓑ ③ ⓒ ④ ⓓ ⑤ ⓔ

12 대화의 내용과 일치하지 않는 것을 모두 고르시오.

① Anna는 더 이상 안 읽는 아동용 도서를 가지고 있지 않다.
② 수호와 Anna는 한국어로 된 책을 영어로 번역할 것이다.
③ 수호와 Anna는 아프리카의 아이들에게 줄 책을 모으기 위해 선생님에게 도움을 청할 것이다.
④ 수호는 아프리카의 아이들에게 줄 책을 구하고 있다.
⑤ 수호의 이모는 아프리카의 아이들이 읽을 책이 필요하다고 말했다.

13 두 문장을 같은 의미의 한 문장이 되도록 관계대명사 what을 사용하여 빈칸을 알맞게 채우시오.

(1) • I can't read the strange letters.
   • Sullivan wrote them in his note.
   = I can't read _____.

(2) • Gale says the thing.
   • It is not important.
   = _____ is not important.

14 다음 〈보기〉에 주어진 두 문장을, 각각의 조건에 맞게 한 문장으로 바꾸어 영작할 때, 빈칸에 적절한 말을 쓰시오.

┌─ 보기 ─
• Peter가 지난 수업에 결석을 했다.
• Peter가 오늘 본 시험에서 만점을 받았다.
(단, score, from, get, absence를 활용할 것)
└

(1) 접속사 but 사용
= _____ _____ _____
   the last class, _____ _____
   _____ _____ _____ _____
   on the exam today.

(2) 접속사 Although 사용
= _____ _____ _____ _____
   _____ the last class, _____
   _____ _____ _____ _____
   on the exam today.

(3) 전치사 despite, 대명사 his 사용
= _____ _____ _____ from the
   last class, _____ _____ _____
   _____ _____ on the exam today.

15 우리말과 일치하도록 괄호 안의 어구를 바르게 배열하시오. (대문자로 주어진 말로 문장을 시작할 것)

(1) 이것이 바로 Frank가 지난 일요일에 일본인 어부로부터 구매한 것이다. (from, last Sunday, Frank, a, what, This, fisherman, is, purchased, Japanese)
➡ _____
_____

(2) 그는 많이 아팠지만, 직장에 갔다. (although, to, He, very, work, sick, was, he, went)
➡ _____
_____

(3) John이 그 복사기를 수리했는데도, 다음날 그것이 작동하지 않았다. (it, next, fixed, Although, photocopier, the, John, work, the, didn't, day)
➡ _____
_____

16 다음 문장을 〈보기〉와 같이 다시 쓰되, 접속사 though의 위치는 문두에 쓰지 말고, 특히 명사와 대명사도 〈보기〉를 참고하여 알맞게 바꿔 쓰시오.

┌─ 보기 ─
Math problems are difficult, but I like to try to solve them.
→ I like to try to solve math problems, though they are difficult.
└

(1) Jason didn't have to read the magazine, but he bought it.
➡ _____
_____

(2) This watch is much older than my grandfather, but it still works well.
➡ _____
_____

(3) Ray has been my classmate for 4 years, but I don't know much about her.
➡ _____
_____

(4) The strawberry looked fine on the surface, but it had a nasty smell.

➡ _____

_____

(5) Many people climbed up on the paper desk, but it didn't break.

➡ _____

_____

17 다음 중 빈칸에 들어갈 것이 <u>다른</u> 하나는?

① Peter sold _____ his family regarded as a treasure to the collector.

② Uncle Joe forgot to tell me _____ he had heard about my lost cat.

③ Did Luke show the police officer _____ I had given him?

④ Mary didn't like the doll _____ her uncle had brought.

⑤ I'll tell you _____ you wanted to hear.

18 다음 밑줄 친 우리말에 맞게 괄호 안에 주어진 단어를 알맞게 배열하시오.

• Reporter: Who or what would you like to give credit to for winning the award tonight?

• Winner: <u>오늘의 저를 만든 것은 내 어머니의 사랑입니다.</u>

(I, my, me, mother's, made, today, what, who, is, am, love)

➡ _____

[19~21] 다음 글을 읽고 물음에 답하시오.

When I was five, my little sister Olivia and I each adopted a cheetah. Did we raise cheetahs at home? No, ⓐ<u>우리는 남아프리카 공화국에 있는 야생 치타를 보호하는 자선단체에 기부했다.</u> Our parents told us that ⓑ<u>if we did not protect them</u>, we might not be able to see cheetahs in the near future.

We soon became interested in helping other endangered animals. A few years later, with help from our parents, we created a non-profit organization to protect them. We wanted the next generation to be able to see these animals, so we named our organization One More Generation. We also studied endangered animals and educated our friends about them.

<I: Carter>

19 위 글의 밑줄 친 ⓐ의 우리말에 맞게 주어진 어휘를 알맞게 배열하시오.

wild cheetahs / donated / in / protects / South Africa / we / to / that / a charity

➡ _____

_____

20 위 글의 밑줄 친 ⓑ를 unless를 사용하여 고치시오.

➡ _____

21 Carter와 Olivia가 그들이 만든 비영리 단체의 이름을 One More Generation이라고 지은 이유를 우리말로 쓰시오.

➡ _____

_____

[22~23] 다음 글을 읽고 물음에 답하시오.

Then one day, a terrible oil spill occurred in the Gulf of Mexico. A lot of sea animals were completely covered with oil, and they were dying. We had to do something. We started collecting animal rescue supplies such as pet carrying cages and rubber gloves from everyone in our neighborhood. Four months later, our family drove to the Gulf of Mexico to deliver what we collected and helped to save (A)the animals. While we were working there, we learned something very useful. When we put mayonnaise into a turtle's throat, the turtle threw up. That way, we were able to get oil out of turtles. I never knew mayonnaise could ____ⓐ____ to save animals!

22 위 글의 빈칸 ⓐ에 use를 알맞은 형태로 쓰시오.

➡ _____

23 다음 빈칸 (A)와 (B)에 알맞은 단어를 넣어 (A)the animals 에 대한 소개를 완성하시오.

They were dying because they were completely covered with (A)_____ due to a terrible oil spill which occurred in (B)_____ _____ _____ _____ .

[24~26] 다음 글을 읽고 물음에 답하시오.

Air pollution is one of the most serious environmental problems these days. Although cars make our lives convenient, (A)they produce a lot of smoke that pollutes the air. That is a big problem. Here is what we can do. We can take the bus or subway more. We can also buy local products because (B)they do not need to ____ⓐ____ very far. Even simple actions like these can help.

24 위 글의 빈칸 ⓐ에 ship을 알맞은 형태로 쓰시오.

➡ _____

25 위 글의 밑줄 친 (A)they, (B)they가 가리키는 것을 본문에서 찾아 쓰시오.

➡ (A)they가 가리키는 것: _____ ,
(B)they가 가리키는 것: _____

26 According to the passage, which is NOT true?

① Air pollution is one of the most serious environmental problems these days.
② Cars make our lives convenient.
③ Cars produce a lot of smoke that pollutes the air.
④ We can buy local products to solve environmental problems.
⑤ Local products need to be shipped very far.

[27~29] 다음 글을 읽고 물음에 답하시오.

Asian black bears have a white V-shape on their chests. They mostly live in forests in Asia. They've become endangered because people hunt them for their body parts and destroy forests. ⓐWe'll tell you what you can do for them. First, use less paper to protect forests. Second, you should not buy any Asian black bear products.

27 위 글의 밑줄 친 ⓐ를 다음과 같이 바꿔 쓸 때 빈칸에 들어갈 알맞은 말을 두 단어로 쓰시오.

➡ We'll tell you what _____ _____ for them.

28 본문의 내용과 일치하도록 다음 빈칸 (A)~(C)에 알맞은 단어를 쓰시오.

> You should use less (A)_____ to protect forests because Asian black bears mostly live in (B)_____ in Asia, and you should not buy any Asian black bear products because people hunt them for their (C)_____ _____ .

29 위 글을 읽고 아시아흑곰에 대해 알 수 없는 것을 고르시오.

① What is special about them?
② Where do they live?
③ Why are they endangered?
④ What should we do for them?
⑤ What products can be made from Asian black bears?

[30~31] 다음 글을 읽고 물음에 답하시오.

Plastic pollution is one of the most serious environmental problems these days. Although plastic makes our lives convenient, a lot of plastic waste goes into the ocean and many sea animals eat it. ⓐThat is a big problem. Here is what we can do. We can reuse and recycle plastic products. We can also bring our own bottle and shopping bag. Even simple actions like these can help.

30 위 글의 밑줄 친 ⓐThat이 가리키는 것을 본문에서 찾아 쓰시오.

➡ _____

_____

31 What are the two solutions to the plastic pollution? Fill in the blanks (A)~(D) with suitable words.

> One of the solutions is (A)_____ _____ and (B)_____ _____ plastic products and to bring our own (C)_____ and (D)_____ _____ .

Lesson

2

Timeless Tales of Gods and Heroes

 의사소통 기능

- 이유 묻기
  What makes you want to go there?

- 허락 요청하기
  A: Do you mind if I sit here?
  B: No, not at all. Go ahead.

 언어 형식

- It ~ that 강조 구문
  It is we **that** are the finest smiths.

- '계속적 용법'의 관계대명사
  Thor soon found Loki, **who** was drinking at home.

교과서

Words & Expressions

Key Words

- accept [æksépt] 동 받아들이다, 수락하다
- adventure [ædvéntʃər] 명 모험
- angrily [æŋɡrəli] 부 화가 나서
- bet [bet] 동 단언하다, 돈을 걸다
- bloom [blu:m] 동 꽃이 피다, 꽃을 피우다
- borrow [bárou] 동 빌리다
- carriage [kǽridʒ] 명 마차, 객차
- challenge [tʃǽlindʒ] 명 도전, 결투 신청
- choose [tʃu:z] 동 선택하다
- cloth [klɔ:θ] 명 옷감, 천
- control [kəntróul] 동 조절하다
- decide [disáid] 동 결정하다
- decision [disíʒən] 명 결정, 판결
- dwarf [dwɔ:rf] 명 난쟁이
- elf [elf] 명 요정
- enemy [énəmi] 명 적, 적군
- fine [fain] 형 질 좋은, 좋은
- flowing [flóuiŋ] 형 흐르는 듯한, 유창한
- golden [ɡóuldən] 형 금빛의
- giant [dʒáiənt] 명 거인
- hammer [hǽmər] 명 망치
- harvest [háːrvist] 명 수확, 추수 동 수확하다, 거둬들이다
- immediately [imíːdiətli] 부 즉시, 곧
- kingdom [kíŋdəm] 명 왕국, 왕조
- magical [mǽdʒikəl] 형 마법 같은
- mind [maind] 형 언짢아하다, 상관하다
- miss [mis] 동 놓치다
- moreover [mɔːróuvər] 부 게다가
- mysterious [mistíəriəs] 형 신비로운

- myth [miθ] 명 신화
- order [ɔ́ːrdər] 동 주문하다
- outside [áutsáid] 부 바깥에
- piece [pi:s] 명 조각, 일부, 한 가지
- poem [póuəm] 명 시
- powerful [páuərfəl] 형 강력한
- precious [préʃəs] 형 귀중한, 값어치 있는
- produce [prədjúːs] 동 만들어 내다, 제조하다
- promise [prámis] 동 약속하다
- protect [prətékt] 동 지키다, 보호하다
- prove [pru:v] 동 증명하다
- pull [pul] 동 당기다
- reply [riplái] 동 대답하다
- scared [skɛərd] 형 두려워하는, 겁먹은
- seafood [síːfud] 명 해산물
- skin [skin] 명 가죽
- smith [smiθ] 명 대장장이, 금속 세공인
- soon [su:n] 부 곧
- southeastern [sàuθíːstərn] 형 동남의
- spear [spiər] 명 창
- target [táːrɡit] 명 목표, 표적
- terrible [térəbl] 형 끔찍한
- throw [θrou] 동 던지다
- treasure [tréʒər] 명 보물
- trick [trik] 명 장난, 묘기
- turn [təːrn] 명 차례
- undo [əndú] 동 원상태로 돌리다
- weather [wéðər] 명 날씨
- wisdom [wízdəm] 명 지혜, 슬기, 현명함

Key Expressions

- be famous for ~ ~로 유명하다
- be gone 사라지다, 없어지다
- be into ~에 관심이 많다
- come along 함께 가다, 동행하다
- come up with ~ ~을 생각해 내다
- fall asleep 잠들다
- give up 포기하다
- had better ~ ~하는 편이 더 낫다

- How do you like ~? ~가 마음에 드니?
- I bet ~. 틀림없이 ~이다.
- in that case 그렇다면, 그런 경우에는
- of one's own 자기 자신의
- play tricks (on) 농간을 부리다, 장난을 치다
- take root 뿌리를 내리다
- turn into ~ ~로 되다

Word Power

※ 서로 비슷한 뜻을 가진 어휘

- ☐ **harvest** 수확, 추수 : **yield** 수확
- ☐ **moreover** 게다가 : **furthermore** 게다가
- ☐ **precious** 귀중한, 값어치 있는 : **priceless** 대단히 귀중한

- ☐ **reply** 응답하다 : **respond** 응답하다
- ☐ **immediately** 즉시 : **instantly** 즉시
- ☐ **protect** 보호하다 : **shield** 보호하다

※ 서로 반대의 뜻을 가진 어휘

- ☐ **accept** 받아들이다 ↔ **refuse** 거절하다
- ☐ **powerful** 강력한 ↔ **weak** 약한
- ☐ **pull** 당기다 ↔ **push** 밀다

- ☐ **scared** 겁먹은 ↔ **brave** 용감한
- ☐ **precious** 소중한 ↔ **worthless** 가치 없는
- ☐ **reply** 응답하다 ↔ **question** 질문하다

※ 형용사 – 부사

- ☐ **actual** 사실의 – **actually** 사실
- ☐ **careful** 조심스러운 – **carefully** 신중하게
- ☐ **easy** 쉬운 – **easily** 쉽게
- ☐ **immediate** 즉각적인 – **immediately** 즉각적으로
- ☐ **mysterious** 신비로운 – **mysteriously** 신비롭게도

- ☐ **angry** 화난 – **angrily** 화가 나서
- ☐ **complete** 완전한 – **completely** 완전하게
- ☐ **happy** 행복한 – **happily** 행복하게
- ☐ **lucky** 운이 좋은 – **luckily** 운 좋게도
- ☐ **powerful** 강력한 – **powerfully** 강력하게

※ **take**와 함께 쓰이는 표현

- ☐ **take a break** 쉬다
- ☐ **take a seat** 자리에 앉다
- ☐ **take care** 조심하다

- ☐ **take a look** 보다
- ☐ **take a test** 시험을 보다
- ☐ **take notes** 필기하다

- ☐ **take a picture** 사진을 찍다
- ☐ **take a walk** 산책하다
- ☐ **take root** 뿌리를 내리다

English Dictionary

- ☐ **bet** 돈을 걸다
  - → to risk money on the result of a race, game, competition, or other future event
  - 경주, 경기, 시합, 또는 다른 미래의 사건의 결과에 돈을 거는 위험을 감수하다

- ☐ **carriage** 마차, 수레
  - → a vehicle with wheels that is pulled by a horse
  - 말이 끄는 바퀴 달린 탈것

- ☐ **challenge** 도전
  - → something new and difficult which requires great effort and determination
  - 엄청난 노력과 결심을 요구하는 새롭고 어려운 어떤 것

- ☐ **enemy** 적
  - → someone who hates you and wants to harm you
  - 당신을 싫어하고 해치고 싶어 하는 사람

- ☐ **hammer** 망치
  - → a tool with a heavy metal part on a long handle, used for hitting nails into wood
  - 나무에 못을 박을 때 사용하는 긴 손잡이에 무거운 금속이 있는 도구

- ☐ **smith** 대장장이
  - → someone who makes and repairs things made of iron
  - 철로 된 물건을 만들거나 수리하는 사람

- ☐ **spear** 창
  - → a pole with a sharp pointed blade at one end, used as a weapon in the past
  - 과거에 무기로 사용된 한쪽 끝에 뾰족하고 날카로운 날이 달린 긴 막대기

- ☐ **treasure** 보물
  - → a group of valuable things such as gold, silver, jewels. etc.
  - 금, 은, 보석 같은 귀중한 것들

- ☐ **trick** 장난, 속임수
  - → something you do to surprise someone and to make other people laugh
  - 누군가를 놀라게 하고 다른 사람들을 웃게 하려고 하는 어떤 것

- ☐ **wisdom** 지혜
  - → the ability to use your experience and knowledge in order to make sensible decisions or judgments
  - 분별 있는 결정이나 판단을 하기 위해 경험과 지식을 사용하는 능력

01 다음 영영풀이에 해당하는 말로 가장 적절한 것은?

> a vehicle with wheels that is pulled by a horse

① game
② race
③ spear
④ carriage
⑤ blade

02 주어진 문장의 밑줄 친 부분과 같은 의미로 쓰인 것은?

> I want to <u>order</u> a coke and a sandwich.

① They used to <u>order</u> me to bring some food for them.
② It was time that she put her life in <u>order</u>.
③ We need to obey social <u>order</u> to live in harmony.
④ She gave <u>orders</u> for the work to be started.
⑤ He will <u>order</u> himself a noodle soup as usual.

03 다음 중 밑줄 친 부분의 뜻풀이가 바르지 <u>않은</u> 것은?

① <u>How do you like</u> the new car? (~가 마음에 드니?)
② This place <u>is famous for</u> its scenery. (~으로 유명하다)
③ I <u>bet</u> she won't come. (틀림없이 ~이다)
④ You <u>had better</u> keep practicing it. (~하는 편이 낫다)
⑤ The man <u>turned into</u> an old man. (~에게로 돌아섰다)

04 다음 우리말에 맞게 빈칸에 알맞은 말을 쓰시오.

> 그가 이미 한 일을 원상태로 되돌릴 수 없어.
> ➡ You can't _____ what he already did.

05 다음 짝지어진 단어의 관계가 같도록 빈칸에 알맞은 말을 주어진 철자로 시작하여 쓰시오.

> reply : respond = precious : p_____

[06~07] 다음 영영풀이에 해당하는 말을 쓰시오.

06

> to prevent something or someone from being harmed or damaged

➡ _____

07

> the gathering of a crop

➡ _____

08 다음 단어의 뜻풀이로 가장 적절한 것은?

> spear

① to plant seeds in the ground
② a pole with a sharp pointed blade at one end, used as a weapon in the past
③ to say someone that you will definitely do something
④ a collection of valuable old objects
⑤ to agree to take an offer

01 다음 빈칸에 알맞은 말을 〈보기〉에서 찾아 쓰시오. 필요하다면 어형을 바꾸시오.

> | 보기 |
> play   give   like   come

(1) He didn't _____ up the work when he was busy taking care of her mother.

(2) If you want to _____ along with us, you have to pay.

(3) Kathy always _____ tricks on her friends.

(4) How do you _____ your new digital camera?

02 다음 빈칸에 들어갈 말을 순서대로 쓰시오.

> (A) She loves cats so much that she has five cats _____ her own.
> (B) I will try to come _____ with some ideas to solve the problem.
> (C) Is the street famous _____ plays and performances?

03 다음 우리말과 일치하도록 주어진 단어를 바르게 배열하시오.

(1) 아이들은 그 방에서 잠들 거야.
(the / will / children / asleep / in / room / fall)
  ➡ _____

(2) 너는 집에 일찍 가는 편이 나아.
(early / better / had / go / you / home)
  ➡ _____

(3) 게다가, 그는 겁먹었어.
(scared / was / moreover / he)
  ➡ _____

04 다음 우리말에 맞게 빈칸에 알맞은 말을 쓰시오.

> 우리가 꿈꾸던 휴가가 악몽으로 변했어요.
> ➡ Our dream holiday _____ _____ a nightmare.

05 다음 영영풀이에 해당하는 말을 〈보기〉에서 골라 바르게 쓰시오.

> | 보기 |
> throw   ask   poem

(1) _____: a piece of writing in which the words are chosen for their beauty and sound and are carefully arranged

(2) _____: to tell someone that you want them to do it

(3) _____: to move your hand or arm quickly and let go of an object, so that it moves through the air

06 다음 밑줄 친 부분과 의미가 통하는 하나의 단어를 쓰시오.

> While you are moving, please handle the violin with care.

➡ _____

Conversation

1 이유 묻기

> • **What makes you want to go there?** 무엇 때문에 거기에 가고 싶으세요?

■ 상대방이 왜 그렇게 말하는지, 혹은 왜 그렇게 생각하는지 등에 대해 이유를 물을 때는 의문사 why를 써서 'Why do you say that?(왜 그렇게 말하니?)'처럼 물어볼 수도 있지만 의문사 what을 사용해서 'What makes you say that?'이라고 물어보기도 한다.

■ 의문사 what을 사용하여 이유를 물어볼 때는 '무엇이 ~하도록 만드느냐?'의 의미로 'What makes you+동사원형 ~?'의 형태가 된다. 행위의 이유를 물어보는 것이므로 '무엇'이라고 해석할 수도 있지만 '왜'라고 해석하기도 한다. 이유를 물어볼 때는 주로 다음과 같은 표현들을 사용할 수 있다.

■ 의문사로 시작하는 이유를 묻는 말 앞에 'Can you tell me'나 'I'd like to know', 'I wonder' 등을 붙여, 간접의문문의 형식으로 좀 더 격식을 갖춰 물어볼 수도 있다. 이유를 말할 때에는 문장 앞에 'I think'나 'In my opinion' 등을 덧붙일 수도 있다.

이유 묻기

- What makes you ~? 무엇이 ~하도록 만드니?
- What makes you want to ~? 무엇이 ~하고 싶도록 만드니?
- What makes you think so? 무엇 때문에 그렇게 생각하니?
- Why is that? 왜 그렇지?
- Why do you ~? 왜 ~하니?
- Why do you think so? 왜 그렇게 생각하니?
- Can you tell me (the reason) why ~? ~의 이유를 설명해 주겠니?

이유 말하기

- I did it because ~. ~ 때문에 그것을 했어요.
- Because ~. 왜냐하면 ~ 때문이야.
- That's because ~. 그것은 ~ 때문입니다.
- Because of ~. ~ 때문이야.

핵심 Check

1. 다음 우리말과 일치하도록 주어진 단어를 이용해 빈칸에 알맞은 말을 쓰시오.

A: I want to visit Iceland.

B: <u>왜 거기에 가고 싶으니?</u> (make)

A: I want to see the northern lights.

➡ _____ _____ _____ want to go there?

② 허락 요청하기

A Do you mind if I sit here? 여기에 앉아도 될까요?

B No, not at all. Go ahead. 물론입니다. 앉으세요.

■ 다른 사람이 같이 있는 상황에서 어떤 일을 하기 전에 상대방에게 허락을 요청할 때는 허락을 요청하는 조동사를 사용하여 'May I ~?', 'Can I ~?', 또는 'Is it okay if I ~?' 등을 사용할 수 있다. 이런 표현 이외에도 좀 더 공손하게 나타내는 표현으로는 'Do you mind if ~?'를 사용할 수 있다.

■ 그 외에 상대방의 허락을 구하는 말은 'Would you mind if ~?', 'I'm wondering if I could ~.', 'Is it okay (with you) if I ~?', 'Would it be all right if I ~?' 등으로 표현할 수도 있다.

■ 'Do you mind if ~?'에서 'mind'는 '꺼리다, 신경 쓰다'라는 의미이기 때문에 'Yes'라고 답변하면 '꺼린다, 신경 쓴다'는 의미가 되어, 허락하지 않는 것을 나타낸다. 상대방에게 괜찮다고 허락할 때는 '신경 쓰지 않으니까 하고 싶은 대로 하세요.'라는 의미로 'Not at all.', 'Of course not.' 'Certainly not.', 'No problem.', 'Sure.', 'Go ahead.' 등을 사용한다. 상대방에게 허락해 주지 않을 경우에는 'I'm afraid I do.(죄송하지만, 안됩니다.)'라고 대답한다.

허락 요청하기와 대답하기

• Do you mind if I ~? ~해도 되겠습니까?

　허락할 때 No, not at all. / Certainly not. / Of course not.
　　　　　　No, I don't. / No problem. / Sure. / Go ahead. 네, 괜찮습니다.
　금지할 때 Yes, I do. / Sorry, but ~. / I'm afraid I ~. 미안하지만 안 됩니다.

• May I ~? ~해도 됩니까?　　　　　　허락할 때 Yes, you may. 네, 괜찮습니다.

• Can I ~? ~해도 될까요?　　　　　　허락할 때 Yes, you can. 네, 괜찮습니다.

• Is it okay if I ~? ~해도 괜찮을까요?　허락할 때 Yes, it is. / Sure. / Of course.

핵심 Check

2. 다음 빈칸에 들어가기에 적절하지 <u>않은</u> 것은?

G: Dad, do you mind if I change the channel?

M: _____

G: Thank you. I need to watch a program about Norway.

M: Norway? Why?

G: Well, we're learning about Norway in class.

M: Oh, I see.

① No, not at all.　　　② Certainly not.　　　③ No, I don't.

④ Go ahead.　　　　　⑤ I'm afraid I do.

Listen and Speak 1 A-1

W: Is it your first time ❶to visit Korea, Mike?

M: Yes, it is. ❷I've always wanted to come to Seoul.

W: ❸What made you come here?

M: I'm really into Korean TV shows. ❹I'm going to go to the places I saw on TV.

W: Have fun!

W: 한국엔 처음 방문하는 거야, Mike?

M: 맞아. 나는 언제나 서울에 오고 싶었어.

W: 이곳에 온 이유가 뭐니?

M: 나는 한국의 TV 프로그램들을 정말 좋아해. TV에서 봤던 장소들에 갈 거야.

W: 재미있게 지내!

❶ to부정사의 형용사적 용법으로 time 수식
❷ 과거부터 지금까지 쭉 원해 왔다는 의미의 현재완료
❸ 이유를 묻는 표현(= What brought you here?, Why did you come here?)
❹ be going to V: V할 예정이다

Check(√) True or False

(1) Mike is not interested in Korea. T ☐ F ☐

(2) Mike wants to visit the places that he saw on TV. T ☐ F ☐

(3) The woman is wondering how many places Mike will visit. T ☐ F ☐

Listen and Speak 2 A-1

G: Dad, ❶do you mind if I change the channel?

M: ❷No, not at all.

G: Thank you. I need to watch a program about Norway.

M: Norway? Why?

G: Well, we're learning about Norway in class.

M: Oh, I ❸see.

G: 아빠, 제가 채널을 돌려도 될까요?

M: 물론이지.

G: 고마워요. 노르웨이에 대한 프로그램을 봐야 해서요.

M: 노르웨이? 왜?

G: 그게, 수업 시간에 노르웨이에 대해 배우고 있거든요.

M: 오, 그렇구나.

❶ 허락을 요청하는 표현(= I'm wondering if I could change the channel.)
❷ 'Do you mind ~?'에 대한 허락 표현(= Certainly not., Of course not., Go ahead.)
❸ '이해하다'라는 의미로 쓰임. (= understand)

Check(√) True or False

(4) Dad is watching TV now. T ☐ F ☐

(5) The girl wants to learn about Norway for fun. T ☐ F ☐

(6) Dad doesn't get the reason why she needs to change the channel. T ☐ F ☐

Listen and Speak 1 A-2

B: April is the ❶worst month of the year.

G: ❷What makes you say so?

B: Flowers are blooming, but I ❸have to stay inside ❹to study for my exams.

G: Oh, ❺I know what you mean.

❶ bad의 최상급
❷ 이유를 묻는 표현(=Why is that?)
❸ '~해야 한다'
❹ to부정사의 부사적 용법 중 목적 (~하기 위해서)
❺ 상대의 말에 공감하거나 이해할 때 쓰는 표현

 Listen and Speak 2 A-2

M: Jane, ❶do you mind if I open the window?

W: Sorry, but I have a cold, and it's ❷pretty windy today.

M: O.K. No problem. ❸Would you like some hot tea? It'd be good for your cold.

W: That would be great. Thanks.

❶ 허락을 요청하는 표현
❷ '꽤'라는 의미의 부사
❸ 'Would you like ~?' 권유하는 말

 Communicate A

Jaden: Hi, Yuri, What're you doing?

Yuri: Hi, Jaden. I'm reading a book on Norse ❶ myths. I'm really into them these days.

Jaden: ❷What makes you like them so much?

Yuri: The stories are very interesting, and there are lots of movies about Norse myths.

Jaden: Are they ❸any good?

Yuri: Yes. There's actually a new movie about ❹ Thor, a famous god in Norse myths.

Jaden: Oh, I know him. He's my favorite online game character.

Yuri: ❺In that case, we should go see the movie together.

Jaden: ❻Do you mind if I borrow your book when you're finished? I want to read it before we see the movie.

Yuri: ❼No, not at all. I'm sure you'll like this book, too.

❶ myth: 신화(= mythology)
❷ 이유를 묻는 표현
❸ any: 부사로 부정문이나 의문문에서 형용사나 부사를 강조함
❹ 토르(북유럽 신화에서 천둥, 전쟁, 농업을 주관하는 신)
❺ 그렇다면, 그런 경우에는
❻ 'Do you mind if ~?' 허락을 요청하는 표현
❼ 'Do you mind if ~?'에 대한 긍정의 대답

 Progress Check 1

B: April is the best month of the year.

G: ❶What makes you say so?

B: The weather is not cold, and flowers are ❷ blooming.

G: I love April because my birthday is in April.

B: Really? We should ❸throw you a party.

❶ 이유를 묻는 표현
❷ bloom: (꽃이) 피다
❸ throw a party: 파티를 열다

 Progress Check 2

M: Excuse me, ❶do you mind if I take this chair? We need ❷one more.

W: ❸I'm sorry, but I'm waiting for my friend. She'll be here soon.

M: Oh, I see. Never mind.

W: You can ❹ask the waiter to bring more chairs.

❶ 'Do you mind if ~?' 허락을 요청하는 표현
❷ one more: 하나 더
❸ 허락을 요청하는 물음에 대한 거절의 표현
❹ ask+목적어+to부정사: 목적어에게 V하도록 요청하다

● 다음 우리말과 일치하도록 빈칸에 알맞은 말을 쓰시오.

Listen & Speak 1 A-1

W: Is _____ your first time _____ _____ Korea, Mike?

M: Yes, it _____. I've always _____ _____ _____ _____ Seoul.

W: _____ _____ you come here?

M: I'm really _____ Korean TV shows. I'm going to _____ _____ the places _____ _____ on TV.

W: _____ fun!

Listen & Speak 1 A-2

B: April is _____ _____ _____ _____ _____ the year.

G: _____ makes you _____ so?

B: Flowers are _____, but I have to _____ _____ to study for my exams.

G: Oh, I know _____ _____ _____.

Listen & Speak 2 A-1

G: Dad, do you mind _____ _____ _____ the channel?

M: No, _____ _____ _____.

G: Thank you. I need _____ _____ a program _____ Norway.

M: Norway? _____?

G: Well, we're _____ _____ Norway in class.

M: Oh, I _____.

Listen & Talk 2 A-2

M: Jane, do you _____ _____ _____ _____ _____ the window?

W: Sorry, but I _____ _____ _____ _____, and it's _____ windy today.

M: O.K. No problem. _____ _____ _____ some hot tea? It'd be good for your cold.

W: That _____ _____ great. Thanks.

해석

W: 한국엔 처음 방문하는 거야, Mike?
M: 응. 나는 언제나 서울에 오고 싶었어.
W: 이곳에 온 이유가 뭐니?
M: 나는 한국의 TV 프로그램들을 정말 좋아해. TV에서 봤던 장소들에 갈 거야.
W: 재미있게 지내!

B: 4월은 1년 중 최악의 달이야.
G: 왜 그렇게 생각해?
B: 꽃은 피는데, 나는 시험 공부를 하느라 집에 있어야 해.
G: 오, 무슨 소린지 알겠어.

G: 아빠, 제가 채널을 돌려도 될까요?
M: 물론이지.
G: 고마워요. 노르웨이에 대한 프로그램을 봐야 해서요.
M: 노르웨이? 왜?
G: 그게, 수업 시간에 노르웨이에 대해 배우고 있거든요.
M: 오, 그렇구나.

M: Jane, 내가 창문을 열어도 되겠니?
W: 미안, 내가 감기에 걸려서, 그리고 오늘 바람이 꽤 많이 불거든.
M: 그래. 괜찮아. 따뜻한 차 좀 줄까? 감기에 도움이 될 거야.
W: 그거 좋겠다. 고마워.

Communicate A

Jaden: Hi, Yuri, What're you _____?

Yuri: Hi, Jaden. I'm _____ a book _____ Norse myths. I'm really _____ _____ these days.

Jaden: _____ makes you _____ so much?

Yuri: The stories are very _____, and there are _____ _____ movies about Norse myths.

Jaden: Are they _____ _____?

Yuri: Yes. There's actually a new movie _____ Thor, a _____ _____ in Norse myths.

Jaden: Oh, I know him. He's my _____ online game _____.

Yuri: _____ _____ _____, we should _____ _____ the movie together.

Jaden: Do you mind _____ _____ _____ your book when you're _____? I want to read _____ _____ we see the movie.

Yuri: No, not at all. I'm sure you'll _____ _____ _____, _____.

Progress Check 1

B: April is the best month _____ _____ _____.

G: What _____ you _____ so?

B: The weather is not cold, and _____ _____ _____.

G: I love April _____ my birthday is in April.

B: Really? We should _____ you _____ _____.

Progress Check 2

M: Excuse me, do you _____ _____ _____ _____ this chair? We need one _____.

W: I'm sorry, but I'm _____ _____ my friend. She'll be here _____.

M: Oh, I see. _____ _____.

W: You can _____ the waiter _____ _____ more chairs.

해석

Jaden: 안녕, 유리야. 뭐 하고 있니?
유리: 안녕, Jaden. 난 북유럽 신화들에 관한 책을 읽고 있어. 요즘 이 신화들에 정말 푹 빠졌어.
Jaden: 네가 그것들을 그렇게 좋아하게 만드는 게 뭐니?
유리: 이야기들이 정말 흥미롭고, 북유럽 신화에 대한 영화들도 많이 있거든.
Jaden: 영화들이 좀 괜찮니?
유리: 응. 사실 북유럽 신화에서 유명한 신인 Thor에 관한 새 영화가 나왔어.
Jaden: 오, 그를 알아. 그는 내가 제일 좋아하는 온라인 게임 캐릭터야.
유리: 그렇다면, 우린 같이 그 영화를 보러 가야겠다.
Jaden: 네가 네 책을 다 읽으면 내가 빌려도 될까? 우리가 그 영화를 보기 전에 그걸 읽고 싶어.
유리: 그럼, 당연하지. 너도 이 책을 좋아할 것이라고 확신해.

B: 4월은 1년 중 최고의 달이야.
G: 왜 그렇게 생각해?
B: 날씨도 춥지 않고, 꽃도 피어나잖아.
G: 나는 내 생일이 4월에 있어서 4월을 아주 좋아해.
B: 정말? 우리 너를 위해 파티를 열어야겠다.

M: 실례합니다, 제가 이 의자를 가져가도 괜찮을까요? 하나가 더 필요해서요.
W: 죄송합니다만, 제 친구를 기다리고 있어서요. 곧 올 거예요.
M: 오, 그렇군요. 신경 쓰지 마세요.
W: 웨이터에게 의자를 더 가져다 달라고 부탁해 보세요.

01 다음 대화의 빈칸에 알맞은 것은?

> A: April is the worst month of the year.
> B: _____
> A: Flowers are blooming, but I have to stay inside to study for my exams.

① Who says like that?
② What makes you go there?
③ Why do you think it does?
④ What makes you say so?
⑤ How can you say like that?

02 다음 대화의 밑줄 친 부분과 바꾸어 쓸 수 있는 것은?

> M: Jane, do you mind if I open the window?
> W: Sorry, but I have a cold, and it's pretty windy today.

① do you want me to open the window?
② I'm wondering if I can open the window.
③ do you mind opening the door?
④ would it be alright if you open the window?
⑤ can I close the window?

[03~04] 다음 대화의 빈칸에 알맞은 것을 고르시오.

> G: Dad, do you mind ___(A)___ I change the channel?
> M: No, not at all.
> G: Thank you. I need to watch a program about Norway.
> M: Norway? Why?
> G: Well, we're learning about Norway in class.
> M: Oh, I see.

03 다음 중 빈칸 (A)에 들어갈 말로 가장 적절한 것은?

① what   ② that   ③ if   ④ why   ⑤ how

04 What is the girl learning about in class? Answer in English with a full sentence.

➡ _____

01 다음 대화의 빈칸에 들어갈 말로 가장 적절한 것은?

> A: I want to visit Iceland.
> B: _____
> A: I want to see the northern lights.

① What made you go there?
② Why do you want to see her?
③ What makes you want to go there?
④ How do you get there?
⑤ What brings you here?

[02~04] 다음 대화를 읽고 물음에 답하시오.

> G: ⓐDad, do you mind if I change the channel?
> M: No, not at all.
> G: Thank you. I need to watch a program about Norway.
> M: Norway? Why?
> G: Well, we're learning about Norway in class.
> M: Oh, I see.

02 밑줄 친 ⓐ의 의미로 가장 적절한 것은?

① 통보하기 ② 길 묻기 ③ 허락 구하기
④ 동의하기 ⑤ 거절하기

03 위 대화의 내용과 일치하지 <u>않는</u> 것은?

① The girl needs to change the channel.
② The man doesn't allow his daughter to change the channel.
③ There is a reason why the girl needs to change the channel.
④ The man is wondering why his daughter needs to watch the program.
⑤ The man understands why his daughter wants to change the channel.

04 Write the reason why the girl needs to change the channel. Use the phrase 'It's because.'

> ➡ _____
>
> _____

[05~06] 다음 대화를 읽고 물음에 답하시오.

> (A) What makes you say so?
> (B) Oh, I know what you mean.
> (C) April is the worst month of the year.
> (D) Flowers are ⓐblooming, but I have to stay inside to study for my exams.

05 자연스러운 대화가 되도록 (A)~(D)를 바르게 배열하시오.

> ➡ _____

06 다음 중 밑줄 친 ⓐ를 대신하여 쓸 수 있는 말은?

① beautiful   ② exciting
③ opening   ④ coloring
⑤ closing

07 다음 대화의 빈칸에 들어갈 말로 알맞지 <u>않은</u> 것은?

> A: Do you mind if I sit here?
> B: _____
> A: Oh, thanks.

① Certainly not.
② No, not at all.
③ Sure, go ahead.
④ Yes, I do.
⑤ Of course not.

[08~10] 다음 대화를 읽고 물음에 답하시오.

> M: Jane, ⓐ<u>do you mind if I open the window?</u>
>
> W: Sorry, but I have a cold, and ⓑ오늘은 바람이 꽤 불어.
>
> M: O.K. No problem. Would you like some hot tea? It'd be good for your cold.
>
> W: That would be great. Thanks.

08 다음 중 밑줄 친 ⓐ를 대신하여 쓸 수 있는 것은?

① do you want to open the window?

② is it okay to close the window?

③ can you open the window?

④ don't you want to close the window?

⑤ would it be alright if I open the window?

서답형

09 주어진 단어를 활용하여 밑줄 친 우리말 ⓑ를 영어로 쓰시오.

> (it / pretty)

➡ _____

중요

10 What is the man likely to do after the conversation?

① He will bring Jane a blanket.

② He will open the window.

③ He will make some hot tea for Jane.

④ He will bring some cold tea.

⑤ He will go see a doctor.

[11~13] 다음 대화를 읽고 물음에 답하시오.

> Jaden: Hi, Yuri, ①<u>What're you doing?</u>
>
> Yuri: Hi, Jaden. I'm reading a book on Norse myths. I'm really into them these days.
>
> Jaden: What makes you like them so much?

> Yuri: ②<u>The stories are very interesting, and there are lots of movies about Norse myths.</u>
>
> Jaden: ③<u>Are they any good?</u>
>
> Yuri: Yes. There's actually a new movie about Thor, a famous god in Norse myths.
>
> Jaden: Oh, ④<u>I know him.</u> He's my favorite online game character.
>
> Yuri: In that case, we should go see the movie together.
>
> Jaden: Do you mind if I borrow your book when you're finished? I want to read it before we see the movie.
>
> Yuri: ⑤<u>I'm afraid I do.</u> I'm sure you'll like this book, too.

서답형

11 ①~⑤ 중 대화의 흐름상 어색한 것을 바르게 고쳐 쓰시오.

_____ ➡ _____

서답형

12 According to the dialogue, what does Jaden want to do before he sees the movie? Answer in English with a full sentence.

➡ _____

_____

중요

13 위 대화의 내용과 일치하는 것은?

① Yuri is not interested in Norse myths at all.

② There are few movies about Norse myths.

③ Yuri is watching a movie about Thor.

④ Jaden likes Norse myths so much.

⑤ Jaden wants Yuri to lend her book to him.

[01~02] 다음 대화를 읽고 물음에 답하시오.

W: Is it your first time to visit Korea, Mike?

M: Yes, it is. I've always wanted to come to Seoul.

W: What made you come ⓐhere?

M: I'm really into Korean TV shows. I'm going to go to the places I saw on TV.

W: Have fun!

01 밑줄 친 ⓐ가 가리키는 것을 위 대화에서 찾아 쓰시오.

➡ _____

02 What is Mike interested in? Answer in English with a full sentence.

➡ _____

[03~04] 다음 대화를 읽고 물음에 답하시오.

M: Excuse me, _____(A)_____?
We need one more.

W: I'm sorry, but I'm waiting for my friend. She'll be here soon.

M: Oh, I see. Never mind.

W: You can ask the waiter to bring more chairs.

03 주어진 단어를 바르게 나열하여 빈칸 (A)에 들어갈 말을 완성하시오.

(mind / chair / take / if / you / do / this / I)

➡ _____

04 What is the man likely to do after the conversation?

➡ _____

05 자연스러운 대화가 되도록 (A)~(D)를 바르게 나열하시오.

(A) O.K. No problem. Would you like some hot tea? It'd be good for your cold.

(B) Jane, do you mind if I open the window?

(C) That would be great. Thanks.

(D) Sorry, but I have a cold, and it's pretty windy today.

➡ _____

[06~07] 다음 대화를 읽고 물음에 답하시오.

B: April is the best month of the year.

G: What ___ⓐ___ you ___ⓑ___ so?

B: The weather is not cold, and flowers are blooming.

G: I love April because my birthday is in April.

B: Really? We should ___ⓒ___ you a party.

06 주어진 단어를 빈칸 ⓐ~ⓒ에 각각 쓰시오. 필요하다면 어형을 바꾸시오.

(throw / say / make)

➡ ⓐ _____ ⓑ _____ ⓒ _____

07 Write the reason why the boy thinks April is the best month of the year. Use the phrase 'It's because.'

➡ _____
_____

Grammar

1 It is[was] ~ that 강조구문

- **It was** a hammer **that** they liked most. 그들이 가장 좋아했던 것은 (바로) 망치였다.
- **It was** in Seoul **that** the concert by BTS took place.
  방탄 소년단의 콘서트가 개최된 것은 (바로) 서울에서였다.

■ It+be동사+[명사]+that+불완전한 절: 주어, 목적어인 명사를 강조한다.
  - **Steve** invented **the machine**.
    → It was **Steve** that invented the machine. 그 기계를 발명한 것은 (바로) Steve였다.
    → It was **the machine** that Steve invented. Steve가 발명한 것은 (바로) 그 기계였다.

■ It+be동사+[부사(구/절)]+that+완전한 절: 부사(구/절)를 강조한다.
  - I met her at the party when she was visiting New York.
    → It was **at the party** that I met her when she was visiting New York.
      그녀가 New York을 방문 중이었을 때, 내가 그녀를 만난 것은 (바로) 파티에서였다.
    → It was **when she was visiting New York** that I met her at the party.
      파티에서 내가 그녀를 만난 것은, (바로) 그녀가 New York을 방문 중이었을 때였다.

■ 'It ~ that' 강조구문에서 강조 대상이 명사일 경우, that을 관계대명사 who(사람일 경우) 또는 which(사물이나 동물일 경우)로 대체할 수 있다.
  - Dr. King took care of my ants.
    → **It was** Dr. King **that[who]** took care of my ants. 나의 개미들을 돌봤던 이는 (바로) King 박사였다.
    → **It was** my ants **that[which]** Dr. King took care of. King 박사가 돌봤던 것은 (바로) 나의 개미들이었다.

핵심 Check

1. 다음 괄호 안에서 알맞은 단어를 고르시오.
   (1) It was Susan's car (who / which) Rooney bought last week.
   (2) It was at the theater (that / which) Mom met Daddy for the first time.

② '계속적 용법'의 관계대명사 which / who

> - The first treasure was for Odin, **who** had only one eye.
>   첫 번째 보물은 Odin을 위한 것이었는데, 그는 눈이 하나뿐이었다.
>
> - This is the novel *Animal Farm*, **which** everyone should read.
>   이것은 소설 동물 농장인데, 모든 사람이 이 책을 읽어야 한다.

■ 계속적 용법은 형태상으로 콤마(,)를 쓰며, 관계대명사가 받는 '선행사의 범위'가 다르다.

- I have two friends **who** are good at playing soccer. - 콤마(×), 축구를 잘하는 친구 두 명(친구들이 더 많을 수 있다)을 지칭 → 제한적 용법

- I have two friends, **who** are good at playing soccer. - 콤마(○), 친구들이 두 명 있는데(친구들은 두 명뿐), 그들은 축구를 잘한다. → 계속적 용법

■ 계속적 용법의 관계대명사는 '접속사+대명사'로 전환 가능하다. (and, but, for, though 등)

- I purchased a monitor, **which** was broken.

  = I purchased a monitor, **but** it was broken. 나는 모니터 한 대를 구매했지만, 그것은 고장났다.

- My son has always had many worries, **most of which** were silly.

  = My son has always had many worries, **and most of them** were silly.
  내 아들은 늘 많은 걱정을 해왔는데, 그것들 대부분은 한심한 것들이었다.

■ 선행사는 앞에 나온 명사, 대명사뿐 아니라, 구, 절, 앞 문장 전체 등이 모두 가능하다.

- Michelle tried to solve the problem, **which** I was proud of.

  = Michelle tried to solve the problem, **and** I was proud of **that**. Michelle은 그 문제를 해결하려고 애썼는데, 나는 그것을 자랑스럽게 여겼다. → 선행사는 앞 문장 전체(Michelle이 노력한 일)이며, '접속사 and와 대명사 it/that'으로 받을 수 있다.

- It is good for the students not to give up their dream, **which** a few think to be natural.

  = It is good for the students not to give up their dream, though a few think it to be natural. 학생들이 자신들의 꿈을 포기하지 않는 것은 좋은 일이다, 비록 소수의 학생들이 그것[꿈을 포기하지 않는 것]이 당연하다고 생각하지만 → 선행사는 not to give up their dream이며, 문맥상 '접속사 though와 대명사 it'으로 받을 수 있다.

■ that, what은 계속적 용법으로 쓸 수 없고, '전치사+관계대명사'는 관계부사로 바꿀 수 있다.

- We visited the house, **which** Einstein once lived in. 우리는 그 집을 방문했는데, 그 집은 Einstein이 한 때 살았었다.

  = We visited the house, **in which** Einstein once lived. (= , **where**)

핵심 Check

2. 다음 괄호 안에서 알맞은 단어를 고르시오.

(1) She worked hard day and night, (that / which) made her a success.

(2) His parents only praise his sisters, (which / who) makes him angry.

01 다음 문장에서 어법상 <u>어색한</u> 단어를 한 개씩만 찾아 고치시오.

(1) Let me see the pictures which you took them in London.

_____ ➡ _____

(2) Karl and his wife, whom I met in Seoul, is going to leave today.

_____ ➡ _____

(3) Robert mentioned her problem, that made her sad.

_____ ➡ _____

(4) Lucy's younger sister, Sue, who age is 3, is a clever girl.

_____ ➡ _____

02 다음 중 어법상 바르지 <u>않은</u> 것은?

① It was David who broke the computer yesterday.
② It was in October that the girl first saw the fireworks.
③ It was four years ago that Chris wrote that novel.
④ It is when people praise his talent that the actor feels happy.
⑤ It was the bus that Sam lost his watch.

03 다음 빈칸에 들어갈 말로 알맞은 것은?

> I like the girl, _____ has recently changed her hair style.

① she   ② which   ③ that
④ who   ⑤ what

04 다음 문장의 밑줄 친 부분을 강조하여 문장을 다시 쓰시오.

> Veronika has always wanted to have <u>those necklaces</u>.

➡ _____

01 다음 중 어법상 <u>어색한</u> 것을 <u>모두</u> 골라 기호를 쓰고 알맞게 고치시오.

> ⓐ My mom grows some herb plants in the living room, which produce good scent.
> ⓑ Those are the houses, where they lived in.
> ⓒ My cat, Mimi, has odd eyes, that have beautiful blue and brown colors.
> ⓓ Tom bought a horse, which run quite fast.
> ⓔ I don't know the way which she got accepted to Harvard University.

➡ _____

_____

02 다음 중 밑줄 친 부분의 쓰임이 나머지와 <u>다른</u> 것은?

① It was the bathroom light <u>that</u> Maggie turned off this morning.
② It is my cat Lulu <u>that</u> always cries out too loud for my family to sleep.
③ I supported Paul's plan <u>that</u> Kevin should join his rugby club.
④ It was at the market <u>that</u> Elsa bought the stationery.
⑤ It was Juliet <u>that</u> met the mayor at the party last weekend.

서답형

03 다음 대화의 문맥에 맞게 괄호 안에 주어진 단어를 강조하는 'It ~ that' 구문의 문장을 영작하시오. (7 단어)

> Father: Did you tear the newspaper?
> Jonathan: No, _____. (Tom)

➡ _____

중요

04 다음 중 어법상 <u>어색한</u> 문장은?

① His wife, whom he loves dearly, is young and beautiful.
② I don't know where my bag is, which was put on the table a minute ago.
③ Sarah had her car fixed by the mechanic, who cost her lots of money.
④ The crowd applauded the little girl playing the piano, which was touching.
⑤ Sumin helped the old lady cross the street, who had trouble walking fast.

서답형

05 다음 '가'와 '나'에서 서로 관련된 표현을 찾아 관계대명사 또는 관계부사를 사용하여 한 문장으로 완성하시오. ('나'의 순서대로)

가	• I learned Chinese from Lily. • All villagers in town like the bridge. • They will go to Jagalchi market. • There lived a hero named Hercules.
나	• It was built 100 years ago. • She made me speak freely in Beijing. • He was the son of Zeus. • They will buy fresh seafood there.

➡ (1) _____

_____

(2) _____

_____

(3) _____

_____

(4) _____

_____

[06~07] 다음 중 'It ~ that'의 쓰임이 나머지 넷과 <u>다른</u> 것은?

06 ① It was my twin brother that you saw in that picture.

② It was 20 years ago that Mr. Berkins came here to settle down.

③ It is certain that Sandra fell in love with the stranger at a glance.

④ It was on her way home that Sophia bought the food which made her sick.

⑤ It was a shirt that Matthew's aunt made for his graduation ceremony.

07 ① It is playing the online game that Nicholas usually enjoys in his free time.

② It was no wonder that Brandon got fired from his company.

③ It was in Daniel's garage that the secret meeting was held.

④ It was Comet Halley that I happened to witness last night.

⑤ It was an hour ago that the train Tom was on left for New York.

08 다음 중 어법상 <u>어색한</u> 문장은?

① The professor called Sam Hamington, who didn't answer right away.

② Bill Gates invented the operating program, which made him rich.

③ The Simpsons moved to Springfield, where their first baby Bart was born.

④ Cooper met his wife in 2002, which the world cup was held in Seoul.

⑤ My parents like this restaurant, which is known for the special pork dish.

09 다음 문장의 빈칸 (A)~(C)에 들어갈 말로 가장 적절한 것은?

- The car had a wheel, ___(A)___ let it run faster than people thought.
- Tiffany's aunt lives in Los Angeles, ___(B)___ became a jewelry designer last year.
- My family was having a party with a couple from another city, ___(C)___ had two daughters.

	(A)	(B)	(C)
①	which	who	which
②	who	who	who
③	that	who	which
④	that	which	who
⑤	which	who	who

10 다음 중 어법상 옳은 문장은?

① Jordan is a famous athlete, who often come to Korea to eat *Bulgogi*.

② There is a chair in the room, of which is made of iron.

③ It was raining, that made me stay all day long.

④ The film, which I borrowed from the library, was so boring.

⑤ The president announced that he would resign, who was shocking to me.

서답형

11 다음 우리말을 조건에 맞게 영작하시오.

> 나의 삼촌들은 Sarah를 아는데, 그녀는 중국어를 원어민처럼 말한다.
> (like, speak, a native 사용, 반드시 총 10단어로 영작할 것)

➡ _____

_____

12 다음 그림을 보고 아래의 대화가 자연스럽게 이뤄지도록 주어진 단어를 모두 활용하여 문장을 완성하시오. (단어들 중 1 단어만 변형할 것.)

Mom: Has anyone done something to my flower? I think someone must have watered them too much.

Kathy: _____. (Jonathan / responsible / care / for / it / the flower / take / is / is / of / who)

➡ _____

_____

13 다음 중 밑줄 친 that의 쓰임이 나머지와 다른 하나는?

① It was in this spaghetti that Peter put the Vietnamese spice by mistake.

② It was his mom's laptop that Yumi's little brother broke this morning.

③ It is in 2019 that the movie *Parasite* won the Best Picture Award.

④ It is my puppy Momo that wakes my daddy up every day.

⑤ His wife concealed the fact that he was seriously ill.

14 다음 중 어법상 올바른 문장의 개수는?

ⓐ I met the girl living next door, and who had the refrigerator fixed.

ⓑ Brian asked his sister to clean her desk, which were messy with pieces of paper.

ⓒ Sophia watched the boys dancing on the street, that led her to decide to be a dancer.

ⓓ The man helped an old lady to cross the street, who was a rare thing nowadays.

ⓔ It was her boss which got Emily to pick up the delivered box.

ⓕ It was my puppy that bit Abigail's toe.

ⓖ Stephen was wounded in the leg, which was the reason he wasn't on time.

① 1개　② 2개　③ 3개　④ 4개　⑤ 5개

15 다음 중 밑줄 친 that을 다른 단어로 대체하여 바꿔 쓸 수 없는 문장은?

① It was the drug dealer that met the FBI agent last night.

② It is no wonder that the team finally made a successful contract.

③ It was the robot arm that carried out the difficult operation.

④ That is the house that I spoke of the other day.

⑤ This is not the book that I am looking for.

16 다음 중 어법상 어색한 문장을 모두 고르시오.

① We respect Mother Theresa, who devoted her whole life to poor people.

② I visited a traditional market in Busan, which sell fresh seafood.

③ Soyeon recently attended Mr. King's lecture, who was impressive.

④ Cathy is proud of her mother, who is good at dancing.

⑤ My sister read the letter, that made all of us cry.

01 다음 문장의 밑줄 친 부분을 강조하여, 각각 It으로 시작하는 문장으로 바꾸어 쓰시오.

> Lucas is going to wear a mask at the
> (A)   (B)   (C)
> party this weekend.

➡ (A) _____

_____

(B) _____

_____

(C) _____

_____

02 다음 문장에 대한 각 질문에 'It ~ that' 강조 구문을 사용하여 답하시오. 답할 수 없는 질문은 '답변 불가'라고 쓰시오.

> Ellen had Grace's car repaired at the shop three weeks ago.

(1) Who repaired Grace's car?

➡ _____

_____

(2) Who got Grace's car repaired?

➡ _____

_____

(3) When did Ellen have Grace's car repaired?

➡ _____

_____

(4) For how many weeks did it take to repair Grace's car?

➡ _____

_____

(5) Where was Grace's car repaired three weeks ago?

➡ _____

_____

03 다음 각 문장에서 어법상 어색한 부분을 모두 찾아 바르게 고치시오. 단, 강조구문 자체가 어색할 경우, 전체를 다시 쓰시오.

(1) It was the auditorium that the girls were watching a musical.

➡ _____

(2) It was my coworker's mistake who she didn't recognize.

➡ _____

(3) It was chairman of the council who Anthony was.

➡ _____

(4) It was the evening that the band gave a street performance at Hongdae street.

➡ _____

(5) It was carefully that he rescued the injured.

➡ _____

04 다음 문장을 관계대명사의 계속적 용법을 이용하여 한 문장으로 만드시오.

(1) • All the people there were so selfish.
    • It made the two parties even farther away.

➡ _____

_____

(2) • Thomas is widely known for dancing.
    • But it is not true.

➡ _____

_____

(3) • Emma fell in love with Alex.
    • Emma met him only once.

➡ _____

_____

05 강조구문을 이용하여 다음 주어진 문장과 뜻이 같도록 빈칸을 알맞게 채우시오.

> January 20, 1993 was the day Audrey Hepburn was dead.
> → It was _____ dead.

➡ _____

06 다음 각 문장에서 어법상 <u>어색한</u> 부분을 한 곳씩 찾아 <u>모두</u> 고치시오.

(1) Genie's father allowed her to meet the handsome guy, that made her so happy.

_____ ➡ _____

(2) Susan was practicing the ballet movement, who was very important to her.

_____ ➡ _____

(3) The customs officers don't have all the baggage checked, but which is ordinary.

_____ ➡ _____

(4) The English teacher praised Dylan, which he made feel good.

_____ ➡ _____

07 다음 〈보기〉와 같이 두 문장이 같은 의미가 되도록 관계대명사 또는 관계부사를 활용하여 영작하시오.

> ┌─ 보기 ├─
> I met Irene but she said nothing about it.
> → I met Irene, who said nothing about it.

(1) The teacher blamed Susan, though she didn't mean to be late.

➡ _____
_____

(2) Jackson's father looked a lot younger than she thought but Jackson was ashamed of it.

➡ _____
_____

(3) Almost everyone in the factory stops working at noon, and they go out for lunch then.

➡ _____
_____

(4) Isabella received a letter of apology from her boyfriend, but she hasn't opened it yet.

➡ _____
_____

(5) Bentley's family went to Mexico, and they saw some Mayan ruins there.

➡ _____
_____

08 다음 그림을 보고, 우리말에 맞게 괄호 안의 단어를 활용하여 영작하시오.

> Camila는 아빠와 함께 15장이 넘는 팬케이크를 만들었는데, 그것은 너무나 재미있었다.
> (make, be, over, so, with, dad, pancake, her, fun, which 등 반드시 사용, 변형 가능, 총 12단어)

➡ _____
_____

Treasures for Three Gods

Important Norse Gods

고유명사 뒤에 쉼표와 함께 쓰이는 who: 관계대명사의 계속적
용법으로 바로 앞의 사람에 대한 추가적인 설명을 덧붙일 때 쓴다.

Odin, who is the highest god, gave up his eye for wisdom. Thor is

Odin's son and the strongest god of all. Frey, who is the god of the

Frey controls the weather.라는 문장에 He is the god of the harvest.를 삽입한 형태.

harvest, controls the weather. Loki is a god who plays tricks on others.

= other people

Thor woke and knew immediately something was wrong. His wife's

V1   V2   앞에 접속사 that 생략

beautiful golden hair was gone. He knew only Loki could do such a

사라졌다   knew 뒤에는 접속사 that이 생략   such, so, really: 다른 어구를 강조하는
역할을 한다.

terrible thing. Thor soon found Loki, who was drinking at home.

= and he

"You'd better undo what you did, or you'll be sorry," Thor said

You had better의 축약된 표현.   what은 선행사를 포함하는   명령문 뒤에 쉼표와 함께   '후회하다'
'~하는 편이 좋다.   관계대명사: '~한 것'   쓰이는 or: '그렇지 않으면'

angrily to Loki.

Loki was scared. He promised that he would get golden hair for

명사절을 이끄는 접속사

Thor's wife.

Loki knew only the sons of Ivaldi could make fine golden hair. He

went to them and said, "I heard Brokk and his brother are the finest

the sons of Ivaldi   '…라고 하던데': 전해 들은 것을 전달하는 표현

smiths. Is that true?"

---

treasure 보물

give up 포기하다

wisdom 지혜, 슬기, 현명함

harvest 수확, 수확물; 수확하다, 거둬들이다

trick 장난, 묘기

play tricks on ~에게 농간을 부리다,
~에게 장난을 치다

wake 잠에서 깨다 (wake-woke-woken)

immediately 즉시, 곧

golden 금빛의

had better (= 'd better) ~하는 편이 좋다

undo 원상태로 돌리다

scared 두려워하는, 겁먹은

promise 약속하다

📎 **확인문제**

● 다음 문장이 본문의 내용과 일치하면 T, 일치하지 <u>않으면</u> F를 쓰시오.

1 Odin gave up his eye for wisdom. ☐

2 Frey is a god who plays tricks on others. ☐

3 Thor's wife's beautiful golden hair was gone. ☐

4 Thor didn't know who could do such a terrible thing. ☐

5 Loki promised that he would get golden hair for Thor's wife. ☐

6 Loki didn't know who could make fine golden hair. ☐

"No, it is we who are the finest smiths," the sons of Ivaldi replied.
'It is ~ that ...'을 사용한 강조 구문. It is와 that[who/which] 사이에 강조하고자 하는 말을 넣는다.

"They're making three treasures for Odin, Thor, and Frey," said Loki.

"Do you think you can make treasures better than theirs?"
'Brokk 형제의 보물들'을 가리키는 소유대명사

"Of course we can," they answered.

"O.K., then you should also make three treasures for them," said

Loki. "The gods will decide on the best treasure."
decide on: '~에 관해 결정을 하다'   the: 최상급 형용사 앞에 붙는 한정사

Loki also told them that one of the treasures had to be golden hair.
'주어+tell+목적어+that 구문'   must의 과거형

They went to work immediately.
= at once

Loki then went to see Brokk and his brother. "Ivaldi's sons are

making three treasures for Odin, Thor, and Frey," said Loki. "I bet that
= I am certain (that): '내 의견으로는 틀림없이 ~할 것이다'

you can never make treasures as fine as theirs."
as ... as ~: '~만큼 ...한'. 형용사 원급을 사용하여 두 대상을 비교하는 구문

Brokk became angry and accepted the challenge. He and his brother
angrily(×)

produced three treasures of their own.
'그들 자신의'

Loki went to see the three gods with all the treasures. Brokk came
~을 가지고

along. Loki showed them the treasures from Ivaldi's sons. The first
수여동사

treasure was for Odin, who had only one eye. It was a spear that never
선행사에 대한 추가적인 정보를 주는 절에 사용하며, '접속사+대명사(and he)'의 의미   주격 관계대명사. 앞에 오는 명사 a spear를 수식

missed its target. The second treasure was a big ship that could turn
주격 관계대명사. 앞에 오는 명사 a big ship을 수식

into a piece of cloth. It was for Frey.

---

fine 질 좋은, 좋은

s m i t h 대장장이, 금속 세공인 (= blacksmith)

reply 대답하다

bet 단언하다

accept 받아들이다, 수락하다

challenge 도전, 결투 신청

produce 만들어 내다, 제조하다

come along 함께 가다, 동행하다

spear 창

target 목표, 표적

piece 조각, 일부, 한 가지

📎 확인문제

● 다음 문장이 본문의 내용과 일치하면 T, 일치하지 않으면 F를 쓰시오.

1 The sons of Ivaldi replied that they were the finest smiths. ☐

2 The sons of Ivaldi should make three treasures for Loki. ☐

3 Loki told the sons of Ivaldi that one of the treasures had to be golden hair. ☐

4 Brokk and his brother refused to accept the challenge. ☐

5 Loki went to see the three gods with all the treasures. ☐

6 The first treasure for Odin was a big ship that could turn into a piece of cloth. ☐

The third treasure was for Thor. Loki showed Thor the flowing
수여동사　　I.O.

golden hair for his wife. Thor put the hair on his wife's head, and it
D.O.　　　　　　　　　　　　　　　　　　　　the hair를 가리킨다.

took root and became real hair.
'뿌리를 내렸다'

It was now Brokk's turn to show the gods his gifts. He gave Odin
turn을 꾸며 주며, '보여 줄 차례'라는 의미, show+I.O.(the gods)+D.O.(his gifts)'　　I.O.

a gold arm ring that produced eight more gold rings every ninth night.
D.O.': ~에게 …를 주다'　　　　　　　　　　　'아홉 번째 밤이 될 때마다' = every nine nights

Brokk then gave Frey a pig. It could pull his carriage faster than any
'비교급+than any (other)+단수 명사'(최상급의 뜻).
any: 비교 대상이 같은 그룹에 속해 있지 않은 경우
any other: 비교 대상이 같은 그룹에 속한 경우

horse.

"My third treasure is for you, Thor," said Brokk. "This is the hammer
콤마(,) which로 연결되는 관계대명사절: 앞의 명사.

Mjolnir, which you'll love. If you throw it, it'll always come back to
앞 문장 전체에 대한 추가적인 설명을 할 때 사용된다.　　if는 조건을 나타내는 접속사, 미래시제 대신 현재시제를 사용한다.

you. Moreover, nothing can ever break it."

It was an easy decision to choose the greatest treasure. It was Mjolnir
가주어　　　　　　　　　진주어　　　　　　　　It was ~that 강조구문

that the three gods liked most. They thought the hammer would

protect the gods from their enemies.
protect A from B: B로부터 A를 보호하다

"Brokk and his brother," said Odin, "are the better smiths."
of the two가 생략되어 있고, of the two가 있는 경우 비교급 앞에 the를 쓴다.

Brokk proved that Loki was wrong, and the three gods now had

precious treasures.

---

flowing 흐르는 듯한. 유창한, 미끈하게
처진
take root 뿌리를 내리다. 정착하다
pull 끌다. 당기다
carriage 마차. 객차
hammer 망치
moreover 게다가
decision 결정. 판결
protect 지키다, 보호하다
enemy 적. 적군 (pl. enemies)
prove 증명하다
precious 귀중한, 값어치 있는

📎 **확인문제**

- 다음 문장이 본문의 내용과 일치하면 T, 일치하지 않으면 F를 쓰시오.

1 Loki showed Thor the flowing golden hair for his wife. ☐

2 Brokk gave Odin a gold arm ring that produced nine more gold rings every eighth
   night. ☐

3 The pig that Brokk gave Frey could pull his carriage faster than any horse. ☐

4 If Thor throws Mjolnir, it will never come back to him. ☐

5 The three gods liked Mjolnir most. ☐

6 Brokk proved that Loki was right. ☐

● 우리말을 참고하여 빈칸에 알맞은 말을 쓰시오.

1 _____ for Three Gods

2 **Important** _____ **Gods**

3 Odin, who is the _____ god, _____ _____ his eye for wisdom.

4 Thor is Odin's son and _____ _____ _____ of all.

5 Frey, who is the god of the harvest, _____ _____ _____.

6 Loki is a god who _____ _____ _____ others.

7 Thor woke and knew immediately _____ _____ _____.

8 His wife's beautiful golden hair _____ _____.

9 He knew only Loki could do _____ _____ _____ _____.

10 Thor soon found Loki, _____ _____ _____ at home.

11 "_____ _____ _____ what you did, or you'll be sorry," Thor said angrily to Loki.

12 Loki was _____.

13 He promised that he _____ _____ golden hair for Thor's wife.

14 Loki knew only the sons of Ivaldi could make _____ _____ _____.

15 He went to them and said, "I heard Brokk and his brother are _____ _____ _____. Is that true?"

16 "No, _____ _____ we _____ are the finest smiths," the sons of Ivaldi replied.

1 세 명의 신을 위한 보물

2 북유럽 신화의 주요 신들

3 Odin은 가장 높은 신이며, 지혜를 위해 한쪽 눈을 포기했다.

4 Thor는 Odin의 아들이며 모든 신들 중에서 가장 강한 신이다.

5 Frey는 수확의 신으로 날씨를 다스린다.

6 Loki는 다른 신들에게 농간을 부리는 신이다.

7 Thor는 잠에서 깨어 즉시 무엇인가가 잘못되었다는 것을 알았다.

8 그의 아내의 아름다운 금발머리가 사라졌다.

9 그는 오직 Loki만이 이런 끔찍한 일을 할 수 있다는 것을 알고 있었다.

10 Thor는 곧 Loki를 찾았는데, 그는 집에서 술을 마시고 있었다.

11 "네가 한 짓을 되돌려 놓는 것이 좋을 거야. 그렇지 않으면 후회하게 될 거야." Thor는 노하여 Loki에게 말했다.

12 Loki는 겁이 났다.

13 그는 Thor의 아내를 위해 금발머리를 얻어 오겠다고 약속했다.

14 Loki는 Ivaldi의 아들들만이 훌륭한 금발머리를 만들 수 있다는 것을 알고 있었다.

15 그는 그들에게 가서 "내가 듣기로 Brokk와 그의 남동생이 가장 훌륭한 대장장이라고 하던데. 그것이 사실인가?"라고 말했다.

16 "아니요, 가장 훌륭한 대장장이는 바로 우리들이요." Ivaldi의 아들들이 대답했다.

17 "They're making _____ _____ for Odin, Thor, and Frey," said Loki.

18 "Do you think you can make treasures _____ _____ _____?"

19 "_____ _____ we can," they answered.

20 "O.K., then you should also _____ three treasures _____ _____," said Loki.

21 "The gods will _____ _____ the best treasure."

22 Loki also told them that one of the treasures _____ _____ _____ golden hair.

23 They went to work _____.

24 Loki then _____ _____ _____ Brokk and his brother.

25 "Ivaldi's sons _____ _____ three treasures _____ Odin, Thor, and Frey," said Loki.

26 "_____ _____ that you can never make treasures _____ _____ _____ _____ _____."

27 Brokk became angry and _____ _____ _____.

28 He and his brother produced three treasures _____ _____ _____.

29 Loki went to see the three gods _____ _____ _____ _____.

30 Brokk _____ _____.

31 Loki _____ them the treasures _____ Ivaldi's sons.

32 The first treasure was _____ Odin, who had _____ _____ _____.

33 _____ _____ a spear _____ never missed its target.

17 "그들은 Odin과 Thor와 Frey 를 위해서 보물을 만들고 있네." Loki는 말했다.

18 "너희들이 그들의 보물보다 더 나은 보물을 만들 수 있다고 생각하는가?"

19 "물론 할 수 있소." 그들이 대답했다.

20 "좋아, 그러면 너희도 그들을 위해 세 개의 보물을 만들어야 한다." Loki가 말했다.

21 "그 신들이 가장 훌륭한 보물을 결정할 것이다."

22 Loki는 또한 그들에게 보물 중 하나는 금발머리이어야 한다고 말했다.

23 그들은 즉시 일에 착수했다.

24 Loki는 그 다음에 Brokk와 그의 남동생을 보러 갔다.

25 "Ivaldi의 아들들이 Odin과 Thor, 그리고 Frey를 위해 세 개의 보물을 만들고 있어." Loki 가 말했다.

26 "너희들은 절대 그들의 보물만큼 훌륭한 보물을 만들 수 없다는 것을 내 장담하지."

27 Brokk는 화가 나서 그 도전을 받아들였다.

28 그와 그의 남동생은 그들만의 세 가지 보물을 만들었다.

29 Loki는 모든 보물을 가지고 세 신을 만나러 갔다.

30 Brokk가 같이 갔다.

31 Loki는 그들에게 Ivaldi의 아들들이 만든 보물들을 보여 주었다.

32 첫 번째 보물은 Odin을 위한 것으로, 그는 눈이 한쪽밖에 없었다.

33 그것은 목표물을 절대로 빗나가지 않는 창이었다.

34 The second treasure was a big ship that could _____ _____ a piece of cloth.

35 It was _____ Frey.

36 _____ _____ _____ was for Thor.

37 Loki showed Thor the _____ _____ _____ for his wife.

38 Thor _____ the hair _____ his wife's head, and it _____ _____ and became real hair.

39 It was now _____ _____ to show the gods his gifts.

40 He gave Odin a gold arm ring that produced _____ _____ gold rings _____ _____ _____.

41 Brokk then gave _____ _____ _____.

42 It could pull his carriage _____ _____ _____ _____.

43 "_____ _____ _____ is for you, Thor," said Brokk.

44 "This is the hammer Mjolnir, _____ you'll love.

45 If you throw it, it'll always _____ _____ _____ you.

46 Moreover, nothing can ever _____ _____."

47 It was an easy decision to choose _____ _____ _____.

48 It was Mjolnir that _____ _____ _____ _____ _____.

49 They thought the hammer would _____ the gods _____ their enemies.

50 "Brokk and his brother," said Odin, "are _____ _____."

51 Brokk _____ that Loki was wrong, and the three gods now had _____ _____.

34 두 번째 보물은 천 조각으로 변할 수 있는 큰 배였다.

35 그것은 Frey를 위한 것이었다.

36 세 번째 보물은 Thor를 위한 것이었다.

37 Loki는 Thor에게 그의 아내를 위한 매끈하게 늘어진 금발머리를 보여 주었다.

38 Thor가 그 머리카락을 그의 아내의 머리에 얹었더니 그것이 뿌리를 내려서 진짜 머리카락이 되었다.

39 이제 Brokk가 신들에게 그의 선물들을 보여 줄 차례였다.

40 그는 Odin에게 아홉 번째 밤이 될 때마다 8개의 금팔찌를 더 만들어 내는 금팔찌를 주었다.

41 그러고 나서 Brokk는 Frey에게 돼지를 한 마리 주었다.

42 그것은 어떤 말보다도 그의 마차를 더 빨리 끌 수 있었다.

43 "나의 세 번째 보물은 당신을 위한 것입니다. Thor." Brokk가 말했다.

44 "이것은 몰니르라는 망치인데 당신은 마음에 드실 겁니다.

45 그것을 던지면, 그것은 항상 당신에게 되돌아 올 것입니다.

46 게다가, 그 무엇도 이것을 부술 수 없지요."

47 가장 훌륭한 보물을 선택하는 것은 쉬운 결정이었다.

48 세 명의 신들이 가장 마음에 든 것은 몰니르였다.

49 그들은 그 망치가 신들을 그들의 적들로부터 보호해 줄 것이라고 생각했다.

50 "Brokk와 그의 남동생이 더 훌륭한 대장장이다." Odin이 말했다.

51 Brokk는 Loki가 틀렸다는 것을 증명해 냈고, 세 신들은 이제 소중한 보물을 가지게 되었다.

● 우리말을 참고하여 본문을 영작하시오.

1 세 명의 신을 위한 보물

➡ _____

2 북유럽 신화의 주요 신들

➡ _____

3 Odin은 가장 높은 신이며, 지혜를 위해 한쪽 눈을 포기했다.

➡ _____

4 Thor는 Odin의 아들이며 모든 신들 중에서 가장 강한 신이다.

➡ _____

5 Frey는 수확의 신으로 날씨를 다스린다.

➡ _____

6 Loki는 다른 신들에게 농간을 부리는 신이다.

➡ _____

7 Thor는 잠에서 깨어 즉시 무엇인가가 잘못되었다는 것을 알았다.

➡ _____

8 그의 아내의 아름다운 금발머리가 사라졌다.

➡ _____

9 그는 오직 Loki만이 이런 끔찍한 일을 할 수 있다는 것을 알고 있었다.

➡ _____

10 Thor는 곧 Loki를 찾았는데, 그는 집에서 술을 마시고 있었다.

➡ _____

11 "네가 한 짓을 되돌려 놓는 것이 좋을 거야, 그렇지 않으면 후회하게 될 거다." Thor는 노하여 Loki에게 말했다.

➡ _____

12 Loki는 겁이 났다.

➡ _____

13 그는 Thor의 아내를 위해 금발머리를 얻어 오겠다고 약속했다.

➡ _____

14 Loki는 Ivaldi의 아들들만이 훌륭한 금발머리를 만들 수 있다는 것을 알고 있었다.

➡ _____

15 그는 그들에게 가서 "내가 듣기로 Brokk와 그의 남동생이 가장 훌륭한 대장장이라고 하던데, 그것이 사실인가?"라고 말했다.

➡ _____

16 "아니요, 가장 훌륭한 대장장이는 바로 우리들이요." Ivaldi의 아들들이 대답했다.

➡ _____

17 "그들은 Odin과 Thor와 Frey를 위해서 보물을 만들고 있네." Loki는 말했다.

➡ _____

18 "너희들이 그들의 보물보다 더 나은 보물을 만들 수 있다고 생각하는가?"

➡ _____

19 "물론 할 수 있소." 그들이 대답했다.

➡ _____

20 "좋아, 그러면 너희도 그들을 위해 세 개의 보물을 만들어야 한다." Loki가 말했다.

➡ _____

21 "그 신들이 가장 훌륭한 보물을 결정할 것이다."

➡ _____

22 Loki는 또한 그들에게 보물 중 하나는 금발머리이어야 한다고 말했다.

➡ _____

23 그들은 즉시 일에 착수했다.

➡ _____

24 Loki는 그 다음에 Brokk와 그의 남동생을 보러 갔다.

➡ _____

25 "Ivaldi의 아들들이 Odin과 Thor, 그리고 Frey를 위해 세 개의 보물을 만들고 있어." Loki가 말했다.

➡ _____

26 "너희들은 절대 그들의 보물만큼 훌륭한 보물을 만들 수 없다는 것을 내 장담하지."

➡ _____

27 Brokk는 화가 나서 그 도전을 받아들였다.

➡ _____

28 그와 그의 남동생은 그들만의 세 가지 보물을 만들었다.

➡ _____

29 Loki는 모든 보물을 가지고 세 신을 만나러 갔다.

➡ _____

30 Brokk가 같이 갔다.

➡ _____

31 Loki는 그들에게 Ivaldi의 아들들이 만든 보물들을 보여 주었다.

➡ _____

32 첫 번째 보물은 Odin을 위한 것으로, 그는 눈이 한쪽밖에 없었다.

➡ _____

33 그것은 목표물을 절대로 빗나가지 않는 창이었다.

➡ _____

34 두 번째 보물은 천 조각으로 변할 수 있는 큰 배였다.

➡ _____

35 그것은 Frey를 위한 것이었다.

➡ _____

36 세 번째 보물은 Thor를 위한 것이었다.

➡ _____

37 Loki는 Thor에게 그의 아내를 위한 매끈하게 늘어진 금발머리를 보여 주었다.

➡ _____

38 Thor가 그 머리카락을 그의 아내의 머리에 얹었더니 그것이 뿌리를 내려서 진짜 머리카락이 되었다.

➡ _____

39 이제 Brokk가 신들에게 그의 선물들을 보여 줄 차례였다.

➡ _____

40 그는 Odin에게 아홉 번째 밤이 될 때마다 8개의 금팔찌를 더 만들어 내는 금팔찌를 주었다.

➡ _____

41 그러고 나서 Brokk는 Frey에게 돼지를 한 마리 주었다.

➡ _____

42 그것은 어떤 말보다도 그의 마차를 더 빨리 끌 수 있었다.

➡ _____

43 "나의 세 번째 보물은 당신을 위한 것입니다, Thor." Brokk가 말했다.

➡ _____

44 "이것은 몰니르라는 망치인데 당신은 마음에 드실 겁니다.

➡ _____

45 그것을 던지면, 그것은 항상 당신에게 되돌아 올 것입니다.

➡ _____

46 게다가, 그 무엇도 이것을 부술 수 없지요."

➡ _____

47 가장 훌륭한 보물을 선택하는 것은 쉬운 결정이었다.

➡ _____

48 세 명의 신들이 가장 마음에 든 것은 몰니르였다.

➡ _____

49 그들은 그 망치가 신들을 그들의 적들로부터 보호해 줄 것이라고 생각했다.

➡ _____

50 "Brokk와 그의 남동생이 더 훌륭한 대장장이야." Odin이 말했다.

➡ _____

51 Brokk는 Loki가 틀렸다는 것을 증명해 냈고, 세 신들은 이제 소중한 보물을 가지게 되었다.

➡ _____

[01~04] 다음 글을 읽고 물음에 답하시오.

Important ⓐ Gods

Odin, who is the highest god, gave up his eye for wisdom.

Thor is Odin's son and the strongest god of all.

Frey, who is the god of the harvest, controls the weather.

Loki is a god who plays tricks ⓑ others.

Thor woke and knew immediately something was wrong. His wife's beautiful golden hair was gone. He knew only Loki could do such a terrible thing. Thor soon found Loki, who was drinking at home.

"You'd better undo what you did, or you'll be sorry," Thor said angrily to Loki.

Loki was scared. He promised that he would get golden hair ⓒ Thor's wife.

서답형

01 주어진 영영풀이를 참고하여 빈칸 ⓐ에 철자 N으로 시작하는 단어를 쓰시오.

1. belonging or relating to Scandinavian countries in medieval times
2. of or relating to Norway or its people or culture or language

➡ _____

02 위 글의 빈칸 ⓑ와 ⓒ에 들어갈 전치사가 바르게 짝지어진 것은?

ⓑ	ⓒ		ⓑ	ⓒ
① for	– to		② in	– for
③ on	– for		④ for	– from
⑤ on	– from			

03 이야기의 구성 단계 중에서 본문의 내용이 속하는 단계를 고르시오.

① 발단 ② 전개
③ 위기 ④ 절정
⑤ 결말

04 According to the passage, which is NOT true?

① Odin is the highest god and gave up his eye for wisdom.
② Thor, who is Odin's son, is the strongest god of all.
③ Frey is the god of the harvest and controls the weather.
④ Thor's wife's beautiful golden hair was gone.
⑤ Thor promised that he would get his wife golden hair.

[05~07] 다음 글을 읽고 물음에 답하시오.

Loki knew only the sons of Ivaldi could make fine golden hair. He went to ①them and said, "I heard Brokk and his brother are the finest smiths. Is that true?"

ⓐ"No, it is we who is the finest smiths," the sons of Ivaldi replied.

"②They're making three treasures for Odin, Thor, and Frey," said Loki. "Do you think you can make treasures better than theirs?"

"Of course ③we can," they answered.

"O.K., then ④you should also make three treasures for them," said Loki. "The gods will decide on the best treasure."

Loki also told ⑤them that ⓑ보물 중 하나는 금발머리이어야 한다. They went to work immediately.

서답형

05 밑줄 친 ①~⑤ 중에서 가리키는 대상이 나머지 넷과 <u>다른</u> 것은?

①   ②   ③   ④   ⑤

서답형

06 위 글의 밑줄 친 @에서 어법상 <u>틀린</u> 부분을 찾아 고치시오.

_____ ➡ _____

서답형

07 위 글의 밑줄 친 ⓑ의 우리말에 맞게 9단어로 영작하시오.

➡ _____

[08~10] 다음 글을 읽고 물음에 답하시오.

Loki then went to see Brokk and his brother. "Ivaldi's sons are making three treasures for Odin, Thor, and Frey," said Loki. "(A)I bet that you can never make treasures ___@___ fine ___ⓑ___ theirs."
Brokk became angry and accepted (B)the challenge. He and his brother produced three treasures of their own.

서답형

08 위 글의 빈칸 @와 ⓑ에 공통으로 들어갈 알맞은 단어를 쓰시오.

➡ _____

09 위 글의 밑줄 친 (A)I bet that과 바꿔 쓸 수 <u>없는</u> 말을 <u>모두</u> 고르시오.

① It is certain that   ② I am sure that
③ It is doubtful if   ④ It is unlikely that
⑤ I am certain that

서답형

10 위 글의 밑줄 친 (B)the challenge가 가리키는 내용을 동명사를 포함하여 영어로 쓰시오.

➡ _____

[11~14] 다음 글을 읽고 물음에 답하시오.

Loki went to see the three gods with all the treasures. Brokk came along. Loki showed them the treasures from Ivaldi's sons. The first treasure was for Odin, who had only one eye. It was a spear that never missed its target. The second treasure was a big ship that could turn into a piece of cloth. It was for Frey. The third treasure was for Thor. Loki showed Thor the flowing golden hair for his wife. Thor put the hair on his wife's head, and it took root and became real hair.

It was now Brokk's turn to show the gods his gifts. He gave Odin a gold arm ring that produced eight more gold rings (A)every ninth night. Brokk then gave Frey a pig. It could pull his carriage faster than any horse.

"My third treasure is for you, Thor," said Brokk. "This is the hammer Mjolnir, ___@___ you'll love. If you throw it, it'll always come back to you. ___ⓑ___, nothing can ever break it."

It was an easy decision to choose the greatest treasure. It was Mjolnir that the three gods liked most. They thought the hammer would protect the gods from their enemies.

"Brokk and his brother," said Odin, "are the better smiths."

Brokk proved that Loki was wrong, and the three gods now had precious treasures.

11 빈칸 @에 들어갈 알맞은 말을 쓰시오.

➡ _____

서답형

12 빈칸 ⓑ에 들어갈 알맞은 말을 고르시오.

① However
② Moreover
③ Therefore
④ In other words
⑤ For example

서답형

13 위 글의 밑줄 친 (A)를 다음과 같이 바꿔 쓸 때 빈칸에 들어갈 알맞은 단어를 쓰시오.

➡ every _____ nights

 위 글의 제목으로 알맞은 것을 고르시오.

① How to Make Treasures for Three Gods
② What Treasures Did Ivaldi's Sons Make?
③ What Is the Greatest Treasure Shown to the Gods?
④ What Treasures Did Brokk and His Brother Make?
⑤ Who Made Treasures in the Norse Myths?

[15~17] 다음 글을 읽고 물음에 답하시오.

Important Norse Gods

Odin, who is the highest god, gave up his eye for wisdom.

Thor is Odin's son and the strongest god of all.

Frey, who is the god of the harvest, controls the weather.

Loki is a god who plays tricks on others.

Thor woke and knew (A)immediately something was wrong. His wife's beautiful golden hair was gone. He knew only Loki could do such a terrible thing. Thor soon found Loki, who was drinking at home.

"You'd better _____ⓐ_____, or you'll be sorry," Thor said angrily to Loki.

Loki was scared. He promised that he would get golden hair for Thor's wife.

15 위 글의 빈칸 ⓐ에 들어갈 알맞은 말을 고르시오.

① repeat what you did
② not play tricks on others
③ undo what you did
④ have the hair removed
⑤ not drink heavily

16 위 글의 밑줄 친 (A)immediately와 바꿔 쓸 수 없는 말을 고르시오.

① instantly   ② at once
③ right away   ④ gradually
⑤ without delay

 Which question CANNOT be answered after reading the passage?

① Who is the highest god?
② Who is the strongest god of all?
③ Who is the god of the harvest?
④ What does Frey control?
⑤ Why does Loki play tricks on others?

[18~20] 다음 글을 읽고 물음에 답하시오.

Loki knew only the sons of Ivaldi could make fine golden hair. He went to them and said, "I heard Brokk and his brother are the finest smiths. Is that true?"

"No, ⓐit is we who are the finest smiths," the sons of Ivaldi replied.

"They're making three treasures for Odin, Thor, and Frey," said Loki. "Do you think you can make treasures better than theirs?"

"Of course we can," they answered.

"O.K., then you should also make three treasures for them," said Loki. "The gods will decide on the best treasure."

ⓑLoki also told them that one of the treasure had to be golden hair. They went to work immediately.

18 위 글의 밑줄 친 ⓐit과 문법적 쓰임이 같은 것을 고르시오.

① Was it yesterday that you met him?

② Have you seen it already?

③ It is said that the earth is round.

④ How's it going with you?

⑤ I think it necessary that you should do it at once.

[서답형]

19 위 글의 밑줄 친 ⓑ에서 어법상 틀린 부분을 찾아 고치시오.

⟶ _____ ➡ _____

[중요]

20 According to the passage, which is NOT true?

① Loki knew that the sons of Ivaldi could make fine golden hair.

② The sons of Ivaldi didn't agree that Brokk and his brother were the finest smiths.

③ Loki said that Brokk and his brother were making three treasures for him.

④ The sons of Ivaldi said that they could make treasures better than Brokk and his brother's.

⑤ The sons of Ivaldi went to work on the spot.

[21~24] 다음 글을 읽고 물음에 답하시오.

Loki went to see the three gods with all the treasures. Brokk came along. Loki showed them the treasures from Ivaldi's sons. The first treasure was for Odin, who had only one eye. It was a spear that never ⓐmissed its target. The second treasure was a big ship that could turn into a piece of cloth. It was for Frey. The third treasure was for Thor. Loki showed Thor the flowing golden hair for his wife. Thor put the hair on his wife's head, and it took root and became real hair.

It was now Brokk's turn to show the gods his gifts. He gave Odin a gold arm ring that produced eight more gold rings every ninth night. Brokk then gave Frey a pig. ⓑIt could pull his carriage faster than any horse.

"My third treasure is for you, Thor," said Brokk. "This is the hammer Mjolnir, which you'll love. If you throw it, it'll always come back to you. (①) Moreover, nothing can ever break it." (②)

It was an easy decision to choose the greatest treasure. (③) They thought the hammer would protect the gods from their enemies. (④)

"Brokk and his brother," said Odin, "are the better smiths." (⑤)

Brokk proved that Loki was wrong, and the three gods now had precious treasures.

21 위 글의 밑줄 친 ⓐmissed와 같은 의미로 쓰인 것을 고르시오.

① He completely missed the joke.

② It was an opportunity not to be missed.

③ You missed a good party last night.

④ She will be greatly missed when she leaves.

⑤ The bullet missed her by about six inches.

22 위 글의 밑줄 친 ⓑ와 의미가 같지 <u>않은</u> 문장을 <u>모두</u> 고르시오.

① No horse could pull his carriage so fast as it.

② Any horse could pull his carriage as fast as it.

③ No horse could pull his carriage faster than it.

④ Any horse could pull his carriage faster than it.

⑤ No horse could pull his carriage as fast as it.

23 위 글의 흐름으로 보아, 주어진 문장이 들어가기에 가장 적절한 곳은?

> It was Mjolnir that the three gods liked most.

①　　　　②　　　　③　　　　④　　　　⑤

24 According to the passage, which is NOT true?

① The first treasure from Ivaldi's sons for Odin was a spear.

② The treasures for Frey were a big ship and a gold arm ring.

③ The treasure from Ivaldi's sons for Thor was the flowing golden hair for his wife.

④ The treasure from Brokk for Thor was Mjolnir.

⑤ The three gods liked Mjolnir most.

[25~27] 다음 글을 읽고 물음에 답하시오.

Loki knew only the sons of Ivaldi could make fine golden hair. He went to them and said, "I heard ①Brokk and his brother are the finest smiths. Is that true?"

"No, it is we who are the finest smiths," the sons of Ivaldi replied.

"②They're making three treasures for Odin, Thor, and Frey," said Loki. "Do you think you can make treasures better than theirs?"

"Of course we can," they answered.

"O.K., then you should also make three treasures for them," said Loki. "The gods will decide on the best treasure."

Loki also told them that one of the treasures had to be golden hair. They went to work immediately.

Loki then went to see Brokk and his brother. "③Ivaldi's sons are making three treasures for Odin, Thor, and Frey," said Loki. "I bet that ④you can never make treasures as fine as theirs."

Brokk became angry and accepted the challenge. He and his brother produced three treasures of ⑤their own.

서답형

25 밑줄 친 ①~⑤ 중에서 가리키는 대상이 나머지 넷과 <u>다른</u> 것은?

①　　　　②　　　　③　　　　④　　　　⑤

26 위 글에서 알 수 있는 Loki의 성격으로 가장 알맞은 것을 고르시오.

① sincere　　② cunning　　③ arrogant

④ generous　　⑤ patient

서답형

27 다음 빈칸 (A)와 (B)에 알맞은 단어를 넣어 Loki가 Ivaldi의 아들들에게 Brokk와 그의 남동생을 언급한 이유를 완성하시오.

> Loki wanted (A)_____ _____ _____, which only the sons of Ivaldi could make. Thus, he mentioned Brokk and his brother to make the sons of Ivaldi feel a sense of rivalry and accept (B)_____ _____.

[01~03] 다음 글을 읽고 물음에 답하시오.

Important Norse Gods

Odin, who is the highest god, gave up his eye for wisdom.

ⓐThor is Odin's son and the strongest god of all.

Frey, who is the god of the harvest, controls the weather.

Loki is a god who plays tricks on others.

Thor woke and knew immediately something was wrong. His wife's beautiful golden hair was (A)[disappeared / gone]. He knew only Loki could do ⓑsuch a terrible thing. Thor soon found Loki, who was drinking at home.

"You'd better undo ⓒwhat you did, or you'll be sorry," Thor said (B)[angry / angrily] to Loki.

Loki was (C)[scaring / scared]. He promised that he would get golden hair for Thor's wife.

01 위 글의 괄호 (A)~(C)에서 어법상 알맞은 낱말을 골라 쓰시오.

➡ (A) _____ (B) _____ (C) _____

02 밑줄 친 ⓐ를 다음과 같이 바꿔 쓸 때 빈칸에 들어갈 알맞은 말을 두 단어로 쓰시오.

➡ Thor is Odin's son and _____ _____ any other god.

03 위 글의 밑줄 친 ⓑ와 ⓒ가 공통으로 가리키는 내용을 우리 말로 쓰시오.

➡ _____

[04~06] 다음 글을 읽고 물음에 답하시오.

Loki knew only the sons of Ivaldi could make fine golden hair. He went to them and said, "I heard Brokk and his brother are the finest smiths. Is that true?"

"No, it is we who are the finest smiths," the sons of Ivaldi replied.

"They're making three treasures for Odin, Thor, and Frey," said Loki. "Do you think you can make treasures better than (A)theirs?"

"Of course we can," they answered.

"O.K., then you should also make three treasures for them," said Loki. "The gods will decide ⓐ the best treasure."

Loki also told them that one of the treasures had to be golden hair. They went to work immediately.

04 빈칸 ⓐ에 들어갈 알맞은 전치사를 쓰시오.

➡ _____

05 위 글의 밑줄 친 (A)theirs가 가리키는 것을 영어로 쓰시오.

➡ _____

06 위 글의 내용을 다음과 같이 정리하고자 한다. 빈칸에 compete를 알맞은 형태로 쓰시오.

> The Loki triggered* the _____ spirit of the sons of Ivaldi to have them make fine golden hair. *trigger: 촉발시키다

[07~09] 다음 글을 읽고 물음에 답하시오.

Loki went to see the three gods with all the treasures. Brokk came along. Loki showed them the treasures from Ivaldi's sons. The first treasure was for Odin, who had only one eye. It was a spear that never missed its target. The second treasure was a big ship that could turn into a piece of cloth. It was for Frey. The third treasure was for Thor. Loki showed Thor the flowing golden hair for his wife. Thor put the hair on his wife's head, and it took root and became real hair.

It was now Brokk's turn to show the gods his gifts. He gave Odin a gold arm ring that produced eight more gold rings every ninth night. Brokk then gave Frey a pig. It could pull his carriage faster than any horse.

"My third treasure is for you, Thor," said Brokk. "This is the hammer Mjolnir, which you'll love. If you throw it, it'll always come back to you. Moreover, nothing can ever break it."

It was an easy decision to choose the greatest treasure. It was Mjolnir that the three gods liked most. They thought the hammer would protect the gods from their enemies.

"Brokk and his brother," said Odin, "are the better smiths."

Brokk proved that Loki was wrong, and the three gods now had precious treasures.

07 다음 빈칸 (A)~(C)에 알맞은 단어를 넣어 Ivaldi의 아들들이 세 명의 신을 위해 만든 보물들을 소개하시오.

> Ivaldi's sons made (A)_____ _____
> for Odin, (B)_____ _____ _____
> for Frey, and (C)_____ _____
> _____ _____ for Thor's wife.

08 What treasure did the three gods like most? Answer in English in a full sentence. (4 words)

➡ _____

09 Between 'Ivaldi's sons' and 'Brokk and his brother', which did Odin think were the better smiths? Answer in English in a full sentence.

➡ _____

_____

[10~12] 다음 글을 읽고 물음에 답하시오.

Important Norse Gods

Odin, who is the highest god, gave up his eye for wisdom.

Thor is Odin's son and the strongest god of all.

Frey, who is the god of the harvest, controls the weather.

Loki is a god who plays tricks on others.

Thor woke and knew immediately something was wrong. His wife's beautiful golden hair was gone. He knew only Loki could do such a terrible thing. Thor soon found Loki, ⓐwho was drinking at home.

"You'd better undo what you did, or you'll be sorry," Thor said angrily to Loki.

Loki was scared. He promised that ⓑhe would get golden hair for Thor's wife.

10 본문의 내용과 일치하도록 다음 빈칸에 알맞은 단어를 쓰시오.

> Odin is the highest god and got his wisdom at the expense of _____ _____.

11 위 글의 밑줄 친 ⓐ를 접속사를 사용하여 두 단어로 고치시오.

➡ _____

12 위 글의 밑줄 친 ⓑ를 4형식 문장으로 고치시오.

➡ _____

해석

After You Read A

(1) Loki took the beautiful golden hair of Thor's wife, so Thor became angry
그래서

at him. Loki promised to get golden hair for Thor's wife.
getting(×)

(2) Loki asked the sons of Ivaldi to make three treasures for Odin, Thor, and
ask+목적어+to부정사

Frey. He also had Brokk and his brother produce three treasures for the
have+사람+동사원형: A가 B를 하도록 시키다

gods. Loki bet that Ivaldi's sons would make better treasures.
단언했다

(3) Loki showed the three gods the treasures from Ivaldi's sons.
→ (3형식) showed the treasures from Ivaldi's sons to the three gods

They were a spear, a big ship, and golden hair. The treasures from Brokk
The treasures from Ivaldi's sons

and his brother were a gold arm ring, a pig, and a hammer.

(4) The gods liked the hammer most. They each had their own precious
The gods   They와 동격

treasures.

구문해설 • golden: 금빛의 • promise: 약속하다 • bet: 단언하다 • produce: 만들어 내다, 제조하다
• spear: 창 • hammer: 망치 • precious: 귀중한, 값어치 있는

Link – Create

I have always been friends with Sif, who is the wife of the strongest god. A
└ 현재완료(계속) ┘   관계대명사(계속적 용법)

few days ago, I cut her golden hair just for fun, and her husband became angry

at me. I came up with a good idea to get her hair back. I asked the sons of
부정사 형용사적 용법 (idea 수식)

Ivaldi to make fine golden hair.
목적격보어

구문해설 • just for fun: 단지 재미로 • come up with: ~을 생각해 내다 • get back: 되돌리다

Culture Project

The Strongest Gods and Heroes in the World
strong의 최상급

Hercules, who was the son of Zeus, is famous for his many adventures.
주격 관계대명사(계속적 용법)

Brave and powerful Hercules killed the Nemean lion and wore the lion's skin
네메아의 사자   wear의 과거(and로 killed와 병렬)

as a coat. He also fought the many-headed Hydra. I think it is Hercules who is
전치사(~으로)   It ~ that[who] 강조   = that

the strongest hero in the world.

구문해설 • be famous for ~으로 유명하다 • brave: 용감한 • powerful: 강력한 • skin: 가죽, 피부
• many-headed: 머리가 여럿달린 • Hydra: 히드라(머리가 9개 달린 뱀)

(1) Loki가 Thor의 아내의 아름다운 금발머리를 가져 가서, Thor는 그에게 화가 났다. Loki는 Thor의 아내를 위해 금발머리를 얻어 오겠다고 약속했다.

(2) Loki는 Ivaldi의 아들들에게 Odin과 Thor와 Frey를 위해서 보물을 만들어 달라고 부탁했다. 그는 또한 Brokk와 그의 남동생에게 신들을 위한 세 개의 보물을 만들게 시켰다. Loki는 Ivaldi의 아들들이 더 훌륭한 보물을 만들 것이라고 장담했다.

(3) Loki는 세 명의 신들에게 Ivaldi의 아들들이 만든 보물들을 보여 주었다. 그것들은 창과 큰 배와 금발머리였다. Brokk와 그의 남동생이 만든 보물들은 금팔찌와 돼지 한 마리와 망치였다.

(4) 신들이 가장 마음에 든 것은 망치였다. 그들은 각자 그들의 소중한 보물을 가지게 되었다.

나는 가장 강한 신의 아내인 Sif와 항상 친구로 지내왔다. 며칠 전에 나는 그녀의 금발을 단지 재미로 잘랐고 그녀의 남편은 나에게 화가 났다. 나는 그녀의 머리를 되돌릴 좋은 생각이 났다. 나는 Ivaldi의 아들들에게 훌륭한 금발머리를 만들어 달라고 부탁했다.

세상에서 가장 강한 신들과 영웅들

제우스의 아들인 헤라클레스는 그의 많은 모험들로 유명하다. 용감하고 강한 헤라클레스는 네메아의 사자를 죽이고, 그 가죽을 외투로 입었다. 그는 또한 머리가 여러 개 달린 히드라와 싸웠다. 나는 헤라클레스가 세상에서 가장 강한 영웅이라고 생각한다.

영역별 핵심문제

01 다음 빈칸에 공통으로 들어갈 말로 가장 적절한 것은?

> • It will _____ root.
> • I _____ a walk every morning.
> • Why don't you _____ a break?

① get   ② make   ③ take
④ help   ⑤ have

02 다음 중 짝지어진 단어의 관계가 다른 하나는?

① immediate – immediately
② actual – actually
③ easy – easily
④ friend – friendly
⑤ precious – preciously

03 다음 중 밑줄 친 단어의 뜻풀이가 잘못된 것은?

① You need to accept her apology. (받아들이다)
② She will prove it true. (증명하다)
③ We need more cloth to make it. (옷)
④ The book is full of mysterious stories. (신비로운)
⑤ She made the decision. (결정)

04 다음 영영풀이에 해당하는 단어를 쓰시오.

> to choose to do something, after having thought carefully about other possibilities

➡ _____

05 주어진 문장의 밑줄 친 단어와 같은 의미로 쓰인 것은?

> The sale prices were too good to miss.

① We will miss you when you leave.
② Don't miss meals when you study.
③ We may miss your joke.
④ You should not miss the opportunity.
⑤ When did you first miss the watch?

06 다음 문장의 빈칸에 들어갈 말을 〈보기〉에서 골라 알맞은 형태로 쓰시오.

> ┤ 보기 ├
> be gone / come along / turn into

(1) The money in the safe _____ _____ the other day.
(2) Please _____ _____ with me. I need some help with my bag.
(3) The milk _____ _____ cheese, so I ate it.

07 주어진 단어를 활용하여 다음 우리말을 영어로 쓰시오.

(1) 너는 어떻게 그 아이디어를 생각해 냈니? (come)
➡ _____

(2) 너의 여동생에게 장난치지 마라. (play / little)
➡ _____

(3) 그는 대장장이로 유명해요. (famous)
➡ _____

Conversation

08 주어진 단어를 활용하여 다음 밑줄 친 우리말을 영어로 쓰시오.

> A: Oh, you have a guitar. I really like to play it. 내가 그것을 연주해 봐도 되겠니? (mind / play) (7 words)
> B: Sure, go ahead.

➡ _____

09 Choose an UNnatural dialogue.

① A: Do you mind if I use your phone?
   B: Certainly not.
② A: What made you come here?
   B: I came here to visit my uncle.
③ A: Is it okay if I turn the radio on?
   B: Of course.
④ A: I think the movie is a disaster.
   B: Why do you say so?
⑤ A: Would you mind if I go home early?
   B: Sure, I do.

10 자연스러운 대화가 되도록 (A)~(E)를 바르게 나열한 것은?

> (A) The weather is not cold, and flowers are blooming.
> (B) What makes you say so?
> (C) Really? We should throw you a party.
> (D) April is the best month of the year.
> (E) I love April because my birthday is in April.

① (B) – (C) – (A) – (E) – (D)
② (D) – (B) – (A) – (E) – (C)
③ (D) – (E) – (B) – (A) – (C)
④ (E) – (A) – (B) – (C) – (D)
⑤ (E) – (B) – (A) – (D) – (C)

[11~12] 다음 대화를 읽고 물음에 답하시오.

> M: Excuse me, _____ (A) _____ We need one more.
> W: I'm sorry, but I'm waiting for my friend. She'll be here soon.
> M: Oh, I see. Never mind.
> W: You can ask the waiter to bring more chairs.

11 다음 중 빈칸 (A)에 들어갈 말로 적절하지 <u>않은</u> 것은?

① do you mind if I take this chair?
② is it okay if I take this chair?
③ would you like to take this chair?
④ I'm wondering if I can take this chair.
⑤ would it be alright if I take this chair?

12 Write the reason why the woman doesn't allow the man to take the chair. Use the phrase 'It's because.'

➡ _____
_____

13 다음 대화를 읽고 답할 수 있는 것은?

> W: Is it your first time to visit Korea, Mike?
> M: Yes, it is. I've always wanted to come to Seoul.
> W: What made you come here?
> M: I'm really into Korean TV shows. I'm going to go to the places I saw on TV.
> W: Have fun!

① Where is Mike from?
② Where are Mike and the woman now?
③ What is Mike interested in?
④ How many places is Mike going to visit?
⑤ How long is Mike going to stay in Korea?

14 다음 중 어법상 올바른 문장은?

① The person on the far left of the picture is my father, which is the smartest one in the world.
② Samantha had three sons, that all became politicians.
③ Paparazzi, what is the plural form of paparazzo, is now an ordinary term around the world.
④ A word derived from a person's name is sandwich, which was the name of the 4th Earl of Sandwich.
⑤ My friends were envious of my bag what my aunt bought me from Italy.

15 다음 중 우리말을 영작한 것이 어색한 것을 고르면?

① 어젯밤 만화방에서 Peter를 만난 사람은 바로 Victoria였다.
→ It was Victoria that met Peter at the comic book cafe last night.
② 엄마가 아빠를 처음 만난 것은 바로 엄마가 고등학교 신입생 때였다.
→ It was when she was a highschool freshman that Mom first met Dad.
③ Steve Jobs가 Apple Computer를 설립한 해는 1976년이었다.
→ It was 1976 that Steve Jobs founded Apple Computer.
④ 그 버스를 고장낸 것은 Damian이었다.
→ It was Damian that broke the bus.
⑤ 오늘 아침에 그녀가 교장선생님께 받은 것은 바로 하버드 대학교 입학 통지서였다.
→ It was an acceptance letter to Harvard that she received from the principal this morning.

16 다음 중 성격이 다른 한 문장을 고르시오.

① It was my daddy and I that saw a clown juggling at the amusement park.
② It was a clown that was juggling with red balls on the platform.
③ It was on the platform that a clown was performing the show.
④ It was exciting that my daddy and I watched a clown at the amusement park.
⑤ It was my daddy that was holding me up to watch the clown.

17 다음 중 밑줄 친 부분의 쓰임이 〈보기〉와 같지 않은 것은?

> 보기
> Joey hired new employees in spite of the financial crisis, which worsened the situation.

① The seafood, which you ordered for me, tasted fantastic.
② Tom saw the sports complex building, which had a central heating system.
③ Charlie had difficulty choosing which employee he would give awards to.
④ Simon was trying to stay awake, which was to no avail in the end.
⑤ We bought the blue car which Mom had always wanted to get.

[18~19] 주어진 우리말에 알맞게 영작할 때 어법상 어색한 문장을 하나 고르시오.

18

Pual은 Ailey가 어제 산 책과 매우 비슷한 책을 한 권 가지고 있다.

① Paul has a book, and it is very similar to the one what Ailey bought yesterday.

② Paul has a book, which is very similar to the one which Ailey bought yesterday.

③ Paul has a book very similar to the one that Ailey bought yesterday.

④ Paul has a book, which is very similar to what Ailey bought yesterday.

⑤ Paul has a book, and it is very similar to the one that Ailey bought yesterday.

19

Stella가 운동을 싫어한다는 것은 그녀의 다섯 명의 친구들 모두 알고 있다.

① Stella doesn't like exercise, and all of her five friends know it.

② Stella doesn't like exercise, which all of her five friends know.

③ All of her five friends know that Stella doesn't like exercise.

④ Stella doesn't like exercise, and all five of whose friends know it.

⑤ Stella has five friends, all of whom know she doesn't like exercise.

20 다음 중 밑줄 친 that의 쓰임이 나머지와 다른 하나는?

① It was on the white snow that my pet dogs left their footprints.

② It is so important that you should never forget it.

③ It was last year that you graduated from Munwha elementary school.

④ It was the persuasion skill that made me a lot of money.

⑤ It was the shrimp pizza that my daddy often cooked for me.

21 다음 중 어법상 어색한 문장은?

① This is Sam's book published a month ago, which I've read 4 times.

② Has anyone seen my pen, which was on the desk?

③ Patrick was talking about New York, which is his wife's home city.

④ Everybody voted for Clara, which she was proud of.

⑤ The kids in your kindergarten like Sonia's English class, which are fun.

Reading

[22~23] 다음 글을 읽고 물음에 답하시오.

Loki knew only the sons of Ivaldi could make fine golden hair. He went to them and said, "I heard Brokk and his brother are the finest ⓐ . Is that true?"

"No, it is we who are the finest ⓑ ," the sons of Ivaldi replied.

"They're making three treasures for Odin, Thor, and Frey," said Loki. "Do you think you can make treasures better than theirs?"

"Of course we can," they answered.

"O.K., then you should also make three treasures for them," said Loki. "The gods will decide on the best treasure."

Loki also told them that one of the treasures had to be golden hair. They went to work immediately.

22 주어진 영영풀이를 참고하여 빈칸 ⓐ와 ⓑ에 공통으로 들어갈 단어를 철자 s로 시작하여 쓰시오.

> people who work in metal, especially those who shape metal by hammering

➡ _____

23 위 글의 주제로 알맞은 것을 고르시오.

① to introduce the superior ability of the finest craftsmen
② to utilize others' competitive spirit to achieve one's purpose
③ to determine who can make three treasures
④ to take advantage of one's generosity
⑤ to emphasize the importance of hard work

[24~27] 다음 글을 읽고 물음에 답하시오.

Loki went to see the three gods with all the treasures. Brokk came along. Loki showed them the treasures from Ivaldi's sons. The first treasure was for Odin, who had only one eye. It was a spear that never missed its target. The second treasure was a big ship that could turn into a piece of cloth. It was for Frey. The third treasure was for Thor. Loki showed Thor the flowing golden hair for his wife. Thor put the hair on his wife's head, ⓐand it took root and became real hair.

It was now Brokk's turn ⓑto show the gods his gifts. He gave Odin a gold arm ring that produced eight more gold rings every ninth night. Brokk then gave Frey a pig. It could pull his carriage faster than any horse.

"My third treasure is for you, Thor," said Brokk. "This is the hammer Mjolnir, which you'll love. If you throw it, it'll always come back to you. Moreover, nothing can ever break it."

It was an easy decision ⓒto choose the greatest treasure. ⓓ세 명의 신들이 가장 마음에 든 것은 묠니르였다. They thought the hammer would protect the gods from their enemies.

"Brokk and his brother," said Odin, "are the better smiths."

Brokk proved that Loki was wrong, and the three gods now had precious treasures.

24 위 글의 밑줄 친 ⓐand it을 한 단어로 바꿔 쓰시오.

➡ _____

25 다음 〈보기〉 중에서 위 글의 밑줄 친 ⓑto show, ⓒto choose와 to부정사의 용법이 같은 것을 각각 모두 고르시오.

> ① I want to show it to you.
> ② There are plenty of restaurants to choose from.
> ③ Why is it difficult to show your heart?
> ④ My role is to show a person the way to the station.
> ⑤ He is the last person to choose it.

➡ ⓑ와 같은 것: _____
　ⓒ와 같은 것: _____

26 위 글의 밑줄 친 ⓓ의 우리말에 맞게 한 단어를 보충하여, 주어진 어휘를 알맞게 배열하시오.

> the three gods / Mjolnir / most / liked / was / it

➡ _____

27 다음 중 대장장이와 신의 이름과 선물의 연결이 옳지 <u>않은</u> 것을 고르시오.

smiths	for whom	what

① Ivaldi's sons – Odin – a spear
② Ivaldi's sons – Frey – a big ship
③ Brokk bros. – Odin – a gold arm ring
④ Brokk bros. – Frey – a carriage
⑤ Brokk bros. – Thor – Mjolnir

[28~29] 다음 글을 읽고 물음에 답하시오.

(1) Loki took the beautiful golden hair of Thor's wife, so Thor became angry at him. Loki promised to get golden hair for Thor's wife.

(2) Loki asked the sons of Ivaldi to make three treasures for Odin, Thor, and Frey. He also had Brokk and his brother produce three treasures for the gods. Loki bet that Ivaldi's sons would make better treasures.

(3) Loki showed the three gods the treasures from Ivaldi's sons. They were a spear, a big ship, and golden hair. The treasures from Brokk and his brother were a gold arm ring, a pig, and a hammer.

(4) The gods liked the hammer most. They each had their own precious treasures.

28 이야기의 구성 단계 중에서 본문 (3)번의 내용이 속하는 단계를 고르시오.

① 발단   ② 전개
③ 위기   ④ 절정
⑤ 결말

29 위 글을 읽고 알 수 없는 것을 고르시오.

① 등장인물이 누구인가?
② 사건의 발단은 무엇인가?
③ 등장인물이 무엇을 했는가?
④ 어떻게 이야기가 끝났는가?
⑤ 대장장이들은 각각 어떤 보상을 받았는가?

[30~31] 다음 글을 읽고 물음에 답하시오.

I have always been friends with Sif, who is the wife of the strongest god. A few days ago, I cut her golden hair just for fun, and her husband became angry at me.

I came up with ⓐa good idea to get her hair back. I asked the sons of Ivaldi to make fine golden hair.

30 다음 각각의 신들의 특징을 참고하여 위 글의 'I'는 다음 중 어떤 신에 해당할지를 고르시오.

- Odin: the highest god who gave up his eye for wisdom
- Thor: Odin's son and the strongest god of all
- Frey: the god of the harvest who controls the weather
- Loki: a god who plays tricks on others

① Odin   ② Thor   ③ Frey
④ Loki   ⑤ None

31 위 글의 밑줄 친 ⓐa good idea가 가리키는 것을 동명사를 사용하여 영어로 쓰시오.

➡ _____

(3) It is when my daughters smile at me that I feel the happiest. (　　)

(4) I can't remember when it was that I visited my grandma in Incheon. (　　)

(5) It is Harold's Idea that all the employees gather at the gate. (　　)

(6) What was it that motivated Gerald to major in genetic engineering? (　　)

① It was Emma who broke Joe's computer.

② It was coffee which Emma spilled.

③ It was her credit card that Emma gave Joe.

④ It was Emma that paid for the repair of computer.

⑤ It was at the shop which Joe's computer was repaired.

출제율 95%

15 다음 밑줄 친 ⓐ~ⓓ를 각각 순서대로 'It'으로 시작하는 강조 구문으로 바꿔 쓰시오.

> Tom bought a tablet at the mall 3 weeks ago.
> ⓐ　　　ⓑ　　　ⓒ　　　ⓓ

➡ ⓐ _____

　　ⓑ _____

　　ⓒ _____

　　ⓓ _____

출제율 100%

13 다음 중 밑줄 친 관계대명사가 가리키는 것으로 바르지 않은 것은?

① Elizabeth is a teacher at Balsan middle school, which is located in Ilsan.
(→ Balsan middle school)

② The old lady should take the subway line 3, which crosses the Han River.
(→ the subway line 3)

③ Norah is a nurse at the general hospital, which was her first work place.
(→ the general hospital)

④ Fred was not afraid of sea water, which allowed him to be a professional diver.
(→ sea water)

⑤ The host of the show forgot the boy band's name, which started with F.
(→ the boy band's name)

출제율 90%

16 다음 주어진 세 문장을 관계대명사의 계속적 용법과 제한적 용법을 활용하여, 〈조건〉에 맞게 한 문장으로 표현하시오.

> • Our school introduced a new system.
> • The new system would help improve the students' math grade.
> • Our school students' math grade had always been under average.

┌── 조건 ──┐
that과 which를 반드시 사용할 것. 본문에 있는 표현만을 활용할 것. (변형불가)

➡ _____

_____

_____

출제율 90%

14 다음의 내용을 'It ~ that' 강조구문으로 쓴 문장들 중 어법상 어색한 것을 고르시오.

> Emma accidentally spilled her coffee, which broke Joe's computer down. She gave Joe her credit card and he had the computer repaired at the shop.

[17~20] 다음 글을 읽고 물음에 답하시오.

Loki knew only the sons of Ivaldi could make fine golden hair. He went to them and said, "I heard Brokk and his brother are the finest smiths. Is ⓐthat true?"

"No, ⓑ가장 훌륭한 대장장이는 바로 우리들이요," the sons of Ivaldi replied.

"They're making three treasures for Odin, Thor, and Frey," said Loki. "Do you think you can make treasures better than theirs?"

"Of course we can," they answered.

"O.K., then you should also make three treasures for them," said Loki. "The gods will decide on the best treasure."

Loki also told them that one of the treasures had to be golden hair. They went to work immediately.

출제율 90%

17 위 글의 밑줄 친 ⓐthat이 가리키는 것을 본문에서 찾아 쓰시오.

➡ _____

출제율 90%

18 위 글의 밑줄 친 ⓑ의 우리말에 맞게 주어진 어휘를 이용하여 8 단어로 영작하시오.

who, finest

➡ _____

출제율 95%

19 Why did Loki go to the sons of Ivaldi first, not to Brokk and his brother? Fill in the blanks with the suitable words.

Because Loki knew that the sons of Ivaldi were the only smiths who could make _____ _____ _____ .

출제율 100%

20 Which question CANNOT be answered after reading the passage?

① Why did Loki go to the sons of Ivaldi?
② What did Loki say to the sons of Ivaldi?
③ What did the sons of Ivaldi think about their craftsmanship?
④ Did the sons of Ivaldi think they could make treasures better than Brokk and his brother's treasures?
⑤ What treasures did the sons of Ivaldi make for the three gods?

[21~24] 다음 글을 읽고 물음에 답하시오.

Loki went to see the three gods with all the treasures. Brokk came along. Loki showed them the treasures from Ivaldi's sons. The first treasure was for Odin, who had only one eye. It was a spear that never missed its target. The second treasure was a big ship that could turn into a piece of cloth. It was for Frey. The third treasure was for Thor. Loki showed Thor the flowing golden hair for his wife. Thor put the hair on his wife's head, and it took root and became real hair.

It was now Brokk's turn to show the gods his gifts. He gave Odin a gold arm ring that produced eight more gold rings every ninth night. Brokk then gave Frey a pig. It could pull his carriage faster than any horse.

"My third treasure is for you, Thor," said Brokk. "This is the hammer Mjolnir, ⓐwhich you'll love. If you throw it, it'll always come back to you. Moreover, nothing can ever break it."

It was an easy decision to choose the greatest treasure. It was Mjolnir that the three gods liked most. They thought the hammer would protect the gods from their enemies.

"Brokk and his brother," said Odin, "are the better smiths."

Brokk proved that Loki was wrong, and the three gods now had ⓑprecious treasures.

21 위 글의 종류로 알맞은 것을 고르시오.

① article ② essay
③ biography ④ myth
⑤ review

22 위 글의 주제로 알맞은 것을 고르시오.

① the wonderful skill of Ivaldi's sons
② treasures for three gods and choosing the greatest treasure among them
③ the way to become a better smith
④ the brilliant skill of Brokk and his brother
⑤ the close relationship between gods and the smiths

23 위 글의 밑줄 친 ⓐwhich you'll love를 접속사를 사용하여 고치시오.

➡ _____

24 위 글의 밑줄 친 ⓑ가 가리키는 것을 본문에서 찾아 쓰시오.

➡ Odin의 소중한 보물:

_____

➡ Frey의 소중한 보물:

_____

➡ Thor의 소중한 보물:

_____

[25~27] 다음 글을 읽고 물음에 답하시오.

Long ago, there were no ①kings in the southeastern part of Korea. One day, a strange voice was heard from Gujibong, which was a small hill. ⓐIt said that a new country would be built there. When people were singing and dancing for their future king, a golden box came from the sky. They found ②six golden eggs in the box. Twelve days later, the six eggs turned into ③six boys. The boys became ④the kings of the six Gayas. It was King Kim Suro who was the strongest of ⑤them. His kingdom became the center of the six Gayas.

25 밑줄 친 ①~⑤ 중에서 가리키는 대상이 나머지 넷과 다른 것은?

① ② ③ ④ ⑤

26 위 글의 밑줄 친 ⓐIt이 가리키는 것을 본문에서 찾아 쓰시오.

➡ _____

27 위 글을 읽고 알 수 없는 것을 고르시오.

① Where were the six Gayas located?
② What was Gujibong?
③ Where did a golden box come from?
④ How did the six eggs turn into six boys?
⑤ Who was the strongest of the kings of the six Gayas?

01 주어진 단어를 문맥에 맞게 빈칸에 쓰시오. 필요하다면 어형을 바꾸시오.

> angry / happy / easy

(1) 그는 그녀를 화가 나서 쳐다보았다.
➡ He looked at her _____.

(2) 그것은 쉬운 결정이었어.
➡ It was an _____ decision.

(3) 나는 기꺼이 너를 도울 거야.
➡ I will _____ help you.

[02~03] 다음 대화를 읽고 물음에 답하시오.

> W: Is it your first time to visit Korea, Mike?
> M: Yes, it is. I've always wanted to come to Seoul.
> W: ⓐWhat made you to come here?
> M: I'm really into Korean TV shows. I'm going to go to the places I saw on TV.
> W: Have fun!

02 밑줄 친 ⓐ를 어법에 맞게 바르게 고쳐 쓰시오.

➡ _____

03 What is Mike going to do in Seoul? Answer in English with a full sentence.

➡ _____

04 다음 문장을 읽고, 글의 빈칸에 들어갈 알맞은 말을 괄호 안에서 골라 순서대로 쓰시오. (필요할 경우 변형가능.)

> Lucas usually listens to the international radio channels online from various countries and enjoys talking to the foreigner about each other's life and culture. He wants to go to a foreign language high school, _____ _____ _____ _____ _____ _____.
>
> (mean, culture, like, which, he, foreign)

05 다음 주어진 단어를 알맞게 배열하여 문맥에 맞게 대화를 완성하시오. (단, 부사구를 강조하는 문장으로 쓰시오.)

> Reporter: What do you believe the biggest contribution to your winning this award tonight is?
> Winner: It _____.
> (award / that / because / won / was / of / my mother / I / the)

➡ _____

[06~08] 다음 글을 읽고 물음에 답하시오.

> Thor woke and knew immediately ⓐsomething was wrong. His wife's beautiful golden hair was gone. He knew only Loki could do ⓑ이런 끔찍한 일. Thor soon found Loki, who was drinking at home.
>
> "ⓒYou'd better undo what you did, or you'll be sorry," Thor said angrily to Loki.
>
> Loki was scared. He promised that he would get golden hair for Thor's wife.

06 위 글의 밑줄 친 ⓐ가 가리키는 것을 본문에서 찾아 쓰시오.

➡ _____

07 위 글의 밑줄 친 ⓑ의 우리말에 맞게 4 단어로 영작하시오.

➡ _____

08 위 글의 밑줄 친 ⓒ를 다음과 같이 바꿔 쓸 때 빈칸에 들어갈 알맞은 말을 쓰시오.

➡ I _____ you to undo what you did.

= You _____ undo what you did.

= It would be better for you _____ _____ what you did.

[09~10] 다음 글을 읽고 물음에 답하시오.

Loki went to see the three gods with all the treasures. Brokk came along. Loki showed them the treasures from Ivaldi's sons. The first treasure was for Odin, who had only one eye. It was a spear that never missed its target. The second treasure was a big ship that could turn into a piece of cloth. It was for Frey. The third treasure was for Thor. Loki showed Thor the flowing golden hair for his wife. Thor put the hair on his wife's head, and it took root and became real hair.

It was now Brokk's turn to show the gods his gifts. He gave Odin a gold arm ring that produced eight more gold rings every ninth night. Brokk then gave Frey a pig. It could pull his carriage faster than any horse.

"My third treasure is for you, Thor," said Brokk. "This is the hammer Mjolnir, which you'll love. If you throw it, it'll always come back to you. Moreover, nothing can ever break it."

It was an easy decision to choose the greatest treasure. It was Mjolnir that the three gods liked most. They thought the hammer would protect the gods from their enemies.

"Brokk and his brother," said Odin, "are the better smiths."

Brokk proved that Loki was wrong, and the three gods now had precious treasures.

09 다음 빈칸 (A)~(C)에 알맞은 단어를 넣어 Ivaldi의 아들들이 세 명의 신을 위해 만든 보물들을 소개하시오.

The treasure for Odin was a spear that never (A)_____ its target, and the treasure for Frey was a big ship that could turn into (B)_____ _____ _____ _____. The treasure for Thor was the flowing golden hair for his wife, and when Thor put the hair on his wife's head, it took root and became (C)_____ _____.

10 다음 빈칸 (A)~(C)에 알맞은 단어를 넣어 Brokk와 그의 남동생이 세 명의 신을 위해 만든 보물들을 소개하시오.

Brokk and his brother made (A)_____ _____ _____ _____ for Odin, (B)_____ _____ for Frey, and (C)_____ _____ _____ for Thor.

01 다음 상황을 읽고 대화의 빈칸에 알맞은 말을 쓰시오.

Jessica is learning about Norway in class, so she needs to watch a program about Norway. She goes out to the living room and sees her father watching TV. She asks her father if she changes the channel. Her father allows her to do so.

G: Dad, do you mind _____?

M: No, _____.

G: Thank you. I need to _____.

M: Norway? Why?

G: Well, we're _____.

M: Oh, I see.

02 다음 내용을 바탕으로 가야의 건국 신화를 쓰시오.

1. There were no kings in the southeastern part of Korea. One day, a strange voice was heard from Gujibong. "I'll build a new country."
2. People were singing and dancing for their future king.
3. A golden box came from the sky.
4. There were six golden eggs in the box.
5. The six eggs turned into six boys. The boys became the kings of the six Gayas.
6. King Kim Suro was the strongest of them.

Long ago, there were no kings in the (A)_____ of Korea. One day, a strange voice was heard from (B)_____, which was a small hill. It said that a new country would be built there. When people were (C)_____ for their future king, a golden box came from the sky. They found (D)_____ in the box. Twelve days later, the six eggs turned into six boys. The boys became the kings of the (E)_____. It was (F)_____ who was the strongest of them. His kingdom became the center of the six Gayas.

단원별 모의고사

01 다음 주어진 단어의 관계와 <u>다른</u> 하나는?

> immediate – immediately

① actual – actually

② careful – carefully

③ gentle – gently

④ comfortable – comfortably

⑤ fast – fastly

02 빈칸에 공통으로 들어갈 말을 쓰시오.

> • Can you _____ a picture of us?
> • Frank, _____ care not to cut your fingers.
> • Would you please _____ a look at this?

➡ _____

03 다음 우리말의 의미에 맞게 빈칸에 알맞은 말을 쓰시오.

(1) 그녀는 잠자리에 들어 즉시 잠들었다.

　➡ She went to bed and _____ _____.

(2) 바깥은 완전히 어두웠다. 나는 아무것도 볼 수 없었다.

　➡ It was _____ _____ _____. I could not see anything.

[04~05] 다음 대화를 읽고 물음에 답하시오.

B: April is the worst month of the year.
G: (A)<u>What makes you say so?</u>
B: Flowers are blooming, but I have to stay inside to study for my exams.
G: Oh, I know what you mean.

04 Write the reason why the boy has to stay inside in April. Use the phrase 'It's because.'

➡ _____

05 위 대화의 밑줄 친 (A)를 대신하여 쓸 수 있는 것은?

① What brings you here?

② How could you say like that?

③ What did you say?

④ Why is that?

⑤ Can you tell me how you say so?

06 다음 중 대화의 내용이 <u>어색한</u> 것은?

① A: Can I borrow your book?
　B: Yes, you can. Use it as much as you want.

② A: I think they won't come to the party.
　B: Why do you think so?

③ A: Can you tell me why you were late?
　B: It's because I woke up late.

④ A: Do you mind if I park my car here?
　B: Certainly not. Parking here is not allowed.

⑤ A: What makes you drink so much water?
　B: Because I feel thirsty a lot.

07 자연스러운 대화가 되도록 (A)~(D)를 바르게 나열하시오.

> (A) You can ask the waiter to bring more chairs.
> (B) Excuse me, do you mind if I take this chair? We need one more.
> (C) Oh, I see. Never mind.
> (D) I'm sorry, but I'm waiting for my friend. She'll be here soon.

➡ _____

[08~11] 다음 대화를 읽고 물음에 답하시오.

Jaden: Hi, Yuri, What're you doing?

Yuri: Hi, Jaden. I'm reading a book on Norse myths. I'm really into them these days.

Jaden: What makes you like them so much?

Yuri: The stories are very interesting, and there are lots of movies about Norse myths.

Jaden: Are they any good?

Yuri: Yes. There's actually a new movie about Thor, a famous god in Norse myths.

Jaden: Oh, I know him. He's my favorite online game character.

Yuri: In that case, we should go see (A)the movie together.

Jaden: Do you mind if I borrow your book when you're finished? I want to read it before we see the movie.

Yuri: _____ ⓐ _____ . I'm sure you'll like this book, too.

08 빈칸 ⓐ에 들어갈 말로 알맞지 <u>않은</u> 것은?

① No, not at all.　② Of course not.

③ Certainly not.　④ Sure, go ahead.

⑤ Of course, I do.

09 밑줄 친 (A)가 의미하는 것을 위 대화에서 찾아 다섯 단어의 영어로 쓰시오.

➡ _____

10 위 대화의 내용과 일치하지 <u>않는</u> 것은?

① Yuri is reading a book.

② Yuri thinks the stories of Norse myths are interesting.

③ Thor is one of gods in Norse myths.

④ Jaden doesn't know who Thor is.

⑤ Yuri suggests that Jaden go see the movie with her.

11 What does Jaden want to do before he sees the movie? Answer in English with a full sentence.

➡ _____

12 다음 상황을 읽고 빈칸에 알맞은 말을 5 단어로 쓰시오.

You visit your friend's place. He has a new piano in his room. You want to play the piano. So you say, "Do you mind _____?

➡ _____

13 다음 내용을 읽고, 질문에 대한 답을 조건에 맞게 영작하시오.

- Today, Raina and April watched *Frozen 2*.
- The movie is the second episode of *Frozen*.
- TY sang its Korean version of the OST.

(1) What movie did Raina and April watch today, and what was it specifically? ('계속적' 용법의 관계대명사 which, the movie, they 등을 반드시 사용할 것, 총 12 단어 - 영화 제목은 1 단어로 취급)

➡ _____
　 _____

(2) What was sung by the singer TY? (the Korean version, *Frozen* 2, which 등을 반드시 사용할 것, 'It ~ that 강조구문' 형식으로 영작할 것, 총 17 단어)

➡ _____
　 _____

14 다음 밑줄 친 부분과 어법상 쓰임이 같은 것은?

> The students chose to go on a field trip to Gyeongju, <u>which</u> is a historic city in Korea.

① What he says doesn't annoys me, but the way in <u>which</u> he says it annoys me.
② The manager announced <u>which</u> of the applicants his company would hire.
③ I'll do volunteer work, <u>which</u> is baking cookies for people in need.
④ If there are three ways for you to use in that situation, <u>which</u> do you prefer?
⑤ This is the town in <u>which</u> Robert's daughters were born.

15 다음 그림과 우리말 설명을 보고 괄호 안에 주어진 단어를 활용하여 영작하시오.

> 엄마는 나에게 상자에 쓰지 않는 물건들을 담으라고 부탁하셨는데, 우리는 그것들을 자선단체에 기부할 것이다.
> (me / donate / the unused things / Mom / in / will / charity / asked / put / the boxes / we / to)

(1) 접속사 and를 이용하시오. (필요시 단어 추가)
➡ _____
_____

(2) 콤마와 관계대명사를 이용하시오. (필요시 단어 추가)
➡ _____
_____

16 주어진 문장의 밑줄 친 부분을 강조하는 문장으로 어법상 옳은 것은?

> Philip didn't help the rich old man <u>with the desire in mind</u>.

① It was with the desire in mind which Philip didn't help the rich old man.
② It was the desire in mind that Philip didn't help the rich old man with.
③ It wasn't with the desire in mind that Philip didn't help the rich old man.
④ It wasn't with the desire in mind that Philip helped the rich old man.
⑤ It was with the desire in mind that Philip helped the rich old man.

17 다음 각각의 그림을 보고 우리말과 조건에 맞게 영작하시오. (어형 변화 가능)

(1)

> 내가 혼자서 이를 닦았는데, 엄마는 그것을 칭찬하셨다.
> (my, I, Mom, praise, brush, myself, teeth, for, which 활용, 총 9 단어)

➡ _____
_____

(2)

Jason의 개 Brown은 너무 영리해서 많은 그릇을 닦을 수 있는데, 이것이 세상을 놀라게 할 것이다.
(dishes, smart, surprise, dog, he, wash, so, which, many, that, is, can 활용, 총 17단어)

➡ _____

_____

[18~21] 다음 글을 읽고 물음에 답하시오.

Loki went to see the three gods with all the treasures. Brokk came along. Loki showed them the treasures from Ivaldi's sons. The first treasure was for Odin, who had only one eye. ①It was a spear that never missed its target. The second treasure was a big ship that could turn into a piece of cloth. It was for Frey. The third treasure was for Thor. Loki showed Thor the flowing golden hair for his wife. Thor put the hair on his wife's head, and it took root and became real hair.

It was now Brokk's turn ⓐto show the gods his gifts. He gave Odin a gold arm ring that produced eight more gold rings every ninth night. ②Brokk then gave Frey a pig. It could pull his carriage faster than any horse.

"My third treasure is for you, Thor," said Brokk. "This is the hammer Mjolnir, which you'll love. ③If you throw it, it'll always come back to you. Moreover, nothing can ever break it."

④It was an easy decision to choose the greatest treasure. It was Mjolnir that the three gods liked most. They thought the hammer would protect the gods from their enemies.

"⑤Brokk and his brother," said Odin, "are the better smiths."

Brokk proved that Loki was wrong, and the three gods now had precious treasures.

18 위 글의 밑줄 친 ⓐ를 3형식 문장으로 고치시오.

➡ _____

19 다음 빈칸 (A)~(C)에 알맞은 단어를 넣어 Brokk와 그의 남동생이 세 명의 신을 위해 만든 보물들의 특징을 소개하시오.

The treasure for Odin was a gold arm ring that produced (A)_____ _____ _____ _____ every ninth night, and the treasure for Frey was a pig which could pull his carriage (B)_____ than any horse. The treasure for Thor was the hammer Mjolnir, which would always (C)_____ _____ to him whenever he threw it and could never be broken by anything.

20 다음 중 위 글의 밑줄 친 ①~⑤에 대한 설명이 옳지 <u>않은</u> 것을 고르시오.

① 'It was ~ that ...'을 사용한 강조 구문이다.
② 3형식으로 고치면, Brokk then gave a pig to Frey이다.
③ If는 조건의 부사절을 이끄는 접속사로, 주절의 시제가 미래의 일이더라도 if절에서는 현재시제를 사용한다.
④ It은 가주어이고 to choose the greatest treasure가 진주어이다.
⑤ 뒤에 of the two가 생략되어 있고, of the two가 있는 경우에는 비교급 앞에 the를 쓴다.

21 Which question CANNOT be answered after reading the passage?

① What was the treasure from Ivaldi's sons for Odin?

② What was the treasure from Ivaldi's sons for Frey?

③ For whom was the third treasure from Ivaldi's sons?

④ Why did the three gods like Mjolnir most?

⑤ What was the treasure that Loki liked most?

[22~23] 다음 글을 읽고 물음에 답하시오.

This morning, I found my wife's beautiful golden hair was gone. I knew only Loki could do such a terrible thing. I got very ⓐ_____ and shouted at him. Loki promised that he would get golden hair for my wife. I guess he may go to the sons of Ivaldi, ⓑwho are the finest smiths.

22 위 글의 빈칸 ⓐ에 들어갈 알맞은 말을 고르시오.

① excited ② bored

③ relieved ④ upset

⑤ indifferent

23 위 글의 밑줄 친 ⓑwho와 바꿔 쓸 수 있는 말을 고르시오.

① because he ② but they

③ and he ④ for they

⑤ though they

[24~25] 다음 글을 읽고 물음에 답하시오.

Long ago, there were no kings in the southeastern part of Korea. One day, a strange voice was heard from Gujibong, which was a small hill. It said that a new country would be built there. When people were singing and dancing for their future king, a golden box came from the sky. They found six golden eggs in the box. Twelve days later, the six eggs turned into six boys. The boys became the kings of the six Gayas. It was King Kim Suro who was the strongest of them. His kingdom became the center of the six Gayas.

24 위 글의 종류로 알맞은 것을 고르시오.

① a fable

② nonfiction

③ the fantasy novel

④ science fiction

⑤ the birth myth of a nation

25 본문의 내용과 일치하도록 다음 빈칸 (A)와 (B)에 알맞은 단어를 쓰시오.

King Kim Suro was born from one of the (A)_____ _____ that came from the sky in a golden box. Twelve days later, the six eggs turned into six boys, who became the kings of the (B)_____ _____. King Kim Suro was the strongest of them.

MEMO

Lesson 3

Plants That Feed Us

 의사소통 기능

- **안부 묻고 답하기**
  A: Is something wrong?
  B: I have a bad fever.

- **조언 구하기**
  What do you think I should do?

언어 형식

- **분사**
  He ate a basket of tomatoes in front of many people **watching** him.

- **동사의 강조**
  Spinach **does have** a lot of nutrients.

Words & Expressions

Key Words

- □ **absorb** [əbsɔ́:rb] 동 흡수하다
- □ **actually** [ǽktʃuəli] 부 실제로
- □ **article** [á:rtikl] 명 기사, 논문
- □ **battleship** [bǽtlʃìp] 명 전함
- □ **bean** [bi:n] 명 콩
- □ **bloom** [blu:m] 동 꽃을 피우다
- □ **British** [brítiʃ] 형 영국의
- □ **capital** [kǽpətl] 명 수도
- □ **cartoon** [kɑ:rtú:n] 명 만화
- □ **character** [kǽriktər] 명 등장인물
- □ **characteristic** [kæriktərístik] 명 특성, 특징 형 특징적인
- □ **consider** [kənsídər] 동 고려하다, 여기다
- □ **contain** [kəntéin] 동 포함하다, 담고 있다
- □ **crush** [krʌʃ] 동 으스러뜨리다
- □ **defeat** [difí:t] 동 물리치다, 패배시키다
- □ **discover** [diskʌ́vər] 동 발견하다
- □ **erase** [iréis] 동 지우다
- □ **expect** [ikspékt] 동 기대하다
- □ **face** [feis] 동 향하다
- □ **fighter** [fáitər] 명 전투기, 투사
- □ **German** [dʒə́:rmən] 형 독일의 명 독일어
- □ **government** [gʌ́vərnmənt] 명 정부, 국가
- □ **happen** [hǽpən] 동 일어나다
- □ **healthy** [hélθi] 형 건강한
- □ **hidden** [hídn] 형 숨겨진
- □ **hide** [haid] 동 숨다, 숨기다
- □ **however** [hauévər] 부 그러나
- □ **improve** [imprú:v] 동 개선하다, 향상시키다
- □ **insect** [ínsekt] 명 곤충, 벌레

- □ **lower** [lóuər] 동 낮추다
- □ **material** [mətíəriəl] 명 물질, 재료
- □ **nutrient** [njú:triənt] 명 영양소, 영양분
- □ **pilot** [páilət] 명 비행사, 조종사
- □ **place** [pleis] 동 두다, 놓다
- □ **planet** [plǽnit] 명 행성, 혹성
- □ **poisonous** [pɔ́izənəs] 형 유독한, 독성의
- □ **prove** [pru:v] 동 증명하다
- □ **publish** [pʌ́bliʃ] 동 출판하다
- □ **radar** [réidɑ:r] 명 레이더, 전파 탐지기
- □ **researcher** [risə́:rtʃər] 명 연구원, 조사원
- □ **Scottish** [skátiʃ] 형 스코틀랜드의
- □ **secret** [sí:krit] 명 비밀
- □ **sensor** [sénsər] 명 감지기, 센서
- □ **snowboard** [snóubɔ̀:rd] 명 스노보드
- □ **soak** [souk] 동 담그다, 적시다
- □ **soil** [sɔil] 명 흙, 토양
- □ **solve** [sɑlv] 동 해결하다
- □ **spinach** [spínitʃ] 명 시금치
- □ **statue** [stǽtʃu:] 명 조각상, 동상
- □ **stomachache** [stʌ́məkèik] 명 복통
- □ **system** [sístəm] 명 시스템, 체계, 장치
- □ **surprising** [sərpráiziŋ] 형 놀라운
- □ **technology** [teknálədʒi] 명 기술
- □ **trace** [treis] 명 흔적 동 추적하다
- □ **truth** [tru:θ] 명 사실, 진실
- □ **vision** [víʒən] 명 시력
- □ **vitamin** [váitəmin] 명 비타민
- □ **world-famous** [wə̀:rldféiməs] 형 세계적으로 유명한

Key Expressions

- □ **be afraid of** ~을 두려워하다
- □ **be good for** ~에 유익하다
- □ **be scared of** ~을 무서워하다
- □ **by -ing** ~함으로써
- □ **get some fresh air** 신선한 공기를 마시다
- □ **give it a try** 시도해 보다
- □ **have a fever** 몸에 열이 있다
- □ **in addition** 게다가
- □ **keep a secret** 비밀을 지키다

- □ **keep ~ away from ...** ~을 …로부터 멀리하다
- □ **Royal Air Force** 영국 공군
- □ **lose weight** 살을 빼다
- □ **no longer** 더 이상 ~가 아닌
- □ **soak up** 흡수하다, 빨아들이다
- □ **sore throat** 인후염
- □ **stay full** 포만감을 가지다
- □ **take medicine** 약을 먹다
- □ **turn A into B** A를 B로 바꾸다

Word Power

※ 서로 비슷한 뜻을 가진 어휘

- □ **absorb** 흡수하다 : **soak up** 빨아들이다, 적시다
- □ **cartoon** 만화 : **comic strip** 만화
- □ **consider** 여기다 : **regard** 간주하다

- □ **improve** 개선하다 : **upgrade** 개선하다
- □ **contain** 포함하다 : **involve** 포함하다
- □ **improve** 개선하다 : **get better** 좋아지다

※ 서로 반대되는 뜻을 가진 어휘

- □ **hide** 숨기다 ↔ **uncover** 밝혀내다

- □ **defeat** 물리치다 ↔ **yield** 굴복하다

※ 동사 – 동사+er/or = 명사(사람)

- □ **act** 행동하다 – **actor** 배우
- □ **fight** 싸우다 – **fighter** 전사, 전투기
- □ **invent** 발명하다 – **inventor** 발명가
- □ **research** 조사하다 – **researcher** 조사원

- □ **direct** 감독하다, 지휘하다 – **director** 감독
- □ **interview** 인터뷰하다 – **interviewer** 면접관
- □ **paint** 그리다 – **painter** 화가
- □ **visit** 방문하다 – **visitor** 방문자

※ 명사 – 명사+ist = 명사(사람)

- □ **art** 예술 – **artist** 예술가
- □ **science** 과학 – **scientist** 과학자

- □ **cartoon** 만화 – **cartoonist** 만화가
- □ **tour** 여행 – **tourist** 여행자

※ **keep**을 포함한 표현

- □ **keep ~ a secret** ~을 비밀로 하다
- □ **keep away** 멀리하다
- □ **keep in touch** 연락하다

- □ **keep a diary** 일기를 쓰다
- □ **keep ~ in mind** ~을 명심하다
- □ **keep track of** ~을 기록하다

English Dictionary

- □ **battleship** 전함
  - → the largest type of ship used in war, with very big guns and heavy armour
  - 중무장을 하고 대형 대포를 가진 전쟁에 사용되는 가장 큰 형태의 선박

- □ **carrot** 당근
  - → a long pointed orange vegetable that grows under the ground
  - 땅 밑에서 자라는 길고 뾰족한 오렌지색 채소

- □ **cartoon** 만화
  - → a funny drawing in a newspaper or magazine
  - 신문이나 잡지에 실린 우스운 그림

- □ **character** 등장인물
  - → a person in a book, play, film etc.
  - 책, 연극, 영화 등에 등장하는 사람

- □ **hide** 숨기다
  - → to cover something so that it cannot be seen clearly
  - 명확하게 보이지 않도록 감추다

- □ **insect** 곤충
  - → a small creature such as a fly or ant, that has six legs
  - 여섯 개의 다리를 가진 파리나 개미 같은 작은 생물

- □ **nutrient** 영양분
  - → a chemical or food that provides what is needed for plants or animals to live and grow
  - 식물이나 동물이 살고 성장하기 위하여 필요한 것을 제공해 주는 화학 물질이나 음식

- □ **secret** 비밀
  - → a fact that is known by only a small number of people, and is not told to anyone else
  - 소수의 사람들에 의해서만 알려진 사실이며 다른 누구에게도 말해지지 않는 어떤 것

- □ **statue** 동상
  - → an image of a person or animal that is made in solid material such as stone or metal
  - 돌이나 금속 같은 단단한 재료로 만들어진 사람이나 동물의 이미지

01 다음 중 주어진 단어의 관계와 같은 것은?

> lower – raise

① similar – alike
② necessary – essential
③ truth – falsehood
④ unusual – uncommon
⑤ advantage – benefit

02 다음 영영풀이에 해당하는 단어로 가장 적절한 것은?

> a fact that is known by only a small number of people, and is not told to anyone else

① diary
② newspaper
③ secret
④ politician
⑤ news

03 다음 중 밑줄 친 단어의 쓰임이 바르지 <u>않은</u> 것은?

① Jamie is a <u>dancer</u>. He dances very well.
② Polly is a <u>diver</u>. She can dive deep in the sea.
③ Chris is a <u>swimmer</u>. He swims like a fish.
④ Dave is an <u>actor</u>. He acts in a movie.
⑤ Jill is a <u>composor</u>. She composes beautiful music.

서답형
04 다음 우리말에 맞게 빈칸에 알맞은 말을 쓰시오. (3 단어)

> 그 곰을 두려워하지 마.
> ➡ Don't _____ the bear.

➡ _____

05 다음은 각 영영풀이에 알맞은 단어를 빈칸으로 표시한 것이다. 모형 '★' 안에 들어갈 알파벳을 순서대로 배열한 것은?

> • ____ ____ ____ ____ ★ : a person who is trained to fly an aircraft
> • ____ ★ ____ ____ : to put something into a liquid and leave it there
> • ____ ____ ★ ____ ____ : to press something very hard to break it into pieces
> • ____ ____ ____ ____ ★ : someone whose job is acting in plays or films

① hide
② tone
③ town
④ hold
⑤ tour

서답형
06 다음 문장의 빈칸에 들어갈 말을 〈보기〉에서 골라 쓰시오.

> ┤ 보기 ├
> material statue bloom character

(1) Flowers _____ every April.
(2) The white _____ of Kim Koo looks good.
(3) The _____ can be divided into two parts, iron and plastic.
(4) The main _____ in this book is very famous all around the world.

중요
07 다음 빈칸에 공통으로 들어갈 말로 가장 적절한 것은? (대 · 소문자 무시)

> • Do you see the house _____ the river?
> • He used to travel _____ train.
> • _____ doing this, I can help her.

① on
② in
③ at
④ about
⑤ by

01 주어진 단어의 관계와 같도록 빈칸에 알맞은 말을 쓰시오.

fight – fighter : invent – _____

02 다음 영영풀이에 해당하는 단어를 〈보기〉에서 찾아 쓰시오.

보기
statue   insect   expect

(1) _____ : to believe that something will happen

(2) _____ : an image of a person or animal that is made in solid material such as stone or metal

(3) _____ : a small creature such as a fly or ant, that has six legs

03 우리말 의미에 맞게 주어진 단어를 바르게 나열하시오. (필요하다면 어형을 바꾸시오.)

(1) 졸업 후에, 나는 조사원으로서 NASA에 직장을 얻었다.
(research / graduation / with NASA / got / after / a job / I / as / a)
➡ _____
_____

(2) 그 면접관은 내게 나의 미래 계획에 관해 물었다.
(plans / asked / about / the / future / me / my / interview)
➡ _____
_____

(3) 나는 만화가인 것이 자랑스러워.
(cartoon / I / proud / being / a / am / of)
➡ _____
_____

04 (A)~(C)에 각각 공통으로 들어가는 말을 순서대로 쓰시오.

(A) I think I _____ a fever.
They _____ difficulty in reading books.
(B) I want you to _____ it a secret.
Dave used to _____ a diary.
(C) I will _____ the medicine tonight.
Shall we _____ a walk?

➡ (A) _____ (B) _____ (C) _____

05 주어진 우리말에 맞게 빈칸에 알맞은 말을 쓰시오.

(1) 운동은 우리의 몸과 마음에 유익하다.
➡ Exercise _____ _____ _____ our body and mind.

(2) 그 법은 더 이상 효력이 없습니다.
➡ The law is _____ _____ effective.

(3) 게다가, 나는 너무 어려요.
➡ _____ _____, I am too young.

(4) 여러분은 매일 계획을 세움으로써 이것을 할 수 있습니다.
➡ You can do this _____ _____ plans every day.

(5) 그것은 독성이 강한 물질로 만들어졌어요.
➡ It was made with a _____ _____.

06 다음 빈칸에 알맞은 말을 쓰시오.

A: What do you want to be in the future?
B: I want to be an _____. I like inventing things. Edison is my role model.

① 안부 묻고 답하기

> **A** Is something wrong? 무슨 문제 있어?
> **B** I have a bad fever. 열이 심하게 나요.

- 상대방의 안부를 묻는 표현에는 우리가 잘 알고 있는 'How are you?'(잘 지내니?) 이외에도 'How have you been?'(어떻게 지냈니?) 또는 'What's up?', 'What's going on?'(무슨 일 있니?) 등의 다양한 표현들이 있다.

- 안부를 물을 때 상대방이 좋지 않아 보여서 걱정이 되는 상황일 때는 '무슨 문제가 있니?'라는 의미로 'Is something wrong?'(무슨 일 있니?), 'Is there anything wrong with you?' 또는 'What's wrong (with you)?' 등으로 물어본다.

- 상대방의 안부를 물을 때 대답은 본인의 상황에 따라서 'Great, very well. Thank you.', 'Fine, thanks.', 'Not bad.', 'I hurt ~.' 등으로 하면 되고, 'How about you?'로 되물을 수도 있다. 'How have you been?'(어떻게 지냈니?)에 대하여 응답할 때는 'I've been'은 생략하고 '(I've been) Good.', 'Fine.', 'Great.' 등을 쓸 수 있다.

안부 묻기

- Is something wrong? 무슨 문제 있어?
- What's wrong with you? 무슨 일 있니?
- How are you doing? 어떻게 지내니?

- What's the matter? 무슨 일 있어?
- How have you been? 그동안 어떻게 지냈어?
- How's it going? 어떻게 지내니?

핵심 Check

1. 다음 대화의 빈칸에 들어가기에 적절하지 <u>않은</u> 것은?

> **B:** Bomi, do you have some medicine?
> **G:** Why? _____
> **B:** I have a stomachache. I think I ate too much for lunch.
> **G:** Why don't you go for a walk?
> **B:** O.K. I'll give it a try.

① What's the matter?
② Is something wrong?
③ What's wrong?
④ Where have you been?
⑤ Is there anything wrong with you?

② 조언 구하기

> • **What do you think I should do?** 내가 뭘 해야 한다고 생각해?

- 어려운 일이나 안 좋은 일이 있어서 상대에게 조언을 구해야 할 때는 '무엇을 해야 할까요?'의 의미로 'What do you think I should do?'(제가 무엇을 해야 한다고 생각하세요?) 또는 'How can I ~?'(어떻게 ~할까요?) 등으로 물어본다.

- 조언을 구할 때 방법을 물어보는 의미로 'How can I ~?', 'What can I ~?'라고 할 수 있고, 'What can I do to ~?', 'What should I do to ~?'라고 하거나 'What's your advice?', 'What do you suggest?' 등으로 물어볼 수도 있다.

- 상대방에게 조언을 할 때는 '(I think) You should ~.', 'Make sure you ~.', 'I suggest (that) you ~.', 'You need to ~.', 'You have to ~.' 등으로 대답할 수 있으며, 'Why don't you ~?' 또는 'How/What about ~?' 등의 제안하는 표현을 이용하여 조언을 할 수도 있다.

조언 구하기

- What do you think I should do? 내가 뭘 해야 한다고 생각해요?
- What should I do to ~? ~하려면 뭘 해야 할까요?
- What do you suggest? 제안하는 게 뭔가요?
- What do you advise me to do? 무엇을 할지 조언해 주시겠습니까?
- If you were me, what would you do? 만약 제 입장이면 어떻게 하실 겁니까?

조언하기

- (I think) You should ~. ~해야 한다고 생각해.
- I suggest you ~. ~하라고 하고 싶어.
- Why don't you ~? ~하는 것이 어떠니?
- Make sure you ~. 반드시 ~해라.
- You need to ~. / You have to ~. 너는 ~해야 해.
- How about ~? / What about ~? ~하면 어때?

핵심 Check

2. 다음 대화의 내용에 어울리도록 빈칸에 주어진 단어를 적절하게 배열하시오.

B: It's so hard to lose weight. (you, I, what, do, do, think, should)?

G: Well, why don't you walk your dog every day?

B: My dog would love it, but would it help me lose weight?

G: Sure. When you walk your dog, you're actually exercising, too.

B: O.K. I'll think about it.

➡ _____

Listen and Speak 1 A-1

B: Bomi, do you have ❶some medicine?

G: Why? ❷Is something wrong?

B: I ❸have a stomachache. I think I ate too much for lunch.

G: ❹Why don't you go for a walk?

B: O.K. I'll ❺give it a try.

B: 보미야, 약 좀 있니?
G: 왜? 무슨 문제 있어?
B: 배가 아파. 점심을 너무 많이 먹었나 봐.
G: 산책을 좀 하는 게 어때?
B: 알겠어. 한번 해 볼게.

❶ some은 셀 수 있는 명사와 없는 명사를 모두 수식할 수 있다.
❷ 주로 상대방이 좋지 않아 보여서 걱정이 되는 상황일 때 쓰는 말로 'What's the matter?', 'Is anything wrong with you?'와 같다.
❸ 병이 있다고 말할 때는 주로 동사 have를 사용하여 말한다.
❹ 조언하는 말로 'How about ~?', '(I think) You should ~.' 등으로 대체하여 쓸 수 있다.
❺ give it a try: 시도하다, 한번 해 보다

Check(√) True or False

(1) Bomi ate too much for lunch. T ☐ F ☐

(2) The boy will try going for a walk. T ☐ F ☐

Listen and Speak 2 A-1

B: It's so hard to lose weight. ❶What do you think I should do?

G: Well, ❷why don't you walk your dog every day?

B: My dog would love it, but would it help me ❸lose weight?

G: Sure. When you walk your dog, you're actually exercising, ❹too.

B: O.K. I'll think about it.

B: 몸무게를 줄이는 건 너무 어려워. 내가 뭘 해야 한다고 생각해?
G: 글쎄, 매일 너의 개를 산책시키는 건 어때?
B: 우리 개는 좋아하겠지만, 그게 살을 빼는 데 도움이 될까?
G: 물론이지. 네가 개를 산책시키면, 사실은 너도 운동하는 거잖아.
B: 좋아. 생각해 볼게.

❶ 조언을 구하는 말로 'What should I do to ~?', 'What do you advise me to do?' 등으로 대체하여 쓸 수 있다.
❷ 조언하는 말로 'How about ~?', '(I think) You should ~.' 등으로 대체하여 쓸 수 있다.
❸ help는 목적격보어로 to부정사나 동사원형을 취하는 동사이다. lose weight: 체중을 줄이다
❹ 긍정에 대한 동의는 too를 쓴다.

Check(√) True or False

(3) The boy wants the girl to lose some weight. T ☐ F ☐

(4) The girl suggests an idea that will help the boy lose weight. T ☐ F ☐

(5) The boy will walk his dog in order to lose his weight. T ☐ F ☐

Listen and Speak 1 A-2

B: ❶Is something wrong? You don't look so good.

G: ❷I have a sore throat. I think it's because of the fine dust these days.

B: ❸Put some plants in your room. They take bad air in and produce fresh air.

G: Really? I'll get ❹a few plants right away.

❶ 주로 상대방이 좋지 않아 보여서 걱정이 되는 상황일 때 쓰는 말로 'What's the matter?', 'Is anything wrong with you?'와 같다.
❷ 병이 있다고 말할 때는 주로 동사 have를 사용하여 말한다.
❸ 명령문을 사용하여 조언하는 말을 할 수 있다.
❹ 셀 수 있는 명사를 수식하는 수량형용사이다.

Listen and Speak 2 A-2

B: ❶How are your tomatoes doing? Are they growing well?

G: No. I've gotten only a few tomatoes ❷so far. ❸What do you think I should do?

B: Where do you have the pot?

G: In the kitchen.

B: Well, tomato plants need about 7 hours of sunlight a day.

G: Oh, ❹I see. I'll move the pot over to the window.

❶ 'How is[are] ~ doing?'은 안부를 묻는 말이다.
❷ 현재완료와 함께 쓰여 '지금까지'라는 의미로 사용된다.
❸ 조언을 구하는 말로 'What should I do to ~?', 'What do you advise me to do?' 등으로 대체하여 쓸 수 있다.
❹ I see는 I understand라는 의미로 사용된다.

Communicate A

Anna: Suho, ❶is something wrong? You're very quiet today.

Suho: I'm just a bit tired. I slept very little last night.

Anna: Did you do something late last night?

Suho: Yes, I watched a movie on my phone until 2 a.m. That's what I often do these days.

Anna: Oh, ❷that's why you have red eyes. You should go to bed before midnight for your health.

Suho: I think my eyes are getting worse. What do you think I should do?

Anna: ❸Try eating lots of carrots and tomatoes. They're rich in vitamin A, so they'll keep your eyes healthy.

Suho: I see. Thank you, Anna.

❶ 'Is anything wrong with you?'라고 말해도 좋다.
❷ 'That's why ~.'는 결과를 이끄는 말이다.
❸ 'What about eating lots of carrots and tomatoes?'라고 말해도 좋다.

Progress Check 1

B: ❶Is something wrong?

G: I'm just a little tired. I've watched a movie on my phone ❷for two hours.

B: ❸That's why you have red eyes. Try putting a warm towel over your eyes.

G: O.K. Thanks.

❶ 'What's the matter?'라고 물을 수 있다.
❷ '~ 동안'이라는 의미로 쓰인다.
❸ 'That is the reason why ~.'로 풀어 쓸 수 있다.

Progress Check 2

G: What's wrong? You look worried.

B: Well, I broke my mom's favorite plate. ❶What do you think I should do?

G: ❷Tell her the truth. She will understand.

B: I hope you're right.

❶ 'What should I do?'라고 말해도 좋다.
❷ 'Why don't you tell her the truth?'라고 말할 수 있다.

다음 우리말과 일치하도록 빈칸에 알맞은 말을 쓰시오.

Listen & Speak 1 A-1

B: Bomi, do you have _____ _____?

G: Why? Is _____ _____?

B: I have _____ _____. I think I ate _____ _____ for lunch.

G: Why don't you _____ _____ _____ _____?

B: O.K. I'll give _____ _____ _____.

B: 보미야, 약 좀 있니?
G: 왜? 무슨 문제 있어?
B: 배가 아파. 점심을 너무 많이 먹었나 봐.
G: 산책을 좀 하는 게 어때?
B: 알겠어. 한번 해 볼게.

Listen & Speak 1 A-2

B: Is _____ _____? You don't look _____ _____.

G: I have _____ _____ _____. I think it's _____ _____ the fine dust these days.

B: _____ some plants in your room. They _____ bad air _____ and _____ fresh air.

G: Really? I'll _____ _____ _____ _____ right away.

B: 어디 안 좋아? 안색이 나빠 보이는데.
G: 목이 아파. 최근의 미세먼지 때문인 것 같아.
B: 방에 식물을 좀 놓아 봐. 나쁜 공기를 흡수하고 신선한 공기를 만들어 내.
G: 정말? 당장 식물을 몇 그루 가져와야 겠어.

Listen & Speak 2 A-1

B: It's _____ _____ _____ _____ weight. What _____ _____ _____ I should do?

G: Well, why don't you _____ _____ _____ every day?

B: My dog would love _____, but would _____ _____ me _____ _____?

G: Sure. When you walk your dog, you're _____ _____, _____.

B: O.K. I'll _____ _____ _____.

B: 몸무게를 줄이는 건 너무 어려워. 내가 뭘 해야 한다고 생각해?
G: 글쎄, 매일 너의 개를 산책시키는 건 어때?
B: 우리 개는 좋아하겠지만, 그게 살을 빼는 데 도움이 될까?
G: 물론이지. 네가 개를 산책시키면, 사실은 너도 운동하는 거잖아.
B: 좋아. 생각해 볼게.

Listen & Talk 2 A-2

B: _____ _____ your tomatoes _____? Are they _____ well?

G: No. I've _____ only _____ _____ tomatoes _____ _____. What do you think _____ _____ _____?

B: _____ do you have the pot?

G: _____ the kitchen.

B: Well, tomato plants _____ _____ 7 hours of sunlight _____ _____.

G: Oh, I see. I'll _____ the pot _____ to the window.

B: 네 토마토들 어떠니? 잘 자라고 있어?
G: 아니. 지금까지 토마토 몇 개밖에 못 얻었어. 내가 뭘 해야 한다고 생각하니?
B: 화분을 어디에 두는데?
G: 부엌에.
B: 음, 토마토는 하루에 7시간 정도 햇빛을 받아야 해.
G: 오, 그렇구나. 화분을 창문 쪽으로 옮겨야겠다.

Communicate A

Anna: Suho, _____ _____ _____? You're very _____ today.

Suho: I'm just _____ _____ _____. I slept very _____ last night.

Anna: Did you do _____ _____ last night?

Suho: Yes, I watched a movie _____ my phone _____ 2 a.m. That's _____ _____ _____ _____ these days.

Anna: Oh, _____ _____ you have red eyes. You should go to bed _____ midnight for your health.

Suho: I think my eyes are _____ _____. What do you think _____ _____ _____?

Anna: Try _____ _____ _____ _____ and tomatoes. They're _____ _____ _____ A, so they'll _____ your eyes _____.

Suho: I _____. Thank you, Anna.

해석

Anna: 수호야, 무슨 일 있어? 오늘 굉장히 조용하네.
수호: 조금 피곤한 것뿐이야. 어젯밤에 정말 조금 잤거든.
Anna: 어제 밤 늦게까지 뭔가 했니?
수호: 응, 새벽 2시까지 휴대폰으로 영화를 봤어. 요즘 종종 하는 일이야.
Anna: 오, 그래서 눈이 충혈됐구나. 건강을 위해 자정 전에는 잠자리에 들어야 해.
수호: 눈이 점점 나빠지는 것 같아. 내가 뭘 해야 한다고 생각해?
Anna: 당근이랑 토마토를 많이 먹어 봐. 그것들은 비타민 A가 많아서, 네 눈을 건강하게 유지해 줄 거야.
수호: 알겠어. 고마워, Anna.

Progress Check 1

B: _____ something _____?

G: I'm just _____ _____ tired. I've _____ a movie on my phone _____ two hours.

B: That's _____ you have _____ _____. Try _____ a warm towel _____ your eyes.

G: O.K. Thanks.

B: 무슨 문제 있어?
G: 조금 피곤한 것뿐이야. 휴대전화로 영화를 두 시간 동안 봤거든.
B: 그래서 눈이 충혈됐구나. 따뜻한 수건으로 눈을 덮어 봐.
G: 알겠어. 고마워.

Progress Check 2

G: What's _____? You look _____.

B: Well, I _____ my mom's favorite _____. What _____ _____ _____ I should do?

G: _____ her the truth. She will _____.

B: I _____ you're _____.

G: 무슨 문제 있어? 걱정이 있는 것 같은데.
B: 그게, 어머니께서 가장 아끼시는 접시를 깨뜨렸어. 내가 뭘 해야 한다고 생각하니?
G: 솔직히 말씀 드려. 이해하실 거야.
B: 네 말이 맞길 바라.

01 다음 대화의 빈칸에 알맞은 것은?

> B: _____ You don't look so good.
> G: I have a sore throat.

① How do you care your neck?
② Is there something interesting?
③ What are you doing?
④ What is the matter?
⑤ How long have you been here?

02 다음 대화의 밑줄 친 부분과 바꾸어 쓸 수 있는 것은?

> B: I lost my wallet that my father gave me. <u>What do you think I should do</u>?
> G: I think you should tell him the truth. He will understand you.

① What should I find?
② What did I do?
③ What do you suggest?
④ How can you help me?
⑤ What can you say to him?

[03~04] 다음 대화를 읽고 물음에 답하시오.

> B: Is something wrong?
> G: I'm just a little ___(A)___ . I've watched a movie on my phone for two hours.
> B: That's why you have red eyes. Try putting a warm towel over your eyes.
> G: O.K. Thanks.

03 빈칸 (A)에 들어갈 말로 가장 적절한 것은?

① boring　　　② upset　　　③ tired
④ excited　　　⑤ sleepy

04 How long has the girl watched a movie on her phone?

➡ _____

01 다음 대화의 밑줄 친 부분의 목적으로 가장 적절한 것은?

> **A:** I have a cold. <u>What do you think I should do?</u>
>
> **B:** Why don't you drink some hot honey tea?

① 안부 묻기   ② 길 묻기
③ 조언 구하기   ④ 제안에 응하기
⑤ 승낙하기

02 다음 짝지어진 대화 중 <u>어색한</u> 것은?

① A: I lied to my mom. What should I do?
   B: I think you should tell her the truth.
② A: Is something wrong?
   B: I forgot to bring my umbrella.
③ A: How have you been?
   B: Great. I have a soar throat.
④ A: What's wrong? You look upset.
   B: I can't find my bicycle.
⑤ A: How are you doing?
   B: Not bad. How are you?

[03~04] 다음 대화를 읽고 물음에 답하시오.

> **B:** Bomi, do you have some medicine?
>
> **G:** Why? Is something wrong?
>
> **B:** I have a stomachache. I think I ate too much for lunch.
>
> **G:** Why don't you go for a walk?
>
> **B:** O.K. (A)<u>I'll give it a try.</u>

03 다음 중 밑줄 친 (A)의 의미로 가장 적절한 것은?

① I will take the medicine.
② I will eat less next time.
③ I will try to exercise more often.
④ I will try walking.
⑤ I will go see a doctor.

04 Write the reason why the boy wants some medicine. Use the phrase below.

> It's because

➡ _____

[05~07] 다음 대화를 읽고 물음에 답하시오.

> **B:** It's so ①<u>hard</u> to lose weight. (A)<u>What do you think I should do?</u>
>
> **G:** Well, why don't you ②<u>walk</u> your dog every day?
>
> **B:** My dog would love it, but would it help me ③<u>losing</u> weight?
>
> **G:** Sure. When you walk your dog, you're actually ④<u>exercising</u>, ⑤<u>too</u>.
>
> **B:** O.K. I'll think about it.

05 다음 중 밑줄 친 (A)를 대신하여 쓸 수 있는 것은?

① What do you think I am doing?
② What can I do for you?
③ How come I should lose weight?
④ What do you advise me to do?
⑤ What do you think I am doing?

06 ①~⑤ 중 어법상 바르지 <u>않은</u> 것은?

①   ②   ③   ④   ⑤

07 위 대화를 읽고 답할 수 있는 것은?

① How does the girl think about the boy?
② What is the girl's suggestion for the boy's problem?
③ How long have they known each other?
④ Why does the boy want to lose weight?
⑤ How old is the boy's dog?

서답형

08 자연스러운 대화가 되도록 (A)~(D)를 바르게 나열하시오.

> (A) Well, I broke my mom's favorite plate. What do you think I should do?
> (B) I hope you're right.
> (C) What's wrong? You look worried.
> (D) Tell her the truth. She will understand.

➡ _____

서답형

09 다음 상황을 읽고 빈칸에 들어갈 말을 조건에 맞게 쓰시오.

> You fought with one of your friend, Mina, today. On your way home, you thought you were sorry to have blamed her. So you wanted some advice from your best friend, Mike. In this situation, what would you say to Mike?
> You: "Mike, _____"
> (should / say sorry)

➡ _____

[10~11] 다음 대화를 읽고 물음에 답하시오.

> B: How are your tomatoes doing? Are they growing well?
> G: No. I've gotten only a few tomatoes so far. What do you think I should do?
> B: Where do you have the pot?
> G: In the kitchen.
> B: Well, tomato plants need about 7 hours of sunlight a day.
> G: Oh, I see. I'll move the pot over to the window.

서답형

10 Where does the girl have the tomato pot? Answer in English with a full sentence.

➡ _____

중요

11 위 대화의 내용과 일치하는 것은?

① The boy doesn't know if the girl is growing tomatoes.
② The girl has gotten lots of tomatoes.
③ The boy wants some tomatoes.
④ The boy gives the girl a tip about growing tomatoes.
⑤ The girl will put the pot in the kitchen.

[12~13] 다음 대화를 읽고 물음에 답하시오.

> Anna: Suho, is something wrong? You're very ①quiet today.
> Suho: I'm just a bit tired. I slept very ②little last night.
> Anna: Did you do something ③late last night?
> Suho: Yes, I watched a movie on my phone until 2 a.m. That's what I often do these days.
> Anna: Oh, that's why you have red eyes. You should go to bed ④before midnight for your health.
> Suho: I think my eyes are getting worse. What do you think I should do?
> Anna: Try eating lots of carrots and tomatoes. They're rich in vitamin A, so they'll keep your eyes ⑤unhealthy.
> Suho: I see. Thank you, Anna.

12 ①~⑤ 중 대화의 흐름상 어색한 것은?

① ② ③ ④ ⑤

서답형

13 What does Suho often do these days? Answer in English with a full sentence.

➡ _____

01 주어진 단어를 활용하여 다음 우리말을 영어로 쓰시오.

> A: I'm tired because of my neighbor. She keeps playing the piano at night. <u>내가 무엇을 해야 한다고 생각해?</u>
> (what / you / think / should)
> B: Why don't you ask her to stop playing the piano at night?

➡ _____

[02~04] 다음 대화를 읽고 물음에 답하시오.

> B: Is something wrong, Jane? You don't look so good.
> G: I ___(A)___ a sore throat. I think it's because of the fine dust these days.
> B: Put some plants in your room. They ___(B)___ bad air in and produce fresh air.
> G: Really? I'll ___(C)___ a few plants right away.

02 주어진 단어를 빈칸 (A)~(C)에 적절하게 쓰시오.

> take / have / get

➡ (A) _____ (B) _____ (C) _____

03 대화의 내용에 맞게 빈칸에 알맞은 말을 쓰시오.

> Jane thinks that _____ _____ _____ makes her throat _____.

04 What is Jane likely to do after the conversation? Answer in English.

➡ _____

[05~06] 다음 대화를 읽고 물음에 답하시오.

> B: (A)<u>Is something wrong?</u>
> G: I'm just a little tired. I've watched a movie on my phone for two hours.
> B: That's why you have red eyes. Try putting a warm towel over your eyes.
> G: O.K. Thanks.

05 주어진 단어를 활용하여 밑줄 친 (A)와 같은 의미의 말을 4 단어로 쓰시오.

> (what / wrong)

➡ _____

06 Write the reason why the girl is tired. Use the phrase 'It's because.'

➡ _____

➡ _____

07 자연스러운 대화가 되도록 (A)~(E)를 바르게 나열하시오.

> (A) I have a stomachache. I think I ate too much for lunch.
> (B) O.K. I'll give it a try.
> (C) Bomi, do you have some medicine?
> (D) Why don't you go for a walk?
> (E) Why? Is something wrong?

➡ _____

08 다음 상황을 읽고 빈칸에 알맞은 말을 쓰시오. 한 칸에 하나의 단어만 쓰시오.

> You meet your friend, Yumi, and find that she looks a little sad. You want to ask her if she is okay. In this situation, what do you say to her?
> You: Yumi, _____ _____ _____ ?
> You look sad.

Grammar

① 분사

> • Peter is a boy **throwing** a big ball. Peter는 큰 공을 던지는 소년이다.
> • I know the dog **barking** at Joseph. 나는 Joseph을 향해 짖는 개를 안다.

■ 현재분사는 '동사원형+-ing' 형태로 형용사처럼 명사를 앞 또는 뒤에서 꾸며준다. 일반적으로는 명사 앞에서, 다른 어구와 함께 구(phrase)를 이룰 때는 명사를 뒤에서 꾸민다.
  • **The crying baby** stopped kicking. 울고 있는 아기가 발차기를 멈췄다.
  • Did you see **the baby crying for the toy**? 장난감을 달라고 울고 있는 아기를 봤니?

■ 현재분사(-ing)는 능동/진행의 의미, 과거분사(p.p.)는 수동/완료의 의미를 갖는다.
  • The researchers are **searching** for the cause of storms. 연구진들은 폭풍우의 원인을 찾고 있는 중이다.
  • John saw the girl **dancing** on the stage. John은 무대에서 춤추고 있는 소녀를 봤다.
  • Watch out the **broken** pieces of glasses! 깨진 유리잔 조각들을 조심하세요!
  • The actors **invited** to the film festival showed up. 영화제에 초대된 배우들이 등장했다.

■ 명사를 뒤에서 꾸미는 분사구는 '주격 관계대명사+be동사'가 생략된 것으로 볼 수 있다.
  • The girl (**who was**) **wearing** Hanbok was Sophia. 한복을 입고 있는 그 소녀는 Sophia였다.
  • The students wanted to read the books (**which were**) **written** by O. Henry. 학생들은 O. Henry에 의해 쓰인 책들을 읽고 싶어했다.

■ 분사는 명사를 꾸며주는 한정 용법 외에, 주어나 목적어의 보충 설명을 하는 서술 용법이 있다. 이 경우, 분사가 주격 보어 또는 목적격 보어가 된다.
  • A gentleman stood **looking** at the picture. 한 신사가 그림을 보며 서 있었다.
  • The injured sheep lay **surrounded** by the wolves. 다친 양이 늑대들에게 둘러싸인 채로 누워 있었다.
  • He was sorry to keep me **waiting**. 그가 나를 기다리게 해서 미안해했다.
  • He heard his name **called**. 그는 그의 이름이 불리는 것을 들었다.
  • Susan had her dream house **built** in her hometown. Susan은 그녀의 고향에 자신의 꿈의 집이 건축되도록 했다.

핵심 Check

1. 다음 괄호 안에서 알맞은 단어를 고르시오.
   (1) A man (named / naming) Robert wanted to prove that tomatoes were safe to eat.
   (2) James had his arms (breaking / broken) while playing soccer.

2 동사 강조

> • I **do love** swimming in the lake. 나는 호수에서 수영하는 것을 정말 좋아한다.
> • James **does prefer** to eat spinach. James는 시금치 먹기를 정말 선호한다.

■ 문장에서 동사의 앞에 do를 써서 동사의 의미를 강조할 수 있다. 주어의 인칭과 시제에 맞춰 do/does/did 등을 활용하며, really(정말)의 의미로 해석한다.

   • Popeye **did get** his superpower by eating spinach. Popeye는 시금치를 먹음으로써 그의 막강한 힘을 정말 얻었다.

   • Sam doesn't like horror movies, but he **does like** comedies. Sam은 공포영화를 좋아하지 않지만, 코미디는 정말 좋아한다.

■ Be로 시작하는 명령문도, Be 앞에 Do를 써서 강조할 수 있다.

   • Be nice to others! = **Do** be nice to others! 다른 사람들에게 정말 착하게 대하라!

■ do는 동사를 강조하는데 반해, 재귀대명사는 (대)명사를 강조한다.

   • Emma **did play** the piano. Emma가 피아노를 정말 연주했다.

   • Emma played the piano **herself**. = Emma **herself** played the piano. Emma가 직접 피아노를 연주했다.

■ It ~ that 강조구문에서는 명사 또는 부사(구/절)를 강조한다. 강조하려는 대상에 따라 that을 관계대명사 who(사람), which(사물)로, 또는 관계부사 when(시간), where(장소) 등으로 대체할 수 있다.

   • Clara broke the toy car at her cousin's house yesterday. Clara가 어제 사촌네 집에서 그 장난감 차를 부쉈다.

   → **It was** Clara **that[who]** broke the toy car at her cousin's house yesterday. 어제 사촌네 집에서 그 장난감 차를 부순 것은 바로 Clara였다.

   → **It was** the toy car **that[which]** Clara broke at her cousin's house yesterday. Clara가 어제 사촌네 집에서 부순 것은 바로 그 장난감 차였다.

   → **It was** yesterday **that[when]** Clara broke the toy car at her cousin's house. Clara가 사촌네 집에서 그 장난감 차를 부순 것은 바로 어제였다.

   → **It was** at her cousin's house **that[where]** Clara broke the toy car yesterday. 어제 Clara가 그 장난감 차를 부순 것은 바로 사촌네 집에서였다.

핵심 Check

2. 다음 괄호 안에서 알맞은 단어를 고르시오.

   (1) I (was / did) feel bad when I was passing by the smoking guys.

   (2) Carrots (does / do) contain a lot of vitamin A.

01 다음 문장에서 어법상 <u>어색한</u> 부분을 바르게 고쳐 쓰시오.

(1) In the future, carrots may actually be using in wars.

_____ ➡ _____

(2) I did called you the day before yesterday.

_____ ➡ _____

(3) Hannah is the one eats tomatoes right now.

_____ ➡ _____

(4) The manager received a letter writing in Latin.

_____ ➡ _____

02 다음 중 어법상 바르지 <u>않은</u> 것은?

① The villagers did build the castle about 100 years ago.
② Potatoes does help you in many ways.
③ Oliver does love what she cooks.
④ Patrick did come back home.
⑤ All of his family do like Anna's novel.

03 다음 대화의 밑줄 친 부분 중에서 어법상 <u>잘못된</u> 곳을 고르시오.

A: ①<u>Aren't</u> you ②<u>tiring</u> ③<u>of</u> eating spinach every day?
B: No, I'm not. I ④<u>do</u> ⑤<u>feel</u> healthy.

04 다음 우리말에 맞게 주어진 단어를 알맞게 배열하시오.

(1) 대부분의 미국인들은 토마토가 독성이 있다고 정말 생각했다. (did, were, poisonous, that, Americans, tomatoes, most, think)

➡ _____

(2) Lily가 찍은 사진들은 인상적이었다. (were, by, the, Lily, pictures, taken, impressive)

➡ _____

138 Lesson 3. Plants That Feed Us

01 다음 괄호 안의 단어가 올바른 형태로 순서대로 짝지어진 것은?

> • The boy (pick) up the flower is my son.
> • The money (spend) for her tour in Europe was too much.
> • Some insects are (scare) of tomatoes.

① picking – spending – scaring
② picking – spent – scaring
③ picking – spent – scared
④ picked – spending – scared
⑤ picked – spent – scaring

02 다음 빈칸에 공통으로 들어갈 말로 알맞은 것은?

> • Kate _____ like her doll.
> • Sophie always _____ the laundry right after she comes home.

① does   ② has   ③ do
④ have   ⑤ don't

서답형

03 다음 예시와 같이 두 문장을 한 문장으로 연결할 때, 빈칸에 알맞은 말을 넣으시오.

> • British pilots improved their night vision.
> • They ate carrots.
> → British pilots eating carrots improved their night vision.

(1) • There were many people.
   • They were watching the pet contest.
   → There _____ _____ _____
      _____ the pet contest.
(2) • The swimming pool is very large.
   • It was built by my grandfather.
   → The swimming pool _____
      _____ _____ _____
      very large.

중요

04 밑줄 친 부분이 어법상 올바른 것은?

① The researcher did warned the people.
② Do be polite to the elderly!
③ The boy did changed his choice.
④ She does believed it is a dream.
⑤ My uncle does looks happy.

서답형

05 다음 문장에서 어법상 틀린 부분을 찾아 바르게 고쳐 쓰시오.

> He bought a shirt making in Vietnam.

_____ ➡ _____

06 다음 중 두 문장의 뜻이 같지 않은 것은?

① I do spend much time playing chess.
   → I really spend much time playing chess.
② Jenny did show me what she drew.
   → Jenny really showed me the picture that was drawn by her.
③ It was Ann that cooked me pizza.
   → It was Ann who cooked me pizza.
④ Sarah did break her leg.
   → Sarah really broke her leg.
⑤ He did find the missing kid in the amusement park.
   → He was able to find the missing kid in the amusement park.

중요

07 밑줄 친 부분의 쓰임이 다른 하나는?

① My dad hearing the news got disappointed.
② The kids tried locking the safe.
③ I want to raise a talking parrot.
④ The girl passing by them is Joan.
⑤ The barking wolf seemed like a puppy.

08 다음 우리말에 맞게 괄호 안에 주어진 단어를 알맞게 배열하시오.

> 꿀이 섞인 감자 주스가 당신의 피부를 부드럽게 만들어 준다.
> (honey, juice, potato, skin, with, soft, mixed, your, makes)

➡ _____
_____

09 다음 빈칸에 알맞은 말이 순서대로 바르게 짝지어진 것은?

> • Emily _____ love eating vegetables.
> • Peter and Mary _____ hope to be famous when they first made the group.

① did – does
② do – did
③ does – did
④ did – do
⑤ does – do

10 다음 밑줄 친 ⓐ, ⓑ를 어법상 알맞게 고친 것이 차례대로 짝지어진 것은?

> • She warned the little kid not to touch the ⓐburn fire.
> • The students ⓑsing by the tree were our school choir members.

① burning – sang
② burning – singing
③ burnt – are singing
④ burnt – being sung
⑤ burning – be singing

11 다음 빈칸에 들어갈 말로 어색한 것은?

> A: Scott, you don't eat spinach any longer, do you?
> B: No, but I _____ when I was watching Popeye on TV.

① used to eat it a lot
② ate it a lot
③ did ate it a lot
④ used to do
⑤ did eat it a lot

12 다음 중 어법상 어색한 것을 모두 고르면?

① The little girl eats tomatoes on the chair is Sally.
② Spinach is actually considered one of the ten healthiest foods on the planet.
③ The researcher developing new material from carrots was Jenny.
④ Olivia was lied to all of us.
⑤ The people her family meeting in New York were so kind and gentle.

13 다음 밑줄 친 부분 중 어법상 어색한 것은?

① She did hide the book under the desk.
② All the jury do think she is innocent.
③ The poor do need the public support.
④ She does learn design 11 years ago.
⑤ Tom did repair his car this morning.

14 다음 중 어법상 옳은 것은?

① He sat surrounding by his friends.
② The old woman sat next to Mr. Brown was the mayor of the city.
③ Spinach can be using in a surprising way in the near future.
④ There was no pizza leaving for Mary.
⑤ The road leading to the city hall was full of traffic.

15 다음 문장의 밑줄 친 부분을 강조하는 문장으로 가장 알맞은 것은?

> Robert ate a basket of tomatoes.

① Robert ate so a basket of tomatoes.
② Robert did ate a basket of tomatoes.
③ Robert ate only a basket of tomatoes.
④ Robert did eat a basket of tomatoes.
⑤ Robert eating a basket of tomatoes.

16 다음 각 문장에서 어법상 어색한 부분을 하나씩 찾아서 알맞게 고치시오.

(1) Bill bought a book writing in Greek.

_____ ➡ _____

(2) Kate likes the potato juice mixing with honey.

_____ ➡ _____

(3) The volunteers took care of the cry babies in the orphanage.

_____ ➡ _____

17 다음 중 각 밑줄 친 부분의 쓰임이 주어진 문장의 밑줄 친 did와 같은 것은?

> The Americans <u>did</u> believe that something poisonous was in tomatoes.

① Everyone admitted Tom <u>did</u> his best.
② I <u>did</u> not have much information.
③ He <u>did</u> his role as a photographer.
④ I don't like it, but he <u>does</u> like it.
⑤ Monica has lots of things to <u>do</u>.

18 다음 중 밑줄 친 부분의 쓰임이 어색한 것을 모두 고르면?

① The students thought the story had lots of <u>touched</u> scenes.
② The dancing class may be the most <u>interesting</u> one here.
③ It was the most <u>excited</u> day of his life.
④ They were so curious that they tried to open the <u>locked</u> safe.
⑤ The clock is something <u>shown</u> you the time of the day.

19 다음 중 어법상 옳은 문장은?

① Spinach do keep our eyes healthy.
② Tim finally did made a sandwich cookie.
③ Liz does love seeing her pets.
④ Michael does plays the violin.
⑤ Barbara did called you yesterday.

20 다음 〈보기〉에 주어진 동사를 한 번씩만 사용하여 어법에 맞게 분사 형태로 빈칸을 완성하시오.

> ┌─ 보기 ─┐
> know, cover, mean, name, use, make

> I'd like to introduce you to the snowboard (A)_____ from carrots. Carrots are well (B)_____ for having a lot of vitamin A. The Scottish researchers made a light and strong material (C)_____ carrots. The snowboard is so strong and light that it is (D)_____ Crosscarros, (E)_____ that carrots cross the steep mountain (F)_____ with snow.

21 Which of the following has the same usage as the underlined part below?

> The twins don't enjoy most vegetables, but they <u>do</u> like potatoes.

① Mary folds her arms and so <u>do</u> I.
② I'm sure that she <u>did</u> do her work.
③ Matt teaches math, <u>doesn't</u> he?
④ The students are <u>doing</u> some research on exercise.
⑤ What she <u>did</u> was fix the roof.

22 다음 괄호 안의 어휘들을 배열하여, 우리말을 영작할 때 5번째와 10번째 단어를 쓰시오.

> 이것은 해바라기의 특성을 이용한다는 아이디어로부터 발명된 배터리이다.
> (using / a battery / of / the idea / sunflowers / this / the characteristic / invented from / of / is).

➡ _____, _____

01 다음 각 문장을 밑줄 친 부분을 강조하는 문장으로 바꿔 쓰시오.

(1) Sofia <u>found</u> her missing cat.

➡ _____

(2) Gordon <u>knows</u> many K-pop songs.

➡ _____

(3) Grace <u>wrote</u> these essays last week.

➡ _____

02 다음 괄호 안의 단어들을 바르게 배열하여 문장을 완성하시오. (단, 동사를 어법상 알맞은 형태로 변형할 것.)

(1) The _____ is waiting for her boy friend. (stand / girl / the street / across)

(2) Do you know the music _____ _____? (by / on / play / the band / the stage)

(3) Luna is the one _____. (a / wear / shirt / red)

03 다음 대화의 빈칸을 채우되, 동사를 강조하는 'do'를 활용하시오.

(1) A: It's amazing. I can't believe David really built the huge tower.

B: Yeah, but he _____ _____ it.

(2) A: Don't you think she should stop running?

B: I _____ _____ so. I've been worried about her.

(3) A: Can you believe Evelyn wrote the classical music only at the age of 3?

B: She _____ _____ the music at the age of 3.

04 다음 문장에서 어법상 어색한 부분을 찾아 바르게 고쳐 다시 쓰시오.

(1) This is the thing placing on the wall.

➡ _____

(2) Sarah is the one wore glasses.

➡ _____

(3) Mary is erasing the scores writing on the board.

➡ _____

(4) I do love Susan, the girl drunk water.

➡ _____

(5) The news was really shocked.

➡ _____

05 다음 두 문장을 '분사'를 활용하여 한 문장으로 만들 때, 분사에 대한 조건에 맞게 빈칸에 적절한 단어를 넣으시오.

(1) Lily tried to play with the baby. The baby was crying. (명사 앞에서 수식)

→ Lily tried to play _____ _____ _____ _____.

(2) They watched the birds. The birds were flying southwards. (명사 뒤에서 수식)

→ They watched _____ _____ _____ _____.

(3) There is a taxi. It is illegally parked. (명사 앞에서 수식)

→ There is _____ _____ _____ _____.

06 다음 우리말에 맞게 빈칸을 채우되, 괄호 안의 어휘를 이용하시오.

Unlike Sarah (A)_____(sit) on a chair, the other members of the band played their instruments (B)_____(stand) on the stage, with Joy's eyes (C)_____ (clsoe).

(의자에 앉아 있는 Sarah와 달리, 다른 멤버들은 무대 위에 서서 그들의 악기를 연주했는데, Joy는 눈을 감고 있었다.)

---

07 다음 문장을 각각의 주어진 조건에 맞게 강조하는 문장으로 바꿔 쓰시오.

Alex called you yesterday.

---

(1) Alex 강조. 재귀대명사 사용.

➡ _____

(2) you 강조. It ~ that 구문 사용.

➡ _____

(3) called 강조.

➡ _____

(4) yesterday 강조.

➡ _____

08 다음 괄호 안의 어휘를 배열하여 우리말에 맞게 빈칸을 채우시오.

_____,
(Ethan이 정말로 두통을 느꼈기 때문에), he went to the clinic for treatment. (feel, did, as, a, headache, Ethan)

---

09 다음 우리말에 맞게 영작할 때, 빈칸에 알맞은 단어를 〈보기〉에서 찾아, 어법에 맞게 활용하여 쓰시오.

┌─ 보기 ─┐
kill call hide do
└────────┘

(1) Stella는 재즈 음악을 정말 좋아한다.
→ Stella _____ like Jazz music.

(2) 어떤 과학자들은 시금치의 특성을 이용해서 땅 속에 숨겨진 폭탄을 찾았다.
→ Some scientists used the characteristic of spinach to find bombs _____ in the ground.

(3) 그 곰이 개를 정말 죽였다.
→ The bear did _____ the dog.

(4) 코끼리 귀라고 불리는 식물은 독성이 있는 식물들 중 하나이다.
→ A plant _____ elephant ear is one of the poisonous plants.

10 다음 그림을 보고, 괄호 안의 어휘를 배열하여 우리말에 맞게 빈칸을 채우시오.

If you want to keep insects away from your room, _____ in a corner of your room.

당신이 만약 당신의 방에서 벌레들을 쫓아내고 싶다면, 으깬 토마토 한 컵을 당신의 방 구석에 놓아두시오.

(crushed / tomatoes / a cup / place / of)

➡ _____

Hidden Stories about Plants

Popeye and the Great Spinach

Popeye is a world-famous cartoon character. He gets his super power by eating spinach. When Popeye became popular in the 1930s in the United States, a lot of children began to eat spinach. Crystal City in Texas, which is called the spinach capital of the world, even built a statue of Popeye. Although eating spinach will not give us super powers, spinach does have a lot of nutrients. It is actually considered one of the ten healthiest foods on the planet.

Spinach can be used in a surprising way. When it absorbs water, spinach also absorbs many other things from the soil. Some scientists have used this characteristic of spinach to find bombs hidden in the ground. They make special spinach plants with sensors on their leaves. When these plants soak up traces from bombs, the sensors light up.

hide 숨기다 (hide–hid–hidden)

spinach 시금치

cartoon 만화

capital 수도

statue 조각상, 동상

although ~임에도 불구하고, 비록 ~이지만

nutrient 영양소

consider 고려하다, 여기다

planet 행성, 세상

absorb 흡수하다, 빨아들이다

characteristic 특성, 특징

soak up 흡수하다, 빨아들이다

trace 흔적, 자취

📎 확인문제

● 다음 문장이 본문의 내용과 일치하면 T, 일치하지 <u>않으면</u> F를 쓰시오.

1 Popeye gets his super power by eating spinach. ☐

2 Crystal City in Texas, which is called the spinach center of the world, even built a statue of Popeye. ☐

3 Spinach is actually considered one of the ten healthiest foods on the planet. ☐

4 When it absorbs water, spinach also absorbs many other things from the air. ☐

5 Some scientists make special spinach plants with sensors on their leaves. ☐

6 When these special spinach plants soak up water from soils, the sensors light up. ☐

Carrots in World War II

In 1940, the Royal Air Force defeated German fighters during World War II by using a radar system. The British government wanted to keep this technology a secret, so it published an article in the newspaper. It said that British pilots improved their night vision because they ate a lot of carrots. Everybody believed the story and began to eat a lot more carrots than before. Can we really improve night vision by eating lots of carrots? Not really, but carrots contain a lot of vitamin A, which does keep our eyes healthy.

In the future, carrots may actually be used in wars. Scottish researchers have discovered a way to turn carrots into a very strong and light material. It can even be used to make battleships. This new material has already been used to make snowboards and bicycles.

Tomatoes, the Scariest Vegetables

We all know that tomatoes are good for our health. Up until the 1800s, however, most Americans thought that tomatoes were poisonous. In 1820, a man named Robert Johnson wanted to prove that tomatoes were safe to eat. So, he ate a basket of tomatoes in front of many people watching him. They all expected him to die, but nothing happened to him. Ever since then, Americans have enjoyed eating tomatoes.

We are no longer afraid of tomatoes, but some insects are still scared of them. If you want to keep insects away from your room, place a bowl of crushed tomatoes in a corner of your room. Insects will not come near the tomatoes.

---

defeat 물리치다, 패배시키다

radar 레이더, 전파 탐지기

system 시스템, 체계, 장치

government 정부, 국가

keep a secret 비밀을 지키다

article 기사

pilot 비행사, 조종사

improve 개선하다, 향상시키다

vision 시력

contain 함유하다, 들어 있다

researcher 연구원, 조사원

snowboard 스노보드

poisonous 유독한, 독성의

insect 곤충, 벌레

crush 으스러뜨리다

📎 **확인문제**

● 다음 문장이 본문의 내용과 일치하면 T, 일치하지 않으면 F를 쓰시오.

1 In 1940, the Royal Air Force won against German fighters during World War II by using a radar system. ☐

2 British pilots improved their night vision because they ate a lot of carrots. ☐

3 Up until the 1800s, most Americans thought that tomatoes were safe. ☐

4 Some insects are still scared of tomatoes. ☐

5 If you place a bowl of crushed tomatoes in a corner of your room, insects will come near the tomatoes. ☐

● 우리말을 참고하여 빈칸에 알맞은 말을 쓰시오.

1 _____ **Stories about Plants**

2 **Popeye and the Great** _____

3 Popeye is a world-famous _____ _____.

4 He gets his super power _____ _____ _____.

5 When Popeye _____ _____ in the 1930s in the United States, a lot of children began to eat spinach.

6 Crystal City in Texas, which is called _____ _____ of the world, even built _____ _____ of Popeye.

7 _____ eating spinach will not give us super powers, spinach _____ _____ a lot of nutrients.

8 It is actually considered _____ _____ _____ _____ on the planet.

9 Spinach can be used _____ _____ _____ _____.

10 When it absorbs water, spinach _____ _____ many other things _____ the soil.

11 Some scientists have used this characteristic of spinach to find bombs _____ _____ _____ _____.

12 They make special spinach plants _____ _____ _____ _____ _____.

13 When these plants _____ _____ traces from bombs, the sensors _____ _____.

14 **Carrots in** _____ _____ _____

15 In 1940, the Royal Air Force _____ German fighters _____ World War II _____ _____ a radar system.

16 The British government wanted to _____ this technology a _____, so it published _____ _____ in the newspaper.

17 It said that British pilots _____ _____ _____ _____ because they ate a lot of carrots.

---

1 식물에 대한 숨겨진 이야기

2 Popeye와 위대한 시금치

3 Popeye는 세계적으로 유명한 만화 캐릭터다.

4 그는 시금치를 먹음으로써 초인적인 힘을 얻는다.

5 Popeye가 1930년대 미국에서 인기를 얻었을 때, 많은 어린이들이 시금치를 먹기 시작했다.

6 텍사스의 크리스털 시티는 세계의 시금치 수도라고 불리는데, 이곳에서는 Popeye의 동상을 세우기까지 했다.

7 비록 시금치를 먹는 것이 우리에게 초인적인 힘을 주지는 않지만, 시금치는 정말로 많은 영양분을 가지고 있다.

8 이것은 실제로 지구상에서 가장 건강한 식품 10개 중 하나로 여겨진다.

9 시금치는 놀라운 용도로 사용될 수 있다.

10 그것이 물을 흡수할 때, 시금치는 흙으로부터 다른 많은 것들도 흡수한다.

11 몇몇 과학자들은 시금치의 이 특성을 땅에 숨겨진 폭탄을 찾는 데 사용했다.

12 그들은 잎에 감지기가 있는 특별한 시금치를 만든다.

13 이 식물들이 폭탄의 흔적을 흡수하면, 감지기가 빛난다.

14 제2차 세계대전에서의 당근

15 1940년, 영국 공군은 제2차 세계 대전에서 레이더 시스템을 사용해 독일군을 패배시켰다.

16 영국 정부는 이 기술을 비밀로 하기를 원했기 때문에, 신문에 기사를 하나 냈다.

17 그것은 영국 비행사들이 당근을 많이 먹어 야간 시력이 좋아졌다는 내용이었다.

18 Everybody believed the story and began to eat a lot more carrots _____ _____.

19 Can we really improve night vision _____ _____ lots of carrots?

20 Not really, but carrots contain a lot of vitamin A, _____ _____ _____ our eyes healthy.

21 In the future, carrots _____ _____ _____ _____ in wars.

22 Scottish researchers have discovered a way to _____ carrots _____ a very strong and light material.

23 It _____ _____ _____ _____ to make battleships.

24 This new material _____ _____ _____ _____ to make snowboards and bicycles.

25 **Tomatoes, the _____ Vegetables**

26 We all know that tomatoes _____ _____ _____ our health.

27 _____ _____ the 1800s, however, most Americans thought that tomatoes were _____.

28 In 1820, a man _____ Robert Johnson wanted to prove that tomatoes were _____ _____ _____.

29 So, he ate _____ _____ _____ tomatoes in front of many people _____ him.

30 They all expected him to die, but nothing _____ _____ him.

31 Ever since then, Americans _____ _____ _____ tomatoes.

32 We are _____ _____ afraid of tomatoes, but some insects are still _____ _____ them.

33 If you want to _____ insects _____ _____ your room, _____ a bowl of _____ tomatoes in a corner of your room.

34 Insects will not _____ _____ the tomatoes.

---

18 모두가 그 이야기를 믿었고 전보다 훨씬 많은 당근을 먹기 시작했다.

19 우리는 정말 당근을 많이 먹어서 야간 시력을 높일 수 있을까?

20 실제로 그렇지는 않지만, 당근은 많은 비타민 A를 함유하는데, 그것은 정말로 우리 눈을 건강하게 유지해 준다.

21 미래에는, 당근이 실제로 전쟁에 이용될지도 모른다.

22 스코틀랜드의 연구원들은 당근을 매우 강하고 가벼운 물질로 바꾸는 방법을 발견했다.

23 그것은 심지어 전함을 만드는 데 사용될 수도 있다.

24 이 새로운 소재는 이미 스노보드와 자전거를 만드는 데 사용되었다.

25 토마토, 가장 무서운 채소

26 우리는 모두 토마토가 건강에 좋다는 것을 안다.

27 그러나, 1800년대까지 대부분의 미국인들은 토마토에 독성이 있다고 생각했다.

28 1820년에, Robert Johnson이라는 이름의 남자가 토마토가 먹기에 안전하다는 것을 증명하기를 원했다.

29 그래서, 그는 그를 지켜보는 많은 사람들 앞에서 한 바구니의 토마토를 먹었다.

30 그들은 모두 그가 죽을 것이라고 예상했으나 그에게는 아무 일도 일어나지 않았다.

31 그 이후로, 미국인들은 토마토를 먹는 것을 즐겼다.

32 우리는 더 이상 토마토를 두려워하지 않지만, 몇몇 곤충들은 여전히 그것을 무서워한다.

33 만약 곤충들이 방에 들어오지 않게 하고 싶다면, 으깬 토마토 한 그릇을 방구석에 놓아 두어라.

34 곤충들은 토마토 가까이 오지 않을 것이다.

● 우리말을 참고하여 본문을 영작하시오.

1 식물에 대한 숨겨진 이야기

➡ _____

2 Popeye와 위대한 시금치

➡ _____

3 Popeye는 세계적으로 유명한 만화 캐릭터다.

➡ _____

4 그는 시금치를 먹음으로써 초인적인 힘을 얻는다.

➡ _____

5 Popeye가 1930년대 미국에서 인기를 얻었을 때, 많은 어린이들이 시금치를 먹기 시작했다.

➡ _____

6 텍사스의 크리스털 시티는 세계의 시금치 수도라고 불리는데, 이곳에서는 Popeye의 동상을 세우기까지 했다.

➡ _____

_____

7 비록 시금치를 먹는 것이 우리에게 초인적인 힘을 주지는 않지만, 시금치는 정말로 많은 영양분을 가지고 있다.

➡ _____

8 이것은 실제로 지구상에서 가장 건강한 식품 10개 중 하나로 여겨진다.

➡ _____

9 시금치는 놀라운 용도로 사용될 수 있다.

➡ _____

10 그것이 물을 흡수할 때, 시금치는 흙으로부터 다른 많은 것들도 흡수한다.

➡ _____

11 몇몇 과학자들은 시금치의 이 특성을 땅에 숨겨진 폭탄을 찾는 데 사용했다.

➡ _____

12 그들은 잎에 감지기가 있는 특별한 시금치를 만든다.

➡ _____

13 이 식물들이 폭탄의 흔적을 흡수하면, 감지기가 빛난다.

➡ _____

14 제2차 세계대전에서의 당근

➡ _____

15 1940년, 영국 공군은 제2차 세계 대전에서 레이더 시스템을 사용해 독일군을 패배시켰다.

➡ _____

16 영국 정부는 이 기술을 비밀로 하기를 원했기 때문에, 신문에 기사를 하나 냈다.

➡ _____

17 그것은 영국 비행사들이 당근을 많이 먹어 야간 시력이 좋아졌다는 내용이었다.

➡ _____

18 모두가 그 이야기를 믿었고 전보다 훨씬 많은 당근을 먹기 시작했다.

➡ _____

19 우리는 정말 당근을 많이 먹어서 야간 시력을 높일 수 있을까?

➡ _____

20 실제로 그렇지는 않지만, 당근은 많은 비타민 A를 함유하는데, 그것은 정말로 우리 눈을
건강하게 유지해 준다.

➡ _____

21 미래에는, 당근이 실제로 전쟁에 이용될지도 모른다.

➡ _____

22 스코틀랜드의 연구원들은 당근을 매우 강하고 가벼운 물질로 바꾸는 방법을 발견했다.

➡ _____

23 그것은 심지어 전함을 만드는 데 사용될 수도 있다.

➡ _____

24 이 새로운 소재는 이미 스노보드와 자전거를 만드는 데 사용되었다.

➡ _____

25 토마토, 가장 무서운 채소

➡ _____

26 우리는 모두 토마토가 건강에 좋다는 것을 안다.

➡ _____

27 그러나, 1800년대까지 대부분의 미국인들은 토마토에 독성이 있다고 생각했다.

➡ _____

28 1820년에, Robert Johnson이라는 이름의 남자가 토마토가 먹기에 안전하다는 것을 증명하기를 원했다.

➡ _____

29 그래서, 그는 그를 지켜보는 많은 사람들 앞에서 한 바구니의 토마토를 먹었다.

➡ _____

30 그들은 모두 그가 죽을 것이라고 예상했으나 그에게는 아무 일도 일어나지 않았다.

➡ _____

31 그 이후로, 미국인들은 토마토를 먹는 것을 즐겼다.

➡ _____

32 우리는 더 이상 토마토를 두려워하지 않지만, 몇몇 곤충들은 여전히 그것을 무서워한다.

➡ _____

33 만약 곤충들이 방에 들어오지 않게 하고 싶다면, 으깬 토마토 한 그릇을 방구석에 놓아 두어라.

➡ _____
_____

34 곤충들은 토마토 가까이 오지 않을 것이다.

➡ _____

[01~03] 다음 글을 읽고 물음에 답하시오.

Popeye is a world-famous cartoon ⓐ character. (①) He gets his super power by eating spinach. (②) When Popeye became popular in the 1930s in the United States, a lot of children began to eat spinach. (③) Crystal City in Texas, which is called the spinach capital of the world, even built a statue of Popeye. (④) It is actually considered one of the ten healthiest foods on the planet. (⑤)

01 위 글의 흐름으로 보아, 주어진 문장이 들어가기에 가장 적절한 곳은?

Although eating spinach will not give us super powers, spinach does have a lot of nutrients.

①   ②   ③   ④   ⑤

02 위 글의 밑줄 친 ⓐcharacter와 같은 의미로 쓰인 것을 고르시오.

① She is my sister, but we have very different character.
② He was a minor character in the book, but everyone loved him.
③ This Chinese character means good luck.
④ The climate of this city plays a big role in the city's character.
⑤ He is a man of fine character.

03 According to the passage, which is NOT true?

① Popeye gets his super power by eating spinach.

② Many children began to eat spinach when Popeye became popular in the 1930s in the United States.
③ People call Crystal City in Texas the spinach capital of the world.
④ In fact, eating spinach will give us super powers.
⑤ Spinach is actually considered one of the ten healthiest foods on the earth.

[04~06] 다음 글을 읽고 물음에 답하시오.

Spinach can be used in a surprising way. When it absorbs water, spinach also absorbs many other things ____ⓐ____ the soil. Some scientists have used (A)this characteristic of spinach to find bombs hidden in the ground. They make special spinach plants ____ⓑ____ sensors on their leaves. (B)When these plants soak up traces from bombs, the sensors go out.

04 위 글의 빈칸 ⓐ와 ⓑ에 들어갈 전치사가 바르게 짝지어진 것은?

    ⓐ   ⓑ   ⓐ   ⓑ
① from – with   ② on – to
③ on – from   ④ from – at
⑤ to – with

서답형
05 위 글의 밑줄 친 (A)this characteristic이 가리키는 것을 우리말로 쓰시오.

➡ _____

_____

서답형
06 위 글의 밑줄 친 (B)에서 흐름상 어색한 부분을 찾아 고치시오.

_____ ➡ _____

[07~09] 다음 글을 읽고 물음에 답하시오.

In 1940, the Royal Air Force defeated German fighters during World War II by using a radar system. The British government wanted to keep this technology a secret, so (A)it published an article in the newspaper. It said that British pilots improved their night ⓐ_____ because they ate a lot of carrots. Everybody believed the story and began to eat a lot more carrots than before. Can we really improve night ⓑ_____ by eating lots of carrots? Not really, but carrots contain a lot of vitamin A, which does keep our eyes healthy.

07 위 글의 빈칸 ⓐ와 ⓑ에 공통으로 들어갈 알맞은 말을 고르시오.

① version   ② sense of touch
③ hearing   ④ vision
⑤ sense of smell

08 위 글의 밑줄 친 (A)it이 가리키는 것을 본문에서 찾아 쓰시오.

➡ _____

위 글의 제목으로 알맞은 것을 고르시오.

① Hidden Stories about Nature
② Carrots in World War II
③ How to Eat a Lot More Carrots
④ A Radar System of the Royal Air Force
⑤ Carrots, Good for the Night Vision

[10~12] 다음 글을 읽고 물음에 답하시오.

In the future, ⓐ당근이 실제로 전쟁에 이용될지도 모른다. Scottish researchers have discovered a way to turn carrots into a very strong and light material. It can even be used to make battleships. This new material ⓑhas already been used to make snowboards and bicycles.

10 위 글의 밑줄 친 ⓐ의 우리말에 맞게 주어진 어휘를 이용하여 7 단어로 영작하시오.

> actually, used

➡ _____

11 위 글의 밑줄 친 ⓑ의 현재완료 용법과 같은 용법으로 쓰인 것을 모두 고르시오.

① How long has he been ill in bed?
② I have just finished my homework.
③ They have never seen such a horrible movie.
④ Has she met him yet?
⑤ I have lost my pen.

12 Which question CANNOT be answered after reading the passage?

① In the future, is it possible for carrots to be used in wars?
② What have Scottish researchers discovered?
③ How do Scottish researchers turn carrots into a very strong and light material?
④ Can the very strong and light material made from carrots be used to make battleships?
⑤ Has the very strong and light material made from carrots been used yet?

[13~15] 다음 글을 읽고 물음에 답하시오.

We all know that tomatoes are good for our health. Up until the 1800s, ____ⓐ____, most Americans thought that tomatoes were poisonous. In 1820, a man named Robert Johnson wanted to prove that tomatoes were safe to eat. So, he ate a basket of tomatoes in front of many people watching him. They all expected him to die, but nothing happened to him. Ever since then, Americans have enjoyed eating tomatoes.

We are no longer afraid of tomatoes, but some insects are still scared of them. If you want to keep insects away from your room, place a bowl of crushed tomatoes in a corner of your room. Insects will not come near the tomatoes.

13 위 글의 빈칸 ⓐ에 들어갈 알맞은 말을 고르시오.

① as a result
② furthermore
③ that is
④ for example
⑤ however

중요
14 위 글의 주제로 알맞은 것을 고르시오.

① eating tomatoes to be healthy
② the spread of tomatoes in America
③ the myth and truth about tomatoes
④ the danger of eating poisonous tomatoes
⑤ how to keep insects away from the room

서답형
15 본문의 내용과 일치하도록 다음 빈칸 (A)와 (B)에 알맞은 단어를 쓰시오.

If you place a bowl of (A)_____ _____ in a corner of your room,

you can keep insects away from your room. It's because some insects are still (B)_____ of tomatoes, they will not come near the tomatoes.

[16~18] 다음 글을 읽고 물음에 답하시오.

ⓐSpinach can be used in a surprising way. When it absorbs water, spinach also absorbs many other things from the soil. Some scientists have used this characteristic of spinach ⓑto find bombs hidden in the ground. They make special spinach plants with sensors on their leaves. When these plants ⓒsoak up traces from bombs, the sensors light up.

서답형
16 위 글의 밑줄 친 문장 ⓐ의 구체적인 용도에 해당하는 문장을 본문에서 찾아, 첫 단어와 마지막 단어를 쓰시오

➡ 첫 단어: _____, 마지막 단어: _____

17 위 글의 밑줄 친 ⓑto find와 to부정사의 용법이 다른 것을 모두 고르시오.

① I've worked hard to find bombs.
② But I don't know how to find bombs.
③ Is it easy to find bombs hidden in the ground?
④ Who is the best person to find bombs?
⑤ Let's start to find bombs together.

서답형
18 위 글의 밑줄 친 ⓒsoak up을 본문에 나오는 어휘를 사용하여 한 단어로 바꿔 쓰시오.

➡ _____

[19~21] 다음 글을 읽고 물음에 답하시오.

Popeye is a world-famous cartoon character. He gets his super power by eating spinach. When Popeye became popular in the 1930s in the United States, a lot of children began to eat spinach. Crystal City in Texas, which is (A)[calling / called] the spinach (B)[capital / capitol] of the world, even built a statue of Popeye. Although ⓐeating spinach will not give us super powers, spinach (C)[did / does] have a lot of nutrients. It is actually considered one of the ten healthiest foods on the planet.

서답형

19 위 글의 괄호 (A)~(C)에서 문맥이나 어법상 알맞은 낱말을 골라 쓰시오.

➡ (A) _____ (B) _____ (C) _____

20 아래 〈보기〉에서 위 글의 밑줄 친 ⓐeating과 문법적 쓰임이 같은 것의 개수를 고르시오.

┌─── 보기 ───┐
① Eating spinach will keep you healthy.
② I saw her eating spinach.
③ He is fond of eating spinach.
④ Is eating spinach really good for your health?
⑤ When I met her, she was eating spinach.
└─────────────┘

① 1개　② 2개　③ 3개　④ 4개　⑤ 5개

서답형

21 How does Popeye get his super power? Answer in English in a full sentence. (6 words)

➡ _____

[22~24] 다음 글을 읽고 물음에 답하시오.

We all know that tomatoes are good for our health. Up until the 1800s, however, most Americans thought that tomatoes were poisonous. In 1820, a man named Robert Johnson wanted to prove that tomatoes were safe to eat. So, he ate a basket of tomatoes in front of many people watching him. They all expected him to die, but nothing happened to him. Ever since then, Americans have enjoyed eating tomatoes.

We are no longer afraid of tomatoes, but some insects are still scared of ⓐthem. If you want to keep insects away from your room, place a bowl of crushed tomatoes in a corner of your room. Insects will not come near the tomatoes.

서답형

22 위 글의 밑줄 친 ⓐthem이 가리키는 것을 본문에서 찾아 쓰시오.

서답형 ➡ _____

23 다음 문장에서 위 글의 내용과 다른 부분을 찾아서 고치시오.

┌──────────────────────┐
In 1820, a man named Robert Johnson ate a basket of tomatoes in front of many people watching him and died against their expectations.
└──────────────────────┘

중요 _____ ➡ _____

24 위 글을 읽고 알 수 없는 것을 고르시오.

① Up until the 1800s, what did most Americans think about tomatoes?
② What did Robert Johnson want to prove?
③ Since when, have Americans enjoyed eating tomatoes?
④ What insects are scared of tomatoes?
⑤ If you place a bowl of crushed tomatoes in a corner of your room, what will happen?

[01~03] 다음 글을 읽고 물음에 답하시오.

Popeye is a world-famous cartoon character. He gets his super power by eating spinach. When Popeye became popular in the 1930s in the United States, a lot of children began to eat spinach. Crystal City in Texas, which is called the spinach capital of the world, even built a statue of Popeye. ⓐAs eating spinach will not give us super powers, spinach does have a lot of nutrients. ⓑIt actually considers one of the ten healthiest foods on the planet.

01 위 글의 밑줄 친 ⓐ에서 흐름상 어색한 부분을 찾아 고치시오.

➡ _____

02 위 글의 밑줄 친 ⓑ에서 어법상 틀린 부분을 찾아 고치시오.

➡ _____

03 본문의 내용과 일치하도록 다음 빈칸 (A)와 (B)에 알맞은 단어를 쓰시오.

Popeye, who gets his super power by eating spinach, is a world-famous (A)_____ _____. Thanks to Popeye, a lot of children in the United States began (B)_____ in the 1930s.

[04~06] 다음 글을 읽고 물음에 답하시오.

Spinach can ___ⓐ___ in a surprising way. When it absorbs water, spinach also absorbs many other things from the soil. Some scientists have used this characteristic of spinach to find bombs ___ⓑ___ in the ground. ⓒThey make special spinach plants with sensors on ⓓtheir leaves. When these plants soak up traces from bombs, the sensors light up.

04 위 글의 빈칸 ⓐ에 use를, ⓑ에 hide를 각각 알맞은 형태로 쓰시오.

➡ ⓐ _____ ⓑ _____

05 위 글의 밑줄 친 ⓒThey와 ⓓtheir가 가리키는 것을 본문에서 찾아 쓰시오.

➡ ⓒ _____ ⓓ _____

06 다음 빈칸 (A)와 (B)에 알맞은 단어를 넣어 땅에 숨겨진 폭탄을 찾는 데 시금치를 사용하는 방법을 완성하시오.

Spinach absorbs many other things in addition to water from the soil. When the special spinach plants with (A)_____ on their leaves soak up traces from bombs, the sensors light up and help people find (B)_____ under the ground.

[07~10] 다음 글을 읽고 물음에 답하시오.

In 1940, the Royal Air Force (A)[defeated / was defeated] German fighters (B)[during / while] ⓐWorld War II by using a radar system. The British government wanted to keep this technology a secret, so it published an article in the newspaper. ⓑIt said that British pilots improved their night vision because they ate a lot of carrots. Everybody believed the story and began to eat a lot more carrots than before. Can we really improve night vision by eating lots of carrots? Not really, but carrots contain a lot of vitamin A, which does keep our eyes (C)[healthy / healthily].

07 위 글의 괄호 (A)~(C)에서 문맥이나 어법상 알맞은 낱말을 골라 쓰시오.

➡ (A) _____ (B) _____ (C) _____

08 위 글의 밑줄 친 ⓐWorld War II를 읽는 법을 영어로 쓰시오.

➡ _____

09 위 글의 밑줄 친 ⓑIt이 가리키는 것을 본문에서 찾아 쓰시오.

➡ _____

10 위 글을 읽고, (1) 영국 정부가 신문기사로 당근의 효능에 관해 발표한 것과 (2) 당근의 실제 효능을 우리말로 쓰시오.

➡ (1) _____
　　 _____
　 (2) _____
　　 _____

[11~14] 다음 글을 읽고 물음에 답하시오.

We all know that tomatoes are good for our health. Up until the 1800s, however, most Americans thought that tomatoes were poisonous. In 1820, a man named Robert Johnson wanted to prove that tomatoes were safe to eat. So, he ate a basket of tomatoes in front of many people watching him. They all expected him to die, but nothing happened to him. ⓐ그 이후로, 미국인들은 토마토를 먹는 것을 즐겼다.

ⓑWe are no longer afraid of tomatoes, but some insects are still scared of them. ⓒIf you want to keep insects away from your room, place a bowl of crushing tomatoes in a corner of your room. Insects will not come near the tomatoes.

11 위 글의 밑줄 친 ⓐ의 우리말에 맞게 주어진 어휘를 이용하여 8 단어로 영작하시오.

> Ever, then, have enjoyed

➡ _____

12 위 글의 밑줄 친 ⓑ를 다음과 같이 바꿔 쓸 때 빈칸에 들어갈 알맞은 말을 두 단어로 쓰시오.

➡ We are not afraid of tomatoes _____
_____,

13 위 글의 밑줄 친 ⓒ에서 어법상 틀린 부분을 찾아 고치시오.

_____ ➡ _____

14 Why did Robert Johnson eat a basket of tomatoes in front of many people watching him? Answer in English beginning with "Because". (11 words)

➡ _____
_____

Inventions from Plants

The Sunflower Battery is a good way to produce energy. It is a battery

_{to부정사의 형용사적 용법}
invented from the idea of using the characteristic of sunflowers. Like

_{battery를 수식하는 과거분사(수동)}　　　　　　　　　_{소유를 나타내는 of}　　　_{전치사로 사용}
sunflowers, it faces the sun during the day, so it produces more electricity than

_{= the Sunflower Battery}　　　　　_{결과를 이끄는 접속사}
other batteries.

_{other+복수 명사}

구문해설 • way: 방법　• characteristic: 특성, 특징　• face: ~을 향하다

　　　　　• produce: 만들다, 생산하다

After You Read A Read and Match

1. Spinach

• the secret of Popeye's super power

• one of the ten healthiest foods on the planet

_{one of the+복수 명사: ~ 중의 하나}

• used with sensors to find bombs hidden in the ground

　　　　　　　　_{to부정사의 부사적 용법(목적)　과거분사(수동)}

2. Carrots

• used to make snowboards and bicycles

_{to부정사의 부사적 용법(목적)}

• made into a very strong and light material

_{~으로(변화)}

• containing a lot of vitamin A, which keeps our eyes healthy

　　　　_{= and it(계속적 용법의 관계대명사)　keep+목적어+목적격보어(형용사) healthily(×)}

3. Tomatoes

• good for keeping insects away

　　　_{keep ~ away: ~을 가까이 오지 못하게 하다}

• considered poisonous until the 1800s

구문해설 • spinach: 시금치　• snowboard: 스노보드　• contain: 함유하다, 들어 있다

　　　　　• insect: 곤충, 벌레　• consider: 고려하다, 여기다

Write

Potatoes are good for your health. They keep your heart healthy because they

　　　　　　　　　　　　　　_{5형식 V +목적어+목적보어　종속접속사(이유)}
lower blood pressure. They also solve your skin problems. Potato juice mixed

　　　　　　　　　　　　　　　　　　　　　　　　　　_{과거분사}
with honey makes your skin soft and clear. In addition, they help you lose

　　　_{단수 동사에 유의　　목적보어1　목적보어2 (병렬구조)　to lose도 가능(help: 준사역동사)}
weight. If you eat potatoes, you will stay full for a long time. Potatoes help

　　　　　　　　　　　　　　　_{2형식 V+형용사(주격보어)}
you stay healthy in many ways.

구문해설 • be good for: ~에 좋다　• keep+A+형용사: A를 ~한 상태로 유지시켜 주다　• lower: 낮추다

　　　　　• blood pressure: 혈압　• in addition: 게다가　• stay full: 배부른 상태를 유지하다

해석

해바라기 배터리는 에너지를 만드는 좋은 방법입니다. 그것은 해바라기의 특징을 이용한다는 생각에서 만들어진 배터리입니다. 해바라기처럼, 그것은 낮 동안에 태양을 향해서, 다른 배터리보다 더 많은 전기를 만들어 냅니다.

1. 시금치
• Popeye의 초인적인 힘의 비밀
• 지구상에서 가장 건강한 식품 10개 중 하나
• 땅에 숨겨진 폭탄을 찾기 위해 감지기와 함께 사용된다.

2. 당근
• 스노보드와 자전거를 만드는 데 사용된다.
• 매우 강하고 가벼운 물질이 된다.
• 많은 비타민 A를 함유하는데, 그것은 정말로 우리 눈을 건강하게 유지해 준다.

3. 토마토
• 곤충들이 가까이 오지 못하게 하는 데 좋다.
• 1800년대까지 독성이 있다고 여겨졌다.

감자는 당신의 건강에 좋다. 감자는 혈압을 낮춰주기 때문에 당신의 심장을 건강하게 지켜준다. 감자는 또한 당신의 피부 문제를 해결해 준다. 꿀을 넣은 감자 주스는 당신의 피부를 부드럽고 깨끗하게 만들어 준다. 게다가, 감자는 당신이 살을 빼도록 도와준다. 당신이 감자를 먹으면, 오랜 시간 배부른 상태를 유지할 것이다. 감자는 여러 가지 면에서 당신을 건강하게 지내도록 도와준다.

01 다음 중 단어의 관계가 <u>다른</u> 하나는?

① improve – get better
② absorb – soak up
③ contain – involve
④ consider – regard
⑤ defeat – yield

02 다음 중 주어진 단어를 풀이하는 말로 가장 적절한 것은?

> nutrient

① someone who is asking questions at an interview
② an occasion when people sit down and eat, usually at a regular time
③ a chemical or food that provides what is needed for plants for animals to live and grow
④ all the different foods you use when you are cooking a particular dish
⑤ taste of a food or drink

03 주어진 단어를 활용하여 다음 우리말을 영어로 쓰시오.

(1) 그 마법사는 모자를 토끼로 바꾸었다.
  (magician / turn)
  ➡ _____

(2) 내가 무엇을 하도록 조언하시겠어요?
  (advise)
  ➡ _____

(3) 신선한 공기를 마시는 건 어때?
  (why / you / some)
  ➡ _____

04 다음 빈칸에 공통으로 들어갈 말로 가장 적절한 것은?

> • Yesterday the ship disappeared without _____.
> • They could finally _____ him to an address in New York.

① happen   ② email   ③ trace
④ rule   ⑤ notice

05 다음 중 주어진 단어의 밑줄 친 부분과 같은 의미로 쓰인 것은?

> Crystal City in Texas is called the spinach <u>capital</u> of the world.

① English is written with a <u>capital</u> 'E'.
② A large amount of <u>capital</u> is invested in the company.
③ Paris is the fashion <u>capital</u> of the world.
④ The firm is having difficulty raising <u>capital</u>.
⑤ The cause of business failure is a lack of <u>capital</u>.

06 다음 우리말에 맞게 빈칸에 알맞은 말을 쓰시오.

(1) 그 감독과 배우 둘 다 정말 놀라운 사람들이야.
  ➡ Both _____ _____ and _____
  _____ are really _____ people.

(2) 몇몇 방문객들은 그 개를 두려워했습니다.
  ➡ Some _____ _____ _____
  _____ the dog.

Conversation

07 다음 대화의 빈칸에 들어갈 말로 적절하지 <u>않은</u> 것은?

> A: I forgot my promise with Sumi. I think she is really upset. _____
>
> B: Why don't you just say sorry to her? She will accept your apology.

① What do you think I should do?
② What do you suggest?
③ How I should keep the promise?
④ What's your advice?
⑤ What do you advise me to do?

[08~09] 다음 대화를 읽고 물음에 답하시오.

> B: Is ①<u>something wrong</u>? You don't look so ②<u>good</u>.
>
> G: I have a sore throat. I think ③<u>it's</u> because of the fine dust these days.
>
> B: Put ④<u>some plants</u> in your room. They take bad air in and produce fresh air.
>
> G: Really? I'll get ⑤<u>a little</u> plants right away.

08 ①~⑤ 중 어법상 바르지 <u>않은</u> 것을 찾아 바르게 고쳐 쓰시오.

_____ ➡ _____

09 다음 중 대화의 내용과 일치하는 것은?

① The boy doesn't care if something is wrong with the girl.
② The girl feels great because of the fresh air.
③ The boy thinks that the fine dust made the girl's throat sore.
④ The girl is going to get some plants after a long time.
⑤ The boy advises the girl to get some plants in her room.

[10~11] 다음 대화를 읽고 물음에 답하시오.

> B: How are your tomatoes doing? Are they growing well? (①)
>
> G: No. I've gotten only a few tomatoes so far. (②)
>
> B: Where do you have the pot? (③)
>
> G: In the kitchen.
>
> B: Well, tomato plants need about 7 hours of sunlight a day. (④)
>
> G: Oh, I see. I'll move the pot over to the window. (⑤)

10 ①~⑤ 중 주어진 문장이 들어가기에 가장 적절한 곳은?

> What do you think I should do?

① ② ③ ④ ⑤

11 대화의 내용에 맞게 빈칸에 알맞은 말을 여섯 단어로 쓰시오.

> For the pot to get enough sunlight, the girl will _____.

➡ _____

12 다음 대화의 밑줄 친 부분을 대신하여 쓸 수 있는 것은?

> B: Is something wrong?
>
> G: I'm just a little tired. I've watched a movie on my phone for two hours.
>
> B: That's why you have red eyes. Try putting a warm towel over your eyes.
>
> G: <u>O.K. Thanks.</u>

① Alright. Never mind.
② Okay, but I'm sorry.
③ I'll give it a try.
④ You should keep that in mind.
⑤ O.K. You're welcome.

Grammar

13 다음 중 어법상 올바른 문장은?

① A man naming Popeye is so strong.
② The teacher recommended vegetables growing by the farmers.
③ This is the material made out of carrots.
④ I love eating carrots contained a lot of vitamin A.
⑤ Those inviting to the party didn't show up.

14 다음 중 어법상 올바른 문장은?

① Vegetables does make you healthy.
② He does says she's crazy.
③ Jason is looks handsome on the stage.
④ Shelly did make a decision.
⑤ The Smiths do met them last year.

15 다음 빈칸에 알맞은 말이 바르게 짝지어진 것은?

> • In the future, carrots may actually be _____ in wars.
> • Some kinds of insects are still _____ of tomatoes.

① used – scared ② using – scaring
③ using – scared ④ used – scary
⑤ use – scaring

16 다음 우리말을 괄호 안의 단어를 활용하여 영작하고, 주어진 조건에 맞는 문장으로 바꾸시오.

> Robert가 자신을 지켜보는 많은 사람들 앞에서 한 바구니의 토마토를 먹었다.

(1) 영작
  = Robert _____
  _____.
  (tomatoes / many people / watch / eat / a basket of / him / in front of)
(2) '먹었다'를 강조, '관계대명사+be동사' 추가
  = Robert _____
  _____.

17 다음 밑줄 친 부분의 쓰임이 나머지와 다른 것은?

① Potatoes <u>do</u> help you in many ways.
② They <u>do</u> eat tomatoes every morning.
③ Angela <u>does</u> work for the company.
④ Maybe you can <u>do</u> some laundry once in a while.
⑤ Ron <u>did</u> play the superhero character.

18 다음 밑줄 친 부분의 쓰임이 나머지 셋과 다른 것은? (2개)

① Carrots <u>containing</u> a lot of vitamin A help keep you healthy.
② The researchers were busy <u>developing</u> the new material from carrots.
③ Many people <u>watching</u> 'Popeye' on TV liked to eat spinach.
④ People <u>reading</u> the article believed that carrots improved night vision.
⑤ Popeye gets his super power by <u>eating</u> spinach.

19 다음 그림을 보고 괄호 안의 단어를 활용해서 빈칸에 알맞게 채우시오.

(1)

➡ When I finished reading *The Little Prince*, it _____(do) make me impressed.

(2)

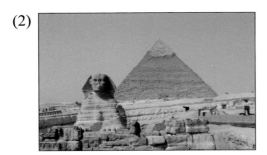

➡ The most famous Egyptian pyramids are those _____(find) at Giza, Egypt.

20 다음 문장들에서 우리말을 영어로 옮긴 것 중 어법상 어색한 것을 고르시오.

① 선생님은 팔짱을 낀 채로 학생들에게 얘기를 시작했다.
   → The teacher began talking to the students with his arms folded.

② 그는 창문을 열어 놓은 채로 잠이 들었다.
   → He fell asleep with the window open.

③ Scarlet은 다리를 꼰 채로 경찰관을 쳐다보았다.
   → Scarlet looked at the police officer with her legs crossing.

④ 나는 셔츠가 완전히 젖은 채로 집에 왔다.
   → I came home with my shirt all wet.

⑤ Elsa는 눈을 감은 채로 노래를 불렀다.
   → Elsa sang with her eyes closed.

21 다음 중 각각의 (A)와 (B)에서 밑줄 친 부분의 쓰임이 서로 같은 것을 고르시오.

① (A) Frank <u>did</u> keep his promise.
   (B) They <u>did</u> something to correct it.

② (A) What should he <u>do</u> now?
   (B) Emma <u>does</u> believe what he says.

③ (A) Peter <u>does</u> eat a lot of spinach.
   (B) Susan knows that I <u>do</u> believe her.

④ (A) Everyone wonders how he <u>did</u> it.
   (B) <u>Do</u> be nice to others.

⑤ (A) <u>Do</u> you know when she will come?
   (B) People don't trust him even if he <u>does</u> good things.

22 다음 중 어법상 <u>어색한</u> 것을 <u>모두</u> 고르시오.

① The room does feel too cold.
② His uncle do likes playing with him.
③ Sandy did believe what you said.
④ Do be careful when you drive.
⑤ Mom did forced me to eat tomatoes.

23 다음 두 문장을 현재분사를 이용하여, 한 문장으로 만드시오.

• The man was Robert Johnson.
• He wanted to prove that tomatoes were safe to eat.

➡ The man _____
   _____.

[24~26] 다음 글을 읽고 물음에 답하시오.

Popeye is a world-famous cartoon character. He gets his super power by eating spinach. When Popeye became popular in the 1930s in the United States, a lot of children began to eat spinach. Crystal City in Texas, which is called the spinach ⓐcapital of the world, even built a statue of Popeye. Although eating spinach will not give us super powers, spinach does have a lot of nutrients. ⓑ이것은 실제로 지구상에서 가장 건강한 식품 10개 중 하나로 여겨진다.

24 위 글의 밑줄 친 ⓐcapital과 같은 의미로 쓰인 것을 고르시오.

① We need capital investment.
② Please write in capital letters.
③ Cairo is the capital of Egypt.
④ He set up a business with a starting capital of £100,000.
⑤ He was sentenced to a capital punishment.

25 위 글의 밑줄 친 ⓑ의 우리말에 맞게 주어진 어휘를 이용하여 13 단어로 영작하시오.

actually, consider, healthiest, planet

➡ _____

_____

26 본문의 내용과 일치하도록 다음 빈칸 (A)~(C)에 알맞은 단어를 쓰시오.

We won't get super powers by eating (A)_____, but it really has lots of (B)_____. In fact, people consider it one of the ten (C)_____ foods on the planet.

[27~29] 다음 글을 읽고 물음에 답하시오.

In 1940, the Royal Air Force defeated German fighters during World War II by using a radar system. (①) The British government wanted to keep ⓐthis technology a secret, so it published an article in the newspaper. (②) Everybody believed the story and began to eat a lot more carrots than before. (③) Can we really improve night vision by eating lots of carrots? (④) Not really, but carrots contain a lot of vitamin A, which does keep our eyes healthy. (⑤)

27 위 글의 흐름으로 보아, 주어진 문장이 들어가기에 가장 적절한 곳은?

It said that British pilots improved their night vision because they ate a lot of carrots.

①   ②   ③   ④   ⑤

28 위 글의 밑줄 친 ⓐthis technology가 가리키는 것을 본문에서 찾아 쓰시오.

➡ _____

29 According to the passage, which is NOT true?

① In 1940, German fighters were defeated by the Royal Air Force during World War II.
② The British government published an article in the newspaper, which said that British pilots improved their night vision by eating a lot of carrots.
③ Everybody believed the article and began to eat a lot more carrots than before.
④ We can really improve night vision by eating lots of carrots.
⑤ Vitamin A contained a lot in carrots does keep our eyes healthy.

01 출제율 95%

다음 중 단어의 관계가 나머지 넷과 <u>다른</u> 하나는?

① edit – editor
② teach – teacher
③ cook – cooker
④ sail – sailor
⑤ visit – visitor

02 출제율 100%

다음 중 밑줄 친 단어의 우리말 의미가 바르지 <u>않은</u> 것은?

① I am afraid of darkness. (~을 두려워하다)
② Why don't you get some fresh air? (신선한 공기를 마시다)
③ I think I have a fever. (열이 나다)
④ In addition, you should try harder. (게다가)
⑤ You should keep away from it. (~에 가까워지다)

03 출제율 90%

다음과 같이 풀이되는 단어로 가장 적절한 것은?

> a person in a book, play, film etc.

① actor   ② director
③ character   ④ founder
⑤ writer

04 출제율 95%

주어진 단어를 활용하여 다음 우리말을 아홉 단어로 이루어진 한 문장의 영어로 쓰시오

> 너는 여전히 너의 친구들과 연락하고 지내니?
> (keep / still)

➡ _____

05 출제율 100%

자연스러운 대화가 되도록 (A)~(D)를 바르게 나열하시오.

> (A) I have a sore throat. I think it's because of the fine dust these days.
> (B) Really? I'll get a few plants right away.
> (C) Put some plants in your room. They take bad air in and produce fresh air.
> (D) Is something wrong? You don't look so good.

➡ _____

[06~08] 다음 대화를 읽고 물음에 답하시오.

> G: What's wrong? You look worried.
> B: Well, I broke my mom's favorite plate.
>   (A)
> _____
> G: (B)Tell her the truth. She will understand.
> B: I hope you're right.

06 출제율 95%

다음 중 빈칸 (A)에 들어갈 말로 적절하지 <u>않은</u> 것은?

① What do you think I should do?
② What do you suggest?
③ What do you advise me to do?
④ What is your advise?
⑤ What can you do for me?

07 출제율 90%

주어진 단어를 활용하여 밑줄 친 (B)와 같은 의미의 문장을 쓰시오.

> what about

➡ _____

08 출제율 95%

Write the reason why the boy looks worried. Use the phrase 'It's because.'

➡ _____

09 다음 대화의 내용과 일치하는 것은?

> B: Bomi, do you have some medicine?
> G: Why? Is something wrong?
> B: I have a stomachache. I think I ate too much for lunch.
> G: Why don't you go for a walk?
> B: O.K. I'll give it a try.

① Bomi is suffering from a stomachache.
② There is a matter with Bomi.
③ Bomi will go for a walk.
④ Bomi wants to know why the boy needs some medicine.
⑤ Bomi doesn't give any advice to the boy.

10 다음 중 빈칸에 들어갈 말로 적절하지 않은 것은?

> A: I've found some money on the street. What do you think I should do?
> B: _____

① You should take it to the police station.
② How about taking it to the police station?
③ I suggest you should take it to the police station.
④ If I were you, I would take it to the police station.
⑤ Make sure taking it to the police station.

11 다음 중 밑줄 친 단어의 바로 앞에 '주격 관계대명사+be동사'가 생략되어 있다고 볼 수 없는 것을 모두 고르면?

① Spinach is the vegetable <u>considered</u> one of the 10 healthiest foods.
② What is the language <u>spoken</u> in Mali?
③ I'm <u>interested</u> in Mexican artworks.
④ Don't touch the baby bears <u>sleeping</u> with their mother.

⑤ Is there anyone who saw the <u>sleeping</u> beauty in the woods?
⑥ There are many school buses <u>parked</u> at the parking lot.
⑦ Jason's presentation was not impressive at all and even <u>boring</u>.
⑧ The cameras <u>made</u> in Taiwan are quite inexpensive and good in quality.

12 다음 중 어법상 어색한 문장을 모두 고르시오.

① You are make me happy.
② Carrots do contains vitamin A.
③ Sean did take good care of his dogs.
④ Munch did paint *The Scream*.
⑤ The kid did believe what the magician showed.
⑥ The citizens did understood what the mayor announced.
⑦ It were the books that he bought there.

13 다음 중 밑줄 친 부분의 용법이 나머지 넷과 다른 것은?

① She liked collecting the leaves <u>fallen</u> on the road.
② Some students went to see the works of Picasso <u>displayed</u> in the art museum.
③ Kelly was so proud of <u>being</u> the fan of BTS that she couldn't help crying.
④ My dad came home with a huge box <u>filled</u> with toys.
⑤ Do you know that pretty girl <u>smiling</u> at a lady?

14 다음 중 괄호 안의 단어를 분사로 바꾸어 빈칸에 넣을 때, 분사의 종류가 나머지 셋과 <u>다른</u> 두 개를 고르시오.

① Cathy likes to help _____ dogs. (abandon)

② The boys saw grey smoke _____ out of the chimney. (come)

③ Brandon must make himself _____ in Japanese. (understand)

④ She kept him _____ while she took some pictures. (wait)

⑤ Sofia didn't see the boy _____ at her at the meeting. (smile)

15 다음 두 문장을 접속사 Although로 시작하는 한 문장으로 고쳐 쓰되, 밑줄 친 부분을 강조하여 쓰시오.

• Eating spinach won't give us super powers.
• But spinach <u>has</u> a lot of nutrients.

➡ Although _____
_____ .

[16~18] 다음 글을 읽고 물음에 답하시오.

Popeye is a world-famous cartoon character. He gets his super power by eating spinach. When Popeye became popular in the 1930s in the United States, a lot of children began to eat spinach. Crystal City in Texas, which is called the spinach capital of the world, even built a statue of Popeye. ⓐAlthough eating spinach will not give us super powers, spinach ⓑdoes have a lot of nutrients. It is actually considered one of the ten healthiest foods on the planet.

16 위 글의 밑줄 친 ⓐ를 3형식 문장으로 고치시오.

➡ _____
_____

17 위 글의 밑줄 친 ⓑdoes와 문법적 쓰임이 같은 것을 고르시오.

① She does not like fish.
② Not only does she speak Spanish, she's also good with computers.
③ Mom does the dishes.
④ What does he do in his free time?
⑤ He does look tired.

18 위 글을 읽고, (1) Popeye가 준 시금치의 이미지와 (2) 시금치에 관한 실제 사실을 우리말로 쓰시오.

➡ (1) Popeye가 준 시금치의 이미지: _____
_____

(2) 시금치에 관한 실제 사실: _____
_____
_____

[19~21] 다음 글을 읽고 물음에 답하시오.

In the future, carrots may actually be used in wars. Scottish researchers have discovered a way to turn carrots into a very strong and light material. ⓐIt can even be used to making battleships. ⓑThis new material has already been used to make snowboards and bicycles.

19 위 글의 밑줄 친 ⓐ에서 어법상 틀린 부분을 찾아 고치시오.

_____ ➡ _____

20 다음 빈칸 (A)와 (B)에 알맞은 단어를 넣어 위 글의 밑줄 친 ⓑ에 대한 소개를 완성하시오.

<출제율 90%>

> It is a very (A)_____ _____
> _____ material made from
> (B)_____ by Scottish researchers.

21 위 글의 주제로 알맞은 것을 고르시오.

<출제율 100%>

① the way to turn carrots into a very strong and light material
② the advantage of a very strong and light material
③ the uses of carrots in wars in the future
④ the products made from the same raw material
⑤ the material used to make snowboards and bicycles

[22~24] 다음 글을 읽고 물음에 답하시오.

We all know that tomatoes are good for our health. (①) Up until the 1800s, however, most Americans thought that tomatoes were poisonous. (②) In 1820, ⓐRobert Johnson이라는 이름의 남자가 토마토가 먹기에 안전하다는 것을 증명하기를 원했다. (③) So, he ate a basket of tomatoes in front of many people watching him. (④) Ever since then, Americans have enjoyed eating tomatoes. (⑤)

We are no longer afraid of tomatoes, but some insects are still scared of them. If you want to keep insects away from your room, place a bowl of crushed tomatoes in a corner of your room. Insects will not come near the tomatoes.

22 위 글의 흐름으로 보아, 주어진 문장이 들어가기에 가장 적절한 곳은?

<출제율 95%>

> They all expected him to die, but nothing happened to him.

① ② ③ ④ ⑤

23 위 글의 밑줄 친 ⓐ의 우리말에 맞게 주어진 어휘를 알맞게 배열하시오.

<출제율 90%>

> that / to eat / Robert Johnson / safe / tomatoes / a man / were / wanted / named / to prove

➡ _____
_____

24 According to the passage, which is NOT true?

<출제율 100%>

① All of us know that tomatoes are healthy food.
② Up until the 1800s, most Americans thought that it was safe to eat tomatoes.
③ Robert Johnson ate a basket of tomatoes while many people were watching him.
④ We are not afraid of tomatoes any more.
⑤ You can keep insects away from your room by placing a bowl of crushed tomatoes in a corner of your room.

[25~26] 다음 글을 읽고 물음에 답하시오.

Potatoes are good for your health. They keep your heart healthy because they lower blood pressure. They also solve your skin problems. Potato juice mixed with honey makes your skin soft and clear. ___ⓐ___, they help you lose weight. If you eat potatoes, you will stay full for a long time. ⓑPotatoes help you stay healthy in many ways.

25 위 글의 빈칸 ⓐ에 들어갈 알맞은 말을 고르시오.

<출제율 95%>

① In addition ② Therefore ③ However
④ By contrast ⑤ For example

26 위 글의 밑줄 친 ⓑ의 내용을 본문에서 찾아 우리말로 쓰시오. (세 가지)

<출제율 90%>

➡ (1) _____
(2) _____
(3) _____

[01~02] 다음 대화를 읽고 물음에 답하시오.

> B: (A)몸무게를 줄이는 건 너무 어려워. What do you think I should do?
> G: Well, why don't you walk your dog every day?
> B: My dog would love it, but would it help me lose weight?
> G: Sure. When you walk your dog, you're actually exercising, too.
> B: O.K. I'll think about it.

01 주어진 단어를 활용하여 밑줄 친 우리말 (A)를 영어로 쓰시오.

> (it / so / hard)

➡ _____

02 대화의 내용에 맞게 빈칸에 알맞은 말을 쓰시오.

> The girl suggests that the boy walk his dog every day because she thinks it will help him _____ _____.

03 다음 상황을 읽고 빈칸에 알맞은 말을 쓰시오. 한 칸에 하나의 단어만 쓰시오.

> You come home from school and find that your mom is sitting on a chair. She looks like she is sick. You want to ask her if she is all right. What do you say to her?
> You: Mom, _____ _____ _____?

04 다음 중 밑줄 친 부분을 어법에 맞게 고치고, 고친 단어의 종류가 다른 두 개를 찾아, 그 이유를 설명하시오.

> ⓐ Spinach can be used in a surprise way.
> ⓑ They are waiting for the train leave at 7:00.
> ⓒ Popeye gets his power by eat spinach.
> ⓓ We saw a beautiful wall of a building cover with ivy.
> ⓔ She memorized a poem write by Ralph Waldo Emerson.
> ⓕ Since Robert's experiment, Americans have enjoyed eat tomatoes.

➡ ⓐ _____ ⓑ _____ ⓒ _____
　 ⓓ _____ ⓔ _____ ⓕ _____
　 이유: _____

05 다음 주어진 문장을 밑줄 친 부분을 강조하는 문장으로 바꾸어 쓰시오.

(1) British pilots ate a lot of carrots.
　 ➡ _____

(2) Place a bowl of crushed tomatoes in a corner of your room.
　 ➡ _____
　 _____

(3) People in Hong Kong love freedom.
　 ➡ _____

06 다음 그림을 보고 괄호 안의 단어를 알맞게 배열하여 빈칸에 넣으시오. (동사는 어법에 맞게 변형 가능)

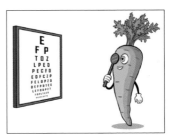

➡ Can we really improve night vision by eating lots of carrots? Not really, but carrots contain a lot of vitamin A, _____.

(keep, eyes, which, our, healthy, do)

09 위 글을 읽고, (1) 1800년대까지 대부분의 미국인들의 토마토에 대한 생각과 (2) 1820년 이후의 미국인들의 토마토에 대한 태도를 우리말로 쓰시오.

➡ (1) 1800년대까지 대부분의 미국인들의 토마토에 대한 생각: _____

(2) 1820년 이후의 미국인들의 토마토에 대한 태도: _____

[07~09] 다음 글을 읽고 물음에 답하시오.

We all know that tomatoes are good for our health. Up until the 1800s, however, most Americans thought that tomatoes were poisonous. In 1820, a man (A)[naming / named] Robert Johnson wanted to prove that tomatoes were safe to eat. So, he ate a basket of tomatoes in front of many people (B) [watching / watched] him. They all expected him ___ⓐ___, but nothing (C)[happened / was happened] to him. Ever since then, Americans have enjoyed eating tomatoes.

We are no longer afraid of tomatoes, but some insects are still scared of them. If you want to keep insects away from your room, place a bowl of crushed tomatoes in a corner of your room. Insects will not come near the tomatoes.

[10~11] 다음 글을 읽고 물음에 답하시오.

In 1940, the Royal Air Force defeated German fighters during World War II by using a radar system. ⓐ영국 정부는 이 기술을 비밀로 하기를 원했기 때문에, 신문에 기사를 하나 냈다. It said that British pilots improved their night vision because they ate a lot of carrots. Everybody believed ⓑthe story and began to eat a lot more carrots than before. Can we really improve night vision by eating lots of carrots? Not really, but carrots contain a lot of vitamin A, which does keep our eyes healthy.

07 위 글의 빈칸 ⓐ에 die를 알맞은 형태로 쓰시오.

➡ _____

10 위 글의 밑줄 친 ⓐ의 우리말에 맞게 주어진 어휘를 알맞게 배열하시오.

a secret / published / to keep / so / wanted / the British government / it / in the newspaper / this technology / an article / ,

➡ _____
_____

11 위 글의 밑줄 친 ⓑthe story가 가리키는 것을 본문에서 찾아 쓰시오.

➡ _____
_____

08 위 글의 괄호 (A)~(C)에서 어법상 알맞은 낱말을 골라 쓰시오.

➡ (A) _____ (B) _____ (C) _____

01 다음 대화를 참고하여 빈칸에 알맞은 말을 쓰시오.

> Brian: How are your tomatoes doing? Are they growing well?
>
> Grace: No. I've gotten only a few tomatoes so far. What do you think I should do?
>
> Brian: Where do you have the pot?
>
> Grace: In the kitchen.
>
> Brian: Well, tomato plants need about 7 hours of sunlight a day.
>
> Grace: Oh, I see. I'll move the pot over to the window.

> Brain wonders if Grace's tomatoes are _____. However, Grace says _____ so far. Grace wants Brain to give _____, so he asks her _____. Grace answers she has it _____. Brian tells her that _____, so Grace says that _____ _____.

02 다음 그림들을 보고, 괄호 안에 주어진 어휘들을 필요한 만큼 활용하여, 분사가 들어가는 문장을 영작하시오. (두 문장 모두 Unlike 로 시작하고 인칭과 시제 등에 유의하여 활용할 것.)

(boss, sleep, man, present the plan)

(I, my sister, read a book, sofa, clean, table, on)

(1) _____.

(2) _____.

03 다음 내용을 바탕으로 감자의 이로운 점을 설명하는 글을 쓰시오.

> **Main Idea**
> Potatoes are good for your health.
> **Supporting Detail 1**
> keep your heart healthy
>
> • lower blood pressure
> **Supporting Detail 2**
> solve your skin problems
> • make your skin soft and clear

> Potatoes are good for (A)_____. They keep your heart healthy because they (B)_____. They also solve your (C)_____. Potato juice mixed with honey makes your skin (D)_____.

단원별 모의고사

01 다음 중 빈칸에 들어갈 말이 <u>다른</u> 하나는?

① I can't promise I can _____ it a secret.
② Kate, _____ away from the edge of the cliff.
③ After our summer class ends, let's _____ in touch!
④ We can _____ better use of our resources.
⑤ I told the driver to _____ the change.

02 다음 중 주어진 단어와 같은 관계가 <u>아닌</u> 것은?

> library – librarian

① call – caller
② play – player
③ science – scientist
④ economic – economist
⑤ visit – visitor

03 다음 중 단어의 영영풀이가 바르지 <u>않은</u> 것은?

① hide: to cover something so that you cannot be seen clearly
② cartoon: funny drawing in a newspaper or magazine
③ carrot: a long pointed orange vegetable that grows under the ground
④ defeat: not to succeed in winning the battle
⑤ discover: to become aware of something that you didn't know about before

04 자연스러운 대화가 되도록 (A)~(E)를 바르게 나열하시오.

> (A) Well, why don't you walk your dog every day?
> (B) O.K. I'll think about it.
> (C) It's so hard to lose weight. What do you think I should do?
> (D) Sure. When you walk your dog, you're actually exercising, too.
> (E) My dog would love it, but would it help me lose weight?

➡ _____

[05~06] 다음 대화를 읽고 물음에 답하시오.

> B: _____(A)_____ You don't look so good.
> G: I have a sore throat. I think it's because of the fine dust these days.
> B: Put some plants in your room. They take bad air in and produce fresh air.
> G: Really? I'll get a few plants right away.

05 다음 중 빈칸 (A)에 들어갈 말로 적절하지 <u>않은</u> 것은?

① Is something wrong?
② Did anything go wrong?
③ What's the matter with you?
④ What did you do that was wrong?
⑤ Did something happen?

06 대화의 내용에 맞게 빈칸에 알맞은 말을 쓰시오.

> The girl thinks that because there is _____ _____ these days, she has a sore throat. So the boy advises her to _____ _____ in her room.

07 다음 대화 중 자연스럽지 <u>않은</u> 것은?

① A: What's wrong?
   B: I made a few mistakes in the math test.

② A: I have a headache. What do you think I should do?
   B: Why don't you go see a doctor?

③ A: Is something wrong?
   B: I can't sleep well these days. What should I do?

④ A: I lied to my friend, Sumi. Please give me advice.
   B: I think you should apologize to her.

⑤ A: I can't save any money. What do you suggest?
   B: How about buying more clothes?

08 다음 대화의 빈칸에 들어갈 말로 적절하지 <u>않은</u> 것은?

A: Is something wrong?
B: This problem is too hard to solve. What do you think I should do?
A: _____

① Why don't you ask the teacher for help?
② How about asking the teacher for help?
③ Make sure the teacher asks you for help.
④ I suggest you should ask the teacher for help.
⑤ You should ask the teacher for help.

09 다음 대화의 밑줄 친 우리말을 일곱 단어로 이루어진 한 문장의 영어로 쓰시오.

A: Is something wrong?
B: I am so nervous about tomorrow's contest. 내가 뭘 해야 한다고 생각해?
A: Why don't you relax and practice more?

➡ _____

[10~12] 다음 대화를 읽고 물음에 답하시오.

Anna: Suho, is something ①<u>wrong</u>? You're very quiet today.
Suho: I'm just a bit tired. I slept very little last night.
Anna: Did you do something ②<u>late</u> last night?
Suho: Yes, I watched a movie on my phone until 2 a.m. That's what I often do these days.
Anna: Oh, ③<u>that's because</u> you have red eyes. You should go to bed before midnight for your health.
Suho: I think my eyes are getting ④<u>worse</u>. What do you think I should do?
Anna: Try eating lots of carrots and tomatoes. They're rich in vitamin A, so they'll keep your eyes healthy.
Suho: ⑤<u>I see.</u> Thank you, Anna.

10 ①~⑤ 중 글의 흐름상 어색한 것은?

①   ②   ③   ④   ⑤

11 Write the reason why Anna advises Suho to try eating lots of carrots and tomatoes. Use the phrase 'It's because.'

➡ _____
_____

12 위 대화를 읽고 답할 수 <u>없는</u> 것은?

① Why is Suho very quiet today?
② Why did Suho sleep very little last night?
③ What does Suho often do these days?
④ What does Anna advise Suho to do for his health?
⑤ How long does Suho watch a movie on his phone?

13 다음 밑줄 친 부분 중 어법상 어색한 것을 고르시오.

① The new material <u>using</u> carrots can even be used to make battleships.
② Kevin felt <u>interested</u> in the healthy effects of spinach.
③ She likes the sound of <u>falling</u> rain.
④ Clocks are something <u>showing</u> you the time.
⑤ Olivia bought some vegetables <u>included</u> spinach, carrots, and tomatoes.

14 다음 중 주어진 문장의 밑줄 친 부분과 쓰임이 같은 것을 모두 고르시오.

> When it takes in water, spinach also <u>does</u> absorb many other things.

① <u>Do</u> we really improve night vision by eating a lot of carrots?
② She <u>doesn't</u> have any food to eat.
③ They <u>do</u> think it's even healthier to eat tomatoes every day.
④ <u>Do</u> not expect the man to help us.
⑤ Susan <u>did</u> the dishes by herself.
⑥ We all <u>do</u> know that tomatoes are good for our health.
⑦ I wonder how he <u>did</u> the trick.

15 괄호 안의 단어를 사용하여 어법에 맞게 주어진 문장의 빈칸을 쓸 때, 빈칸에 들어갈 말과 쓰임이 같지 <u>않은</u> 것을 고르시오.

> Scottish scientists turned carrots into a very strong and light material, which is already _____ (use) to make snowboards and bicycles.

① My father has invented a box _____ (design) to keep tomatoes fresh.
② She can't attend the meeting _____ (schedule) on Thursday.
③ Many people eat carrots _____ (contain) a lot of vitamin A.
④ Don't touch the tomato _____ (crush) to make insect repellent.
⑤ Sue gathered the dishes _____ (break) by her mistake.

16 우리말과 일치하도록 괄호 안의 어구를 바르게 배열하시오.

(1) 이 새로운 물질이 벌써 자전거를 만들기 위해 사용되어져 왔다.
(bicycles, material, been, has, to, new, this, used, make, already).

➡ _____

(2) 어떤 과학자들은 땅 속에 숨겨진 폭탄을 찾기 위해 시금치의 이러한 특성을 이용해 왔다.
(this characteristic, bombs, to find, used, of, some scientists, have, spinach, in the ground, hidden).

➡ _____

17 다음 중 밑줄 친 단어의 쓰임이 나머지 넷과 <u>다른</u> 것은?

① Crystal City in Texas <u>called</u> the spinach capital of the world is a small town.
② Vitamin A <u>contained</u> in carrots does keep our eyes healthy.
③ Some insects <u>scared</u> of tomatoes don't come near tomato crush.
④ Chinese do love eating <u>boiled</u> vegetables.
⑤ The female pop singer, IU, has <u>composed</u> a lot of good songs.

[18~19] 다음 글을 읽고 물음에 답하시오.

Popeye is a world-famous cartoon character. He gets his super power by eating spinach. When Popeye became popular in the 1930s in the United States, a lot of children began to eat spinach. Crystal City in Texas, which is called the spinach capital of the world, even built a statue of Popeye. Although eating spinach will not give us super powers, spinach does have a lot of nutrients. ⓐIt is actually considered one of the ten healthiest foods on the planet.

18 다음 문장에서 위 글의 내용과 <u>다른</u> 부분을 찾아서 고치시오.

Popeye is a real person.

➡ _____

19 위 글의 밑줄 친 ⓐIt이 가리키는 것을 본문에서 찾아 쓰시오.

➡ _____

[20~22] 다음 글을 읽고 물음에 답하시오.

In 1940, the Royal Air Force defeated German fighters during World War II by using a radar system. The British government wanted to keep this technology a secret, so it published an (A)article in the newspaper. It said that British pilots improved their night vision because they ate a lot of carrots. Everybody believed the story and began to eat a lot more carrots than before. Can we really improve night vision by eating lots of carrots? Not really, but carrots contain a lot of vitamin A, (B)which ____ⓐ____ our eyes healthy.

20 위 글의 빈칸 ⓐ에 keeps를 강조하는 형태로 바꿔 쓰시오.

➡ _____

21 위 글의 밑줄 친 (A)article과 같은 의미로 쓰인 것을 고르시오.

① We need an article of clothing.
② Have you seen that article about young fashion designers?
③ She didn't pay for the article she had bought.
④ According to the article 3, it is against the law.
⑤ This shampoo is a first class article.

22 위 글의 밑줄 친 (B)를 접속사를 사용하여 고치시오.

➡ _____

[23~25] 다음 글을 읽고 물음에 답하시오.

We all know that tomatoes are good for our health. Up until the ⓐ1800s, however, most Americans thought that tomatoes were poisonous. In ⓑ1820, a man named Robert Johnson wanted to prove that tomatoes were safe ⓒto eat. So, he ate a basket of tomatoes in front of many people watching him. They all expected him to die, but nothing happened to him. Ever since then, Americans have enjoyed eating tomatoes.

We are no longer afraid of tomatoes, but some insects are still scared of them. If you want to keep insects away from your room, place a bowl of crushed tomatoes in a corner of your room. Insects will not come near the tomatoes.

23 위 글의 밑줄 친 ⓐ1800s와 ⓑ1820을 읽는 법을 영어로 쓰시오.

➡ ⓐ _____ ⓑ _____

24 위 글의 밑줄 친 ⓒto eat과 to부정사의 용법이 다른 것을 모두 고르시오.

① It was safe to eat tomatoes.
② What is the best way to eat tomatoes?
③ I'm too young to eat tomatoes well.
④ Who chose to eat tomatoes?
⑤ Robert Johnson was brave enough to eat tomatoes.

25 위 글의 제목으로 알맞은 것을 고르시오.

① Tomatoes, Good for Our Health
② The Reason Americans Were Afraid of Tomatoes
③ Robert Johnson Proved the Safety of Tomatoes
④ Tomatoes, the Scariest Vegetables
⑤ The Kind of Insects Which Are Scared of Tomatoes

[26~27] 다음 글을 읽고 물음에 답하시오.

We all know that tomatoes are good for our health. Up until the 1800s, however, most Americans thought that tomatoes were ___ⓐ___ . In 1820, a man named Robert Johnson wanted to prove that tomatoes were ___ⓑ___ to eat. So, he ate a basket of tomatoes in front of many people watching him. They all expected him to die, but nothing happened to him. Ever since then, Americans ⓒhave enjoyed eating tomatoes.

26 위 글의 빈칸 ⓐ와 ⓑ에 들어갈 알맞은 말을 고르시오.

① safe – harmless
② poisonous – safe
③ precious – harmful
④ harmless – precious
⑤ evil – poisonous

27 위 글의 밑줄 친 ⓒhave enjoyed와 현재완료의 용법이 다른 것을 모두 고르시오.

① I have studied English since the second grade of elementary school.
② They have lived in this house for 10 years.
③ She has never visited the National Museum of Korea.
④ His father has been dead for ten years.
⑤ I have watched the movie twice.

[28~29] 다음 글을 읽고 물음에 답하시오.

Garlic is good for your health. It keeps your heart healthy because it lowers blood pressure. It also helps you get over a cold. ⓐGarlic tea mixed with honey makes you get better faster. In addition, it helps you prevent future sickness. Eating garlic helps your body fight against bad viruses. Garlic helps you stay healthy in many ways.

28 How can garlic keep your heart healthy? Answer in English beginning with "By". (4 words)

➡ _____

29 위 글의 밑줄 친 문장 ⓐ에 생략된 단어들을 넣어 문장을 다시 쓰시오.

➡ _____

_____

MEMO

Lesson 4

This is Korea

🌷 의사소통 기능

- 궁금한 것 묻고 답하기
  A: I wonder why he is running.
  B: I think he is late for school.

- 설명 요청하기
  A: Could you explain what this is?
  B: It's a traditional Korean hat. It's called a gat.

🌷 언어 형식

- '과거완료' had + 과거분사
  She kept laughing even after she **had been** in the water for over five hours.

- 간접의문문
  They didn't understand **why I wanted to take their pictures**.

Words & Expressions

Key Words

- **ad** [æd] 명 광고 (= advertisement)
- **attend** [əténd] 동 참석하다
- **audience** [ɔ́:diəns] 명 청중
- **audio guide** 음성 안내기
- **bakery** [béikəri] 명 빵집
- **beat** [bi:t] 명 (북 등을 치는) 소리, (심장의) 고동
- **black-and-white** 형 (사진, TV 등) 흑백의
- **bookstore** [búkstər] 명 서점
- **breadwinner** [brédwinər] 명 생계를 책임지는 사람, 가장
- **breathe** [bri:ð] 동 호흡하다
- **bridge** [bridʒ] 명 교량, 다리
- **community** [kəmjú:nəti] 명 지역 공동체
- **complete** [kəmplí:t] 동 완성[완료]하다
- **continue** [kəntínju:] 동 계속하다
- **copy machine** 복사기
- **destroy** [distrɔ́i] 동 파괴하다
- **device** [diváis] 명 기구
- **diver** [dáivər] 명 잠수부
- **environment** [inváiərənmənt] 명 환경
- **exhibition** [èksəbíʃən] 명 전시회, 박람회
- **female** [fí:meil] 형 여성의
- **good harvest** 풍년
- **greenhouse** [grí:nhàus] 명 온실
- **harvest** [háːrvist] 동 수확하다
- **heritage** [héritidʒ] 명 유산
- **intangible** [intǽndʒəbl] 형 무형의, 만질 수 없는

- **jellyfish** [dʒélifiʃ] 명 해파리
- **marine** [mərí:n] 형 해양의, 바다의
- **moved** [mu:vd] 형 감동받은
- **nationwide** [néiʃənwàid] 형 전국적인
- **overseas** [óuvərsìz] 부 해외로, 해외에
- **overwork** [óuvərwərk] 동 과로하다
- **past** [pæst] 형 지나간 명 과거
- **path** [pæθ] 명 경로, 길
- **photographer** [fətágrəfər] 명 사진작가
- **press** [pres] 동 누르다 명 언론, 기자
- **promote** [prəmóut] 동 홍보하다, 촉진하다
- **realize** [rí:làiz] 동 깨닫다, 인식하다
- **seafood** [sí:fud] 명 해산물
- **several** [sévərəl] 형 몇몇의
- **suitable** [sú:təbl] 형 적합한, 적절한
- **sunshine** [sʌ́nʃain] 명 햇빛
- **tightly** [táitli] 부 단단히, 꽉
- **traditional** [trədíʃənl] 형 전통적인
- **trail** [treil] 명 좁은 길
- **underground** [ʌndərgráund] 형 지하의
- **underwater** [ʌndərwɔ́tər] 형 수중의, 물속에서
- **volcanic** [vɑlkǽnik] 형 화산의, 화산 작용에 의한
- **waterfall** [wɔ́tərfɔl] 명 폭포
- **wetsuit** [wétsuːt] 명 잠수용 고무옷, 잠수복
- **worldwide** [wə́rldwaid] 부 세계적으로

Key Expressions

- **a couple of** 두 서너 개의
- **a little bit** 조금, 약간
- **an intangible cultural treasure** 무형문화재
- **be good for** ~에 유익하다
- **be suitable for** ~에 적절하다
- **check ~ out** ~을 확인하다, ~를 조사하다
- **cheer up** 힘을 북돋아 주다, 격려하다
- **get into** ~에 들어가다
- **give (someone) a call** 전화를 걸다
- **give (someone) a hand** 거들어 주다, 돕다
- **give a presentation** 발표하다

- **give a talk** 강의하다, 연설하다
- **go on vacation** 휴가 가다
- **happen to** 우연히 ~하다
- **keep -ing** 계속해서 ~하다
- **make double-sided copies** 양면 복사를 하다
- **take a photo** 사진을 찍다
- **walk along** ~을 따라 걷다
- **Why don't we ~?** ~하는 것이 어때?
- **Why not?** 왜 안 되겠어?, 좋고말고.
- **wish for** ~을 기원하다
- **would like to** ~하고 싶다

Word Power

※ 서로 비슷한 뜻을 가진 어휘

- □ **ad** 광고(**advertisement**) : **commercial** 광고
- □ **device** 기구 : **tool** 도구
- □ **moved** 감동받은 : **touched** 감동받은
- □ **several** 몇몇의 : **a few** 몇몇의

- □ **borrow** 빌리다 : **rent** 임대하다
- □ **environment** 환경 : **surrounding** 환경
- □ **path** 경로, 길 : **trail** 좁은 길
- □ **suitable** 적합한, 적절한 : **proper** 적절한

※ 서로 반대되는 뜻을 가진 어휘

- □ **borrow** 빌리다 ↔ **lend** 빌려주다
- □ **nationwide** 전국적인 ↔ **local** 지역적인

- □ **female** 여성의 ↔ **male** 남성의
- □ **suitable** 적합한 ↔ **unsuitable** 부적절한

※ 동사 – 명사

- □ **attend** 참석하다 – **attendance** 참석
- □ **continue** 계속하다 – **continuity** 연속
- □ **explain** 설명하다 – **explanation** 설명
- □ **realize** 깨닫다 – **realization** 깨달음

- □ **breathe** 호흡하다 – **breath** 호흡
- □ **destroy** 파괴하다 – **destruction** 파괴
- □ **promote** 홍보하다 – **promotion** 홍보

※ 형용사 – 명사

- □ **good** 좋은 – **goodness** 선량함
- □ **aware** 알고 있는 – **awareness** 인식
- □ **weak** 약한 – **weakness** 약함
- □ **polite** 예의 바른 – **politeness** 예의 바름
- □ **sad** 슬픈 – **sadness** 슬픔

- □ **ill** 아픔 – **illness** 질병
- □ **fair** 공정한 – **fairness** 공정함
- □ **kind** 친절한 – **kindness** 친절
- □ **happy** 행복한 – **happiness** 행복
- □ **dark** 어두운 – **darkness** 어둠

English Dictionary

- □ **ad** 광고 (= **advertisement**)
  → a picture, set of words, or a short film, intended to persuade people to buy
  사람들이 사도록 설득하려고 의도된 사진, 어구, 또는 짧은 영상

- □ **beat** (북 등을 치는) 소리
  → one of a series of regular movements or hitting actions 일련의 규칙적인 움직임 또는 치는 동작 중의 하나

- □ **breadwinner** 생계를 책임지는 사람, 가장
  → the member of a family who earns the money to support the others 가족을 부양하려고 돈을 버는 가족 구성원

- □ **breathe** 호흡하다
  → to take air into your lungs and send it out again
  폐로 공기를 들여보내고 그것을 다시 내보내다

- □ **community** 지역 공동체
  → the people who live in the same area, town, etc.
  같은 지역이나 마을 등에 사는 사람들

- □ **heritage** 유산
  → the traditional beliefs, values, customs of a family, country, or society
  한 가족, 국가, 사회의 전통적인 믿음, 가치관, 관습

- □ **intangible** 무형의, 만질 수 없는
  → having value but not existing physically
  가치가 있지만 물리적으로 존재하지는 않는

- □ **overseas** 해외의
  → to or in a foreign country that is across the sea
  바다 건너 있는 외국으로 가거나 외국에 있는

01 다음 짝지어진 단어의 관계가 같도록 빈칸에 알맞은 말을 쓰시오.

> female : male = _____ : borrow

02 다음 영영풀이가 가리키는 것을 고르시오.

> having value but not existing physically

① underground   ② traditional

③ volcanic   ④ marine

⑤ intangible

03 다음 중 밑줄 친 부분의 뜻풀이가 바르지 <u>않은</u> 것은?

① All the <u>audience</u> stood up and gave the performer a big hand. (청중)

② We can't <u>breathe</u> in outer space. (호흡하다)

③ It is an important part of <u>community</u> life. (공동체)

④ She invited me to her photo <u>exhibition</u>. (전시회)

⑤ The trip was a great <u>experience</u>. (실험)

서답형
04 다음 우리말에 맞게 빈칸에 알맞은 말을 쓰시오. (철자가 주어진 경우, 그 철자로 시작하여 쓸 것.)

(1) 심해 잠수를 위해 잠수복을 가져와라.
➡ Bring a w_____ for deep sea diving.

(2) 그 영화는 전세계적으로 유명해졌다.
➡ The movie has become famous w_____.

(3) 그들은 지역 신문에 광고를 실었다.
➡ They put an _____ in the local paper.

(4) 우리는 강 위에 놓인 다리를 건넜다.
➡ We crossed the _____ over the river.

서답형
05 다음 문장의 빈칸에 들어갈 말을 〈보기〉에서 골라 알맞은 형태로 쓰시오.

> ┤ 보기 ├
> cheer up / wish for / get into / be good for / walk along

(1) Walking _____ your health.

(2) I _____ lots of interests for our new products.

(3) _____! You can do better next time.

(4) If you _____ the street, you can find the post office.

(5) It is hard to _____ the medical school.

06 다음 주어진 문장의 밑줄 친 press와 같은 의미로 쓰인 것은?

> Please <u>press</u> the start button.

① Jack blamed the <u>press</u> photographers for violating his privacy.

② Which switch should I <u>press</u> to turn it off?

③ Some people don't believe the <u>press</u> reports.

④ They are fighting for the freedom of the <u>press</u>.

⑤ The car accident in my town was reported in the <u>press</u>.

01 다음 짝지어진 단어의 관계가 같도록 빈칸에 알맞은 말을 쓰시오.

> thin : thick = future : _____

02 다음 우리말에 맞게 빈칸에 알맞은 말을 쓰시오. (철자가 주어진 경우, 그 철자로 시작하여 쓸 것.)

(1) 길은 단풍잎으로 덮여 있었다.

➡ The p_____ was covered with colorful leaves.

(2) 전 지역 공동체가 바이러스에 대해 걱정했다.

➡ The whole _____ was concerned about the virus.

(3) 그 밴드는 그들의 새로운 앨범을 홍보할 필요가 있다.

➡ The band needs to p_____ their new album.

(4) 해파리를 본 적이 있나요?

➡ Have you ever seen the _____?

03 다음 우리말과 일치하도록 주어진 단어를 모두 배열하여 완성하시오.

(1) 우리는 작년에 풍년이 들었다.

(last / harvest / had / we / a / good / year)

➡ _____

(2) 돈이 항상 행복을 가져다주지는 않는다.

(does / happiness / money / not / bring / always)

➡ _____

(3) 우리의 국가적 유산이 화재에 의해 파괴되었다.

(was / by / the / our / heritage / destroyed / fire / national)

➡ _____

04 다음 우리말을 주어진 단어를 이용하여 영작하시오.

(1) 우리는 한 시간 동안 길을 따라 걸었다. (along, for, street)

➡ _____

(2) 이 책은 초등학생들에게 적합하다. (suitable, elementary)

➡ _____

(3) 종이를 절약하기 위해 양면 복사를 하자. (let's, save)

➡ _____

05 다음 문장의 빈칸에 들어갈 말을 〈보기〉에서 골라 쓰시오.

> ┤ 보기 ├
> realize / promote / underwater / volcanic / several

(1) This campaign will _____ the education for all ages.

(2) He didn't _____ that he was acting differently.

(3) I go hiking _____ times a month.

(4) The _____ photographer is diving into the sea.

(5) Dokdo was created from _____ activity.

Conversation

A I wonder why he is running. 왜 그가 달리고 있는지 궁금해.

B I think he is late for school. 내 생각엔 그가 학교에 늦은 것 같아.

■ 궁금증을 표현할 때 wonder(궁금하다), curious(궁금한, 호기심이 많은), want to know(알고 싶다) 등의 표현을 이용하여 'I wonder ~.'라고 말한다. 이때 어순은 'I wonder+의문사+주어+동사 ~.', 'I wonder+if/whether+주어+동사 ~.'이다. 또한 궁금한 내용을 'I want to know ~.', 'I don't know why ~.'로 표현할 수 있다.

■ 'Can I ~?', 'Can/Could you ~?' 등과 같이 요구/요청을 나타내는 조동사 표현을 사용하여 'Can I ask you ~?' 또는 'Can you tell me ~?'와 같이 궁금한 점에 대하여 물어볼 수 있다. 그 외에 궁금증을 나타낼 때는 'Do you know ~?' 등을 사용할 수도 있다.

■ 궁금함을 나타낼 때 'I wonder ~.' 대신에 쓸 수 있는 표현으로 'I'm curious ~.' 또는 'I want to know ~.' 등이 있다. 'I'm curious'와 명사구를 같이 쓸 때는 'I'm curious about+명사구'이고, 명사절과 함께 쓸 때는 'I'm curious if/whether ~.' 또는 'I'm curious 의문사+주어+동사'이다.

궁금한 것 묻고 답하기

- I'm wondering + if/whether 주어+동사/의문사절. ~인지 궁금하다.
- Can you tell me ~? ~에 대해 말해 줄 수 있니?
- Can I ask you + 의문사절? ~에 대하여 물어봐도 되니?
- I'm curious if/whether 주어+동사. ~가 궁금하다.
- I want to know 명사구/명사절. ~을 알고 싶다.
- I'd be very interested to ~. 나는 ~에 매우 관심이 많다.

핵심 Check

1. 밑줄 친 우리말을 괄호 안에 주어진 어휘를 이용하여 영작하시오.

G: Wow, look at the bridge in this ad.

<u>어디에서 찍은 사진인지 궁금하네.</u> (the photo, taken)

B: That's Gwangandaegyo in Busan.

G: How do you know that?

B: I went there with my family last summer.

➡ _____

2 설명 요청하기

> **A** Could you explain what this is? 이게 무엇인지 설명해 줄 수 있니?
>
> **B** It's a traditional Korean hat. It's called a gat. 그것은 한국의 전통적인 모자야. 갓이라고 불러.

■ 상대방에게 궁금한 내용에 대한 설명을 요청할 때는 '설명하다, 말하다'의 의미를 가지는 동사 'explain', 'tell' 또는 'give information' 등의 표현을 사용하여 'Could/Can you explain 의문사절?', 'Could/Can you tell me more about ~?'라고 표현한다. Could 대신 Would, Can, Will 등을 사용할 수 있고, 'Do you mind if I ask you to explain ~?'이라고 말할 수도 있다.

■ 상대방의 말을 듣고 추가로 더 많이 설명해 달라고 할 때는 'Could/Can you tell me more about it?' 이라고 한다. 좀 더 공손하게 표현하여 Can 대신에 Could나 Would를 사용할 수도 있다. tell 대신에 explain을 써서 'Could/Can you explain that more, please?'라고 할 수 있다.

■ 상대방이 말하는 의도를 모르거나 사용하는 단어의 뜻을 몰라서 설명을 요청할 때 쓰는 표현은 'What does that mean?(그것이 무슨 뜻입니까?)', 'What do you mean by that?(그것이 무슨 뜻이니?)' 등 이다. 상대방의 말을 알아듣지 못했을 때는 'I'm not following you.(잘 알아듣지 못하겠습니다.)', 'I don't get it.(제대로 이해를 못하겠어요.)' 등의 표현을 사용하여 상대방이 다시 설명을 하도록 요청할 수도 있다.

설명 요청하기

- Could/Can you explain what this is? 이게 무엇인지 설명해 줄 수 있니?
- Could/Can you tell me more about it? 그것에 대해 좀 더 말해 줄 수 있니?
- I think I need some more information about it. 그것에 대해 정보가 더 필요한 것 같아.
- Could you give me more information? 좀 더 정보를 주시겠습니까?
- Could you be more specific? 좀 더 구체적으로 말해 주시겠습니까?
- What is the meaning of that exactly? 그게 정확하게 무슨 뜻입니까?

핵심 Check

2. 다음 대화를 자연스러운 순서로 배열하시오.

B: Excuse me, I'd like to use a copy machine.

(A) Sure. Press the button for double-sided copies, and then press the start button.

(B) Could you explain how to make double-sided copies?

(C) O.K. You can use this machine.

B: Thank you.

➡ _____

Listen & Speak 1 A-2

> B: Look over there. ❶I wonder why there are so many people waiting in line.
>
> G: They're waiting to ❷get into the new bakery there.
>
> B: Why? Is ❸it famous?
>
> G: Yes. ❸It was on a TV program.
>
> B: Really? We should try their bread then.
>
> G: Sure.

> B: 저기 좀 봐. 왜 저렇게 많은 사람들이 줄을 서서 기다리고 있는지 궁금하네.
>
> G: 새로 생긴 제과점에 들어가려고 기다리고 있는 거야.
>
> B: 왜? 유명한 곳이야?
>
> G: 맞아. TV 프로그램에 나왔어.
>
> B: 정말? 그럼 우리 저곳의 빵을 먹어 봐야겠다.
>
> G: 그래.

❶ 궁금한 것을 묻는 표현으로 'I want to know why there are so many people waiting in line.' 등으로 바꾸어 쓸 수 있다.
❷ get into: ~에 들어가다
❸ It은 The new bakery를 가리킨다.

Check(√) True or False

(1) The boy wants to know why there are lots of people waiting in line.　　　　T ☐ F ☐

(2) The new bakery became famous after it was on a TV program.　　　　T ☐ F ☐

 Communicate A

> Jaden: Do you hear that? I wonder where that music is coming from.
>
> Yuri: I think it's coming from over there. Do you want to go and ❶check it out?
>
> Jaden: Yes, I love that strong beat. Is it ❷traditional Korean music?
>
> Yuri: Yes, it's called nongak. It's a kind of ❸community band music.
>
> Jaden: Nongak? ❹Could you explain a little bit more about it?
>
> Yuri: It's traditionally used to ❺cheer up farmers and ❻wish for a good harvest.
>
> Jaden: I see. Look! Some people are dancing to the rhythm.
>
> Yuri: Yes, that's a big part of nongak. Dancing together completes the music.
>
> Jaden: Let's join them.
>
> Yuri: Sure. Why not?

> Jaden: 저거 들리니? 저 음악이 어디서 오는 것인지 궁금하네.
>
> 유리: 저기서 나오는 것 같은데. 가서 확인해 볼래?
>
> Jaden: 그래. 저 강한 비트가 마음에 들어. 이게 한국의 전통 음악이니?
>
> 유리: 맞아. 농악이라고 해. 공동체 악단 음악의 한 종류야.
>
> Jaden: 농악? 그것에 대해 좀 더 설명해 줄래?
>
> 유리: 그건 전통적으로 농부들의 힘을 북돋아 주고 풍년을 기원하기 위해 사용되었어.
>
> Jaden: 그렇구나. 봐! 몇몇 사람들이 리듬에 맞춰 춤추고 있어.
>
> 유리: 그래. 그게 농악의 큰 부분이야. 함께 춤추는 것이 음악을 완성하지.
>
> Jaden: 저들과 함께 하자.
>
> 유리: 물론이야. 왜 안 되겠어?

❶ check (something) out: ~을 확인하다, 조사하다　　❷ traditional: 전통적인　　❸ community: 지역 공동체
❹ 상대방에게 궁금한 내용에 대한 설명을 요청할 때 쓰는 표현으로 'Could you tell me a little bit more about it?' 등으로 바꾸어 쓸 수 있다.
❺ cheer up: 격려하다　　❻ wish for: ~을 기원하다

Check(√) True or False

(3) Jaden and Yuri are listening to nongak.　　　　T ☐ F ☐

(4) The strong beat is a big part of nongak.　　　　T ☐ F ☐

Listen & Speak 1 A-1

G: Wow, look at the ❶bridge in this ❷ad. I wonder where the photo was taken.

B: That's Gwangandaegyo in Busan.

G: How do you know that?

B: I went ❸there with my family last summer.

❶ bridge: 다리
❷ ad(= advertisement): 광고
❸ there는 Gwangandaegyo in Busan을 가리킨다.

Listen & Speak 2 A-1

W: Excuse me, ❶I'd like to ❷borrow ❸an audio guide.

M: Here you are.

W: ❹Could you explain how to use ❺it?

M: Sure. Press this button, and it'll tell you what to do.

❶ would like to ～: ～하고 싶다
❷ borrow: 빌리다
❸ audio guide: 음성 안내기
❹ 'Could you tell me how to use it?' 등으로 바꾸어 표현할 수 있다.
❺ it은 the audio guide를 가리킨다.

Listen & Speak 2 A-2

B: Are you going somewhere this summer?

G: I'm going to Jejudo to ❶walk along the Jeju Olle Trail.

B: The Jeju Olle Trail? Could you explain what ❷that is?

G: It's a long hiking ❸path around Jejudo.

B: Oh, I see. I hope you enjoy your trip!

❶ walk along: ～을 따라 걷다
❷ that은 the Jeju Olle Trail을 가리킨다.
❸ path: 길

Progress Check 1

W: Look over there. ❶I wonder why there are so many cars on the road.

M: Lots of people are ❷going on vacation this weekend.

W: Really? Then, ❸why don't we go somewhere, too?

M: O.K.

❶ 궁금한 것을 묻는 표현으로 'Could you tell me why there are so many cars on the road?'로 바꾸어 표현할 수 있다.
❷ go on vacation: 휴가를 가다
❸ why don't we ～? = how about ～? = what about ～? = ～하는 게 어때?

Progress Check 2

B: Excuse me, I'd like to use a ❶copy machine.

W: O.K. You can use ❷this machine.

B: Could you explain how to ❸make double-sided copies?

W: Sure. ❹Press the button for double-sided copies, and then press the start button.

B: Thank you.

❶ copy machine: 복사기
❷ this machine은 복사기를 가리킨다.
❸ make double-sided copies: 양면 복사를 하다
❹ press: 누르다

● 다음 우리말과 일치하도록 빈칸에 알맞은 말을 쓰시오.

Listen & Speak 1 A-1

G: Wow, look at the _____ in this _____. I wonder _____ _____ _____ _____ _____.

B: That's Gwangandaegyo in Busan.

G: _____ do you know that?

B: I went there _____ my family _____ _____.

Listen & Speak 1 A-2

B: Look over there. _____ _____ _____ there are so many people _____ _____ _____.

G: They're waiting to _____ _____ the new bakery there.

B: Why? Is it _____?

G: Yes. It was _____ a TV program.

B: Really? We should _____ their bread then.

G: Sure.

Listen & Speak 2 A-1

W: Excuse me, _____ _____ _____ _____ _____ an audio guide.

M: Here you are.

W: Could you _____ _____ _____ _____ _____?

M: Sure. _____ this button, and it'll tell you _____ _____ _____.

Listen & Speak 2 A-2

B: Are you going _____ this summer?

G: I'm going to Jejudo to _____ _____ the Jeju Olle Trail.

B: The Jeju Olle Trail? _____ _____ _____ what that is?

G: It's a _____ _____ _____ around Jejudo.

B: Oh, I see. I hope you _____ _____ _____!

해석

G: 와, 이 광고에 나오는 다리 좀 봐. 어디에서 찍은 사진인지 궁금하네.
B: 부산의 광안대교야.
G: 그걸 어떻게 아니?
B: 작년 여름에 우리 가족들과 그곳에 갔었거든.

B: 저기 좀 봐. 왜 저렇게 많은 사람들이 줄을 서서 기다리고 있는지 궁금하네.
G: 새로 생긴 제과점에 들어가려고 기다리고 있는 거야.
B: 왜? 유명한 곳이야?
G: 맞아. TV 프로그램에 나왔어.
B: 정말? 그럼 우리 저곳의 빵을 먹어 봐야겠다.
G: 그래.

W: 실례합니다. 음성 가이드를 대여하고 싶은데요.
M: 여기 있습니다.
W: 어떻게 사용하는지 설명해 주실 수 있나요?
M: 물론이죠. 이 버튼을 누르면, 무엇을 해야 할지 말해 줄 겁니다.

B: 이번 여름에 어디 갈 거야?
G: 제주 올레길을 따라 걸으러 제주도에 갈 거야.
B: 제주 올레길? 그게 무엇인지 설명해 줄래?
G: 제주도 둘레에 있는 긴 하이킹 코스야.
B: 오, 그렇구나. 즐거운 여행이 되길 바랄게!

Communicate A

Jaden: Do you hear that? _____ _____ _____ that music is coming from.

Yuri: I think it's coming from over there. Do you want to go and _____ _____ _____?

Jaden: Yes, I love that _____ _____. Is it _____ Korean music?

Yuri: Yes, it's called nongak. It's a kind of _____ band music.

Jaden: Nongak? _____ _____ _____ a little bit more about it?

Yuri: It's _____ used to _____ _____ farmers and wish for a _____ _____.

Jaden: I see. Look! Some people are dancing to the _____.

Yuri: Yes, that's a big part of nongak. Dancing together _____ the music.

Jaden: Let's join them.

Yuri: Sure. _____ _____?

해석

Jaden: 저거 들리니? 저 음악이 어디서 오는 것인지 궁금하네.
유리: 저기서 나오는 것 같은데. 가서 확인해 볼래?
Jaden: 그래. 저 강한 비트가 마음에 들어. 그게 한국의 전통 음악이니?
유리: 맞아, 농악이라고 해. 공동체 악단 음악의 한 종류야.
Jaden: 농악? 그것에 대해 좀 더 설명해 줄래?
유리: 그건 전통적으로 농부들의 힘을 북돋아 주고 풍년을 기원하기 위해 사용되었어.
Jaden: 그렇구나. 봐! 몇몇 사람들이 리듬에 맞춰 춤추고 있어.
유리: 그래, 그게 농악의 큰 부분이야. 함께 춤추는 것이 음악을 완성하지.
Jaden: 저들과 함께 하자.
유리: 물론이야. 왜 안 되겠어?

Progress Check 1

W: Look over there. _____ _____ _____ _____ _____ _____ _____ _____ on the road.

M: Lots of people are _____ _____ _____ this weekend.

W: Really? Then, _____ _____ _____ go somewhere, too?

M: O.K.

W: 저기 좀 봐요. 도로에 왜 저렇게 차가 많은지 궁금하네요.
M: 많은 사람들이 이번 주말에 휴가를 가거든요.
W: 정말로요? 그럼, 우리도 어디 가는 게 어떤가요?
M: 좋아요.

Progress Check 2

B: Excuse me, I'd like to use a _____ _____.

W: O.K. You can use this machine.

B: Could you explain _____ _____ _____ _____ _____?

W: Sure. _____ the button for double-sided copies, and then _____ the start button.

B: Thank you.

B: 실례합니다, 복사기를 좀 쓰고 싶은데요.
W: 알겠어요. 이 기계를 써도 돼요.
B: 어떻게 양면 복사를 하는지 설명해 주실 수 있나요?
W: 물론이죠. 양면 복사 버튼을 누르고, 시작 버튼을 누르세요.
B: 감사합니다.

[01~02] 다음 대화를 읽고 물음에 답하시오.

G: Wow, look at the bridge in this ad. (A)<u>I wonder where was the photo taken.</u>

B: That's Gwangandaegyo in Busan.

G: (B)<u>그걸 어떻게 아니?</u>

B: I went there with my family last summer.

01 위 대화의 밑줄 친 (A)를 어법상 바르게 고치시오.

➡ _____

02 위 대화의 밑줄 친 우리말 (B)를 5 단어로 영작하시오.

➡ _____

[03~04] 다음 대화를 읽고 물음에 답하시오.

Tom: Are you going somewhere this summer?

Jane: I'm going to Jejudo to walk along the Jeju Olle Trail.

Tom: The Jeju Olle Trail? (A)<u>Could you explain what that is?</u> (tell)

Jane: It's a long hiking path around Jejudo.

Tom: Oh, I see. I hope you enjoy your trip!

03 위 대화의 밑줄 친 (A)와 의미가 같도록 주어진 단어를 사용하여 바꿔 쓰시오.

➡ _____

04 위 대화의 내용과 일치하지 <u>않는</u> 것은?

① Jane은 이번 여름에 제주도에 갈 예정이다.
② Jane은 제주도에서 올레길을 걸을 것이다.
③ 올레길은 제주도 둘레에 있는 긴 하이킹 코스이다.
④ Tom은 Jane이 즐거운 여행을 하길 바란다.
⑤ Tom은 이미 올레길에 대해 잘 알고 있다.

01 다음 대화가 자연스럽게 이어지도록 순서대로 배열하시오.

> Look over there. I wonder why there are so many people waiting in line.

> (A) Sure.
> (B) Yes. It was on a TV program.
> (C) Why? Is it famous?
> (D) Really? We should try their bread then.
> (E) They're waiting to get into the new bakery there.

➡ _____

02 다음 대화의 빈칸 (A)에 들어갈 말로 적절하지 <u>않은</u> 것은?

> W: Excuse me, I'd like to borrow an audio guide.
> M: Here you are.
> W: _____ (A)
> M: Sure. Press this button, and it'll tell you what to do.

① Could you explain how to use it?
② Can you tell me how to use it?
③ Could you give me more information about how to use it?
④ Could you be more specific about how to use it?
⑤ What do you mean by that?

[03~04] 다음 대화를 읽고 물음에 답하시오.

> G: Wow, ⓐ<u>look</u> at the bridge in this ad. I wonder where the photo ⓑ<u>took</u>.
> B: That's Gwangandaegyo ⓒ<u>in</u> Busan.
> G: How do you know ⓓ<u>that</u>?
> B: I went ⓔ<u>there</u> with my family last summer.

03 위 대화의 밑줄 친 ⓐ~ⓔ 중 어법상 틀린 것을 찾아 바르게 고치시오.

➡ _____

04 위 대화의 내용과 일치하지 <u>않는</u> 것은?

① The girl and the boy are watching the ad.
② There is a bridge in the ad.
③ The girl wants to know where the photo of the bridge was taken.
④ The boy visited Busan with his family last summer.
⑤ The girl wants to take a photo of the bridge.

[05~06] 다음 대화를 읽고 물음에 답하시오.

> Brian: Look over there. I wonder why there are so many people (A)[waited / waiting] in line.
> Sujin: They're waiting to (B)[get into / get out] the new bakery there.
> Brian: Why? Is it famous?
> Sujin: Yes. It was (C)[on / off] a TV program.
> Brian: Really? We should try their bread then.
> Sujin: Sure.

05 위 대화의 (A)~(C)에 들어갈 말로 바르게 짝지어진 것은?

	(A)	(B)	(C)
①	waited	get into	on
②	waited	get out	off
③	waiting	get out	on
④	waiting	get out	off
⑤	waiting	get into	on

06 위 대화의 내용과 일치하지 <u>않는</u> 것은?

① Brian은 왜 많은 사람들이 줄을 서서 기다리고 있는지 궁금하다.

② 새로 생긴 제과점에 들어가려고 많은 사람들이 줄을 서 있다.

③ 새로 생긴 제과점이 TV 프로그램에 나왔다.

④ Brian은 새로 생긴 제과점의 빵을 먹어 보고 싶다.

⑤ Brian과 수진은 함께 제과점 앞에서 줄을 서서 기다리고 있었다.

서답형

07 다음 대화가 자연스럽게 이어지도록 순서대로 배열하시오.

> (A) Thank you.
> (B) O.K. You can use this machine.
> (C) Excuse me, I'd like to use a copy machine.
> (D) Could you explain how to make double-sided copies?
> (E) Sure. Press the button for double-sided copies, and then press the start button.

➡ _____

[08~09] 다음 대화를 읽고 물음에 답하시오.

> Jaden: Do you hear that? (a)<u>I wonder where that music is coming from.</u>
> Yuri: I think it's coming from over there. Do you want to go and check it out?
> Jaden: Yes, I love that strong beat. Is it traditional Korean music?
> Yuri: Yes, it's called nongak. It's a kind of community band music.
> Jaden: Nongak? Could you explain a little bit more about it?
> Yuri: It's traditionally used to cheer up farmers and wish for a good harvest.
> Jaden: I see. Look! Some people are dancing to the rhythm.

> Yuri: Yes, that's a big part of nongak. (b)<u>함께 춤추는 것이 음악을 완성하지</u>. (together)
> Jaden: Let's join them.
> Yuri: Sure. Why not?

08 위 대화의 밑줄 친 (a)와 바꾸어 쓸 수 있는 것을 고르시오.

① I don't know where that music is coming from.

② I'm sure where that music is coming from.

③ It's not certain where that music is coming from.

④ I want to know where that music is coming from.

⑤ I've been told where that music is coming from.

09 위 대화의 밑줄 친 (b)를 주어진 단어를 사용하여 5 단어로 영작하시오.

➡ _____

10 다음 짝지어진 대화가 <u>어색한</u> 것은?

① A: Look at the boy. I wonder why he is running.
　 B: I think he is late for school.

② A: Look at her. I wonder why she looks surprised.
　 B: I think she saw a celebrity.

③ A: Could you explain what this is?
　 B: It's a traditional Korean hairpin. It's called a binyeo.

④ A: Can you tell me how to use this machine?
　 B: Sure. Press this button first.

⑤ A: I want to know where the photo was taken.
　 B: Thank you for your great efforts.

[01~02] 다음 대화를 읽고 물음에 답하시오.

W: Excuse me, I'd like to borrow an audio guide.

M: Here you are.

W: _____

M: Sure. Press this button, and it'll tell you what to do.

01 위 대화의 빈칸에 들어갈 말을 주어진 단어를 배열하여 영작하시오.

> you / how / it / could / to / explain / use

➡ _____

02 What does the woman get to know after pressing the button?

➡ _____

03 다음 대화의 내용과 일치하도록 빈칸을 완성하시오.

Brian: Look over there. I wonder why there are so many people waiting in line.

Sujin: They're waiting to get into the new bakery there.

Brian: Why? Is it famous?

Sujin: Yes. It was on a TV program.

Brian: Really? We should try their bread then.

Sujin: Sure.

Brian and Sujin saw many people (A) _____ in front of (B) _____. People wanted to (C) _____ there. The new bakery was so popular because (D) _____. Brian and Sujin wanted to try its bread together.

[04~05] 다음 대화를 읽고 물음에 답하시오.

Jaden: Do you hear that? I wonder where that music is coming from.

Yuri: I think it's coming from over there. Do you want to go and check it out?

Jaden: Yes, I love that strong beat. Is it traditional Korean music?

Yuri: Yes, it's called nongak. It's a kind of community band music.

Jaden: Nongak? Could you explain a little bit more about it?

Yuri: It's traditionally used to cheer up farmers and wish for a good harvest.

Jaden: I see. Look! Some people are dancing to the rhythm.

Yuri: Yes, that's a big part of nongak. Dancing together completes the music.

Jaden: Let's join them.

Yuri: Sure. Why not?

04 위 대화를 읽고 빈칸에 알맞은 말을 써 넣으시오.

VISIT Korea

About Korea | **Culture** | Food | Travel | More

Nongak ...
- is a community ___(1)___ music
- has ___(2)___ beats
- cheers up ___(3)___
- wishes for a good ___(4)___

➡ (1) _____ (2) _____ (3) _____
(4) _____

05 What are Jaden and Yuri going to do after the conversation?

➡ _____

_____

Grammar

---

1 '과거완료' had + 과거분사

- Until then, I **had** only **seen** black-and-white photos of haenyeo.

  그때까지, 나는 흑백 사진 속의 해녀만 보았었다.   그녀는 다섯 시간이 넘도록 물속에 있은 후에도 계속 웃었다.

- She kept laughing even after she **had been** in the water for over five hours.

■ 과거완료시제는 'had+과거분사' 형태로 표현하며, 과거의 어느 시점을 기준으로 그 이전에 일어난 동작이나 상태를 나타낸다.

- Somi went shopping at the local market after she **had gone** swimming at Hyeopjae Beach.
  소미는 협재 해변으로 수영하러 간 후, 지역 시장으로 쇼핑하러 갔다.

■ 과거의 특정 시점을 기준으로 그 이전에 일어난 동작의 완료, 경험, 계속, 결과를 나타낸다.

(1) 완료: '막 ~했었다'는 의미로 과거 이전에 시작된 동작이 과거의 어느 시점에 완료된 일을 나타낸다. 보통 already, yet 등의 부사와 함께 쓰인다.

- When I arrived, the class **had** already **begun**. 내가 도착했을 때, 수업이 벌써 시작됐다.

(2) 경험: '~한 적이 있었다'는 의미로 과거 이전부터 과거의 어느 시점까지의 경험을 나타낸다. 보통 never, ever, once, twice, before 등의 부사(구)와 함께 쓰인다.

- Barbara recognized the suspect immediately, for she **had met** him online before.
  Barbara는 그 용의자를 즉시 알아봤는데, 전에 온라인상에서 그를 만난 적이 있었기 때문이었다.

(3) 결과: '(과거 이전에) ~해서, 그 결과 …했다'는 의미로 과거 이전의 동작이 과거의 어느 시점의 결과에 영향을 미치는 것을 나타낸다.

- He **had gone** to work when I called. 내가 전화했을 때, 그는 (이미) 출근했다.

(4) 계속: '계속 ~하고 있었다'는 의미로 과거 이전부터 과거의 어느 시점까지 계속되는 동작이나 상태를 나타낸다. 보통 since, for 등과 함께 쓰인다.

- Tiffany **had waited** for her brother for 2 years when he returned.
  그녀의 오빠가 돌아왔을 때, Tiffany는 오빠를 2년 동안이나 기다렸었다.

■ 부정문은 'had+not[never]+과거분사', 의문문은 'Had+주어+과거분사 ~?', 과거 어느 시점을 기준으로 전부터 진행 중인 동작을 강조할 때는 과거완료진행형 'had+been+V-ing'을 쓴다.

- She **had never won** an Academy Award by then. 그녀는 그 때까지 아카데미상을 탄 적이 없었다.
- **Had they met** the director before? 그들이 전에 감독을 만난 적이 있었나요?
- I **had been watching** a movie until you came to see me. 당신이 나를 보러올 때까지 나는 영화를 보고 있었다.

핵심 Check

1. 괄호 안에서 알맞은 말을 고르시오.

(1) My family (has / had) lived in Seoul before we moved to Busan.

(2) Suji had never seen wild animals until she (visits / visited) the zoo.

2 간접의문문

• They didn't understand **why I wanted to take their pictures.**

그들은 내가 왜 그들의 사진을 찍으려고 하는지 이해하지 못했다.

• Please tell us **what you're planning to do in the future.**

앞으로 계획하고 있는 것에 대해 말씀해 주세요.

■ 간접의문문은 의문문이 다른 문장의 일부가 된 형태로 '의문사+주어+동사' 형태로 쓰며, 이때 의문사가 접속사 역할을 한다.

• I want to know. + Where is he from?

→ I want to know **where he is from**. 나는 그가 어디에서 왔는지 알고 싶다.

• I wonder. + Why did she leave so early?

→ I wonder **why she left so early**. 나는 그녀가 왜 그렇게 빨리 떠났는지 궁금하다.

■ 의문문의 '동사+주어'의 어순이, 간접의문문에서 '주어+동사'의 어순이 되지만, 의문사가 주어인 의문문은 어순의 변화가 생길 수 없다.

• My teacher will tell us. + Who called the police?

→ My teacher will tell us **who called the police**.

나의 선생님은 누가 경찰에게 전화를 했는지 우리에게 말해 줄 것이다.

■ 의문사가 없는 경우, **if** 또는 **whether**가 '~인지 (아닌지)'라는 의미의 명사절을 이끈다.

• I don't know. + Does she like me?

→ I don't know **if[whether] she likes me**. 나는 그녀가 나를 좋아하는지 알지 못한다.

• Tell us. + Is the lady married or not?

→ Tell us **if[whether] the lady is married or not**. 그 숙녀분이 결혼했는지 안 했는지를 우리에게 말해 주시오.

■ 생각이나 추측, 상상, 믿음 등을 나타내는 동사들(think, believe, guess, suppose, imagine)이 쓰인 문장에서 의문사가 이끄는 간접의문문이 목적어가 될 때, 간접의문문의 의문사를 문장 맨 앞으로 보낸다. 이 경우, 의문사가 문두로 가도, 어순은 '주어+동사'이다.

• Do you believe? + What does he have in his bag?

→ **What** do you believe **he has in his bag**? 당신은 그의 가방 속에 그가 무엇을 가지고 있다고 생각합니까?

• Do you think? + Who is going to marry you?

→ **Who** do you think **is going to marry you**? 당신은 누가 당신과 결혼할 것이라고 생각합니까?

핵심 Check

2. 다음 문장에서 어법상 틀린 부분을 찾아 바르게 고쳐 쓰시오.

(1) I wonder when will she make us the cookie. ➡ _____

(2) Nobody knows why was Sarah so upset. ➡ _____

Grammar 시험대비 기본평가

01 다음 빈칸에 들어갈 말로 알맞은 것은?

> Parker was sure he _____ his laptop on the table last night, but he couldn't find it.

① put   ② puts   ③ has put
④ to put   ⑤ had put

02 다음 두 문장을 한 문장으로 바꿔 쓸 때, 빈칸에 들어갈 말로 가장 적절한 것은?

> • Does Andy know?
> • Is that bus going to the airport?
> → Does Andy know _____ that bus is going to the airport?

① where   ② but   ③ if   ④ how   ⑤ so

03 다음 밑줄 친 부분 중 어법상 옳은 것을 고르시오.

① The old man had lived in the town for 40 years until now.
② The plane has already taken off when I reached the airport.
③ The police had found his wallet that was left under the desk.
④ She opened the box that Miles had sent a week before.
⑤ Nora has gone to London before her husband came back.

04 다음 두 문장을 간접의문문을 이용하여 한 문장으로 만들 때, 빈칸에 알맞은 말을 써 넣으시오.

(1) The reporter asked.
   How did she become interested in taking photos?
   ➡ The reporter _____ _____ _____ _____ _____ in taking photos.

(2) Could you tell us?
   What is so special about haenyeo?
   ➡ Could you _____ _____ _____ _____ _____ _____ about haenyeo?

01 밑줄 친 부분이 어법상 <u>어색한</u> 것은?

① After all the animals <u>had left</u> the burning woods, she felt relieved.

② The violinist <u>had played</u> such a beautiful song that the audience gave her an endless applause that night.

③ Lucy asked the man how to fix the phone that <u>has broken</u> down.

④ The professor <u>had</u> just <u>left</u> the hall when the politician appeared.

⑤ Caroline ate the cookies that her grandma <u>had made</u> for her.

[02~03] 다음 우리말을 어법상 알맞게 영작한 것을 고르시오.

02 그게 무엇인지 설명해 주시겠어요?

① Could you explain that what it is?

② Could you explain that what that is?

③ Could you explain what is that?

④ Could you explain that what is that?

⑤ Could you explain what that is?

03 왜 저렇게 많은 사람들이 줄을 서서 기다리고 있는지 궁금하다.

① I wonder why so many people there waiting in line.

② I wonder why are there so many people waiting in line.

③ I wonder why do so many people are waiting in line.

④ I wonder why there are so many people waiting in line.

⑤ I wonder why there are so many people are waiting in line.

[04~05] 다음 중 어법상 옳은 것을 고르시오.

04 ① Jinsu had read the article about the history of Jeju for the last 3 years.

② William lived in New York before he had moved to San Francisco.

③ Kevin required Minsu that he had completed the report.

④ He lost the watch which he had bought the day before.

⑤ I am hungry since I had not eaten anything so far.

05 ① Could you tell us more about what so special is about haenyeo?

② Does Julie know which subject do I like?

③ Do you imagine how old she is?

④ Tell me what is your favorite food.

⑤ Do you want to ask your English teacher what the sentence means?

서답형

06 다음 문장에서 어법상 <u>어색한</u> 단어 한 개를 찾아서 고치시오.

It had been raining since Miranda went to Spain to learn tango.

➡

07 다음 두 문장을 의미가 같도록 한 문장으로 바꿔 쓸 때 적절하지 않은 것은?

① I'd like to know. + When did Louise apply for the scholarship?
　→ I'd like to know when Louise applied for the scholarship.
② May I ask you? + How much are the souvenir photos?
　→ May I ask you how much the souvenir photos are?
③ David asked Emma. + Why was she angry with him?
　→ David asked Emma why she was angry with him.
④ Could you tell us? + What did Frank buy at the mall?
　→ Could you tell us what Frank bought at the mall?
⑤ Susan is wondering. + Who took away her kids' toys?
　→ Susan is wondering who her kids' toys took away.

08 다음 중 밑줄 친 과거완료의 용법이 〈보기〉와 같은 것은?

┌─ 보기 ─────────────────┐
He <u>had</u> already <u>found</u> out the secret of the mystery cube when I asked him.
└──────────────────────┘

① Tiffany <u>had lived</u> in Busan for 7 months before she moved to Daegu.
② Anna <u>had</u> never <u>been</u> fat by the time she started learning swimming.
③ My cousin <u>had been</u> sick in bed for a week when I visited him.
④ I didn't know how long he <u>had waited</u> for me at the gate the other day.
⑤ Jordan <u>had</u> not <u>finished</u> the work when everyone was about to go out.

09 다음 중 밑줄 친 부분의 쓰임이 〈보기〉와 같은 것은?

┌─ 보기 ─────────────────┐
Chanho should not miss such a good opportunity <u>if</u> he wants to win the game.
└──────────────────────┘

① Does anybody know <u>if</u> the handsome guy over there has a girlfriend?
② I'm sure the company will succeed <u>if</u> it expands their market in Asia.
③ All of us were not sure <u>if</u> Peter's answer was right or wrong.
④ Taste the food to determine <u>if</u> more salt is required.
⑤ Sarah wondered <u>if</u> Ted would come to the party without the invitation.

10 다음 두 문장을 한 문장으로 만들 때 가장 적절한 것은?

┌────────────────────────┐
• Do you think?
• Why did the haenyeo look happy?
└────────────────────────┘

① Do you think why did the haenyeo look happy?
② Do you think why the haenyeo looked happy?
③ Why do you think did the haenyeo look happy?
④ Why do you think the haenyeo looked happy?
⑤ Why do you think the haenyeo did looked happy?

[11~12] 다음 중 어법상 옳은 문장은?

11
① Cecilia had lost the necklace which I bought for her.
② You can't see the snowman anymore as it had melted this morning.
③ When we were about to leave home, my uncle had already arrived.
④ The passengers have been seated before the plane took off.
⑤ William has never seen the wallaby until he visited Australia.

12 중요
① Do you think where Clara first met her husband?
② Could you please tell us what did your action mean?
③ I wonder whether did anyone see the boy walking along the beach.
④ Do you know how the writer of these books old is?
⑤ Let me know what they are drinking.

서답형
[13~14] 우리말과 일치하도록 괄호 안에 주어진 어구를 바르게 배열하시오.

13
기자는 많은 고객들이 돈가스를 먹으려고 줄을 서서 상당한 시간을 보냈다고 말했다. (돈가스: pork cutlet)
→ The reporter said that (lining up, time, had spent, in order to, quite a long, many, eat, customers, pork cutlet).

➡ The reporter said that _____
_____
_____.

14
당신은 그 절들이 왜 유명하다고 생각합니까?
(the temples, you, famous, why, are, do, think)?

➡ _____

서답형
15 다음 그림을 보고 자연스러운 문장이 되도록 괄호 안에 주어진 어구를 바르게 배열하여 빈칸을 완성하시오.

(1)

➡ Jiho _____
_____. (fly, could, asked, people, in the sky, his sister, why, not)

(2)

➡ Pooh _____
_____. (a hive, told, touched, he, that morning, his friend, had, that)

01 다음 우리말과 일치하도록 괄호 안에 주어진 어구를 바르게 배열하여 문장을 완성하시오.

(1) 그 기업은 몇몇 프랑스인들이 전에 훔쳐갔었던 한국의 많은 보물들을 수집했다.

➡ The company _____

_____.

(before, French, stolen, collected, many, that, had, Korean treasures, some)

(2) 수민이는 어떻게 자신이 해녀를 전 세계적으로 홍보할 수 있을지 궁금하다.

➡ Sumin _____

_____. (the haenyeo, wonders, can, worldwide, promote, how, she)

(3) Jim이 출장에서 돌아왔을 때, 그는 누군가가 자신의 집에 침입했었던 것을 발견했다.

➡ When Jim came back from a business trip, _____

_____. (his house, found, broken, he, someone, into, had)

(4) 그 사진 작가가 어디에서 이 사진들을 찍었는지 추측할 수 있습니까?

➡ _____

these pictures? (guess, took, can, the photographer, where, you)

02 다음 〈보기〉와 같이 간접의문문을 활용하여 빈칸을 채우시오.

┌─ 보기 ┐

When does the post office close?

→ Do you know when the post office closes?

└──────────────────────┘

(1) How could they get to the meeting on time?

➡ Do you know _____

_____?

(2) Which boy did the girl next to Jane choose at the blind date?

➡ Can you tell me _____

_____?

(3) Hasn't Shrek learned German yet?

➡ Do you know _____

_____?

(4) Where did Alex find the baby tiger?

➡ Let her figure out _____

_____.

(5) How old does the new employee look?

➡ How old do you think _____

_____?

03 다음 사진을 참고하여 우리말에 맞게, 괄호 안에 주어진 어구를 활용하되, 과거완료시제를 써서 빈칸을 채우시오.

그 날까지 나는 흑백 사진들 속의 아주 지친 모습의 해녀만 봤었다. (who, haenyeo, photos, only see, black-and-white photos)

➡ Until the day, I _____

_____

looked very tired.

04 다음 문장에서 어법상 <u>어색한</u> 것을 바르게 고쳐 다시 쓰시오.

(1) Can you tell me where was the magician when he disappeared?

➡ _____

_____

(2) Does the young student know how the hotel is far?

➡ _____

_____

(3) Do you know could I take pictures of haenyeo?

➡ _____

_____

(4) They didn't understand why did the girl want to take their pictures.

➡ _____

_____

(5) Tell me what did Zin Kim promise the haenyeo.

➡ _____

_____

(6) I wonder why is Jejudo not suitable for farming.

➡ _____

_____

05 주어진 우리말을 〈조건〉에 맞게 영작하시오.

┌─── 조건 ───
1. 부정 의미의 과거완료시제를 쓸 것.
2. The haenyeo를 포함, 총 18 단어로 쓸 것.
3. 숫자도 영어로 쓸 것.
4. the photographer, think, her picture, pretty, until, that, she, take 등을 활용할 것.
5. ago를 가장 마지막 단어로 할 것.
└─────────────

그 사진작가가 12년 전에 그녀의 사진을 찍을 때까지, 그 해녀는 자신이 예쁘다고 생각하지 않았었다.

➡ _____

_____

_____

06 괄호 안에 주어진 어휘를 활용하여 글자 수대로 다음 우리말을 영작하시오.

(1) Tom은 해녀들이 어떤 호흡장치도 없이 어떻게 물속에 그렇게나 오래 머무를 수 있는지 궁금했다. (how, stay, wonder, so long, without, breathing devices, haenyeo, for, any, could, 16 단어)

➡ _____

_____

(2) 그들은 너무 많은 해양 생물을 채취하는 것이 바다를 어떻게 파괴할 수 있는지 연구하고 있다. (how, can, are, study, marine life, destroy, catching, too much, the ocean, 13 단어)

➡ _____

_____

(3) 마녀는 거울에게 세상에서 가장 아름다운 여자가 누구인지 물었다. (who, woman, the witch, in the world, beautiful, was, ask, the mirror, 14 단어)

➡ _____

_____

(4) 엄마 염소는 아기들이 늑대에게 언제 문을 열어 준 것인지 몰랐다. (when, to, the door, the mother goat, open, not know, the wolf, the babies, 15 단어)

➡ _____

_____

Haenyeo, Female Divers of Korea

For the past several years, the underwater photographer Zin Kim has promoted the culture of Jeju haenyeo worldwide. Haenyeo are Korean female divers who harvest seafood without any breathing devices. Their culture made UNESCO's Intangible Cultural Heritage list in 2016. At her studio last week, Zin Kim was interviewed about her experience of taking pictures of haenyeo.

Q. How did you become interested in taking photos of haenyeo?

One day, I happened to take pictures of a haenyeo. I was surprised to find that she was enjoying her job. Until then, I had only seen black-and-white photos of haenyeo who looked very tired. However, she kept laughing even after she had been in the water for over five hours. I realized then that I should take pictures of haenyeo.

Q. You take beautiful pictures of them, but isn't it difficult to take pictures of haenyeo?

At first, they didn't understand why I wanted to take their pictures. They didn't think they looked pretty in their wetsuits. So, I said to them, "You're very special. I want to show your culture to the world." They opened up to me then. Of course, I also promised them that I would make them look beautiful in my pictures.

---

female 여성의, 암컷의

past 지나간

several 몇몇의

underwater 수중의, 물속에서

photographer 사진작가

promote 홍보하다, 촉진하다

worldwide 세계적으로

breathe 호흡하다

intangible 무형의, 만질 수 없는

heritage 유산

experience 경험

happen to 우연히 ~하다

black-and-white (사진, TV 등) 흑백의

realize 깨닫다, 인식하다

wetsuit 잠수용 고무 옷

📎 **확인문제**

● 다음 문장이 본문의 내용과 일치하면 T, 일치하지 않으면 F를 쓰시오.

1 Zin Kim is the underwater photographer. ☐

2 Haenyeo are Korean female divers who harvest seafood with breathing devices. ☐

3 At first, haenyeo understood why Zin Kim wanted to take their pictures. ☐

4 Haenyeo didn't think they looked pretty in their wetsuits. ☐

5 Zin Kim wants to show the culture of Korea to the world. ☐

Q. Could you tell us more about haenyeo? What's so special about them?

I can tell you three things. First, haenyeo are a symbol of strong women. Jejudo, which is a volcanic island, is not suitable for farming,
계속적 용법의 관계대명사. which가 Jejudo를 받아서 그에 대한 추가 설명을 덧붙이고 있다.
so many haenyeo have become the breadwinners for their families. Second, haenyeo form their own communities and help each other. For example, more-experienced haenyeo train less-experienced haenyeo.
more(부사)+experienced(형용사)가 haenyeo를 꾸며 주고 있음.   less(부사)+experienced(형용사)가 haenyeo를 꾸며 주고 있음.
Third, because they stay in the water without any breathing devices, haenyeo can't catch a lot of seafood. This is good for the underwater
be good for: ~에 좋다
environment. Catching too much marine life at one time in one place
동명사 주어   = It can destroy the ocean to catch too much marine life at one time
can destroy the ocean.   in one place.

Q. Lastly, please tell us what you're planning to do in the future.
'What are you planning to do ~?'라는 의문문이 tell의 직접목적어로 쓰여 간접의문문이 된 형태
I once attended an overseas exhibition with a couple of haenyeo
attended at(×)   2~3명[개]
to give a talk about their lives. When I finished my talk, one of the
to부정사의 부사적 용법(목적)
haenyeo held my hand tightly. She said to me, "Thank you so much.
= me by the
I've never known in my whole life that I was such a special person."
경험 용법   such+a+형용사+명사
She was crying with happiness. Everyone in the audience was deeply moved. I can never forget that moment, so I'll continue to take pictures
= touched   = taking
of haenyeo. I want to tell more beautiful stories about them to many
tell은 to를 사용하여 3형식으로 바꿀 수 있다.
more people in the world.

volcanic 화산의, 화산 작용에 의한

suitable 적합한, 적절한

breadwinner 생계를 책임지는 사람, 가장

experienced 경험이 있는

marine 해양의, 바다의

once 한 번, 한때, 옛날

attend 참석하다

overseas 해외의

exhibition 전시회, 박람회

give a talk 강의하다, 연설하다

tightly 단단히, 꽉

audience 청중

📎 **확인문제**

● 다음 문장이 본문의 내용과 일치하면 T, 일치하지 <u>않으면</u> F를 쓰시오.

1 Many haenyeo have become the breadwinners for their families. ☐

2 Haenyeo can catch a lot of seafood at one time. ☐

3 Catching too much marine life at one time in one place can destroy the ocean. ☐

4 A couple of haenyeo attendeded an overseas exhibition and gave a talk about their lives. ☐

5 One of the haenyeo said that she had never known in her whole life that she was such a special person. ☐

● 우리말을 참고하여 빈칸에 알맞은 말을 쓰시오.

1 Haenyeo, _____ _____ of Korea

2 For the past several years, the _____ _____ Zin Kim _____ _____ the culture of Jeju haenyeo worldwide.

3 Haenyeo are Korean female divers who harvest seafood _____ _____ _____ _____.

4 Their culture _____ _____ _____ _____ _____ in 2016.

5 At her studio last week, Zin Kim _____ _____ about her experience of taking pictures of haenyeo.

6 Q. How did you _____ _____ _____ taking photos of haenyeo?

7 One day, I _____ _____ take pictures of a haenyeo.

8 I _____ _____ _____ _____ that she was enjoying her job.

9 Until then, I had only seen black-and-white photos of haenyeo who _____ _____ _____.

10 However, she _____ _____ even after she had been in the water for over five hours.

11 I realized then that I _____ _____ pictures of haenyeo.

12 Q. You take beautiful pictures of them, but _____ _____ _____ to take pictures of haenyeo?

13 At first, they didn't understand _____ _____ _____ to take their pictures.

14 They didn't think they looked pretty _____ _____ _____.

15 So, I said to them, "You're _____ _____.

16 I want to _____ your culture _____ the world."

17 They _____ _____ to me then.

18 Of course, I also promised them that I would _____ _____ look _____ in my pictures.

1 해녀, 한국의 여성 잠수부

2 지난 몇 년 동안, 수중 사진작가 Zin Kim은 제주 해녀 문화를 전 세계에 홍보해 왔다.

3 해녀는 어떤 호흡 장치도 사용하지 않고 해산물을 채취하는 한국의 여성 잠수부들이다.

4 그들의 문화는 2016년에 유네스코 무형문화유산에 등재되었다.

5 지난주 그녀의 작업실에서, Zin Kim과 해녀의 사진을 찍는 그녀의 경험에 대해 인터뷰를 했다.

6 Q. 어떻게 해녀의 사진을 찍는 것에 관심을 가지게 되었나요?

7 어느 날, 저는 우연히 한 해녀의 사진을 찍게 되었어요.

8 저는 그녀가 자신의 일을 즐겁게 하는 것을 보고 놀랐습니다.

9 그때까지, 저는 흑백 사진 속의 아주 지친 모습의 해녀만 봐 왔죠.

10 하지만, 그녀는 다섯 시간이 넘도록 물속에 있은 후에도 계속 웃었어요.

11 저는 그때 해녀의 사진을 찍어야겠다고 깨달았어요.

12 Q. 작가님은 아름다운 해녀 사진들을 찍으시는데, 그들의 사진을 찍는 것이 어렵진 않으신가요?

13 처음에, 그들은 제가 왜 자신들의 사진을 찍으려고 하는지 이해하지 못했어요.

14 그들은 잠수복을 입은 자신들의 모습이 예뻐 보인다고 생각하지 않았으니까요.

15 그래서, 제가 그들에게 말했죠, "여러분은 아주 특별해요.

16 저는 여러분의 문화를 세계에 알리고 싶어요."

17 그들은 그때 제게 마음을 열었어요.

18 물론, 저 또한 그들에게 제 사진 속에서 그들을 아름답게 보이도록 하겠다고 약속했지요.

19 Q. Could you tell us _____ _____ haenyeo?

20 What's _____ _____ about them?

21 I _____ _____ _____ three things.

22 First, haenyeo are a symbol of _____ _____.

23 Jejudo, which is a volcanic island, _____ _____ _____ _____ farming, so many haenyeo have become _____ _____ _____ their families.

24 Second, haenyeo _____ their own communities and help _____ _____.

25 For example, _____ haenyeo train _____ haenyeo.

26 Third, because they stay in the water _____ any breathing devices, haenyeo _____ _____ a lot of seafood.

27 This _____ _____ _____ the underwater environment.

28 Catching too much marine life _____ _____ _____ _____ _____ _____ can destroy the ocean.

29 Q. Lastly, please tell us what you're _____ _____ in the future.

30 I once _____ an overseas exhibition with a couple of haenyeo to _____ _____ _____ about their lives.

31 When I finished my talk, one of the haenyeo _____ _____ _____ tightly.

32 She said to me, "Thank you _____ _____.

33 I've never known in my whole life that I was _____ _____ _____ _____."

34 She was crying _____ _____.

35 Everyone in the audience _____ _____ _____.

36 I _____ _____ _____ that moment, so I'll continue to take pictures of haenyeo.

37 I want to tell _____ _____ _____ _____ _____ to many more people in the world.

19 Q. 해녀에 대해서 더 말씀해 주시겠어요?

20 그들은 무엇이 그렇게 특별한가요?

21 세 가지를 말씀 드릴게요.

22 첫 번째로, 해녀들은 강인한 여성의 상징이에요.

23 제주도는 화산섬이고, 이는 농사에 적합하지 않아서 많은 해녀들이 가족들의 생계비를 버는 가장이 되어 왔어요.

24 둘째로, 해녀들은 그들 자신의 공동체를 조직하고 서로 도와요.

25 예를 들어, 경험이 더 많은 해녀들이 경험이 적은 해녀들을 훈련시키지요.

26 세 번째로, 어떤 호흡 장치도 사용하지 않고 물속에 머물기 때문에, 해녀는 많은 해산물을 채취할 수가 없어요.

27 이것은 수중 환경에 좋은 것이지요.

28 한 번에 한 장소에서 너무 많은 해양생물을 채취하는 것은 바다를 파괴할 수 있으니까요.

29 Q. 마지막으로, 앞으로 계획하고 있는 것에 대해 말씀해 주세요.

30 예전에 두 명의 해녀들과 함께 그들의 삶에 대해 이야기하기 위해 해외에서 열리는 박람회에 참가한 적이 있어요.

31 제가 연설을 마쳤을 때, 해녀 중 한 분이 제 손을 꼭 잡았어요.

32 그분이 말했죠. "너무 고마워.

33 내 평생 내가 이렇게 특별한 사람이라는 걸 미처 알지 못했어."

34 그녀는 행복해서 울고 있었어요.

35 청중들 모두가 깊은 감동을 받았어요.

36 전 그 순간을 절대 잊을 수가 없기 때문에 해녀의 사진을 계속해서 찍을 거예요.

37 저는 그들에 대한 더 많은 아름다운 이야기들을 세계의 더 많은 사람들에게 알려 주고 싶어요.

● 우리말을 참고하여 본문을 영작하시오.

1 해녀, 한국의 여성 잠수부
➡ _____

2 지난 몇 년 동안, 수중 사진작가 Zin Kim은 제주 해녀 문화를 전 세계에 홍보해 왔다.
➡ _____
_____

3 해녀는 어떤 호흡 장치도 사용하지 않고 해산물을 채취하는 한국의 여성 잠수부들이다.
➡ _____

4 그들의 문화는 2016년에 유네스코 무형문화유산에 등재되었다.
➡ _____

5 지난주 그녀의 작업실에서, Zin Kim과 해녀의 사진을 찍는 그녀의 경험에 대해 인터뷰를 했다.
➡ _____

6 Q. 어떻게 해녀의 사진을 찍는 것에 관심을 가지게 되었나요?
➡ _____

7 어느 날, 저는 우연히 한 해녀의 사진을 찍게 되었어요.
➡ _____

8 저는 그녀가 자신의 일을 즐겁게 하는 것을 보고 놀랐습니다.
➡ _____

9 그때까지, 저는 흑백 사진 속의 아주 지친 모습의 해녀만 봐 왔죠.
➡ _____

10 하지만, 그녀는 다섯 시간이 넘도록 물속에 있은 후에도 계속 웃었어요.
➡ _____

11 저는 그때 해녀의 사진을 찍어야겠다고 깨달았어요.
➡ _____

12 Q. 작가님은 아름다운 해녀 사진들을 찍으시는데, 그들의 사진을 찍는 것이 어렵진 않으신가요?
➡ _____

13 처음에, 그들은 제가 왜 자신들의 사진을 찍으려고 하는지 이해하지 못했어요.
➡ _____

14 그들은 잠수복을 입은 자신들의 모습이 예뻐 보인다고 생각하지 않았으니까요.
➡ _____

15 그래서, 제가 그들에게 말했죠, "여러분들은 아주 특별해요.
➡ _____

16 저는 여러분의 문화를 세계에 알리고 싶어요."
➡ _____

17 그들은 그때 제게 마음을 열었어요.
➡ _____

18 물론, 저 또한 그들에게 제 사진 속에서 그들을 아름답게 보이도록 하겠다고 약속했지요.
➡ _____

19 Q. 해녀에 대해서 더 말씀해 주시겠어요?
➡ _____

20 그들은 무엇이 그렇게 특별한가요?
➡ _____

21 세 가지를 말씀 드릴게요.
➡ _____

22 첫 번째로, 해녀들은 강인한 여성의 상징이에요.
➡ _____

23 제주도는 화산섬이고, 이는 농사에 적합하지 않아서 많은 해녀들이 가족들의 생계비를 버는 가장이 되어 왔어요.
➡ _____
_____

24 둘째로, 해녀들은 그들 자신의 공동체를 조직하고 서로 도와요.
➡ _____

25 예를 들어, 경험이 더 많은 해녀들이 경험이 적은 해녀들을 훈련시키지요.
➡ _____

26 세 번째로, 어떤 호흡 장치도 사용하지 않고 물속에 머물기 때문에, 해녀는 많은 해산물을 채취할 수가 없어요.
➡ _____
_____

27 이것은 수중 환경에 좋은 것이지요.
➡ _____

28 한 번에 한 장소에서 너무 많은 해양생물을 채취하는 것은 바다를 파괴할 수 있으니까요.
➡ _____

29 Q. 마지막으로, 앞으로 계획하고 있는 것에 대해 말씀해 주세요.
➡ _____

30 예전에 두 명의 해녀들과 함께 그들의 삶에 대해 이야기하기 위해 해외에서 열리는 박람회에 참가한 적이 있어요.
➡ _____

31 제가 연설을 마쳤을 때, 해녀 중 한 분이 제 손을 꼭 잡았어요.
➡ _____

32 그분이 말했죠, "너무 고마워.
➡ _____

33 내 평생 내가 이렇게 특별한 사람이라는 걸 미처 알지 못했어."
➡ _____

34 그녀는 행복해서 울고 있었어요.
➡ _____

35 청중들 모두가 깊은 감동을 받았어요.
➡ _____

36 전 그 순간을 절대 잊을 수가 없기 때문에 해녀의 사진을 계속해서 찍을 거예요.
➡ _____

37 저는 그들에 대한 더 많은 아름다운 이야기들을 세계의 더 많은 사람들에게 알려 주고 싶어요.
➡ _____

[01~03] 다음 글을 읽고 물음에 답하시오.

For the past several years, the underwater photographer Zin Kim has promoted the culture of Jeju haenyeo worldwide. Haenyeo are Korean female divers ⓐ_____ harvest seafood without any breathing devices. Their culture ⓑmade UNESCO's Intangible Cultural Heritage list in 2016. At her studio last week, Zin Kim was interviewed about her experience of taking pictures of haenyeo.

01 위 글의 빈칸 ⓐ에 들어갈 알맞은 말을 <u>모두</u> 고르시오.

① which   ② who   ③ what
④ that   ⑤ whom

02 위 글의 밑줄 친 ⓑmade와 같은 의미로 쓰인 것을 고르시오.

① She <u>made</u> her own clothes.
② He always <u>made</u> me laugh.
③ She <u>made</u> him her assistant.
④ They <u>made</u> me repeat the whole story.
⑤ Jones <u>made</u> a professor in five years.

03 According to the passage, which is NOT true?

① Zin Kim is an underwater photographer.
② Zin Kim has promoted the culture of Jeju haenyeo worldwide for the past several years.
③ Haenyeo are Korean female divers.
④ Haenyeo harvest seafood with the help of breathing devices.
⑤ Haenyeo's culture has been UNESCO's Intangible Cultural Heritage since 2016.

[04~06] 다음 글을 읽고 물음에 답하시오.

Q. _____ⓐ_____

One day, I happened to take pictures of a haenyeo. I was surprised to find that she was enjoying her job. Until then, I had only seen black-and-white photos of haenyeo who looked very tired. However, she kept _____ⓑ_____ even after she ⓒhad been in the water for over five hours. I realized then that I should take pictures of haenyeo.

04 위 글의 빈칸 ⓐ에 들어갈 알맞은 질문을 고르시오.

① Could you tell us more about haenyeo?
② What's so special about haenyeo?
③ How did you become interested in taking photos of haenyeo?
④ What do you want to do in the future?
⑤ Is it difficult to take pictures of haenyeo?

서답형
05 위 글의 빈칸 ⓑ에 laugh를 알맞은 형태로 쓰시오.

➡ _____

06 아래 〈보기〉에서 위 글의 밑줄 친 ⓒhad been과 과거완료의 용법이 다른 것의 개수를 고르시오.

┌─ 보기 ┐
① I <u>had</u> just <u>finished</u> my homework when she came.
② He <u>had lived</u> there for ten years when his father died.
③ I found that I <u>had lost</u> my wallet on the subway.
④ The train <u>had</u> already <u>left</u> when he got to the station.
⑤ They <u>had</u> never <u>met</u> a student like him before.
└─────────────────┘

① 1개   ② 2개   ③ 3개   ④ 4개   ⑤ 5개

[07~09] 다음 글을 읽고 물음에 답하시오.

> Q. You take beautiful pictures of them, but isn't it difficult to take pictures of haenyeo?
>
> (①) At first, ⓐ그들은 제가 왜 자신들의 사진을 찍으려고 하는지 이해하지 못했어요. (②) They didn't think they looked pretty in their wetsuits. (③) So, I said to them, "You're very special. (④) I want to show your culture to the world." (⑤) Of course, I also promised them that I would make them look beautiful in my pictures.

07 위 글의 흐름으로 보아, 주어진 문장이 들어가기에 가장 적절한 곳은?

> They opened up to me then.

①　　　②　　　③　　　④　　　⑤

08 위 글의 제목으로 알맞은 것을 고르시오.

① Why Do You Want to Take Pictures of Haenyeo?

② Wow! Haenyeo Let Me Show Their Culture through Pictures!

③ Why Is It Important to Show Haenyeo's Culture?

④ Are You Interested in Taking Pictures of Haenyeo?

⑤ How Can You Make Haenyeo Look Beautiful in Your Pictures?

09 위 글의 밑줄 친 ⓐ의 우리말에 맞게 주어진 어휘를 이용하여 10 단어로 영작하시오.

> why, their pictures

➡ _____

_____

[10~13] 다음 글을 읽고 물음에 답하시오.

> Q. Lastly, please tell us what you're planning to do in the future.
>
> I once (A)[attended / attended to] an overseas exhibition with a couple of haenyeo to give a talk about their lives. When I finished my talk, one of the haenyeo held my hand tightly. She said to me, "Thank you so much. ⓐI've never known in my whole life that I was (B)[so / such] a special person." She was crying with happiness. Everyone in the audience was deeply moved. I can never forget that moment, (C)[as / so] I'll continue to take pictures of haenyeo. I want to tell more beautiful stories about them to many more people in the world. <I: Zin Kim>

서답형

10 위 글의 괄호 (A)~(C)에서 문맥이나 어법상 알맞은 낱말을 골라 쓰시오.

➡ (A) _____ (B) _____ (C) _____

11 위 글의 분위기로 가장 알맞은 것을 고르시오.

① confusing　　② interesting

③ depressing　　④ boring

⑤ touching

12 Which question CANNOT be answered after reading the passage?

① With whom did Zin Kim attend an overseas exhibition?

② Why did Zin Kim attend an overseas exhibition?

③ When Zin Kim finished her talk, what did one of the haenyeo tell her?

④ How long has Zin Kim taken pictures of haenyeo?

⑤ What does Zin Kim want to tell to many more people in the world?

13 위 글의 밑줄 친 ⓐ의 현재완료와 용법이 같은 것을 모두 고르시오.

① I have just bought my watch.

② I have been to England twice.

③ Have you ever seen a panda?

④ Have you finished it yet?

⑤ Alice has lived in New York since January.

[14~17] 다음 글을 읽고 물음에 답하시오.

Q. Could you tell us more about haenyeo? What's so special about them?

  I can tell you three things. First, haenyeo are a symbol of strong women. (A)Jejudo, that is a volcanic island, is not suitable for farming, so many haenyeo have become the _____ⓐ_____ for their families. Second, haenyeo form their own communities and help each other. For example, more-experienced haenyeo train less-experienced haenyeo. Third, because they stay in the water without any breathing devices, haenyeo can't catch a lot of seafood. (B)This is good for the underwater environment. Catching too much marine life at one time in one place can destroy the ocean.

14 주어진 영영풀이를 참고하여 빈칸 ⓐ에 철자 b로 시작하는 단어를 쓰시오.

> the people who earn the money that the family need for essential things

➡ _____

15 위 글의 밑줄 친 (A)에서 어법상 틀린 부분을 찾아 고치시오.

_____ ➡ _____

16 위 글의 밑줄 친 (B)This가 가리키는 것을 본문에서 찾아 쓰시오.

➡ _____

17 위 글의 주제로 알맞은 것을 고르시오.

① haenyeo as the subject of pictures

② what is special about haenyeo

③ haenyeo as a symbol of strong women

④ the hard lives of the breadwinners

⑤ the way haenyeo form their own communities

[18~21] 다음 글을 읽고 물음에 답하시오.

Q. ①You take beautiful pictures of them, but isn't it difficult to take pictures of haenyeo?

  At first, ②they didn't understand why I wanted to take ③their pictures. They didn't think they looked pretty _____ⓐ_____ their wetsuits. So, I said to ④them, "⑤You're very special. I want to show your culture _____ⓑ_____ the world." They opened up to me then. Of course, ⓒI also promised them that I would make them looking beautiful in my pictures.

<I: Zin Kim>

18 위 글의 빈칸 ⓐ와 ⓑ에 들어갈 전치사가 바르게 짝지어진
것은?

ⓐ	ⓑ		ⓐ	ⓑ
① for	– from		② in	– by
③ in	– to		④ on	– to
⑤ for	– by			

19 밑줄 친 ①~⑤ 중에서 가리키는 대상이 나머지 넷과 다른
것은?

①   ②   ③   ④   ⑤

서답형
20 위 글의 밑줄 친 ⓒ에서 어법상 틀린 부분을 찾아 고치시오.

➡ _____

중요
21 자신들의 사진을 찍는 것에 대한 해녀들의 심경 변화로 가
장 알맞은 것을 고르시오.

① hopeful → nervous
② delighted → upset
③ bored → agreeing
④ puzzled → consenting
⑤ confused → disappointed

[22~25] 다음 글을 읽고 물음에 답하시오.

**Q. Could you tell us more about haenyeo?
What's so special about them?**

  I can tell you three things. First, haenyeo
are a symbol of strong women. (A)Jejudo,
which is a volcanic island, is suitable for
farming, so many haenyeo have become
the breadwinners for their families. Second,
haenyeo form their own communities and

help each other.   ⓐ , more-experienced
haenyeo train less-experienced haenyeo.
Third, because they stay in the water without
any (B)breathing devices, haenyeo can't
catch a lot of seafood. This is good for the
underwater environment. (C)Catching too
much marine life at one time in one place can
destroy the ocean.

22 위 글의 빈칸 ⓐ에 들어갈 알맞은 말을 고르시오.

① Therefore   ② However
③ For example   ④ Moreover
⑤ As a result

서답형
23 위 글의 밑줄 친 (A)에서 흐름상 어색한 부분을 찾아 고치시오.

➡ _____

중요
24 위 글의 밑줄 친 (B)breathing과 문법적 쓰임이 다른 것을
모두 고르시오.

① He is a walking dictionary.
② Where is my sleeping bag?
③ She is in the waiting room.
④ If you want to smoke, you need to go to
   a smoking room in the lobby.
⑤ Look at the dancing girl over there.

서답형
25 위 글의 밑줄 친 (C)를 다음과 같이 바꿔 쓸 때 빈칸에 들어
갈 알맞은 말을 두 단어로 쓰시오.

➡ It can destroy the ocean _____
   too much marine life at one time in one
   place.

[01~03] 다음 글을 읽고 물음에 답하시오.

> **Q. How did you become interested in taking photos of haenyeo?**
>
> ⓐOne day, I happened to take pictures of a haenyeo. I was surprised to find that she was enjoying her job. ⓑUntil then, I have only seen black-and-white photos of haenyeo who looked very tired. However, she kept laughing even after she had been in the water for over five hours. I realized then that I should take pictures of haenyeo. <I: Zin Kim>

01 위 글의 밑줄 친 ⓐ를 다음과 같이 바꿔 쓸 때 빈칸에 들어갈 알맞은 말을 두 단어로 쓰시오.

➡ One day, I took pictures of a haenyeo _____ (또는 _____).

02 위 글의 밑줄 친 ⓑ에서 어법상 **틀린** 부분을 찾아 고치시오.

_____ ➡ _____

03 다음 빈칸 (A)와 (B)에 알맞은 단어를 넣어 Zin Kim이 해녀의 사진을 찍는 것에 관심을 가지게 된 계기를 완성하시오.

> When Zin Kim happened to take pictures of a haenyeo, she was (A)_____ her job and kept (B)_____ even after she had been in the water for over five hours. Zin Kim was surprised at that and decided to take pictures of haenyeo.

[04~06] 다음 글을 읽고 물음에 답하시오.

> (A)[During / For] the past several years, the underwater photographer Zin Kim has promoted the culture of Jeju haenyeo worldwide. Haenyeo are Korean female divers who harvest seafood without (B)[any / no] breathing devices. ⓐTheir culture made UNESCO's (C)[Tangible / Intangible] Cultural Heritage list in ⓑ2016. At her studio last week, Zin Kim was interviewed about her experience of taking pictures of haenyeo.

04 위 글의 괄호 (A)~(C)에서 문맥이나 어법상 알맞은 낱말을 골라 쓰시오.

➡ (A) _____ (B) _____ (C) _____

05 위 글의 밑줄 친 ⓐTheir가 가리키는 것을 본문에서 찾아 쓰시오.

➡ _____

06 위 글의 밑줄 친 ⓑ2016을 영어로 읽는 법을 쓰시오.

➡ _____

[07~09] 다음 글을 읽고 물음에 답하시오.

> **Q. Could you tell us more about haenyeo? What's so special about them?**
>
> I can tell you three things. First, haenyeo are a symbol of strong women. Jejudo, which is a volcanic island, is not suitable for farming, so many haenyeo have become the breadwinners for their families. Second, haenyeo form their own communities and

help each other. For example, more-experienced haenyeo train less-experienced haenyeo. Third, because they stay in the water without any breathing devices, haenyeo can't catch a lot of seafood. This is good for the underwater environment. Catching too much ____ⓐ____ life at one time in one place can destroy the ocean.

07 주어진 영영풀이를 참고하여 빈칸 ⓐ에 철자 m으로 시작하는 단어를 쓰시오.

> relating to the sea or to the animals and plants that live in the sea

➡ _____

08 Why is the way haenyeo catch seafood good for the underwater environment? Fill in the blanks (A) and (B) with suitable words.

> Because they stay in the water without any (A)_____ _____, haenyeo (B)_____ _____ a lot of seafood.

09 해녀에 대한 특별한 점 3가지를 우리말로 쓰시오.

➡ (1) _____
   (2) _____
   (3) _____
   _____

[10~13] 다음 글을 읽고 물음에 답하시오.

Q. Lastly, please tell us ____ⓐ____ .
  I once attended an overseas exhibition with a couple of haenyeo to give a talk about their lives. When I finished my talk, ⓑone of the haenyeo held my hand tightly. She

said to me, "Thank you so much. I've never known in my whole life that I was such a special person." She was crying with happiness. Everyone in the audience was deeply ⓒmoved. I can never forget that moment, so I'll continue to take pictures of haenyeo. I want to tell more beautiful stories about them to many more people in the world.   <I: Zin Kim>

10 다음 주어진 의문문을 위 글의 빈칸 ⓐ에 알맞은 순서로 배열하여 쓰시오.

> What are you planning to do in the future?

➡ _____

11 위 글의 밑줄 친 ⓑ를 다음과 같이 바꿔 쓸 때 빈칸에 들어갈 알맞은 단어를 쓰시오.

➡ one of the haenyeo held _____ by the hand tightly

12 위 글의 밑줄 친 ⓒmoved와 바꿔 쓸 수 있는 말을 쓰시오.

➡ _____

13 위 글의 내용과 일치하도록 다음 빈칸 (A)와 (B)에 알맞은 단어를 쓰시오.

> Zin Kim will continue to (A)_____ _____ of haenyeo as she can never forget the moment when one of the haenyeo thanked her. She wants to tell (B)_____ _____ _____ about haenyeo to many more people in the world.

Communicate – B Talk and Play

A: I wonder what these are.
간접의문문 어순으로 '의문사+주어+동사'의 순서로 이어진다.
B: They're called songpyeon.

A: Could you explain more about them?
= songpyeon
B: They're traditional Korean rice cakes.

구문해설 • traditional: 전통적인

A: 나는 이것들이 무엇인지 궁금해.

B: 그것들은 송편이라고 불려.

A: 이것에 대해 좀 더 설명해 줄래?

B: 그것들은 전통적인 한국 떡이야.

After You Read A

A Photographer Who Loves Haenyeo

Zin Kim, an underwater photographer, has promoted the culture of Jeju
현재완료(계속적 용법)
haenyeo worldwide. She decided to take pictures of them when she met a
= take their pictures
haenyeo who was enjoying her job. It was not easy taking their pictures at
관계대명사(주격)   가주어   진주어(동명사)
first. However, when she told them that she wanted to show their culture to the
접속사(명사절)
world, the haenyeo finally opened their minds. At an overseas exhibition, she
부사(동사 수식)   → its(×) 주의 haenyeo는 복수(a haenyeo는 단수)
gave a talk about the lives of haenyeo. After her speech, one of the haenyeo
one of the 복수명사+단수동사
was crying with happiness. Zin Kim said that she would continue to take
시제 일치(will과거)
pictures of haenyeo.

구문해설 • underwater: 수중의, 물속의   • promote: 홍보하다, 촉진하다   • overseas: 해외의
• exhibition: 전시회

해녀를 사랑하는 사진작가

수중 사진작가 김진은 전 세계에 제주의 해녀 문화를 홍보해 왔다. 그녀는 자신의 일을 즐기고 있었던 한 해녀를 만났을 때, 그들의 사진을 찍기로 결심했다. 처음에는 그들의 사진을 찍는 것이 쉽지 않았다. 그러나, 그녀가 세상 사람들에게 그들의 문화를 보여주고 싶다고 그들에게 말했을 때, 마침내 해녀들은 마음을 열었다. 한 해외 전시회에서 그녀는 해녀들의 삶에 대해 강연했다. 그녀의 연설이 끝나자 해녀들 중 한 사람은 기쁨의 눈물을 흘렸다. 김진은 앞으로도 해녀들의 사진 찍는 일을 계속할 것이라고 말했다.

Write

Kim Minho is a barista. He makes coffee drinks for a living. He became a
for a living: 밥벌이로, 생계 수단으로
barista after he had found out about his passion for coffee. His favorite part of
바리스타가 되기 전에 발견한 것이므로, 과거완료시제를 사용
his job is decorating coffee with hot milk and watching his customers enjoying
동명사 보어   동명사 보어   지각동사 whatching의
목적격보어로 쓰인 현재분사
it. He is planning to open his own coffee shop.
opening(×)

구문해설 • barista: 바리스타, 커피 내리는 사람   • find out: 발견하다, 찾다   • passion: 열정, 흥미
• decorate: 장식하다, 꾸미다   • customer: 손님

김민호는 바리스타이다. 그의 직업은 커피 음료를 만드는 것이다. 그는 커피에 대한 그의 열정을 발견한 후에 바리스타가 되었다. 그의 직업에서 그가 가장 좋아하는 부분은 뜨거운 우유로 커피를 장식하고 그의 손님들이 그것을 즐기는 것을 보는 것이다. 그는 자신의 커피점을 열 계획이다.

01 다음 짝지어진 단어의 관계가 같도록 빈칸에 알맞은 말을 쓰시오.

> dark : darkness = happy : _____

02 다음 영영풀이가 가리키는 것을 고르시오.

> the member of a family who earns the money to support the others

① baker   ② breadwinner
③ diver   ④ audience
⑤ presenter

03 다음 중 밑줄 친 부분의 뜻풀이가 바르지 않은 것은?

① Could you explain more about it? (설명하다)
② There are a lot of female teachers in Korea. (여성의)
③ I'm planning an overseas trip. (해외의)
④ I have been on a trip for the past few days. (지나간)
⑤ She is walking along the path. (신뢰)

04 다음 우리말에 맞게 빈칸에 알맞은 말을 쓰시오.

(1) 너는 어디로 휴가를 가고 싶니?
➡ Where do you want to _____?
(2) 제가 두 서너 개의 질문을 하겠습니다.
➡ I'm going to ask _____ questions.
(3) 이 음악은 군인들을 격려하기 위해 만들어졌다.
➡ This music was made to _____ soldiers.

(4) 질문이 있다면 제게 전화주세요.
➡ _____ me _____ if you have any questions.

05 다음 문장의 빈칸에 들어갈 말을 〈보기〉에서 골라 쓰시오.

> ┤ 보기 ├
> heritage / greenhouse / device / breathe / overwork

(1) Her _____ and stress caused her to be ill.
(2) In winter, farmers grow vegetables in their _____.
(3) Cotton clothing allows your skin to _____.
(4) They tried to invent a _____ to measure brain activity during sleep.
(5) We should protect our national _____.

[06~07] 다음 대화를 읽고 물음에 답하시오.

> Jack: Excuse me, I'd like to use a copy machine.
> Sue: O.K. You can use this machine.
> Jack: Could you explain how to make double-sided copies?
> Sue: Sure. Press the button for double-sided copies, and then press the start button.
> Jack: Thank you.

06 What does Jack want to make?

➡ _____

07 What will Jack do before pressing the start button?

➡ _____

[08~09] 다음 대화를 읽고 물음에 답하시오.

Tom: Are you going somewhere this summer? (A)

Jane: I'm going to Jejudo to walk along the Jeju Olle Trail. (B)

Tom: The Jeju Olle Trail? (C)

Jane: It's a long hiking path around Jejudo. (D)

Tom: Oh, I see. I hope you enjoy your trip! (E)

08 위 대화의 (A)~(E) 중 주어진 문장이 들어가기에 가장 적절한 곳은?

Could you explain what that is?

① (A)　② (B)　③ (C)　④ (D)　⑤ (E)

09 위 대화를 읽고 대답할 수 없는 것은?

① Where is Jane going to visit this summer?

② What is the Jeju Olle Trail?

③ Why does Jane want to visit Jejudo?

④ What does Tom hope for Jane?

⑤ What does Tom want to do in Jejudo?

[10~12] 다음 대화를 읽고 물음에 답하시오.

Jaden: Do you hear that? I wonder where that music is coming from.

Yuri: I think it's coming from over there. Do you want to go and ⓐcheck out it?

Jaden: Yes, I love ⓑthat strong beat. Is it traditional Korean music?

Yuri: Yes, it's ⓒcalled nongak. It's a kind of community band music.

Jaden: Nongak? Could you explain a little bit more about it?

Yuri: It's traditionally used to cheer up farmers and ⓓwish for a good harvest.

Jaden: I see. Look! Some people are dancing to the rhythm.

Yuri: Yes, that's a big part of nongak. Dancing together ⓔcompletes the music.

Jaden: Let's join them.

Yuri: Sure. Why not?

10 위 대화의 밑줄 친 ⓐ~ⓔ 중 어법상 어색한 것을 찾아 바르게 고치시오.

➡ _____

11 위 대화에서 다음 주어진 영영풀이가 가리키는 말을 찾아 쓰시오.

one of a series of regular movements or hitting actions

➡ _____

12 위 대화의 내용과 일치하지 않는 것은?

① Jaden은 들려오는 음악의 강한 비트가 마음에 든다.

② Jaden과 유리는 농악을 듣고 있다.

③ 농악은 공동체 악단 음악의 한 종류이다.

④ 농악은 전통적으로 농부들의 힘을 북돋아 주고 풍년을 기원하기 위해 사용되었다.

⑤ 리듬은 농악의 큰 부분으로서 음악을 완성한다.

13 다음 대화를 참고하여 주어진 빈칸에 적절한 단어를 쓰시오.

Philip: Sam, have you ever eaten cheese fondue made with Swiss style?

Sam: Yes, two times.

Philip: When did you first eat it?

Sam: Before I graduated from the college.

➡ Sam _____ _____ cheese fondue before he graduated from the college.

[14~15] 다음 중 어법상 어색한 문장을 모두 고르시오.

14 ① The people can't even guess where are the monsters from.

② The participants don't understand why the speaker is interested in.

③ Mom doesn't know whether Jamie and Esther are coming.

④ When do you think the researcher will complete the project?

⑤ There's no one knowing when the car accident happened.

15 ① I wonder why she didn't choose me as her colleague.

② Do you know who made these yummy cookies and drinks?

③ Would you tell me when did he leave the office?

④ Do you think when Tracy will come back for her original position?

⑤ Do you have any idea how long it will take to get to the wedding?

16 다음 그림을 보고 괄호 안의 단어를 배열하여 빈칸을 알맞게 채우시오.

(1)

➡ Junho is _____

_____. (which, go, thinking, should, he, to, about, university)

(2)

➡ Ye-eun is _____

_____. (when, stop, will, the, wondering, rain)

17 다음 괄호 안에서 어법상 알맞은 것을 고르시오.

(1) Sven dropped the carrot that Olaf (had pulled / has pulled) out of the field in the snow.

(2) Last week, we learned that Kennedy (had been killed / was killed) by gunshot in 1963.

(3) The rock band (has already gone / had already gone) to New York before their fans got informed of the news.

(4) Some film lovers around the world said that they (have been / had been) learning Korean to watch *Parasite* without subtitles.

(5) An invitation was sent to the girl after the prince (had seen / has seen) her dancing on the street.

(6) I wonder when the angels (had appeared / appeared / has appeared) to the nuns.

18 다음 쇼핑몰의 안내 페이지와 〈보기〉의 질문을 참고하여 알맞은 내용을 골라 빈칸에 간접의문문을 써 넣으시오.

> Fresh Daddy Grocery
> • Open Hours: 10a.m. ~ 8p.m.
> • Address: 123 Ilsan, Goyang
> • Nearby Station: Daewha (line 3)
> • Contact: mngr@freshdaddy.co.kr

> ┤ 보기 ├
> • Is there any subway station near the store?
> • What time does the store open?
> • How can we contact the store manager?
> • Where is the store located?

(1) Do you know _____?
→ The store opens at 10 a.m.

(2) Can you tell me _____
_____?
→ By e-mail. mngr@freshdaddy.co.kr.

(3) Tell me _____.
→ Fresh Daddy Grocery is at 123 Ilsan, Goyang.

(4) Do you know _____
_____?
→ Yes, the nearest subway station from the store is Daewha on line 3.

19 다음 각 문장의 밑줄 친 부분이 과거완료시제의 용법 중 어떤 것에 해당하는지 〈보기〉에서 찾아 기호를 쓰시오.

> ┤ 보기 ├
> ⓐ 완료   ⓑ 경험   ⓒ 결과   ⓓ 계속

(1) I had never seen the desert until I went to Sahara last year. (_____)

(2) As soon as she came back to her desk, she felt something had gone from her drawer. (_____)

(3) Before the boss came up, Jessica had finished her report. (_____)

(4) The lady couldn't notice the old man since she had lost her sight. (_____)

(5) By the time the teacher found something strange, Michael had already completed his reading. (_____)

(6) Jacob had lived in Daejeon for 4 years by last year. (_____)

(7) Bong had won several awards before winning the Academy Award. (_____)

(8) The girl had stayed in the dormitory until her parents came to visit her. (_____)

20 다음 그림과 스케줄 표를 보고 과거완료시제를 활용하여, 빈칸에 알맞은 말을 써 넣으시오.

> Today's Schedule
> • Vanessa – clean the windows and wash the dishes
> • Sally – give the dog some food and water the plant

(1) When Mom came home, she found
_____
_____.

(2) When Mom came home, she found
_____
_____.

21 다음 우리말에 맞도록 괄호 안에 주어진 어휘를 알맞게 배열하시오.

(1) 수진이는 왜 자신이 다른 나라에 가서 요리법을 배워야 하는지 이해할 수 없었다. (had to, in, how, why, to cook, she, learn, another country)

➡ Sujin couldn't understand _____

_____.

(2) 비행기에 남은 좌석이 있는지 확인해 주시겠어요? (seats, there, the plane, left, any, on, are, if)

➡ Could you check _____

_____?

Reading

[22~24] 다음 글을 읽고 물음에 답하시오.

> **Q. Could you tell us more about haenyeo? What's so special about them?**
>
> I can tell you three things. First, haenyeo are a symbol of strong women. Jejudo, which is a volcanic island, is not suitable ⓐ____ farming, so many haenyeo have become the breadwinners ⓑ____ their families. Second, haenyeo form their own communities and help each other. For example, more-experienced haenyeo train less-experienced haenyeo. Third, because they stay in the water without any breathing devices, haenyeo can't catch a lot of seafood. This is good for the underwater environment. ⓒCatching too much marine life at one time in one place can destroy the ocean.

22 위 글의 빈칸 ⓐ와 ⓑ에 공통으로 들어갈 알맞은 전치사를 고르시오.

① to   ② on   ③ for
④ in   ⑤ at

23 위 글의 밑줄 친 ⓒCatching과 문법적 쓰임이 같은 것을 모두 고르시오.

① Our cat is good at catching mice.
② Do you know the man catching fish?
③ I think I'm catching a cold.
④ My hobby is catching the fish.
⑤ I saw a woman catching a butterfly.

24 According to the passage, which is NOT true?

① Haenyeo are a symbol of strong women.
② Jejudo is a volcanic island.
③ Haenyeo form their own communities.
④ Haenyeo stay in the water with no breathing devices.
⑤ Haenyeo can catch a lot of seafood at one time.

[25~26] 다음 글을 읽고 물음에 답하시오.

> **Q. Lastly, please tell us what you're planning to do in the future.**
>
> I once attended an overseas exhibition with a couple of haenyeo to give a talk about their lives. When I finished my talk, one of the haenyeo held my hand tightly. She said to me, "Thank you so much. I've never known in my whole life that I was such a special person." She was crying with happiness. Everyone in the audience was deeply ⓐmoved. I can never forget that moment, so I'll continue to take pictures of haenyeo. I want to tell more beautiful stories about them to many more people in the world.   <I: Zin Kim>.

25 위 글의 밑줄 친 ⓐmoved와 같은 의미로 쓰인 것을 고르시오.

① He moved towards the window.

② The sight moved me to tears.

③ We moved to the country last week.

④ The ship moved before the wind.

⑤ I moved that a vote should be taken on this.

26 위 글의 주제로 알맞은 것을 고르시오.

① an overseas exhibition Zin Kim attended

② giving a talk about haenyeo's lives

③ Zin Kim's plan in the future

④ the happiness of one of the haenyeo

⑤ beautiful stories about haenyeo

[27~29] 다음 글을 읽고 물음에 답하시오.

A Photographer Who Loves Haenyeo

Zin Kim, an underwater photographer, has promoted the culture of Jeju haenyeo worldwide. She decided to take pictures of them when she met a haenyeo who was enjoying her job.

It was not easy taking their pictures at first. _____ⓐ_____, when she told them that she wanted to show their culture to the world, the haenyeo finally opened their minds.

At an overseas exhibition, she gave a talk about the lives of haenyeo. After her speech, one of the haenyeo was crying with happiness. Zin Kim said that she would continue to take pictures of haenyeo.

27 위 글의 빈칸 ⓐ에 들어갈 알맞은 말을 고르시오.

① That is   ② Moreover

③ Thus   ④ For example

⑤ However

28 위 글의 종류로 알맞은 것을 고르시오.

① review   ② book report

③ diary   ④ article

⑤ autobiography

29 Which question CANNOT be answered after reading the passage?

① What does Zin Kim do?

② How did Zin Kim take pictures of haenyeo?

③ When did Zin Kim decide to take pictures of haenyeo?

④ Was it easy to take pictures of haenyeo at first?

⑤ What did Zin Kim want to show to the world?

01 다음 문장의 빈칸에 공통으로 들어갈 말을 고르시오.

> • The manager will _____ a presentation on the new items.
> • Can you _____ me your hand?
> • I usually _____ a call to my grandmother every week.

① give　　② take　　③ keep
④ like　　⑤ check

02 다음 대화가 자연스럽게 이어지도록 순서대로 배열하시오.

> (A) Really? Then, why don't we go somewhere, too?
> (B) O.K.
> (C) Lots of people are going on vacation this weekend.
> (D) Look over there. I wonder why there are so many cars on the road.

➡ _____

[03~04] 다음 대화를 읽고 물음에 답하시오.

Jaden: Do you hear that? I wonder where that music is coming from.

Yuri: (A) I think it's coming from over there. Do you want to go and check it out?

Jaden: Yes, I love that strong beat. Is it traditional Korean music?

Yuri: (B) It's a kind of community band music.

Jaden: Nongak? Could you explain a little bit more about it?

Yuri: (C) It's traditionally used to cheer up farmers and wish for a good harvest.

Jaden: (D)I see. Look! Some people are dancing to the rhythm.

Yuri: Yes, that's a big part of nongak. Dancing together completes the music.

Jaden: (E) Let's join them.

Yuri: Sure. Why not?

03 위 대화의 (A)~(E) 중 주어진 문장이 들어가기에 적절한 곳은?

> Yes, it's called nongak.

① (A)　② (B)　③ (C)　④ (D)　⑤ (E)

04 위 대화를 읽고 대답할 수 <u>없는</u> 것은?

① Where is the strong beat coming from?
② What is nongak?
③ What are some people doing to the rhythm?
④ What is a big part of nongak?
⑤ What kind of dancing can complete the music?

[05~06] 다음 대화를 읽고 물음에 답하시오.

W: Excuse me, I'd like to borrow an audio guide.

M: Here you are.

W: Could you explain how to use it?

M: Sure. Press this button, and it'll tell you what to do.

05 What does the woman want to do?

➡ _____

06 What should the woman do to use the audio guide?

➡ _____

[07~08] 다음 대화를 읽고 물음에 답하시오.

Emma: Look over there. (A)도로에 왜 저렇게 차가 많은지 궁금하네요.

Mike: Lots of people are going on vacation this weekend.

Emma: Really? Then, (B)why don't we go somewhere, too? (how)

Mike: O.K.

출제율 95%

07 위 대화의 밑줄 친 (A)의 우리말을 〈보기〉에 주어진 단어들을 <u>모두</u> 배열하여 영작하시오.

┌─ 보기 ┤
there / wonder / on / I / the / cars / so / are / road / why /many
└─

➡ _____

출제율 90%

08 위 대화의 밑줄 친 (B)와 의도가 같도록 주어진 단어를 사용하여 다시 쓰시오.

➡ _____

출제율 95%

09 다음 대화가 자연스럽게 이어지도록 순서대로 배열하시오.

(A) How do you know that?
(B) That's Gwangandaegyo in Busan.
(C) I went there with my family last summer.
(D) Wow, look at the bridge in this ad. I wonder where the photo was taken.

➡ _____

[10~11] 다음 대화를 읽고 물음에 답하시오.

Jack: Excuse me, I'd like to use a copy machine.

Sue: O.K. You can use this machine.

Jack: 어떻게 양면 복사를 하는지 설명해 주실 수 있나요?

Sue: Sure. Press the button for double-sided copies, and then press the start button.

Jack: Thank you.

출제율 95%

10 위 대화의 밑줄 친 우리말을 〈보기〉에 주어진 단어를 알맞게 배열하여 영작하시오.

┌─ 보기 ┤
how / you / copies / explain / could / make / double-sided / to
└─

➡ _____

_____

출제율 100%

11 위 대화의 내용과 일치하지 <u>않는</u> 것은?

① Jack wants to use a copy machine.
② Jack wants to make double-sided copies.
③ Sue knows how to make double-sided copies.
④ Jack should press the two buttons to make double-sided copies.
⑤ Jack should press the start button at first.

출제율 95%

12 다음 우리말을 바르게 영작한 것은?

당신은 Paul이 무슨 음악을 듣고 있다고 생각합니까?

① What music do you suppose Paul is listening to?
② What do you suppose music is Paul listening to?
③ Do you suppose what music is Paul listening to?
④ Is what music you suppose Paul listening to?
⑤ What music do you suppose is Paul listening to?

13 〈보기〉와 같이 과거완료시제를 이용하여, 두 문장을 괄호 안에 주어진 접속사로 시작하는 한 문장으로 만드시오.

┌ 보기 ┐
All the Korean film fans shouted for joy. Bong won the Academy Awards. (because)
→ Because Bong had won the Academy Awards, all the Korean film fans shouted for joy.

(1) Susan promised her teacher not to throw away used batteries. She learned the importance of recycling. (after)

➡ _____
_____
_____

(2) Sunwoo lay in his room all day long. He sprained his ankle during the basketball game. (before)

➡ _____
_____
_____

14 다음 빈칸에 들어가기에 <u>어색한</u> 문장을 <u>모두</u> 골라 번호를 쓰고 알맞게 고쳐 다시 쓰시오.

┌─────────────────────────┐
Do you know _____ ?
└─────────────────────────┘

ⓐ when does the shopping mall close
ⓑ where the nearest subway station is
ⓒ what kind of movie was she watching
ⓓ what does she usually do on Sundays
ⓔ how many toys there are in the room
ⓕ what time does the show begin

➡ _____
_____
_____

15 다음 중 어법상 올바른 문장을 <u>모두</u> 고르면? (정답 2개)

① His family happened to know that Brian has worked hard only to be taken to hospital the day before.
② The first half of the match already started when we had arrived at the stadium.
③ Most Asians felt proud that Director Bong has won the grand prize at the Cannes Film Festival for the film.
④ Marty returned the umbrella which she had borrowed from the restaurant.
⑤ The flower looked much fresher than before because it had rained yesterday.

16 다음 그림을 보고, 내용에 맞게 〈보기〉에서 알맞은 단어를 각각 선택하여 어법에 맞게 빈칸에 채워 넣으시오.

┌ 보기 ┐
• already / much / often / how → 1회씩 사용
• gain / eat / weigh → 1회씩 사용, 어형변화 가능
• had / he → 2회씩 사용

┌─────────────────────────┐
The bulldog wanted to know _____ _____ _____ _____. He was surprised to find that _____ _____ _____ weight before he stood on the scale. He regretted that he _____ some snacks before going to bed.
└─────────────────────────┘

17 다음 우리말과 그 영작이 바르게 짝지어지지 <u>않은</u> 것은?

① 네가 몇 시에 올 것인지 궁금하다.
→ I wonder what time you will come.

② 누가 그 강아지를 내게 줬는지 말해줘.
→ Tell me who gave me the puppy.

③ 그녀가 무슨 드레스를 입었는지 기억이 안 난다.
→ I can't remember what dress she put on.

④ 그녀가 몇 살이라고 짐작하니?
→ Do you guess how old she is?

⑤ 수민이가 왜 날 싫어하는지 몰라.
→ I don't know why Sumin hates me.

19 위 글의 주제로 알맞은 것을 고르시오.

① how to take pictures of haenyeo
② the hard lives of haenyeo
③ the reason Zin Kim became interested in taking photos of haenyeo
④ the difficulty of taking pictures of haenyeo
⑤ the most beautiful picture that has ever been taken

20 Until she happened to take pictures of a haenyeo, what kind of photos of haenyeo had Zin Kim only seen? Answer in English in a full sentence.

➡ _____

_____

[18~20] 다음 글을 읽고 물음에 답하시오.

Q. How did you become interested in taking photos of haenyeo?

One day, I happened to take pictures of a haenyeo. I was surprised to find that she was enjoying her job. Until then, I had only seen black-and-white photos of haenyeo who looked very tired. ___ⓐ___, she kept laughing even after she had been in the water for over five hours. I realized then that I should take pictures of haenyeo. <I: Zin Kim>

18 위 글의 빈칸 ⓐ에 들어갈 알맞은 말을 고르시오.

① In addition   ② For example
③ That is   ④ However
⑤ Therefore

[21~22] 다음 글을 읽고 물음에 답하시오.

Q. You take beautiful pictures of them, but isn't ⓐit difficult to take pictures of haenyeo?

At first, they didn't understand why I wanted to take their pictures. They didn't think they looked pretty in their wetsuits. So, I said to them, "You're very special. I want to show your culture to the world." They opened up to me then. Of course, I also promised them that I would make them look beautiful in my pictures. <I: Zin Kim>

21 위 글의 밑줄 친 ⓐit과 문법적 쓰임이 같은 것을 고르시오.

① I make it a rule to eat breakfast.
② It is 2 miles from here to the airport.
③ It is I that am to blame.
④ Did you see it?
⑤ It is important for you to have a dream.

22 According to the passage, which is NOT true?

① Zin Kim takes beautiful pictures of haenyeo.

② From the beginning, Zin Kim had no difficulty in taking pictures of haenyeo.

③ Haenyeo didn't think they looked pretty in their wetsuits.

④ Zin Kim wanted to show haenyeo's culture to the world.

⑤ Zin Kim promised haenyeo that she would make them look beautiful in her pictures.

[23~25] 다음 글을 읽고 물음에 답하시오.

Q. ⓐ**Lastly, please tell us what you're planning to do in the future.**

I once attended an overseas exhibition with a couple of haenyeo ⓑto give a talk about their lives. (①) She said to me, "Thank you so much. (②) I've never known in my whole life that I was such a special person." (③) She was crying with happiness. (④) Everyone in the audience was deeply moved. (⑤) I can never forget that moment, so I'll continue to take pictures of haenyeo. I want to tell more beautiful stories about them to many more people in the world.

23 위 글의 흐름으로 보아, 주어진 문장이 들어가기에 가장 적절한 곳은?

When I finished my talk, one of the haenyeo held my hand tightly.

①   ②   ③   ④   ⑤

24 위 글의 밑줄 친 ⓐLastly와 바꿔 쓸 수 있는 말을 고르시오.

① Eventually   ② Immediately
③ Extremely   ④ Finally
⑤ At last

25 위 글의 밑줄 친 ⓑto give와 to부정사의 용법이 다른 것의 개수를 고르시오.

── 보기 ──
① She went there to give a talk about it.
② It's your turn to give a talk about it.
③ He is wise enough to give a talk about it.
④ I felt proud to give a talk about it.
⑤ It was exciting to give a talk about it.

① 1개   ② 2개   ③ 3개   ④ 4개   ⑤ 5개

[26~28] 다음 글을 읽고 물음에 답하시오.

Kim Minho is a barista. He makes coffee drinks ⓐ a living. He became a barista after he had found out about his passion ⓑ coffee. His favorite part of his job is decorating coffee with hot milk and watching his customers enjoying it. He is planning to open his own coffee shop.

26 위 글의 빈칸 ⓐ와 ⓑ에 공통으로 들어갈 알맞은 전치사를 쓰시오.

➡ _____

27 주어진 영영풀이에 해당하는 단어를 본문에서 찾아 쓰시오.

a person who makes and serves coffee in a coffee bar

➡ _____

28 What's Kim Minho's favorite part of his job? Answer in English beginning with "It's".

➡ _____

단원별 예상문제 **221**

[01~03] 다음 대화를 읽고 물음에 답하시오.

Brian: Look over there. I wonder why there are so many people waiting in line.
Sujin: They're waiting to get into the new bakery there.
Brian: Why? Is it famous?
Sujin: Yes. It was on a TV program.
Brian: Really? We should try their bread then.
Sujin: Sure.

01 Why are so many people waiting in line?

➡ _____

02 Why is the new bakery famous? (7 words)

➡ _____

03 What does Brian want to try?

➡ _____

[04~05] 다음 중에서 틀린 문장을 찾아 번호를 쓰고, 바르게 고쳐 문장을 다시 쓰시오.

04 ① The film director had been tired because he spoke in front of so many people.
② The mechanic told her that someone had touched the tires of her car.
③ Emilia found out that she had lost her smartphone.
④ Julie decided to marry Jake as she had liked him for a long time.
⑤ The accounting manager said he had already completed his financial report.

➡ _____
_____

05 ① The president wants to know what his secretary bought a week ago.
② I have no idea why the super hero is blamed for the accident.
③ Could you tell us if the injured soldier will come tomorrow morning?
④ Do you think where the police officer caught the thief?
⑤ Does Michael know how you could escape from the prison?

➡ _____
_____

06 〈보기〉처럼 괄호 안에 주어진 접속사와 과거완료시제를 이용하여 두 문장을 한 문장으로 쓰시오.

┌─ 보기 ─┐
James was too full to eat more. He ate all three meals by himself. (Because로 시작)
→ Because James had eaten all three meals by himself, he was too full to eat more.

(1) Mary fought off a strange man's attack. She learned taekwondo before. (Because로 시작)

➡ _____
_____
_____

(2) Kevin never thought of quitting drinking. He saw a video of himself being a heavy drinker. (Until로 시작)

➡ _____
_____

Q. **You take beautiful pictures of them, but isn't it difficult to take pictures of haenyeo?**

At first, they didn't understand why I wanted to take their pictures. ⓐThey didn't think they looked prettily in their wetsuits. So, I said to them, "You're very special. I want to show your culture to the world." They opened up to me then. Of course, I also promised them that ⓑ내 사진 속에서 그들을 아름답게 보이도록 하겠다.   <I: Zin Kim>

07 위 글의 밑줄 친 ⓐ에서 어법상 틀린 부분을 찾아 고치시오.

_____ ➡ _____

08 위 글의 밑줄 친 ⓑ의 우리말에 맞게 주어진 어휘를 알맞게 배열하시오.

them / pictures / beautiful / make / I / in / would / my / look

➡ _____

09 Why did Zin Kim want to take pictures of haenyeo? Fill in the blanks (A) and (B) with suitable words.

Because haenyeo are (A)_____ _____ and she wanted to (B)_____ _____ _____ to the world.

Q. **Could you tell us more about haenyeo? What's so special about them?**

I can tell you three things. First, haenyeo are a symbol of strong women. Jejudo, which is a volcanic island, is not suitable for farming, so many haenyeo have become the breadwinners for their families. Second, haenyeo form their own communities and help each other. For example, more-experienced haenyeo train less-experienced haenyeo. Third, because they stay in the water (A)[with / without] any breathing devices, haenyeo can't catch a lot of seafood. This is good (B)[at / for] the underwater environment. Catching too much marine life at one time in one place can (C)[destroy / protect] the ocean.

10 위 글의 괄호 (A)~(C)에서 문맥상 알맞은 낱말을 골라 쓰시오.

➡ (A) _____ (B) _____ (C) _____

11 다음 빈칸 (A)와 (B)에 알맞은 단어를 넣어 해녀들이 그들 자신의 공동체를 조직하고 서로 돕는 한 예를 완성하시오.

(A)_____ haenyeo are trained by (B)_____ haenyeo.

12 Why is it impossible for haenyeo to catch a lot of seafood at one time? Answer in English beginning with "Because".

➡ _____

_____

01 다음 대화를 읽고 대화의 내용과 일치하도록 Jaden의 일기를 완성하시오.

> **Jaden:** Do you hear that? I wonder where that music is coming from.
>
> **Yuri:** I think it's coming from over there. Do you want to go and check it out?
>
> **Jaden:** Yes, I love that strong beat. Is it traditional Korean music?
>
> **Yuri:** Yes, it's called nongak. It's a kind of community band music.
>
> **Jaden:** Nongak? Could you explain a little bit more about it?
>
> **Yuri:** It's traditionally used to cheer up farmers and wish for a good harvest.
>
> **Jaden:** I see. Look! Some people are dancing to the rhythm.
>
> **Yuri:** Yes, that's a big part of nongak. Dancing together completes the music.
>
> **Jaden:** Let's join them.
>
> **Yuri:** Sure. Why not?

> Walking down the street, I heard music with a (A)_____. I wanted to know (B)_____. Yuri and I found that it was traditional Korean music, called (C)_____. Yuri explained that it's a kind of (D)_____ and traditionally used to (E)_____. It was impressive for me that some people were dancing to the rhythm because dancing was a big part of nongak. Yuri and I joined them and completed the music together.

02 다음 그림을 보고, 그림의 상황에 맞게 〈보기〉와 같이 간접의문문을 사용하여 어법에 맞게 자유롭게 영작하시오.

> ⎡ 보기 ⎤
> Do you know when you should feed the puppy?
> Tell me if you checked our mailbox.

(1) _____

(2) _____

(3) _____

단원별 모의고사

01 다음 영영풀이가 가리키는 것을 고르시오.

> a picture, set of words, or a short film, intended to persuade people to buy

① advertisement
② audio guide
③ jellyfish
④ beat
⑤ sunshine

02 다음 주어진 문장의 밑줄 친 beat와 같은 의미로 쓰인 것은?

> This type of music has a strong beat.

① I like the steady beat of the drums.
② He beat me at chess.
③ Hailstones beat against the window.
④ My mother beat dust out of the carpet.
⑤ I heard the sound of beating the door.

03 다음 우리말에 맞게 주어진 단어를 활용하여 영작하시오.

(1) 나는 사진작가가 되고 싶다. (photo)
➡ _____

(2) 그녀는 가장 적절한 후보였다. (suit)
➡ _____

(3) 그는 내 손을 꽉 잡았다. (hold, tight)
➡ _____

(4) 나는 소설을 빌리고 싶습니다. (like)
➡ _____

[04~05] 다음 대화를 읽고 물음에 답하시오.

G: Wow, look at the bridge in this ad.
_____
B: That's Gwangandaegyo in Busan.
G: How do you know that?
B: I went there with my family last summer.

04 위 대화의 빈칸에 들어갈 말로 적절하지 <u>않은</u> 것은?

① I wonder where the photo was taken.
② Can you tell me where the photo was taken?
③ Can I ask you where the photo was taken?
④ I want to know where the photo was taken.
⑤ I'm sure where the photo was taken.

05 Where did the boy visit last summer?

➡ _____

[06~07] 다음 대화를 읽고 물음에 답하시오.

Brian: Look over there. _____
Sujin: They're waiting to get into the new bakery there.
Brian: Why? Is it famous?
Sujin: Yes. It was on a TV program.
Brian: Really? We should try their bread then.
Sujin: Sure.

06 위 대화의 빈칸에 들어갈 말을 〈보기〉에 주어진 단어들을 배열하여 완성하시오.

┌─ 보기 ├─
many / in / why / are / wonder / so / I / people / waiting / line / there

➡ _____

07 위 대화를 읽고 대답할 수 <u>없는</u> 것은?

① What is Brian wondering?
② Why are many people waiting in line?
③ Why is the new bakery famous?
④ What does Brian want to try?
⑤ When was the new bakery on the TV program?

08 다음 대화가 자연스럽게 이어지도록 순서대로 배열하시오.

(A) It's a long hiking path around Jejudo.

(B) Oh, I see. I hope you enjoy your trip!

(C) Are you going somewhere this summer?

(D) I'm going to Jejudo to walk along the Jeju Olle Trail.

(E) The Jeju Olle Trail? Could you explain what that is?

➡ _____

[09~10] 다음 대화를 읽고 물음에 답하시오.

Emma: Look over there. I wonder why there are so many cars on the road.

Mike: Lots of people are going on vacation this weekend.

Emma: Really? Then, why don't we go somewhere, too?

Mike: O.K.

09 Why are so many cars on the road?

➡ _____
_____

10 What did Emma suggest to Mike?

➡ _____

11 다음 짝지어진 대화가 <u>어색한</u> 것은?

① A: I'm wondering why he got upset.
   B: I think he had a fight with his brother.

② A: Can you tell me what they are?
   B: They're called songpyeon.

③ A: Could you tell me about them?
   B: They're traditional Korea rice cakes.

④ A: Would you give me more information?
   B: Sure. Let's take a look at this book together.

⑤ A: I'm curious why she looks so sad.
   B: I'm not following you.

12 다음 주어진 우리말을 영작한 것으로 옳은 것은?

이것이 무엇인지 설명해 주시겠어요?

① Can you explain what is this?

② Could you explain what this is?

③ Could you explain that what this?

④ What could you explain this is?

⑤ What could you explain is this?

13 다음 두 문장을 한 문장으로 만들 때 빈칸에 들어갈 말로 가장 알맞은 것은?

• He was infected by the virus.

• He stayed at the center of the disease for 3 months.

→ He was infected by the virus because _____

① he might stay at the center of the disease for 3 months.

② had he stayed at the center of the disease for 3 months.

③ he has stayed at the center of the disease for 3 months.

④ he had stayed at the center of the disease for 3 months.

⑤ he could have stayed at the center of the disease for 3 months.

14 다음 중 밑줄 친 부분의 쓰임이 나머지 넷과 <u>다른</u> 것은?

① Mr. Baker doesn't know <u>where the post office is located</u>.

② Mina asked me <u>what time the bank would close</u>.

③ I wonder <u>when my girlfriend will come France</u>.

④ The executives of the company don't understand <u>why the facility is required</u>.

⑤ Let everybody know about the man <u>who won the Oscars</u> yesterday.

15 다음 그림을 보고, 주어진 단어들을 알맞게 배열하여 영작하되, 과거완료시제를 반드시 포함하시오. (동사를 변형)

(the woman, put, the fish, really, if)

➡ James wondered _____

_____ in the fish-shaped bun.

16 다음에 등장하는 사람과 직업에 대한 안내문을 읽고 괄호 안에 주어진 어휘를 알맞게 배열하여 빈칸 (A)와 (B)를 채우시오.

Yori became a content creator (A)_____
_____(gotten, she, after, views, had, 20,000) on her first video clip on WeTube. Her favorite part of her job is (B)_____
_____(about, what, sharing, special, Korean food, is) with many people around the world.

[17~18] 다음 글을 읽고 물음에 답하시오.

> **Q. How did you become interested in taking photos of haenyeo?**
>
> One day, I happened to take pictures of a haenyeo. I was surprised ⓐ<u>to find</u> that she was enjoying her job. Until then, I had only seen black-and-white photos of haenyeo who looked very tired. However, she kept laughing even after she had been in the water for over five hours. I realized then that I should take pictures of haenyeo. <I: Zin Kim>

17 위 글의 밑줄 친 ⓐ<u>to find</u>와 to부정사의 용법이 같은 것을 <u>모두</u> 고르시오.

① She was too tired <u>to find</u> it.

② Do you know how <u>to find</u> it?

③ I was eager <u>to find</u> it.

④ Tell me the way <u>to find</u> it.

⑤ Is it difficult <u>to find</u> it?

18 According to the passage, which is NOT true?

① Zin Kim happened to take pictures of a haenyeo.

② The haenyeo was enjoying her job.

③ Before Zin Kim took pictures of a haenyeo, she had seen many colorful photos of haenyeo.

④ The haenyeo Zin Kim took pictures of kept laughing even after she had been in the water for over five hours.

⑤ At that time, Zin Kim realized that she should take pictures of haenyeo.

[19~21] 다음 글을 읽고 물음에 답하시오.

Q. Could you tell us more about haenyeo?
ⓐ

I can tell you three things. First, haenyeo are a symbol of strong women. Jejudo, which is a volcanic island, is not suitable for farming, so ⓑ<u>많은 해녀들이 가족들의 생계비를 버는 가장이 되어 왔어요.</u> (①) Second, haenyeo form their own communities and help each other. (②) For example, more-experienced haenyeo train less-experienced haenyeo. (③) Third, because they stay in the water without any breathing devices, haenyeo can't catch a lot of seafood. (④) Catching too much marine life at one time in one place can destroy the ocean. (⑤)

19 위 글의 빈칸 ⓐ에 들어갈 알맞은 질문을 고르시오.

① What's so special about them?
② How did you become interested in taking photos of them?
③ Isn't it difficult to take their pictures?
④ What's the secret of holding their breath?
⑤ What are you planning to do in the future?

20 위 글의 흐름으로 보아, 주어진 문장이 들어가기에 가장 적절한 곳은?

> This is good for the underwater environment.

①   ②   ③   ④   ⑤

21 위 글의 밑줄 친 ⓑ의 우리말에 맞게 9 단어로 영작하시오.
➡ _____
_____

[22~24] 다음 글을 읽고 물음에 답하시오.

Yori is a content creator about traditional Korean food. She posts her video clips about making and eating Korean food. She became a content creator after she had gotten ⓐ<u>20,000</u> views on her first video clip on WeTube. Her favorite part of her job is sharing ⓑ<u>what</u> is special about Korean food with many people around the world. She is planning to write a cookbook on Korean food.

22 위 글의 밑줄 친 ⓐ를 영어로 읽는 법을 쓰시오.
➡ _____

23 위 글의 밑줄 친 ⓑwhat과 바꿔 쓸 수 있는 말을 세 단어로 쓰시오.
➡ _____

24 위 글을 읽고 답할 수 <u>없는</u> 질문을 고르시오.

① What does Yori do?
② How did Yori become a content creator?
③ When did Yori get 20,000 views on her first video clip on WeTube?
④ What is Yori's favorite part of her job?
⑤ What is Yori planning to do in the future?

Middle School 3-1
학교시험 완벽 대비

1학기 전과정
적중100 plus
영어 기출문제집

영어 중 3

미래 | 최연희

Best Collection

내용문의 중등영어발전소 적중100 편집부 TEL 070-4416-3636

INSIGHT
on the textbook
교과서 파헤치기

영어 기출 문제집

1학기 전과정

적중 100 plus

영어 중 3

미래 | 최연희

INSIGHT
on the textbook
교과서 파헤치기

※ 다음 영어를 우리말로 쓰시오.

01 marine		22 spill
02 adopt		23 donate
03 endangered		24 charity
04 fix		25 rescue
05 generation		26 specialist
06 child-care center		27 supply
07 deliver		28 teenager
08 actually		29 non-profit organization
09 educate		30 occur
10 throat		31 waste
11 various		32 volunteer
12 expression		33 gulf
13 book review		34 signature
14 rubber		35 die from
15 neighborhood		36 run into
16 translate		37 be able to 동사원형
17 collect		38 throw up
18 raise		39 in addition to
19 although		40 break down
20 probably		41 be covered with
21 reduce		42 read A to B
		43 ask for help

Step2

※ 다음 우리말을 영어로 쓰시오.

01	자선단체, 자선		22	멸종 위기의
02	전문가		23	구조, 구출
03	다양한, 여러 가지의		24	입양하다
04	일어나다, 발생하다		25	표현
05	쓰레기		26	가르치다, 교육하다
06	해양의		27	서명
07	모으다, 수집하다		28	만
08	아마도		29	고무
09	기부하다, 기증하다		30	탁아소, 보육원
10	공급		31	마요네즈
11	줄이다		32	십 대, 청소년
12	목구멍, 목		33	자원봉사자; 자원하다
13	전달하다, 배달하다		34	주차 공간
14	번역하다		35	~으로 죽다
15	유출		36	더 이상, 이제는
16	이웃, 근처		37	A를 B에게 읽어주다
17	비록 ~이지만		38	토하다
18	고치다		39	~으로 뒤덮여 있다
19	세대		40	고장나다
20	실제로		41	(곤경, 어려움 등을) 만나다[겪다]
21	기르다		42	~ 이외에, ~에 더하여
			43	A를 B와 나누다, 공유하다

※ 다음 영영풀이에 알맞은 단어를 <보기>에서 골라 쓴 후, 우리말 뜻을 쓰시오.

1 _____ : to happen: _____

2 _____ : in danger of extinction: _____

3 _____ : a large area of sea partly enclosed by land: _____

4 _____ : to repair something that is broken or not working properly: _____

5 _____ : to save somebody/something from a dangerous or harmful situation: _____

6 _____ : to teach a child at a school, college, or university: _____

7 _____ : relating to the sea and the creatures that live there: _____

8 _____ : to care for a child or young animal until it is able to take care of itself: _____

9 _____ : something you say, write, or do that shows what you think or feel: _____

10 _____ : to change written or spoken words into another language: _____

11 _____ : to make something smaller or less in size, amount, or price: _____

12 _____ : to take goods, letters, packages etc. to a particular place or person: _____

13 _____ : your name written in the way you usually write it, for example at the end of a letter, or on a cheque etc, to show that you have written it: _____

14 _____ : someone who knows a lot about a particular subject, or is very skilled at it: _____

15 _____ : to give something, especially money, to a person or an organization in order to help them: _____

16 _____ : an organization which raises money in order to help people who are sick or very poor, or who have a disability: _____

보기

donate	marine	reduce	fix
signature	rescue	specialist	gulf
charity	raise	deliver	occur
expression	educate	translate	endangered

※ 다음 우리말과 일치하도록 빈칸에 알맞은 말을 쓰시오.

Listen and Speak 1 A

1. **G:** What are you _____ _____ _____?
   B: I'm _____ _____ _____ some _____ _____ at the child-care center.
   G: _____ would you do there?
   B: I would _____ _____ some books _____ the children.
   G: That _____ interesting. Can I _____ you?
   B: Of _____.

2. **B:** What _____ _____ going _____ _____ for the book _____ _____?
   G: I'm _____ of reading a book about _____ _____.
   B: Good idea. I _____ the _____ _____ for you.
   G: Oh, could you _____ it to me?
   B: Sure. I'll _____ it tomorrow.

1. **G:** 이번 주말에 뭐 하니?
   B: 나는 보육원에서 봉사 활동을 좀 하려고 해.
   G: 거기서 뭘 할 것 같아?
   B: 아마 아이들에게 책을 좀 읽어 줄 것 같아.
   G: 그거 흥미로워 보인다. 나도 함께 가도 될까?
   B: 물론이지.

2. **B:** 너는 독후감 숙제로 뭘 읽을 거니?
   G: 나는 젊은 지도자들에 관한 책을 읽을까 해.
   B: 좋은 생각이야. 나한테 너에게 딱 맞는 책이 있어.
   G: 오, 내게 빌려줄 수 있어?
   B: 그럼. 내일 그걸 가져올게.

Listen and Speak 1 B

1. **A:** _____ your plan for _____ _____?
   B: I'm _____ of watching a movie _____ _____.

2. **A:** _____ your _____ for this year?
   B: I'm _____ _____ learning _____ _____ play baduk.

3. **A:** _____ your _____ _____ this year?
   B: I'm _____ _____ _____ _____ swimming _____.

1. **A:** 올해 너의 계획이 뭐니?
   B: 나는 주말마다 영화를 볼까 해.

2. **A:** 올해 너의 계획이 뭐니?
   B: 나는 바둑 두는 걸 배울까 해.

3. **A:** 올해 너의 계획이 뭐니?
   B: 나는 수영 강습을 받을까 해.

Listen and Speak 2 A

1. **G:** Dad, I'm _____ bit hungry. Is _____ anything _____ eat?
   M: Do you _____ _____ _____ cook tteokbokki for you?
   G: That'd be great. I love tteokbokki.
   M: O.K. Give me _____ _____ _____.

2. **B:** Sujin, can you help us?
   G: Sure. _____ _____ _____ _____ for you?
   B: We're going to _____ the school _____ _____ _____ a _____ _____ for bicycles.
   G: That's a great idea. Do you _____ _____ _____ _____ you _____ _____ from students?
   B: That would help us _____ _____. Thanks!

1. **G:** 아빠, 저 배가 좀 고파요. 먹을 게 좀 있나요?
   M: 네게 떡볶이를 만들어 줄까?
   G: 그거 정말 좋겠어요. 전 떡볶이를 매우 좋아해요.
   M: 알겠다. 잠시만 시간을 주렴.

2. **B:** 수진아, 우리를 좀 도와줄 수 있니?
   G: 물론이야. 무엇을 해 줄까?
   B: 우리는 학교에 자전거 주차 공간을 만들어 달라고 요청하려 해.
   G: 그거 멋진 생각이다. 학생들에게 사인을 받는 것을 도와줄까?
   B: 그건 우리에게 큰 도움이 될 거야. 고마워!

Listen and Speak 2 B

1. **A:** My bike _____ _____.

   B: Do you _____ _____ _____ _____ it?

   A: Yes, please.

2. **A:** I didn't _____ an umbrella.

   B: Do you want me to _____ my _____ _____ you?

   A: Yes, please.

3. **A:** _____ box is _____ _____.

   B: Do you _____ _____ _____ _____ you _____ it?

   A: Yes, please.

4. **A:** My _____ is too short.

   B: Do you _____ _____ _____ _____ a picture of you?

   A: Yes, please.

1. **A:** 내 자전거가 고장 났어.
   B: 내가 그것을 고쳐 줄까?
   A: 응, 부탁해.

2. **A:** 나 우산을 안 가져왔어.
   B: 내가 우산을 너와 함께 쓸까?
   A: 응, 부탁해.

3. **A:** 이 상자는 너무 무거워.
   B: 내가 그것을 나르는 걸 도와줄까?
   A: 응, 부탁해.

4. **A:** 내 팔이 너무 짧아.
   B: 내가 네 사진을 찍어줄까?
   A: 응, 부탁해.

Communicate A

Suho: Anna, do you have any children's books _____ _____ read _____ _____?

Anna: Sure. Why?

Suho: _____ _____ _____ _____ _____ some books to children in Africa. My aunt _____ _____ _____ they need books _____ _____.

Anna: Good idea, Suho! Wait, _____ your books in Korean?

Suho: Oh, that's a problem.

Anna: Well, how _____ _____ them _____ English?

Suho: _____? That's a great idea, Anna.

Anna: _____ _____ _____ _____ _____ _____ _____?

Suho: Sure. If we _____ _____ any _____ _____, let's ask our English teacher _____ _____.

Anna: O.K. It's really great _____ _____ can _____ the children in Africa.

수호: Anna, 너는 더 이상 읽지 않는 아동용 도서들을 가지고 있니?
Anna: 물론이지. 왜?
수호: 나는 아프리카의 아이들에게 책을 좀 보낼 생각을 하고 있어. 우리 이모가 내게 그 아이들이 읽을 책이 필요하다고 말씀하셨어.
Anna: 좋은 생각이야, 수호야! 잠깐만, 네 책들은 한글로 되어 있지 않니?
수호: 오, 그게 문제구나.
Anna: 음. 그것들을 영어로 번역하는 건 어때?
수호: 번역? 그거 좋은 생각이다, Anna.
Anna: 너는 내가 너를 도와주기를 원하니?
수호: 물론이지. 만약 어려운 표현들이 나오면, 영어 선생님께 도움을 요청하자.
Anna: 알겠어. 우리가 아프리카의 아이들을 도울 수 있어서 정말 좋다.

Communicate B

A: (춤추는 동작을 한다.)

B: Are you _____ _____ _____ taekwondo?

A: No.

C: _____ _____ _____ _____ learning _____ _____?

A: Yes. _____ _____ _____ _____ K-pop dancing.

C: Do you _____ _____ _____ _____ you?

A: Sure. That'd be great.

A: (춤추는 동작을 한다.)
B: 너 태권도 배우려고 하니?
A: 아니야.
C: 춤추는 걸 배우려고 하니?
A: 그래. K-pop 춤을 배우려고 해.
C: 내가 가르쳐 줄까?
A: 그래. 그거 좋겠다.

Progress Check 1

B: _____ _____ you _____ this weekend?

G: _____ _____ _____ going for a _____ _____.

B: Sounds good. _____ I _____ you?

G: Sure. _____ meet _____ _____ _____ _____ the park at ten.

B: O.K.

B: 이번 주말에 뭐 하니?
G: 자전거를 타러 가려고 해.
B: 좋겠구나. 나도 함께 해도 되니?
G: 물론이야. 공원 앞에서 10시에 보자.
B: 그래.

Progress Check 2

M: _____ _____ have pancakes _____ breakfast?

W: Sure. Oh, we _____ have any eggs.

M: Do you _____ _____ _____ _____ to the store and _____ some?

W: Thanks, Mike. Can you get _____ _____, _____?

M: Sure.

M: 아침으로 팬케이크를 먹을까요?
W: 좋아요. 오, 달걀이 없네요.
M: 가게에 가서 좀 사올까요?
W: 고마워요, Mike. 블루베리 시럽도 사와 줄래요?
M: 물론이죠.

※ 다음 우리말에 맞도록 대화를 영어로 쓰시오.

Listen and Speak 1 A

1. G: _____

   B: _____

   G: _____

   B: _____

   G: _____

   B: _____

2. B: _____

   G: _____

   B: _____

   G: _____

   B: _____

1. G: 이번 주말에 뭐 하니?
   B: 나는 보육원에서 봉사 활동을 좀 하려고 해.
   G: 거기서 뭘 할 것 같아?
   B: 아마 아이들에게 책을 좀 읽어 줄 것 같아.
   G: 그거 흥미로워 보인다. 나도 함께 가도 될까?
   B: 물론이지.

2. B: 너는 독후감 숙제로 뭘 읽을 거니?
   G: 나는 젊은 지도자들에 관한 책을 읽을까 해.
   B: 좋은 생각이야. 나한테 너에게 딱 맞는 책이 있어.
   G: 오, 내게 빌려줄 수 있어?
   B: 그럼. 내일 그걸 가져올게.

Listen and Speak 1 B

1. A: _____

   B: _____

2. A: _____

   B: _____

3. A: _____

   B: _____

1. A: 올해 너의 계획이 뭐니?
   B: 나는 주말마다 영화를 볼까 해.

2. A: 올해 너의 계획이 뭐니?
   B: 나는 바둑 두는 걸 배울까 해.

3. A: 올해 너의 계획이 뭐니?
   B: 나는 수영 강습을 받을까 해.

Listen and Speak 2 A

1. G: _____

   M: _____

   G: _____

   M: _____

2. B: _____

   G: _____

   B: _____

   G: _____

   B: _____

1. G: 아빠, 저 배가 좀 고파요. 먹을 게 좀 있나요?
   M: 네게 떡볶이를 만들어 줄까?
   G: 그거 정말 좋겠어요. 전 떡볶이를 매우 좋아해요.
   M: 알겠다. 잠시만 시간을 주렴.

2. B: 수진아, 우리를 좀 도와줄 수 있니?
   G: 물론이야. 무엇을 해 줄까?
   B: 우리는 학교에 자전거 주차 공간을 만들어 달라고 요청하려 해.
   G: 그거 멋진 생각이다. 학생들에게 사인을 받는 것을 도와줄까?
   B: 그건 우리에게 큰 도움이 될 거야. 고마워!

Listen and Speak 2 B

1. A: _____

   B: _____

   A: _____

2. A: _____

   B: _____

   A: _____

3. A: _____

   B: _____

   A: _____

4. A: _____

   B: _____

   A: _____

1. A: 내 자전거가 고장 났어.
   B: 내가 그것을 고쳐 줄까?
   A: 응, 부탁해.

2. A: 나 우산을 안 가져왔어.
   B: 내가 우산을 너와 함께 쓸까?
   A: 응, 부탁해.

3. A: 이 상자는 너무 무거워.
   B: 내가 그것을 나르는 걸 도와줄까?
   A: 응, 부탁해.

4. A: 내 팔이 너무 짧아.
   B: 내가 네 사진을 찍어줄까?
   A: 응, 부탁해.

Communicate A

Suho: _____

Anna: _____

Suho: _____

Anna: _____

Suho: _____

Anna: _____

Suho: _____

Anna: _____

Suho: _____

Anna: _____

수호: Anna, 너는 더 이상 읽지 않는 아동용 도서들을 가지고 있니?
Anna: 물론이지. 왜?
수호: 나는 아프리카의 아이들에게 책을 좀 보낼 생각을 하고 있어. 우리 이모가 내게 그 아이들이 읽을 책이 필요하다고 말씀하셨어.
Anna: 좋은 생각이야, 수호야! 잠깐만, 네 책들은 한글로 되어 있지 않니?
수호: 오, 그게 문제구나.
Anna: 음. 그것들을 영어로 번역하는 건 어때?
수호: 번역? 그거 좋은 생각이다, Anna.
Anna: 너는 내가 너를 도와주기를 원하니?
수호: 물론이지. 만약 어려운 표현들이 나오면, 영어 선생님께 도움을 요청하자.
Anna: 알겠어. 우리가 아프리카의 아이들을 도울 수 있어서 정말 좋다.

Communicate B

A: (춤추는 동작을 한다.)

B: _____

A: _____

C: _____

A: _____

C: _____

A: _____

A: (춤추는 동작을 한다.)
B: 너 태권도 배우려고 하니?
A: 아니야.
C: 춤추는 걸 배우려고 하니?
A: 그래. K-pop 춤을 배우려고 해.
C: 내가 가르쳐 줄까?
A: 그래. 그거 좋겠다.

Progress Check 1

B: _____

G: _____

B: _____

G: _____

B: _____

B: 이번 주말에 뭐 하니?
G: 자전거를 타러 가려고 해.
B: 좋겠구나. 나도 함께 해도 되니?
G: 물론이야. 공원 앞에서 10시에 보자.
B: 그래.

Progress Check 2

M: _____

W: _____

M: _____

W: _____

M: _____

M: 아침으로 팬케이크를 먹을까요?
W: 좋아요. 오, 달걀이 없네요.
M: 가게에 가서 좀 사올까요?
W: 고마워요, Mike. 블루베리 시럽도 사와 줄래요?
M: 물론이죠.

※ 다음 우리말과 일치하도록 빈칸에 알맞은 것을 골라 쓰시오.

1 _____ in _____

   A. Action　　　　B. Teens

2 Many young people are _____ the _____ a _____
_____.

   A. better　　　B. making　　　C. place　　　D. world

3 _____ _____, Carter and Olivia Ries have become leaders _____ _____ animals.

   A. saving　　　B. example　　　C. in　　　D. for

4 _____ they are only teenagers, they _____ actually _____ a _____ in the world.

   A. difference　　B. although　　C. made　　D. have

5 _____ were they _____ _____ do that?

   A. able　　　B. how　　　C. to

6 _____ _____ _____ Carter.

   A. hear　　　B. let's　　　C. from

7 _____ I was five, my _____ sister Olivia and I _____ a cheetah.

   A. each　　　B. little　　　C. adopted　　　D. when

8 Did we _____ cheetahs _____ _____?

   A. at　　　B. raise　　　C. home

9 No, we _____ _____ a _____ that _____ wild cheetahs in South Africa.

   A. protects　　B. donated　　C. charity　　D. to

10 Our parents told us that if we did not _____ them, we _____ not be _____ to see cheetahs in the _____ future.

   A. able　　　B. near　　　C. might　　　D. protect

11 We soon _____ _____ _____ helping other _____ animals.

   A. endangered　　B. interested　　C. in　　D. became

12 A few years _____, with help from our parents, we _____ a _____ _____ to protect them.

   A. created　　B. later　　C. organization　　D. non-profit

13 We wanted the next _____ to be able to see these animals, _____ we _____ our _____ One More Generation.

   A. generation　　B. named　　C. organization　　D. so

14 We also _____ _____ animals and _____ our _____ about them.

   A. educated　　B. studied　　C. friends　　D. endangered

15 Then one day, a _____ _____ _____ _____ in the Gulf of Mexico.

   A. spill　　　B. terrible　　　C. occurred　　　D. oil

---

1 활약하는 십 대들

2 많은 젊은 사람들이 세상을 더 좋은 곳으로 만들고 있다.

3 예를 들어, Carter Ries와 Olivia Ries는 동물을 구하는 일에 리더가 되어 왔다.

4 비록 그들은 십 대일 뿐이지만, 실제로 세상에 변화를 일으켜 왔다.

5 그들은 어떻게 그것을 할 수 있었을까?

6 Carter의 이야기를 들어보자.

7 내가 다섯 살이었을 때, 나의 여동생 Olivia와 나는 각자 치타를 입양했다.

8 우리가 치타를 집에서 길렀을까?

9 아니, 우리는 남아프리카 공화국에 있는 야생 치타를 보호하는 자선단체에 기부했다.

10 부모님께서는 우리에게 우리가 그들을 보호하지 않으면, 가까운 미래에 치타를 볼 수 없을지도 모른다고 말씀하셨다.

11 우리는 곧 다른 멸종 위기의 동물들을 도와주는 것에 관심을 갖게 되었다.

12 몇 년 후에, 부모님의 도움으로, 우리는 그들을 보호하기 위해 비영리 단체를 만들었다.

13 우리는 다음 세대가 이러한 동물들을 볼 수 있기를 원했기에, 우리 단체를 One More Generation이라고 이름 붙였다.

14 우리는 또한 멸종 위기의 동물들을 연구했고 친구들에게 그들에 대해 가르쳐 주었다.

15 그러던 어느 날, 끔찍한 석유 유출 사건이 멕시코만에서 발생했다.

16 A lot of sea animals were _____ _____ _____ oil, and they were _____.

    A. covered   B. dying   C. with   D. completely

17 We _____ _____ _____ something.

    A. to   B. had   C. do

18 We started collecting animal _____ _____ such _____ pet carrying cages and rubber gloves from everyone in our _____.

    A. supplies   B. neighborhood   C. as   D. rescue

19 Four months later, our family drove to the Gulf of Mexico to _____ _____ we _____ and helped to _____ the animals.

    A. collected   B. deliver   C. save   D. what

20 _____ we were _____ there, we learned _____ very _____.

    A. something   B. working   C. useful   D. while

21 When we put mayonnaise _____ a turtle's _____, the turtle _____ _____.

    A. throat   B. up   C. into   D. threw

22 That _____, we were able to _____ oil _____ _____ turtles.

    A. out   B. get   C. of   D. way

23 I never knew mayonnaise could _____ _____ _____ animals!

    A. save   B. be   C. to   D. used

24 On our _____ day, we met a _____ _____ _____.

    A. life   B. last   C. specialist   D. marine

25 She told us that plastic _____ is more _____ to sea animals _____ oil _____ are.

    A. dangerous   B. spills   C. waste   D. than

26 A lot of sea animals and sea birds _____ _____ _____ plastic _____.

    A. from   B. eating   C. die   D. waste

27 After we came home, we _____ an _____ project about _____ to _____ plastic waste.

    A. reduce   B. educational   C. how   D. created

28 In _____ to this, our organization _____ to do _____ projects to _____ animals.

    A. various   B. addition   C. save   D. continues

29 _____ we started small, we are _____ a _____ _____.

    A. big   B. although   C. difference   D. making

30 _____ you do today can _____ the world, so _____ that first _____!

    A. take   B. change   C. step   D. what

16 많은 해양 동물들이 완전히 기름을 뒤집어썼고, 죽어가고 있었다.

17 우리는 무엇인가를 해야만 했다.

18 우리는 애완동물 수송용 우리와 고무장갑과 같은 동물 구조 물품들을 동네의 모든 사람으로부터 모으기 시작했다.

19 4개월 후에, 우리 가족은 우리가 모았던 것들을 전달하기 위해서 멕시코만으로 운전해 갔으며 동물들을 구하는 일을 도왔다.

20 거기서 일하는 동안에, 우리는 매우 유용한 것을 배웠다.

21 마요네즈를 거북이의 목구멍에 집어넣으면, 거북이가 토했다.

22 그런 식으로, 우리는 거북이들에게서 기름을 빼낼 수 있었다.

23 나는 마요네즈가 동물을 구하는 데 사용될 수 있다는 것을 전혀 알지 못했다!

24 마지막 날에, 우리는 해양 생물 전문가를 만났다.

25 그녀는 우리에게 석유 유출보다 플라스틱 쓰레기가 해양 동물에게 더 위험하다고 말했다.

26 많은 해양 동물과 바다 새들이 플라스틱 쓰레기를 먹어서 죽는다.

27 집으로 돌아온 후, 우리는 플라스틱 쓰레기를 줄일 수 있는 방법에 관한 교육 프로젝트를 만들었다.

28 이것 외에도, 우리 단체는 동물들을 구하기 위한 다양한 프로젝트들을 계속하고 있다.

29 비록 우리는 작은 것부터 시작했지만, 큰 변화를 만들어 내고 있는 중이다.

30 당신이 오늘 하는 일이 세상을 바꿀 수 있기에, 첫발을 내디뎌라!

Step2

※ 다음 우리말과 일치하도록 빈칸에 알맞은 말을 쓰시오.

1   Teens _____ _____

2   _____ young people are making the world _____ _____
    _____.

3   _____ _____, Carter and Olivia Ries have become leaders
    _____ _____ _____.

4   _____ they are only _____, they _____ _____ _____
    _____ in the world.

5   _____ were they _____ _____ do that?

6   _____ _____ Carter.

7   When I was five, my _____ _____ Olivia and I _____
    _____ a cheetah.

8   Did we _____ cheetahs _____ _____?

9   No, we _____ _____ _____ _____ that _____ wild
    cheetahs in _____ _____.

10 Our parents told us that if we did not protect them, we _____
    _____ _____ _____ _____ _____ in the
    near future.

11 We soon _____ _____ _____ helping _____ _____
    _____.

12 _____ _____ _____ later, with help from our parents, we
    _____ _____ _____ _____ to protect them.

13 We wanted _____ _____ _____ to _____
    _____ see these animals, so we named our organization One
    More Generation.

14 We also studied _____ _____ and _____ _____
    _____ about them.

15 Then one day, _____ _____ _____ _____ _____ in
    the Gulf of Mexico.

1   활약하는 십 대들

2   많은 젊은 사람들이 세상을 더 좋은 곳으로 만들고 있다.

3   예를 들어, Carter Ries와 Olivia Ries는 동물을 구하는 일에 리더가 되어 왔다.

4   비록 그들은 십 대일 뿐이지만, 실제로 세상에 변화를 일으켜 왔다.

5   그들은 어떻게 그것을 할 수 있었을까?

6   Carter의 이야기를 들어보자.

7   내가 다섯 살이었을 때, 나의 여동생 Olivia와 나는 각자 치타를 입양했다.

8   우리가 치타를 집에서 길렀을까?

9   아니, 우리는 남아프리카 공화국에 있는 야생 치타를 보호하는 자선단체에 기부했다.

10 부모님께서는 우리에게 우리가 그들을 보호하지 않으면, 가까운 미래에 치타를 볼 수 없을지도 모른다고 말씀하셨다.

11 우리는 곧 다른 멸종 위기의 동물들을 도와주는 것에 관심을 갖게 되었다.

12 몇 년 후에, 부모의 도움으로, 우리는 그들을 보호하기 위해 비영리 단체를 만들었다.

13 우리는 다음 세대가 이러한 동물들을 볼 수 있기를 원했기에, 우리 단체를 One More Generation이라고 이름 붙였다.

14 우리는 또한 멸종 위기의 동물들을 연구했고 친구들에게 그들에 대해 가르쳐 주었다.

15 그러던 어느 날, 끔찍한 석유 유출 사건이 멕시코만에서 발생했다.

16 A lot of sea animals _____ _____ _____ _____ _____, and they _____ _____.

17 We _____ _____ _____ something.

18 We started _____ _____ _____ _____ such as pet carrying cages and rubber gloves from everyone _____ _____ _____.

19 Four months _____, our family drove to the Gulf of Mexico to deliver _____ _____ _____ and helped _____ _____ _____ _____.

20 _____ we were _____ there, we learned _____ _____ _____.

21 When we _____ mayonnaise _____ a turtle's throat, the turtle _____ _____.

22 That way, we were able to _____ oil _____ _____ turtles.

23 I never knew mayonnaise _____ _____ _____ _____ _____ animals!

24 On our last day, we met a _____ _____ _____.

25 She told us that plastic waste is _____ _____ to sea animals _____ _____ _____ are.

26 A lot of sea animals and sea birds _____ _____ _____ _____.

27 After we came home, we _____ _____ _____ _____ about _____ _____ _____ plastic waste.

28 _____ _____ _____ _____ this, our organization continues to do various _____ _____ _____ animals.

29 _____ we started small, we are _____ _____ _____ _____.

30 _____ you do today can change the world, so _____ _____ _____ _____!

16 많은 해양 동물들이 완전히 기름을 뒤집어썼고, 죽어가고 있었다.

17 우리는 무엇인가를 해야만 했다.

18 우리는 애완동물 수송용 우리와 고무장갑과 같은 동물 구조 물품들을 동네의 모든 사람으로부터 모으기 시작했다.

19 4개월 후에, 우리 가족은 우리가 모았던 것들을 전달하기 위해서 멕시코만으로 운전해 갔으며 동물들을 구하는 일을 도왔다.

20 거기서 일하는 동안에, 우리는 매우 유용한 것을 배웠다.

21 마요네즈를 거북이의 목구멍에 집어넣으면, 거북이가 토했다.

22 그런 식으로, 우리는 거북이들에게서 기름을 빼낼 수 있었다.

23 나는 마요네즈가 동물을 구하는 데 사용될 수 있다는 것을 전혀 알지 못했다!

24 마지막 날에, 우리는 해양 생물 전문가를 만났다.

25 그녀는 우리에게 석유 유출보다 플라스틱 쓰레기가 해양 동물에게 더 위험하다고 말했다.

26 많은 해양 동물과 바다 새들이 플라스틱 쓰레기를 먹어서 죽는다.

27 집으로 돌아온 후, 우리는 플라스틱 쓰레기를 줄일 수 있는 방법에 관한 교육 프로젝트를 만들었다.

28 이것 외에도, 우리 단체는 동물들을 구하기 위한 다양한 프로젝트들을 계속하고 있다.

29 비록 우리는 작은 것부터 시작했지만, 큰 변화를 만들어 내고 있는 중이다.

30 당신이 오늘 하는 일이 세상을 바꿀 수 있기에, 첫발을 내디뎌라!

※ 다음 문장을 우리말로 쓰시오.

1 Teens in Action

➡ _____

2 Many young people are making the world a better place.

➡ _____

3 For example, Carter and Olivia Ries have become leaders in saving animals.

➡ _____

4 Although they are only teenagers, they have actually made a difference in the world.

➡ _____

5 How were they able to do that?

➡ _____

6 Let's hear from Carter.

➡ _____

7 When I was five, my little sister Olivia and I each adopted a cheetah.

➡ _____

8 Did we raise cheetahs at home?

➡ _____

9 No, we donated to a charity that protects wild cheetahs in South Africa.

➡ _____

10 Our parents told us that if we did not protect them, we might not be able to see cheetahs in the near future.

➡ _____

11 We soon became interested in helping other endangered animals.

➡ _____

12 A few years later, with help from our parents, we created a non-profit organization to protect them.

➡ _____

13 We wanted the next generation to be able to see these animals, so we named our organization One More Generation.

➡ _____

_____

14 We also studied endangered animals and educated our friends about them.

➡ _____

15 Then one day, a terrible oil spill occurred in the Gulf of Mexico.

➡ _____

16 A lot of sea animals were completely covered with oil, and they were dying.

➡ _____

17 We had to do something.

➡ _____

18 We started collecting animal rescue supplies such as pet carrying cages and rubber gloves from everyone in our neighborhood.

➡ _____

19 Four months later, our family drove to the Gulf of Mexico to deliver what we collected and helped to save the animals.

➡ _____

_____

20 While we were working there, we learned something very useful.

➡ _____

21 When we put mayonnaise into a turtle's throat, the turtle threw up.

➡ _____

22 That way, we were able to get oil out of turtles.

➡ _____

23 I never knew mayonnaise could be used to save animals!

➡ _____

24 On our last day, we met a marine life specialist.

➡ _____

25 She told us that plastic waste is more dangerous to sea animals than oil spills are.

➡ _____

26 A lot of sea animals and sea birds die from eating plastic waste.

➡ _____

27 After we came home, we created an educational project about how to reduce plastic waste.

➡ _____

28 In addition to this, our organization continues to do various projects to save animals.

➡ _____

29 Although we started small, we are making a big difference.

➡ _____

30 What you do today can change the world, so take that first step!

➡ _____

※ 다음 괄호 안의 단어들을 우리말에 맞도록 바르게 배열하시오.

1 (in / Teens / Action)
➡ _____

2 (young / many / are / people / making / world / the / better / a / place.)
➡ _____

3 (example, / for / Olivia / and / Ries / Carter / become / have / leaders / in / animals. / saving)
➡ _____

4 (they / although / are / teenagers, / only / have / they / made / actually / difference / a / the / world. / in)
➡ _____

5 (were / how / able / they / do / that? / to)
➡ _____

6 (hear / let's / Carter. / from)
➡ _____

7 (I / when / five, / was / little / my / Olivia / sister / I / and / adopted / each / cheetah. / a)
➡ _____

8 (we / did / cheetahs / raise / home? / at)
➡ _____

9 (we / no, / donated / a / to / charity / protects / that / cheetahs / wild / South / in / Africa.)
➡ _____

10 (parents / our / us / told / if / that / did / we / protect / not / them, / might / we / be / not / to / able / cheetahs / see / the / in / future. / near)
➡ _____

11 (soon / we / interested / became / helping / in / endangered / other / animals.)
➡ _____

12 (few / a / later, / years / help / with / our / from / parents, / created / we / non-profit / a / organization / protect / to / them.)
➡ _____

13 (wanted / we / next / the / to / generation / be / to / able / these / see / so / animals, / we / our / named / organization / More / One / Generation.)
➡ _____

14 (also / we / endangered / studied / and / animals / our / educated / friends / them. / about)
➡ _____

15 (one / then / day, / terrible / a / spill / oil / in / occurred / the / of / Mexico. / Gulf)
➡ _____

1　활약하는 십 대들

2　많은 젊은 사람들이 세상을 더 좋은 곳으로 만들고 있다.

3　예를 들어, Carter Ries와 Olivia Ries는 동물을 구하는 일에 리더가 되어 왔다.

4　비록 그들은 십 대일 뿐이지만, 실제로 세상에 변화를 일으켜 왔다.

5　그들은 어떻게 그것을 할 수 있었을까?

6　Carter의 이야기를 들어보자.

7　내가 다섯 살이었을 때, 나의 여동생 Olivia와 나는 각자 치타를 입양했다.

8　우리가 치타를 집에서 길렀을까?

9　아니, 우리는 남아프리카 공화국에 있는 야생 치타를 보호하는 자선단체에 기부했다.

10　부모님께서는 우리에게 우리가 그들을 보호하지 않으면, 가까운 미래에 치타를 볼 수 없을지도 모른다고 말씀하셨다.

11　우리는 곧 다른 멸종 위기의 동물들을 도와주는 것에 관심을 갖게 되었다.

12　몇 년 후에, 부모님의 도움으로, 우리는 그들을 보호하기 위해 비영리 단체를 만들었다.

13　우리는 다음 세대가 이러한 동물들을 볼 수 있기를 원했기에, 우리 단체를 One More Generation이라고 이름 붙였다.

14　우리는 또한 멸종 위기의 동물들을 연구했고 친구들에게 그들에 대해 가르쳐 주었다.

15　그러던 어느 날, 끔찍한 석유 유출 사건이 멕시코만에서 발생했다.

16 (lot / a / sea / of / animals / completely / were / with / covered / oil, / they / and / dying. / were)
➡ _____

17 (had / we / do / to / something.)
➡ _____

18 (started / we / animal / collecting / supplies / rescue / as / such / carrying / pet / cages / and / gloves / rubber / from / in / everyone / neighborhood. / our)
➡ _____

19 (months / four / laters, / family / our / to / drove / the / of / Gulf / to / Mexico / deliver / we / what / and / collected / to / helped / save / animals. / the)
➡ _____
_____

20 (we / while / working / were / there, / learned / we / very / useful. / something)
➡ _____

21 (we / when / mayonnaise / put / a / into / throat, / turtle's / the / threw / turtle / up.)
➡ _____

22 (way, / that / were / we / to / able / get / out / oil / turtles. / of)
➡ _____

23 (never / I / mayonnaise / knew / be / could / to / used / save / animals!)
➡ _____

24 (our / on / day, / last / met / we / marine / a / specialist. / life)
➡ _____

25 (told / she / that / us / waste / plastic / is / dangerous / more / sea / to / than / animals / oil / are. / spills)
➡ _____
_____

26 (lot / a / sea / of / animals / sea / and / birds / eating / from / die / waste. / plastic)
➡ _____

27 (we / after / home, / came / created / we / educational / an / about / project / how / reduce / to / waste. / plastic)
➡ _____
_____

28 (addition / in / this, / to / organization / our / to / continues / various / do / projects / save / to / animals.)
➡ _____
_____

29 (we / although / started / small, / are / we / a / making / big / difference.)
➡ _____

30 (you / what / today / do / change / can / world, / the / take / so / first / step! / that)
➡ _____

16 많은 해양 동물들이 완전히 기름을 뒤집어썼고, 죽어가고 있었다.

17 우리는 무엇인가를 해야만 했다.

18 우리는 애완동물 수송용 우리와 고무장갑과 같은 동물 구조 물품들을 동네의 모든 사람으로부터 모으기 시작했다.

19 4개월 후에, 우리 가족은 우리가 모았던 것들을 전달하기 위해서 멕시코만으로 운전해 갔으며 동물들을 구하는 일을 도왔다.

20 거기서 일하는 동안에, 우리는 매우 유용한 것을 배웠다.

21 마요네즈를 거북이의 목구멍에 집어넣으면, 거북이가 토했다.

22 그런 식으로, 우리는 거북이들에게서 기름을 빼낼 수 있었다.

23 나는 마요네즈가 동물을 구하는 데 사용될 수 있다는 것을 전혀 알지 못했다!

24 마지막 날에, 우리는 해양 생물 전문가를 만났다.

25 그녀는 우리에게 석유 유출보다 플라스틱 쓰레기가 해양 동물에게 더 위험하다고 말했다.

26 많은 해양 동물과 바다 새들이 플라스틱 쓰레기를 먹어서 죽는다.

27 집으로 돌아온 후, 우리는 플라스틱 쓰레기를 줄일 수 있는 방법에 관한 교육 프로젝트를 만들었다.

28 이것 외에도, 우리 단체는 동물들을 구하기 위한 다양한 프로젝트들을 계속하고 있다.

29 비록 우리는 작은 것부터 시작했지만, 큰 변화를 만들어 내고 있는 중이다.

30 당신이 오늘 하는 일이 세상을 바꿀 수 있기에, 첫발을 내디뎌라!

※ 다음 우리말을 영어로 쓰시오.

1 활약하는 십 대들

➡ _____

2 많은 젊은 사람들이 세상을 더 좋은 곳으로 만들고 있다.

➡ _____

3 예를 들어, Carter Ries와 Olivia Ries는 동물을 구하는 일에 리더가 되어 왔다.

➡ _____

4 비록 그들은 십 대일 뿐이지만, 실제로 세상에 변화를 일으켜 왔다.

➡ _____

5 그들은 어떻게 그것을 할 수 있었을까?

➡ _____

6 Carter의 이야기를 들어보자.

➡ _____

7 내가 다섯 살이었을 때, 나의 여동생 Olivia와 나는 각자 치타를 입양했다.

➡ _____

8 우리가 치타를 집에서 길렀을까?

➡ _____

9 아니, 우리는 남아프리카 공화국에 있는 야생 치타를 보호하는 자선단체에 기부했다.

➡ _____

10 부모님께서는 우리에게 우리가 그들을 보호하지 않으면, 가까운 미래에 치타를 볼 수 없을지도 모른다고 말씀하셨다.

➡ _____

_____

11 우리는 곧 다른 멸종 위기의 동물들을 도와주는 것에 관심을 갖게 되었다.

➡ _____

12 몇 년 후에, 부모님의 도움으로, 우리는 그들을 보호하기 위해 비영리 단체를 만들었다.

➡ _____

13 우리는 다음 세대가 이러한 동물들을 볼 수 있기를 원했기에, 우리 단체를 One More Generation 이라고 이름 붙였다.

➡ _____

_____

14 우리는 또한 멸종 위기의 동물들을 연구했고 친구들에게 그들에 대해 가르쳐 주었다.

➡ _____

15 그러던 어느 날, 끔찍한 석유 유출 사건이 멕시코만에서 발생했다.

➡ _____

16 많은 해양 동물들이 완전히 기름을 뒤집어썼고, 죽어가고 있었다.

➡ _____

17 우리는 무엇인가를 해야만 했다.

➡ _____

18 우리는 애완동물 수송용 우리와 고무장갑과 같은 동물 구조 물품들을 동네의 모든 사람으로부터 모으기 시작했다.

➡ _____

_____

19 4개월 후에, 우리 가족은 우리가 모았던 것들을 전달하기 위해서 멕시코만으로 운전해 갔으며 동물들을 구하는 일을 도왔다.

➡ _____

_____

20 거기서 일하는 동안에, 우리는 매우 유용한 것을 배웠다.

➡ _____

21 마요네즈를 거북이의 목구멍에 집어넣으면, 거북이가 토했다.

➡ _____

22 그런 식으로, 우리는 거북이들에게서 기름을 빼낼 수 있었다.

➡ _____

23 나는 마요네즈가 동물을 구하는 데 사용될 수 있다는 것을 전혀 알지 못했다!

➡ _____

24 마지막 날에, 우리는 해양 생물 전문가를 만났다.

➡ _____

25 그녀는 우리에게 석유 유출보다 플라스틱 쓰레기가 해양 동물에게 더 위험하다고 말했다.

➡ _____

26 많은 해양 동물과 바다 새들이 플라스틱 쓰레기를 먹어서 죽는다.

➡ _____

27 집으로 돌아온 후, 우리는 플라스틱 쓰레기를 줄일 수 있는 방법에 관한 교육 프로젝트를 만들었다.

➡ _____

28 이것 외에도, 우리 단체는 동물들을 구하기 위한 다양한 프로젝트들을 계속하고 있다.

➡ _____

29 비록 우리는 작은 것부터 시작했지만, 큰 변화를 만들어 내고 있는 중이다.

➡ _____

30 당신이 오늘 하는 일이 세상을 바꿀 수 있기에, 첫발을 내디뎌라!

➡ _____

※ 다음 우리말과 일치하도록 빈칸에 알맞은 말을 쓰시오.

After You Read B

1. A: _____ _____ _____ _____ One More Generation?

2. B: _____ is _____?

3. A: It is a _____ _____ that _____ _____ animals.

4. B: What _____ One More Generation _____?

5. A: The organization wants the next _____ _____ _____ _____ _____ _____ those animals.

6. B: That's a great _____. I'll _____ it.

1. A: One More Generation에 가입하는 것이 어때?
2. B: 그게 무엇이니?
3. A: 그것은 멸종 위기의 동물들을 보호하는 비영리 단체야.
4. B: One More Generation이 무슨 뜻이니?
5. A: 그 단체는 다음 세대가 그러한 동물들을 볼 수 있기를 원해.
6. B: 그것은 멋진 단체구나. 나는 거기에 가입할게.

Link Science – Share

1. Asian black bears have a _____ _____ _____ _____ _____.

2. They _____ _____ _____ _____ in Asia.

3. They've _____ _____ _____ people _____ them for their _____ and _____ _____.

4. We'll tell you _____ _____ _____ _____ for them.

5. First, _____ _____ paper _____ _____ _____.

6. Second, you _____ _____ any Asian _____ _____.

1. 아시아흑곰은 가슴에 흰색의 V 모양을 갖고 있습니다.
2. 그들은 주로 아시아의 숲에서 삽니다.
3. 그들은 사람들이 그들의 신체 부분을 얻으려고 사냥을 하고 숲을 파괴하기 때문에 멸종 위기에 처했습니다.
4. 우리는 그들을 위해 여러분이 무엇을 할 수 있는지 말하고자 합니다.
5. 첫째, 숲을 보호하기 위해서 종이를 덜 사용하세요.
6. 둘째, 어떤 아시아의 흑곰 제품도 사지 말아야 합니다.

Write

1. Air pollution is _____ of the _____ _____ _____ _____ these days.

2. _____ cars _____ our lives _____, they produce _____ _____ _____ that _____ the air.

3. That is a _____ _____.

4. Here is _____ _____ _____ _____ _____.

5. We can _____ _____ _____ or _____ more.

6. We can also _____ _____ _____ because they _____ _____ _____ _____ _____ very far.

7. _____ _____ _____ _____ these can help.

1. 공해는 요즘 가장 심각한 환경 문제들 중의 하나이다.
2. 비록 자동차가 우리의 생활을 편리하게 하지만, 자동차는 공기를 오염시키는 매연을 많이 만들어낸다.
3. 그것은 커다란 문제이다.
4. 우리가 할 수 있는 일이 있다.
5. 우리는 버스나 지하철을 더 많이 이용할 수 있다.
6. 우리는 또한 현지에서 생산된 상품은 멀리까지 배송될 필요가 없기 때문에 지역의 제품들을 구매할 수 있다.
7. 이런 일들과 같은 간단한 행동들조차 환경에는 도움이 될 수 있다.

※ 다음 우리말을 영어로 쓰시오.

After You Read B

1. A: One More Generation에 가입하는 것이 어때?
   ➡ _____

2. B: 그게 무엇이니?
   ➡ _____

3. A: 그것은 멸종 위기의 동물들을 보호하는 비영리 단체야.
   ➡ _____

4. B: One More Generation이 무슨 뜻이니?
   ➡ _____

5. A: 그 단체는 다음 세대가 그러한 동물들을 볼 수 있기를 원해.
   ➡ _____

6. B: 그것은 멋진 단체구나. 나는 거기에 가입할게.
   ➡ _____

Link Science – Share

1. 아시아흑곰은 가슴에 흰색의 V 모양을 갖고 있습니다.
   ➡ _____

2. 그들은 주로 아시아의 숲에서 삽니다.
   ➡ _____

3. 그들은 사람들이 그들의 신체 부분을 얻으려고 사냥을 하고 숲을 파괴하기 때문에 멸종 위기에 처했습니다.
   ➡ _____

4. 우리는 그들을 위해 여러분이 무엇을 할 수 있는지 말하고자 합니다.
   ➡ _____

5. 첫째, 숲을 보호하기 위해서 종이를 덜 사용하세요.
   ➡ _____

6. 둘째, 어떤 아시아의 흑곰 제품도 사지 말아야 합니다.
   ➡ _____

Write

1. 공해는 요즘 가장 심각한 환경 문제들 중의 하나이다.
   ➡ _____

2. 비록 자동차가 우리의 생활을 편리하게 하지만, 자동차는 공기를 오염시키는 매연을 많이 만들어낸다.
   ➡ _____

3. 그것은 커다란 문제이다.
   ➡ _____

4. 우리가 할 수 있는 일이 있다.
   ➡ _____

5. 우리는 버스나 지하철을 더 많이 이용할 수 있다.
   ➡ _____

6. 우리는 또한 현지에서 생산된 상품은 멀리까지 배송될 필요가 없기 때문에 지역의 제품들을 구매할 수 있다.
   ➡ _____

7. 이런 일들과 같은 간단한 행동들조차 환경에는 도움이 될 수 있다.
   ➡ _____

※ 다음 영어를 우리말로 쓰시오.

01 accept

02 treasure

03 bloom

04 produce

05 borrow

06 mysterious

07 adventure

08 myth

09 dwarf

10 bet

11 golden

12 giant

13 harvest

14 smith

15 undo

16 kingdom

17 moreover

18 poem

19 carriage

20 challenge

21 choose

22 precious

23 enemy

24 prove

25 magical

26 seafood

27 wisdom

28 immediately

29 decision

30 protect

31 spear

32 order

33 control

34 trick

35 be into

36 give up

37 turn into ~

38 come up with ~

39 had better ~

40 in that case

41 be famous for ~

42 fall asleep

43 come along

※ 다음 우리말을 영어로 쓰시오.

01 모험 _____

02 지혜, 슬기, 현명함 _____

03 마차, 객차 _____

04 도전, 결투 신청 _____

05 수확, 추수 _____

06 받아들이다, 수락하다 _____

07 창 _____

08 선택하다 _____

09 시 _____

10 놓치다 _____

11 강력한 _____

12 게다가 _____

13 조절하다 _____

14 결정, 판결 _____

15 난쟁이 _____

16 꽃이 피다 _____

17 결정하다 _____

18 만들어 내다, 제조하다 _____

19 보물 _____

20 마법 같은 _____

21 언짢아하다, 상관하다 _____

22 지키다, 보호하다 _____

23 적, 적군 _____

24 망치 _____

25 즉시, 곧 _____

26 왕국, 왕조 _____

27 거인 _____

28 신비로운 _____

29 신화 _____

30 귀중한, 값어치 있는 _____

31 장난, 묘기 _____

32 원상태로 돌리다 _____

33 증명하다 _____

34 해산물 _____

35 잠들다 _____

36 ~하는 편이 더 낫다 _____

37 ~을 생각해 내다 _____

38 ~ 자신의 _____

39 뿌리를 내리다 _____

40 ~로 유명하다 _____

41 포기하다 _____

42 그렇다면, 그런 경우에는 _____

43 ~로 되다 _____

※ 다음 영영풀이에 알맞은 단어를 <보기>에서 골라 쓴 후, 우리말 뜻을 쓰시오.

1 _____ : to produce flowers: _____

2 _____ : to request food or drinks from a restaurant: _____

3 _____ : a group of valuable things such as gold, silver, jewels, etc.: _____

4 _____ : a creature like a small person with pointed ears, who has magic powers: _____

5 _____ : someone who makes and repairs things made of iron: _____

6 _____ : fish and shellfish that live in the ocean and are used for food: _____

7 _____ : a vehicle with wheels that is pulled by a horse: _____

8 _____ : someone who hates you and wants to harm you: _____

9 _____ : a pole with a sharp pointed blade at one end, used as a weapon in the past: _____

10 _____ : something you do to surprise someone and to make other people laugh: _____

11 _____ : to decide which thing or person you want out of the ones that are available: _____

12 _____ : to risk money on the result of a race, game, competition, or other future event: _____

13 _____ : something new and difficult which requires great effort and determination: _____

14 _____ : a tool with a heavy metal part on a long handle, used for hitting nails into wood: _____

15 _____ : to send something from your hand through the air by moving your hand or arm quickly: _____

16 _____ : the ability to use your experience and knowledge in order to make sensible decisions or judgments: _____

보기			
throw	bet	choose	elf
hammer	trick	smith	order
enemy	spear	seafood	treasure
bloom	carriage	wisdom	challenge

※ 다음 우리말과 일치하도록 빈칸에 알맞은 말을 쓰시오.

Listen & Speak 1 A-1

W: Is _____ your first time _____ _____ Korea, Mike?

M: Yes, it _____. I've _____ _____ _____ _____ Seoul.

W: _____ _____ you come here?

M: I'm really _____ Korean TV shows. I'm _____ _____ _____ _____ the places _____ _____ on TV.

W: _____ fun!

Listen & Speak 1 A-2

B: April is _____ _____ _____ _____ the year.

G: _____ _____ you _____ so?

B: Flowers are _____, but I _____ _____ _____ _____ to study for my exams.

G: Oh, I know _____ _____ _____.

Listen & Speak 2 A-1

G: Dad, do you mind _____ _____ _____ the channel?

M: No, _____ _____ _____.

G: Thank you. I _____ _____ _____ a program _____ Norway.

M: Norway? _____?

G: Well, we're _____ _____ Norway _____ _____.

M: Oh, I _____.

Listen & Speak 2 A-2

M: Jane, do you _____ _____ _____ _____ _____ the window?

W: Sorry, but I _____ _____ _____, and it's _____ _____ today.

M: O.K. No _____. _____ _____ _____ some hot tea? It'd be _____ _____ your cold.

W: That _____ _____ great. Thanks.

W: 한국엔 처음 방문하는 거야, Mike?
M: 응. 나는 언제나 서울에 오고 싶었어.
W: 이곳에 온 이유가 뭐니?
M: 나는 한국의 TV 프로그램들을 정말 좋아해. TV에서 봤던 장소들에 갈 거야.
W: 재미있게 지내!

B: 4월은 1년 중 최악의 달이야.
G: 왜 그렇게 생각해?
B: 꽃은 피는데, 나는 시험 공부를 하느라 집에 있어야 해.
G: 오, 무슨 소린지 알겠어.

G: 아빠, 제가 채널을 돌려도 될까요?
M: 물론이지.
G: 고마워요. 노르웨이에 대한 프로그램을 봐야 해서요.
M: 노르웨이? 왜?
G: 그게, 수업 시간에 노르웨이에 대해 배우고 있거든요.
M: 오, 그렇구나.

M: Jane, 내가 창문을 열어도 되겠니?
W: 미안, 내가 감기에 걸려서, 그리고 오늘 바람이 꽤 많이 불거든.
M: 그래. 괜찮아. 따뜻한 차 좀 줄까? 감기에 도움이 될 거야.
W: 그거 좋겠다. 고마워.

Communicate A

Jaden: Hi, Yuri, What're you _____?

Yuri: Hi, Jaden. I'm _____ a book _____ Norse myths. I'm really _____ _____ _____ _____.

Jaden: _____ makes you _____ _____ so much?

Yuri: The stories are very _____, and there are _____ _____ movies about Norse myths.

Jaden: Are they _____ _____?

Yuri: Yes. There's actually a new movie _____ Thor, a _____ _____ in Norse myths.

Jaden: Oh, I know him. He's my _____ online game _____.

Yuri: _____ _____ _____, we should _____ _____ the movie _____.

Jaden: Do you mind _____ _____ _____ your book when you're _____? I want to read _____ _____ we see the movie.

Yuri: No, not _____ _____. I'm sure you'll _____ _____ _____, _____.

Jaden: 안녕, 유리야. 뭐 하고 있니?

유리: 안녕, Jaden. 난 북유럽 신화들에 관한 책을 읽고 있어. 요즘 이 신화들에 정말 푹 빠졌어.

Jaden: 네가 그것들을 그렇게 좋아하게 만드는 게 뭐니?

유리: 이야기들이 정말 흥미롭고, 북유럽 신화에 대한 영화들도 많이 있거든.

Jaden: 영화들이 좀 괜찮니?

유리: 응. 사실 북유럽 신화에서 유명한 신인 Thor에 관한 새 영화가 나왔어.

Jaden: 오, 그를 알아. 그는 내가 제일 좋아하는 온라인 게임 캐릭터야.

유리: 그렇다면, 우린 같이 그 영화를 보러 가야겠다.

Jaden: 네가 네 책을 다 읽으면 내가 빌려도 될까? 우리가 그 영화를 보기 전에 그걸 읽고 싶어.

유리: 그럼, 당연하지. 너도 이 책을 좋아할 것이라고 확신해.

Progress Check 1

B: April is the best month _____ _____ _____.

G: What _____ you _____ so?

B: The weather is not _____, and _____ _____.

G: I love April _____ my birthday is _____ _____.

B: Really? We should _____ you _____.

B: 4월은 1년 중 최고의 달이야.

G: 왜 그렇게 생각해?

B: 날씨도 춥지 않고, 꽃도 피어나잖아.

G: 나는 내 생일이 4월에 있어서 4월을 아주 좋아해.

B: 정말? 우리 너를 위해 파티를 열어야겠다.

Progress Check 2

M: Excuse me, do you _____ _____ _____ this chair? We need one _____.

W: I'm sorry, but I'm _____ _____ my friend. She'll be here _____.

M: Oh, I see. _____ _____.

W: You can _____ the waiter _____ _____ more chairs.

M: 실례합니다, 제가 이 의자를 가져가도 괜찮을까요? 하나가 더 필요해서요.

W: 죄송합니다만, 제 친구를 기다리고 있어서요. 곧 올 거예요.

M: 오, 그렇군요. 신경 쓰지 마세요.

W: 웨이터에게 의자를 더 가져다 달라고 부탁해 보세요.

※ 다음 우리말에 맞도록 대화를 영어로 쓰시오.

Listen & Speak 1 A-1

W: _____

M: _____

W: _____

M: _____

W: _____

W: 한국엔 처음 방문하는 거야, Mike?
M: 응. 나는 언제나 서울에 오고 싶었어.
W: 이곳에 온 이유가 뭐니?
M: 나는 한국의 TV 프로그램들을 정말 좋아해. TV에서 봤던 장소들에 갈 거야.
W: 재미있게 지내!

Listen & Speak 1 A-2

B: _____

G: _____

B: _____

G: _____

B: 4월은 1년 중 최악의 달이야.
G: 왜 그렇게 생각해?
B: 꽃은 피는데, 나는 시험 공부를 하느라 집에 있어야 해.
G: 오, 무슨 소린지 알겠어.

Listen & Speak 2 A-1

G: _____

M: _____

G: _____

M: _____

G: _____

M: _____

G: 아빠, 제가 채널을 돌려도 될까요?
M: 물론이지.
G: 고마워요. 노르웨이에 대한 프로그램을 봐야 해서요.
M: 노르웨이? 왜?
G: 그게, 수업 시간에 노르웨이에 대해 배우고 있거든요.
M: 오, 그렇구나.

Listen & Speak 2 A-2

M: _____

W: _____

M: _____

W: _____

M: Jane, 내가 창문을 열어도 되겠니?
W: 미안, 내가 감기에 걸려서, 그리고 오늘 바람이 꽤 많이 불거든.
M: 그래. 괜찮아. 따뜻한 차 좀 줄까? 감기에 도움이 될 거야.
W: 그거 좋겠다. 고마워.

Communicate A

Jaden: _____

Yuri: _____

Jaden: _____

Yuri: _____

_____

Jaden: _____

Yuri: _____

Jaden: _____

Yuri: _____

Jaden: _____

_____

Yuri: _____

Jaden: 안녕, 유리야. 뭐 하고 있니?

유리: 안녕, Jaden. 난 북유럽 신화들에 관한 책을 읽고 있어. 요즘 이 신화들에 정말 푹 빠졌어.

Jaden: 네가 그것들을 그렇게 좋아하게 만드는 게 뭐니?

유리: 이야기들이 정말 흥미롭고, 북유럽 신화에 대한 영화들도 많이 있거든.

Jaden: 영화들이 좀 괜찮니?

유리: 응. 사실 북유럽 신화에서 유명한 신인 Thor에 관한 새 영화가 나왔어.

Jaden: 오, 그를 알아. 그는 내가 제일 좋아하는 온라인 게임 캐릭터야.

유리: 그렇다면, 우린 같이 그 영화를 보러 가야겠다.

Jaden: 네가 네 책을 다 읽으면 내가 빌려도 될까? 우리가 그 영화를 보기 전에 그걸 읽고 싶어.

유리: 그럼, 당연하지. 너도 이 책을 좋아할 것이라고 확신해.

Progress Check 1

B: _____

G: _____

B: _____

G: _____

B: _____

B: 4월은 1년 중 최고의 달이야.

G: 왜 그렇게 생각해?

B: 날씨도 춥지 않고, 꽃도 피어나잖아.

G: 나는 내 생일이 4월에 있어서 4월을 아주 좋아해.

B: 정말? 우리 너를 위해 파티를 열어야겠다.

Progress Check 2

M: _____

W: _____

M: _____

W: _____

M: 실례합니다, 제가 이 의자를 가져가도 괜찮을까요? 하나가 더 필요해서요.

W: 죄송합니다만, 제 친구를 기다리고 있어서요. 곧 올 거예요.

M: 오, 그렇군요. 신경 쓰지 마세요.

W: 웨이터에게 의자를 더 가져다 달라고 부탁해 보세요.

※ 다음 우리말과 일치하도록 빈칸에 알맞은 것을 골라 쓰시오.

1 _____ **for** _____ _____
A. Gods   B. Three   C. Treasures

2 _____ _____ **Gods**
A. Norse   B. Important

3 Odin, who is the _____ god, _____ _____ his eye for _____.
A. wisdom   B. gave   C. highest   D. up

4 Thor is Odin's son and _____ _____ _____ of all.
A. strongest   B. the   C. god

5 Frey, who is the _____ of the _____, _____ the _____.
A. controls   B. harvest   C. weather   D. god

6 Loki is a god who _____ _____ _____ _____.
A. tricks   B. on   C. others   D. plays

7 Thor _____ and knew immediately _____ was _____.
A. something   B. wrong   C. woke

8 His _____ beautiful golden hair _____ _____.
A. gone   B. was   C. wife's

9 He knew only Loki could do _____ _____ _____ _____.
A. a   B. thing   C. such   D. terrible

10 Thor soon _____ Loki, _____ _____ _____ at home.
A. was   B. found   C. drinking   D. who

11 "You'd _____ _____ _____ you did, or you'll be sorry," Thor said _____ to Loki.
A. undo   B. angrily   C. better   D. what

12 Loki _____ _____.
A. scared   B. was

13 He _____ that he _____ _____ golden hair for Thor's _____.
A. get   B. promised   C. wife   D. would

14 Loki knew _____ the _____ of Ivaldi could make _____ _____ hair.
A. fine   B. only   C. sons   D. golden

15 He went to them and said, "I _____ Brokk and his brother are the _____ _____. Is that _____?"
A. smiths   B. heard   C. finest   D. true

16 "No, _____ _____ we _____ are the finest smiths," the sons of Ivaldi _____.
A. who   B. replied   C. is   D. it

---

1 세 명의 신을 위한 보물

2 북유럽 신화의 주요 신들

3 Odin은 가장 높은 신이며, 지혜를 위해 한쪽 눈을 포기했다.

4 Thor는 Odin의 아들이며 모든 신들 중에서 가장 강한 신이다.

5 Frey는 수확의 신으로 날씨를 다스린다.

6 Loki는 다른 신들에게 농간을 부리는 신이다.

7 Thor는 잠에서 깨어 즉시 무엇인가가 잘못되었다는 것을 알았다.

8 그의 아내의 아름다운 금발머리가 사라졌다.

9 그는 오직 Loki만이 이런 끔찍한 일을 할 수 있다는 것을 알고 있었다.

10 Thor는 곧 Loki를 찾았는데, 그는 집에서 술을 마시고 있었다.

11 "네가 한 짓을 되돌려 놓는 것이 좋을 거야. 그렇지 않으면 후회하게 될 거야." Thor는 노하여 Loki에게 말했다.

12 Loki는 겁이 났다.

13 그는 Thor의 아내를 위해 금발머리를 얻어 오겠다고 약속했다.

14 Loki는 Ivaldi의 아들들만이 훌륭한 금발머리를 만들 수 있다는 것을 알고 있었다.

15 그는 그들에게 가서 "내가 듣기로 Brokk와 그의 남동생이 가장 훌륭한 대장장이라고 하던데. 그것이 사실인가?"라고 말했다.

16 "아니요, 가장 훌륭한 대장장이는 바로 우리들이요." Ivaldi의 아들들이 대답했다.

17 "They're _____ _____ _____ for Odin, Thor, and Frey," said Loki.

A. treasures   B. making   C. three

18 "Do you think you can _____ _____ _____ _____ theirs?"

A. treasures   B. than   C. make   D. better

19 "_____ _____ we can," they _____.

A. answered   B. course   C. of

20 "O.K., then you _____ also _____ three _____ them," said Loki.

A. for   B. make   C. should   D. treasures

21 "The gods will _____ the best _____."

A. treasure   B. on   C. decide

22 Loki also told them that _____ of the treasures _____ _____ golden hair.

A. be   B. one   C. to   D. had

23 They went _____ _____ _____.

A. immediately   B. to   C. work

24 Loki then _____ _____ _____ Brokk and his brother.

A. to   B. went   C. see

25 "Ivaldi's sons _____ _____ three treasures _____ Odin, Thor, and Frey," _____ Loki.

A. for   B. making   C. said   D. are

26 "I _____ that you can never make treasures _____ _____ theirs."

A. as   B. bet   C. fine   D. as

27 Brokk _____ angry and _____ the _____.

A. accepted   B. became   C. challenge

28 He and his brother _____ three treasures _____.

A. of   B. produced   C. own   D. their

29 Loki went to see the three gods _____ _____.

A. all   B. treasures   C. the   D. with

30 Brokk _____ _____.

A. along   B. came

31 Loki _____ them the _____ _____ Ivaldi's _____.

A. from   B. treasures   C. showed   D. sons

32 The first treasure was _____ Odin, who had _____ _____.

A. one   B. for   C. eye   D. only

33 It was a _____ that never _____ its _____.

A. missed   B. spear   C. target

17 "그들은 Odin과 Thor와 Frey를 위해서 보물을 만들고 있네." Loki는 말했다.

18 "너희들이 그들의 보물보다 더 나은 보물을 만들 수 있다고 생각하는가?"

19 "물론 할 수 있소." 그들이 대답했다.

20 "좋아. 그러면 너희도 그들을 위해 세 개의 보물을 만들어야 한다." Loki가 말했다.

21 "그 신들이 가장 훌륭한 보물을 결정할 것이다."

22 Loki는 또한 그들에게 보물 중 하나는 금발머리이어야 한다고 말했다.

23 그들은 즉시 일에 착수했다.

24 Loki는 그 다음에 Brokk와 그의 남동생을 보러 갔다.

25 "Ivaldi의 아들들이 Odin과 Thor, 그리고 Frey를 위해 세 개의 보물을 만들고 있어." Loki가 말했다.

26 "너희들은 절대 그들의 보물만큼 훌륭한 보물을 만들 수 없다는 것을 내 장담하지."

27 Brokk는 화가 나서 그 도전을 받아들였다.

28 그와 그의 남동생은 그들만의 세 가지 보물을 만들었다.

29 Loki는 모든 보물을 가지고 세 신을 만나러 갔다.

30 Brokk가 같이 갔다.

31 Loki는 그들에게 Ivaldi의 아들들이 만든 보물들을 보여 주었다.

32 첫 번째 보물은 Odin을 위한 것으로, 그는 눈이 한쪽밖에 없었다.

33 그것은 목표물을 절대로 빗나가지 않는 창이었다.

34 The second treasure was a big ship that could _____ _____ a _____ of _____.

    A. into   B. cloth   C. piece   D. turn

35 It _____ _____ Frey.

    A. for   B. was

36 The _____ _____ was _____ Thor.

    A. treasure   B. for   C. third

37 Loki _____ Thor the _____ _____ _____ for his wife.

    A. golden   B. showed   C. hair   D. flowing

38 Thor _____ the hair _____ his wife's head, and it _____ _____ and became real hair.

    A. root   B. on   C. put   D. took

39 It was now Brokk's _____ to _____ the gods his _____.

    A. show   B. turn   C. gifts

40 He gave Odin a gold arm ring that produced _____ _____ gold rings _____ _____ night.

    A. more   B. ninth   C. eight   D. every

41 Brokk then _____ _____ a _____.

    A. pig   B. gave   C. Frey

42 It could _____ his _____ _____ than _____ horse.

    A. carriage   B. pull   C. any   D. faster

43 "_____ _____ _____ is for you, Thor," said Brokk.

    A. treasure   B. third   C. my

44 "This is the _____ Mjolnir, _____ you'll _____.

    A. love   B. hammer   C. which

45 If you _____ it, it'll always _____ to you.

    A. back   B. throw   C. come

46 _____, _____ can ever _____ it."

    A. break   B. nothing   C. moreover

47 It was an easy _____ to _____ the _____ _____.

    A. choose   B. decision   C. treasure   D. greatest

48 _____ was Mjolnir that the three _____ _____ _____.

    A. most   B. gods   C. it   D. liked

49 They _____ the hammer would _____ the gods _____ their _____.

    A. protect   B. enemies   C. from   D. thought

50 "Brokk and his brother," said Odin, "are _____ _____ _____."

    A. smiths   B. better   C. the

51 Brokk _____ that Loki was _____, and the three gods now had _____ _____.

    A. wrong   B. treasures   C. proved   D. precious

---

34 두 번째 보물은 천 조각으로 변할 수 있는 큰 배였다.

35 그것은 Frey를 위한 것이었다.

36 세 번째 보물은 Thor를 위한 것이었다.

37 Loki는 Thor에게 그의 아내를 위한 매끈하게 늘어진 금발머리를 보여 주었다.

38 Thor가 그 머리카락을 그의 아내의 머리에 얹었더니 그것이 뿌리를 내려서 진짜 머리카락이 되었다.

39 이제 Brokk가 신들에게 그의 선물들을 보여 줄 차례였다.

40 그는 Odin에게 아홉 번째 밤이 될 때마다 8개의 금팔찌를 더 만들어 내는 금팔찌를 주었다.

41 그리고 나서 Brokk는 Frey에게 돼지를 한 마리 주었다.

42 그것은 어떤 말보다도 그의 마차를 더 빨리 끌 수 있었다.

43 "나의 세 번째 보물은 당신을 위한 것입니다. Thor." Brokk가 말했다.

44 "이것은 묠니르라는 망치인데 당신은 마음에 드실 겁니다.

45 그것을 던지면, 그것은 항상 당신에게 되돌아 올 것입니다.

46 게다가, 그 무엇도 이것을 부술 수 없지요."

47 가장 훌륭한 보물을 선택하는 것은 쉬운 결정이었다.

48 세 명의 신들이 가장 마음에 든 것은 묠니르였다.

49 그들은 그 망치가 신들을 그들의 적들로부터 보호해 줄 것이라고 생각했다.

50 "Brokk와 그의 남동생이 더 훌륭한 대장장이다." Odin이 말했다.

51 Brokk는 Loki가 틀렸다는 것을 증명해 냈고, 세 신들은 이제 소중한 보물을 가지게 되었다.

Step2

※ 다음 우리말과 일치하도록 빈칸에 알맞은 말을 쓰시오.

1 _____ for Three _____

2 _____ _____ **Gods**

3 Odin, who is the _____ god, _____ _____ his eye for wisdom.

4 Thor is Odin's son and _____ _____ _____ all.

5 Frey, who is the god of the _____, _____ _____ _____.

6 Loki is a god who _____ _____ _____ others.

7 Thor woke and knew immediately _____ _____ _____.

8 His wife's beautiful _____ hair _____ _____.

9 He knew only Loki could do _____ _____ _____.

10 Thor soon _____ Loki, _____ _____ _____ at home.

11 "_____ _____ _____ what you did, or you'll be sorry," Thor said _____ to Loki.

12 Loki was _____.

13 He _____ that he _____ _____ golden hair for Thor's wife.

14 Loki knew only the sons of Ivaldi could make _____ _____ _____.

15 He went to them and said, "I heard Brokk and his brother are _____ _____ _____. Is that _____?"

16 "No, _____ _____ we _____ are the finest smiths," the sons of Ivaldi _____.

1 세 명의 신을 위한 보물

2 북유럽 신화의 주요 신들

3 Odin은 가장 높은 신이며, 지혜를 위해 한쪽 눈을 포기했다.

4 Thor는 Odin의 아들이며 모든 신들 중에서 가장 강한 신이다.

5 Frey는 수확의 신으로 날씨를 다스린다.

6 Loki는 다른 신들에게 농간을 부리는 신이다.

7 Thor는 잠에서 깨어 즉시 무엇인가가 잘못되었다는 것을 알았다.

8 그의 아내의 아름다운 금발머리가 사라졌다.

9 그는 오직 Loki만이 이런 끔찍한 일을 할 수 있다는 것을 알고 있었다.

10 Thor는 곧 Loki를 찾았는데, 그는 집에서 술을 마시고 있었다.

11 "네가 한 짓을 되돌려 놓는 것이 좋을 거야. 그렇지 않으면 후회하게 될 거다." Thor는 노하여 Loki에게 말했다.

12 Loki는 겁이 났다.

13 그는 Thor의 아내를 위해 금발머리를 얻어 오겠다고 약속했다.

14 Loki는 Ivaldi의 아들들만이 훌륭한 금발머리를 만들 수 있다는 것을 알고 있었다.

15 그는 그들에게 가서 "내가 듣기로 Brokk와 그의 남동생이 가장 훌륭한 대장장이라고 하던데. 그것이 사실인가?"라고 말했다.

16 "아니요. 가장 훌륭한 대장장이는 바로 우리들이요." Ivaldi의 아들들이 대답했다.

17 "They're making _____ _____ for Odin, Thor, and Frey," said Loki.

18 "Do you think you can make _____ _____ _____ _____?"

19 "_____ _____ we can," they _____.

20 "O.K., then you should also _____ three treasures _____ _____," said Loki.

21 "The gods will _____ _____ the _____ _____."

22 Loki also told them that _____ _____ the treasures _____ _____ _____ golden hair.

23 They went _____ _____ _____.

24 Loki then _____ _____ _____ Brokk and his brother.

25 "Ivaldi's sons _____ _____ three treasures _____ Odin, Thor, and Frey," said Loki.

26 "_____ _____ that you can never make treasures _____ _____ _____ _____."

27 Brokk became _____ and _____ _____ _____.

28 He and his brother produced three treasures _____ _____ _____.

29 Loki went to see the three gods _____ _____ _____ _____.

30 Brokk _____ _____.

31 Loki _____ them the treasures _____ Ivaldi's sons.

32 The first treasure was _____ Odin, who had _____ _____ _____.

33 _____ _____ a spear _____ never _____ its target.

17 "그들은 Odin과 Thor와 Frey를 위해서 보물을 만들고 있네." Loki는 말했다.

18 "너희들이 그들의 보물보다 더 나은 보물을 만들 수 있다고 생각하는가?"

19 "물론 할 수 있소." 그들이 대답했다.

20 "좋아, 그러면 너희도 그들을 위해 세 개의 보물을 만들어야 한다." Loki가 말했다.

21 "그 신들이 가장 훌륭한 보물을 결정할 것이다."

22 Loki는 또한 그들에게 보물 중 하나는 금발머리이어야 한다고 말했다.

23 그들은 즉시 일에 착수했다.

24 Loki는 그 다음에 Brokk와 그의 남동생을 보러 갔다.

25 "Ivaldi의 아들들이 Odin과 Thor, 그리고 Frey를 위해 세 개의 보물을 만들고 있어." Loki가 말했다.

26 "너희들은 절대 그들의 보물만큼 훌륭한 보물을 만들 수 없다는 것을 내 장담하지."

27 Brokk는 화가 나서 그 도전을 받아들였다.

28 그와 그의 남동생은 그들만의 세 가지 보물을 만들었다.

29 Loki는 모든 보물을 가지고 세 신을 만나러 갔다.

30 Brokk가 같이 갔다.

31 Loki는 그들에게 Ivaldi의 아들들이 만든 보물들을 보여 주었다.

32 첫 번째 보물은 Odin을 위한 것으로, 그는 눈이 한쪽밖에 없었다.

33 그것은 목표물을 절대로 빗나가지 않는 창이었다.

34 The second treasure was a big ship that could _____ _____ a _____ _____ _____.

35 It was _____ Frey.

36 _____ _____ _____ was for Thor.

37 Loki showed Thor the _____ _____ _____ for his wife.

38 Thor _____ the hair _____ his wife's head, and it _____ _____ and _____ _____ _____.

39 It was now _____ _____ to show the gods his _____.

40 He gave Odin a gold arm ring that produced _____ _____ gold rings _____ _____ _____.

41 Brokk then gave _____ _____ _____.

42 It could pull his carriage _____ _____ _____ _____.

43 "_____ _____ _____ is for you, Thor," said Brokk.

44 "This is the _____ Mjolnir, _____ you'll love.

45 If you throw it, it'll always _____ _____ _____ you.

46 _____, nothing can ever _____ _____."

47 It was an easy decision to choose _____ _____ _____.

48 It was Mjolnir that _____ _____ _____ _____ _____ _____.

49 They thought the hammer would _____ the gods _____ their _____.

50 "Brokk and his brother," said Odin, "are _____ _____."

51 Brokk _____ that Loki was _____, and the three gods now had _____ _____.

---

34 두 번째 보물은 천 조각으로 변할 수 있는 큰 배였다.

35 그것은 Frey를 위한 것이었다.

36 세 번째 보물은 Thor를 위한 것이었다.

37 Loki는 Thor에게 그의 아내를 위한 매끈하게 늘어진 금발머리를 보여 주었다.

38 Thor가 그 머리카락을 그의 아내의 머리에 얹었더니 그것이 뿌리를 내려서 진짜 머리카락이 되었다.

39 이제 Brokk가 신들에게 그의 선물들을 보여 줄 차례였다.

40 그는 Odin에게 아홉 번째 밤이 될 때마다 8개의 금팔찌를 더 만들어 내는 금팔찌를 주었다.

41 그러고 나서 Brokk는 Frey에게 돼지를 한 마리 주었다.

42 그것은 어떤 말보다도 그의 마차를 더 빨리 끌 수 있었다.

43 "나의 세 번째 보물은 당신을 위한 것입니다, Thor." Brokk가 말했다.

44 "이것은 몰니르라는 망치인데 당신은 마음에 드실 겁니다.

45 그것을 던지면, 그것은 항상 당신에게 되돌아 올 것입니다.

46 게다가, 그 무엇도 이것을 부술 수 없지요."

47 가장 훌륭한 보물을 선택하는 것은 쉬운 결정이었다.

48 세 명의 신들이 가장 마음에 든 것은 몰니르였다.

49 그들은 그 망치가 신들을 그들의 적들로부터 보호해 줄 것이라고 생각했다.

50 "Brokk와 그의 남동생이 더 훌륭한 대장장이다." Odin이 말했다.

51 Brokk는 Loki가 틀렸다는 것을 증명해 냈고, 세 신들은 이제 소중한 보물을 가지게 되었다.

※ 다음 문장을 우리말로 쓰시오.

1 ▶ Treasures for Three Gods

➡ _____

2 ▶ Important Norse Gods

➡ _____

3 ▶ Odin, who is the highest god, gave up his eye for wisdom.

➡ _____

4 ▶ Thor is Odin's son and the strongest god of all.

➡ _____

5 ▶ Frey, who is the god of the harvest, controls the weather.

➡ _____

6 ▶ Loki is a god who plays tricks on others.

➡ _____

7 ▶ Thor woke and knew immediately something was wrong.

➡ _____

8 ▶ His wife's beautiful golden hair was gone.

➡ _____

9 ▶ He knew only Loki could do such a terrible thing.

➡ _____

10 ▶ Thor soon found Loki, who was drinking at home.

➡ _____

11 ▶ "You'd better undo what you did, or you'll be sorry," Thor said angrily to Loki.

➡ _____

12 ▶ Loki was scared.

➡ _____

13 ▶ He promised that he would get golden hair for Thor's wife.

➡ _____

14 ▶ Loki knew only the sons of Ivaldi could make fine golden hair.

➡ _____

15 ▶ He went to them and said, "I heard Brokk and his brother are the finest smiths. Is that true?"

➡ _____

_____

16 ▶ "No, it is we who are the finest smiths," the sons of Ivaldi replied.

➡ _____

17 "They're making three treasures for Odin, Thor, and Frey," said Loki.

➡ _____

18 "Do you think you can make treasures better than theirs?"

➡ _____

19 "Of course we can," they answered.

➡ _____

20 "O.K., then you should also make three treasures for them," said Loki.

➡ _____

21 "The gods will decide on the best treasure."

➡ _____

22 Loki also told them that one of the treasures had to be golden hair.

➡ _____

23 They went to work immediately.

➡ _____

24 Loki then went to see Brokk and his brother.

➡ _____

25 "Ivaldi's sons are making three treasures for Odin, Thor, and Frey," said Loki.

➡ _____

26 "I bet that you can never make treasures as fine as theirs."

➡ _____

27 Brokk became angry and accepted the challenge.

➡ _____

28 He and his brother produced three treasures of their own.

➡ _____

29 Loki went to see the three gods with all the treasures.

➡ _____

30 Brokk came along.

➡ _____

31 Loki showed them the treasures from Ivaldi's sons.

➡ _____

32 The first treasure was for Odin, who had only one eye.

➡ _____

33 It was a spear that never missed its target.

➡ _____

34 The second treasure was a big ship that could turn into a piece of cloth.

➡ _____

35 It was for Frey.

➡ _____

36 The third treasure was for Thor.

➡ _____

37 Loki showed Thor the flowing golden hair for his wife.

➡ _____

38 Thor put the hair on his wife's head, and it took root and became real hair.

➡ _____

39 It was now Brokk's turn to show the gods his gifts.

➡ _____

40 He gave Odin a gold arm ring that produced eight more gold rings every ninth night.

➡ _____

41 Brokk then gave Frey a pig.

➡ _____

42 It could pull his carriage faster than any horse.

➡ _____

43 "My third treasure is for you, Thor," said Brokk.

➡ _____

44 "This is the hammer Mjolnir, which you'll love.

➡ _____

45 If you throw it, it'll always come back to you.

➡ _____

46 Moreover, nothing can ever break it."

➡ _____

47 It was an easy decision to choose the greatest treasure.

➡ _____

48 It was Mjolnir that the three gods liked most.

➡ _____

49 They thought the hammer would protect the gods from their enemies.

➡ _____

50 "Brokk and his brother," said Odin, "are the better smiths."

➡ _____

51 Brokk proved that Loki was wrong, and the three gods now had precious treasures.

➡ _____

※ 다음 괄호 안의 단어들을 우리말에 맞도록 바르게 배열하시오.

1 (for / Treasures / Gods / Three)
➡ _____

2 (Norse / Important / Gods)
➡ _____

3 (who / Odin, / the / is / god, / highest / up / gave / for / eye / his / wisdom.)
➡ _____

4 (is / Thor / son / Odin's / the / and / god / strongest / all. / of)
➡ _____

5 (who / Frey, / the / is / of / god / harvest, / the / the / weather. / controls)
➡ _____

6 (is / Loki / god / a / plays / who / on / others. / tricks)
➡ _____

7 (woke / Thor / knew / and / something / immediately / wrong. / was)
➡ _____

8 (wife's / his / golden / beautiful / hair / gone. / was)
➡ _____

9 (knew / he / Loki / only / do / could / a / such / thing. / terrible)
➡ _____

10 (soon / Thor / Loki, / found / was / who / at / drinking / home.)
➡ _____

11 (better / "you'd / what / undo / did, / you / or / be / you'll / sorry," / said / Thor / to / angrily / Loki.)
➡ _____

12 (was / Loki / scared.)
➡ _____

13 (promised / he / that / would / he / golden / get / for / hair / wife. / Thor's)
➡ _____

14 (knew / Loki / the / only / of / sons / Ivaldi / make / could / golden / hair. / fine)
➡ _____

15 (went / he / them / to / said, / and / heard / "I / and / Brokk / brother / his / the / are / smiths. / finest // that / true? / is)
➡ _____
_____

16 ("no, / is / it / who / we / the / are / smiths," / finest / the / of / sons / repiled. / Ivaldi)
➡ _____

1 세 명의 신을 위한 보물

2 북유럽 신화의 주요 신들

3 Odin은 가장 높은 신이며, 지혜를 위해 한쪽 눈을 포기했다.

4 Thor는 Odin의 아들이며 모든 신들 중에서 가장 강한 신이다.

5 Frey는 수확의 신으로 날씨를 다스린다.

6 Loki는 다른 신들에게 농간을 부리는 신이다.

7 Thor는 잠에서 깨어 즉시 무엇인가가 잘못되었다는 것을 알았다.

8 그의 아내의 아름다운 금발머리가 사라졌다.

9 그는 오직 Loki만이 이런 끔찍한 일을 할 수 있다는 것을 알고 있었다.

10 Thor는 곧 Loki를 찾았는데, 그는 집에서 술을 마시고 있었다.

11 "네가 한 짓을 되돌려 놓는 것이 좋을 거야. 그렇지 않으면 후회하게 될 거다." Thor는 노하여 Loki에게 말했다.

12 Loki는 겁이 났다.

13 그는 Thor의 아내를 위해 금발머리를 얻어 오겠다고 약속했다.

14 Loki는 Ivaldi의 아들들만이 훌륭한 금발머리를 만들 수 있다는 것을 알고 있었다.

15 그는 그들에게 가서 "내가 듣기로 Brokk와 그의 남동생이 가장 훌륭한 대장장이라고 하던데. 그것이 사실인가?"라고 말했다.

16 "아니요. 가장 훌륭한 대장장이는 바로 우리들이요." Ivaldi의 아들들이 대답했다.

17 (making / "they're / treasures / three / Odin, / for / and / Thor, / Frey," / Loki. / said)

➡ _____

18 (you / "do / you / think / make / can / better / treasures / than / theirs?")

➡ _____

19 (course / "of / can," / we / answered. / they)

➡ _____

20 ("O.K., / you / then / also / should / three / make / them," / for / treasures / Loki. / said)

➡ _____

21 ("the / will / gods / on / decide / best / the / treasure.")

➡ _____

22 (also / Loki / them / told / one / that / the / of / had / treasures / be / to / hair. / golden)

➡ _____

23 (went / they / work / to / immediately.)

➡ _____

24 (then / Loki / to / went / Brokk / see / his / and / brother.)

➡ _____

25 (sons / Ivaldi's / are / three / making / for / treasures / Odin, / and / Thor, / Frey," / Loki. / said)

➡ _____

26 (bet / "I / you / that / never / can / treasures / make / fine / as / theirs." / as)

➡ _____

27 (became / Brokk / and / accepted / angry / challenge. / the)

➡ _____

28 (his / and / he / brother / three / produced / of / treasures / own. / their)

➡ _____

29 (went / Loki / see / to / the / gods / three / all / with / treasures. / the)

➡ _____

30 (came / Brokk / along.)

➡ _____

31 (showed / Loki / the / them / treasures / Ivaldi's / from / sons.)

➡ _____

32 (first / the / was / treasure / Odin, / for / had / who / one / eye. / only)

➡ _____

33 (was / it / spear / a / never / that / its / missed / target.)

➡ _____

17 "그들은 Odin과 Thor와 Frey를 위해서 보물을 만들고 있네." Loki는 말했다.

18 "너희들이 그들의 보물보다 더 나은 보물을 만들 수 있다고 생각하는가?"

19 "물론 할 수 있소." 그들이 대답했다.

20 "좋아, 그러면 너희도 그들을 위해 세 개의 보물을 만들어야 한다." Loki가 말했다.

21 "그 신들이 가장 훌륭한 보물을 결정할 것이다."

22 Loki는 또한 그들에게 보물 중 하나는 금발머리이어야 한다고 말했다.

23 그들은 즉시 일에 착수했다.

24 Loki는 그 다음에 Brokk와 그의 남동생을 보러 갔다.

25 "Ivaldi의 아들들이 Odin과 Thor, 그리고 Frey를 위해 세 개의 보물을 만들고 있어." Loki가 말했다.

26 "너희들은 절대 그들의 보물만큼 훌륭한 보물을 만들 수 없다는 것을 내 장담하지."

27 Brokk는 화가 나서 그 도전을 받아들였다.

28 그와 그의 남동생은 그들만의 세 가지 보물을 만들었다.

29 Loki는 모든 보물을 가지고 세 신을 만나러 갔다.

30 Brokk가 같이 갔다.

31 Loki는 그들에게 Ivaldi의 아들들이 만든 보물들을 보여 주었다.

32 첫 번째 보물은 Odin을 위한 것으로, 그는 눈이 한쪽밖에 없었다.

33 그것은 목표물을 절대로 빗나가지 않는 창이었다.

34 (second / the / was / treasure / a / ship / big / could / that / into / turn / piece / a / cloth. / of)

➡ _____

35 (was / it / Frey. / for)

➡ _____

36 (third / the / was / treasure / Thor. / for)

➡ _____

37 (showed / Loki / the / Thor / golden / flowing / for / hair / wife. / his)

➡ _____

38 (put / Thor / hair / the / his / on / head, / wife's / and / took / it / and / root / real / became / hair.)

➡ _____

39 (was / it / Brokk's / now / to / turn / show / gods / the / gifts. / his)

➡ _____

40 (gave / he / a / Odin / gold / ring / arm / produced / that / eight / gold / more / every / rings / night. / ninth)

➡ _____

41 (then / Brokk / Frey / gave / pig. / a)

➡ _____

42 (could / it / his / pull / faster / carriage / than / horse. / any)

➡ _____

43 (third / "my / is / treasure / for / you, / said / Brokk. / Thor,")

➡ _____

44 (is / "this / hammer / the / which / Mjolnir, / love. / you'll)

➡ _____

45 (you / if / it, / throw / always / it'll / back / come / you. / to)

➡ _____

46 (nothing / moreover, / ever / can / it." / break)

➡ _____

47 (was / it / easy / to / an / decision / choose / greatest / the / treasure.)

➡ _____

48 (was / it / that / Mjolnir / three / the / gods / most. / liked)

➡ _____

49 (thought / they / hammer / the / protect / would / gods / the / their / from / enemies.)

➡ _____

50 (and / "Brokk / brother," / his / Odin, / said / the / "are / smiths." / better)

➡ _____

51 (proved / Brokk / Loki / that / wrong, / was / the / and / gods / three / had / now / treasures. / precious)

➡ _____
_____

---

34 두 번째 보물은 천 조각으로 변할 수 있는 큰 배였다.

35 그것은 Frey를 위한 것이었다.

36 세 번째 보물은 Thor를 위한 것이었다.

37 Loki는 Thor에게 그의 아내를 위한 매끈하게 늘어진 금발머리를 보여 주었다.

38 Thor가 그 머리카락을 그의 아내의 머리에 얹었더니 그것이 뿌리를 내려서 진짜 머리카락이 되었다.

39 이제 Brokk가 신들에게 그의 선물들을 보여 줄 차례였다.

40 그는 Odin에게 아홉 번째 밤이 될 때마다 8개의 금팔찌를 더 만들어 내는 금팔찌를 주었다.

41 그러고 나서 Brokk는 Frey에게 돼지를 한 마리 주었다.

42 그것은 어떤 말보다도 그의 마차를 더 빨리 끌 수 있었다.

43 "나의 세 번째 보물은 당신을 위한 것입니다. Thor." Brokk가 말했다.

44 "이것은 묠니르라는 망치인데 당신은 마음에 드실 겁니다.

45 그것을 던지면, 그것은 항상 당신에게 되돌아 올 것입니다.

46 게다가, 그 무엇도 이것을 부술 수 없지요."

47 가장 훌륭한 보물을 선택하는 것은 쉬운 결정이었다.

48 세 명의 신들이 가장 마음에 든 것은 묠니르였다.

49 그들은 그 망치가 신들을 그들의 적들로부터 보호해 줄 것이라고 생각했다.

50 "Brokk와 그의 남동생이 더 훌륭한 대장장이다." Odin이 말했다.

51 Brokk는 Loki가 틀렸다는 것을 증명해 냈고, 세 신들은 이제 소중한 보물을 가지게 되었다.

※ 다음 우리말을 영어로 쓰시오.

1 세 명의 신을 위한 보물

➡ _____

2 북유럽 신화의 주요 신들

➡ _____

3 Odin은 가장 높은 신이며, 지혜를 위해 한쪽 눈을 포기했다.

➡ _____

4 Thor는 Odin의 아들이며 모든 신들 중에서 가장 강한 신이다.

➡ _____

5 Frey는 수확의 신으로 날씨를 다스린다.

➡ _____

6 Loki는 다른 신들에게 농간을 부리는 신이다.

➡ _____

7 Thor는 잠에서 깨어 즉시 무엇인가가 잘못되었다는 것을 알았다.

➡ _____

8 그의 아내의 아름다운 금발머리가 사라졌다.

➡ _____

9 그는 오직 Loki만이 이런 끔찍한 일을 할 수 있다는 것을 알고 있었다.

➡ _____

10 Thor는 곧 Loki를 찾았는데, 그는 집에서 술을 마시고 있었다.

➡ _____

11 "네가 한 짓을 되돌려 놓는 것이 좋을 거야, 그렇지 않으면 후회하게 될 거다." Thor는 노하여 Loki에게 말했다.

➡ _____

12 Loki는 겁이 났다.

➡ _____

13 그는 Thor의 아내를 위해 금발머리를 얻어 오겠다고 약속했다.

➡ _____

14 Loki는 Ivaldi의 아들들만이 훌륭한 금발머리를 만들 수 있다는 것을 알고 있었다.

➡ _____

15 그는 그들에게 가서 "내가 듣기로 Brokk와 그의 남동생이 가장 훌륭한 대장장이라고 하던데, 그것이 사실인가?"라고 말했다.

➡ _____

16 "아니요, 가장 훌륭한 대장장이는 바로 우리들이요." Ivaldi의 아들들이 대답했다.

➡ _____

17 "그들은 Odin과 Thor와 Frey를 위해서 보물을 만들고 있네." Loki는 말했다.

➡ _____

18 "너희들이 그들의 보물보다 더 나은 보물을 만들 수 있다고 생각하는가?"

➡ _____

19 "물론 할 수 있소." 그들이 대답했다.

➡ _____

20 "좋아, 그러면 너희도 그들을 위해 세 개의 보물을 만들어야 한다." Loki가 말했다.

➡ _____

21 "그 신들이 가장 훌륭한 보물을 결정할 것이다."

➡ _____

22 Loki는 또한 그들에게 보물 중 하나는 금발머리이어야 한다고 말했다.

➡ _____

23 그들은 즉시 일에 착수했다.

➡ _____

24 Loki는 그 다음에 Brokk와 그의 남동생을 보러 갔다.

➡ _____

25 "Ivaldi의 아들들이 Odin과 Thor, 그리고 Frey를 위해 세 개의 보물을 만들고 있어." Loki가 말했다.

➡ _____

26 "너희들은 절대 그들의 보물만큼 훌륭한 보물을 만들 수 없다는 것을 내 장담하지."

➡ _____

27 Brokk는 화가 나서 그 도전을 받아들였다.

➡ _____

28 그와 그의 남동생은 그들만의 세 가지 보물을 만들었다.

➡ _____

29 Loki는 모든 보물을 가지고 세 신을 만나러 갔다.

➡ _____

30 Brokk가 같이 갔다.

➡ _____

31 Loki는 그들에게 Ivaldi의 아들들이 만든 보물들을 보여 주었다.

➡ _____

32 첫 번째 보물은 Odin을 위한 것으로, 그는 눈이 한쪽밖에 없었다.

➡ _____

33 그것은 목표물을 절대로 빗나가지 않는 창이었다.

➡ _____

34 두 번째 보물은 천 조각으로 변할 수 있는 큰 배였다.

➡ _____

35 그것은 Frey를 위한 것이었다.

➡ _____

36 세 번째 보물은 Thor를 위한 것이었다.

➡ _____

37 Loki는 Thor에게 그의 아내를 위한 매끈하게 늘어진 금발머리를 보여 주었다.

➡ _____

38 Thor가 그 머리카락을 그의 아내의 머리에 얹었더니 그것이 뿌리를 내려서 진짜 머리카락이 되었다.

➡ _____

39 이제 Brokk가 신들에게 그의 선물들을 보여 줄 차례였다.

➡ _____

40 그는 Odin에게 아홉 번째 밤이 될 때마다 8개의 금팔찌를 더 만들어 내는 금팔찌를 주었다.

➡ _____

41 그러고 나서 Brokk는 Frey에게 돼지를 한 마리 주었다.

➡ _____

42 그것은 어떤 말보다도 그의 마차를 더 빨리 끌 수 있었다.

➡ _____

43 "나의 세 번째 보물은 당신을 위한 것입니다, Thor." Brokk가 말했다.

➡ _____

44 "이것은 묠니르라는 망치인데 당신은 마음에 드실 겁니다.

➡ _____

45 그것을 던지면, 그것은 항상 당신에게 되돌아 올 것입니다.

➡ _____

46 게다가, 그 무엇도 이것을 부술 수 없지요."

➡ _____

47 가장 훌륭한 보물을 선택하는 것은 쉬운 결정이었다.

➡ _____

48 세 명의 신들이 가장 마음에 든 것은 묠니르였다.

➡ _____

49 그들은 그 망치가 신들을 그들의 적들로부터 보호해 줄 것이라고 생각했다.

➡ _____

50 "Brokk와 그의 남동생이 더 훌륭한 대장장이야." Odin이 말했다.

➡ _____

51 Brokk는 Loki가 틀렸다는 것을 증명해 냈고, 세 신들은 이제 소중한 보물을 가지게 되었다.

➡ _____

※ 다음 우리말과 일치하도록 빈칸에 알맞은 말을 쓰시오.

After You Read A

1. (1) Loki _____ the beautiful _____ _____ of Thor's wife, _____ Thor _____ him.
2. Loki _____ _____ _____ _____ _____ _____ for Thor's wife.
3. (2) Loki _____ the sons of Ivaldi _____ _____ _____ _____ Odin, Thor, and Frey.
4. He also _____ Brokk and his brother _____ _____ _____ _____.
5. Loki _____ that Ivaldi's sons _____ _____ _____ _____ _____.
6. (3) Loki _____ the _____ _____ the _____ Ivaldi's sons.
7. They were a _____, a _____ _____, and _____ _____.
8. _____ _____ _____ _____ Brokk and his brother _____ a _____ _____, a pig, _____ _____ _____ _____.
9. (4) The gods _____ _____ _____ _____.
10. They each had _____ _____ _____ _____.

Link Create

1. I _____ always _____ friends with Sif, _____ is the wife of _____ _____ _____.
2. A _____ _____ ago, I cut her golden hair _____ _____ _____, and her husband _____ _____ _____ me.
3. I _____ _____ _____ a good idea _____ _____ her hair _____.
4. I asked the sons of Ivaldi _____ _____ _____ _____ _____.

Culture Project

1. The _____ _____ _____ _____ in the World
2. Hercules, _____ was the son of Zeus, _____ _____ _____ _____ _____.
3. _____ _____ _____ Hercules killed the Nemean lion and _____ the _____ _____ _____ _____.
4. He _____ _____ the _____ Hydra.
5. I think _____ is Hercules _____ is _____ _____ in the world.

1. (1) Loki가 Thor의 아내의 아름다운 금발머리를 가져가서, Thor는 그에게 화가 났다.
2. Loki는 Thor의 아내를 위해 금발머리를 얻어 오겠다고 약속했다.
3. (2) Loki는 Ivaldi의 아들들에게 Odin과 Thor와 Frey를 위해서 보물을 만들어 달라고 부탁했다.
4. 그는 또한 Brokk와 그의 남동생에게 신들을 위한 세 개의 보물을 만들게 시켰다.
5. Loki는 Ivaldi의 아들들이 더 훌륭한 보물을 만들 것이라고 장담했다.
6. (3) Loki는 세 명의 신들에게 Ivaldi의 아들들이 만든 보물들을 보여 주었다.
7. 그것들은 창과 큰 배와 금발머리였다.
8. Brokk와 그의 남동생이 만든 보물들은 금팔찌와 돼지 한 마리와 망치였다.
9. (4) 신들이 가장 마음에 든 것은 망치였다.
10. 그들은 각자 그들의 소중한 보물을 가지게 되었다.

1. 나는 가장 강한 신의 아내인 Sif와 항상 친구로 지내왔다.
2. 며칠 전에 나는 그녀의 금발을 단지 재미로 잘랐고 그녀의 남편은 나에게 화가 났다.
3. 나는 그녀의 머리를 되돌릴 좋은 생각이 났다.
4. 나는 Ivaldi의 아들들에게 훌륭한 금발머리를 만들어 달라고 부탁했다.

1. 세상에서 가장 강한 신들과 영웅들
2. 제우스의 아들인 헤라클레스는 그의 많은 모험들로 유명하다.
3. 용감하고 강한 헤라클레스는 네메아의 사자를 죽이고, 그 가죽을 외투로 입었다.
4. 그는 또한 머리가 여러 개 달린 히드라와 싸웠다.
5. 나는 헤라클레스가 세상에서 가장 강한 영웅이라고 생각한다.

구석구석 지문 Test

※ 다음 우리말을 영어로 쓰시오.

After You Read A

1. (1) Loki가 Thor의 아내의 아름다운 금발머리를 가져가서, Thor는 그에게 화가 났다.
➡ _____

2. Loki는 Thor의 아내를 위해 금발머리를 얻어 오겠다고 약속했다.
➡ _____

3. (2) Loki는 Ivaldi의 아들들에게 Odin과 Thor와 Frey를 위해서 보물을 만들어 달라고 부탁했다.
➡ _____

4. 그는 또한 Brokk와 그의 남동생에게 신들을 위한 세 개의 보물을 만들게 시켰다.
➡ _____

5. Loki는 Ivaldi의 아들들이 더 훌륭한 보물을 만들 것이라고 장담했다.
➡ _____

6. (3) Loki는 세 명의 신들에게 Ivaldi의 아들들이 만든 보물들을 보여 주었다.
➡ _____

7. 그것들은 창과 큰 배와 금발머리였다.
➡ _____

8. Brokk와 그의 남동생이 만든 보물들은 금팔찌와 돼지 한 마리와 망치였다.
➡ _____

9. (4) 신들이 가장 마음에 든 것은 망치였다.
➡ _____

10. 그들은 각자 그들의 소중한 보물을 가지게 되었다.
➡ _____

Link Create

1. 나는 가장 강한 신의 아내인 Sif와 항상 친구로 지내왔다.
➡ _____

2. 며칠 전에 나는 그녀의 금발을 단지 재미로 잘랐고 그녀의 남편은 나에게 화가 났다.
➡ _____

3. 나는 그녀의 머리를 되돌릴 좋은 생각이 났다.
➡ _____

4. 나는 Ivaldi의 아들들에게 훌륭한 금발머리를 만들어 달라고 부탁했다.
➡ _____

Culture Project

1. 세상에서 가장 강한 신들과 영웅들
➡ _____

2. 제우스의 아들인 헤라클레스는 그의 많은 모험들로 유명하다.
➡ _____

3. 용감하고 강한 헤라클레스는 네메아의 사자를 죽이고, 그 가죽을 외투로 입었다.
➡ _____

4. 그는 또한 머리가 여러 개 달린 히드라와 싸웠다.
➡ _____

5. 나는 헤라클레스가 세상에서 가장 강한 영웅이라고 생각한다.
➡ _____

※ 다음 영어를 우리말로 쓰시오.

01	prove	
02	absorb	
03	publish	
04	bloom	
05	capital	
06	secret	
07	actually	
08	solve	
09	discover	
10	soak	
11	erase	
12	expect	
13	spinach	
14	face	
15	defeat	
16	character	
17	statue	
18	article	
19	battleship	
20	government	
21	bean	

22	hidden	
23	consider	
24	happen	
25	hide	
26	characteristic	
27	improve	
28	lower	
29	contain	
30	nutrient	
31	world-famous	
32	crush	
33	trace	
34	poisonous	
35	lose weight	
36	soak up	
37	keep ~ away from …	
38	turn A into B	
39	no longer	
40	be scared of	
41	give it a try	
42	keep a secret	
43	in addition	

※ 다음 우리말을 영어로 쓰시오.

01 흡수하다

02 기사, 논문

03 전함

04 꽃을 피우다

05 수도

06 등장인물

07 기대하다

08 고려하다, 여기다

09 물리치다, 패배시키다

10 특성, 특장; 특징적인

11 으스러뜨리다

12 유독한, 독성의

13 포함하다, 담고 있다

14 숨다, 숨기다

15 출판하다

16 조각상, 동상

17 개선하다, 향상시키다

18 낮추다

19 사실, 진실

20 흔적; 추적하다

21 시금치

22 물질, 재료

23 숨겨진

24 영양소, 영양분

25 증명하다

26 세계적으로 유명한

27 담그다, 적시다

28 행성

29 시력

30 비밀

31 해결하다

32 만화

33 연구원, 조사원

34 정부, 국가

35 포만감을 가지다

36 게다가

37 ~에 유익하다

38 살을 빼다

39 비밀을 지키다

40 더 이상 ~가 아닌

41 흡수하다, 빨아들이다

42 시도해 보다

43 약을 먹다

※ 다음 영영풀이에 알맞은 단어를 <보기>에서 골라 쓴 후, 우리말 뜻을 쓰시오.

1 _____ : a person in a book, play, film, etc.: _____

2 _____ : a funny drawing in a newspaper or magazine: _____

3 _____ : to cover something so that it cannot be seen clearly: _____

4 _____ : to use facts, evidence, etc. to show that something is true: _____

5 _____ : a small creature such as a fly or ant, that has six legs: _____

6 _____ : to prepare and produce a book, magazine, etc. for sale: _____

7 _____ : to put something in a liquid for a period of time: _____

8 _____ : a long pointed orange vegetable that grows under the ground: _____

9 _____ : a plant with dark green leaves that are eaten as a vegetable: _____

10 _____ : the largest type of ship used in war, with very big guns and heavy armour: _____

11 _____ : a fact that is known by only a small number of people, and is not told to anyone else: _____

12 _____ : a chemical or food that provides what is needed for plants or animals to live and grow: _____

13 _____ : an image of a person or animal that is made in solid material such as stone or metal: _____

14 _____ : a seed that is eaten as a vegetable and that comes from any one of many different kinds of climbing plants: _____

15 _____ : something such as a mark or an object which shows that someone or something was in a particular place: _____

16 _____ : a board like a wide ski that is used for sliding down hills of snow while standing: _____

보기			
snowboard	secret	battleship	hide
statue	bean	insect	character
trace	nutrient	prove	carrot
publish	spinach	soak	cartoon

※ 다음 우리말과 일치하도록 빈칸에 알맞은 말을 쓰시오.

Listen & Speak 1 A-1

B: Bomi, do you have _____ _____?

G: Why? Is _____ _____?

B: I have _____ _____. I think I ate _____ _____ for lunch.

G: _____ _____ you _____ _____ _____ _____ _____?

B: O.K. I'll give _____ _____ _____.

B: 보미야, 약 좀 있니?
G: 왜? 무슨 문제 있어?
B: 배가 아파. 점심을 너무 많이 먹었나 봐.
G: 산책을 좀 하는 게 어때?
B: 알겠어. 한번 해 볼게.

Listen & Speak 1 A-2

B: Is _____ _____? You don't _____ _____ _____.

G: I have _____ _____ _____. I think it's _____ _____ the fine dust _____ _____.

B: _____ some plants in your room. They _____ bad air _____ and _____ _____ _____.

G: Really? I'll _____ _____ _____ _____ right away.

B: 어디 안 좋아? 안색이 나빠 보이는데.
G: 목이 아파. 최근의 미세먼지 때문인 것 같아.
B: 방에 식물을 좀 놓아 봐. 나쁜 공기를 흡수하고 신선한 공기를 만들어 내.
G: 정말? 당장 식물을 몇 그루 가져와야 겠어.

Listen & Speak 2 A-1

B: It's _____ _____ _____ _____. What _____ _____ _____ I should do?

G: Well, why don't you _____ _____ _____ every day?

B: My dog would love _____, but would _____ _____ me _____ _____?

G: Sure. _____ you _____ your dog, you're _____ _____, _____.

B: O.K. I'll _____ _____ _____.

B: 몸무게를 줄이는 건 너무 어려워. 내가 뭘 해야 한다고 생각해?
G: 글쎄, 매일 너의 개를 산책시키는 건 어때?
B: 우리 개는 좋아하겠지만, 그게 살을 빼는 데 도움이 될까?
G: 물론이지. 네가 개를 산책시키면, 사실은 너도 운동하는 거잖아.
B: 좋아. 생각해 볼게.

Listen & Speak 2 A-2

B: _____ _____ your tomatoes _____? Are they _____ well?

G: No. I've _____ only _____ tomatoes _____ _____. What do you think _____ _____ _____?

B: _____ do you have the pot?

G: _____ the kitchen.

B: Well, tomato plants _____ _____ 7 hours of sunlight _____ _____.

G: Oh, I see. I'll _____ the pot _____ to the window.

B: 네 토마토들 어떠니? 잘 자라고 있어?
G: 아니. 지금까지 토마토 몇 개밖에 못 얻었어. 내가 뭘 해야 한다고 생각하니?
B: 화분을 어디에 두는데?
G: 부엌에.
B: 음, 토마토는 하루에 7시간 정도 햇빛을 받아야 해.
G: 오, 그렇구나. 화분을 창문 쪽으로 옮겨야겠다.

Communicate A

Anna: Suho, _____ _____ _____? You're very _____ today.

Suho: I'm just _____ _____ _____. I slept very _____ last night.

Anna: Did you do _____ _____ last night?

Suho: Yes, I watched a movie _____ my phone _____ 2 a.m. That's _____ _____ _____ _____ _____ _____ _____.

Anna: Oh, _____ _____ you have red eyes. You should go to bed _____ _____ for your health.

Suho: I think my eyes are _____ _____. What do you think _____ _____ _____?

Anna: Try _____ _____ _____ _____ and tomatoes. They're _____ _____ _____ A, so they'll _____ your eyes _____.

Suho: I _____. Thank you, Anna.

Anna: 수호야, 무슨 일 있어? 오늘 굉장히 조용하네.

수호: 조금 피곤한 것뿐이야. 어젯밤에 정말 조금 잤거든.

Anna: 어젯밤 늦게까지 뭔가 했니?

수호: 응, 새벽 2시까지 휴대폰으로 영화를 봤어. 요즘 종종 하는 일이야.

Anna: 오, 그래서 눈이 충혈됐구나. 건강을 위해 자정 전에는 잠자리에 들어야 해.

수호: 눈이 점점 나빠지는 것 같아. 내가 뭘 해야 한다고 생각해?

Anna: 당근이랑 토마토를 많이 먹어 봐. 그것들은 비타민 A가 많아서, 네 눈을 건강하게 유지해 줄 거야.

수호: 알겠어. 고마워, Anna.

Progress Check 1

B: _____ something _____?

G: I'm just _____ _____ _____. I've _____ a movie on my phone _____ _____ _____.

B: That's _____ you have _____ _____. Try _____ a warm towel _____ your eyes.

G: O.K. Thanks.

B: 무슨 문제 있어?

G: 조금 피곤한 것뿐이야. 휴대전화로 영화를 두 시간 동안 봤거든.

B: 그래서 눈이 충혈됐구나. 따뜻한 수건으로 눈을 덮어 봐.

G: 알겠어. 고마워.

Progress Check 2

G: What's _____? You _____ _____.

B: Well, I _____ my mom's favorite _____. What _____ _____ I should do?

G: _____ her the _____. She will _____.

B: I _____ you're _____.

G: 무슨 문제 있어? 걱정이 있는 것 같은데.

B: 그게, 어머니께서 가장 아끼시는 접시를 깨뜨렸어. 내가 뭘 해야 한다고 생각하니?

G: 솔직히 말씀 드려. 이해하실 거야.

B: 네 말이 맞길 바라.

※ 다음 우리말에 맞도록 대화를 영어로 쓰시오.

Listen & Speak 1 A-1

B: _____

G: _____

B: _____

G: _____

B: _____

B: 보미야, 약 좀 있니?
G: 왜? 무슨 문제 있어?
B: 배가 아파. 점심을 너무 많이 먹었나 봐.
G: 산책을 좀 하는 게 어때?
B: 알겠어. 한번 해 볼게.

Listen & Speak 1 A-2

B: _____

G: _____

B: _____

G: _____

B: 어디 안 좋아? 안색이 나빠 보이는데.
G: 목이 아파. 최근의 미세먼지 때문인 것 같아.
B: 방에 식물을 좀 놓아 봐. 나쁜 공기를 흡수하고 신선한 공기를 만들어 내.
G: 정말? 당장 식물을 몇 그루 가져와야겠어.

Listen & Speak 2 A-1

B: _____

G: _____

B: _____

G: _____

B: _____

B: 몸무게를 줄이는 건 너무 어려워. 내가 뭘 해야 한다고 생각해?
G: 글쎄, 매일 너의 개를 산책시키는 건 어때?
B: 우리 개는 좋아하겠지만, 그게 살을 빼는 데 도움이 될까?
G: 물론이지. 네가 개를 산책시키면, 사실은 너도 운동하는 거잖아.
B: 좋아. 생각해 볼게.

Listen & Speak 2 A-2

B: _____

G: _____

B: _____

G: _____

B: _____

G: _____

B: 네 토마토들 어떠니? 잘 자라고 있어?
G: 아니. 지금까지 토마토 몇 개밖에 못 얻었어. 내가 뭘 해야 한다고 생각하니?
B: 화분을 어디에 두는데?
G: 부엌에.
B: 음, 토마토는 하루에 7시간 정도 햇빛을 받아야 해.
G: 오, 그렇구나. 화분을 창문 쪽으로 옮겨야겠다.

Communicate A

Anna: _____

Suho: _____

Anna: _____

Suho: _____

_____

Anna: _____

_____

Suho: _____

Anna: _____

_____

Suho: _____

Anna: 수호야, 무슨 일 있어? 오늘 굉장히 조용하네.

수호: 조금 피곤한 것뿐이야. 어젯밤에 정말 조금 잤거든.

Anna: 어젯밤 늦게까지 뭔가 했니?

수호: 응, 새벽 2시까지 휴대폰으로 영화를 봤어. 요즘 종종 하는 일이야.

Anna: 오, 그래서 눈이 충혈됐구나. 건강을 위해 자정 전에는 잠자리에 들어야 해.

수호: 눈이 점점 나빠지는 것 같아. 내가 뭘 해야 한다고 생각해?

Anna: 당근이랑 토마토를 많이 먹어 봐. 그것들은 비타민 A가 많아서, 네 눈을 건강하게 유지해 줄 거야.

수호: 알겠어. 고마워, Anna.

Progress Check 1

B: _____

G: _____

B: _____

G: _____

B: 무슨 문제 있어?

G: 조금 피곤한 것뿐이야. 휴대전화로 영화를 두 시간 동안 봤거든.

B: 그래서 눈이 충혈됐구나. 따뜻한 수건으로 눈을 덮어 봐.

G: 알겠어. 고마워.

Progress Check 2

G: _____

B: _____

G: _____

B: _____

G: 무슨 문제 있어? 걱정이 있는 것 같은데.

B: 그게, 어머니께서 가장 아끼시는 접시를 깨뜨렸어. 내가 뭘 해야 한다고 생각하니?

G: 솔직히 말씀 드려. 이해하실 거야.

B: 네 말이 맞길 바라.

※ 다음 우리말과 일치하도록 빈칸에 알맞은 것을 골라 쓰시오.

1 _____ **Stories about** _____
A. Plants   B. Hidden

2 **Popeye and the** _____
A. Great   B. Spinach

3 Popeye is a _____ _____ _____ .
A. character   B. cartoon   C. world-famous

4 He _____ his super power _____ _____ _____ .
A. eating   B. by   C. gets   D. spinach

5 _____ Popeye _____ _____ in the 1930s in the United States, a _____ of children began to eat spinach.
A. popular   B. lot   C. became   D. when

6 Crystal City in Texas, which is _____ the spinach _____ of the world, even _____ a _____ of Popeye.
A. built   B. called   C. statue   D. capital

7 _____ eating spinach will not give us super _____ , _____ does have a lot of _____ .
A. spinach   B. although   C. nutrients   D. powers

8 It is actually _____ one of the ten _____ _____ on the _____ .
A. healthiest   B. planet   C. considered   D. foods

9 Spinach can be _____ in a _____ _____ .
A. surprising   B. used   C. way

10 _____ it absorbs water, spinach also _____ many _____ things from the _____ .
A. absorbs   B. soil   C. other   D. when

11 Some scientists have used this _____ of spinach to find _____ _____ in the _____ .
A. characteristic   B. ground   C. bombs   D. hidden

12 They make special spinach plants _____ _____ their _____ .
A. ensors   B. leaves   C. on   D. with

13 When these plants _____ up traces from _____ , the sensors _____ _____ .
A. light   B. bombs   C. up   D. soak

14 **Carrots in** _____ _____ _____
A. War   B. World   C. II

15 In 1940, the Royal Air Force _____ German fighters _____ World War II _____ _____ a radar system.
A. by   B. defeated   C. using   D. during

16 The British government wanted to _____ this technology a _____ , so it _____ an _____ in the newspaper.
A. secret   B. keep   C. published   D. article

17 It _____ that British pilots _____ their night _____ because they _____ a lot of carrots.
A. vision   B. said   C. ate   D. improved

---

1 식물에 대한 숨겨진 이야기

2 Popeye와 위대한 시금치

3 Popeye는 세계적으로 유명한 만화 캐릭터다.

4 그는 시금치를 먹음으로써 초인적인 힘을 얻는다.

5 Popeye가 1930년대 미국에서 인기를 얻었을 때, 많은 어린이들이 시금치를 먹기 시작했다.

6 텍사스의 크리스털 시티는 세계의 시금치 수도라고 불리는데, 이곳에서는 Popeye의 동상을 세우기까지 했다.

7 비록 시금치를 먹는 것이 우리에게 초인적인 힘을 주지는 않지만, 시금치는 정말로 많은 영양분을 가지고 있다.

8 이것은 실제로 지구상에서 가장 건강한 식품 10개 중 하나로 여겨진다.

9 시금치는 놀라운 용도로 사용될 수 있다.

10 그것이 물을 흡수할 때, 시금치는 흙으로부터 다른 많은 것들도 흡수한다.

11 몇몇 과학자들은 시금치의 이 특성을 땅에 숨겨진 폭탄을 찾는 데 사용했다.

12 그들은 잎에 감지기가 있는 특별한 시금치를 만든다.

13 이 식물들이 폭탄의 흔적을 흡수하면, 감지기가 빛난다.

14 제2차 세계대전에서의 당근

15 1940년, 영국 공군은 제2차 세계 대전에서 레이더 시스템을 사용해 독일군을 패배시켰다.

16 영국 정부는 이 기술을 비밀로 하기를 원했기 때문에, 신문에 기사를 하나 냈다.

17 그것은 영국 비행사들이 당근을 많이 먹어 야간 시력이 좋아졌다는 내용이었다.

18 Everybody _____ the story and began to eat a _____ more carrots _____ _____.

    A. than   B. lot   C. before   D. believed

19 Can we really _____ night vision _____ _____ lots of _____?

    A. improve   B. eating   C. by   D. carrots

20 Not really, but carrots _____ a lot of _____ A, which does _____ our eyes _____.

    A. vitamin   B. healthy   C. contain   D. keep

21 In the _____, carrots _____ actually be _____ in _____.

    A. used   B. future   C. wars   D. may

22 Scottish researchers have _____ a way to _____ carrots _____ a very strong and _____ material.

    A. turn   B. discovered   C. light   D. into

23 It can _____ _____ to make _____.

    A. be   B. battleships   C. used   D. even

24 This new material _____ _____ _____ _____ to make snowboards and bicycles.

    A. been   B. has   C. used   D. already

25 **Tomatoes, the _____ _____**

    A. Vegetables   B. Scariest

26 We all know that tomatoes _____ _____ _____ our _____.

    A. good   B. health   C. are   D. for

27 _____ _____ the 1800s, _____, most Americans thought that tomatoes were _____.

    A. until   B. poisonous   C. up   D. however

28 In 1820, a man _____ Robert Johnson wanted to _____ that tomatoes were _____ to _____.

    A. prove   B. eat   C. named   D. safe

29 So, he _____ a _____ of tomatoes in _____ of many people _____ him.

    A. front   B. basket   C. watching   D. ate

30 They all _____ him to die, but _____ _____ _____ him.

    A. nothing   B. expected   C. to   D. happened

31 Ever _____ then, Americans _____ _____ _____ tomatoes.

    A. enjoyed   B. since   C. eating   D. have

32 We are _____ _____ afraid of tomatoes, but some insects are still _____ _____ them.

    A. scared   B. no   C. of   D. longer

33 If you want to _____ insects _____ from your room, _____ a bowl of _____ tomatoes in a corner of your room.

    A. away   B. crushed   C. keep   D. place

34 _____ will not _____ _____ the tomatoes.

    A. come   B. insects   C. near

---

18 모두가 그 이야기를 믿었고 전보다 훨씬 많은 당근을 먹기 시작했다.

19 우리는 정말 당근을 많이 먹어서 야간 시력을 높일 수 있을까?

20 실제로 그렇지는 않지만, 당근은 많은 비타민 A를 함유하는데, 그것은 정말로 우리 눈을 건강하게 유지해 준다.

21 미래에는, 당근이 실제로 전쟁에 이용될지도 모른다.

22 스코틀랜드의 연구원들은 당근을 매우 강하고 가벼운 물질로 바꾸는 방법을 발견했다.

23 그것은 심지어 전함을 만드는 데 사용될 수도 있다.

24 이 새로운 소재는 이미 스노보드와 자전거를 만드는 데 사용되었다.

25 토마토, 가장 무서운 채소

26 우리는 모두 토마토가 건강에 좋다는 것을 안다.

27 그러나, 1800년대까지 대부분의 미국인들은 토마토에 독성이 있다고 생각했다.

28 1820년에, Robert Johnson이라는 이름의 남자가 토마토가 먹기에 안전하다는 것을 증명하기를 원했다.

29 그래서, 그는 그를 지켜보는 많은 사람들 앞에서 한 바구니의 토마토를 먹었다.

30 그들은 모두 그가 죽을 것이라고 예상했으나 그에게는 아무 일도 일어나지 않았다.

31 그 이후로, 미국인들은 토마토를 먹는 것을 즐겼다.

32 우리는 더 이상 토마토를 두려워하지 않지만, 몇몇 곤충들은 여전히 그것을 무서워한다.

33 만약 곤충들이 방에 들어오지 않게 하고 싶다면, 으깬 토마토 한 그릇을 방구석에 놓아 두어라.

34 곤충들은 토마토 가까이 오지 않을 것이다.

※ 다음 우리말과 일치하도록 빈칸에 알맞은 것을 골라 쓰시오.

1 _____ **Stories about** _____

2 **Popeye and the Great** _____

3 Popeye is a _____ _____ _____.

4 He gets his super power _____ _____ _____.

5 When Popeye _____ _____ in the 1930s in the United States, _____ _____ _____ children began to eat spinach.

6 Crystal City in Texas, _____ is called _____ _____ _____ of the world, even built _____ _____ of Popeye.

7 _____ _____ spinach will not give us super powers, spinach _____ _____ a lot of _____.

8 It is actually considered _____ _____ _____ _____ _____ _____ on the planet.

9 Spinach can be used _____ _____ _____ _____.

10 _____ it _____ water, spinach _____ _____ many other things _____ the soil.

11 Some scientists have used this characteristic of spinach _____ _____ bombs _____ _____ _____ _____.

12 They make special spinach plants _____ _____ _____ _____ _____ _____.

13 When these plants _____ _____ _____ from bombs, the sensors _____ _____.

14 **Carrots in** _____ _____ _____ _____

15 In 1940, the Royal Air Force _____ German fighters _____ World War II _____ _____ a radar system.

16 The British government wanted to _____ this technology a _____, so it _____ _____ _____ in the newspaper.

17 It said that British pilots _____ _____ _____ _____ they ate a lot of carrots.

---

1 식물에 대한 숨겨진 이야기

2 Popeye와 위대한 시금치

3 Popeye는 세계적으로 유명한 만화 캐릭터다.

4 그는 시금치를 먹음으로써 초인적인 힘을 얻는다.

5 Popeye가 1930년대 미국에서 인기를 얻었을 때, 많은 어린이들이 시금치를 먹기 시작했다.

6 텍사스의 크리스털 시티는 세계의 시금치 수도라고 불리는데, 이곳에서는 Popeye의 동상을 세우기까지 했다.

7 비록 시금치를 먹는 것이 우리에게 초인적인 힘을 주지는 않지만, 시금치는 정말로 많은 영양분을 가지고 있다.

8 이것은 실제로 지구상에서 가장 건강한 식품 10개 중 하나로 여겨진다.

9 시금치는 놀라운 용도로 사용될 수 있다.

10 그것이 물을 흡수할 때, 시금치는 흙으로부터 다른 많은 것들도 흡수한다.

11 몇몇 과학자들은 시금치의 이 특성을 땅에 숨겨진 폭탄을 찾는 데 사용했다.

12 그들은 잎에 감지기가 있는 특별한 시금치를 만든다.

13 이 식물들이 폭탄의 흔적을 흡수하면, 감지기가 빛난다.

14 제2차 세계대전에서의 당근

15 1940년, 영국 공군은 제2차 세계 대전에서 레이더 시스템을 사용해 독일군을 패배시켰다.

16 영국 정부는 이 기술을 비밀로 하기를 원했기 때문에, 신문에 기사를 하나 냈다.

17 그것은 영국 비행사들이 당근을 많이 먹어 야간 시력이 좋아졌다는 내용이었다.

18 Everybody believed the story and began to eat _____ _____ more carrots _____ _____.

19 Can we really _____ night vision _____ _____ lots of carrots?

20 Not really, but carrots contain a lot of vitamin A, _____ _____ _____ our eyes _____.

21 In the future, carrots _____ _____ _____ _____ _____ in wars.

22 Scottish researchers have discovered a way to _____ carrots _____ a very strong and _____ _____.

23 It _____ _____ _____ _____ to make battleships.

24 This new material _____ _____ _____ _____ to make snowboards and bicycles.

25 **Tomatoes, the _____ Vegetables**

26 We all know that tomatoes _____ _____ _____ _____ our health.

27 _____ _____ the 1800s, _____, most Americans thought that tomatoes were _____.

28 In 1820, a man _____ Robert Johnson wanted _____ _____ that tomatoes were _____ _____ _____.

29 So, he ate _____ _____ _____ tomatoes _____ _____ many people _____ him.

30 They all expected him to die, but nothing _____ _____ him.

31 Ever _____ then, Americans _____ _____ _____ _____ tomatoes.

32 We are _____ _____ afraid of tomatoes, but some insects are still _____ _____ them.

33 If you want to _____ insects _____ _____ your room, _____ a bowl of _____ tomatoes in a corner of your room.

34 Insects will not _____ _____ the tomatoes.

18 모두가 그 이야기를 믿었고 전보다 훨씬 많은 당근을 먹기 시작했다.

19 우리는 정말 당근을 많이 먹어서 야간 시력을 높일 수 있을까?

20 실제로 그렇지는 않지만, 당근은 많은 비타민 A를 함유하는데, 그것은 정말로 우리 눈을 건강하게 유지해 준다.

21 미래에는, 당근이 실제로 전쟁에 이용될지도 모른다.

22 스코틀랜드의 연구원들은 당근을 매우 강하고 가벼운 물질로 바꾸는 방법을 발견했다.

23 그것은 심지어 전함을 만드는 데 사용될 수도 있다.

24 이 새로운 소재는 이미 스노보드와 자전거를 만드는 데 사용되었다.

25 토마토, 가장 무서운 채소

26 우리는 모두 토마토가 건강에 좋다는 것을 안다.

27 그러나, 1800년대까지 대부분의 미국인들은 토마토에 독성이 있다고 생각했다.

28 1820년에, Robert Johnson이라는 이름의 남자가 토마토가 먹기에 안전하다는 것을 증명하기를 원했다.

29 그래서, 그는 그를 지켜보는 많은 사람들 앞에서 한 바구니의 토마토를 먹었다.

30 그들은 모두 그가 죽을 것이라고 예상했으나 그에게는 아무 일도 일어나지 않았다.

31 그 이후로, 미국인들은 토마토를 먹는 것을 즐겼다.

32 우리는 더 이상 토마토를 두려워하지 않지만, 몇몇 곤충들은 여전히 그것을 무서워한다.

33 만약 곤충들이 방에 들어오지 않게 하고 싶다면, 으깬 토마토 한 그릇을 방구석에 놓아 두어라.

34 곤충들은 토마토 가까이 오지 않을 것이다.

※ 다음 문장을 우리말로 쓰시오.

1 ▸ Hidden Stories about Plants

➡ _____

2 ▸ Popeye and the Great Spinach

➡ _____

3 ▸ Popeye is a world-famous cartoon character.

➡ _____

4 ▸ He gets his super power by eating spinach.

➡ _____

5 ▸ When Popeye became popular in the 1930s in the United States, a lot of children began to eat spinach.

➡ _____

6 ▸ Crystal City in Texas, which is called the spinach capital of the world, even built a statue of Popeye.

➡ _____

7 ▸ Although eating spinach will not give us super powers, spinach does have a lot of nutrients.

➡ _____

8 ▸ It is actually considered one of the ten healthiest foods on the planet.

➡ _____

9 ▸ Spinach can be used in a surprising way.

➡ _____

10 ▸ When it absorbs water, spinach also absorbs many other things from the soil.

➡ _____

11 ▸ Some scientists have used this characteristic of spinach to find bombs hidden in the ground.

➡ _____

12 ▸ They make special spinach plants with sensors on their leaves.

➡ _____

13 ▸ When these plants soak up traces from bombs, the sensors light up.

➡ _____

14 ▸ Carrots in World War II

➡ _____

15 ▸ In 1940, the Royal Air Force defeated German fighters during World War II by using a radar system.

➡ _____

16 ▸ The British government wanted to keep this technology a secret, so it published an article in the newspaper.

➡ _____

17 It said that British pilots improved their night vision because they ate a lot of carrots.

➡ _____

18 Everybody believed the story and began to eat a lot more carrots than before.

➡ _____

19 Can we really improve night vision by eating lots of carrots?

➡ _____

20 Not really, but carrots contain a lot of vitamin A, which does keep our eyes healthy.

➡ _____

21 In the future, carrots may actually be used in wars.

➡ _____

22 Scottish researchers have discovered a way to turn carrots into a very strong and light material.

➡ _____

23 It can even be used to make battleships.

➡ _____

24 This new material has already been used to make snowboards and bicycles.

➡ _____

25 Tomatoes, the Scariest Vegetables

➡ _____

26 We all know that tomatoes are good for our health.

➡ _____

27 Up until the 1800s, however, most Americans thought that tomatoes were poisonous.

➡ _____

28 In 1820, a man named Robert Johnson wanted to prove that tomatoes were safe to eat.

➡ _____

29 So, he ate a basket of tomatoes in front of many people watching him.

➡ _____

30 They all expected him to die, but nothing happened to him.

➡ _____

31 Ever since then, Americans have enjoyed eating tomatoes.

➡ _____

32 We are no longer afraid of tomatoes, but some insects are still scared of them.

➡ _____

33 If you want to keep insects away from your room, place a bowl of crushed tomatoes in a corner of your room.

➡ _____

34 Insects will not come near the tomatoes.

➡ _____

※ 다음 괄호 안의 단어들을 우리말에 맞도록 바르게 배열하시오.

1 (Stories / Hidden / Plants / about)
➡ _____

2 (and / Popeye / the / Spinach / Great)
➡ _____

3 (is / Popeye / a / cartoon / world-famous / character.)
➡ _____

4 (gets / he / his / power / super / eating / by / spinach.)
➡ _____

5 (Popeye / when / popular / became / the / in / 1930s / the / in / States, / United / lot / a / of / began / children / eat / to / spinach.)
➡ _____

6 (City / Crystal / Texas, / in / is / which / the / called / spinach / of / capital / world, / the / bulit / even / statue / a / Popeye. / of)
➡ _____

7 (eating / although / will / spinach / give / not / super / us / powers, / does / spinach / have / lot / a / nutrients. / of)
➡ _____

8 (is / it / considered / actually / of / one / the / healthiest / ten / on / foods / planet. / the)
➡ _____

9 (can / spinach / be / used / a / in / way. / surprising)
➡ _____

10 (it / when / water, / absorbs / also / spinach / many / absorbs / things / other / the / from / soil.)
➡ _____

11 (scientists / some / used / have / characteristic / this / spinach / of / find / to / hidden / bombs / the / in / ground.)
➡ _____

12 (make / they / spinach / special / with / plants / on / sensors / leaves. / their)
➡ _____

13 (these / when / soak / plants / traces / up / bombs, / from / sensors / the / up. / light)
➡ _____

14 (in / Carrots / War / World / II)
➡ _____

15 (1940, / in / Royal / the / Force / Air / German / defeated / during / fighters / War / World / by / II / using / radar / system. / a)
➡ _____

16 (British / the / wanted / government / keep / to / this / a / technology / secret, / it / so / an / published / article / the / in / newspaper.)
➡ _____

17 (said / it / British / that / improved / pilots / night / their / because / vision / ate / they / lot / a / carrots. / of)
➡ _____

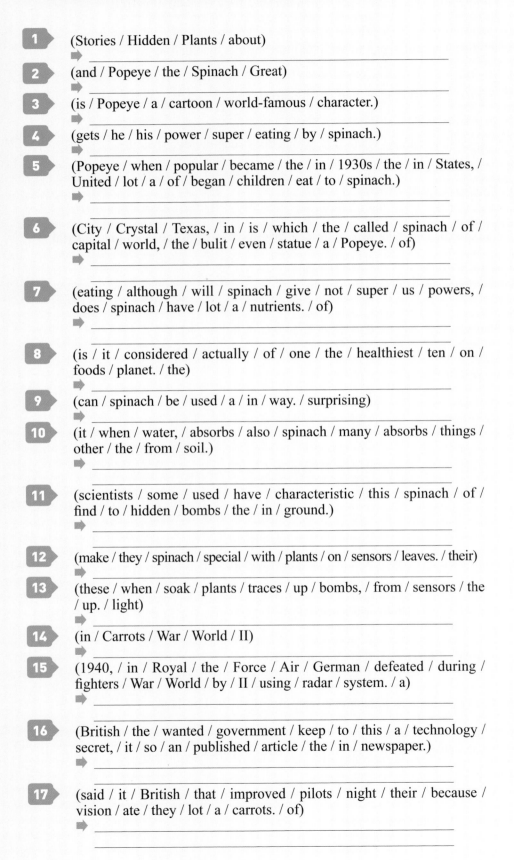

1 식물에 대한 숨겨진 이야기

2 Popeye와 위대한 시금치

3 Popeye는 세계적으로 유명한 만화 캐릭터다.

4 그는 시금치를 먹음으로써 초인적인 힘을 얻는다.

5 Popeye가 1930년대 미국에서 인기를 얻었을 때, 많은 어린이들이 시금치를 먹기 시작했다.

6 텍사스의 크리스털 시티는 세계의 시금치 수도라고 불리는데, 이곳에서는 Popeye의 동상을 세우기까지 했다.

7 비록 시금치를 먹는 것이 우리에게 초인적인 힘을 주지는 않지만, 시금치는 정말로 많은 영양분을 가지고 있다.

8 이것은 실제로 지구상에서 가장 건강한 식품 10개 중 하나로 여겨진다.

9 시금치는 놀라운 용도로 사용될 수 있다.

10 그것이 물을 흡수할 때, 시금치는 흙으로부터 다른 많은 것들도 흡수한다.

11 몇몇 과학자들은 시금치의 이 특성을 땅에 숨겨진 폭탄을 찾는 데 사용했다.

12 그들은 잎에 감지기가 있는 특별한 시금치를 만든다.

13 이 식물들이 폭탄의 흔적을 흡수하면, 감지기가 빛난다.

14 제2차 세계대전에서의 당근

15 1940년, 영국 공군은 제2차 세계 대전에서 레이더 시스템을 사용해 독일군을 패배시켰다.

16 영국 정부는 이 기술을 비밀로 하기를 원했기 때문에, 신문에 기사를 하나 냈다.

17 그것은 영국 비행사들이 당근을 많이 먹어 야간 시력이 좋아졌다는 내용이었다.

18 (believed / everybody / story / the / and / to / began / eat / lot / a / carrots / more / before. / than)
➡ _____

19 (we / can / improve / really / vision / night / eating / by / of / carrots? / lots)
➡ _____

20 (really, / not / carrots / but / a / contain / of / lot / A, / vitamin / does / which / our / keep / healthy. / eyes)
➡ _____

21 (the / in / future, / may / carrots / be / actually / used / be / wars. / in)
➡ _____

22 (researchers / Scottish / discovered / have / way / a / turn / to / into / carrots / very / a / strong / and / material. / light)
➡ _____

23 (can / it / be / even / to / used / battleships. / make)
➡ _____

24 (new / this / has / material / been / already / to / used / make / and / snowboards / bycycles.)
➡ _____

25 (the / Tomatoes, / Vegetables / Scariest)
➡ _____

26 (all / we / that / know / are / tomatoes / good / our / for / health.)
➡ _____

27 (until / up / 1800s, / the / most / however, / thought / Americans / that / were / tomatoes / poisonous.)
➡ _____

28 (1820, / in / man / a / named / Johnson / Robert / to / wanted / that / prove / tomatoes / safe / were / eat. / to)
➡ _____

29 (he / so, / ate / of / basket / a / tomatoes / front / in / many / of / watching / people / him.)
➡ _____

30 (all / they / him / expected / die, / to / nothing / but / to / happened / him.)
➡ _____

31 (since / ever / then, / have / Americans / eating / enjoyed / tomatoes.)
➡ _____

32 (are / we / longer / no / of / afraid / tomatoes, / some / but / are / insects / still / of / scared / them.)
➡ _____

33 (you / if / to / want / insects / keep / from / away / room, / your / a / place / of / bowl / tomatoes / crushed / a / in / of / corner / room. / your)
➡ _____

34 (will / insects / come / not / the / near / tomatoes.)
➡ _____

---

18 모두가 그 이야기를 믿었고 전보다 훨씬 많은 당근을 먹기 시작했다.

19 우리는 정말 당근을 많이 먹어서 야간 시력을 높일 수 있을까?

20 실제로 그렇지는 않지만, 당근은 많은 비타민 A를 함유하는데, 그것은 정말로 우리 눈을 건강하게 유지해 준다.

21 미래에는, 당근이 실제로 전쟁에 이용될지도 모른다.

22 스코틀랜드의 연구원들은 당근을 매우 강하고 가벼운 물질로 바꾸는 방법을 발견했다.

23 그것은 심지어 전함을 만드는 데 사용될 수도 있다.

24 이 새로운 소재는 이미 스노보드와 자전거를 만드는 데 사용되었다.

25 토마토, 가장 무서운 채소

26 우리는 모두 토마토가 건강에 좋다는 것을 안다.

27 그러나, 1800년대까지 대부분의 미국인들은 토마토에 독성이 있다고 생각했다.

28 1820년에, Robert Johnson이라는 이름의 남자가 토마토가 먹기에 안전하다는 것을 증명하기를 원했다.

29 그래서, 그는 그를 지켜보는 많은 사람들 앞에서 한 바구니의 토마토를 먹었다.

30 그들은 모두 그가 죽을 것이라고 예상했으나 그에게는 아무 일도 일어나지 않았다.

31 그 이후로, 미국인들은 토마토를 먹는 것을 즐겼다.

32 우리는 더 이상 토마토를 두려워하지 않지만, 몇몇 곤충들은 여전히 그것을 무서워한다.

33 만약 곤충들이 방에 들어오지 않게 하고 싶다면, 으깬 토마토 한 그릇을 방구석에 놓아 두어라.

34 곤충들은 토마토 가까이 오지 않을 것이다.

※ 다음 우리말을 영어로 쓰시오.

1 식물에 대한 숨겨진 이야기

➡ _____

2 Popeye와 위대한 시금치

➡ _____

3 Popeye는 세계적으로 유명한 만화 캐릭터다.

➡ _____

4 그는 시금치를 먹음으로써 초인적인 힘을 얻는다.

➡ _____

5 Popeye가 1930년대 미국에서 인기를 얻었을 때, 많은 어린이들이 시금치를 먹기 시작했다.

➡ _____

6 텍사스의 크리스털 시티는 세계의 시금치 수도라고 불리는데, 이곳에서는 Popeye의 동상을 세우기까지 했다.

➡ _____

7 비록 시금치를 먹는 것이 우리에게 초인적인 힘을 주지는 않지만, 시금치는 정말로 많은 영양분을 가지고 있다.

➡ _____

8 이것은 실제로 지구상에서 가장 건강한 식품 10개 중 하나로 여겨진다.

➡ _____

9 시금치는 놀라운 용도로 사용될 수 있다.

➡ _____

10 그것이 물을 흡수할 때, 시금치는 흙으로부터 다른 많은 것들도 흡수한다.

➡ _____

11 몇몇 과학자들은 시금치의 이 특성을 땅에 숨겨진 폭탄을 찾는 데 사용했다.

➡ _____

12 그들은 잎에 감지기가 있는 특별한 시금치를 만든다.

➡ _____

13 이 식물들이 폭탄의 흔적을 흡수하면, 감지기가 빛난다.

➡ _____

14 제2차 세계대전에서의 당근

➡ _____

15 1940년, 영국 공군은 제2차 세계 대전에서 레이더 시스템을 사용해 독일군을 패배시켰다.

➡ _____

16 영국 정부는 이 기술을 비밀로 하기를 원했기 때문에, 신문에 기사를 하나 냈다.

➡ _____

17 그것은 영국 비행사들이 당근을 많이 먹어 야간 시력이 좋아졌다는 내용이었다.
➡ _____

18 모두가 그 이야기를 믿었고 전보다 훨씬 많은 당근을 먹기 시작했다.
➡ _____

19 우리는 정말 당근을 많이 먹어서 야간 시력을 높일 수 있을까?
➡ _____

20 실제로 그럴지는 않지만, 당근은 많은 비타민 A를 함유하는데, 그것은 정말로 우리 눈을 건강하게 유지해 준다.
➡ _____

21 미래에는, 당근이 실제로 전쟁에 이용될지도 모른다.
➡ _____

22 스코틀랜드의 연구원들은 당근을 매우 강하고 가벼운 물질로 바꾸는 방법을 발견했다.
➡ _____

23 그것은 심지어 전함을 만드는 데 사용될 수도 있다.
➡ _____

24 이 새로운 소재는 이미 스노보드와 자전거를 만드는 데 사용되었다.
➡ _____

25 토마토, 가장 무서운 채소
➡ _____

26 우리는 모두 토마토가 건강에 좋다는 것을 안다.
➡ _____

27 그러나, 1800년대까지 대부분의 미국인들은 토마토에 독성이 있다고 생각했다.
➡ _____

28 1820년에, Robert Johnson이라는 이름의 남자가 토마토가 먹기에 안전하다는 것을 증명하기를 원했다.
➡ _____

29 그래서, 그는 그를 지켜보는 많은 사람들 앞에서 한 바구니의 토마토를 먹었다.
➡ _____

30 그들은 모두 그가 죽을 것이라고 예상했으나 그에게는 아무 일도 일어나지 않았다.
➡ _____

31 그 이후로, 미국인들은 토마토를 먹는 것을 즐겼다.
➡ _____

32 우리는 더 이상 토마토를 두려워하지 않지만, 몇몇 곤충들은 여전히 그것을 무서워한다.
➡ _____

33 만약 곤충들이 방에 들어오지 않게 하고 싶다면, 으깬 토마토 한 그릇을 방구석에 놓아 두어라.
➡ _____
_____

34 곤충들은 토마토 가까이 오지 않을 것이다.
➡ _____

※ 다음 우리말과 일치하도록 빈칸에 알맞은 말을 쓰시오.

Inventions from Plants

1. The Sunflower Battery is a _____ _____ _____ _____ energy.

2. It is a _____ _____ _____ the idea _____ _____ the _____ _____ _____.

3. _____ sunflowers, it _____ the sun _____ _____ _____, so it produces _____ _____ _____ _____ _____.

1. 해바라기 배터리는 에너지를 만드는 좋은 방법입니다.
2. 그것은 해바라기의 특징을 이용한다는 생각에서 만들어진 배터리입니다.
3. 해바라기처럼, 그것은 낮 동안에 태양을 향해서, 다른 배터리보다 더 많은 전기를 만들어 냅니다.

After You Read A Read and Match

1. 1. _____

2. • the _____ of Popeye's _____ _____

3. • _____ _____ _____ _____ _____ _____ on the planet

4. • used _____ sensors _____ _____ _____ _____ in the ground

5. 2. _____

6. • used _____ _____ _____ and bicycles

7. • made _____ a very strong and _____ _____

8. • containing a lot of vitamin A, _____ _____ _____ _____ _____ _____

9. 3. _____

10. • good for _____ _____ _____

11. • considered _____ _____ the 1800s

1. 1. 시금치
2. • Popeye의 초인적인 힘의 비밀
3. • 지구상에서 가장 건강한 식품 10개 중 하나
4. • 땅에 숨겨진 폭탄을 찾기 위해 감지기와 함께 사용된다.
5. 2. 당근
6. • 스노보드와 자전거를 만드는 데에 사용된다.
7. • 매우 강하고 가벼운 물질이 된다.
8. • 많은 비타민 A를 함유하는데, 그것은 정말로 우리 눈을 건강하게 유지해 준다.
9. 3. 토마토
10. • 곤충들이 가까이 오지 못하게 하는데 좋다.
11. • 1800년대까지 독성이 있다고 여겨졌다.

Write

1. Potatoes _____ _____ _____ your health.

2. They _____ _____ _____ _____ because they _____ _____ _____.

3. They also _____ _____ _____ _____ _____.

4. Potato juice _____ _____ honey _____ your skin _____ and _____.

5. _____ _____, they _____ you _____ _____.

6. If you eat potatoes, you will _____ _____ _____ _____ _____ _____.

7. Potatoes _____ you _____ _____ in many ways.

1. 감자는 당신의 건강에 좋다.
2. 감자는 혈압을 낮춰주기 때문에 당신의 심장을 건강하게 지켜준다.
3. 감자는 또한 당신의 피부 문제를 해결해 준다.
4. 꿀을 넣은 감자 주스는 당신의 피부를 부드럽고 깨끗하게 만들어 준다.
5. 게다가, 감자는 당신이 살을 빼도록 도와준다.
6. 당신이 감자를 먹으면, 오랜 시간 배부른 상태를 유지할 것이다.
7. 감자는 여러 가지 면에서 당신을 건강하게 지내도록 도와준다.

※ 다음 우리말을 영어로 쓰시오.

Inventions from Plants

1. 해바라기 배터리는 에너지를 만드는 좋은 방법입니다.
➡ _____

2. 그것은 해바라기의 특징을 이용한다는 생각에서 만들어진 배터리입니다.
➡ _____

3. 해바라기처럼, 그것은 낮 동안에 태양을 향해서, 다른 배터리보다 더 많은 전기를 만들어 냅니다.
➡ _____

After You Read A Read and Match

1. 1. 시금치
➡ _____

2. • Popeye의 초인적인 힘의 비밀
➡ _____

3. • 지구상에서 가장 건강한 식품 10개 중 하나
➡ _____

4. • 땅에 숨겨진 폭탄을 찾기 위해 감지기와 함께 사용된다.
➡ _____

5. 2. 당근
➡ _____

6. • 스노보드와 자전거를 만드는 데에 사용된다.
➡ _____

2. • 매우 강하고 가벼운 물질이 된다.
➡ _____

3. • 많은 비타민 A를 함유하는데, 그것은 정말로 우리 눈을 건강하게 유지해 준다.
➡ _____

4. 3. 토마토
➡ _____

5. • 곤충들이 가까이 오지 못하게 하는데 좋다.
➡ _____

6. • 1800년대까지 독성이 있다고 여겨졌다.
➡ _____

Write

1. 감자는 당신의 건강에 좋다.
➡ _____

2. 감자는 혈압을 낮춰주기 때문에 당신의 심장을 건강하게 지켜준다.
➡ _____

3. 감자는 또한 당신의 피부 문제를 해결해 준다.
➡ _____

4. 꿀을 넣은 감자 주스는 당신의 피부를 부드럽고 깨끗하게 만들어 준다.
➡ _____

5. 게다가, 감자는 당신이 살을 빼도록 도와준다.
➡ _____

6. 당신이 감자를 먹으면, 오랜 시간 배부른 상태를 유지할 것이다.
➡ _____

7. 감자는 여러 가지 면에서 당신을 건강하게 지내도록 도와준다.
➡ _____

※ 다음 영어를 우리말로 쓰시오.

01	greenhouse	22	breathe
02	harvest	23	destroy
03	ad(= advertisement)	24	waterfall
04	exhibition	25	trail
05	underwater	26	intangible
06	marine	27	jellyfish
07	nationwide	28	press
08	overseas	29	underground
09	promote	30	suitable
10	bridge	31	audience
11	community	32	overwork
12	moved	33	path
13	heritage	34	realize
14	environment	35	wish for
15	seafood	36	happen to
16	several	37	walk along
17	breadwinner	38	a couple of
18	female	39	get into
19	volcanic	40	be suitable for
20	worldwide	41	give a talk
21	complete	42	a little bit
		43	be good for

※ 다음 우리말을 영어로 쓰시오.

01 폭포 _____

02 광고 _____

03 경로, 길 _____

04 과로하다 _____

05 교량, 다리 _____

06 좁은 길 _____

07 지하의 _____

08 세계적으로 _____

09 화산의, 화산 작용에 의한 _____

10 온실 _____

11 파괴하다 _____

12 전시회, 박람회 _____

13 홍보하다, 촉진하다 _____

14 완성[완료]하다 _____

15 몇몇의 _____

16 생계를 책임지는 사람, 가장 _____

17 적합한, 적절한 _____

18 여성의 _____

19 누르다; 언론, 기자 _____

20 지역 공동체 _____

21 무형의, 만질 수 없는 _____

22 수중의, 물속에서 _____

23 해파리 _____

24 해양의, 바다의 _____

25 수확하다 _____

26 청중 _____

27 유산 _____

28 호흡하다 _____

29 전국적인 _____

30 해외의 _____

31 깨닫다, 인식하다 _____

32 단단히, 꽉 _____

33 (북 등을 치는) 소리, (심장의) 고동 _____

34 풍년 _____

35 휴가가다 _____

36 ~에 들어가다 _____

37 우연히 ~하다 _____

38 ~을 따라 걷다 _____

39 ~에 유익하다 _____

40 계속해서 ~하다 _____

41 힘을 북돋아 주다, 격려하다 _____

42 거들어 주다, 돕다 _____

43 발표하다 _____

※ 다음 영영풀이에 알맞은 단어를 <보기>에서 골라 쓴 후, 우리말 뜻을 쓰시오.

1 _____ : to gather a crop: _____

2 _____ : under the surface of the ground: _____

3 _____ : to finish making or doing something: _____

4 _____ : one of a series of regular movements or hitting actions: _____

5 _____ : a place where a stream or river falls from a high place: _____

6 _____ : right or appropriate for a particular purpose or occasion: _____

7 _____ : to take air into your lungs and send it out again: _____

8 _____ : the people who live in the same area, town, etc.: _____

9 _____ : the traditional beliefs, values, customs of a family, country, or society: _____

10 _____ : having value but not existing physically: _____

11 _____ : to or in a foreign country that is across the sea: _____

12 _____ : fish and shellfish that live in the ocean and are used for food: _____

13 _____ : to damage something so badly that it no longer exists, works, etc.: _____

14 _____ : a picture, set of words, or a short film, intended to persuade people to buy: _____

15 _____ : a structure built over something such as a river so that people or vehicles can get across: _____

16 _____ : the member of a family who earns the money to support the others: _____

보기			
destroy	breadwinner	community	suitable
intangible	overseas	harvest	seafood
bridge	complete	waterfall	ad
heritage	breathe	beat	underground

※ 다음 우리말과 일치하도록 빈칸에 알맞은 말을 쓰시오.

Listen & Speak 1 A-1

G: Wow, _____ _____ the _____ in this _____. I wonder _____ _____ _____ _____.

B: That's Gwangandaegyo in Busan.

G: _____ _____ you _____ that?

B: I _____ _____ _____ my family _____ _____.

Listen & Speak 1 A-2

B: _____ _____ there. _____ _____ _____ _____ there are so many people _____ _____ _____.

G: They're _____ _____ _____ _____ the new bakery there.

B: Why? Is it _____?

G: Yes. It was _____ a TV program.

B: Really? We _____ _____ their bread _____.

G: Sure.

Listen & Speak 2 A-1

W: Excuse me, _____ _____ _____ _____ an audio guide.

M: _____ you _____.

W: Could you _____ _____ _____ _____ _____?

M: Sure. _____ this button, and it'll tell you _____ _____ _____.

Listen & Speak 2 A-2

B: _____ you _____ _____ this summer?

G: I'm _____ _____ Jejudo to _____ _____ the Jeju Olle Trail.

B: The Jeju Olle Trail? _____ _____ _____ _____ _____?

G: It's a _____ _____ _____ _____ Jejudo.

B: Oh, I see. I hope you _____ _____ _____!

Communication A

Jaden: Do you hear that? _____ _____ _____ that music is _____ _____.

Yuri: I think it's coming from _____ _____. Do you want to go and _____ _____ _____?

Jaden: Yes, I love that _____ _____. Is it _____ Korean music?

Yuri: Yes, it's _____ nongak. It's _____ _____ _____ _____ band music.

Jaden: Nongak? _____ _____ _____ _____ _____ _____ more about it?

Yuri: It's _____ used to _____ _____ farmers and _____ _____ a _____ _____.

Jaden: I see. Look! Some people _____ _____ _____ the _____.

Yuri: Yes, that's a big _____ _____ nongak. Dancing together _____ the music.

Jaden: _____ _____ them.

Yuri: Sure. _____ _____?

Jaden: 저거 들리니? 저 음악이 어디서 오는 것인지 궁금하네.
유리: 저기서 나오는 것 같은데. 가서 확인해 볼래?
Jaden: 그래, 저 강한 비트가 마음에 들어. 그게 한국의 전통 음악이니?
유리: 맞아, 농악이라고 해. 공동체 악단 음악의 한 종류야.
Jaden: 농악? 그것에 대해 좀 더 설명해 줄래?
유리: 그건 전통적으로 농부들의 힘을 북돋아 주고 풍년을 기원하기 위해 사용되었어.
Jaden: 그렇구나. 봐! 몇몇 사람들이 리듬에 맞춰 춤추고 있어.
유리: 그래, 그게 농악의 큰 부분이야. 함께 춤추는 것이 음악을 완성하지.
Jaden: 저들과 함께 하자.
유리: 물론이야. 왜 안 되겠어?

Progree Check 1

W: Look over there. _____ _____ _____ _____ _____ on the road.

M: _____ _____ people are _____ _____ _____ this weekend.

W: Really? Then, _____ _____ _____ go somewhere, _____?

M: O.K.

W: 저기 좀 봐요. 도로에 왜 저렇게 차가 많은지 궁금하네요.
M: 많은 사람들이 이번 주말에 휴가를 가거든요.
W: 정말로요? 그럼, 우리도 어디 가는 게 어떤가요?
M: 좋아요.

Progree Check 2

B: _____ me, I'd like to use a _____ _____.

W: O.K. You can use this machine.

B: Could you explain _____ _____ _____ _____ _____ _____?

W: Sure. _____ the button for _____ _____, and then _____ the start button.

B: Thank you.

B: 실례합니다, 복사기를 좀 쓰고 싶은데요.
W: 알겠어요. 이 기계를 써도 돼요.
B: 어떻게 양면 복사를 하는지 설명해 주실 수 있나요?
W: 물론이죠. 양면 복사 버튼을 누르고, 시작 버튼을 누르세요.
B: 감사합니다.

※ 다음 우리말에 맞도록 대화를 영어로 쓰시오.

Listen & Speak 1 A-1

G: _____

B: _____

G: _____

B: _____

G: 와, 이 광고에 나오는 다리 좀 봐. 어디에서 찍은 사진인지 궁금하네.
B: 부산의 광안대교야.
G: 그걸 어떻게 아니?
B: 작년 여름에 우리 가족들과 그곳에 갔었거든.

Listen & Speak 1 A-2

B: _____

G: _____

B: _____

G: _____

B: _____

G: _____

B: 저기 좀 봐. 왜 저렇게 많은 사람들이 줄을 서서 기다리고 있는지 궁금하네.
G: 새로 생긴 제과점에 들어가려고 기다리고 있는 거야.
B: 왜? 유명한 곳이야?
G: 맞아. TV 프로그램에 나왔어.
B: 정말? 그럼 우리 저곳의 빵을 먹어 봐야겠다.
G: 그래.

Listen & Speak 2 A-1

W: _____

M: _____

W: _____

M: _____

W: 실례합니다, 음성 가이드를 대여하고 싶은데요.
M: 여기 있습니다.
W: 어떻게 사용하는지 설명해 주실 수 있나요?
M: 물론이죠. 이 버튼을 누르면, 무엇을 해야 할지 말해 줄 겁니다.

Listen & Speak 2 A-2

B: _____

G: _____

B: _____

G: _____

B: _____

B: 이번 여름에 어디 갈 거야?
G: 제주 올레길을 따라 걸으러 제주도에 갈 거야.
B: 제주 올레길? 그게 무엇인지 설명해 줄래?
G: 제주도 둘레에 있는 긴 하이킹 코스야.
B: 오, 그렇구나. 즐거운 여행이 되길 바랄게!

Communication A

Jaden: _____

Yuri: _____

Jaden: _____

Yuri: _____

Jaden: _____

Yuri: _____

Jaden: _____

Yuri: _____

Jaden: _____

Yuri: _____

Jaden: 저거 들리니? 저 음악이 어디서 오는 것인지 궁금하네.
유리: 저기서 나오는 것 같은데. 가서 확인해 볼래?
Jaden: 그래. 저 강한 비트가 마음에 들어. 그게 한국의 전통 음악이니?
유리: 맞아, 농악이라고 해. 공동체 악단 음악의 한 종류야.
Jaden: 농악? 그것에 대해 좀 더 설명해 줄래?
유리: 그건 전통적으로 농부들의 힘을 북돋아 주고 풍년을 기원하기 위해 사용되었어.
Jaden: 그렇구나. 봐! 몇몇 사람들이 리듬에 맞춰 춤추고 있어.
유리: 그래, 그게 농악의 큰 부분이야. 함께 춤추는 것이 음악을 완성하지.
Jaden: 저들과 함께 하자.
유리: 물론이야. 왜 안 되겠어?

Progree Check 1

W: _____

M: _____

W: _____

M: _____

W: 저기 좀 봐요. 도로에 왜 저렇게 차가 많은지 궁금하네요.
M: 많은 사람들이 이번 주말에 휴가를 가거든요.
W: 정말로요? 그럼, 우리도 어디 가는 게 어떤가요?
M: 좋아요.

Progree Check 2

B: _____

W: _____

B: _____

W: _____

B: _____

B: 실례합니다, 복사기를 좀 쓰고 싶은데요.
W: 알겠어요. 이 기계를 써도 돼요.
B: 어떻게 양면 복사를 하는지 설명해 주실 수 있나요?
W: 물론이죠. 양면 복사 버튼을 누르고, 시작 버튼을 누르세요.
B: 감사합니다.

※ 다음 우리말과 일치하도록 빈칸에 알맞은 것을 골라 쓰시오.

1 _____, _____ _____ of Korea

A. Divers　　　　B. Female　　　　C. Haenyeo

2 For the past _____ years, the _____ photographer Zin Kim has _____ the culture of Jeju haenyeo _____.

A. promoted　　B. several　　C. worldwide　　D. underwater

3 Haenyeo are Korean _____ divers who _____ seafood _____ any _____ devices.

A. without　　B. female　　C. breathing　　D. harvest

4 Their culture _____ UNESCO's _____ Cultural _____ in 2016.

A. Heritage　　B. Intangible　　C. made　　D. list

5 At her studio _____ week, Zin Kim was _____ about her _____ of _____ pictures of haenyeo.

A. interviewed　　B. taking　　C. last　　D. experience

6 Q. How did you _____ _____ _____ _____ photos of haenyeo?

A. interested　　B. in　　C. become　　D. taking

7 _____ _____, I _____ _____ take pictures of a haenyeo.

A. happened　　B. day　　C. to　　D. one

8 I _____ _____ _____ _____ that she was enjoying her job.

A. to　　B. was　　C. find　　D. surprised

9 _____ then, I had only _____ black-and-white photos of haenyeo who _____ very _____.

A. looked　　B. until　　C. tired　　D. seen

10 However, she _____ _____ even after she had _____ in the water for _____ five hours.

A. over　　B. kept　　C. been　　D. laughing

11 I _____ then that I _____ _____ pictures of haenyeo.

A. should　　B. realized　　C. take

12 Q. You take beautiful pictures of them, but _____ _____ _____ _____ take pictures of haenyeo?

A. to　　B. isn't　　C. difficult　　D. it

13 _____ first, they didn't understand _____ _____ to take their pictures.

A. wanted　　B. why　　C. I　　D. at

14 They didn't think they _____ _____ their _____.

A. pretty　　B. wetsuits　　C. looked　　D. in

15 _____, I said to them, "You're _____ _____.

A. very　　B. so　　C. special

16 I want to _____ your _____ _____ the _____."

A. to　　B. show　　C. culture　　D. world

17 They _____ _____ to me _____.

A. up　　B. opened　　C. then

18 Of course, I also promised them that I would _____ _____ _____ _____ in my pictures.

A. them　　B. beautiful　　C. make　　D. look

1 해녀, 한국의 여성 잠수부

2 지난 몇 년 동안, 수중 사진작가 Zin Kim은 제주 해녀 문화를 전 세계에 홍보해 왔다.

3 해녀는 어떤 호흡 장치도 사용하지 않고 해산물을 채취하는 한국의 여성 잠수부들이다.

4 그들의 문화는 2016년에 유네스코 무형문화유산에 등재되었다.

5 지난주 그녀의 작업실에서, Zin Kim과 해녀의 사진을 찍는 그녀의 경험에 대해 인터뷰를 했다.

6 Q. 어떻게 해녀의 사진을 찍는 것에 관심을 가지게 되었나요?

7 어느 날, 저는 우연히 한 해녀의 사진을 찍게 되었어요.

8 저는 그녀가 자신의 일을 즐겁게 하는 것을 보고 놀랐습니다.

9 그때까지, 저는 흑백 사진 속의 아주 지친 모습의 해녀만 봐 왔죠.

10 하지만, 그녀는 다섯 시간이 넘도록 물속에 있은 후에도 계속 웃었어요.

11 저는 그때 해녀의 사진을 찍어야겠다고 깨달았어요.

12 Q. 작가님은 아름다운 해녀 사진들을 찍으시는데, 그들의 사진을 찍는 것이 어렵진 않으신가요?

13 처음에, 그들은 제가 왜 자신들의 사진을 찍으려고 하는지 이해하지 못했어요.

14 그들은 잠수복을 입은 자신들의 모습이 예뻐 보인다고 생각하지 않았으니까요.

15 그래서, 제가 그들에게 말했죠, "여러분들은 아주 특별해요.

16 저는 여러분의 문화를 세계에 알리고 싶어요."

17 그들은 그때 제게 마음을 열었어요.

18 물론, 저 또한 그들에게 제 사진 속에서 그들을 아름답게 보이도록 하겠다고 약속했지요.

19 Q. Could you _____ _____ _____ haenyeo?
  A. more   B. tell   C. about   D. us

20 What's _____ _____ them?
  A. special   B. about   C. so

21 I _____ _____ three _____ .
  A. things   B. tell   C. you   D. can

22 First, haenyeo are a _____ of _____ .
  A. strong   B. symbol   C. women

23 Jejudo, which is a _____ island, is not _____ for _____ ,
so many haenyeo have become the _____ for their families.
  A. suitable   B. breadwinners   C. farming   D. volcanic

24 Second, haenyeo _____ their _____ communities and help
_____ .
  A. each   B. form   C. other   D. own

25 For _____ , _____ haenyeo train _____ haenyeo.
  A. example   B. less-experienced   C. more-experienced

26 Third, because they _____ in the water _____ any _____
devices, haenyeo can't _____ a lot of seafood.
  A. without   B. stay   C. catch   D. breathing

27 This is _____ _____ the _____ .
  A. good   B. environment   C. for   D. underwater

28 Catching too much _____ life at one _____ in one _____
can _____ the ocean.
  A. destroy   B. marine   C. place   D. time

29 Q. Lastly, please tell us _____ you're _____ to _____ in
the _____ .
  A. what   B. future   C. planning   D. do

30 I once _____ an overseas _____ with a couple of haenyeo to
give a _____ about their _____ .
  A. talk   B. attended   C. lives   D. exhibition

31 When I _____ my talk, one of the haenyeo _____ my
_____ .
  A. held   B. tightly   C. finished   D. hand

32 She _____ _____ me, "Thank you _____ .
  A. much   B. so   C. to   D. said

33 I've never known in my whole life that I was _____
_____ ."
  A. special   B. a   C. person   D. such

34 She was _____ _____ _____ .
  A. with   B. crying   C. happiness

35 Everyone in the audience _____ _____ _____ .
  A. deeply   B. was   C. moved

36 I can _____ _____ that _____ , so I'll _____ to take
pictures of haenyeo.
  A. continue   B. forget   C. never   D. moment

37 I want to tell _____ _____ _____ them to many
more people in the world.
  A. beautiful   B. about   C. more   D. stories

19 Q. 해녀에 대해서 더 말씀해 주 시겠어요?

20 그들은 무엇이 그렇게 특별한가요?

21 세 가지를 말씀 드릴게요.

22 첫 번째로, 해녀들은 강인한 여 성의 상징이에요.

23 제주도는 화산섬이고, 이는 농 사에 적합하지 않아서 많은 해 녀들이 가족들의 생계비를 버는 가장이 되어 왔어요.

24 둘째로, 해녀들은 그들 자신의 공동체를 조직하고 서로 도와요.

25 예를 들어, 경험이 더 많은 해녀 들이 경험이 적은 해녀들을 훈 련시키지요.

26 세 번째로, 어떤 호흡 장치도 사 용하지 않고 물속에 머물기 때 문에, 해녀는 많은 해산물을 채 취할 수가 없어요.

27 이것은 수중 환경에 좋은 것이 지요.

28 한 번에 한 장소에서 너무 많은 해양생물을 채취하는 것은 바다 를 파괴할 수 있으니까요.

29 Q. 마지막으로, 앞으로 계획하고 있는 것에 대해 말씀해 주세요.

30 예전에 두 명의 해녀들과 함께 그들의 삶에 대해 이야기하기 위해 해외에서 열리는 박람회에 참가한 적이 있어요.

31 제가 연설을 마쳤을 때, 해녀 중 한 분이 제 손을 꼭 잡았어요.

32 그분이 말했죠, "너무 고마워.

33 내 평생 내가 이렇게 특별한 사 람이라는 걸 미처 알지 못했어."

34 그녀는 행복해서 울고 있었어요.

35 청중들 모두가 깊은 감동을 받 았어요.

36 전 그 순간을 절대 잊을 수가 없 기 때문에 해녀의 사진을 계속 해서 찍을 거예요.

37 저는 그들에 대한 더 많은 아름 다운 이야기들을 세계의 더 많은 사람들에게 알려 주고 싶어요.

※ 다음 우리말과 일치하도록 빈칸에 알맞은 말을 쓰시오.

1 Haenyeo, _____ _____ of Korea

2 For the past several years, the _____ _____ Zin Kim _____ _____ the culture of Jeju haenyeo _____.

3 Haenyeo are Korean _____ _____ who harvest seafood _____ _____ _____ _____.

4 Their culture _____ _____ _____ _____ _____ _____ in 2016.

5 At her studio last week, Zin Kim _____ _____ about her _____ _____ _____ _____ of haenyeo.

6 Q. How did you _____ _____ _____ _____ photos of haenyeo?

7 _____ _____, I _____ _____ take pictures of a haenyeo.

8 I _____ _____ _____ that she _____ _____ her job.

9 _____ _____, I _____ _____ black-and-white photos of haenyeo who _____ _____ _____ _____.

10 However, she _____ _____ even after she had been in the water _____ _____ _____ _____ _____.

11 I _____ then that I _____ _____ _____ of haenyeo.

12 Q. You take beautiful pictures of them, but _____ _____ _____ _____ _____ _____ of haenyeo?

13 _____ _____, they didn't understand _____ _____ to take their pictures.

14 They didn't think they _____ _____ _____ _____.

15 So, I said to them, "You're _____ _____.

16 I want to _____ your culture _____ the world."

17 They _____ _____ to me _____.

18 _____ _____, I also promised them that I would _____ _____ look _____ in my pictures.

---

1 해녀, 한국의 여성 잠수부

2 지난 몇 년 동안, 수중 사진작가 Zin Kim은 제주 해녀 문화를 전 세계에 홍보해 왔다.

3 해녀는 어떤 호흡 장치도 사용하지 않고 해산물을 채취하는 한국의 여성 잠수부들이다.

4 그들의 문화는 2016년에 유네스코 무형문화유산에 등재되었다.

5 지난주 그녀의 작업실에서, Zin Kim과 해녀의 사진을 찍는 그녀의 경험에 대해 인터뷰를 했다.

6 Q. 어떻게 해녀의 사진을 찍는 것에 관심을 가지게 되었나요?

7 어느 날, 저는 우연히 한 해녀의 사진을 찍게 되었어요.

8 저는 그녀가 자신의 일을 즐겁게 하는 것을 보고 놀랐습니다.

9 그때까지, 저는 흑백 사진 속의 아주 지친 모습의 해녀만 봐 왔죠.

10 하지만, 그녀는 다섯 시간이 넘도록 물속에 있은 후에도 계속 웃었어요.

11 저는 그때 해녀의 사진을 찍어야겠다고 깨달았어요.

12 Q. 작가님은 아름다운 해녀 사진들을 찍으시는데, 그들의 사진을 찍는 것이 어렵진 않으신가요?

13 처음에, 그들은 제가 왜 자신들의 사진을 찍으려고 하는지 이해하지 못했어요.

14 그들은 잠수복을 입은 자신들의 모습이 예뻐 보인다고 생각하지 않았으니까요.

15 그래서, 제가 그들에게 말했죠, "여러분은 아주 특별해요.

16 저는 여러분의 문화를 세계에 알리고 싶어요."

17 그들은 그때 제게 마음을 열었어요.

18 물론, 저 또한 그들에게 제 사진 속에서 그들을 아름답게 보이도록 하겠다고 약속했지요.

19 Q. Could you tell us _____ _____ haenyeo?

20 What's _____ _____ about them?

21 I _____ _____ _____ three things.

22 First, haenyeo are a _____ _____ _____ _____ .

23 Jejudo, _____ is a volcanic island, _____ _____ _____ farming, so many haenyeo _____ _____ _____ _____ their families.

24 Second, haenyeo _____ their _____ _____ and help _____ _____ .

25 For example, _____ haenyeo train _____ haenyeo.

26 Third, _____ they stay in the water _____ any _____ _____ , haenyeo _____ _____ a lot of seafood.

27 This _____ _____ _____ the _____ _____ .

28 _____ too much marine life _____ _____ _____ _____ _____ _____ _____ _____ the ocean.

29 Q. Lastly, please tell us _____ you're _____ in the future.

30 I once _____ an _____ _____ with a couple of haenyeo to _____ _____ _____ about their lives.

31 When I finished my talk, one of the haenyeo _____ _____ _____ _____ .

32 She said to me, "Thank you _____ _____ .

33 I've never known in my _____ _____ that I was _____ _____ _____ ."

34 She was _____ _____ _____ .

35 Everyone in the audience _____ _____ _____ .

36 I _____ _____ _____ _____ that moment, so I'll _____ _____ _____ pictures of haenyeo.

37 I want to tell _____ _____ _____ _____ _____ to many more people in the world.

19 Q. 해녀에 대해서 더 말씀해 주시겠어요?

20 그들은 무엇이 그렇게 특별한가요?

21 세 가지를 말씀 드릴게요.

22 첫 번째로, 해녀들은 강인한 여성의 상징이에요.

23 제주도는 화산섬이고, 이는 농사에 적합하지 않아서 많은 해녀들이 가족들의 생계비를 버는 가장이 되어 왔어요.

24 둘째로, 해녀들은 그들 자신의 공동체를 조직하고 서로 도와요.

25 예를 들어, 경험이 더 많은 해녀들이 경험이 적은 해녀들을 훈련시키지요.

26 세 번째로, 어떤 호흡 장치도 사용하지 않고 물속에 머물기 때문에, 해녀는 많은 해산물을 채취할 수가 없어요.

27 이것은 수중 환경에 좋은 것이지요.

28 한 번에 한 장소에서 너무 많은 해양생물을 채취하는 것은 바다를 파괴할 수 있으니까요.

29 Q. 마지막으로, 앞으로 계획하고 있는 것에 대해 말씀해 주세요.

30 예전에 두 명의 해녀들과 함께 그들의 삶에 대해 이야기하기 위해 해외에서 열리는 박람회에 참가한 적이 있어요.

31 제가 연설을 마쳤을 때, 해녀 중 한 분이 제 손을 꼭 잡았어요.

32 그분이 말했죠, "너무 고마워.

33 내 평생 내가 이렇게 특별한 사람이라는 걸 미처 알지 못했어."

34 그녀는 행복해서 울고 있었어요.

35 청중들 모두가 깊은 감동을 받았어요.

36 전 그 순간을 절대 잊을 수가 없기 때문에 해녀의 사진을 계속해서 찍을 거예요.

37 저는 그들에 대한 더 많은 아름다운 이야기들을 세계의 더 많은 사람들에게 알려 주고 싶어요.

※ 다음 문장을 우리말로 쓰시오.

1 ▸ Haenyeo, Female Divers of Korea
➡ _____

2 ▸ For the past several years, the underwater photographer Zin Kim has promoted the culture of Jeju haenyeo worldwide.
➡ _____

3 ▸ Haenyeo are Korean female divers who harvest seafood without any breathing devices.
➡ _____

4 ▸ Their culture made UNESCO's Intangible Cultural Heritage list in 2016.
➡ _____

5 ▸ At her studio last week, Zin Kim was interviewed about her experience of taking pictures of haenyeo.
➡ _____

6 ▸ Q. How did you become interested in taking photos of haenyeo?
➡ _____

7 ▸ One day, I happened to take pictures of a haenyeo.
➡ _____

8 ▸ I was surprised to find that she was enjoying her job.
➡ _____

9 ▸ Until then, I had only seen black-and-white photos of haenyeo who looked very tired.
➡ _____

10 ▸ However, she kept laughing even after she had been in the water for over five hours.
➡ _____

11 ▸ I realized then that I should take pictures of haenyeo.
➡ _____

12 ▸ Q. You take beautiful pictures of them, but isn't it difficult to take pictures of haenyeo?
➡ _____

13 ▸ At first, they didn't understand why I wanted to take their pictures.
➡ _____

14 ▸ They didn't think they looked pretty in their wetsuits.
➡ _____

15 ▸ So, I said to them, "You're very special.
➡ _____

16 ▸ I want to show your culture to the world."
➡ _____

17 ▸ They opened up to me then.
➡ _____

18 ▸ Of course, I also promised them that I would make them look beautiful in my pictures.
➡ _____

19 ▸ Q. Could you tell us more about haenyeo?w
➡ _____

20 What's so special about them?

➡ _____

21 I can tell you three things.

➡ _____

22 First, haenyeo are a symbol of strong women.

➡ _____

23 Jejudo, which is a volcanic island, is not suitable for farming, so many haenyeo have become the breadwinners for their families.

➡ _____

24 Second, haenyeo form their own communities and help each other.

➡ _____

25 For example, more-experienced haenyeo train less-experienced haenyeo.

➡ _____

26 Third, because they stay in the water without any breathing devices, haenyeo can't catch a lot of seafood.

➡ _____

27 This is good for the underwater environment.

➡ _____

28 Catching too much marine life at one time in one place can destroy the ocean.

➡ _____

29 Q. Lastly, please tell us what you're planning to do in the future.

➡ _____

30 I once attended an overseas exhibition with a couple of haenyeo to give a talk about their lives.

➡ _____

31 When I finished my talk, one of the haenyeo held my hand tightly.

➡ _____

32 She said to me, "Thank you so much.

➡ _____

33 I've never known in my whole life that I was such a special person."

➡ _____

34 She was crying with happiness.

➡ _____

35 Everyone in the audience was deeply moved.

➡ _____

36 I can never forget that moment, so I'll continue to take pictures of haenyeo.

➡ _____

37 I want to tell more beautiful stories about them to many more people in the world.

➡ _____

※ 다음 괄호 안의 단어들을 우리말에 맞도록 바르게 배열하시오.

1 (Female / Haenyeo, / of / Divers / Korea)
➡ _____

2 (the / for / past / years, / several / underwater / the / Zin / photographer / Kim / promoted / has / culture / the / Jeju / of / worldwide. / haenyeo)
➡ _____

3 (are / haenyeo / Korean / divers / female / harvest / who / without / seafood / breathing / any / devices.)
➡ _____

4 (culture / their / UNESCO's / made / Cultural / Intangible / Heritage / in / list / 2016.)
➡ _____

5 (her / at / last / studio / week, / Kim / Zin / interviewed / was / her / about / of / experience / taking / of / pictures / haenyeo.)
➡ _____
_____

6 (Q. / did / how / become / you / in / interested / photos / taking / haenyeo? / of)
➡ _____

7 (day, / one / happened / I / take / to / of / pictures / haenyeo. / a)
➡ _____

8 (was / I / to / surprised / find / she / that / enjoying / was / job. / her)
➡ _____

9 (then, / until / had / I / seen / only / photos / black-and-white / haenyeo / of / looked / who / tired. / very)
➡ _____

10 (she / however, / laughing / kept / after / even / she / been / had / the / in / water / over / for / hours. / five)
➡ _____
_____

11 (realized / I / that / then / should / I / pictures / take / haenyeo. / of)
➡ _____

12 (Q. / take / you / pictures / beautiful / them, / of / isn't / but / difficult / it / take / to / of / pictures / haenyeo?)
➡ _____
_____

1 해녀, 한국의 여성 잠수부

2 지난 몇 년 동안, 수중 사진작가 Zin Kim은 제주 해녀 문화를 전 세계에 홍보해 왔다.

3 해녀는 어떤 호흡 장치도 사용하지 않고 해산물을 채취하는 한국의 여성 잠수부들이다.

4 그들의 문화는 2016년에 유네스코 무형문화유산에 등재되었다.

5 지난주 그녀의 작업실에서, Zin Kim과 해녀의 사진을 찍는 그녀의 경험에 대해 인터뷰를 했다.

6 Q. 어떻게 해녀의 사진을 찍는 것에 관심을 가지게 되었나요?

7 어느 날, 저는 우연히 한 해녀의 사진을 찍게 되었어요.

8 저는 그녀가 자신의 일을 즐겁게 하는 것을 보고 놀랐습니다.

9 그때까지, 저는 흑백 사진 속의 아주 지친 모습의 해녀만 봐 왔죠.

10 하지만, 그녀는 다섯 시간이 넘도록 물속에 있은 후에도 계속 웃었어요.

11 저는 그때 해녀의 사진을 찍어야겠다고 깨달았어요.

12 Q. 작가님은 아름다운 해녀 사진들을 찍으시는데, 그들의 사진을 찍는 것이 어렵진 않으신가요?

13 (first, / at / didn't / they / why / understand / wanted / I / take / to / pictures. / their)

   ➡ _____

14 (didn't / they / they / think / pretty / looked / their / in / wetsuits.)

   ➡ _____

15 (I / so, / said / them, / to / very / "you're / special.)

   ➡ _____

16 (want / I / show / to / culture / your / the / to / world.")

   ➡ _____

17 (opened / they / to / up / then. / me)

   ➡ _____

18 (course, / of / also / I / them / promised / I / that / make / would / look / them / in / beautiful / pictures. / my)

   ➡ _____

      _____

19 (Q. / you / could / us / tell / about / more / haenyeo?)

   ➡ _____

20 (so / what's / about / special / them?)

   ➡ _____

21 (can / I / you / tell / things. / three)

   ➡ _____

22 (haenyeo / first, / a / are / of / symbol / women. / strong)

   ➡ _____

23 (which / Jejudo, / is / volcanic / a / island, / not / is / for / suitable / farming, / many / so / have / haenyeo / the / become / breadwinners / their / for / families.)

   ➡ _____

      _____

24 (haenyeo / second, / their / form / communities / own / and / each / help / other.)

   ➡ _____

25 (example, / for / haenyeo / more-experienced / less-experienced / train / haenyeo.)

   ➡ _____

13 처음에, 그들은 제가 왜 자신들의 사진을 찍으려고 하는지 이해하지 못했어요.

14 그들은 잠수복을 입은 자신들의 모습이 예뻐 보인다고 생각하지 않았으니까요.

15 그래서, 제가 그들에게 말했죠. "여러분들은 아주 특별해요.

16 저는 여러분의 문화를 세계에 알리고 싶어요."

17 그들은 그때 제게 마음을 열었어요.

18 물론, 저 또한 그들에게 제 사진 속에서 그들을 아름답게 보이도록 하겠다고 약속했지요.

19 Q. 해녀에 대해서 더 말씀해 주시겠어요?

20 그들은 무엇이 그렇게 특별한가요?

21 세 가지를 말씀 드릴게요.

22 첫 번째로, 해녀들은 강인한 여성의 상징이에요.

23 제주도는 화산섬이고, 이는 농사에 적합하지 않아서 많은 해녀들이 가족들의 생계비를 버는 가장이 되어 왔어요.

24 둘째로, 해녀들은 그들 자신의 공동체를 조직하고 서로 도와요.

25 예를 들어, 경험이 더 많은 해녀들이 경험이 적은 해녀들을 훈련시키지요.

26 (because / third, / stay / they / the / in / without / water / breathing / any / devices, / can't / haenyeo / a / catch / of / lot / seafood.)

➡ _____

_____

27 (is / this / for / good / underwater / the / environment.)

➡ _____

28 (too / catching / much / life / marine / one / at / time / one / in / place / destroy / can / ocean. / the)

➡ _____

_____

29 (Q. / please / lastly, / us / tell / you're / what / to / planning / do / the / in / future.)

➡ _____

30 (once / I / an / attneded / overseas / with / exhibition / a / of / couple / haenyeo / a / give / to / talk / their / lives. / about)

➡ _____

_____

31 (I / when / my / finished / talk, / of / one / haenyeo / the / my / held / tightly. / hand)

➡ _____

32 (said / she / me, / to / you / "thank / much. / so)

➡ _____

33 (never / I've / in / known / whole / my / that / life / was / I / a / such / person." / special)

➡ _____

34 (was / she / with / crying / happiness.)

➡ _____

35 (in / everyone / audience / the / was / moved. / deeply)

➡ _____

36 (can / I / forget / never / moment, / that / I'll / so / to / continue / take / of / haenyeo / pictures)

➡ _____

_____

37 (want / I / to / more / tell / stories / beautiful / about / to / them / more / many / people / the / in / world.)

➡ _____

_____

26 세 번째로, 어떤 호흡 장치도 사용하지 않고 물속에 머물기 때문에, 해녀는 많은 해산물을 채취할 수가 없어요.

27 이것은 수중 환경에 좋은 것이지요.

28 한 번에 한 장소에서 너무 많은 해양생물을 채취하는 것은 바다를 파괴할 수 있으니까요.

29 Q. 마지막으로, 앞으로 계획하고 있는 것에 대해 말씀해 주세요.

30 예전에 두 명의 해녀들과 함께 그들의 삶에 대해 이야기하기 위해 해외에서 열리는 박람회에 참가한 적이 있어요.

31 제가 연설을 마쳤을 때, 해녀 중 한 분이 제 손을 꼭 잡았어요.

32 그분이 말했죠. "너무 고마워.

33 내 평생 내가 이렇게 특별한 사람이라는 걸 미처 알지 못했어."

34 그녀는 행복해서 울고 있었어요.

35 청중들 모두가 깊은 감동을 받았어요.

36 전 그 순간을 절대 잊을 수가 없기 때문에 해녀의 사진을 계속해서 찍을 거예요.

37 저는 그들에 대한 더 많은 아름다운 이야기들을 세계의 더 많은 사람들에게 알려 주고 싶어요.

※ 다음 우리말을 영어로 쓰시오.

1 해녀, 한국의 여성 잠수부

➡ _____

2 지난 몇 년 동안, 수중 사진작가 Zin Kim은 제주 해녀 문화를 전 세계에 홍보해 왔다.

➡ _____

_____

3 해녀는 어떤 호흡 장치도 사용하지 않고 해산물을 채취하는 한국의 여성 잠수부들이다.

➡ _____

4 그들의 문화는 2016년에 유네스코 무형문화유산에 등재되었다.

➡ _____

5 지난주 그녀의 작업실에서, Zin Kim과 해녀의 사진을 찍는 그녀의 경험에 대해 인터뷰를 했다.

➡ _____

6 Q. 어떻게 해녀의 사진을 찍는 것에 관심을 가지게 되었나요?

➡ _____

7 어느 날, 저는 우연히 한 해녀의 사진을 찍게 되었어요.

➡ _____

8 저는 그녀가 자신의 일을 즐겁게 하는 것을 보고 놀랐습니다.

➡ _____

9 그때까지, 저는 흑백 사진 속의 아주 지친 모습의 해녀만 봐 왔죠.

➡ _____

10 하지만, 그녀는 다섯 시간이 넘도록 물속에 있은 후에도 계속 웃었어요.

➡ _____

11 저는 그때 해녀의 사진을 찍어야겠다고 깨달았어요.

➡ _____

12 Q. 작가님은 아름다운 해녀 사진들을 찍으시는데, 그들의 사진을 찍는 것이 어렵진 않으신가요?

➡ _____

13 처음에, 그들은 제가 왜 자신들의 사진을 찍으려고 하는지 이해하지 못했어요.

➡ _____

14 그들은 잠수복을 입은 자신들의 모습이 예뻐 보인다고 생각하지 않았으니까요.

➡ _____

15 그래서, 제가 그들에게 말했죠, "여러분들은 아주 특별해요.

➡ _____

16 저는 여러분의 문화를 세계에 알리고 싶어요."

➡ _____

17 그들은 그때 제게 마음을 열었어요.

➡ _____

18 물론, 저 또한 그들에게 제 사진 속에서 그들을 아름답게 보이도록 하겠다고 약속했지요.

➡ _____

19 Q. 해녀에 대해서 더 말씀해 주시겠어요?

➡ _____

20 그들은 무엇이 그렇게 특별한가요?

➡ _____

21 세 가지를 말씀 드릴게요.

➡ _____

22 첫 번째로, 해녀들은 강인한 여성의 상징이에요.

➡ _____

23 제주도는 화산섬이고, 이는 농사에 적합하지 않아서 많은 해녀들이 가족들의 생계비를 버는 가장이 되어 왔어요.

➡ _____

24 둘째로, 해녀들은 그들 자신의 공동체를 조직하고 서로 도와요.

➡ _____

25 예를 들어, 경험이 더 많은 해녀들이 경험이 적은 해녀들을 훈련시키지요.

➡ _____

26 세 번째로, 어떤 호흡 장치도 사용하지 않고 물속에 머물기 때문에, 해녀는 많은 해산물을 채취할 수가 없어요.

➡ _____

27 이것은 수중 환경에 좋은 것이지요.

➡ _____

28 한 번에 한 장소에서 너무 많은 해양생물을 채취하는 것은 바다를 파괴할 수 있으니까요.

➡ _____

29 Q. 마지막으로, 앞으로 계획하고 있는 것에 대해 말씀해 주세요.

➡ _____

30 예전에 두 명의 해녀들과 함께 그들의 삶에 대해 이야기하기 위해 해외에서 열리는 박람회에 참가한 적이 있어요.

➡ _____

31 제가 연설을 마쳤을 때, 해녀 중 한 분이 제 손을 꼭 잡았어요.

➡ _____

32 그분이 말했죠, "너무 고마워.

➡ _____

33 내 평생 내가 이렇게 특별한 사람이라는 걸 미처 알지 못했어."

➡ _____

34 그녀는 행복해서 울고 있었어요.

➡ _____

35 청중들 모두가 깊은 감동을 받았어요.

➡ _____

36 전 그 순간을 절대 잊을 수가 없기 때문에 해녀의 사진을 계속해서 찍을 거예요.

➡ _____

37 저는 그들에 대한 더 많은 아름다운 이야기들을 세계의 더 많은 사람들에게 알려 주고 싶어요.

➡ _____

※ 다음 우리말과 일치하도록 빈칸에 알맞은 말을 쓰시오.

Communicate – B Talk and Play

1. A: I wonder _____ _____ _____.

2. B: They're _____ _____.

3. A: Could you _____ _____ _____ them?

4. B: They're _____ _____ _____ _____.

After You Read A

1. A _____ _____ _____ Haenyeo

2. Zin Kim, _____ _____ _____ _____, _____ _____ the culture of Jeju haenyeo _____.

3. She _____ _____ _____ _____ of them _____ _____ _____ a haenyeo _____ _____ _____ her job.

4. _____ was not _____ _____ their pictures _____ _____.

5. _____, when she told them _____ she wanted to show _____ _____ _____ _____ _____, the haenyeo _____ _____ _____.

6. _____ _____ _____ _____, she _____ _____ _____ about the lives of haenyeo.

7. After her speech, _____ _____ the haenyeo _____ _____ _____.

8. Zin Kim said that she _____ _____ _____ _____ pictures of haenyeo.

Write

1. Kim Minho is a barista. He _____ _____ _____ _____ _____ _____.

2. He _____ _____ _____ after he _____ _____ _____ _____ _____ for coffee.

3. _____ _____ _____ _____ his job is _____ _____ hot milk and _____ his customers _____ it.

4. He is _____ _____ _____ his own coffee shop.

※ 다음 우리말을 영어로 쓰시오.

Communicate – B Talk and Play

1. A: 나는 이것들이 무엇인지 궁금해.
   ➡ _____

2. B: 그것들은 송편이라고 불려.
   ➡ _____

3. A: 이것에 대해 좀 더 설명해 줄래?
   ➡ _____

4. B: 그것들은 전통적인 한국 떡이야.
   ➡ _____

After You Read A

1. 해녀를 사랑하는 사진작가
   ➡ _____

2. 수중 사진작가 김진은 전 세계에 제주의 해녀 문화를 홍보해 왔다.
   ➡ _____

3. 그녀는 자신의 일을 즐기고 있었던 한 해녀를 만났을 때, 그들의 사진을 찍기로 결심했다.
   ➡ _____

4. 처음에는 그들의 사진을 찍는 것이 쉽지 않았다.
   ➡ _____

5. 그러나, 그녀가 세상 사람들에게 그들의 문화를 보여주고 싶다고 그들에게 말했을 때, 마침내 해녀들은 마음을 열었다.
   ➡ _____
   _____

6. 한 해외 전시회에서 그녀는 해녀들의 삶에 대해 강연했다.
   ➡ _____

7. 그녀의 연설이 끝나자 해녀들 중 한 사람은 기쁨의 눈물을 흘렸다.
   ➡ _____

8. 김진은 앞으로도 해녀들의 사진 찍는 일을 계속할 것이라고 말했다.
   ➡ _____

Write

1. 김민호는 바리스타이다. 그의 직업은 커피 음료를 만드는 것이다.
   ➡ _____

2. 그는 커피에 대한 그의 열정을 발견한 후에 바리스타가 되었다.
   ➡ _____

3. 그의 직업에서 그가 가장 좋아하는 부분은 뜨거운 우유로 커피를 장식하고 그의 손님들이 그것을 즐기는 것을 보는 것이다.
   ➡ _____

4. 그는 자신의 커피점을 열 계획이다.
   ➡ _____

MEMO

MEMO

MEMO

영어 기출 문제집

적중100 plus
1학기 전과정

1학기

정답 및 해설

미래 | 최연희

중3

적중100

Young Enough to Change the World

시험대비 실력평가 p.08

01 ① 02 ④ 03 ①
04 (e)ducate 05 ② 06 ④
07 (1) waste (2) marine

01 ① 이외의 보기들은 -ion이나 -tion을 이용해 명사형으로 만든다. ② imagine: 상상하다 imagination: 상상 ③ educate: 교육하다, 가르치다 education: 교육 ④ act: 행동하다 action: 행동 ⑤ collect: 모으다, 수집하다 collection: 수집 ① succeed: 성공하다 success: 성공

02 a bit: 조금, 약간 a little: 약간 / 나는 약간 피곤하다.

03 (A) lend 사물 to 사람: …에게 ~을 빌려주다 / 은행은 우리에게 돈을 빌려주는 것을 거절했다. (B) ask for help: 도움을 청하다 / 도움을 청하는 것을 어려워하지 마세요. (C) be covered with: ~으로 덮여 있다, ~으로 뒤집어쓰다 / 책상은 서류들로 덮여 있었다.

04 educate: 가르치다, 교육하다 / 학교 또는 대학에서 아이들을 가르치다

05 ① occurred, occur: 일어나다, 발생하다 / 오후 4시 30분쯤 사고가 발생했다고 경찰이 말했다. ② donate, donate: 기부하다, 기증하다 / 콘서트 주최자는 그들이 모든 수익을 자선단체에 기부할 것이라고 말했다. ③ educated, educate: 가르치다, 교육하다 / 그는 Bristol 대학에서 교육받았다. ④ fix, fix: 고치다 / Ellis는 문제를 빠르게 발견하고 고칠 수 있다. ⑤ bring, bring: ~을 데려오다 / 나의 부모님은 항상 우리에게 친구들을 집에 데려오도록 격려하셨다.

06 decrease: 줄이다 reduce: 줄이다 / 우리는 비용을 줄이고 더 효과적인 것들에 투자를 하는 중이다.

07 (1) waste: 쓰레기 (2) marine: 해양의

서술형 시험대비 p.09

01 (1) invitation (2) endangered
02 (Al)though / (al)though / (Al)though
03 various
04 (1) Do you want me to close the window?
   (2) She decided to name her dog Mary.
   (3) The mountain is covered with snow.

(4) Many people die from drinking dirty water.
(5) I plan to do volunteer work during the vacation.
(6) The man was asked to quit smoking.
05 (1) translated (2) collecting (3) raised (4) deliver

01 (1) invite: 초대하다 invitation: 초대 (2) danger: 위험 endangered: 멸종 위기의

02 although: ~임에도 불구하고, 비록 ~이지만 / 날씨가 너무 추웠지만 아이들은 놀기 위해 나갔다. 그녀는 너무 배고팠지만 아무것도 먹지 않았다. 모두가 잘 싸웠지만 우리는 그 경기에서 졌다.

03 various: 다양한, 여러 가지의 / 이제 환경 친화적인 다양한 자동차들이 있다.

04 (1) want+목적어+to부정사: ~가 …하는 것을 원하다 (2) name+목적어+목적격보어(명사): ~를 …라고 이름 짓다 (3) be covered with: ~으로 뒤덮여 있다, ~을 뒤집어쓰다 (4) die from: ~으로 죽다 (5) do volunteer work: 자원봉사를 하다

05 (1) translate: 번역하다 / 그 책은 27개의 언어로 번역되었다. (2) collect: 모으다, 수집하다 / Tony의 취미 중 하나는 희귀한 동전을 모으는 것이다. (3) raise: 기르다 / 나는 거북 두 마리를 1년 동안 키워 왔다. (4) deliver: 전달하다, 배달하다 / 우리는 당신의 주문을 정오에서 오후 1시 사이에 배달할 것입니다.

교과서 Conversation

핵심 Check p.10~11

1 I'm, of ordering
2 I'm thinking of buying a scarf.
3 I'm considering buying a car.
4 (B) → (C) → (A)
5 Do you want me to help you with your homework?
6 you want me to wake you up

교과서 대화문 익히기

Check(√) True or False p.12~13

1 F 2 T 3 T 4 T 5 F 6 T 7 T 8 F

Listen & Speak 1 A

1. doing this / thinking of, volunteer / What / read, to / sounds, join
2. are you, to read / thinking, young / have / lend / bring

Listen & Speak 1 B

1. What's / thinking
2. What's, plan / thinking of
3. What's, plan for / thinking of taking

Listen & Speak 2 A

1. a, there, to / want me to / few
2. What can I do / ask, to make / want me to help, collect / a lot

Listen & Speak 2 B

1. broke / want me to
2. bring / share, umbrella with
3. This, too / want me to help, carry
4. arm / want me to take

Communicate A

you don't, any longer / I'm thinking of sending, told me that, to / aren't / about translating, into / Translating / Do you want me to help you / run into, expressions / that we, help

Communicate B

thinking of learning / Are you thinking, to dance / I'm thinking, learning / want me to

Progress Check 1

What, doing / I'm thinking of / Let's

Progress Check 2

Can we, for / don't / want me to go, get

---

01 ④   02 ④   03 ②

01 'I'm thinking of ~.'는 '나는 ~할까 생각 중이다'라는 뜻으로 of 뒤에 동명사를 취해 의도나 계획을 나타낼 때 쓰는 표현이며, 같은 의미로 'I'm considering 동명사 ~.', 'I intend to 동사원형 ~.', 'I'm planning to 동사원형 ~.'등을 사용할 수 있다.

02 여자아이가 책을 다시 읽어야 하는지는 알 수 없다.

03 수진에게 도움을 부탁하는 말을 하고, (B) 수진은 좋다고 대답하며 무엇을 도와줘야 하는지 물어보고, (C) 자전거를 주차해 놓을 장소를 만들자고 학교에 요청할 예정이라고 대답한다. (A) 주차 공간을 요청할 목적으로 서명을 받는 것을 도와주기를 원하는지 질문하자 (D) 그러는 것이 도움이 되겠다고 하면서, 감사를 표현한다.

---

01 ④   02 ②   03 ①, ④   04 ③
05 ⑤   06 ⑤   07 ①   08 ①
09 ②
10 I'm thinking of learning how to play baduk.

01 'Do you want me to+동사원형 ~?(당신은 내가 ~해 주기를 원하십니까?)'으로 상대방에게 도움을 제안하는 말을 하고, 제안하는 말에 대한 대답으로 'That'd be great.(그게 좋겠다.)'라고 대답하는 것이 적절하다.

02 Do you want me to+동사원형 ~?: 당신은 내가 ~해 주기를 원하십니까? 여기서 want는 5형식으로 사용되어 목적어(me)와 목적격보어(to cook tteokbokki)를 취하고 있다.

03 ① 여자아이가 떡볶이를 좋아한다. ④ 'Give me a few minutes.'에서 떡볶이 만드는 데 시간이 많이 걸리지 않는다는 것을 알 수 있다.

04 현장학습에 무엇을 가져갈지 묻는 질문에 현장학습이 기다려진다는 대답은 어색하다.

05 식탁 차리는 것을 도와주기를 원하느냐고 묻는 말에 긍정의 대답을 하고 자신이 한다고 말하는 것은 어색하다.

06 아침식사로 팬케이크를 먹을 수 있는지 질문하자, (C) 물론이라고 대답하며 달걀이 없다고 말한다. (D) 가게에 가서 달걀을 사오는 것을 원하는지 도움을 제안하는 질문을 하자 (B) 고맙다고 대답하며 블루베리 시럽도 사오라고 부탁하자 (A) 알았다고 대답한다.

07 우산을 안 가져왔다는 말에 같이 우산을 쓰는 것을 원하는지 묻는 것이 어울린다.

08 'I'm thinking of ~.'는 '나는 ~할까 생각 중이다'라는 뜻으로 의향을 말할 때 사용한다. ① 'I'd like to+동사원형'을 이용해 바람이나 소원을 말하는 표현이다. ⑤ 'I'm concerned about[for] ~.'는 '~에 대해 걱정하다.'의 의미로 걱정이나 두려움을 말할 때 사용하는 표현이다.

09 ① 보육원 ② 여자아이는 흥미롭다고 생각했지만 남자아이의 생각은 언급되어 있지 않았다. ③ 네 ④ 보육원에 가서 아이들에게 책을 읽어줄 것이다. ⑤ 아이들에게 책을 읽어줄 것이다.

10 I'm thinking of ~: 나는 ~할까 생각 중이다 how to 동사원형: ~하는 방법

---

01 to make
02 Do you want me to help you (to) collect signatures from students?
03 into
04 do you have any children's books you don't read any longer?

3

05 I'm thinking of sending some books to children in Africa.

06 Do you want me to cook tteokbokki for you?

01 ask+목적어+to 동사원형: …가 ~할 것을 요청하다

02 'Do you want me to 동사원형 ~?'은 '당신은 내가 ~해 주기를 원하십니까?'라는 뜻으로 상대방에게 도움이 필요한지 묻는 표현이다. collect: 모으다, 수집하다 signature: 서명

03 translate ~ into 언어: …를 ~로 번역하다 run into: (곤경, 어려움 등을) 만나다[겪다]

04 not ~ any longer: 더 이상 ~ 않다 books와 you 사이에 목적격 관계대명사가 that[which]이 생략되어 있다.

05 I'm thinking of ~: 나는 ~할까 생각 중이다 send A to B: A를 B에게 보내다

06 'Do you want me to+동사원형 ~?'은 '당신은 내가 ~해 주기를 원하십니까?'라는 뜻으로 상대방에게 도움이 필요한지 묻는 표현이다.

교과서 Grammar

핵심 Check p.22~23

1 (1) What are made in the shop are cookies.
　(2) Sandra told me what she knew.

2 (1) Despite　(2) although

시험대비 기본평가 p.24

01 (1) which → what　(2) despite → though[although]
　(3) did → didn't　(4) what → that
02 ③　　**03** ④　　**04** what

01 (1) 전치사 by의 목적어와 held의 목적어 두 개의 명사가 필요한 자리에 관계대명사 what을 쓴다. (2) 전치사 despite는 뒤에 명사 또는 명사구가 오는 반면에, 접속사는 '주어+동사'가 온다. 어색한 한 단어만 찾아 고치는 문제이므로, she had hit이라는 문장을 고려하여, despite를 though[although]로 바꾸는 것이 적절하다. (3) Even though가 이끄는 종속절과 주절의 내용은 서로 상반되어야 하므로, did를 didn't로 쓰는 것이 적절하다. (4) 선행사 all 뒤에는 관계대명사 that을 쓴다. All을 삭제하는 것도 어법상 적절하다.

02 접속사 although가 이끄는 종속절과 주절의 내용은 상반되어야 한다. Mary가 약속을 깼음에도 Tom이 화를 내지 않았다거나, Mary가 약속을 깼기 때문에 Tom이 화났다가 자연스럽다.

03 전치사가 필요한 자리이므로, ①, ②, ⑤는 부적절하며, ③의 전치사 within은 기간 또는 범위 등이 '~ 이내'라는 뜻이므로 문맥상 맞지 않다. 의미와 어법상 전치사 despite가 적절하다.

04 선행사인 the things와 관계대명사 that을 한 단어로 바꾸려면, 선행사를 포함하는 관계대명사 what을 쓰는 것이 적절하다.

시험대비 실력평가 p.25~27

01 ④	**02** ③	**03** ⓐ, ⓑ, ⓒ, ⓔ, ⓖ	
04 ④	**05** that → what		
06 Even though		**07** ④	**08** ④
09 ③	**10** ⑤	**11** ③	**12** ④, ⑤
13 ③	**14** ①	**15** ⑤	**16** 네 번째
17 ④	**18** ④	**19** ⑤	
20 what, was		**21** ⑤	

01 두 문장이 하나가 되었으므로, 앞 문장에서의 보어와 뒤 문장에서의 buy의 목적어로 명사 두 개가 필요한데, 이 조건을 충족시키는 것은 관계대명사 what이다.

02 커피는 마시지만 볶은 커피콩의 향은 좋아하지 않는다는 상반되는 내용을 이끄는 접속사들 중 하나와, 선행사와 관계대명사를 포함하여 명사절을 이끄는 what이 적절하다.

03 ⓐ which → what ⓑ what → which[that] ⓒ The thing → The thing that[which] 또는 What ⓔ that → what ⓖ That → What

04 '비록 Jessy가 읽기 장애가 있지만, 많은 언어를 알고 있다.'라는 문장들이다. ④의 so를 but으로 고치면 다른 문장들과 같은 의미가 된다.

05 what was worse는 '설상가상으로'라는 뜻이다.

06 두 개의 빈칸에 맞는 '양보' 접속사가 적절하다.

07 빈칸 뒤의 '주어+동사' 구조로 보아 접속사가 필요한 자리이므로 ①, ②는 부적절하다. ③의 등위접속사 for와 ⑤ 접속사로서의 since는 이유 또는 원인을 나타내는데 문맥상 적절하지 않다. '양보' 의미의 though를 써야 한다.

08 관계대명사 what과 의문대명사 what의 문장 구조는 동일할 때가 있다. 구분의 기준은 해석으로서 관계대명사는 '~하는 것'으로, 의문대명사는 '무엇(이/을) ~하는지'로 한다. ④ 그녀는 나에게 내가 무엇을 할 것인지 물어보았다.

09 접속사 although가 이끄는 '양보'의 부사절은 주절의 내용과 상반된다. 피곤한 것과 전날 밤을 샌 것은 상반되는 내용이 아니다.

10 돈을 많이 가진 것과, 비싼 물건을 사는 것은 상반되는 내용이 아니다.

11 '숙제가 끝나지 않았는데도 불구하고'라는 양보절 뒤에, '나는 바로 숙제를 해야 한다'는 호응 관계가 어색하다.

12 ④ what → which[that] ⑤ Which → What

13 '양보' 접속사 although와, 주절과 종속절이 상반되는 문장을 찾는다. ① In spite that과 ⑤ despite of는 부적절한 표현이다. ② Even though 또는 but 중 하나 삭제

14 ① 정답을 평서문으로 바꿔 쓰면 what이 옳게 쓰였다는 사실이 쉽게 이해된다. This cat is what she is looking for. ② a new car와 his daughter의 자리를 바꿔야 한다. ③ what → that ④ what → which[that] ⑤ said him → said to him(또는 told him)

15 접속사 뒤에는 '주어+동사'를, 전치사 뒤에는 명사를 쓰는 것이 기본이다. ①, ③, ④는 전치사 despite 또는 in spite of를 알맞게 써야 하고, ②는 접속사 though[although]가 적절하다.

16 Pay attention to what the boss is saying.

17 관계대명사 what과 의문대명사 what을 구분하는 문제이다. 명백하게 '무엇이(을) ~하는지'로 해석되면 의문사이다. ④ 나는 그녀가 내게 무엇을 줄 것인지 궁금했다.

18 선행사를 포함하는 관계대명사 what은 선행사 the game 뒤에 쓸 수 없다. which[that]로 고치는 것이 적절하다.

19 ① In spite → Though ② Although → Despite ③ get → got ④ though worked → though he worked

20 과거의 그: what he was, 과거의 재산: what he had 현재의 그: what he is, 현재의 재산: what he has

21 ① what → which[that] ② which → why[that] ③ which → that[in which], 또는 which 생략 ④ what → where

서술형 시험대비 p.28~29

01 (1) fall asleep, books, read
   (2) it is, playing soccer
   (3) their colors, love each other

02 (1) I don't believe what Eva said to me.
   (2) Show me what you put in your pocket.
   (3) Despite her fear of his attitude, she looked him right in the eye.
   (4) That Josh asked me to help her was not natural.

03 (1) What Sam bought were mystery books.
   (2) Harold couldn't believe what the reporters referred to.
   (3) What was discussed was surprising.

04 Although Jackie was not hungry, she ate what the cook had made for her.

05 (1) Mongol maintains an old tradition although it is a small country.
   (2) Kelly was so easygoing although she was late for the wedding.

   (3) Walter caused a serious car accident although he was a careful driver.
   (4) Michael regularly buys many books although he doesn't read them at all.

06 (1) What Mary found in the cave surprised the villagers.
   (2) Despite the policy of the museum, the kids were not quiet.
   (3) What Candy bought at the market were all inexpensive.

07 (1) Sue finally accepted what Tom gave.
   (2) Despite his wealth, he was lonely.
   (3) That is far different from what Sunny has been waiting for.
   (4) That I met her yesterday is true.
   (5) What people believed in the past is called superstition.

08 Although Audrey Hepburn passed away 25 years ago, her beautiful spirit will remain with us

02 (1) believe의 목적어와 said의 목적어 두 개 역할의 what이 적절하다. (2) 나에게 '당신이 주머니에 넣은 것'을 보여 달라는 문장이므로 접속사 if를 관계대명사 what으로 바꾼다. (3) Though는 접속사이므로 명사구가 올 수 없다. 어법상 또는 내용상 despite나 in spite of가 적절하다. (4) What 뒤에는 불완전한 문장 구조가 와야 한다. 주어 역할을 하는 명사절을 이끄는 접속사 that이 적절하다.

03 관계대명사 what은 문맥에 따라 단/복수 취급에 유의해야 한다. (1) Sam이 산 것들은 미스터리 책들이었다. (2) Harold는 기자들이 언급한 것을 믿을 수 없었다. (3) 논의된 것은 놀라웠다.

04 '양보'의 접속사 although와 관계대명사 what을 적절히 활용한다.

05 although를 후반부에 배치하여, 상반되는 두 문장을 하나로 묶는 문제이다. 대명사에 유의하여 영작한다. easygoing: 태평한, 느긋한

06 (1) 관계대명사 what을 활용한다. (2) 전치사 despite를 활용한다. (3) be동사를 were로 사용하는 것에 주의한다. what은 문맥에 따라 복수 취급이 가능하다.

07 (1) 'Tom이 준 것'이므로 what이 적절하다. (2) 한 단어만 틀렸으므로, 접속사 though를 전치사 despite로 바꿔야 한다. (3) 'Sunny가 기다려왔던 것'이므로 what이 적절하다. (4) What 뒤에 완전한 절이 올 수 없다. 내용상 '내가 어제 그녀를 만난 것'이라는 명사절로서 접속사 That이 적절하다. (5) '사람들이 과거에 믿었던 것'이므로 What이 적절하다.

08 forever가 마지막에 오려면, 접속사 although가 문두에 와야 한다. 내용에 알맞게 주어진 단어들을 배열하도록 한다.

확인문제   p.30

1 T   2 F   3 T   4 F   5 T   6 F

확인문제   p.31

1 T   2 F   3 T   4 F   5 T   6 F

교과서 확인학습 A   p.32~33

01 in Action
02 a better place
03 in saving animals
04 Although, have actually made a difference
05 How, able to
06 hear from
07 each adopted
08 raise, at home
09 donated to a charity
10 might not be able to see cheetahs
11 became interested in, endangered animals
12 created a non-profit organization
13 the next generation
14 educated our friends
15 a terrible oil spill
16 were completely covered with oil
17 had to do
18 animal rescue supplies, in our neighborhood
19 what we collected, to save the animals
20 something very useful
21 threw up
22 get, out of
23 could be used
24 marine life specialist
25 more dangerous, than
26 die from eating
27 created an educational project
28 In addition to
29 making a big difference
30 What, take that first step

교과서 확인학습 B   p.34~35

1 Teens in Action
2 Many young people are making the world a better place.
3 For example, Carter and Olivia Ries have become leaders in saving animals.
4 Although they are only teenagers, they have actually made a difference in the world.
5 How were they able to do that?
6 Let's hear from Carter.

7 When I was five, my little sister Olivia and I each adopted a cheetah.
8 Did we raise cheetahs at home?
9 No, we donated to a charity that protects wild cheetahs in South Africa.
10 Our parents told us that if we did not protect them, we might not be able to see cheetahs in the near future.
11 We soon became interested in helping other endangered animals..
12 A few years later, with help from our parents, we created a non-profit organization to protect them.
13 We wanted the next generation to be able to see these animals, so we named our organization One More Generation.
14 We also studied endangered animals and educated our friends about them.
15 Then one day, a terrible oil spill occurred in the Gulf of Mexico.
16 A lot of sea animals were completely covered with oil, and they were dying.
17 We had to do something.
18 We started collecting animal rescue supplies such as pet carrying cages and rubber gloves from everyone in our neighborhood.
19 Four months later, our family drove to the Gulf of Mexico to deliver what we collected and helped to save the animals.
20 While we were working there, we learned something very useful.
21 When we put mayonnaise into a turtle's throat, the turtle threw up.
22 That way, we were able to get oil out of turtles.
23 I never knew mayonnaise could be used to save animals!
24 On our last day, we met a marine life specialist.
25 She told us that plastic waste is more dangerous to sea animals than oil spills are.
26 A lot of sea animals and sea birds die from eating plastic waste.
27 After we came home, we created an educational project about how to reduce plastic waste.
28 In addition to this, our organization continues to do various projects to save animals.
29 Although we started small, we are making a big difference.
30 What you do today can change the world, so take that first step!

01 ④	02 ①, ③	03 possible	04 ③
05 ①	06 ①	07 ①, ④ / ②, ③, ⑤	
08 ③	09 ②	10 ①, ④	

11 A lot of sea animals and sea birds die from eating plastic waste.

12 Since → Although(Though)　　13 ③

14 difference　15 ⑤　　16 ③　　17 ⑤

18 adopted　19 ③　　20 ④　　21 ④

22 vomited　　　23 ④

01 많은 젊은 사람들이 세상을 더 좋은 곳으로 만들고 있는 예로 Carter와 Olivia Ries를 들고 있으므로, For example이 적절하다. ① 그 결과, ② 게다가, 더욱이, ⑤ 게다가, 더욱이 ④ 예를 들면

02 ⓑ와 ①, ③: actually = in fact = really = in reality = in effect = in practice: 실제로, ② 특히, ④ 극도로, 극히, ⑤ 아마

03 사람+can(=be able to)+동사원형 = It is possible for 사람 to부정사

04 ⓐ donate to: (특히 자선단체에) 기부[기증]하다, ⓑ become interested in: ~에 관심을 갖게 되다

05 ①번은 'wild cheetahs'를 가리키고 나머지는 다 '멸종 위기의 동물들'을 가리킨다.

06 Carter와 Olivia는 야생 치타를 보호하는 자선단체에 치타를 기부했다.

07 ⓐ와 ①, ④: 명사적 용법, ⓑ와 ②, ③, ⑤: 부사적 용법

08 위 글은 '멕시코만에서 발생한 끔찍한 석유 유출 사건으로 죽어가고 있는 많은 해양 동물들을 구조하기 위해 벌인 활동'에 관한 글이므로, 주제로는 ③번 '석유 유출 사건으로 죽어가고 있는 동물들을 구조하기 위한 활동'이 적절하다.

09 전반부의 'A lot of sea animals were completely covered with oil, and they were dying. We had to do something.'을 통해 'sympathetic'을, 하반부의 'I never knew mayonnaise could be used to save animals!'를 통해 'surprised'를 찾을 수 있다. ① delighted: 아주 기뻐[즐거워]하는, puzzled: 어리둥절해하는, ② sympathetic: 동정적인, 동정어린, ③ depressed: 우울한, nervous: 초조한, ④ regretful: 유감스러워[애석해] 하는, confused: 혼란스러워하는, ⑤ relieved: 안도하는, 다행으로 여기는, astonished: 깜짝[크게] 놀란

10 앞에 나오는 내용에 추가하는 내용이 뒤에 이어지므로 Besides(게다가, 뿐만 아니라) 혹은 In addition to(~에 더하여, ~일 뿐 아니라)가 가장 적절하다. ② ~와 대조를 이루어, ③ ~ 대신에, ⑤ ~의 결과로

11 die from: ~으로 죽다

12 '비록' 우리는 작은 것부터 시작했지만, 큰 변화를 만들어 내고 있는 중이라고 해야 하므로, Since를 Although[Though]로 고치는 것이 적절하다.

13 ⓐ와 ③, ④: 동명사, ①, ②, ⑤: 현재분사

14 do that은 앞 문장의 make a difference in the world를 받는다.

15 본문 끝부분에서 '십 대일 뿐이지만, 실제로 세상에 변화를 일으켜 온 사람들이 어떻게 그것을 할 수 있었을까?'라면서 'Carter의 이야기를 들어보자.'라고 했으므로, 다음에 올 내용으로는 '세상에 변화를 일으켜 온 Carter의 이야기'가 적절하다.

16 ⓐ와 ③: 쓰레기, ① 낭비[허비](되는 상황), ② (기회 등을) 놓치다(동사), ④ 이용[활용]되고 있지 않은(형용사), waste talents: 빛을 못 보고 있는 재능, ⑤ (돈·시간·재능 등을) 낭비하다

17 '비록 우리는 작은 것부터 시작했지만, 큰 변화를 만들어 내고 있는 중이다. 당신이 오늘 하는 일이 세상을 바꿀 수 있기에, 첫발을 내디뎌라!'라는 글의 마지막 내용으로 보아, 어울리는 속담으로는 ⑤번 '시작이 반이다.'가 적절하다. ① 잘 생각해 보고 행동하라[돌다리도 두드려 보고 건너라]. ② 안 좋은 일은 겹쳐서 일어나기 마련이다[불운은 한꺼번에 닥친다]. ③ 급할수록 돌아가라. ④ 손 안에 든 새 한 마리는 풀숲에 있는 두 마리 새의 가치가 있다.

18 adopt: 입양하다, 자신의 가족으로 받아들이다

19 ③번 다음 문장의 our organization에 주목한다. 주어진 문장의 a non-profit organization을 받고 있으므로 ③번이 적절하다.

20 위 글은 'Carter와 Olivia가 치타를 입양한 후에 다른 멸종 위기의 동물들을 도와주는 것에도 관심을 갖게 되어 One More Generation을 만들게 되는 과정'에 관한 글이므로, 제목으로는 ④번 'One More Generation의 탄생 배경'이 적절하다.

21 선행사를 포함하는 관계대명사 what을 쓰는 것이 적절하다.

22 throw up = vomit: 토하다.

23 Carter의 가족은 멕시코만으로 비행기를 타고 간 것이 아니라 '운전해 갔다.'

01 endangered

02 with help from our parents, we created a non-profit organization to protect them 또는 we created a non-profit organization to protect them with help from our parents

03 They donated to a charity that protects wild cheetahs in South Africa.

04 was occurred → occurred

05 the things which[that]

01 '가까운 미래에 치타를 볼 수 없을지도 모른다.'는 것은 치타가 '멸종 위기의' 동물이라는 뜻이다.

02 with help from ~: ~의 도움으로

03 그들은 남아프리카 공화국에 있는 야생 치타를 보호하는 자선단체에 기부했다.

04 occur는 수동태로 쓸 수 없는 동사이다.

05 관계대명사 what을 '선행사+관계대명사'로 바꿔 쓸 수 있다. 가족이 전달한 것들은 동네의 모든 사람으로부터 모은 동물 구조 물품들이기 때문에 복수 형태인 the things로 쓰는 것이 적절하다.

06 '마요네즈'를 거북이의 목구명에 집어넣으면, 거북이가 '토한다'는 것을 배웠다..

07 Carter and Olivia가 각자 치타를 입양한 것이기 때문에, 치타 두 마리를 입양하여 자선단체에 기부한 것이다.

08 '그들의 부모님'이 도와주셨다.

09 so 대신 맨 앞에 이유를 나타내는 접속사 As[Because 등]를 쓰는 것이 적절하다.

10 석유 유출이 '해양 동물에게 위험한' 것보다 플라스틱 쓰레기가 해양 동물에게 더 위험하다.

11 In addition to having created an educational project about how to reduce plastic waste로 고칠 수 있다. in addition to ~ing: ~에 더하여, ~일 뿐 아니라

12 Carter의 가족은 석유 유출보다 플라스틱 쓰레기가 해양 동물에게 더 위험하다는 것을 알게 되어서, '플라스틱 쓰레기를 줄일 수 있는' 방법에 관한 교육 프로젝트를 만들었다.

영역별 핵심문제

01 repair: 수리하다, 수선하다 fix: 고치다 / 너는 그들이 그 손상된 것을 수선할 수 있다고 생각하니?

02 ① in addition to: ~ 이외에, ~에 더하여 / 할인에 더하여 그들은 무료 선물을 제공한다. ② share A with B: A를 B와 나누다, 공유하다 / 나는 침실을 동생과 같이 쓴다. ③ read A to B: A를 B에게 읽어 주다 / 그가 우리에게 그 편지를 소리 내어 읽어 주었다. ④ send A to B: A를 B에게 보내다 / 그걸 제게 팩스로 보내 줄 수 있으세요? ⑤ lend 사물to 사람: ~에게 ~을 빌려주다 / 내일까지 나에게 돈을 좀 빌려줄 수 있겠니?

03 주어진 단어는 동사와 명사의 관계이다. marry: 결혼하다 marriage: 결혼 protect: 보호하다 protection: 보호

04 make a difference: 차이를 낳다, 변화를 가져오다 / 저는 운동이 제 삶에 어떤 차이점을 만들어 줬는지 이루 말할 수가 없습니다. make a discovery: 발견하다 / 그들은 화성에서 물의 흔적을 찾는 엄청난 발견을 했다.

05 주어진 문장은 'Can I join you?(나도 함께 할 수 있어?)'의 질문에 긍정의 대답을 한 후 만나는 장소와 시간을 정하는 것이 어울리므로 ⑤가 적절하다.

06 현재진행형의 형태이지만 this weekend라는 미래를 나타내는 어구와 함께 쓰여 가까운 미래를 나타내 이번 주에 무엇을 할 예정인지 묻고 있으므로 ⑤가 적절하다.

07 break down: 고장나다

08 want+목적어+to부정사: ~가 …하는 것을 원하다 'Do you want me to+동사원형 ~?'은 '당신은 내가 ~하기를 원하십니까?'라는 뜻으로 상대방에게 도움이 필요한지 묻는 표현이다.

09 어려운 표현들이 나온다는 말과 영어 선생님께 도움을 요청하자는 말을 연결할 때 조건의 접속사 If를 사용해서 '만약 어려운 표현들이 나오면, 영어 선생님께 도움을 요청하자.'라고 두 문장을 연결하는 것이 적절하다.

10 to read는 명사 books를 꾸며주는 to부정사의 형용사적 용법으로 사용되고 있다. ②는 to부정사의 부사적 용법(~하기 위해서)으로 사용되어 있고 나머지 보기들은 형용사적 용법으로 사용되고 있다. ① 모든 학생은 올해 성취할 한 가지를 썼다. ② 가난한 사람들을 돕기 위해서 학교에서 벼룩시장을 열고 싶다. ③ 나는 밤에 입을 따뜻한 재킷이 필요하다. ④ 나는 비행기에서 읽을 책이 필요하다. ⑤ 나는 써야 할 편지가 많다.

11 translate: 번역하다 / 쓰여지거나 말해진 단어들을 다른 언어로

바꾸다

12 want+목적어+to부정사: ~가 …하는 것을 원하다 'Do you want me to+동사원형 ~?'은 '당신은 내가 ~해 주기를 원하십니까?'라는 뜻으로 상대방에게 도움이 필요한지 묻는 표현이다.

13 ⓐ In spite of → Though[Although] ⓑ Despite → Though[Although] ⓒ Though → Despite[In spite of] ⓓ even though → despite[in spite of] ⓔ Although → Despite[In spite of] ⓕ 고칠 곳 없음

14 첫 번째 문장에서는 '청와대 앞에서 찍힌 것들(사진들)'을 가리키는 말이므로 what이 적절하다. 두 번째 문장에서는 빈칸 앞뒤가 상반되는 내용이므로 접속사 though 또는 although가 적절하다.

15 (1) 책 '노인과 바다'를 3일 동안 읽어오고 있지만, 전혀 이해할 수 없다는 상반된 내용이 있으므로, '양보'의 접속사가 필요한데, 빈칸이 2개이므로 Even though가 적절하다. (2) showed와 believed의 목적어가 들어갈 자리이므로 what이 적절하다.

16 모든 문장이 '양보'의 접속사 Although로 시작하지만, 상반되는 내용을 가진 것은 ③번뿐이다. 각각 Although를 ① 접속사 Because(Since/As)로, ② 접속사 When으로, ④ 접속사 Because(Since/As)로, ⑤ 접속사 Whether로 바꿔야 한다.
immunity: 면역(성), 면역질

17 관계대명사 what은 선행사를 포함하며, 문맥에 따라 단/복수 취급한다. (1) 이것은 Hermione가 항상 원해 왔던 것이 아니다. (2) 이웃들은 두 달 전에 생긴 일들을 알고 있다. (3) Sam의 아버지에게 그를 괴롭혀 온 것들을 말해 주시오.

18 상반되는 내용을 접속사 but으로 연결하는 문장은 '양보' 접속사를 이용하여 바꾸면 같은 의미가 된다.

19 '날이 너무 더워서 부채질을 했는데도 땀이 너무 많이 났다'라는 내용으로, 양보의 접속사 even though를 활용한다.

20 ⓐ는 관계 대명사 ⓑ는 접속사

21 멸종 위기의 동물들을 연구했고 친구들에게 그들에 대해 가르쳐 주었다.

22 ⓐ '목구멍에' 집어넣는 것이므로 into가 적절하다. ⓑ 기름을 몸 '밖으로' 빼낸 것이므로 out of가 적절하다.

23 ③번 다음 문장의 what we collected에 주목한다. 주어진 문장의 'animal rescue supplies'를 받고 있으므로 ③번이 적절하다.

24 끔찍한 석유 유출 사건은 '글쓴이의 동네'에서 발생한 것이 아니라 '멕시코만'에서 발생했다.

25 ⓐ marine: 바다의, 해양의, ⓑ make a difference: 변화를 가져오다, 차이를 낳다, 중요하다, <영영풀이: 행동을 수행하고, 그 결과가 매우 의미심장한 변화를 이루다>

26 관계대명사 what을 보충하여 What you do today를 주어로 쓰는 것이 적절하다.

27 이 글은 '석유 유출보다 플라스틱 쓰레기가 해양 동물에게 더 위험하다는 이야기를 들은 뒤에, 비록 작은 것부터 시작했지만 동

물들을 구하기 위한 다양한 프로젝트들을 계속하여 큰 변화를 만들어 내고 있는 중'이라는 내용의 글이므로, 주제로는 ③번 '동물들을 구하기 위한 다양한 프로젝트들을 행함으로써 큰 변화를 만들어 내기'가 적절하다.

28 Why don't you 동사원형 ~? = How[What] about ~ing?: ~하는 게 어때?

29 ④는 '다음 세대'를 가리키고, 나머지는 다 비영리 단체인 'One More Generation'을 가리킨다.

단원별 예상문제   p.48~51

01 (s)pecialist
02 ask / ask (2) with / with   03 ③
04 (1) to (c)ure (2) (b)reak down (3) (r)an into
    (4) die from
05 ④
06 Do you want me to go to the store and get some?
07 ⑤   08 ⑤   09 ⓐ What ⓑ probably
10 (A) of (B) to   11 ④   12 ④
13 ③, ⑤
14 (1) If (2) Although (3) Since (4) although
    (5) If (6) since
15 ①, ②, ③, ⑥
16 (1) although (2) since (3) Although
17 (A) terrible (B) from (C) something very useful
18 ②, ④, ⑤   19 ②
20 (A) last (B) from (B) In addition to
21 ③   22 ④

---

01 주어진 단어는 동의어 관계이다. occur: 일어나다, 발생하다 happen: 발생하다 expert: 전문가 specialist: 전문가

02 (1) ask for help: 도움을 청하다 / 자녀들이 숙제를 도와 달라고 요청하면 당신은 어떻게 할 건가요? ask+목적어+to 동사원형: …가 ~할 것을 요청하다 / 이 편지 타이핑을 부탁해도 괜찮겠습니까? (2) share A with B: A를 B와 나누다, 공유하다 / 여기 그들이 나와 함께 공유했던 몇 가지 조언들이 있다. be covered with: ~으로 뒤덮여 있다, ~을 뒤집어�다 / 그는 길을 걸어가다가 먼지를 뒤덮어 썼다.

03 (A) in addition to: ~ 이외에, ~에 더하여 / 사망자뿐 아니라, 부상자도 한 명 더 있었다. (B) although: ~임에도 불구하고, 비록 ~이지만 / 비록 그녀가 돈이 많을지라도 행복하지 않다. Despite와 In spite of는 전치사이므로 뒤에 명사나 동명사가 올 수 있다.

04 (1) be able to 동사원형: ~할 수 있다 (2) break down: 고장 나다 (3) run into: (곤경, 어려움 등을) 만나다[겪다] (4) die from: ~으로 죽다 starvation: 기아

9

05 달걀이 없는 상황에서 달걀을 사올 것을 원하는지 도움을 제안하는 말을 먼저하고 블루베리 시럽도 사올 수 있는지 묻는 것이 주어진 문장의 대답인 'Sure.(물론이지.)'와 어울리므로 ⑤가 적절하다.

06 'Do you want me to+동사원형 ~?'은 상대방에게 도움이 필요한지 묻는 표현이다.

07 자전거가 고장났다는 말에, 자전거를 고쳐주는 것을 원하는지에 대한 도움을 제안하는 말이 어울린다.

08 주어진 문장은 '나도 같이 해도 돼?'의 의미로 맥락상 남자아이가 보육원에서 책을 읽어 준다고 얘기하니, 이것에 대해서 여자아이가 흥미롭다며 같이 하고 싶다고 말하는 것이 자연스럽다.

09 ⓐ 이번 주에 무엇을 하는지 묻는 질문과 보육원에서 자원봉사를 할 생각이라는 대답이 어울린다. ⓑ 동사 read를 수식하므로 부사 probably가 어울린다. probably: 아마도

10 (A) 'I'm thinking of ~.'는 '나는 ~할까 생각 중이다'라는 뜻으로 of 뒤에 동명사를 취해 의도나 계획을 나타낼 때 사용한다. (B) read A to B: A를 B에게 읽어 주다

11 ⓐ to read ⓑ thinking ⓒ reading ⓓ lend ⓔ bring I'm thinking of ~: 나는 ~할까 생각 중이다 (= I'm considering 동명사 ~.) 전치사 of가 있으므로 thinking을 사용해야 한다.

12 ④번 다음 문장의 it이 주어진 문장의 the perfect book을 가리키므로 ④번이 적절하다.

13 what이 관계대명사인지 의문대명사사인지 구분하는 것은 해석을 기준으로 한다. 때로, 구분이 모호한 경우도 많지만 일반적으로 의문사 what은 '무엇이[을] ~한지'로, 관계대명사 what은 '~하는 것'으로 해석한다. ① 의문대명사 ② 의문대명사 ③ 관계대명사 ④ 의문대명사 ⑤ 관계대명사 (과거에 도덕적인 것으로 여겨졌던 것이 오늘날 항상 그렇게 여겨지는 것은 아니다.)

14 <보기>의 if는 '조건', although는 '양보', since는 '이유, 원인'의 부사절을 이끈다. 각각 (1) 조건 (2) 양보 (3) 이유 (4) 양보 (5) 조건 (6) 이유의 부사절이다.

15 ① 선행사 the only person 뒤에는 which가 아니라 who 또는 that이 적절하다. ② 관계대명사 what이 이끄는 명사절이 있는데, 목적어 something valuable이 나왔다. 둘 중 하나는 삭제해야 한다. ③ 전치사 Despite 뒤에 절이 나왔다. 접속사 Though[Although]로 바꿔야 한다. ⑥ 'It ~ that 강조 구문'이다. what을 that으로 바꾸는 것이 적절하다. give ~ the cold shoulder: ~를 쌀쌀맞게 대하다

16 (1)과 (3)은 상반된 내용이므로 '양보'의 접속사 although를, (2)는 이유를 나타내는 내용이므로 접속사 since를 쓴다.

17 (A) '끔찍한' 석유 유출 사건이라고 해야 하므로 terrible이 적절하다. terrific: 아주 좋은, 멋진, 훌륭한, (B) 동네의 모든 '사람으로부터' 동물 구조 물품들을 모으기 시작했다고 해야 하므로 from이 적절하다. (C) '-thing'으로 끝나는 말은 형용사가 뒤에서 수식해야 하므로 something very useful이 적절하다.

18 ⓐ와 ②, ④, ⑤: 동명사(목적, 용도를 나타냄), pet carrying cages: 애완동물 수송용 우리, ① 현재분사형 형용사, ③: 현재분사

19 애완동물 수송용 우리를 만든 것이 아니라, 동물 구조 물품들을 동네의 모든 사람으로부터 모으기 시작했다.

20 (A) '마지막' 날이라고 해야 하므로 last가 적절하다. latest: 최근의, (B) '플라스틱 쓰레기를 먹어서 죽는다'고 해야 하므로 from이 적절하다. die from: 상처, 부상으로 인한 사망(최근에는 die from 대신에 die of를 쓰는 일이 많음. die of: 주로 질병, 굶주림, 노령으로 인한 사망에 사용), die for: ~을 위해 죽다, ~하고 싶어 죽다[못 견디다], (C) '이것 외에도', 다양한 프로젝트들을 계속하고 있다고 해야 하므로 In addition to가 적절하다. in spite of: ~에도 불구하고

21 ③번 뒤 문장의 this에 주목한다. 주어진 문장의 내용을 받고 있으므로 ③번이 적절하다.

22 Carter의 가족은 '플라스틱 쓰레기'를 줄일 수 있는 방법에 관한 교육 프로젝트를 만들었다.

서술형 실전문제 p.52~53

01 a little → a few

02 Do you want me to cook tteokbokki for you?

03 I'm considering doing some volunteer work at the child-care center.
I'm planning to do some volunteer work at the child-care center.
I intend to do some volunteer work at the child-care center.

04 (1) Although James made a few mistakes, he succeeded in the project.
(2) Although Mr. Park left for the station earlier than usual, he missed the train.
(3) Although Angela caught a bad cold, she exercised in the morning.
(4) Although Jinho prepared for the civil service exam for 4 years, he failed it.

05 (1) What you do is much more important than what you speak.
(2) Paula must make the most of what she has.

06 what　07 less　08 we should[could]

09 change the world　10 to be

11 (A) adopted　(B) raise　(C) protects

12 (1) 몇 년 후에 부모님의 도움으로, 그들은 멸종 위기의 동물들을 보호하기 위해 비영리 단체를 만들고 One More Generation이라고 이름 붙였다
(2) 멸종 위기의 동물들을 연구했다.
(3) 친구들에게 멸종 위기의 동물들에 대해 가르쳐 주었다.

01 a little 다음에는 셀 수 없는 명사가 오므로 a few로 바꾸어야 한다. a few: 어느 정도, 조금

02 'Do you want me to+동사원형 ~?'은 '당신은 내가 ~해 주기를 원하십니까?'라는 뜻으로 상대방에게 도움이 필요한지 묻는 표현이다. for: ~을 위해

03 'I'm thinking of ~.'는 '나는 ~할까 생각 중이다'라는 뜻으로 of 뒤에 동명사를 취해 의도나 계획을 나타낼 때 쓰는 표현이다. 'I'm thinking of ~.' 대신에 'I'm considering 동명사 ~.', 'I intend to 동사원형 ~.', 'I'm planning to 동사원형 ~.' 등을 사용할 수 있다.

04 '양보'의 부사절 접속사 Although를 사용하여 문장을 바꾸면, 본래 문장의 but은 삭제해야 한다.

05 (1) 관계대명사 what을 활용해야 글자 수에 맞는 영작이 가능하다. (2) make the most of: ~을 최대한 활용하다

06 the thing+that[which] = what.

07 석유 유출이 플라스틱 쓰레기보다 해양 동물에게 '덜' 위험하다

08 의문사+to부정사 = 의문사+주어+조동사 should[can]+동사원형

09 우리가 오늘 하는 일이 '세상을 바꿀 수' 있기 때문이다.

10 'want+목적어+to부정사'로 써야 하므로 to be로 쓰는 것이 적절하다.

11 (A) 치타를 '입양했다'고 해야 하므로 adopted가 적절하다. adapt: (새로운 용도·상황에) 맞다[조정하다], adopt: 입양하다, (B) 치타를 집에서 '길렀을까?'라고 해야 하므로 raise가 적절하다. raise: 기르다, 올리다, rise: 오르다, 올라가다, (C) 야생 치타를 '보호하는' 자선단체라고 해야 하므로 protects가 적절하다. prevent: 막다[예방/방지하다]

12 두 번째 단락 'We soon became interested in helping other endangered animals.' 다음의 내용을 쓰면 된다.

창의사고력 서술형 문제 p.54

|모범답안|

01 they are thinking of going swimming. She is considering visiting an art museum, is planning to read a book at home

02 We love each other although we are different. / Althoug we are different, we love each other.

03 (A) plastic waste   (B) sea animals
   (C) reuse and recycle   (D) bottle
   (E) shopping bag

01 go swimming: 수영하러 가다 visit: 방문하다 art museum: 미술관 at home: 집에서 'I'm thinking of ~.'는 '나는 ~할까 생각 중이다'라는 뜻으로 of 뒤에 동명사를 취해 의도나 계획을 나타낼 때 쓰는 표현이다. 'I'm thinking of ~.' 대신에 'I'm considering (동)명사 ~.', 'I intend to 동사원형 ~.', 'I'm planning to 동사원형 ~.' 등을 사용할 수 있다.

단원별 모의고사 p.55~60

01 ①   02 ④   03 ①
04 (1) (e)ndangered
   (2) Donate, non-profit organization
   (3) (r)escue   (4) problem, (p)robably, (v)arious
05 ⑤   06 (p)lan
07 I'm thinking of watching a movie every weekend.
08 ③   09 translating
10 (A) longer   (B) that   (C) expressions
11 ①   12 ①, ③
13 (1) what Sullivan wrote in his note
   (2) What Gale says
14 (1) Peter was absent from, but he got a perfect score
   (2) Although Peter was absent from, he got a perfect score
   (3) Despite his absence, Peter got a perfect score
15 (1) This is what Frank purchased from a Japanese fisherman last Sunday.
   (2) He went to work although he was very sick.
   (3) Although John fixed the photocopier, it didn't work the next day.
16 (1) Jason bought the magazine though he didn't have to read it.
   (2) This watch still works well though it is much older than my grandfather.
   (3) I don't know much about Ray though she has been my classmate for 4 years.
   (4) The strawberry had a nasty smell though it looked fine on the surface.
   (5) The paper desk didn't break though many people climbed up on it.
17 ④
18 What made me who I am today is my mother's love.
19 we donated to a charity that protects wild cheetahs in South Africa
20 unless we protected them
21 다음 세대가 이러한 멸종 위기의 동물들을 볼 수 있기를 원했기 때문이다.
22 be used   23 (A) oil   (B) the Gulf of Mexico
24 be shipped   25 cars / local products
26 ⑤   27 to do
28 (A) paper   (B) forests   (C) body parts   29 ⑤
30 A lot of plastic waste goes into the ocean and many sea animals eat it.
31 (A) to reuse   (B) to recycle   (C) bottle
   (D) shopping bag

01 actually: 실제로 / 그것은 올림픽 종목이 되었지만 사실은 그렇게 새로운 것은 아닙니다. although: ~임에도 불구하고, 비록 ~이지만 / 그는 비록 어렸지만, 이 수학 문제를 풀 수 있다.

02 spill: 유출 / 기름 유출이 있었고 그 기름이 자연을 파괴했다.

03 donate: 기부하다, 기증하다 charity: 자선단체, 자선 / A: 얼마나 기부했나요? B: 나는 자선단체에 100달러를 보냈어요.

04 (1) endangered: 멸종 위기의 (2) donate: 기부하다, 기증하다 non-profit organization: 비영리 단체 (3) rescue: 구조, 구출 (4) problem: 문제 probably: 아마도 various: 다양한, 여러 가지의

05 (C) 아빠한테 배가 조금 고프다고 말하면서 먹을 것이 있는지 질문하자, (D) 떡볶이를 해주기를 원하느냐고 묻는다. (B) 좋다고 대답하며 떡볶이를 좋아한다고 말하자 (A) 알았다고 말하면서 (떡볶이를 만들) 시간을 조금 달라고 얘기한다.

06 plan: 계획 What's your plan for ~?: ~에 무엇을 할 계획이니? 바꿔 쓸 수 있는 표현으로 'What are you planning to do for ~?', 'What are you going to do for ~?'가 있다.

07 I'm thinking of ~: 나는 ~할까 생각 중이다 watch a movie: 영화를 보다

08 ⓐ too heavy ⓑ want ⓒ to help ⓓ carry ⓔ it / This box는 단수이므로 them이 아니라 it이 어울린다.

09 translate ... into ~: …를 ~로 번역하다

10 (A) any longer: 더 이상, 이제는 (B) told의 직접목적어로 that절이 적절하다. that 다음에 완전한 절이 나온다. (C) expression: 표현 experience: 경험

11 How? → Why?

12 ① Anna는 더 이상 읽지 않는 아동용 도서들을 가지고 있다. ③ 책을 모으기 위해서가 아니라 영어로 번역할 때 어려운 표현들이 나오면 선생님께 도움을 청할 것이다.

13 (1)과 (2) 각각의 선행사와 관계대명사를 써보면, the strange letters which[that], the thing which[that]이다. 문맥상 what으로 바꾸는 데 무리가 없다.

14 (1) be absent from: 결석하다. (2), (3) 접속사와 '주어+be동사'로 양보절을 구로 바꿀 때는 동명사 being을 활용한다. Although he was absent = Despite his being absent 최근 영문법에서는 his 대신 him을 쓰기도 한다. (3)의 종속절에 his가 있으므로, 주절에 Peter를 쓰는 것이 적절하다.

16 접속사 though를 문장 중간에 위치할 때, but을 사용했던 원문의 순서가 반대가 된다. 명사와 그 명사를 지칭하는 대명사를 바뀐 순서에 맞게 적절하게 배치한다.

17 ①, ②, ③, ⑤는 모두 what이 들어가면 된다. ④는 what은 쓸 수 없고, which 또는 that을 써야 한다.

18 기자는 '오늘밤의 수상에 대해 누구 또는 무엇에게 공로를 돌리고 싶은지'를 물었고, 수상자의 대답을 관계대명사 what을 활용하여, 단어를 적절히 배열한다.

19 주격 관계대명사 that이 선행사인 a charity를 수식하도록 배열

하는 것이 적절하다.

20 unless = if ~ not

21 Carter와 Olivia는 다음 세대가 이러한 동물들을 볼 수 있기를 원했기에, 그들의 단체를 One More Generation이라고 이름 붙였다.

22 마요네즈가 동물을 구하는 데 사용되는 것이므로 수동태로 쓰는 것이 적절하다.

23 그들은 '멕시코만'에서 발생한 끔찍한 석유 유출 사건으로 인해 완전히 '기름'을 뒤집어썼기 때문에 죽어가고 있었다.

24 멀리 '수송될' 필요가 없으므로 수동태로 쓰는 것이 적절하다.

25 (A)는 '자동차'를, (B)는 '지역 생산품들'을 가리킨다.

26 지역 생산품들은 그리 멀리 수송될 필요가 '없다.'

27 의문사+to부정사 = 의문사+주어+조동사 should[can]+동사원형

28 아시아흑곰들이 주로 아시아의 '숲'에 살기 때문에 숲을 보호하기 위해 '종이'를 덜 사용해야 하고, 사람들이 그들의 '몸 부위'를 얻기 위해 그들을 사냥하기 때문에 아시아 흑곰으로 만든 제품을 사지 말아야 한다.

29 아시아흑곰으로 무슨 제품을 만들 수 있는지는 알 수 없다. ① A white V-shape on their chests. ② In forests in Asia. ③ Because of hunting and forest destruction. ④ We should use less paper to protect forests. And we should not buy any Asian black bear products.

30 앞부분의 내용을 가리킨다.

31 플라스틱 제품을 '재사용', '재활용'하고 자신의 '병'과 '쇼핑백'을 가지고 오는 것이다.

Timeless Tales of Gods and Heroes

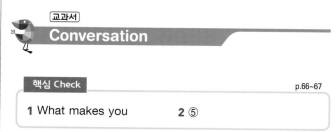

01 ④   02 ⑤   03 ⑤   04 undo
05 (p)riceless   06 protect
07 harvest   08 ②

01 말이 끄는 바퀴 달린 탈것은 '마차(carriage)'이다.

02 주어진 문장의 order는 '주문하다'라는 의미로 쓰였다. ① 명령하다 ② 정돈(된 상태) / 그녀가 생활을 정리해야 할 때였다. ③ 질서 ④ 명령, 지시 ⑤ 주문하다

03 turn into: ~이 되다

04 undo: 무효로 만들다, 원상태로 돌리다

05 reply와 respond는 유의어 관계이다. 따라서 precious와 유의어 관계에 있는 priceless를 쓰는 것이 적절하다.

06 어떤 사물이나 사람이 다치지 않도록 막아준다는 '보호하다(protect)'이다.

07 곡식을 모으는 것은 '추수, 수확(harvest)'이라고 한다.

08 주어진 단어는 '창'이다. 따라서 ②번이 적절하다. 각각 ① sow ③ promise ④ treasure ⑤ accept를 풀이한 말이다.

01 (1) give (2) come (3) plays (4) like
02 (A) of (B) up (C) for
03 (1) Children will fall asleep in the room.
    (2) You had better go home early.
    (3) Moreover, he was scared.
04 turned into
05 (1) poem (2) ask (3) throw
06 carefully

01 give up: ~을 포기하다, come along: 함께 가다, play tricks on: ~에게 장난치다, How do you like ~?: ~가 마음에 드니?

02 of one's own: 자기 자신의, come up with: ~을 생각해 내다, be famous for: ~으로 유명하다

03 (1) fall asleep: 잠들다 (2) had better: ~하는 편이 낫다 (3) moreover: 더욱이, 게다가

04 '~로 되다'는 의미로 쓰이는 것은 'turn into'이다.

05 (1) 단어가 미적 요소와 소리에 따라 선택되고 조심스럽게 배열되는 글은 '시(poem)', (2) 누군가에게 당신이 원하는 무언가

를 하라고 말하는 것은 '요청하다(ask)', (3) 손이나 팔을 빠르게 움직여 어떤 물체를 놓음으로써 그 물체가 공기 중으로 움직이게 하는 것은 '던지다(throw)'이다.

06 'with+명사'는 부사의 의미를 갖는다. 따라서 carefully로 쓰는 것이 적절하다.

Conversation

1 What makes you   2 ⑤

교과서 대화문 익히기

1 F   2 T   3 F   4 T   5 F   6 F

Listen & Speak 1 A-1

it, to visit / is, wanted to come to / What made / into, go to, I saw / Have

Listen & Speak 1 A-2

the worst month of / What, say / blooming, stay inside / what you mean

Listen & Speak 2 A-1

if I change / not at all / to watch, about / Why / learning about / see

Listen & Talk 2 A-2

mind if I open / have a cold, pretty / Would you like / would be

Communicate A

doing / reading, on, into them / What, like them / interesting, lots of / any good / about, famous god / favorite, character / In that case, go see / if I borrow, finished, it before / like this book, too

Progress Check 1

of the year / makes, say / flowers are blooming / because / throw, a party

Progress Check 2

mind if I take, more / waiting for, soon / Never mind / ask, to bring

01 ④   02 ②   03 ③

04 She is learning about Norway in class.

01 왜 그렇게 생각하는지를 묻는 표현이 들어가는 것이 적절하다. 따라서 ④번이 적절하다.

02 허락을 구하는 표현이므로 ②번과 바꾸어 쓸 수 있다. 대화의 밑줄 친 부분은 내가 창문을 열겠다는 것이므로, 창문을 열어달라고 상대에게 요청하는 표현인 ③, ④번은 적절하지 않다.

03 'Do you mind if ~?'는 허락을 구하는 표현이다.

04 소녀는 수업 시간에 노르웨이에 관하여 배우고 있다고 하였다.

시험대비 실력평가   p.73~74

01 ③   02 ③   03 ②

04 It's because she needs to watch a program about Norway.

05 (C)–(A)–(D)–(B)   06 ③   07 ④

08 ⑤   09 it's pretty windy today   10 ③

11 ⑤번 → No, not at all.

12 He wants to read the book before he sees the movie.

13 ⑤

01 답변으로 미루어 보아 아이슬란드로 가고 싶어 하는 이유를 묻는 말이 들어가는 것이 적절하다.

02 'Do you mind if ~?'는 허락을 구하는 표현이다.

03 'Do you mind if ~?'에 대한 대답이 'No, not at all.'이면 승낙한다는 의미이므로 ②번은 글의 내용과 일치하지 않는다.

04 소녀가 채널을 돌려야 하는 이유는 노르웨이에 관한 프로그램을 보아야 하기 때문이다.

05 (C) 4월은 연중 최악의 달이라는 말에 (A) 그렇게 말하는 이유를 묻고 (D) 이유를 답하자 (B) 무슨 말인지 알겠다고 말하는 것이 가장 자연스럽다.

06 bloom은 '꽃이 피다'라는 의미로, opening으로 쓸 수 있다.

07 A의 다음 말로 보아 요청을 허락한 것임을 알 수 있다. 따라서 거절하는 표현인 ④번은 적절하지 않다.

08 ⓐ는 허락을 구하는 표현이므로 ⑤번으로 대신할 수 있다.

09 날씨를 표현할 때 쓰이는 주어는 비인칭 주어 It이다. pretty는 '예쁜'이라는 의미의 형용사 외에도 '꽤'라는 의미의 부사로도 쓰인다.

10 Jane에게 따뜻한 차를 권했고, Jane이 이에 응했으므로 ③번이 가장 적절하다.

11 이어지는 말로 보아 책을 빌려달라는 요청의 말에 승낙했음을 알 수 있다. 'Of course not.', 'Certainly not.', 'No, I don't.', 'No problem.', 'Sure. Go ahead.' 등으로 고쳐도

무방하다.

12 Jaden은 영화를 보러 가기 전에 유리가 읽고 있는 책을 빌려서 읽기를 원한다.

13 Jaden은 유리에게 그녀가 읽고 있는 책을 빌려달라고 하였으므로 ⑤번이 대화의 내용과 일치한다.

서술형 시험대비   p.75

01 Seoul

02 He is interested in Korean TV shows.

03 do you mind if I take this chair

04 He is likely to ask the waiter to bring more chairs.

05 (B)–(D)–(A)–(C)

06 ⓐ makes   ⓑ say   ⓒ throw

07 It's because the weather is not cold and flowers are blooming.

01 Mike는 항상 서울에 와 보고 싶었다고 하였으므로 here는 서울을 가리키는 말이다.

02 남자가 관심 있는 것은 한국 텔레비전 쇼라고 하였다.

03 대답으로 미루어 보아 의자를 사용해도 되는지 허락을 구하는 표현이 들어가는 것이 적절하다.

04 대화가 끝난 후 남자는 웨이터에게 의자를 더 가져다 달라고 요청할 것이다.

05 (B) 창문을 열어도 되느냐고 요청하는 말에, (D) 거절하며 그 이유로 감기에 걸렸다고 설명하자, (A) 따뜻한 차를 마시겠냐고 권하고, (C) 이에 응하는 것이 가장 자연스럽다.

06 이유를 묻는 표현은 'What makes you say so?'이다. throw a party: 파티를 열다

07 소년이 1년 중 4월이 최고의 달이라고 말하는 이유는 날씨가 춥지 않고 꽃이 피기 때문이라고 하였다.

교과서
Grammar

핵심 Check   p.76~77

1 (1) which   (2) that

2 (1) which   (2) which

시험대비 기본평가   p.78

01 (1) them → 생략   (2) is → are   (3) that → which

     (4) who → whose

02 ⑤   03 ④

04 It is those necklaces that[which] Veronika has always wanted to have.

01 (1) 선행사 the pictures를 받는 관계대명사가 있으므로 them은 생략한다. (2) 주어가 복수이므로 are가 적절하다. (3) Robert가 그녀의 문제를 언급한 내용 전체가 선행사가 되는 계속적 용법의 관계대명사 자리이다. that은 계속적 용법으로 쓸 수 없다. (4) 'Sue의 나이'를 가리키는 것이므로 소유격 관계대명사인 whose가 적절하다.

02 강조 구문에서 명사를 강조하면 that 뒤는 불완전한 절이 와야 한다. ⑤에서 the bus를 강조했는데 구조가 완전하다. 내용상 Sam이 그의 시계를 잃어버린 장소를 강조하는 문장이 되어야 하기 때문에 the bus를 in the bus로 바꾸는 것이 적절하다.

03 계속적 용법의 관계대명사로서, 선행사는 사람인 the girl이다. 콤마 뒤에 who가 적절하다.

04 목적어를 강조하는 것이므로, 'It ~ that' 강조구문을 사용한다. 강조되는 대상이 복수라 하더라도 be동사는 is/was만 가능하며, 주절의 문장이 현재완료 시제이므로, 강조구문의 시제도 is로 하는 것에 유의한다.

시험대비 실력평가 p.79~81

01 ⓑ where → which 또는 in 생략, ⓒ that → which, ⓓ run → runs 또는 ran, ⓔ which → that 또는 in which
02 ③   03 it was Tom that tore the newspaper
04 ③
05 (1) All villagers in town like the bridge, which was built 100 years ago.
(2) I learned Chinese from Lily, who made me speak freely in Beijing.
(3) There lived a hero named Hercules, who was the son of Zeus.
(4) They will go to Jagalchi market, where they will buy fresh seafood.
06 ③   07 ②   08 ④   09 ⑤
10 ④
11 My uncles know Sarah, who speaks Chinese like a native.
12 It is Jonathan who is responsible for taking care of the flower.
13 ⑤   14 ②   15 ②
16 ②, ③, ⑤

01 ⓑ 전치사 in이 있으므로, where를 which로 고치거나 in을 생략한다. ⓒ 계속적 용법에서 that 불가 ⓓ 선행사 a horse

단수이므로 runs 또는 ran이 적절하다. ⓔ the way+that[in which]

02 ③의 that은 동격의 접속사로 쓰였다. 나머지는 모두 'It ~ that' 강조구문의 that이다.

03 과거시제 동사 tore 형태에 유의하여, 'It ~ that' 강조구문을 글자 수에 맞게 쓴다.

04 내용상 기술자에게 수리를 맡겼고, '그 기술자가 차를 수리한 것'이 선행사이므로, 관계대명사 which가 적절하다.

05 사람과 사물은 각각 who와 which로 받고, 문장에 나온 there는 장소의 부사이므로 where로 받는다.

06 ③번은 가주어 It과 진주어 명사절을 이끄는 접속사 that이 쓰였다. 나머지는 모두 'It ~ that' 강조구문이다.

07 ②번은 가주어 It과 진주어 명사절을 이끄는 접속사 that이 쓰였다. 나머지는 모두 'It ~ that' 강조구문이다.

08 내용상 '월드컵이 서울에서 개최된' 2002년을 선행사로 받는 관계대명사이므로, 관계대명사 앞에 in이 있어야 한다. Seoul 앞의 in과는 무관하다. which를 in which 또는 관계부사 when으로 바꿔야 한다.

09 빈칸은 모두 계속적 용법의 관계대명사가 들어가는 자리이다. 문장의 선행사는 각각 (A) a wheel, (B) Tiffany's aunt, (C) a couple이다.

10 ①번은 동사의 수의 일치가 부적절, ②, ③, ⑤번은 계속적 용법의 관계대명사 which가 적절하다. ① come → comes, ② of which → which, ③ that → which, ⑤ who → which

11 My uncles know Sarah and she speaks Chinese like a native.에서 and she를 계속적 용법의 관계대명사 who로 바꿔 영작한다.

12 내용상 엄마가 기르는 꽃에 대한 책임을 맡고 있는 사람을 강조하는 문장이므로 'It ~ who' 강조구문을 사용한다. 전치사 for 뒤의 동명사 taking의 형태에 주의한다.

13 ⑤번 문장의 that은 동격의 접속사로 쓰였다. 나머지는 모두 'It ~ that' 강조구문의 that이다.

14 옳은 문장은 ⓕ, ⓖ 2개이다. ⓐ and who → who 또는 and she, ⓑ were → was, ⓒ that → which, ⓓ who → which, ⓔ which → who 또는 that

15 ①, ③ 'It ~ that' 강조구문에서는 강조되는 명사의 성격에 따라 that을 who 또는 which로 대체할 수 있다. ②번은 진주어 명사절을 이끄는 접속사 that이며 다른 단어로 대체 불가하다. ④, ⑤ 선행사가 사물일 때 관계대명사 that은 which로 바꿔 쓸 수 있다.

16 ② 선행사가 단수이므로, which 뒤에 sells가 적절하다. ③ Mr. King's lecture가 선행사이므로 which가 적절하다. ⑤ 계속적 용법이므로 that은 불가능하다. which가 적절하다.

01 (A) It is Lucas that[who] is going to wear a mask at the party this weekend.

   (B) It is a mask that[which] Lucas is going to wear at the party this weekend.

   (C) It is at the party that Lucas is going to wear a mask this weekend.

02 (1) 답변 불가

   (2) It was Ellen that[who] had Grace's car repaired.

   (3) It was three weeks ago that Ellen had Grace's car repaired.

   (4) 답변 불가

   (5) It was at the shop that Grace's car was repaired three weeks ago.

03 (1) the auditorium → in the auditorium

   (2) who → which[that]

   (3) Anthony was chairman of the council.

   (4) the evening → in the evening

   (5) He rescued the injured carefully.

04 (1) All the people there were so selfish, which made the two parties even farther away.

   (2) Thomas is widely known for dancing, which is not true.

   (3) Emma fell in love with Alex, whom she met only once.

05 on January 20, 1993 that Audrey Hepburn was

06 (1) that → which   (2) who → which

   (3) but which → but 삭제 또는 but it

   (4) he made → made him

07 (1) The teacher blamed Susan, who didn't mean to be late.

   (2) Jackson's father looked a lot younger than she thought, which Jackson was ashamed of.

   (3) Almost everyone in the factory stops working at noon, when they go out for lunch.

   (4) Isabella received a letter of apology from her boyfriend, which she hasn't opened yet.

   (5) Bentley's family went to Mexico, where they saw some Mayan ruins.

08 Camila made over 15 pancakes with her dad, which was so fun.

01 It is ~ that 구문을 쓴다. 강조하는 대상이 사람일 때는 that 대신 who, 사물일 때는 that 대신 which를 쓸 수 있다.

02 (1) 5형식 문장의 사역동사 'have+목적어+p.p' 형태에서는 명시적 표현이 없으면 행위자 파악 불가. (4) 주어진 문장만으로는 수리 시점(3주 전)만을 알 수 있고, 수리 기간은 파악할 수 없음. (2), (3), (5)번은 'It ~ that' 강조구문에 맞춰 적절히 영작한다.

03 (1) '부사구'로 장소를 강조하는 것이므로 전치사를 써야 한다. (2) 강조 대상이 사람이 아니므로 who는 쓸 수 없다. which 또는 that이 적절하다. (3) '주격보어'는 'It ~ that' 강조구문의 강조 대상이 될 수 없다. (4) '부사구'로 시간을 강조하는 것이므로 전치사를 써야 한다. (5) 태도를 나타내는 '양태 부사'는 'It ~ that' 강조구문의 강조 대상이 될 수 없다.

04 (1), (2)의 선행사는 앞 문장 전체, (3)은 Alex이다.

05 '1993년 1월 20일이 Audrey Hepburn이 사망한 날'이라는 문장을 '부사구'를 강조하는 'It ~ that 강조구문'으로 표현한다. 전치사 on과 함께 쓰는 것에 유의하여 영작한다.

06 (1) 앞 문장 전체가 선행사이므로, 계속적 용법의 which, (2) 선행사가 발레 동작이므로 which가 적절하다. (3) 앞 문장 전체가 선행사이므로 접속사 but을 삭제하거나, 앞 문장 전체를 받는 대명사로 바꾸는 것이 적절하다. (4) 앞 문장 전체가 선행사이고, 목적어 him으로 바꿔 위치를 수정한다.

07 선행사에 따라 who, which, when, where에 유의하여 영작한다.

08 '계속적' 용법의 관계대명사 which를 사용하여, 앞 문장 전체 내용을 선행사로 하는 문장을 만든다.

확인문제   p.84

1 T   2 F   3 T   4 F   5 T   6 F

확인문제   p.85

1 T   2 F   3 T   4 F   5 T   6 F

확인문제   p.86

1 T   2 F   3 T   4 F   5 T   6 F

01 Treasures   02 Norse

03 highest, gave up   04 the strongest god

05 controls the weather   06 plays tricks on

07 something was wrong   08 was gone

09 such a terrible thing   10 who was drinking

11 You'd better undo   12 scared

13 would get   14 fine golden hair

15 the finest smiths   16 it is, who

17 three treasures

18 better than theirs

19 Of course

20 make, for them

21 decide on

22 had to be

23 immediately

24 went to see

25 are making, for

26 I bet, as fine as theirs

27 accepted the challenge

28 of their own

29 with all the treasures

30 came along

31 showed, from

32 for, only one eye

33 It was, that

34 turn into

35 for

36 The third treasure

37 flowing golden hair

38 put, on, took root

39 Brokk's turn

40 eight more, every ninth night

41 Frey a pig

42 faster than any horse

43 My third treasure

44 which

45 come back to

46 break it

47 the greatest treasure

48 the three gods liked most

49 protect, from

50 the better smiths

51 proved, precious treasures

교과서 확인학습 B   p.90~92

1 Treasures for Three Gods

2 Important Norse Gods

3 Odin, who is the highest god, gave up his eye for wisdom.

4 Thor is Odin's son and the strongest god of all.

5 Frey, who is the god of the harvest, controls the weather.

6 Loki is a god who plays tricks on others.

7 Thor woke and knew immediately something was wrong.

8 His wife's beautiful golden hair was gone.

9 He knew only Loki could do such a terrible thing.

10 Thor soon found Loki, who was drinking at home.

11 "You'd better undo what you did, or you'll be sorry," Thor said angrily to Loki.

12 Loki was scared.

13 He promised that he would get golden hair for Thor's wife.

14 Loki knew only the sons of Ivaldi could make fine golden hair.

15 He went to them and said, "I heard Brokk and his brother are the finest smiths. Is that true?"

16 "No, it is we who are the finest smiths," the sons of Ivaldi replied.

17 "They're making three treasures for Odin, Thor, and Frey," said Loki.

18 "Do you think you can make treasures better than theirs?"

19 "Of course we can," they answered.

20 "O.K., then you should also make three treasures for them," said Loki.

21 "The gods will decide on the best treasure."

22 Loki also told them that one of the treasures had to be golden hair.

23 They went to work immediately.

24 Loki then went to see Brokk and his brother.

25 "Ivaldi's sons are making three treasures for Odin, Thor, and Frey," said Loki.

26 "I bet that you can never make treasures as fine as theirs."

27 Brokk became angry and accepted the challenge.

28 He and his brother produced three treasures of their own.

29 Loki went to see the three gods with all the treasures.

30 Brokk came along.

31 Loki showed them the treasures from Ivaldi's sons.

32 The first treasure was for Odin, who had only one eye.

33 It was a spear that never missed its target.

34 The second treasure was a big ship that could turn into a piece of cloth.

35 It was for Frey.

36 The third treasure was for Thor.

37 Loki showed Thor the flowing golden hair for his wife.

38 Thor put the hair on his wife's head, and it took root and became real hair.

39 It was now Brokk's turn to show the gods his gifts.

40 He gave Odin a gold arm ring that produced eight more gold rings every ninth night.

41 Brokk then gave Frey a pig.

42 It could pull his carriage faster than any horse.

43 "My third treasure is for you, Thor," said Brokk.

44 "This is the hammer Mjolnir, which you'll love.

45 If you throw it, it'll always come back to you.

46 Moreover, nothing can ever break it."

47 It was an easy decision to choose the greatest treasure.

17

48 It was Mjolnir that the three gods liked most.

49 They thought the hammer would protect the gods from their enemies.

50 "Brokk and his brother," said Odin, "are the better smiths."

51 Brokk proved that Loki was wrong, and the three gods now had precious treasures.

시험대비 실력평가

p.93~97

01 Norse　　**02** ③　　**03** ①　　**04** ⑤

05 ②　　**06** who is → who are

07 one of the treasures had to be golden hair

08 as　　**09** ③, ④

10 making treasures as fine as Ivaldi's sons'

11 which　**12** ②　**13** nine　**14** ③

15 ③　　**16** ④　　**17** ⑤　　**18** ①

19 treasure → treasures　**20** ③　**21** ⑤

22 ②, ④　　**23** ③　　**24** ②　　**25** ③

24 ②

24 (A) fine golden hair　(B) the challenge

01 Norse: 고대 스칸디나비아(사람[말])의, 노르웨이(사람[말])의, (특히 고대) 노르웨이[스칸디나비아]어, 영영풀이: 1. 중세 시대 스칸디나비아 국가에 속하는 또는 관련된, 2. 노르웨이의 또는 노르웨이와 관련된 또는 노르웨이 사람, 문화, 언어

02 ⓑ play tricks on: 농간을 부리다, 장난을 치다, ⓒ get: 사다, 구입하다(buy, purchase), 구하다, 얻다(obtain)의 뜻으로, 3형식으로 고칠 때 전치사 for를 사용한다.

03 본문은 인물과 배경이 제시되고, 사건의 실마리를 제공하는 도입 단계에 해당하므로, ① '발단'이 적절하다.

04 'Loki'가 Thor의 아내를 위해 금발머리를 얻어 오겠다고 약속했다.

05 ②는 Brokk and his brother를 가리키고, 나머지는 다 the sons of Ivaldi를 가리킨다.

06 we are the finest smiths에서 주어인 we를 강조한 것이기 때문에 'who are'로 고치는 것이 적절하다..

07 told라는 과거시제에 맞추어 목적절인 that 이하의 시제도 has to(~해야 한다)의 과거인 had to로 쓰는 것이 적절하다.

08 as ... as ~: '~만큼 …한', 형용사 원급을 사용하여 두 대상을 비교하는 구문이다.

09 (A)와 ①, ②, ⑤: 틀림없이 ~하다, 내 의견으로는 틀림없이 ~할 것이다, ③ doubtful: 의심스러운, ④ unlikely: ~할[일] 것 같지 않은, 있음직하지[있을 것 같지] 않은

10 'Ivaldi의 아들들의 보물만큼 훌륭한 보물을 만드는 것'을 가리킨다.

11 선행사가 사물이고 계속적 용법이므로 which가 적절하다.

12 앞에 나오는 내용에 추가하는 내용이 뒤에 이어지므로 Moreover가 가장 적절하다. Moreover: 게다가, 더욱이, ③ 그러므로, ④ 다시 말해서

13 every+서수+단수명사 = every+기수+복수명사: ~마다, every ninth night: 아홉 번째 밤이 될 때마다

14 이 글은 '모든 보물을 세 명의 신에게 보여주고 그 중에서 가장 훌륭한 보물을 선택하는' 내용의 글이므로, 제목으로는 ③번 '무엇이 신들에게 보여진 가장 훌륭한 보물인가?'가 적절하다.

15 Loki가 겁을 내며 Thor의 아내를 위해 금발머리를 얻어 오겠다고 약속했다는 내용이 이어지고 있으므로, "네가 한 짓을 되돌려 놓는 것이 좋을 거야"라고 하는 것이 적절하다. undo 원상태로 돌리다

16 ④ gradually: 서서히, 나머지는 다 '즉시', ⑤ without delay: 지체 없이, 즉시

17 Loki가 왜 다른 신들에게 농간을 부리는지는 대답할 수 없다. ① Odin. ② Thor. ③ Frey. ④ The weather.

18 ⓐ와 ①: It is[was] ... that[who, whom, which, etc.]의 구문으로 문장의 주어·(동사 또는 전치사의) 목적어·부사 어구를 강조하여 쓰인 대명사, ② 그것(앞에 이미 언급되었거나 현재 이야기되고 있는 사물·동물을 가리킴), ③ 가주어, ④ [사정·상황을 막연히 가리키는] 비인칭 주어, ⑤ 가목적어

19 one+of+the+복수명사: ~ 중의 하나

20 Brokk와 그의 남동생이 'Odin과 Thor와 Frey'를 위해서 보물을 만들고 있다고 말했다. ⑤ on the spot: 즉각[즉석에서]

21 ⓐ와 ⑤: 빗나가다, ① 이해[파악]하지 못하다, ② (기회를) 놓치다, ③ (어디에 참석하지 않아서 그 일을) 놓치다, ④ 그리워[아쉬워]하다

22 ⓑ와 ①, ③, ⑤: 최상급의 뜻. '비교급+than any (other)+단수 명사'로 최상급을 나타낼 수 있는데, 비교 대상이 같은 그룹에 속해 있지 않은 경우에는 any other 대신 any만 쓴다. 부정주어+비교급+than = 부정주어+as(so)+원급+as도 최상급의 뜻을 나타낸다.

23 ③번 다음 문장의 They에 주목한다. 주어진 문장의 'the three gods'를 받고 있으므로 ③번이 적절하다.

24 Frey를 위한 보물은 '큰 배'와 '돼지 한 마리'였다.

25 ③은 'Ivaldi의 아들들'을 가리키고, 나머지는 다 'Brokk와 그의 남동생'을 가리킨다.

26 Ivaldi의 아들들과 Brokk와 그의 남동생에게 각각 거짓말로 경쟁을 하도록 부추기는 것으로 보아 '교활한' 성격이라고 하는 것이 적절하다. ① 성실한, ③ 거만한, ④ 관대한, ⑤ 인내심이 있는

27 Loki는 '훌륭한 금발머리'를 원했는데, Ivaldi의 아들들만이 그것을 만들 수 있었다. 그래서 그는 Ivaldi의 아들들이 경쟁심을 느끼고 '도전'을 받아들이도록 하기 위해서 Brokk와 그의 남동생을 언급했다.

01 (A) gone   (B) angrily   (C) scared
02 stronger than
03 Loki가 Thor의 아내의 아름다운 금발머리를 사라지게 한 것
04 on   05 Brokk and his brother's treasures
06 competitive
07 (A) a spear   (B) a big ship
    (C) the flowing golden hair
08 They liked Mjolnir most.
09 He thought 'Brokk and his brother' were the better smiths.
10 his eye   11 and he
12 he would get Thor's wife golden hair

06 (1) was gone   (2) come along   (3) turned into
07 (1) How did you come up with the idea?
    (2) Don't play tricks on your little sister.
    (3) He is famous for a smith.
08 Do you mind if I play it?
09 ⑤   10 ②   11 ③
12 It's because she is waiting for her friend and she'll be here soon.
13 ③   14 ②   15 ③   16 ④
17 ③   18 ①   19 ④   20 ②
21 ⑤   22 smiths   23 ②   24 which
25 ②, ⑤ / ①, ③, ④
26 It was Mjolnir that the three gods liked most.
27 ④   28 ④   29 ⑤   30 ④
31 asking the sons of Ivaldi to make fine golden hair

---

01 (A) disappear는 수동태로 쓸 수 없으므로 gone이 적절하다. be gone = disappear: 사라지다, (B) 동사 said를 수식하는 것이므로, 부사인 angrily가 적절하다. (C) Loki가 '겁이 난' 것이므로 scared가 적절하다. scared: 무서워하는, 겁먹은, scaring: 놀라운, 위협적인
02 비교급+than+any other+단수명사: 최상급의 뜻을 나타낸다.
03 'Loki가 Thor의 아내의 아름다운 금발머리를 사라지게 한' 일을 가리킨다.
04 decide on: ~에 관해 결정을 하다
05 'Brokk와 그의 남동생의 보물'을 가리킨다.
06 Loki는 Ivaldi의 아들들이 훌륭한 금발머리를 만들도록 하기 위해 그들의 '경쟁심'을 촉발시켰다. competitive spirit: 경쟁심
07 Ivaldi의 아들들은 Odin을 위해 '창'을, Frey를 위해 '큰 배'를, Thor의 아내를 위해 '매끈하게 늘어진 금발머리'를 만들었다.
08 세 명의 신들이 가장 마음에 든 것은 '묠니르'였다.
09 'Brokk와 그의 남동생'이 더 훌륭한 대장장이라고 Odin은 생각했다.
10 '지혜를 위해 한쪽 눈을 포기했다'는 것은 '한쪽 눈을 희생하여(대가로 치르고) 지혜를 얻었다'는 뜻이다. at the expense[cost/price] of: ~을 희생하여
11 계속적 용법의 관계대명사는 '접속사+대명사'로 바꿔 쓸 수 있다.
12 get: 사다, 구입하다(buy, purchase), 구하다, 얻다(obtain)의 뜻으로, 3형식으로 고칠 때 전치사 for를 사용한 것을 '간접목적어+직접목적어' 순서로 쓰면 4형식이 된다.

---

01 ③   02 ④   03 ③
04 decide   05 ④

---

01 take root: 뿌리를 내리다, take a walk: 산책하다, take a break: 쉬다
02 '형용사+ly'는 부사로 쓰이지만 '명사+ly'는 형용사로 쓰인다.
03 cloth는 '옷감'이라는 의미로 쓰인다. '옷'은 clothes이다.
04 다른 가능성에 대해 주의 깊게 생각한 후 무언가를 하기로 선택하다는 '결정하다(decide)'이다.
05 주어진 문장에서 miss는 '(기회를) 놓치다'는 의미로 쓰였다. 따라서 ④번이 가장 적절하다. ① 그리워하다 ② (식사를) 거르다 ③ 이해하지 못하다 ⑤ (있어야 할 것이) 없다는 것을 알다[눈치채다]
06 (1) be gone: 사라지다, 없어지다 (2) come along: 함께 가다 (3) turn into: ~으로 되다 (1) safe: 금고
07 come up with: ~을 생각해 내다, play tricks on: ~에게 장난을 치다 (3) be famous for: ~로 유명하다
08 허락을 구하는 표현은 'Do you mind if ~?'이다.
09 'Sure, go ahead.'라고 답하는 것이 적절하다. 'I do'라고 하였으므로 상대가 집으로 일찍 가는 것을 꺼린다는 말이 되므로 Sure와 의미상 맞지 않다.
10 (D) 4월이 가장 좋다고 말하자 (B) 그렇게 말한 이유를 묻고 (A) 이유를 답하고 (E) 자신이 4월을 좋아하는 이유는 생일이 있기 때문이라고 하자 (C) 파티를 열어주겠다고 말하는 것이 가장 자연스럽다.
11 허락을 요청하는 말이 들어가는 것이 적절하다. ③번은 권하는 말이다.
12 여자는 친구를 기다리고 있고 그 친구가 곧 도착할 것이기 때문에 의자를 줄 수 없다고 하였다.
13 Mike는 한국 텔레비전 쇼에 관심이 있다고 하였다. be into ~: ~에 흥미가 있다
14 ① which → who ② that → who ③ what → which ⑤ what → which 또는 that

15 'It ~ that' 강조구문에서 어떤 사건이 일어난 해를 가리키는 부사구 표현은 연도 앞에 in을 쓰는 것이 적절하다.

16 ④번은 가주어 It과 진주어 명사절 접속사 that이 쓰인 문장이다. 나머지는 모두 'It ~ that' 강조구문이 쓰였다.

17 <보기>의 which는 관계대명사로서 '계속적 용법'으로 사용되었다. ③번의 which는 의문형용사로서 '어느'라는 뜻이다. 나머지는 모두 관계대명사 which로 사용되었다. to no avail: 보람 없이, 헛되이

18 ① what → that[which]

19 'Stella는 친구 다섯 명이 있는데, Stella가 운동을 싫어한다는 것을 그들 모두가 알고 있다'는 내용으로 풀어볼 수 있다. ④번은 접속사 and와 관계대명사 whose friends가 같이 있어서 틀렸다. whose를 her로 바꾸거나 and를 삭제해야 한다.

20 ②번의 that은 so ~ that 부사절의 접속사로 쓰였다. 나머지는 모두 'It ~ that' 강조구문의 that이다. persuasion: 설득

21 which are → which is

22 smith: 대장장이, 금속 세공인, <영영풀이: 금속을 다루는 일을 하는 사람들, 특히 망치질로 금속의 형태를 만드는 사람들>

23 이 글은 'Loki가 Ivaldi의 아들들로 하여금 훌륭한 금발머리를 만들도록 하기 위해 그들의 경쟁심을 이용하는' 내용의 글이므로, 주제로는 ②번 '자신의 목적을 성취하기 위해 타인의 경쟁심을 활용하기'가 적절하다. ① craftsman: (숙련된) 장인

24 '접속사+대명사'를 계속적 용법의 관계대명사 which로 바꿔 쓰는 것이 적절하다. it은 the hair를 가리킨다.

25 ⓑ와 ②, ⑤: 형용사적 용법, to show는 turn을 꾸며 주어 '보여 줄 차례'라는 의미로 쓰임, ⓒ와 ①, ③, ④: 명사적 용법, ③번의 to show는 진주어로 쓰인 명사적 용법

26 that이나 which를 보충하면 된다. It was와 that[which]사이에 강조하고자 하는 말을 넣어 배열하는 것이 적절하다.

27 ④ Brokk와 그의 남동생이 Frey를 위해 만들어 준 것은 'a pig'였다.

28 본문 (3)번은 이야기에서 갈등과 긴장이 최고조에 도달하고 주제가 선명하게 부각되는 부분으로, 어떤 결말을 낼 것인가를 결정하는 계기를 제공하는 절정 단계에 해당하므로, ④ '절정'이 적절하다.

29 대장장이들이 각각 어떤 보상을 받았는지는 알 수 없다. ① Loki, Odin, Thor, and Frey. the sons of Ivaldi, Brokk and his brother ② Loki가 Thor의 아내의 아름다운 금발머리를 사라지게 했다. ③ Loki가 세 명의 신들에게 보물을 보여 주었다. ④ 신들은 망치를 가장 마음에 들어 했고, 각자 소중한 보물을 가지게 되었다.

30 단지 재미로 남의 머리를 자르는 것으로 보아, 'I'는 Loki에 해당한다고 하는 것이 적절하다. play tricks (on): 농간을 부리다, 장난을 치다

31 'Ivaldi의 아들들에게 훌륭한 금발머리를 만들어 달라고 부탁하는 것'을 가리킨다.

01 ④, ⑤   02 ③   03 ⑤   04 ④

05 ③   06 Why do you say so?

07 ④   08 ⑤

09 What makes you like them so much?

10 ⑤   11 ⑤

12 (1) ⓐ   (2) ⓑ   (3) ⓐ   (4) ⓐ   (5) ⓑ   (6) ⓐ

13 ④   14 ⑤

15 ⓐ It was Tom that[who] bought a tablet at the mall 3 weeks ago.

   ⓑ It was a tablet that[which] Tom bought at the mall 3 weeks ago.

   ⓒ It was at the mall that Tom bought a tablet 3 weeks ago.

   ⓓ It was 3 weeks ago that Tom bought a tablet at the mall.

16 Our school introduced a new system, which would help improve the students' math grade that had always been under average.

17 Brokk and his brother are the finest smiths

18 it is we who are the finest smiths

19 fine golden hair   20 ⑤

21 ④   22 ②   23 and you'll love it

24 a spear and a gold arm ring / a big ship and a pig / the flowing golden hair for his wife and the hammer Mjolnir

25 ①   26 a strange voice   27 ④

01 주어진 단어는 '명사-형용사'의 관계로 '금 – 금으로 만든, 금빛의'라는 의미이다. ④번은 '흙 – 흙으로 만든', ⑤번은 '나무 – 나무로 만든'이란 의미이다. 나머지는 모두 '형용사-동사'의 관계이다.

02 주어진 문장의 빈칸에는 take가 쓰인다. ① make a noise: 소음을 만들다 ② make a decision: 결정을 내리다 ③ take place: 발생하다 ④ get angry: 화내다 ⑤ get along with: ~와 사이좋게 지내다

03 주어진 단어는 '조각'이라는 의미이므로 ⑤번이 가장 적절하다. ① mysterious ② miss ③ reply ④ skin

04 답변으로 보아 왜 왔는지를 물어보는 말이 들어가는 것이 가장 적절하다.

05 한국을 처음으로 방문한 Mike는 자신이 TV 속에서 보았던 장소들을 둘러볼 것이라고 하였다.

06 밑줄 친 (A)는 왜 그렇게 말하는지를 묻는 말이다. 'Why do you think so?', 'Why is that?' 등으로 써도 무방하다.

07 대답으로 미루어 보아 빈칸에는 거절하는 말이 들어가는 것이 적절하다. ④번은 요청에 응하는 답변이다.

08 주어진 문장의 it은 책을 가리키는 말이며 책을 빌려달라고 말하는 이유를 설명하고 있으므로 ⑤번이 가장 적절하다.

20 정답 및 해설

09 이유를 묻는 표현으로 'What makes you ~?'를 쓴다. 이때 make는 사역동사이므로 목적격 보어로 동사원형을 쓰는 것에 유의한다.

10 두 사람은 새로 나온 토르 영화를 볼 예정이다.

11 관계대명사 '계속적' 용법의 문장들이다. ⑤번의 that을 which로 고쳐야 한다.

12 (2), (5)는 접속사 that이 이끄는 진주어 명사절이 쓰였다. 나머지는 모두 'It ~ that' 강조구문인데, 그 중 (4), (6)은 의문사를 강조하고 있다. genetic engineering: 유전 공학

13 ④번은 선행사가 sea water가 아니라 '앞 문장 전체'이다.

14 장소의 부사구가 강조될 때는 that을 쓴다.

15 강조하는 대상에 따라 that 외에 who, which도 사용한다.

16 본문에 나온 표현만으로 계속적 용법의 관계대명사와 제한적 용법의 관계대명사를 모두 사용해야 하기 때문에, 보충 설명이 필요한 두 번째 문장을 계속적 용법의 'which'로 연결하는 것이 적절하다.

17 'Brokk와 그의 남동생이 가장 훌륭한 대장장이'라는 것을 가리킨다.

18 It is와 that[who/which] 사이에 강조하고자 하는 말을 넣는다. 강조하고자 하는 말이 사람일 경우 that 대신 who를 사용할 수 있다.

19 Loki는 Ivaldi의 아들들만이 '훌륭한 금발머리'를 만들 수 있다는 것을 알고 있었기 때문이다.

20 Ivaldi의 아들들이 세 명의 신들을 위해 무슨 보물들을 만들었는지는 대답할 수 없다. ① Because he knew only they could make fine golden hair. ② He said, "I heard Brokk and his brother are the finest smiths. Is that true?" ③ They felt proud of it. craftsmanship: 손재주, (훌륭한) 솜씨, ④ Yes.

21 위 글은 '신화'이다. ① (신문·잡지의) 글, 기사, ② 수필, ③ 전기, ⑤ (책·연극·영화 등에 대한) 논평[비평], 감상문

22 이 글은 'Ivaldi의 아들들과 Brokk와 그의 남동생이 세 명의 신을 위해 만든 보물들을 소개하면서, 신들이 그 중에서 가장 훌륭한 보물을 선택하는 것'에 관한 내용의 글이므로, 주제로는 ②번 '세 신을 위한 보물과 그들 중 가장 훌륭한 보물을 선택하는 것'이 적절하다.

23 계속적 용법의 관계대명사는 '접속사+대명사'로 바꿔 쓸 수 있다.

24 Odin의 소중한 보물: '창'과 '금팔찌', Frey의 소중한 보물: '큰 배'와 '돼지 한 마리', Thor의 소중한 보물: '그의 아내를 위한 매끈하게 늘어진 금발머리'와 '묠니르라는 망치'

25 ①번은 '일반적인 왕'을 가리키고, 나머지는 다 '6 가야의 왕들'을 가리킨다.

26 '이상한 목소리'를 가리킨다.

27 여섯 개의 알이 어떻게 여섯 명의 소년들로 변했는지는 알 수 없다. ① In the southeastern part of Korea. ② It was a small hill. ③ From the sky. ⑤ King Kim Suro.

서술형 실전문제
p.112~113

01 (1) angrily   (2) easy   (3) happily
02 What made you come here?
03 He is going to go to the places he saw on TV.
04 which means he likes foreign cultures
05 was because of my mother that I won the award
06 His wife's beautiful golden hair was gone.
07 such a terrible thing
08 advise / should / to undo
09 (A) missed   (B) a piece of cloth   (C) real hair
10 (A) a gold arm ring   (B) a pig
   (C) the hammer Mjolnir

01 '성내어, 화가 나서'는 부사이므로 angrily, '쉬운'은 '결정'이라는 명사를 수식하므로 형용사 easy, '기꺼이'는 부사이므로 happily라고 쓰는 것이 적절하다.

02 make는 사역동사로 쓰였으므로 목적격보어로 동사원형을 쓰는 것이 적절하다.

03 그는 TV에서 보았던 장소들을 가볼 것이라고 하였다.

04 Lucas가 평소 다양한 나라의 국제 라디오 방송을 온라인으로 청취하고, 외국인들과 문화에 관한 이야기를 나누는 것을 즐긴다는 내용으로 보아, 그가 외국 문화를 좋아한다는 결론을 내릴 수 있다. 동사의 수의 일치에 주의하여, 단어를 배열한다.

05 기자의 질문이 '수상의 제일 큰 공로자'에 대해 묻는 것이었으므로, 괄호에 나온 어머니와 관련된 답변을 해야 한다. 'because of my mother'를 'It ~ that' 구문으로 강조하는 문장을 쓰는 것이 적절하다.

06 '그의 아내의 아름다운 금발머리가 사라진 것'을 가리킨다.

07 'such+a+형용사+명사'의 순서로 쓰는 것이 적절하다. so terrible a thing도 가능하다.

08 You had better 동사원형 = I advise you to 부정사 = You should 동사원형 = It would be better for you to 부정사: ~해야 하다, ~하는 것이 좋다

09 Odin을 위한 보물은 목표물을 절대로 '빗나가지' 않는 창이었고, Frey를 위한 보물은 '천 조각'으로 변할 수 있는 큰 배였다. Thor를 위한 보물은 그의 아내를 위한 매끈하게 늘어진 금발머리였는데, Thor가 그 머리카락을 그의 아내의 머리에 얹었을 때 그것이 뿌리를 내려서 '진짜 머리카락'이 되었다.

10 Brokk와 그의 남동생은 Odin을 위해 '금팔찌'를, Frey를 위해 '돼지 한 마리'를, Thor를 위해 '묠니르라는 망치'를 만들었다.

창의사고력 서술형 문제
p.114

|모범답안|

01 if I change the channel / not at all / watch a program about Norway / learning about Norway in class

02 (A) southeastern part　(B) Gujibong
　　(C) singing and dancing　(D) six golden eggs
　　(E) six Gayas　(F) King Kim Suro

01 ⑤　　　　　　02 take

03 (1) fell asleep immediately
　　(2) completely dark outside

04 It's because he has to study for his exams.

05 ④　　　　　06 ④　　　　07 (B)-(D)-(C)-(A)

08 ⑤　　　　　09 a new movie about Thor

10 ④　　　　　11 He wants to read Yuri's book.

12 if I play the piano

13 (1) They watched the movie *Frozen 2*, which is the
　　　second episode of *Frozen*
　　(2) It was the Korean version of the OST of *Frozen
　　　2* which was sung by the singer TY.

14 ③

15 (1) Mom asked me to put the unused things in
　　　the boxes, and we will donate them to charity.
　　(2) Mom asked me to put the unused things in the
　　　boxes, which we will donate to charity.

16 ④

17 (1) I brushed my teeth for myself, which mom
　　　praised.
　　(2) Jason's dog Brown is so smart that he can
　　　wash many dishes, which will surprise the
　　　world.

18 to show his gifts to the gods

19 (A) eight more gold rings　(B) faster
　　(C) come back

20 ①　　　21 ⑤　　　22 ④　　　23 ④

24 ⑤　　　25 (A) six eggs　(B) six Gayas

01 모두 '형용사-부사'의 관계이지만 fast의 부사는 fast이다.

02 take a picture: 사진을 찍다, take care: 조심하다, take a
look: 보다

03 fall asleep: 잠들다, completely: 완전히, outside: 바깥에

04 시험을 위해 공부해야 하기 때문이라고 하였다.

05 이유를 묻는 말이므로 ④번이 가장 적절하다.

06 'Do you mind if ~?'는 허락을 구하는 표현으로 'Certainly
not.'이라고 답할 경우 허락에 응하는 것이 된다. 그러나 이어지
는 문장에서는 주차가 안 된다고 하였으므로 대화의 내용이 어색
하다.

07 (B) 의자를 써도 되느냐는 요청 (D) 거절하는 말 (C) 이에 알겠
다고 답함 (A) 웨이터에게 의자를 더 가져다 달라고 말하라고 알
려 줌

08 이어지는 말로 보아 요청에 응하는 말이 들어가는 것이 적절하
다. 따라서 금지하는 답변인 ⑤번은 적절하지 않다.

09 토르에 관한 새 영화를 의미한다.

10 Jaden이 'I know him. He's my favorite online game
character.'라고 하고 있다.

11 Jaden은 영화를 보러 가기 전에 유리가 읽고 있는 책을 읽고 싶
다고 하였다.

12 친구에게 피아노를 연주해 보아도 되는지를 묻는 말을 쓰는 것
이 적절하다. 'Do you mind if ~?'는 허락을 구할 때 쓰이는
표현이다.

13 내용을 정확히 이해하고, 조건에 맞게 질문에 답하도록 한다. (1)
관계대명사의 계속적 용법을 활용한다. (2) It ~ that 강조구문
의 형식으로 영작하되 which를 반드시 사용해야 하기 때문에
which를 놓치지 않아야 한다.

14 '계속적' 용법의 관계대명사이다. ①, ⑤번은 전치사의 목적어
역할(한정적 용법), ②, ④번은 의문대명사 which이다.

15 and we will donate them = , which we will donate

16 'Philip이 그 욕망을 갖고 그 부자 노인을 도운 것은 아니었다.
(부자 노인을 도왔지만, 그 욕망 때문은 아니었다)'라는 내용에
맞게 'It wasn't ~ that'을 적절히 활용한다.

17 (1) for myself: 혼자서(남의 도움 없이) (2) so smart that ~:
너무나 영리해서 그 결과 ~

18 show는 to를 사용하여 3형식으로 고친다.

19 Odin을 위한 보물은 아홉 번째 밤이 될 때마다 '8개의 금팔찌를
더' 만들어 내는 금팔찌였고, Frey를 위한 보물은 어떤 말보다
도 그의 마차를 '더 빨리' 끌 수 있는 돼지였다. Thor를 위한 보
물은 묠니르라는 망치였는데, Thor가 그것을 던질 때마다 그것
은 항상 그에게 '되돌아 올 것'이었고 어떤 것에 의해서도 부서지
지 않을 것이었다.

20 ① It은 The first treasure was for Odin을 가리키고, 주격
관계대명사 that이 이끄는 관계대명사절이 that 앞에 오는 명사
a spear를 수식하고 있다.

21 Loki가 가장 마음에 들어 한 보물이 무엇이었는지는 대답할
수 없다. ① It was a spear. ② It was a big ship. ③ For
Thor. ④ Because they thought it would protect the
gods from their enemies.

22 아내의 아름다운 금발머리가 사라졌기 때문에 '속상하다'고 하는
것이 적절하다. upset: 속상한, ② 지루한, ③ 안도하는, 다행으
로 여기는, ⑤ 무관심한

23 이유를 나타내는 접속사를 쓰고, 선행사가 the sons of Ivaldi
이므로 대명사를 they로 쓰는 것이 적절하다.

24 위 글은 '가야의 건국 신화'이다. ① 우화, ② 논픽션(소설이나
허구의 이야기가 아닌 전기·역사·사건 기록 따위), ③ 공상 소
설, ④ 공상 과학 소설[영화]

25 김수로왕은 황금 상자에 담겨 하늘에서부터 내려온 '여섯 개의
알들' 중 하나에서 태어났다. 12일 뒤에 여섯 개의 알들은 여섯
명의 소년들로 변했고, 그들이 '여섯 가야'의 왕이 되었다. 김수
로왕이 그들 중 가장 강했다.

Lesson 3
Plants That Feed Us

시험대비 실력평가   p.124

01 ③   02 ③   03 ⑤
04 be afraid[scared] of   05 ⑤
06 (1) bloom   (2) statue   (3) material   (4) character
07 ⑤

01 주어진 단어는 반의어 관계에 있다. 모두 유의어지만 ③번은 반의어이다. ① 비슷한 ② 필수적인 ③ 진실 – 거짓 ④ 흔치 않은 ⑤ 이점

02 '소수의 사람들에 의해서만 알려진 사실이며 다른 누구에게도 말해지지 않는 어떤 것'은 '비밀(secret)'이다.

03 ⑤ composer라고 쓰는 것이 적절하다.

04 be scared of 혹은 be afraid of: ~을 두려워하다

05 각각 pilot, soak, crush, actor의 영영풀이이다. 따라서 tour가 적절하다.

06 bloom: (꽃을) 피우다, 피다, statue: 동상, material: 재료, 물질, character: 등장인물

07 '~ 옆에'라는 의미의 by는 교통수단과 함께 쓰여 '~로'라는 의미로도 쓰일 수 있으며 동명사와 함께 쓰이면 '~함으로써'라는 의미로도 쓰인다.

서술형 시험대비   p.125

01 inventor
02 (1) expect   (2) statue   (3) insect
03 (1) After graduation, I got a job with NASA as a researcher.
   (2) The interviewer asked me about my future plans.
   (3) I am proud of being a cartoonist.
04 (A) have   (B) keep   (C) take
05 (1) is good for   (2) no longer   (3) In addition
   (4) by making   (5) poisonous material
06 inventor

01 동사에 '-er'이나 '-or'을 붙여서 명사를 만든 것이다. invent는 직업을 나타내는 명사로 쓰기 위하여 '-or'을 붙인다.

02 (1) 어떤 일이 일어날 것이라고 믿다 (2) 돌이나 금속 같은 단단한 재료로 만들어진 사람이나 동물의 이미지 (3) 여섯 개의 다리를 가진 파리나 개미 같은 작은 생물

03 researcher: 조사원, interviewer: 면접관, cartoonist: 만화가

04 have a fever: 열이 있다, have difficulty in Ving: V 하는 데 어려움이 있다, keep ~ a secret: ~을 비밀로 하다, keep a diary: 일기를 쓰다, take medicine: 약을 먹다, take a walk: 산책하다

05 (1) be good for: ~에 유익하다 (2) no longer: 더 이상 ~가 아닌 (3) in addition: 게다가 (4) by Ving: V함으로써 (5) poisonous: 독성이 강한, material: 재료, 물질

06 에디슨이 롤모델이며 무언가를 발명하는 것을 좋아한다고 하였으므로 '발명가(inventor)'를 빈칸에 쓰는 것이 적절하다.

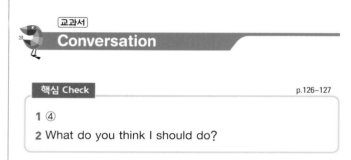

(교과서) Conversation

핵심 Check   p.126~127

1 ④
2 What do you think I should do?

01 Bomi에게 약이 있는지 물어보는 것으로 보아 거기에 대한 대답으로 Bomi는 '왜? 무슨 문제가 있니?'라고 다시 물어보는 것이 적절하다. 'Where have you been?'은 '어디 갔다 왔니?'라는 뜻이다.

교과서 대화문 익히기

Check(√) True or False   p.128

1 F   2 T   3 F   4 T   5 T

교과서 확인학습   p.130~131

Listen & Speak 1 A-1
some medicine / something wrong / a stomachache, too much / go for a walk / it a try

Listen & Speak 1 A-2
something wrong, so good / a sore throat, because of / Put, take, in, produce / get a few plants

Listen & Speak 2 A-1
so hard to lose, do you think / walk your dog / it, it help, lose weight / actually exercising, too / think about it

How are, doing, growing / gotten, a few, so far, I should do / Where / In / need about, a day / move, over

Communicate A

is something wrong, quiet / a bit tired, little / something late / on, until, what I often do / that's why, before / getting worse, I should do / eating lots of carrots, rich in vitamin, keep, healthy / see

Progress Check 1

Is, wrong / a little, watched, for / why, red eyes, putting, over

Progress Check 2

wrong, worried / broke, plate, do you think / Tell, understand / hope, right

---

시험대비 기본평가   p.132

01 ④   02 ③   03 ③

04 She has watched a movie on her phone for two hours.

01 빈칸에는 안부를 묻는 말이 들어가는 것이 자연스럽다. 따라서 ④번이 적절하다.

02 밑줄 친 부분은 조언을 구하는 말이므로 ③번이 가장 적절하다.

03 눈이 충혈되었다는 것으로 보아 tired가 가장 적절하다.

04 소녀는 자신의 휴대전화로 두 시간 동안 영화를 보았다.

시험대비 실력평가   p.133~134

01 ③   02 ③   03 ④

04 It's because he has a stomachache.

05 ④   06 ③   07 ②

08 (C)–(A)–(D)–(B)

09 what should I do to say sorry to Mina?

10 She has the tomato pot in the kitchen.

11 ④   12 ⑤

13 He watches a movie on his phone until late at night.

01 조언을 구하고 조언을 제공하는 대화를 나누고 있으므로 ③번이 가장 적절하다.

02 안부를 묻는 말에 '좋다'고 답하고 목이 아프다는 말이 이어지고 있으므로 어색하다.

03 밑줄 친 (A)는 시도해 보겠다는 의미로, 걷는 것이 어떠냐는 소녀의 조언을 시도해 보겠다는 말이다.

04 소년이 소녀에게 약이 있느냐고 물은 이유는 복통 때문이다.

---

05 (A)는 조언을 구하는 말이므로 ④번이 가장 적절하다.

06 help는 목적격보어로 to부정사나 동사원형을 취한다. 따라서 to lose 혹은 lose라고 쓰는 것이 적절하다.

07 소년의 문제에 소녀는 개를 산책시키라고 조언해 주고 있으므로 ②번을 답할 수 있다.

08 (C) 무슨 일이냐고 묻자 (A) 엄마가 가장 좋아하는 접시를 깼다며 조언을 구하자 (D) 엄마에게 사실대로 말씀드리라며 조언하고 (B) 이에 대한 답이 이어지는 것이 가장 자연스럽다.

09 'What should I do to ~?'는 조언을 구하는 표현이다. '미나에게 사과하기 위해서 무엇을 해야 할까?'라고 묻는 것이 적절하다.

10 소녀는 토마토 화분을 주방에 둔다고 하였다.

11 소년은 소녀에게 조언을 하고 있으므로 ④번이 글의 내용과 일치한다.

12 눈을 건강하게 유지하는 데 도움을 주기 때문에 당근과 토마토를 먹으라고 권하는 것이 적절하다.

13 수호는 새벽 2시까지 휴대폰으로 영화를 본다고 하였으므로 수호가 요즘에 종종 하는 것은 밤늦게까지 영화를 보는 것이라고 답할 수 있다.

서술형 시험대비   p.135

01 What do you think I should do?

02 (A) have   (B) take   (C) get

03 the fine dust, sore

04 She is likely to buy a few plants.

05 What's wrong with you?

06 It's because she has watched a movie on her phone for two hours.

07 (C)–(E)–(A)–(D)–(B)   08 is something wrong

01 의견을 묻는 말로 What do you think I should do?를 쓸 수 있다.

02 (A) '~가 아프다'고 말할 때에는 'have+병명'을 쓰는 것이 일반적이다. (B) 'take ~ in'은 '~을 흡수하다'는 의미이며, (C)에서 'get'은 '사다, 구하다'라는 의미로 쓰인다.

03 Jane은 미세먼지가 자신의 목을 아프게 한다고 생각한다.

04 식물을 몇 개 사야겠다고 하였다.

05 무슨 일이 있는지를 묻는 말이다. 'What's wrong with you?'와 그 의미가 같다.

06 소녀가 피곤한 이유는 휴대전화기로 두 시간 동안 영화를 봤기 때문이다.

07 (C) 약이 있냐고 물음 - (E) 무슨 문제가 있는지 되물음 - (A) 약이 필요한 이유를 설명 - (D) 조언 제공 - (B) 조언을 시도해 보겠다고 말함

08 슬퍼 보이는 친구에게 안부를 묻는 말이 들어가는 것이 적절하다. 'What's the matter?'라고 써도 무방하다.

핵심 Check   p.136~137

1 (1) named (2) broken   **2** (1) did (2) do

시험대비 기본평가   p.138

01 (1) using → used   (2) called → call
   (3) eats → eating   (4) writing → written
02 ②   03 ②
04 (1) Most Americans did think that tomatoes were
       poisonous.
   (2) The pictures taken by Lily were impressive.

01 (1) 당근이 전쟁에서 사용될 수도 있다는 수동이므로 used가 적
   절하다. (2) 강조의 조동사 뒤에는 동사 원형을 쓴다. (3) 능동
   의 현재분사가 뒤에서 꾸미는 것이 적절하다. (4) 라틴어로 쓰여
   진 편지이므로, written이 적절하다.
02 주어가 복수이므로 동사를 강조할 때 do를 써야 한다.
03 싫증을 느끼는 것은 능동이 아니라 수동의 과거분사를 써야 한
   다.
04 (1) 주어가 복수이므로 동사를 강조할 때 do를 써야 한다. (2)
   명사를 뒤에서 꾸미는 과거분사의 활용에 유의하여, 단어를 배
   열한다.

시험대비 실력평가   p.139~141

01 ③   02 ①
03 (1) were many people watching
   (2) built by my grandfather is
04 ②   05 making → made   06 ⑤
07 ②
08 Potato juice mixed with honey makes your skin
   soft.
09 ③   10 ②   11 ③
12 ①, ④, ⑤   13 ④   14 ⑤   15 ④
16 (1) writing → written   (2) mixing → mixed
   (3) cry → crying
17 ④   18 ①, ③, ⑤   19 ③
20 (A) made (B) known (C) using (D) named
   (E) meaning (F) covered
21 ②   22 invented, using

01 (1) 꽃을 꺾는 소년(능동) (2) 여행에 쓰인 돈(수동) (3) 두려워
   하는(수동) 등에 적절하게 분사를 활용한다.
02 첫 번째 빈칸은 동사 강조의 does이며, 두 번째 빈칸은 본동사

이다. do the laundry: 빨래를 하다
03 분사가 명사의 뒤에서 꾸며주는 것을 적절히 활용한다. (1)은
   watching the pet contest가 people을 꾸며주고(능동), (2)
   는 built by my grandfather가 the swimming pool을 뒤
   에서 꾸민다.(수동)
04 ② Be로 시작하는 명령문도 Do로 강조 가능하다. ① warned
   → warn, ③ changed → change, ④ believed →
   believe, ⑤ looks → look
05 베트남에서 제조된 셔츠이므로 과거분사가 적절하다.
06 '그는 잃어버린 아이를 정말로 찾아냈다.'라는 문장과 '잃어버린
   아이를 찾을 수 있었다.'라는 문장은 다르다.
07 ②는 try의 목적어로 쓰인 동명사이고, 나머지는 모두 명사를
   앞 또는 뒤에서 꾸며 주는 현재분사이다.
08 분사가 명사 뒤에서 꾸며주는 것을 활용한다. 수동이므로
   mixed를 사용하고, 본동사는 makes를 쓴다.
09 첫 번째 빈칸은 강조의 does 또는 did를 쓸 수 있다. 두 번째 빈
   칸은 시제가 과거이기 때문에 did만 가능.
10 ⓐ 타는 불, ⓑ 노래하는 학생들 모두 '능동'의 의미를 갖고 있으
   며, 명사를 앞, 뒤에서 꾸며주고 있다.
11 강조의 did를 쓰면 동사는 원형이 와야 한다.
12 ① 토마토를 먹고 있는 소녀이므로 eats → eating ④ '거짓
   말을 하고 있었다'는 뜻의 과거진행형이므로 현재분사가 필요.
   lied → lying, ⑤ 그녀의 가족을 만난 것이면, meeting her
   family가, 그녀의 가족이 만난 사람들이면 meeting → met으
   로 하는 것이 적절하다.
13 11년 전 과거의 일이므로 does를 did로 바꿔야 한다.
14 ① 수동의 의미이므로, 과거분사 surrounded가 온다. ② 명사
   를 뒤에서 꾸미는 분사를 활용한다. 능동이므로 sat → sitting
   ③ using → used ④ 남겨진 케이크가 없는 것이므로 leaving
   → left가 적절하다.
15 과거 시제를 강조하는 'did+동사원형'을 이용한다.
16 (1) 쓰인 책(수동) (2) 꿀과 섞인 감자 주스(수동) (3) 우는 아기
   들(능동)
17 동사 강조의 do(does/did)를 찾는다.
18 ① 감동적인 장면들 touched → touching ③ 신나는
   날 excited → exciting ⑤ 시간을 알려주는 shown →
   showing
19 ① do → does ② made → make ④ plays → play ⑤
   called → call
20 (A) 만들어진 (B) ~로 알려진 (C) (당근)을 이용하여 (D) ~라
   고 이름 불리는 (E) ~를 의미하는 (F) ~로 덮인
21 동사 강조의 do(does/did)를 찾는다.
22 어법에 맞게 배열하면, 'This is a battery invented from
   the idea of using the characteristic of sunflowers.'이다.
   invented는 과거분사, using은 동명사이다.

서술형 시험대비

p.142~143

01 (1) Sofia did find her missing cat.

    (2) Gordon does know many K-pop songs.

    (3) Grace did write these essays last week.

02 (1) girl standing across the street

    (2) played by the band on the stage

    (3) wearing a red shirt

03 (1) did build   (2) do think   (3) did write

04 (1) This is the thing placed on the wall.

    (2) Sarah is the one wearing glasses.

    (3) Mary is erasing the scores written on the board.

    (4) I do love Susan, the girl drinking water.

    (5) The news was really shocking.

05 (1) with the crying baby

    (2) the birds flying southwards

    (3) an illegally parked taxi

06 (A) sitting   (B) standing   (C) closed

07 (1) Alex himself called you yesterday.

    (2) It was you that Alex called yesterday.

    (3) Alex did call you yesterday.

    (4) It was yesterday that Alex called you.

08 As Ethan did feel a headache

09 (1) does   (2) hidden   (3) kill   (4) called

10 place a cup of crushed tomatoes

---

01 수와 시제 등에 유의하여 do/does/did를 활용하되 강조를 위해 사용한 do 뒤에는 본동사의 원형이 와야 한다.

02 명사의 뒤에서 꾸미는 분사 활용 (1) 서 있는 소녀(능동) (2) 연주되는 음악(수동) (3) 셔츠를 입은 사람(능동)

03 수와 시제 등에 유의하여 do를 활용하되 do 뒤에는 동사 원형이 와야 한다.

04 명사를 뒤에서 꾸며주는 분사를 활용한다. 능동/진행은 현재분사, 수동/완료는 과거분사를 쓴다. (1) 벽에 놓이는 물건 placed (2) 안경을 쓰고 있는 사람 wearing (3) 보드에 쓰여진 점수 written (4) 물을 마시는 소녀 drinking (5) 충격적인 뉴스 shocking

05 (1) 울고 있는 아기 (2) 남쪽으로 날아가고 있는 새들 (3) 불법으로 주차된 택시(부정관사 an에 유의한다)

06 (A) 능동 (B) 능동 (C) 'with+목적어' 뒤에 나오는 '현재분사/과거분사' 여부는 목적어의 '능동/수동'을 따진다. 목적어가 eyes이므로, 수동의 과거분사 closed가 적절하다.

07 (1) himself를 문미로 보내도 된다. (2) (대)명사와 부사는 'It ~ that 강조 구문'으로 강조 가능하다. (3) 'did+동사원형'으로 동사를 강조한다. (4) 부사 yesterday는 'It ~ that 강조 구문'으로 강조한다.

08 동사 강조의 'do'를 시제에 맞게 활용한다. 과거시제이므로 did를

쓰는 것에 유의한다.

09 (1) does로 강조 (2) 땅에 숨겨진 폭탄이므로 hide의 과거분사 hidden이 적절하다. (3) 강조의 did 뒤에는 원형동사 kill이 적절하다. (4) '~라고 불리는'이라는 표현은 call의 과거분사를 쓴다.

10 으깬 토마토가 되려면 crush의 과거분사형이 명사의 앞에서 수식하는 형태가 된다. 명령문이므로 place로 시작하는 것이 적절하다.

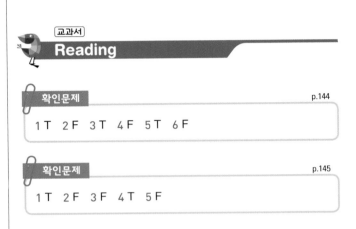

교과서 Reading

확인문제

p.144

1 T   2 F   3 T   4 F   5 T   6 F

확인문제

p.145

1 T   2 F   3 F   4 T   5 F

교과서 확인학습 A

p.146~147

01 Hidden   02 Spinach

03 cartoon character   04 by eating spinach

05 became popular

06 the spinach capital, a statue

07 Although, does have

08 one of the ten healthiest foods

09 in a surprising way

10 also absorbs, from

11 hidden in the ground

12 with sensors on their leaves

13 soak up, light up   14 World War II

15 defeated, during, by using

16 keep, secret, an article

17 improved their night vision

18 than before   19 by eating

20 which does keep   21 may actually be used

22 turn, into   23 can even be used

24 has already been used   25 Scariest

26 are good for   27 Up until, poisonous

28 named, safe to eat   29 a basket of, watching

30 happened to   31 have enjoyed eating

32 no longer, scared of

33 keep, away from, place, crushed

34 come near

1 Hidden Stories about Plants

2 Popeye and the Great Spinach

3 Popeye is a world-famous cartoon character.

4 He gets his super power by eating spinach.

5 When Popeye became popular in the 1930s in the United States, a lot of children began to eat spinach.

6 Crystal City in Texas, which is called the spinach capital of the world, even built a statue of Popeye.

7 Although eating spinach will not give us super powers, spinach does have a lot of nutrients.

8 It is actually considered one of the ten healthiest foods on the planet.

9 Spinach can be used in a surprising way.

10 When it absorbs water, spinach also absorbs many other things from the soil.

11 Some scientists have used this characteristic of spinach to find bombs hidden in the ground.

12 They make special spinach plants with sensors on their leaves.

13 When these plants soak up traces from bombs, the sensors light up.

14 Carrots in World War II

15 In 1940, the Royal Air Force defeated German fighters during World War II by using a radar system.

16 The British government wanted to keep this technology a secret, so it published an article in the newspaper.

17 It said that British pilots improved their night vision because they ate a lot of carrots.

18 Everybody believed the story and began to eat a lot more carrots than before.

19 Can we really improve night vision by eating lots of carrots?

20 Not really, but carrots contain a lot of vitamin A, which does keep our eyes healthy.

21 In the future, carrots may actually be used in wars.

22 Scottish researchers have discovered a way to turn carrots into a very strong and light material.

23 It can even be used to make battleships.

24 This new material has already been used to make snowboards and bicycles.

25 Tomatoes, the Scariest Vegetables

26 We all know that tomatoes are good for our health.

27 Up until the 1800s, however, most Americans thought that tomatoes were poisonous.

28 In 1820, a man named Robert Johnson wanted to prove that tomatoes were safe to eat.

29 So, he ate a basket of tomatoes in front of many people watching him.

30 They all expected him to die, but nothing happened to him.

31 Ever since then, Americans have enjoyed eating tomatoes.

32 We are no longer afraid of tomatoes, but some insects are still scared of them.

33 If you want to keep insects away from your room, place a bowl of crushed tomatoes in a corner of your room.

34 Insects will not come near the tomatoes.

01 ④ 02 ② 03 ④ 04 ①

05 시금치가 물을 흡수할 때, 시금치는 흙으로부터 다른 많은 것들도 흡수하는 것

06 go out → light up 07 ④

08 the British government 09 ②

10 carrots may actually be used in wars

11 ②, ④ 12 ③ 13 ⑤ 14 ③

15 (A) crushed tomatoes (B) scared[afraid]

16 Some / ground 17 ②, ③, ④, ⑤

18 absorb 19 (A) called (B) capital (C) does

20 ③ 21 He gets it by eating spinach.

22 tomatoes 23 died → didn't die 24 ④

01 ④번 다음 문장의 It에 주목한다. 주어진 문장의 spinach를 받고 있으므로 ④번이 적절하다.

02 ⓐ와 ②: 캐릭터, 등장인물, ① 성격, ③ 문자, ④ 특징, ⑤ 인격

03 시금치를 먹는 것이 우리에게 초인적인 힘을 주지는 않는다.

04 ⓐ absorb A from B: B로부터 A를 흡수하다, ⓑ with sensors on their leaves: 잎에 감지기가 있는

05 시금치의 이 특성은 바로 앞 문장의 내용을 가리킨다.

06 시금치의 특성을 사용하여 땅에 숨겨진 폭탄을 찾는다고 했기 때문에, 이 특별한 시금치가 폭탄의 흔적을 흡수하면 감지기가 '빛난다'고 해야 하므로 light up으로 고치는 것이 적절하다. go out: (불·전깃불이) 꺼지다, light up: (빛·색으로) 환하게 되다

07 본문 끝 부분에 '실제로 그렇지는 않지만(야간 시력을 높일 수는 없지만), 당근은 많은 비타민 A를 함유하는데, 그것은 정말로 우리 눈을 건강하게 유지해 준다.'라는 말이 있으므로, 야간 '시력'

이라고 하는 것이 적절하다. vision: 시력, 시야, ① (이전의 것·비슷한 종류의 다른 것들과 약간 다른) 판[형태], ② 촉각, ③ 청력 ⑤ 후각

08 '영국 정부'를 가리킨다.

09 이 글은 '영국 공군이 제2차 세계 대전에서 독일군을 패배시킨 레이더 시스템을 비밀로 하려고, 영국 비행사들이 당근을 많이 먹어 야간 시력이 좋아졌다는 신문 기사를 실었는데, 당근이 야간 시력을 높일 수는 없지만 실제로 많은 비타민 A를 함유하고 있어서 우리 눈을 건강하게 유지해 준다.'는 내용의 글이므로, 제목으로는 ②번 '제2차 세계대전에서의 당근'이 적절하다.

10 추측을 나타내는 조동사 may를 사용하여 수동태로 쓰는 것이 적절하다.

11 ⓑ와 ②, ④: 완료 용법, ① 계속 용법, ③ 경험 용법, ⑤ 결과 용법

12 스코틀랜드의 연구원들은 어떻게 당근을 매우 강하고 가벼운 물질로 바꾸는지는 대답할 수 없다. ① Yes. ② A way to turn carrots into a very strong and light material. ④ Yes. ⑤ Yes, it has already been used to make snowboards and bicycles.

13 앞에 나오는 내용과 상반되는 내용이 뒤에 이어지므로 however가 가장 적절하다. ① 그 결과, ② 뿐만 아니라, 더욱이, ③ 즉, 말하자면 ④ 예를 들면

14 이 글은 '1820년에 Robert Johnson이 토마토가 먹기에 안전하다는 것을 증명하기 전까지는 대부분의 미국인들은 토마토에 독성이 있다고 생각했다는 것과 몇몇 곤충들은 여전히 토마토를 무서워한다.'는 내용의 글이므로, 주제로는 ③번 '토마토에 관한 근거 없는 믿음과 진실'이 적절하다. myth: (많은 사람들의) 근거 없는 믿음

15 몇몇 곤충들은 여전히 토마토를 '무서워해서' 토마토 가까이 오지 않을 것이므로, 만약 '으깬 토마토' 한 그릇을 방구석에 놓아두면 곤충들이 방에 들어오지 않게 할 수 있다.

16 시금치의 놀라운 용도는 '몇몇 과학자들이 시금치의 특성을 사용하여 땅에 숨겨진 폭탄을 찾는 것'을 가리킨다.

17 ⓑ와 ①: 부사적 용법, ②, ③, ⑤: 명사적 용법, ④: 형용사적 용법

18 soak up = absorb: 흡수하다, 빨아들이다

19 (A) 시금치 수도라고 '불린다'고 해야 하므로 called가 적절하다. (B) 시금치 '수도'라고 해야 하므로 capital이 적절하다. capital: 수도, capitol: 미국 국회 의사당, (C) 시금치가 정말로 많은 영양분을 가지고 있다는 것은 일반적인 사실에 해당하므로 현재시제로 쓰는 것이 적절하다.

20 ⓐ와 ①, ③, ④: 동명사, ②, ⑤: 현재분사

21 Popeye는 '시금치를 먹음으로써' 초인적인 힘을 얻는다.

22 '토마토'를 가리킨다.

23 Robert Johnson은 그를 지켜보는 많은 사람들 앞에서 한 바구니의 토마토를 먹었고, 모두 그가 죽을 것이라고 예상했

으나 '그에게는 아무 일도 일어나지 않았다.' against one's expectations: 예상과 달리

24 무슨 곤충들이 토마토를 무서워하는지는 알 수 없다. ① They thought that tomatoes were poisonous. ② He wanted to prove that tomatoes were safe to eat. ③ They have enjoyed eating tomatoes since Robert Johnson proved that they were safe to eat. ⑤ Insects will not come near the tomatoes.

🦉 서술형 시험대비
p.154~155

01 As → Although 또는 Though
02 actually considers → is actually considered
03 (A) cartoon character   (B) eating spinach
04 ⓐ be used   ⓑ hidden
05 ⓒ Some scientists   ⓓ special spinach plants
06 (A) sensors   (B) bombs
07 (A) defeated   (B) during   (C) healthy
08 World War Two 또는 the second World War
09 An article
10 (1) 영국 비행사들이 당근을 많이 먹어 야간 시력이 좋아졌다.
   (2) 당근은 많은 비타민 A를 함유하는데, 그것은 정말로 우리 눈을 건강하게 유지해 준다.
11 Ever since then, Americans have enjoyed eating tomatoes.
12 any longer[more]   13 crushing → crushed
14 Because he wanted to prove that tomatoes were safe to eat.

01 '비록' 시금치를 먹는 것이 우리에게 초인적인 힘을 주지는 않지만, 시금치는 정말로 많은 영양분을 가지고 있다고 해야 하므로, Although 또는 Though로 고치는 것이 적절하다.

02 '가장 건강한 식품 10개 중 하나로 여겨진다.'고 해야 하므로 수동태로 쓰는 것이 적절하다.

03 시금치를 먹음으로써 초인적인 힘을 얻는 Popeye는 세계적으로 유명한 만화 캐릭터다. Popeye 덕분에, 1930년대 미국의 많은 어린이들이 시금치를 먹기 시작했다. 동사 begin은 목적어로 to부정사와 동명사를 모두 다 사용할 수 있다.

04 ⓐ 시금치는 놀라운 용도로 '사용될 수 있다'고 해야 하므로, 수동태로 쓰는 것이 적절하다. ⓑ 땅에 '숨겨진' 폭탄이라고 해야 하므로 hidden으로 쓰는 것이 적절하다.

05 ⓒ '몇몇 과학자들' ⓓ '특별한 시금치'를 가리킨다.

06 시금치는 흙으로부터 물뿐만 아니라 다른 많은 것들도 흡수한다. 잎에 '감지기'가 있는 특별한 시금치가 폭탄의 흔적을 흡수하면, 감지기가 빛나서 땅속에 있는 '폭탄'을 찾도록 도와준다.

07 (A) 영국 공군이 독일군을 '패배시킨' 것이므로 defeated가 적

절하다. (B) '제2차 세계 대전에서'라고 해야 하므로 during이 적절하다. during+기간을 나타내는 명사, while+주어+동사, (C) keep의 목적격보어에 해당하기 때문에 형용사 healthy가 적절하다.

08 'World War+기수', 또는 'the 서수+World War'로 읽는 것이 적절하다.

09 신문의 '기사'를 가리킨다.

10 영국 공군이 제2차 세계 대전에서 독일군을 패배시킨 레이더 시스템을 비밀로 하려고, '영국 비행사들이 당근을 많이 먹어 야간 시력이 좋아졌다'는 신문 기사를 실었는데, 당근이 야간 시력을 높일 수는 없지만 '실제로 많은 비타민 A를 함유하고 있어서 우리 눈을 건강하게 유지해 준다.'

11 과거의 일이 현재까지 영향을 미쳐 현재와 관련이 있을 때 사용하는 현재완료시제로 쓰는 것이 적절하다.

12 no longer = not ~ any longer[more]: 더 이상 … 아닌

13 토마토가 으깨지는 것이므로 crushed가 적절하다.

14 토마토가 먹기에 안전하다는 것을 증명하기를 원했기 때문이다.

영역별 핵심문제
p.157~161

01 ⑤   02 ③

03 (1) The magician turned the hat into a rabbit.
   (2) What do you advise me to do?
   (3) Why don't you get some fresh air?

04 ③   05 ③

06 (1) the director, the actor, surprising
   (2) visitors were scared of

07 ③   08 ⑤번 → a few   09 ⑤

10 ②   11 move it over to the window

12 ③   13 ③   14 ④   15 ①

16 (1) ate a basket of tomatoes in front of many people watching him
   (2) did eat a basket of tomatoes in front of many people who[that] were watching him

17 ④   18 ②, ⑤   19 (1) did (2) found

20 ③   21 ③   22 ②, ⑤

23 wanting to prove that tomatoes were safe to eat was Robert Johnson

24 ③

25 It is actually considered one of the ten healthiest foods on the planet.

26 (A) spinach   (B) nutrients   (C) healthiest

27 ②   28 a radar system   29 ④

01 모두 유의어이지만 ⑤번은 반의어로 '이기다 – 굴복하다'라는 의미로 쓰인다.

02 각각 ① interviewer ② meal ③ nutrient ④ ingredient

⑤ flavor를 풀이한 말이다.

03 (1) turn A into B: A를 B로 바꾸다 (2) advise+목적어+to V: 목적어가 V하도록 조언하다 (3) get some fresh air: 신선한 공기를 마시다

04 trace는 '흔적'이라는 명사와 '추적하다'라는 의미의 동사로 쓰인다. 따라서 ③번이 가장 적절하다.

05 주어진 문장의 밑줄 친 부분은 '수도'라는 의미로 쓰였다. capital은 그 외에도 '자본', '대문자의'라는 의미로도 쓰인다.

06 (1) '놀라운'이라는 의미로 쓰이는 것은 surprising이다. (2) '~을 두려워하다'는 'be scared of' 혹은 'be afraid of'를 쓴다.

07 자신의 잘못에 대한 조언을 구하는 말이 들어가는 것이 적절하다.

08 셀 수 있는 명사를 수식하는 'a few'를 쓰는 것이 적절하다.

09 소년은 소녀에게 방 안에 식물을 두라고 권하고 있다.

10 주어진 문장은 조언을 구하는 말이다. 지금까지 토마토를 몇 개밖에 수확하지 못했다는 말을 하며 조언을 구하는 말을 하는 것이 가장 자연스럽다.

11 해석: 토마토 화분이 충분한 햇빛을 얻도록, 소녀는 화분을 창가로 옮길 것이다.

12 소년의 조언에 알겠다며 고마움을 표시하고 있으므로, 한 번 시도해 보겠다는 ③번이 가장 적절하다.

13 ① Popeye라고 '이름이 불리는' 것이므로 named가 적절하다. ② 그 농부들에 의해 '길러진 채소들'이 되어야 하므로 grown을 써야 한다. ④ 비타민 A를 '함유하고 있는' 것이므로 containing이 적절하다. ⑤ 파티에 '초대 받은 사람들'이므로 invited가 적절하다.

14 ① Vegetables가 복수이므로 do make가 적절하다. ② does say가 적절하다 ③ be동사와 상태를 나타내는 look 본동사가 같이 쓰였다. is를 생략하거나 does look으로 강조한다. ⑤ 과거동사 met을 강조할 때는 did meet이 적절하다.

15 첫 번째 문장에서 '사용될 것(수동)'을 뜻하므로 used가 적절하다. 두 번째 문장에서 '두려워하는'(수동)의 내용이므로 scared가 적절하다. be scary of로는 표현하지 않는다.

16 (1) 과거시제이므로 ate를 써야 하고, 명사를 뒤에서 꾸미는 현재분사 watching에 유의하여 영작한다. (2) ate의 강조는 did eat이며, 명사를 뒤에서 수식하는 분사의 앞에 '관계대명사+be동사'를 넣을 수 있다. who를 that으로 써도 된다.

17 do some laundry는 '빨래를 하다'라는 뜻으로 do는 본동사이다. 다른 문장들의 do는 강조를 위해 사용되었다.

18 ② be busy ~ing는 '~하느라 바쁘다'라는 뜻의 동명사의 관용적 표현이며, ⑤는 전치사 by의 목적어로 쓰인 동명사이다. 다른 문장들에서는 모두 현재분사로 사용되었다.

19 (1) 책 '어린 왕자'는 3인칭 단수이고, 동사원형 make가 쓰였으므로, 강조의 does 또는 did가 가능하지만, 시제가 과거이므로 did가 적절하다. (2) 이집트의 Giza에서 발견된 pyramids(수동)이므로, 과거분사 found가 적절하다.

20 'with+A+형용사/분사' 형태는 A의 능동/수동 여부에 따라 현재분사 또는 과거분사를 활용한다. ③ with one's legs crossed '다리를 꼰 채로', crossing은 부적절하다.

21 ① (A) 강조 (B) 본동사 ② (A) 본동사 (B) 강조 ③ (A) 강조 (B) 강조 ④ (A) 본동사 (B) 강조 ⑤ (A) 의문문을 만드는 조동사 (B) 본동사

22 ② do likes → does like 또는 likes가 적절하다. ⑤ 강조의 did 뒤에는 동사 원형을 써야 한다.

23 분사가 명사의 앞, 뒤에서 꾸미는 것을 적절히 활용하여 영작한다.

24 ⓐ와 ③: 수도, ① 자본의(형용사), investment: 투자, ② 대문자, ④ 자본금, 자금, ⑤ 사형에 처해야 할(형용사), sentence: 선고하다

25 one of the ten healthiest foods: 가장 건강한 식품 10개 중 하나, 수량형용사 ten을 성상 형용사(사물의 성질, 상태, 종류를 나타내는 형용사) healthiest보다 먼저 쓰는 것이 적절하다.

26 '시금치'를 먹는 것으로 우리가 초인적인 힘을 얻지는 못하지만, 시금치는 정말로 많은 '영양분'을 가지고 있다. 실제로 사람들은 그것을 지구상에서 '가장 건강한' 식품 10개 중 하나로 여긴다.

27 주어진 문장의 It에 주목한다. ②번 앞 문장의 an article을 받고 있으므로 ②번이 적절하다.

28 '레이더 시스템'을 가리킨다.

29 실제로 당근을 많이 먹어서 야간 시력을 높일 수 있는 것은 아니라고 했다.

단원별 예상문제
p.162~165

01 ③ 　　　　02 ⑤ 　　　　03 ③
04 Do you still keep in touch with your friends?
05 (D)–(A)–(C)–(B) 　　　06 ⑤
07 What about telling her the truth?
08 It's because he broke his mom's favorite plate.
09 ④ 　　　10 ⑤ 　　　11 ③, ⑤, ⑦
12 ①, ②, ⑥, ⑦ 　　　13 ③
14 ①, ③
15 eating spinach won't give us super powers, spinach does have a lot of nutrients
16 Although eating spinach will not give super powers to us
17 ⑤
18 (1) 시금치를 먹으면 초인적인 힘을 얻는다.
　(2) 시금치는 정말로 많은 영양분을 가지고 있고, 실제로 지구상에서 가장 건강한 식품 10개 중 하나로 여겨진다.
19 making → make
20 (A) strong and light　(B) carrots
21 ③ 　　　　22 ④

23 a man named Robert Johnson wanted to prove that tomatoes were safe to eat
24 ② 　　　　25 ①
26 (1) 혈압을 낮춰 심장을 건강하게 유지시켜 준다.
　(2) 피부 문제를 해결해 준다.
　(3) 살이 빠지도록 도와준다.

01 ①, ②, ④, ⑤는 동사에 '-er'이나 '-or'을 붙여서 사람을 나타내는 명사로 쓰였으나 cooker는 '주방기구'의 뜻으로 사람을 나타내지 않는다.

02 keep away from: ~으로부터 멀어지다

03 '책, 연극, 영화 등에 등장하는 사람'은 '등장인물(character)'이다.

04 keep in touch (with): (~와) 연락하고 지내다

05 (D) 무슨 문제가 있냐고 물음 - (A) 자신의 문제를 말함 - (C) 조언을 제시함 - (B) 조언을 받아들임

06 조언을 구하는 말이 들어가는 것이 자연스러우므로 ⑤번은 적절하지 않다.

07 What about ~?: ~하는 것이 어때?

08 소년이 걱정스러워 보였던 이유는 그의 엄마가 가장 좋아하는 그릇을 깨트려서이다.

09 보미는 소년이 왜 약을 달라고 하는지 궁금해 하고 있으므로 ④번이 대화 내용과 일치한다.

10 Make sure는 that절을 이끈다. 따라서 'Make sure that you take it to the police station.'이라고 말하는 것이 적절하다.

11 명사를 꾸미는 분사가 다른 어구와 결합해서 뒤에서 꾸밀 때는 '관계대명사+be동사'가 생략된 것으로 볼 수 있다. 그러므로, 명사를 앞에서 꾸미거나 서술적 용법으로 사용된 분사를 찾으면, '관계대명사+be동사'가 생략된 것이 아닌 경우에 해당한다. ③, ⑦번은 서술적 용법으로, ⑤번은 명사 앞에서 수식하는 분사로 사용되었다.

12 ① are와 make 두개의 동사가 같이 쓰였다. make만 쓰거나 강조의 do make로 하는 것이 적절하다. ②, ⑥ 강조의 do/does/did 뒤에는 원형동사를 써야 한다. ⑦ 'It ~ that 강조 구문'의 동사는 is와 was 둘 뿐이다.

13 ③번은 전치사의 목적어로 쓰인 동명사이다. 그 외에는 모두 명사의 뒤에서 꾸미는 분사로 사용되었다.

14 분사의 역할이 아니라 종류가 다른 두 개를 찾는 문제이다. ①, ③번만 과거분사로서 ① abandoned dogs, ③ make himself understood이며, 나머지는 모두 현재분사를 써야 한다. ③ smoke coming out, ④ kept him waiting, ⑤ the boy smiling at her

15 has를 강조할 때는 does have로 한다.

16 give는 to를 사용하여 3형식으로 고친다.

17 ⓑ와 ⑤: 강조의 조동사, ① 부정문의 조동사, ② 부사(구) 따위가 문두에 오면서 어순이 도치되는 경우에 쓰이는 조동사, ③

~을 하다(본동사), ④ 의문문의 조동사

18 비록 시금치를 먹는 것이 우리에게 초인적인 힘을 주지는 않지만, 시금치는 정말로 많은 영양분을 가지고 있고, 이것은 실제로 지구상에서 가장 건강한 식품 10개 중 하나로 여겨진다.

19 '전함을 만드는 데 사용될 수도 있다'라고 해야 하므로 to부정사의 부사적 용법(목적)이 되도록, make로 고치는 것이 적절하다. be used to ~ing: ~하는 데 익숙하다

20 그것은 스코틀랜드의 연구원들에 의해 '당근'을 재료로 하여 만들어진 매우 '강하고 가벼운' 물질이다.

21 이 글은 '미래에는, 당근이 실제로 전쟁에 이용될지도 모른다.'는 내용의 글이므로, 주제로는 ③번 '미래에 전쟁에서의 당근의 용도'가 적절하다.

22 주어진 문장의 They에 주목한다. ④번 앞 문장의 many people을 받고 있으므로 ④번이 적절하다.

23 safe to eat: 먹기에 안전한

24 1800년대까지 대부분의 미국인들은 토마토에 '독성이 있다'고 생각했다.

25 앞에 나오는 내용에 추가하는 내용이 뒤에 이어지므로 In addition이 가장 적절하다. ② 그러므로, ④ 그에 반해서

26 (3) 오랜 시간 동안 허기를 느끼지 않고 배부른 상태를 유지하게 하여 살이 빠지도록 도와준다. stay full: 허기를 느끼지 않고 배부른 상태를 유지하다

서술형 실전문제   p.166~167

01 It is so hard to lose weight.

02 lose weight   03 is something wrong

04 ⓐ surprising ⓑ leaving ⓒ eating ⓓ covered
ⓔ written ⓕ eating
이유: ⓒ와 ⓕ 두 개는 동명사이고, 나머지는 모두 분사이다.

05 (1) British pilots did eat a lot of carrots.
(2) Do place a bowl of crushed tomatoes in a corner of your room.
(3) People in Hong Kong do love freedom.

06 which does keep our eyes healthy

07 to die

08 (A) named   (B) watching   (C) happened

09 (1) 토마토에 독성이 있다.
(2) 토마토를 먹는 것을 즐겼다.

10 The British government wanted to keep this technology a secret, so it published an article in the newspaper.

11 British pilots improved their night vision because they ate a lot of carrots.

01 가주어 It과 진주어 to부정사구를 이용하여 문장을 쓸 수 있다. lose weight: 몸무게를 줄이다

02 소녀가 소년에게 개를 매일 산책시키라고 제안한 이유는 그렇게 하는 것이 소년이 살을 빼도록 도움을 줄 것이라고 생각하기 때문이다.

03 엄마에게 무슨 문제가 있는지 묻는 말이 들어가는 것이 적절하다. 'what's the matter'를 써도 좋다.

04 ⓐ '놀라운 방법'(능동) ⓑ '7시에 출발하는 기차'(능동) ⓒ '먹음'으로써, 전치사의 목적어로 쓰인 동명사 ⓓ '담쟁이로 덮인 건물 벽'(수동) ⓔ '에머슨에 의해 쓰여진 시'(수동) ⓕ '먹는 것'을 즐겨왔다. enjoy의 목적어로 쓰인 동명사

05 (1) 과거 시제이므로 did eat이 적절하다. (2) 명령문의 강조는 동사 앞에 Do를 쓴다. (3) 주어가 복수이고 현재시제이므로 do love로 강조한다.

06 선행사 vitamin A를 받으며, 접속사 역할까지 하는 관계대명사 which를 사용하고, 동사 keep을 강조하는 does를 이용해서 알맞게 배열한다.

07 expect+목적어+to부정사

08 (A) Robert Johnson이라는 '이름의(~라고 이름 지어진)' 남자라고 해야 하므로 named가 적절하다. (B) 그를 '지켜보는' 많은 사람들이라고 해야 하므로 watching이 적절하다. (C) happen은 수동태로 만들 수 없으므로 happened가 적절하다.

09 1800년대까지 대부분의 미국인들은 토마토에 독성이 있다고 생각했지만, Robert Johnson이 토마토가 먹기에 안전하다는 것을 증명한 이후로, 미국인들은 토마토를 먹는 것을 즐겼다.

10 keep+목적어+목적격보어: ~을 …한 상태로 유지시키다

11 영국 정부가 신문에 낸 기사의 내용을 가리킨다.

창의사고력 서술형 문제   p.168

|모범답안|

01 growing well, she has gotten only a few tomatoes, her advice, where she has the pot, in the kitchen, tomato plants need about 7 hours of sunlight a day, she will move the pot over to the window

02 (1) Unlike the man presenting the plan, the boss is sleeping in a chair.
(2) Unlike my sister reading a book on the sofa, I am cleaning the table.

03 (A) your health   (B) lower blood pressure
(C) skin problems   (D) soft and clear

단원별 모의고사   p.169~173

01 ④   02 ④   03 ④
04 (C)-(A)-(E)-(D)-(B)

05 ④　　　　06 fine dust, put some plants

07 ⑤　　　　08 ③

09 What do you think I should do?　　　10 ③

11 It's because they are rich in vitamin A, so they'll keep Suho's eyes healthy.

12 ⑤　　　13 ⑤　　　14 ③, ⑥　　　15 ③

16 (1) This new material has already been used to make bicycles.

　　(2) Some scientists have used this characteristic of spinach to find bombs hidden in the ground.

17 ⑤

18 real person → world-famous cartoon character

19 spinach　　　　　　　20 does keep

21 ②　　　　　　　　　　22 and it

23 ⓐ eighteen hundreds　ⓑ eighteen twenty

24 ①, ②, ④　25 ④　　　26 ②　　　27 ③, ⑤

28 By lowering blood pressure.

29 Garlic tea which[that] is mixed with honey makes you get better faster.

01 ① keep ~ a secret: ~을 비밀로 하다 ② keep away: 멀리하다 ③ keep in touch: 연락하다 ④ make use of: ~을 이용하다 ⑤ keep the change: 잔돈을 가지다

02 주어진 단어는 '명사-명사(행위자)'의 관계에 있다. ④번은 '형용사-명사'의 연결이다. economy: 경제의, 경제성이 있는 economist: 경제학자

03 defeat은 '~를 패배시키다'라는 의미이므로 '전투에서 이기는 것에 성공하지 못하다'는 적절한 풀이가 아니다.

04 (C) 체중을 줄이는 것이 힘들다고 말하며 조언을 요청함 (A) 개를 산책시키라고 조언함 (E) 그것이 어떻게 체중을 줄이는데 도움이 되는지 되물음 (D) 이에 대한 설명 (B) 생각해 보겠다고 말함

05 빈칸에는 상대를 걱정하며 안부를 묻는 말이 들어가는 것이 적절하다. ④번은 무엇을 잘못했는지를 묻는 말이다.

06 소녀는 미세먼지 때문에 목이 아프다고 생각하고, 이에 소년은 방 안에 식물을 두라고 조언하고 있다.

07 돈을 저축할 수 없다고 말하며 조언을 요청하고 있으므로 더 많은 옷을 사라는 조언은 적절하지 않다.

08 모두 선생님에게 도움을 요청하라는 의미이지만 ③번은 선생님이 너에게 도움을 요청하는 것을 확실히 하라는 의미이다.

09 조언을 구하는 말로 자주 쓰이는 표현은 'What do you think I should do?'이다.

10 새벽 2시까지 휴대 전화로 영화를 본 결과 눈이 충혈된 것이므로 'that's why'라고 쓰는 것이 적절하다.

11 Anna가 수호에게 당근과 토마토를 많이 먹어 보라고 한 이유는 그것들에 비타민 A가 많아서 눈을 건강하게 유지해 줄 것이기

때문이다.

12 수호가 휴대전화로 영화를 얼마나 오래 보는지는 위 글을 읽고 답할 수 없다.

13 ⑤ included → including

14 ③, ⑥번이 주어진 문장의 밑줄 친 does와 같은 용법인 동사를 강조하는 do/did로 사용되었다. ①, ②, ④번은 모두 조동사로서 각각 ① 의문문, ② 부정문, ④ 명령문을 만들기 위해 사용됐다. ⑤, ⑦번은 본동사로 쓰였다.

15 ③번은 containing(현재분사)이 들어가야 하지만 주어진 문장과 나머지는 모두 수동의 의미로 명사를 뒤에서 꾸미는 과거분사가 들어가야 한다. *repellent: 방충제

16 (1) used는 과거분사의 서술 용법으로, (2) hidden은 과거분사의 한정 용법으로 명사 뒤에서 꾸미는 역할이다.

17 ⑤번만 현재완료시제에 사용되어 동사의 일부가 되었다. 나머지는 모두 형용사적 용법으로 사용된 과거분사이다. *crush: 즙 음료

18 Popeye는 세계적으로 유명한 '만화 캐릭터'다.

19 '시금치'를 가리킨다.

20 조동사 does를 사용하여 고치는 것이 적절하다.

21 (A)와 ②: (신문·잡지의) 글, 기사, ① (같은 종류의 물건 중) 한 개, 한 가지, ③, ⑤: 물품, 물건, ④ (조약·계약 등의) 조항, 조목

22 계속적 용법의 관계대명사 = 접속사+대명사

23 연도는 두 단위씩 끊어서 읽는 것이 적절하다. 단, 2000년이 넘어가면 'two thousand+나머지 숫자'로 읽는 것이 적절하다. ⓐ의 경우는 끝부분을 hundreds로 읽으면 된다.

24 ⓒ와 ③, ⑤: 부사적 용법, ①, ④: 명사적 용법, ②: 형용사적 용법

25 이 글은 '요즘 우리는 토마토를 두려워하지 않지만, 1800년대까지 대부분의 미국인들은 토마토에 독성이 있다고 생각했고, 몇몇 곤충들은 여전히 그것을 무서워한다.'는 내용의 글이므로, 제목으로는 ④번 '토마토, 가장 무서운 채소'가 적절하다.

26 1800년대까지 대부분의 미국인들은 토마토에 '독성이 있다'고 생각했지만, Robert Johnson이 토마토가 먹기에 '안전하다'는 것을 증명하기를 원했다고 하는 것이 문맥상 적절하다. ① harmless: 해가 없는, ③ precious: 귀중한, harmful: 해로운, ⑤ evil: 사악한

27 ⓒ와 ①, ②, ④: 계속 용법, ③, ⑤ 경험 용법

28 '혈압을 낮춤으로써' 심장을 건강하게 유지시켜 준다.

29 mixed 앞에 주격 관계대명사(which/that)와 be동사가 생략되어 있다.

This is Korea

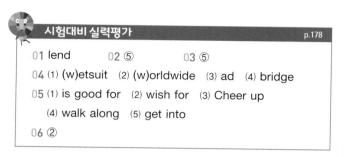

01 lend   02 ⑤   03 ⑤

04 (1) (w)etsuit   (2) (w)orldwide   (3) ad   (4) bridge

05 (1) is good for   (2) wish for   (3) Cheer up

    (4) walk along   (5) get into

06 ②

01 주어진 단어는 반의어 관계이다. lend: 빌려주다, borrow: 빌리다

02 '가치가 있지만 물리적으로 존재하지는 않는'을 의미하는 말은 intangible(무형의)이다.

03 experience: 경험

04 wetsuit: 잠수복, worldwide: 세계적으로, ad: 광고, bridge: 다리

05 cheer up: 격려하다, wish for: 기원하다, get into: ~에 들어가다, be good for: ~에 유익하다, walk along: ~을 따라 걷다

06 주어진 문장에서 press는 '누르다'를 의미하며 이와 같은 의미로 쓰인 것은 ②번이다. 나머지는 모두 '신문, 언론'을 뜻한다.

01 past

02 (1) (p)ath   (2) community   (3) (p)romote

    (4) jellyfish

03 (1) We had a good harvest last year.

    (2) Money does not always bring happiness.

    (3) Our national heritage was destroyed by the fire.

04 (1) We walked along the street for an hour.

    (2) This book is suitable for elementary school students.

    (3) Let's make double-sided copies to save paper.

05 (1) promote   (2) realize   (3) several

    (4) underwater   (5) volcanic

01 주어진 단어는 반의어 관계이다. future: 미래, past: 과거

02 path: 길, community: 지역 공동체, promote: 홍보하다, jellyfish: 해파리

03 good harvest: 풍년, happiness: 행복, heritage: 유산

04 walk along: ~을 따라 걷다, be suitable for: ~에 적절하다, make double-sided copies: 양면 복사를 하다

05 realize: 깨닫다, promote: 홍보하다, underwater: 물속의, 수중의, volcanic: 화산의, several: 몇몇의

1 I wonder where the photo was taken.

2 (C) → (B) → (A)

1 T   2 T   3 T   4 F

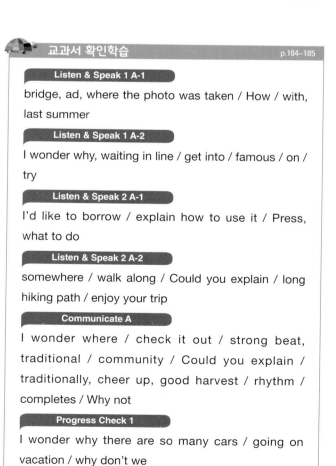

Listen & Speak 1 A-1

bridge, ad, where the photo was taken / How / with, last summer

Listen & Speak 1 A-2

I wonder why, waiting in line / get into / famous / on / try

Listen & Speak 2 A-1

I'd like to borrow / explain how to use it / Press, what to do

Listen & Speak 2 A-2

somewhere / walk along / Could you explain / long hiking path / enjoy your trip

Communicate A

I wonder where / check it out / strong beat, traditional / community / Could you explain / traditionally, cheer up, good harvest / rhythm / completes / Why not

Progress Check 1

I wonder why there are so many cars / going on vacation / why don't we copy machine / how to make double-sided copies / Press, press

시험대비 기본평가 p.186

01 I wonder where the photo was taken.
02 How do you know that?
03 Could you tell me what that is?　04 ⑤

01 간접의문문 어순으로 '의문사+주어+동사'의 어순이 알맞다.
04 Tom이 구체적으로 제주 올레길에 대한 설명을 요청한 것으로 보아 Tom이 이미 올레길에 대해 잘 알고 있다는 설명은 일치하지 않는다.

시험대비 실력평가 p.187~188

01 (E) → (C) → (B) → (D) → (A)　　02 ⑤
03 ⓑ → was taken　　04 ⑤　　05 ⑤
06 ⑤　　　　07 (C) → (B) → (D) → (E) → (A)
08 ④
09 Dancing together completes the music.
10 ⑤

01 (E) 궁금함에 대한 대답 → (C) 유명한지 질문→ (B) 대답 및 이유 설명 → (D) 제안 → (A) 동의
02 ⑤번을 제외한 나머지는 모두 설명을 요청하는 표현이다.
03 사진이 찍혔으므로 수동태가 알맞다.
04 소녀가 다리 사진을 찍고 싶다는 내용은 대화를 통해 알 수 없다.
05 (A)는 진행을 나타내는 현재분사 waiting, (B) get into: 들어가다, get out: 나가다, (C) TV에 나왔음을 나타내는 on이 적절하다.
06 Brian과 수진은 줄을 서 있는 사람들을 보고 있다.
07 (C) 하고 싶은 일 부탁 → (B) 허락 → (D) 양면 복사 방법 질문 → (E) 대답 → (A) 감사 표현
08 궁금함을 나타내는 표현으로 ④번으로 바꾸어 쓸 수 있다.
09 complete: 완성하다
10 궁금한 것을 알고 싶다는 말에 노력에 감사하다는 대답은 어색하다.

서술형 시험대비 p.189

01 Could you explain how to use it?
02 She gets to know what she should do.
03 (A) waiting in line　(B) the new bakery
　　(C) get into　(D) it was on a TV program

04 (1) band　(2) strong　(3) farmers　(4) harvest
05 They are going to join some people dancing to the rhythm.

02 버튼을 누르면 여자는 무엇을 해야 하는지 알 수 있다.
03 Brian과 Sujin은 새로 생긴 제과점 앞에 줄을 서 있는 많은 사람들을 보았다. 사람들은 그곳에 들어가고 싶어 했다. 새로 생긴 제과점은 매우 인기가 있었다. 왜냐하면 TV 프로그램에 나왔었기 때문이다. Brian과 Sujin은 함께 그곳의 빵을 먹어보고 싶어 했다.
05 Jaden과 유리는 대화 후 춤추는 사람들과 함께 할 것이다.

교과서 Grammar

핵심 Check p.190~191

1 (1) had　(2) visited
2 (1) will she make → she will make
　(2) was Sarah → Sarah was

시험대비 기본평가 p.192

01 ⑤　　　02 ③　　　03 ④
04 (1) asked how she became interested
　　(2) tell us what is so special

01 기준이 되는 시점이 과거이고, 그 이전에 일어난 동작이므로 과거완료시제를 찾는다.
02 의문사가 없는 의문문의 간접의문문은 if 또는 whether가 접속사 역할을 한다.
03 ① '지금까지'이므로 현재완료시제로 써야 한다. had lived → has lived, ② has → had ③ had found → found, ⑤ 과거 시점 이전에 일어난 일이므로 had gone이 적절하다. 단, before를 통해 전후 관계가 명확하므로 went도 가능하다.
04 간접의문문을 만들 때, 의문사는 접속사 역할을 하고 '의문사+주어+동사'의 어순이 된다. 시제와 수에 유의하여, 동사를 적절히 쓴다. 의문사가 주어일 때는 순서가 바뀌지 않는 것도 주의한다.

시험대비 실력평가 p.193~195

01 ③　　02 ⑤　　03 ④　　04 ④
05 ⑤　　06 had been → has been　07 ⑤
08 ⑤　　09 ②　　10 ④　　11 ③
12 ⑤

13 many customers had spent quite a long time lining up in order to eat pork cutlet

14 Why do you think the temples are famous?

15 (1) asked his sister why people could not fly in the sky

(2) told his friend that he had touched a hive that morning

---

01 ③ 과거시점(Lucy asked) 이전에 발생한 일이다. has broken → had broken이 적절하다.

02 간접의문문의 어순은 '의문사+주어+동사'이다. 원래의 의문문 'What is that?'에서 What은 주어로 쓰인 것이 아님에 유의하여 'what that is' 어순으로 배열한 정답을 찾는다.

03 '의문사+be+there+주어'는 간접의문문이 될 때, '의문사+there+be+주어'의 어순이 된다.

04 ① had read → has read ② 'San Francisco로 이사를 하기 전에 New York에서 살았다'는 문장이므로 'William lived[had lived] in New York before he moved to San Francisco.'가 적절하다. ③ '민수가 보고서를 완성해야 한다고 요구'한 것이므로 had completed → (should) complete ⑤ had not eaten → have not eaten

05 ① what so special is → what is so special ② do I like → I like ③ Do you imagine how old → How old do you imagine ④ what is your favorite food → what your favorite food is

06 과거의 특정 시점 이전에 발생한 일을 과거완료시제로 표현해야 한다. 종속절이 'since+과거시제'이므로, 주절은 과거완료가 아니라 현재완료시제로 표현하는 것이 적절하다.

07 간접의문문의 접속사 역할을 하는 who가 주어로 사용되었으므로, 어순을 바꿀 필요가 없다. 'who took away her kids' toys' 원래 어순 그대로 쓰는 것이 적절하다.

08 <보기>의 had found는 과거완료시제 중 '완료' 용법으로 쓰였다. ①, ③, ④는 '계속', ②는 '경험' 용법이다.

09 <보기> if는 조건의 '부사절' 접속사이며, ②도 그렇다. 나머지는 모두 '의문사 없는 간접의문문을 이끄는 접속사'이다.

10 본동사가 think일 때, 간접의문문의 의문사는 문두로 보내고 어순은 '주어+동사' 순으로 한다.

11 ① 내용상 '내가 사준 것'이 '그녀가 목걸이를 잃어버린 것'보다 먼저이기 때문에 'Cecilia lost the necklace which I had bought for her.'가 적절하다. ② had melted → melted ④ have → had ⑤ has → had

12 ① Do you think where → Where do you think ② what did your action mean → what your action meant ③ did anyone see → anyone saw ④ how the writer of these books old → how old the writer of these books is

13 과거완료시제(had spent)와, 'spend+시간+V-ing'를 활용하

여, 주어진 어구를 적절히 배열한다.

14 간접의문문을 활용하는 문제이다. 생각 동사 think, believe, imagine 등이 주절에 올 때, 간접의문문의 의문사를 문두로 보내는 것에 유의한다.

15 (1) 의문사 why를 간접의문문으로 활용한 문장이다. '지호는 누나에게 왜 사람이 하늘을 날 수 없는지 물어봤다.' (2) 과거완료시제를 이용하여, 어구를 배열하는 문장이다. 'Pooh는 그의 친구에게 그 날 아침에 벌집을 건드렸었다고 말했다.'

서술형 시험대비

01 (1) collected many Korean treasures that some French had stolen before

(2) wonders how she can promote the haenyeo worldwide

(3) he found someone had broken into his house

(4) Can you guess where the photographer took

02 (1) how they could get to the meeting on time

(2) which boy the girl next to Jane chose at the blind date

(3) if(또는 whether) Shrek hasn't learned German yet

(4) where Alex found the baby tiger

(5) the new employee looks

03 had only seen black-and-white photos of haenyeo who

04 (1) Can you tell me where the magician was when he disappeared?

(2) Does the young student know how far the hotel is?

(3) Do you know if[whether] I could take pictures of haenyeo?

(4) They didn't understand why the girl wanted to take their pictures.

(5) Tell me what Zin Kim promised the haenyeo.

(6) I wonder why Jejudo isn't suitable for farming.

05 The haenyeo had not thought that she was pretty until the photographer took her picture twelve years ago.

06 (1) Tom wondered how haenyeo could stay in the water for so long without any breathing devices.

(2) They are studying how catching too much marine life can destroy the ocean.

(3) The witch asked the mirror who the most beautiful woman in the world was.

(4) The mother goat did not know when the babies opened the door to the wolf.

01 (1), (3) 과거의 특정 시점 이전에 일어난 일은 '과거완료시제'로 쓰는 것에 유의한다. (2), (4) '간접의문문'의 어순은 '의문사＋주어＋동사'이다. 특히, (4)번에서 guess라는 생각 동사가 오지만, yes나 no로 대답이 가능한 의문문의 경우 의문사가 앞으로 가지 않는 것에 유의한다.

02 '간접의문문'의 어순은 '의문사＋주어＋동사'이다. 어순이 바뀔 때는 수와 시제에 유의해야 한다. (5)번에서 think와 같은 생각 동사가 있을 때는 의문사가 문두로 와야 한다.

03 only see를 과거완료시제로 표현하면 had only seen이다. 빈칸 뒤의 looked가 동사이므로 주어 역할의 관계대명사 who를 마지막에 쓴다.

04 (1) was the magician → the magician was (2) how the hotel is far → how far the hotel is (3) could I → if(또는 whether) I could (4) did the girl want → the girl wanted (5) did Zin Kim promise → Zin Kim promised (6) why is Jejudo not → why Jejudo isn't

05 과거의 어느 특정 시점을 기준으로 그 전의 동작은 과거완료시제로 표현한다. 12년 전에 사진작가가 사진을 찍기까지는 자신을 예쁘다고 생각하지 않았으므로, 부정의 과거완료시제를 사용해서 표현하면, 'had not thought that she was pretty'가 적절하다.

06 주어진 단어들 중 동사의 수와 시제에 유의하여, 간접의문문의 어순과 내용에 알맞게 적절한 문장을 영작한다.

교과서
Reading

확인문제　　　　　　　　　　p.198

1 T　2 F　3 F　4 T　5 F

확인문제　　　　　　　　　　p.199

1 T　2 F　3 T　4 F　5 T

교과서 확인학습 A　　　　　p.200~201

01 Female Divers
02 underwater photographer, has promoted
03 without any breathing devices
04 made UNESCO's Intangible Cultural Heritage list
05 was interviewed
06 become interested in
07 happened to
08 was surprised to find
09 looked very tired
10 kept laughing
11 should take
12 isn't it difficult

13 why I wanted
14 in their wetsuits
15 very special
16 show, to
17 opened up
18 make them, beautiful
19 more about
20 so special
21 can tell you
22 strong women
23 is not suitable for, the breadwinners for
24 form, each other
25 more-experienced, less-experienced
26 without, can't catch
27 is good for
28 at one time in one place
29 planning to do
30 attended, give a talk
31 held my hand
32 so much
33 such a special person
34 with happiness
35 was deeply moved
36 can never forget
37 more beautiful stories about them

교과서 확인학습 B　　　　　p.202~203

1 Haenyeo, Female Divers of Korea
2 For the past several years, the underwater photographer Zin Kim has promoted the culture of Jeju haenyeo worldwide.
3 Haenyeo are Korean female divers who harvest seafood without any breathing devices.
4 Their culture made UNESCO's Intangible Cultural Heritage list in 2016.
5 At her studio last week, Zin Kim was interviewed about her experience of taking pictures of haenyeo.
6 Q. How did you become interested in taking photos of haenyeo?
7 One day, I happened to take pictures of a haenyeo.
8 I was surprised to find that she was enjoying her job.
9 Until then, I had only seen black-and-white photos of haenyeo who looked very tired.
10 However, she kept laughing even after she had been in the water for over five hours.
11 I realized then that I should take pictures of haenyeo.
12 Q. You take beautiful pictures of them, but isn't it difficult to take pictures of haenyeo?
13 At first, they didn't understand why I wanted to take their pictures.
14 They didn't think they looked pretty in their wetsuits.

15 So, I said to them, "You're very special.

16 I want to show your culture to the world."

17 They opened up to me then.

18 Of course, I also promised them that I would make them look beautiful in my pictures.

19 Q. Could you tell us more about haenyeo?

20 What's so special about them?

21 I can tell you three things.

22 First, haenyeo are a symbol of strong women.

23 Jejudo, which is a volcanic island, is not suitable for farming, so many haenyeo have become the breadwinners for their families.

24 Second, haenyeo form their own communities and help each other.

25 For example, more-experienced haenyeo train less-experienced haenyeo.

26 Third, because they stay in the water without any breathing devices, haenyeo can't catch a lot of seafood.

27 This is good for the underwater environment.

28 Catching too much marine life at one time in one place can destroy the ocean.

29 Q. Lastly, please tell us what you're planning to do in the future.

30 I once attended an overseas exhibition with a couple of haenyeo to give a talk about their lives.

31 When I finished my talk, one of the haenyeo held my hand tightly.

32 She said to me, "Thank you so much.

33 I've never known in my whole life that I was such a special person."

34 She was crying with happiness.

35 Everyone in the audience was deeply moved.

36 I can never forget that moment, so I'll continue to take pictures of haenyeo.

37 I want to tell more beautiful stories about them to many more people in the world.

시험대비 실력평가

p.204~207

01 ②, ④　　02 ⑤　　03 ④　　04 ③
05 laughing　06 ④　　07 ⑤　　08 ②
09 they didn't understand why I wanted to take their pictures
10 (A) attended　(B) such　(C) so
11 ⑤　　12 ④　　13 ②, ③
14 breadwinners　　15 that → which

16 because they stay in the water without any breathing devices, haenyeo can't catch a lot of seafood

17 ②　　18 ③　　19 ①
20 looking → look　　21 ④　　22 ③
23 suitable → not suitable 또는 unsuitable
24 ①, ⑤　　25 to catch

01 주격 관계대명사 who와 that이 적절하다.

02 ⓑ와 ⑤: ~이 되다, ~의 지위를 얻다; ~으로 승진[승격]하다, 존스는 5년 만에 교수가 되었다. ① 만들다[제작/제조하다], ② (~로 하여금 …하게) 만들다[하다], ③ 선출[임명/지명]하다, ④ (억지로 무엇을 하게) 만들다[시키다]

03 해녀는 어떤 호흡 장치도 '사용하지 않고' 해산물을 채취하는 한국의 여성 잠수부들이다.

04 대답에서 해녀의 사진을 찍는 것에 관심을 가지게 된 이유를 설명하고 있으므로, 빈칸에 들어갈 질문으로는 ③번 '어떻게 해녀의 사진을 찍는 것에 관심을 가지게 되었나요?'가 적절하다.

05 keep -ing: 계속 ~하다

06 (B)와 ②: 계속 용법, ①, ④: 완료 용법, ③: 결과 용법, ⑤: 경험 용법

07 주어진 문장의 then에 주목한다. 그들이 '그때' 제게 마음을 열었다고 했을 때의 '그때'는 ⑤번 앞 문장에서 말한 "여러분들은 아주 특별해요. 저는 여러분의 문화를 세계에 알리고 싶어요."라고 말한 때를 가리키므로 ⑤번이 적절하다.

08 이 글은 '글쓴이가 해녀들을 설득하여 그들의 사진을 찍게 된 과정'을 설명하는 글이므로, 제목으로는 ②번 '와! 해녀들은 내가 사진을 통해 그들의 문화를 알리도록 허락해 주었어!'가 적절하다.

09 why는 의문문의 문두에 쓰이는 의문사이지만 간접의문문에서는 문장 안에 쓰인다. 이때는 보통 주어가 동사 앞에 와서 '의문사+주어+동사'의 순서로 쓰인다.

10 (A) 박람회에 '참가한' 적이 있다고 해야 하므로 attended가 옳다. attend to: ~을 돌보다, 시중들다, (B) 'such+a+형용사+명사'의 순서로 써야 하므로 such가 옳다. 'so+형용사+a+명사', (C) '그 순간을 절대 잊을 수가 없기 때문에 해녀의 사진을 계속해서 찍을 것'이라고 해야 하므로 so가 옳다.

11 중반부의 'She was crying with happiness. Everyone in the audience was deeply moved.'를 통해 'touching'을 찾을 수 있다. touching: 감동적인, ① 혼란스러운, ② 재미있는, 흥미로운, ③ 우울하게 만드는, 우울한, ④ 지루한

12 Zin Kim이 얼마나 오랫동안 해녀들의 사진을 찍어 왔는지는 대답할 수 없다. ① With a couple of haenyeo. ② To give a talk about haenyeo's lives. ③ She said, "Thank you so much. I've never known in my whole life that I was such a special person." ⑤ She wants to tell more

beautiful stories about haenyeo.

13 ⓐ와 ②, ③: 경험 용법, ① 완료 용법, ④ 완료 용법, ⑤ 계속 용법

14 필수적인 것들을 위해 가족이 필요한 돈을 버는 사람들, breadwinner: (집안의) 생계비를 버는 사람, 가장

15 관계대명사 that은 계속적 용법으로 쓸 수 없으므로 which로 바꾸는 것이 적절하다.

16 앞 문장의 내용을 가리킨다.

17 이 글은 '해녀에 대해 무엇이 특별한지'를 설명하는 글이므로, 주제로는 ②번 '해녀에 대한 특별한 점들'이 적절하다. ① subject: (그림·사진 등의) 대상[소재]

18 ⓐ in: '착용'을 나타내는 전치사, ⓑ show는 3형식으로 고칠 때 전치사 to를 사용한다.

19 ①은 Zin Kim을 가리키고, 나머지는 다 '해녀들'을 가리킨다.

20 사역동사 make의 목적격보어이므로 동사원형으로 고치는 것이 적절하다.

21 전반부의 'they didn't understand why I wanted to take their pictures'를 통해 'puzzled'를, 중반부의 'They opened up to me then.'을 통해 'consenting'을 찾을 수 있다. puzzled: 어리둥절하는, 얼떨떨한, consenting: 동의[승낙]하는, ① nervous: 초조한, ② delighted: 아주 기뻐하는, upset: 속상한, ③ agreeing: 동의하는, ⑤ confused: 혼란스러워 하는, disappointed: 실망한

22 앞의 내용의 예가 나오고 있으므로 For example이 가장 적절하다. ① 그러므로, ④ 게다가, ⑤ 그 결과

23 제주도는 화산섬이라서 농사에 '적합하지 않다'로 고치는 것이 적절하다.

24 (B)와 ②, ③, ④: 동명사(목적, 용도), ①, ⑤: 현재분사(동작의 진행)

25 to부정사를 진주어로 하여 고치는 것이 적절하다.

서술형 시험대비

01 by chance (또는 by accident)

02 have → had

03 (A) enjoying   (B) laughing

04 (A) For   (B) any   (C) Intangible

05 Haenyeo 또는 haenyeo

06 two thousand (and) sixteen 또는 twenty sixteen

07 marine

08 (A) breathing devices   (B) can't catch

09 (1) 해녀들은 강인한 여성의 상징이다.
(2) 해녀들은 그들 자신의 공동체를 조직하고 서로 돕는다.
(3) 어떤 호흡 장치도 사용하지 않고 물속에 머물기 때문에, 해녀는 많은 해산물을 채취할 수가 없다.

10 what you're planning to do in the future

11 me   12 touched

13 (A) take pictures   (B) more beautiful stories

01 by chance = by accident = accidentally: 우연히, 뜻밖에, happen to do it = do it by chance[by accident]: 우연히 ~하다

02 Until then이 있으므로 과거완료로 고치는 것이 적절하다.

03 Zin Kim이 우연히 한 해녀의 사진을 찍게 되었을 때, 그녀는 자신의 직업을 '즐겼고 '다섯 시간이 넘도록 물속에 있은 후에도 계속 '웃었다'. Zin Kim은 그것에 놀라서 해녀의 사진을 찍어야겠다고 결심했다.

04 (A) '지난 몇 년 동안'이라고 해야 하므로 For가 옳다. during은 뒤에 기간을 나타내는 명사를 써서, 특정 기간 중의 어느 한 시점을 가리키고, for는 'how long?'에 대한 답을 나타낸다. (B) 부정의 뜻을 가지는 without이 있으므로 any가 옳다. (C) '무형문화유산'이라고 해야 하므로 Intangible이 옳다. tangible: 유형의

05 haenyeo를 복수로 취급했고, 한 명의 해녀는 a haenyeo라고 하는 것이 적절하다.

06 2001년부터 2009년까지는 two thousand (and) ~로 읽는 것이 적절하다.

07 바다 혹은 바다에서 사는 동식물들과 관련된, marine: 바다의, 해양의

08 해녀는 어떤 '호흡 장치'도 사용하지 않고 물속에 머물러서, 많은 해산물을 '채취할 수가 없기' 때문이다.

09 인터뷰 질문에 대한 답 세 가지를 쓰는 것이 적절하다.

10 간접의문문의 순서(의문사+주어+동사)로 쓰는 것이 적절하다.

11 소유격+신체의 일부를 나타내는 명사 = 목적격+전치사+the+신체의 일부를 나타내는 명사

12 moved = touched: 감동한

13 Zin Kim은 해녀 중 한 분이 그녀에게 감사를 표했던 순간을 절대 잊을 수가 없기 때문에 해녀의 '사진을 계속해서 찍을' 것이다. 그녀는 그들에 대한 '더 많은 아름다운 이야기들'을 세계의 더 많은 사람들에게 알려 주고 싶어 한다.

영역별 핵심문제

01 happiness   02 ②   03 ⑤

04 (1) go on (a) vacation   (2) a couple of
(3) cheer up   (4) Give, a call

05 (1) overwork   (2) greenhouse   (3) breathe
(4) device   (5) heritage

06 He wants to make double-sided copies.

07 He will press the button for double-sided copies.

08 ③   09 ⑤   10 ⓐ → check it out

38 정답 및 해설

11 beat   12 ⑤   13 had eaten

14 ①, ②   15 ③, ④

16 (1) thinking about which university he should go to

   (2) wondering when the rain will stop

17 (1) had pulled   (2) was killed

   (3) had already gone   (4) had been

   (5) had seen   (6) appeared

18 (1) what time the store opens

   (2) how we can contact the store manager

   (3) where the store is located

   (4) if[whether] there is any subway station near the store

19 (1) ⓑ (2) ⓒ (3) ⓐ (4) ⓒ (5) ⓐ (6) ⓓ (7) ⓑ

   (8) ⓓ

20 (1) Vanessa had cleaned the windows and (had) washed the dishes

   (2) Sally had given the dog some food and (had) watered the plant

21 (1) why she had to learn how to cook in another country

   (2) if there are any seats left on the plane

22 ③   23 ①, ④   24 ⑤   25 ②

26 ③   27 ⑤   28 ④   29 ②

01 주어진 단어는 형용사와 명사의 관계이다.

02 '가족을 부양하려고 돈을 버는 가족 구성원'을 나타내는 말은 breadwinner(생계를 책임지는 사람, 가장)이다.

03 path: 오솔길, 작은 길

04 go on (a) vacation: 휴가가다, a couple of: 두 서너 개의, cheer up: 힘을 북돋아 주다, 격려하다, give (someone) a call: 전화를 걸다

05 heritage: 유산, greenhouse: 온실, device: 장치, breathe: 호흡하다, overwork: 과로

06 Jack은 양면 복사를 하고 싶다.

07 Jack은 시작 버튼을 누르기 전에 양면 복사 버튼을 누를 것이다.

08 주어진 문장은 구체적인 설명을 요청하는 것이므로 이어지는 문장에서 구체적인 제주 올레길에 대한 설명이 이어지는 (C)에 들어가는 것이 적절하다.

09 Tom이 제주도에서 무엇을 하고 싶은지는 대화를 통해 알 수 없다.

10 '동사+부사'로 이루어진 구동사의 목적어가 인칭대명사일 때 목적어가 동사 바로 뒤에 위치한다.

11 '일련의 규칙적인 움직임 또는 치는 동작 중의 하나'를 가리키는 말은 beat(소리)이다.

12 유리는 함께 춤추는 것이 음악을 완성한다고 설명한다.

13 대학 졸업 전에 처음 치즈 퐁듀를 먹었다고 했으므로, 과거완료 시제이다. before와 같이 명백한 전후 관계를 알 수 있는 접속사가 있을 때는 과거시제로 써도 괜찮다. 그러나 빈칸이 두 개이므로 과거완료시제를 쓰는 것이 적절하다.

14 ① where the monsters are from ② why 뒤에는 완전한 문장 구조가 와야 한다. in 뒤에 특정한 명사를 덧붙이거나 why 대신 의문대명사 who, which, what 등을 써야 한다.

15 간접의문문에서는 '의문사+주어+동사' 구조를 잘 이해하고, think 동사 등의 예외에 주의해야 한다. ③ when did he leave → when he left ④ Do you think when → When do you think

16 (1) 준호는 어느 대학에 갈지 생각 중이다. (2) 예은이는 비가 언제 그칠지 궁금해 하고 있다.

17 (1), (3), (4), (5) 과거의 어느 특정 시점을 기준으로 그 이전에 시작된 일은 과거완료시제로 표현한다. (2) '역사적 사실'은 주절의 동사 시제와 상관없이 과거시제를 쓴다. (6) when은 '시점'을 표현하기 때문에 의문문 또는 간접의문문에서 완료시제로 표현할 수 없다.

18 의문문이 간접의문문이 될 때는 '의문사+주어+동사'의 어순이 된다. 의문사가 없을 경우 if 또는 whether를 써서 접속사 역할을 하도록 한다.

19 과거완료시제는 완료, 경험, 결과, 계속 등의 용법으로 구분할 수 있으며, 해석을 정확하게 하는 것이 중요하다.

20 우리말에 맞게 과거완료시제를 사용하여 쓴다.

21 (1) 간접의문문의 어순은 '의문사+주어+동사'이다. (2) '의문사가 없는 간접의문문'은 if 또는 whether가 접속사 역할을 한다.

22 ⓐ be suitable for: ~에 적합하다, ⓑ the breadwinners for their families: 가족들의 생계비를 버는 가장

23 ⓒ와 ①, ④: 동명사, ②, ③, ⑤ : 현재분사

24 어떤 호흡 장치도 사용하지 않고 물속에 머물기 때문에, 해녀는 한 번에 많은 해산물을 채취할 수가 '없다.'

25 ⓐ와 ②: 감동시키다, ① (몸 등을) 움직이다, ③ (집, 근무지 등을) 옮기다[이사하다], ④ (차·배 따위가) 나아가다, 전진하다, ⑤ (안건 등을) 제안[제출]하다

26 이 글은 'Zin Kim이 앞으로 계획하고 있는 것'을 설명하는 글이므로, 주제로는 ③번 'Zin Kim의 앞으로의 계획'이 적절하다.

27 앞에 나오는 내용과 상반되는 내용이 뒤에 이어지므로 However가 가장 적절하다. ① 즉[말하자면], ② 게다가, 더욱이, ③ 따라서, 그러므로

28 위 글은 '기사문'이다. ① (책·연극·영화 등에 대한) 논평[비평], 감상문, ② 독후감, ⑤ 자서전

29 Zin Kim이 어떻게 해녀들의 사진을 찍었는지는 대답할 수 없다. ① She is an underwater photographer. ③ When she met a haenyeo who was enjoying her job. ④ No. ⑤ Haenyeo's culture.

---

01 ①　**02** (D) → (C) → (A) → (B)　**03** ②

04 ⑤

05 She wants to borrow an audio guide.

06 She should press the button.

07 I wonder why there are so many cars on the road.

08 how about going somewhere, too?

09 (D) → (B) → (A) → (C)

10 Could you explain how to make double-sided copies?

11 ⑤　　**12** ①

13 (1) After Susan had learned the importance of recycling, she promised her teacher not to throw away used batteries.

(2) Before Sunwoo lay in his room all day long, he had sprained his ankle during the basketball game.

14 ⓐ when the shopping mall closes

ⓒ what kind of movie she was watching

ⓓ what she usually does on Sundays

ⓕ what time the show begins

15 ④, ⑤

16 how much he weighed, he had already gained, had often eaten

17 ④　　**18** ④　　**19** ③

20 She had only seen black-and-white photos of haenyeo who looked very tired.

21 ⑤　**22** ②　**23** ①　**24** ④

25 ②　**26** for　**27** barista

28 It's decorating coffee with hot milk and watching his customers enjoying it.

01 give a presentation: 발표하다, give a hand: 돕다, give a call: 전화를 걸다

02 (D) 궁금한 점 말하기 → (C) 궁금한 점에 대한 답변 → (A) 제안 → (B) 수락

03 농악을 소개하는 문장으로 그것은 한국의 전통 음악인지 묻는 대답으로 적절하므로 (B)가 적절하다.

04 대화를 통해 어떤 종류의 춤이 음악을 완성하는지 알 수 없다.

05 여자는 음성 가이드를 빌리고 싶다.

06 여자는 음성 가이드를 사용하기 위해 버튼을 눌러야 한다.

08 'Why don't we ~?'는 '~하는 게 어때?'라고 제안하는 표현으로 'How about ~?'으로 바꾸어 쓸 수 있다.

09 (D) 궁금한 것 말하기 → (B) 궁금한 것에 대한 설명 → (A) 어떻게 알게 되었는지 질문 → (C) 대답

10 double-sided: 양면의

11 Jack은 양면 복사 버튼을 먼저 누르고 시작 버튼을 눌러야 한

12 'Do you suppose?'와 'What music is Paul listening to?'를 한 문장으로 합칠 때 간접의문문의 의문사를 문두로 보내고 '주어+동사'의 어순으로 정리하면 ①과 같다.

13 과거의 특정 시점을 기준으로 전에 일어난 동작이나 상태를 과거완료로 표현한다. before나 after와 같이 '명확한 전후 관계'를 알 수 있는 경우 과거완료를 쓰지 않아도 되지만, 문제의 조건에 맞게 과거완료를 사용하도록 한다.

14 간접의문문의 어순은 '의문사+주어+동사'이다. 시제와 인칭에 맞게 동사의 형태에 유의한다.

15 과거 이전에 발생한 일은 과거완료시제로 표현한다. ① '그의 가족은 Brian이 전날 열심히 일했지만 결국 병원에 실려갔다는 사실을 우연히 알게 되었다' has worked → had worked ② '우리가 경기장에 도착했을 때, 전반전이 벌써 시작되었다'는 The first half of the match had already started when we arrived at the stadium.이 적절하다. ③ '대부분의 아시아인들은 봉감독이 칸 영화제에서 대상을 수상한 것을 자랑스럽게 느꼈다.' has won → had won 또는 felt → feel로 고쳐도 된다.

16 '불독은 몸무게가 얼마나 될지 알고 싶었다. 그는 저울에 오르기 전에 이미 살이 쪘다는 사실을 알게 되어 놀랐다. 그는 자기 전에 간식을 자주 먹었던 것을 후회했다.'

17 간접의문문 앞에 think, believe, imagine, guess 등 생각, 추측 등의 동사가 있을 때는 의문사를 문두로 보낸다. How old do you guess she is?가 적절하다.

18 앞에 나오는 내용과 상반되는 내용이 뒤에 이어지므로 however가 가장 적절하다. ① 게다가, ③ 즉, ⑤ 그러므로

19 이 글은 '어떻게 Zin Kim이 해녀의 사진을 찍는 것에 관심을 가지게 되었는지'를 설명하는 글이므로, 주제로는 ③번 'Zin Kim이 해녀의 사진을 찍는 것에 관심을 가지게 된 이유'가 적절하다.

20 Zin Kim이 우연히 한 해녀의 사진을 찍었을 때까지, '그녀는 흑백 사진 속의 아주 지친 모습의 해녀만 봐 왔다.'

21 ⓐ와 ⑤: 가주어, ① 가목적어, ② 비인칭 주어, ③ 'It is … that'의 구문으로 문장의 주어·목적어·부사구를 강조하는 대명사, ④ 그것(앞에 이미 언급되었거나 현재 이야기되고 있는 사물·동물을 가리킴)

22 처음에, 해녀들은 왜 Zin Kim이 자신들의 사진을 찍으려고 하는지 이해하지 못했다.

23 주어진 문장의 my talk에 주목한다. ①번 앞 문장의 a talk를 받고 있으므로 ①번이 적절하다.

24 lastly = finally: (여러 개를 언급할 때) 마지막으로, ① 결국, 마침내, ② 즉시, ③ 극도로, 극히, ⑤ 마침내[드디어]

25 ⓐ와 ①, ③, ④: 부사적 용법, ②: 형용사적 용법, ⑤: 명사적 용법

26 ⓐ for a living: 밥벌이로, 생계 수단으로, ⓑ passion for: ~

에 대한 열정

27 barista: 바리스타, 커피 내리는 사람

28 '뜨거운 우유로 커피를 장식하고 그의 손님들이 그것을 즐기는 것을 보는 것'이다.

01 They are waiting to get into the new bakery.

02 Because it was on a TV program.

03 He wants to try the new bakery's bread.

04 ① The film director was tired because he spoke[had spoken] in front of so many people.

05 ④ Where do you think the police officer caught the thief?

06 (1) Because Mary had learned taekwondo before, she fought off a strange man's attack.

　 (2) Until Kevin saw a video of himself being a heavy drinker, he had never thought of quitting drinking.

07 prettily → pretty

08 I would make them look beautiful in my pictures.

09 (A) very special   (B) show their culture

10 (A) without   (B) for   (C) destroy

11 (A) Less-experienced   (B) more-experienced

12 Because they stay in the water without any breathing devices.

01 많은 사람들이 새로 생긴 제과점에 들어가려고 줄을 서서 기다리고 있다.

02 새로 생긴 제과점이 TV에 나왔었기 때문이다.

03 Brian은 새로 생긴 제과점의 빵을 먹어 보고 싶어 한다.

04 영화감독이 피곤한 것은 너무나 많은 사람들 앞에서 연설했기 때문이다. 피곤한 상황이 과거완료가 되어서는 전후 관계가 뒤바뀌므로 적절하지 않다.

05 간접의문문 앞에 think, believe, imagine, guess 등 생각, 추측 등의 동사가 있을 때 의문사가 문두에 와야 한다.

06 (1) 'Mary는 전에 태권도를 배웠기 때문에 낯선 남자의 공격을 물리쳤다' (2) 'Kevin이 본인의 주정뱅이 모습을 보기 전까지는 술을 끊는 것을 생각해 본 적이 없었다.'

07 감각동사 looked의 보어로 형용사를 써야 하므로 pretty로 고치는 것이 적절하다.

08 사역동사 make+목적어+목적격보어(동사원형)의 순서로 쓰는 것이 적절하다.

09 해녀들은 '아주 특별하고', 세계에 '그들의 문화를 알리고' 싶었기 때문이다.

10 (A) 어떤 호흡 장치도 '사용하지 않고'라고 해야 하므로 without이 옳다. (B) 이것은 수중 환경에 '좋은' 것이라고 해야

하므로 for가 옳다. be good at: ~을 잘하다, be good for: ~에 좋다, (C) 한 번에 한 장소에서 너무 많은 해양생물을 채취하는 것은 바다를 '파괴할 수 있다'고 해야 하므로 destroy가 옳다. protect: ~을 보호하다

11 '경험이 적은 해녀들'은 '경험이 더 많은 해녀들'에 의해 훈련을 받는다.

12 '어떤 호흡 장치도 사용하지 않고 물속에 머물기' 때문이다.

|모범답안|

01 (A) strong beat   (B) where the music came from
　 (C) nongak   (D) community band music
　 (E) cheer up farmers and wish for a good harvest

02 (1) He wants to know when I fed the puppy.
　 (2) Did you check whether the plant is dried?
　 (3) Tell me where I should empty the waste bin.

01 거리를 걷다가, 나는 강한 비트가 있는 음악을 들었다. 나는 음악이 어디서 오는 것인지 알고 싶었다. 유리와 나는 그것이 농악이라고 불리는 한국의 전통 음악이라는 것을 알게 되었다. 유리는 그것이 공동체 악단 음악의 한 종류로 전통적으로 농부들의 힘을 북돋아 주고 풍년을 기원하기 위해 사용되었다고 설명했다. 나는 몇몇 사람들이 리듬에 맞춰 춤을 추는 것이 인상 깊었다. 왜냐하면 함께 춤추는 것이 음악을 완성했기 때문이다. 유리와 나는 함께 했고 음악을 완성했다.

01 ①　　　　02 ①

03 (1) I want to be a photographer.
　 (2) She was the most suitable candidate.
　 (3) He held my hand tightly.
　 (4) I'd like to borrow the novel.

04 ⑤

05 He visited Gwangandaegyo in Busan (with his family).

06 I wonder why there are so many people waiting in line.

07 ⑤　　　　08 (C) → (D) → (E) → (A) → (B)

09 Because lots of people are going on vacation this weekend.

10 She suggested going somewhere.

11 ⑤　　　12 ②　　　13 ④　　　14 ⑤

15 if the woman had really put(또는 really had put) the fish

41

01 '사람들이 사도록 설득하려고 의도된 사진, 어구 또는 짧은 영상'을 가리키는 말은 advertisement(광고)이다.

02 주어진 문장에서 beat는 '리듬, 비트'를 가리키며 이와 같은 의미로 쓰인 것은 ①번이다. ②번은 '이기다', 나머지는 모두 '때리다, 두드리다'를 뜻한다.

03 photographer: 사진작가, suitable: 적절한, tightly: 단단히, 꽉, novel: 소설, borrow: 빌리다

04 ⑤번을 제외하고는 궁금한 점을 묻는 표현이다.

05 소년은 (그의 가족들과) 부산에 있는 광안대교를 방문했다.

07 위 대화를 통해 새로 생긴 제과점이 언제 TV에 방영되었는지는 알 수 없다.

08 (C) 이번 여름 계획 질문 → (D) 계획 설명 → (E) 올레길에 대한 설명 요청 → (A) 올레길에 대한 설명 → (B) 바람 표현

09 길 위에 많은 차들이 있는 것은 많은 사람들이 이번 주말에 휴가를 가려고 하기 때문이다.

10 Emma는 어딘가 갈 것을 제안했다.

11 궁금한 것을 묻는 질문에 이해가 가지 않는다는 말은 어색하다.

12 간접의문문의 어순은 '의문사+주어+동사'이다. 의문사를 문두로 보낼 이유가 없다.

13 그가 바이러스에 감염된 것은 그 질병의 중심지에서 3개월간 체류했던 것 때문이며, 과거보다 더 앞선 시점의 일이다. 과거완료 시제를 활용하는 것이 적절하다.

14 모두 '명사절로 사용된 간접의문문'인데, ⑤번만 '관계대명사가 이끄는 형용사절'로 쓰였다.

15 James는 그 여자가 붕어빵에 정말로 붕어를 넣었는지 궁금했다. 부사 really는 'had+p.p'의 중간에 와도 좋고, had 앞에 위치해도 괜찮다.

16 (A) Yori는 WeTube에서 그녀의 첫 비디오가 2만 개의 조회수를 얻었을 때 콘텐츠 창작자가 되었다. (B) 그녀가 자신의 직업에서 가장 좋아하는 부분은 한국 음식의 어떤 점이 특별한지 세계의 많은 사람들과 공유하는 것이다.

17 ⓐ와 ①, ③: 부사적 용법, ②, ⑤: 명사적 용법, ④: 형용사적 용법

18 Zin Kim이 우연히 한 해녀의 사진을 찍기 전에 그녀는 '흑백 사진 속의' 아주 지친 모습의 해녀만 봐 왔다.

19 이 글은 '해녀에 대해 무엇이 특별한지'를 설명하는 글이므로, 빈칸에 들어갈 질문으로는 ①번 '그들은 무엇이 그렇게 특별한가요?'가 적절하다. ④ hold one's breath: 숨을 참다

20 주어진 문장의 This에 주목한다. ④번 앞 문장의 내용을 받고 있으므로 ④번이 적절하다.

21 '되어 왔어요'를 현재완료 시제로 쓰는 것이 적절하다.

22 twenty thousands로 읽지 않도록 조심해야 한다.

23 what 다음의 동사가 is이므로, the things which[that]는 적절하지 않다.

24 Yori가 WeTube의 그녀의 첫 번째 동영상에 대해 언제 20,000 뷰를 돌파했는지는 알 수 없다. ① She is a content creator about traditional Korean food. ② By getting 20,000 views on her first video clip on WeTube. ④ It is sharing what is special about Korean food with many people around the world. ⑤ She is planning to write a cookbook on Korean food.

교과서 파헤치기

Lesson 1

1 occur, 일어나다, 발생하다   2 endangered, 멸종 위기의
3 gulf, 만   4 fix, 고치다   5 rescue, 구조, 구출
6 educate, 가르치다, 교육하다   7 marine, 해양의
8 raise, 기르다   9 expression, 표현
10 translate, 번역하다   11 reduce, 줄이다
12 deliver, 전달하다, 배달하다   13 signature, 서명
14 specialist, 전문가   15 donate, 기부하다, 기증하다
16 charity, 자선단체

단어 TEST Step 1   p.02

01 해양의	02 입양하다	03 멸종 위기의
04 고치다	05 세대	06 탁아소, 보육원
07 전달하다, 배달하다		08 실제로
09 가르치다, 교육하다		10 목구멍, 목
11 다양한, 여러 가지의		12 표현
13 서평	14 고무	15 이웃, 근처
16 번역하다	17 모으다, 수집하다	18 기르다
19 ~임에도 불구하고, 비록 ~이지만		20 아마도
21 줄이다	22 유출	23 기부하다, 기증하다
24 자선단체, 자선	25 구조, 구출	26 전문가
27 공급	28 십 대, 청소년	29 비영리 단체
30 일어나다, 발생하다		31 쓰레기
32 자원봉사자; 자원하다		33 만
34 서명	35 ~으로 죽다	
36 (곤경, 어려움 등을) 만나다[겪다]		37 ~할 수 있다
38 토하다	39 ~ 이외에, ~에 더하여	
40 고장나다	41 ~으로 뒤덮여 있다	
42 A를 B에게 읽어주다		43 도움을 청하다

단어 TEST Step 2   p.03

01 charity	02 specialist	03 various
04 occur	05 waste	06 marine
07 collect	08 probably	09 donate
10 supply	11 reduce	12 throat
13 deliver	14 translate	15 spill
16 neighborhood	17 although	18 fix
19 generation	20 actually	21 raise
22 endangered	23 rescue	24 adopt
25 expression	26 educate	27 signature
28 gulf	29 rubber	30 child-care center
31 mayonnaise	32 teenager	33 volunteer
34 parking space	35 die from	36 any longer
37 read A to B	38 throw up	39 be covered with
40 break down	41 run into	42 in addition to
43 share A with B		

대화문 TEST Step 1   p.05~07

Listen & Speak 1 A

1. doing this weekend / thinking of doing, volunteer work / What / probably read, to / sounds, join / course
2. are you, to read, review homework / thinking, young leaders / have, perfect book / lend / bring

Listen & Speak 1 B

1. What's, this year / thinking, every weekend
2. What's, plan / thinking of, how to
3. What's, plan for / thinking of taking, lessons

Listen & Speak 2 A

1. a, there, to / want me to / a few minutes
2. What can I do / ask, to make, parking space / want me to help, collect signatures / a lot

Listen & Speak 2 B

1. broke down / want me to fix
2. bring / share, umbrella with
3. This, too heavy / want me to help, carry
4. arm / want me to take

Communicate A

you don't, any longer / I'm thinking of sending, told me that, to read / aren't / about translating, into / Translating / Do you want me to help you / run into, difficult, expressions, for help / that we, help

Communicate B

thinking of learning / Are you thinking, to dance / I'm thinking of learning / want me to teach

Progress Check 1

What are, doing / I'm thinking of, bike ride / Can, join / Let's, in front of

Progress Check 2

Can we, for / don't / want me to go, get / blueberry syrup, too

Listen & Speak 1 A

1. G: What are you doing this weekend?

B: I'm thinking of doing some volunteer work at the child-care center.

G: What would you do there?

B: I would probably read some books to the children.

G: That sounds interesting. Can I join you?

B: Of course.

2. B: What are you going to read for the book review homework?

G: I'm thinking of reading a book about young leaders.

B: Good idea. I have the perfect book for you.

G: Oh, could you lend it to me?

B: Sure. I'll bring it tomorrow.

Listen & Speak 1 B

1. A: What's your plan for this year?

B: I'm thinking of watching a movie every weekend.

2. A: What's your plan for this year?

B: I'm thinking of learning how to play baduk.

3. A: What's your plan for this year?

B: I'm thinking of taking swimming lessons.

Listen & Speak 2 A

1. G: Dad, I'm a bit hungry. Is there anything to eat?

M: Do you want me to cook tteokbokki for you?

G: That'd be great. I love tteokbokki.

M: O.K. Give me a few minutes.

2. B: Sujin, can you help us?

G: Sure. What can I do for you?

B: We're going to ask the school to make a parking space for bicycles.

G: That's a great idea. Do you want me to help you collect signatures from students?

B: That would help us a lot. Thanks!

Listen & Speak 2 B

1. A: My bike broke down.

B: Do you want me to fix it?

A: Yes, please.

2. A: I didn't bring an umbrella.

B: Do you want me to share my umbrella with you?

A: Yes, please.

3. A: This box is too heavy.

B: Do you want me to help you carry it?

A: Yes, please.

4. A: My arm is too short.

B: Do you want me to take a picture of you?

A: Yes, please.

Communicate A

Suho: Anna, do you have any children's books you don't read any longer?

Anna: Sure. Why?

Suho: I'm thinking of sending some books to children in Africa. My aunt told me that they need books to read.

Anna: Good idea, Suho! Wait, aren't your books in Korean?

Suho: Oh, that's a problem.

Anna: Well, how about translating them into English?

Suho: Translating? That's a great idea, Anna.

Anna: Do you want me to help you?

Suho: Sure. If we run into any difficult expressions, let's ask our English teacher for help.

Anna: O.K. It's really great that we can help the children in Africa.

Communicate B

A: (춤추는 동작을 한다.)

B: Are you thinking of learning taekwondo?

A: No.

C: Are you thinking of learning to dance?

A: Yes. I'm thinking of learning K-pop dancing.

C: Do you want me to teach you?

A: Sure. That'd be great.

Progress Check 1

B: What are you doing this weekend?

G: I'm thinking of going for a bike ride.

B: Sounds good. Can I join you?

G: Sure. Let's meet in front of the park at ten.

B: O.K.

Progress Check 2

M: Can we have pancakes for breakfast?

W: Sure. Oh, we don't have any eggs.

M: Do you want me to go to the store and get some?

W: Thanks, Mike. Can you get blueberry syrup, too?

M: Sure.

01 Teens, Action
02 making, world, better place
03 For example, in saving
04 Although, have, made, difference
05 How, able to   06 Let's hear from
07 When, little, each adopted
08 raise, at home
09 donated to, charity, protects
10 protect, might, able, near
11 became interested in, endangered
12 later, created, non-profit organization
13 generation, so, named, organization
14 studied endangered, educated, friends
15 terrible oil spill occurred
16 completely covered with, dying
17 had to do
18 rescue supplies, as, neighborhood
19 deliver what, collected, save
20 While, working, something, useful
21 into, throat, threw up   22 wat, get, out of
23 be used to save
24 last, marine life specialist
25 waste, dangerous, than, spills
26 die from eating, waste
27 created, educational, how, reduce
28 addition, continues, various, save
29 Although, making, big difference
30 What, change, take, step

19 later, what we collected, to save the animals
20 while, working, something very useful
21 put, into, threw up   22 get, out of
23 could be used to save   24 marine life specialist
25 more dangerous, than oil spils
26 die from eating plastic waste
27 created an educational project, how to reduce
28 In addition to, projects to save
29 Although, making a big difference
30 What, take that first step

1 활약하는 십 대들
2 많은 젊은 사람들이 세상을 더 좋은 곳으로 만들고 있다.
3 예를 들어, Carter Ries와 Olivia Ries는 동물을 구하는 일에 리더가 되어 왔다.
4 비록 그들은 십 대일 뿐이지만, 실제로 세상에 변화를 일으켜 왔다.
5 그들은 어떻게 그것을 할 수 있었을까?
6 Carter의 이야기를 들어보자.
7 내가 다섯 살이었을 때, 나의 여동생 Olivia와 나는 각자 치타를 입양했다.
8 우리가 치타를 집에서 길렀을까?
9 아니, 우리는 남아프리카 공화국에 있는 야생 치타를 보호하는 자선단체에 기부했다.
10 부모님께서는 우리에게 우리가 그들을 보호하지 않으면, 가까운 미래에 치타를 볼 수 없을지도 모른다고 말씀하셨다.
11 우리는 곧 다른 멸종 위기의 동물들을 도와주는 것에 관심을 갖게 되었다.
12 몇 년 후에, 부모님의 도움으로, 우리는 그들을 보호하기 위해 비영리 단체를 만들었다.
13 우리는 다음 세대가 이러한 동물들을 볼 수 있기를 원했기에, 우리 단체를 One More Generation이라고 이름 붙였다.
14 우리는 또한 멸종 위기의 동물들을 연구했고 친구들에게 그들에 대해 가르쳐 주었다.
15 그러던 어느 날, 끔찍한 석유 유출 사건이 멕시코만에서 발생했다.
16 많은 해양 동물들이 완전히 기름을 뒤집어썼고, 죽어가고 있었다.
17 우리는 무엇인가를 해야만 했다.
18 우리는 애완동물 수송용 우리와 고무장갑과 같은 동물 구조 물품들을 동네의 모든 사람으로부터 모으기 시작했다.
19 4개월 후에, 우리 가족은 우리가 모았던 것들을 전달하기 위해서 멕시코만으로 운전해 갔으며 동물들을 구하는 일을 도왔다.
20 거기서 일하는 동안에, 우리는 매우 유용한 것을 배웠다.
21 마요네즈를 거북이의 목구멍에 집어넣으면, 거북이가 토했다.

01 in Action   02 Many, a better place
03 For example, in saving animals
04 Although, teenagers, have actually made a difference
05 How, able to   06 Let's hear from
07 little sister, each adopted 08 raise, at home
09 donated to a charity, protects, South Africa
10 might not be able to see cheetahs
11 became interested in, other endangered animals
12 A few years, created a non-profit organization
13 the next generation, be able to
14 endangered animals, educated our friends
15 a terrible oil spill occurred
16 were completely covered with oil, were dying
17 had to do
18 collecting, animal rescue supplies, in our
    neighborhood

22 그런 식으로, 우리는 거북이들에게서 기름을 빼낼 수 있었다.

23 나는 마요네즈가 동물을 구하는 데 사용될 수 있다는 것을 전혀 알지 못했다!

24 마지막 날에, 우리는 해양 생물 전문가를 만났다.

25 그녀는 우리에게 석유 유출보다 플라스틱 쓰레기가 해양 동물에게 더 위험하다고 말했다.

26 많은 해양 동물과 바다 새들이 플라스틱 쓰레기를 먹어서 죽는다.

27 집으로 돌아온 후, 우리는 플라스틱 쓰레기를 줄일 수 있는 방법에 관한 교육 프로젝트를 만들었다.

28 이것 외에도, 우리 단체는 동물들을 구하기 위한 다양한 프로젝트들을 계속하고 있다.

29 비록 우리는 작은 것부터 시작했지만, 큰 변화를 만들어 내고 있는 중이다.

30 당신이 오늘 하는 일이 세상을 바꿀 수 있기에, 첫발을 내디뎌라!

본문 TEST Step 4-Step 5 p.17~20

1 Teens in Action

2 Many young people are making the world a better place.

3 For example, Carter and Olivia Ries have become leaders in saving animals.

4 Although they are only teenagers, they have actually made a difference in the world.

5 How were they able to do that?

6 Let's hear from Carter.

7 When I was five, my little sister Olivia and I each adopted a cheetah.

8 Did we raise cheetahs at home?

9 No, we donated to a charity that protects wild cheetahs in South Africa.

10 Our parents told us that if we did not protect them, we might not be able to see cheetahs in the near future.

11 We soon became interested in helping other endangered animals..

12 A few years later, with help from our parents, we created a non-profit organization to protect them.

13 We wanted the next generation to be able to see these animals, so we named our organization One More Generation.

14 We also studied endangered animals and educated our friends about them.

15 Then one day, a terrible oil spill occurred in the Gulf of Mexico.

16 A lot of sea animals were completely covered with oil, and they were dying.

17 We had to do something.

18 We started collecting animal rescue supplies such as pet carrying cages and rubber gloves from everyone in our neighborhood.

19 Four months later, our family drove to the Gulf of Mexico to deliver what we collected and helped to save the animals.

20 While we were working there, we learned something very useful.

21 When we put mayonnaise into a turtle's throat, the turtle threw up.

22 That way, we were able to get oil out of turtles.

23 I never knew mayonnaise could be used to save animals!

24 On our last day, we met a marine life specialist.

25 She told us that plastic waste is more dangerous to sea animals than oil spills are.

26 A lot of sea animals and sea birds die from eating plastic waste.

27 After we came home, we created an educational project about how to reduce plastic waste.

28 In addition to this, our organization continues to do various projects to save animals.

29 Although we started small, we are making a big difference.

30 What you do today can change the world, so take that first step!

구석구석지문 TEST Step 1 p.21

After You Read B

1. Why don't you join

2. What, that

3. non-profit organization, protects endangered

4. does, mean

5. generation to be able to see

6. organization, join

Link Science - Share

1. white V-shape on their chests

2. mostly live in forests

3. become endangered because, hunt, body parts, destroy forests

4. what you can do

5. use less, to protect forests

6. should not buy, black bear products

Write

1. one, most serious environmental problems
2. Although, make, convenient, a lot of smoke, pollutes
3. big problem
4. what we can do
5. take the bus, subway
6. buy local products, do not need to be shipped
7. Even simple actions like

단어 TEST Step 1　　　　　p.23

01 받아들이다, 수락하다		02 보물	
03 꽃이 피다, 꽃을 피우다			
04 만들어 내다, 제조하다		05 빌리다	
06 신비로운	07 모험	08 신화	
09 난쟁이	10 단언하다, 돈을 걸다		
11 금빛의	12 거인		
13 수확, 추수; 수확하다, 거둬들이다			
14 대장장이, 금속 세공인		15 원상태로 돌리다	
16 왕국, 왕조	17 게다가	18 시	
19 마차, 객차	20 도전, 결투 신청	21 선택하다	
22 귀중한, 값어치 있는		23 적, 적군	
24 증명하다	25 마법 같은	26 해산물	
27 지혜, 슬기, 현명함	28 즉시, 곧		
29 결정, 판결	30 지키다, 보호하다	31 창	
32 주문하다	33 조절하다	34 장난, 묘기	
35 ~에 관심이 많다	36 포기하다	37 ~로 되다	
38 ~을 생각해 내다	39 ~하는 편이 더 낫다		
40 그렇다면, 그런 경우에는		41 ~로 유명하다	
42 잠들다	43 함께 가다, 동행하다		

구석구석지문 TEST Step 2　　　　p.22

After You Read B

1. A: Why don't you join One More Generation?
2. B: What is that?
3. A: It is a non-profit organization that protects endangered animals.
4. B: What does One More Generation mean?
5. A: The organization wants the next generation to be able to see those animals.
6. B: That's a great organization. I'll join it.

Link Science - Share

1. Asian black bears have a white V-shape on their chests.
2. They mostly live in forests in Asia.
3. They've become endangered because people hunt them for their body parts and destroy forests.
4. We'll tell you what you can do for them.
5. First, use less paper to protect forests.
6. Second, you should not buy any Asian black bear products.

Write

1. Air pollution is one of the most serious environmental problems these days.
2. Although cars make our lives convenient, they produce a lot of smoke that pollutes the air.
3. That is a big problem.
4. Here is what we can do.
5. We can take the bus or subway more.
6. We can also buy local products because they do not need to be shipped very far.
7. Even simple actions like these can help.

단어 TEST Step 2　　　　　p.24

01 adventure	02 wisdom	03 carriage
04 challenge	05 harvest	06 accept
07 spear	08 choose	09 poem
10 miss	11 powerful	12 moreover
13 control	14 decision	15 dwarf
16 bloom	17 decide	18 produce
19 treasure	20 magical	21 mind
22 protect	23 enemy	24 hammer
25 immediately	26 kingdom	27 giant
28 mysterious	29 myth	30 precious
31 trick	32 undo	33 prove
34 seafood	35 fall asleep	36 had better ~
37 come up with ~		38 of one's own
39 take root	40 be famous for ~	
41 give up	42 in that case	43 turn into ~

1 bloom, 꽃이 피다   2 order, 주문하다   3 treasure, 보물

4 elf, 요정   5 smith, 대장장이   6 seafood, 해산물

7 carriage, 마차, 수레   8 enemy, 적   9 spear, 창

10 trick, 장난, 속임수   11 choose, 선택하다

12 bet, 돈을 걸다   13 challenge, 도전

14 hammer, 망치   15 throw, 던지다   16 wisdom, 지혜

Listen & Speak 1 A-1

it, to visit / is, always wanted to come to / What made / into, going to go to, I saw / Have

Listen & Speak 1 A-2

the worst month of / What makes, say / blooming, have to stay inside / what you mean

Listen & Speak 2 A-1

if I change / not at all / need to watch, about / Why / learning about, in class / see

Listen & Talk 2 A-2

mind if I open / have a cold, pretty windy / problem, Would you like, good for / would be

Communicate A

doing / reading, on, into them these days / What, like them / interesting, lots of / any good / about, famous god / favorite, character / In that case, go see / if I borrow, finished, it before / at all, like this book, too

Progress Check 1

of the year / makes, say / cold, flowers are blooming / because, in April / throw, a party

Progress Check 2

mind if I take, more / waiting for, soon / Never mind / ask, to bring

---

Listen & Speak 1 A-1

W: Is it your first time to visit Korea, Mike?

M: Yes, it is. I've always wanted to come to Seoul.

W: What made you come here?

M: I'm really into Korean TV shows. I'm going to go to the places I saw on TV.

W: Have fun!

Listen & Speak 1 A-2

B: April is the worst month of the year.

G: What makes you say so?

B: Flowers are blooming, but I have to stay inside to study for my exams.

G: Oh, I know what you mean.

Listen & Speak 2 A-1

G: Dad, do you mind if I change the channel?

M: No, not at all.

G: Thank you. I need to watch a program about Norway.

M: Norway? Why?

G: Well, we're learning about Norway in class.

M: Oh, I see.

Listen & Talk 2 A-2

M: Jane, do you mind if I open the window?

W: Sorry, but I have a cold, and it's pretty windy today.

M: O.K. No problem. Would you like some hot tea? It'd be good for your cold.

W: That would be great. Thanks.

Communicate A

Jaden: Hi, Yuri, What're you doing?

Yuri: Hi, Jaden. I'm reading a book on Norse myths. I'm really into them these days.

Jaden: What makes you like them so much?

Yuri: The stories are very interesting, and there are lots of movies about Norse myths.

Jaden: Are they any good?

Yuri: Yes. There's actually a new movie about Thor, a famous god in Norse myths.

Jaden: Oh, I know him. He's my favorite online game character.

Yuri: In that case, we should go see the movie together.

Jaden: Do you mind if I borrow your book when you're finished? I want to read it before we see the movie.

Yuri: No, not at all. I'm sure you'll like this book, too.

Progress Check 1

B: April is the best month of the year.

G: What makes you say so?

B: The weather is not cold, and flowers are blooming.

G: I love April because my birthday is in April.

B: Really? We should throw you a party.

Progress Check 2

M: Excuse me, do you mind if I take this chair? We need one more.

W: I'm sorry, but I'm waiting for my friend. She'll be here soon.

M: Oh, I see. Never mind.

W: You can ask the waiter to bring more chairs.

01 Treasures, Three Gods   02 Important Norse
03 highest, gave up, wisdom   04 the strongest god
05 god, harvest, controls, weather
06 plays tricks on others
07 woke, something, wrong   08 wife's, was gone
09 such a terrible thing
10 found, who was drinking
11 better undo what, angrily   12 was scared
13 promised, would get, wife
14 only, sons, fine golden
15 heard, finest smiths, true   16 It is, who, replied
17 making three treasures
18 make treasures better than
19 Of course, answered
20 should, make, treasures for
21 decide on, treasure   22 one, had to be
23 to work immediately   24 went to see
25 are making, for, said
26 bet, as fine as
27 became, accepted, challenge
28 produced, of their own
29 with all the treasures   30 came along
31 showed, treasures from, sons
32 for, only one eye
33 spear, missed, target
34 turn into, piece, cloth
35 was for   36 third treasure, for
37 showed, flowing golden hair
38 put, on, took root
39 turn, show, gifts
40 eight more, every ninth   41 gave Frey, pig
42 pull, carriage faster, any
43 My third treasure
44 hammer, which, love
45 throw, come back
46 Moreover, nothing, break
47 decision, choose, greatest treasure
48 It, gods liked most
49 thought, protect, from, enemies
50 the better smiths
51 proved, wrong, precious treasures

01 Treasures, Gods   02 Important Norse
03 highest, gave up
04 the strongest god of
05 harvest, controls the weather
06 plays tricks on
07 something was wrong
08 golden, was gone
09 such a terrible thing
10 found, who was drinking
11 You'd better undo, angrily   12 scared
13 promised, would get   14 fine golden hair
15 the finest smiths, true   16 it is, who, replied
17 three treasures
18 treasures better than theirs
19 Of course, answered   20 make, for them
21 decide on, best treasure   22 one of, had to be
23 to work immediately   24 went to see
25 are making, for
26 I bet, as fine as theirs
27 angry, accepted the challenge
28 of their own
29 with all the treasures   30 came along
31 showed, from   32 for, only one eye
33 It was, that, missed
34 turn into, piece of cloth
35 for   36 The third treasure
37 flowing golden hair
38 put, on, took root, became real hair
39 Brokk's turn, gifts
40 eight more, every ninth night
41 Frey a pig
42 faster than any horse
43 My third treasure   44 hammer, which
45 come back to   46 Moreover, break it
47 the greatest treasure
48 the three gods liked most
49 protect, from, enemies   50 the better smiths
51 proved, wrong, precious treasures

1 세 명의 신을 위한 보물

2 북유럽 신화의 주요 신들

3 Odin은 가장 높은 신이며, 지혜를 위해 한쪽 눈을 포기했다.

4 Thor는 Odin의 아들이며 모든 신들 중에서 가장 강한 신이다.

5 Frey는 수확의 신으로 날씨를 다스린다.

6 Loki는 다른 신들에게 농간을 부리는 신이다.

7 Thor는 잠에서 깨어 즉시 무엇인가가 잘못되었다는 것을 알았다.

8 그의 아내의 아름다운 금발머리가 사라졌다.

9 그는 오직 Loki만이 이런 끔찍한 일을 할 수 있다는 것을 알고 있었다.

10 Thor는 곧 Loki를 찾았는데, 그는 집에서 술을 마시고 있었다.

11 "네가 한 짓을 되돌려 놓는 것이 좋을 거야, 그렇지 않으면 후회하게 될 거다." Thor는 노하여 Loki에게 말했다.

12 Loki는 겁이 났다.

13 그는 Thor의 아내를 위해 금발머리를 얻어 오겠다고 약속했다.

14 Loki는 Ivaldi의 아들들만이 훌륭한 금발머리를 만들 수 있다는 것을 알고 있었다.

15 그는 그들에게 가서 "내가 듣기로 Brokk와 그의 남동생이 가장 훌륭한 대장장이라고 하던데. 그것이 사실인가?"라고 말했다.

16 "아니요, 가장 훌륭한 대장장이는 바로 우리들이요." Ivaldi의 아들들이 대답했다.

17 "그들은 Odin과 Thor와 Frey를 위해서 보물을 만들고 있네." Loki는 말했다.

18 "너희들이 그들의 보물보다 더 나은 보물을 만들 수 있다고 생각하는가?"

19 "물론 할 수 있소." 그들이 대답했다.

20 "좋아, 그러면 너희도 그들을 위해 세 개의 보물을 만들어야 한다." Loki가 말했다.

21 "그 신들이 가장 훌륭한 보물을 결정할 것이다."

22 Loki는 또한 그들에게 보물 중 하나는 금발머리이어야 한다고 말했다.

23 그들은 즉시 일에 착수했다.

24 Loki는 그 다음에 Brokk와 그의 남동생을 보러 갔다.

25 "Ivaldi의 아들들이 Odin과 Thor, 그리고 Frey를 위해 세 개의 보물을 만들고 있어." Loki가 말했다.

26 "너희들은 절대 그들의 보물만큼 훌륭한 보물을 만들 수 없다는 것을 내 장담하지."

27 Brokk는 화가 나서 그 도전을 받아들였다.

28 그와 그의 남동생은 그들만의 세 가지 보물을 만들었다.

29 Loki는 모든 보물을 가지고 세 신을 만나러 갔다.

30 Brokk가 같이 갔다.

31 Loki는 그들에게 Ivaldi의 아들들이 만든 보물들을 보여 주었다.

32 첫 번째 보물은 Odin을 위한 것으로, 그는 눈이 한쪽밖에 없었다.

33 그것은 목표물을 절대로 빗나가지 않는 창이었다.

34 두 번째 보물은 천 조각으로 변할 수 있는 큰 배였다.

35 그것은 Frey를 위한 것이었다.

36 세 번째 보물은 Thor를 위한 것이었다.

37 Loki는 Thor에게 그의 아내를 위한 매끈하게 늘어진 금발머리를 보여 주었다.

38 Thor가 그 머리카락을 그의 아내의 머리에 얹었더니 그것이 뿌리를 내려서 진짜 머리카락이 되었다.

39 이제 Brokk가 신들에게 그의 선물들을 보여 줄 차례였다.

40 그는 Odin에게 아홉 번째 밤이 될 때마다 8개의 금팔찌를 더 만들어 내는 금팔찌를 주었다.

41 그러고 나서 Brokk는 Frey에게 돼지를 한 마리 주었다.

42 그것은 어떤 말보다도 그의 마차를 더 빨리 끌 수 있었다.

43 "나의 세 번째 보물은 당신을 위한 것입니다, Thor." Brokk가 말했다.

44 "이것은 묠니르라는 망치인데 당신은 마음에 드실 겁니다."

45 그것을 던지면, 그것은 항상 당신에게 되돌아 올 것입니다.

46 게다가, 그 무엇도 이것을 부술 수 없지요."

47 가장 훌륭한 보물을 선택하는 것은 쉬운 결정이었다.

48 세 명의 신들이 가장 마음에 든 것은 묠니르였다.

49 그들은 그 망치가 신들을 그들의 적들로부터 보호해 줄 것이라고 생각했다.

50 "Brokk와 그의 남동생이 더 훌륭한 대장장이야." Odin이 말했다.

51 Brokk는 Loki가 틀렸다는 것을 증명해 냈고, 세 신들은 이제 소중한 보물을 가지게 되었다.

1 Treasures for Three Gods

2 Important Norse Gods

3 Odin, who is the highest god, gave up his eye for wisdom.

4 Thor is Odin's son and the strongest god of all.

5 Frey, who is the god of the harvest, controls the weather.

6 Loki is a god who plays tricks on others.

7 Thor woke and knew immediately something was wrong.

8 His wife's beautiful golden hair was gone.

9 He knew only Loki could do such a terrible thing.

10 Thor soon found Loki, who was drinking at home.

11 "You'd better undo what you did, or you'll be sorry," Thor said angrily to Loki.

12 Loki was scared.

13 He promised that he would get golden hair for Thor's wife.

14 Loki knew only the sons of Ivaldi could make fine golden hair.

15 He went to them and said, "I heard Brokk and his brother are the finest smiths. Is that true?"

16 "No, it is we who are the finest smiths," the sons of Ivaldi replied.

17 "They're making three treasures for Odin, Thor, and Frey," said Loki.

18 "Do you think you can make treasures better than theirs?"

19 "Of course we can," they answered.

20 "O.K., then you should also make three treasures for them," said Loki.

21 "The gods will decide on the best treasure."

22 Loki also told them that one of the treasures had to be golden hair.

23 They went to work immediately.

24 Loki then went to see Brokk and his brother.

25 "Ivaldi's sons are making three treasures for Odin, Thor, and Frey," said Loki.

26 "I bet that you can never make treasures as fine as theirs."

27 Brokk became angry and accepted the challenge.

28 He and his brother produced three treasures of their own.

29 Loki went to see the three gods with all the treasures.

30 Brokk came along.

31 Loki showed them the treasures from Ivaldi's sons.

32 The first treasure was for Odin, who had only one eye.

33 It was a spear that never missed its target.

34 The second treasure was a big ship that could turn into a piece of cloth.

35 It was for Frey.

36 The third treasure was for Thor.

37 Loki showed Thor the flowing golden hair for his wife.

38 Thor put the hair on his wife's head, and it took root and became real hair.

39 It was now Brokk's turn to show the gods his gifts.

40 He gave Odin a gold arm ring that produced eight more gold rings every ninth night.

41 Brokk then gave Frey a pig.

42 It could pull his carriage faster than any horse.

43 "My third treasure is for you, Thor," said Brokk.

44 "This is the hammer Mjolnir, which you'll love.

45 If you throw it, it'll always come back to you.

46 Moreover, nothing can ever break it."

47 It was an easy decision to choose the greatest treasure.

48 It was Mjolnir that the three gods liked most.

49 They thought the hammer would protect the gods from their enemies.

50 "Brokk and his brother," said Odin, "are the better smiths."

51 Brokk proved that Loki was wrong, and the three gods now had precious treasures.

구석구석지문 TEST Step 1 p.45

After You Read A

1. took, golden hair, so, became angry at
2. promised to get golden hair
3. asked, to make three treasures for
4. had, produce three treasures for the gods
5. bet, would make better treasures
6. showed, three gods, treasures from
7. spear, big ship, golden hair
8. The treasures from, were, gold arm ring, and a hammer
9. liked the summer most
10. their own precious treasures

Link Create

1. have, been, who, the strongest god
2. few days, just for fun, became angry at
3. came up with, to get, back
4. to make fine golden hair

Culture Project

1. Strongest Gods and Heroes
2. who, is famous for his many adventures
3. Brave and powerful, wore, lion's skin as a coat
4. also fought, many-headed
5. who, Miss, the strongest hero

After You Read A

1. (1) Loki took the beautiful golden hair of Thor's wife, so Thor became angry at him.
2. Loki promised to get golden hair for Thor's wife.
3. (2) Loki asked the sons of Ivaldi to make three treasures for Odin, Thor, and Frey.
4. He also had Brokk and his brother produce three treasures for the gods.
5. Loki bet that Ivaldi's sons would make better treasures.
6. (3) Loki showed the three gods the treasures from Ivaldi's sons.
7. They were a spear, a big ship, and golden hair.
8. The treasures from Brokk and his brother were a gold arm ring, a pig, and a hammer.
9. (4) The gods liked the summer most.
10. They each had their own precious treasures.

Link Create

1. I have always been friends with Sif, who is the wife of the strongest god.
2. A few days ago, I cut her golden hair just for fun, and her husband became angry at me.
3. I came up with a good idea to get her hair back.
4. I asked the sons of Ivaldi to make fine golden hair.

Culture Project

1. The Strongest Gods and Heroes in the World
2. Hercules, who was the son of Zeus, is famous for his many adventures.
3. Brave and powerful Hercules killed the Nemean lion and wore the lion's skin as a coat.
4. He also fought the many-headed Hydra.
5. I think who is Hercules Miss is the strongest hero in the world.

Lesson 3

01 증명하다	02 흡수하다	03 출판하다
04 꽃을 피우다	05 수도	06 비밀
07 실제로	08 해결하다	09 발견하다
10 담그다, 적시다	11 지우다	12 기대하다
13 시금치	14 향하다	
15 물리치다, 패배시키다		16 등장인물
17 조각상, 동상	18 기사, 논문	19 전함
20 정부, 국가	21 콩	22 숨겨진
23 고려하다, 여기다	24 일어나다	25 숨다, 숨기다
26 특성, 특징; 특징적인		
27 개선하다, 향상시키다		28 낮추다
29 포함하다, 담고 있다		30 영양소, 영양분
31 세계적으로 유명한		32 으스러뜨리다
33 흔적; 추적하다	34 유독한, 독성의	35 살을 빼다
36 흡수하다, 빨아들이다		
37 ~을 …로부터 멀리하다		38 A를 B로 바꾸다
39 더 이상 ~가 아닌	40 ~을 무서워하다	41 시도해 보다
42 비밀을 지키다	43 게다가	

01 absorb	02 article	03 battleship
04 bloom	05 capital	06 character
07 expect	08 consider	09 defeat
10 characteristic	11 crush	12 poisonous
13 contain	14 hide	15 publish
16 statue	17 improve	18 lower
19 truth	20 trace	21 spinach
22 material	23 hidden	24 nutrient
25 prove	26 world-famous	27 soak
28 planet	29 vision	30 secret
31 solve	32 cartoon	33 researcher
34 government	35 stay full	36 in addition
37 be good for	38 lose weight	39 keep a secret
40 no longer	41 soak up	42 give it a try
43 take medicine		

1 character, 등장인물   2 cartoon, 만화   3 hide, 숨기다
4 prove, 증명하다   5 insect, 곤충   6 publish, 출판하다
7 soak, 담그다, 적시다   8 carrot, 당근   9 spinach, 시금치

10 battleship, 전함　11 secret, 비밀
12 nutrient, 영양분　13 statue, 동상　14 bean, 콩
15 trace, 흔적　16 snowboard, 스노보드

대화문 TEST Step 1　　　　　　　　　　p.50~51

Listen & Speak 1 A-1

some medicine / something wrong / a stomachache, too much / Why don't, go for a walk / it a try

Listen & Speak 1 A-2

something wrong, look so good / a sore throat, because of, these days / Put, take, in, produce fresh air / get a few plants

Listen & Speak 2 A-1

so hard to lose weight, do you think / walk your dog / it, it help, lose weight / When, walk, actually exercising, too / think about it

Listen & Talk 2 A-2

How are, doing, growing / gotten, a few, so far, I should do / Where / In / need about, a day / move, over

Communicate A

is something wrong, quiet / a bit tired, little / something late / on, until, what I often do these days / that's why, before midnight / getting worse, I should do / eating lots of carrots, rich in vitamin, keep, healthy / see

Progress Check 1

Is, wrong / a little tired, watched, for two hours / why, red eyes, putting, over

Progress Check 2

wrong, look worried / broke, plate, do you think / Tell, truth, understand / hope, right

대화문 TEST Step 2　　　　　　　　　　p.52~53

Listen & Speak 1 A-1

B: Bomi, do you have some medicine?

G: Why? Is something wrong?

B: I have a stomachache. I think I ate too much for lunch.

G: Why don't you go for a walk?

B: O.K. I'll give it a try.

Listen & Speak 1 A-2

B: Is something wrong? You don't look so good.

G: I have a sore throat. I think it's because of the fine dust these days.

B: Put some plants in your room. They take bad air in and produce fresh air.

G: Really? I'll get a few plants right away.

Listen & Speak 2 A-1

B: It's so hard to lose weight. What do you think I should do?

G: Well, why don't you walk your dog every day?

B: My dog would love it, but would it help me lose weight?

G: Sure. When you walk your dog, you're actually exercising, too.

B: O.K. I'll think about it.

Listen & Talk 2 A-2

B: How are your tomatoes doing? Are they growing well?

G: No. I've gotten only a few tomatoes so far. What do you think I should do?

B: Where do you have the pot?

G: In the kitchen.

B: Well, tomato plants need about 7 hours of sunlight a day.

G: Oh, I see. I'll move the pot over to the window.

Communicate A

Anna: Suho, is something wrong? You're very quiet today.

Suho: I'm just a bit tired. I slept very little last night.

Anna: Did you do something late last night?

Suho: Yes, I watched a movie on my phone until 2 a.m. That's what I often do these days.

Anna: Oh, that's why you have red eyes. You should go to bed before midnight for your health.

Suho: I think my eyes are getting worse. What do you think I should do?

Anna: Try eating lots of carrots and tomatoes. They're rich in vitamin A, so they'll keep your eyes healthy.

Suho: I see. Thank you, Anna.

Progress Check 1

B: Is something wrong?

G: I'm just a little tired. I've watched a movie on my phone for two hours.

B: That's why you have red eyes. Try putting a warm towel over your eyes.

G: O.K. Thanks.

Progress Check 2

G: What's wrong? You look worried.

B: Well, I broke my mom's favorite plate. What do you think I should do?

G: Tell her the truth. She will understand.

B: I hope you're right.

01 Hidden, Plants   02 Great Spinach

03 world-famous cartoon character

04 gets, by eating spinach

05 When, became popular, lot

06 called, capital, built, statue

07 Although, powers, spinach, nutrients

08 considered, healthiest foods, planet

09 used, surprising way

10 When, absorbs, other, soil

11 characteristic, bombs hidden, ground

12 with sensors on, leaves   13 soak, bombs, light up

14 World War II

15 defeated, during, by using

16 keep, secret, published, article

17 said, improved, vision, ate

18 believed, lot, than before

19 improve, by eating, carrots

20 contain, vitamin, keep, healthy

21 future, may, used, wars

22 discovered, turn, into, light

23 even be used, battleships

24 has already been used   25 Scariest Vegetables

26 are good for, health

27 Up until, however, poisonous

28 named, prove, safe, eat

29 ate, basket, front, watching

30 expected, nothing happened to

31 since, have enjoyed eating

32 no longer, scared of

33 keep, away, place, crushed

34 Insects, come near

01 Hidden, Plants   02 Spinach

03 world-famous cartoon character

04 by eating spinach

05 became popular, a lot of

06 which, the spinach capital, a statue

07 Although eating, does have, nutrients

08 one of the ten healthiest foods

09 in a surprising way

10 When, absorbs, also absorbs, from

11 to find, hidden in the ground

12 with sensors on their leaves

13 soak up traces, light up   14 World War II

15 defeated, during, by using

16 keep, secret, published an article

17 improved their night vision because

18 a lot, than before

19 improve, by eating

20 which does keep, healthy

21 may actually be used

22 turn, into, light material   23 can even be used

24 has already been used   25 Scariest

26 are good for

27 Up until, however, poisonous

28 named, to prove, safe to eat

29 a basket of, in front of, watching

30 happened to

31 since, have enjoyed eating

32 no longer, scared of

33 keep, away from, place, crushed

34 come near

1 식물에 대한 숨겨진 이야기

2 Popeye와 위대한 시금치

3 Popeye는 세계적으로 유명한 만화 캐릭터다.

4 그는 시금치를 먹음으로써 초인적인 힘을 얻는다.

5 Popeye가 1930년대 미국에서 인기를 얻었을 때, 많은 어린이들이 시금치를 먹기 시작했다.

6 텍사스의 크리스털 시티는 세계의 시금치 수도라고 불리는데, 이곳에서는 Popeye의 동상을 세우기까지 했다.

7 비록 시금치를 먹는 것이 우리에게 초인적인 힘을 주지는 않지만, 시금치는 정말로 많은 영양분을 가지고 있다.

8 이것은 실제로 지구상에서 가장 건강한 식품 10개 중 하나로 여겨진다.

9 시금치는 놀라운 용도로 사용될 수 있다.

10 그것이 물을 흡수할 때, 시금치는 흙으로부터 다른 많은 것들도 흡수한다.

11 몇몇 과학자들은 시금치의 이 특성을 땅에 숨겨진 폭탄을 찾는 데 사용했다.

12 그들은 잎에 감지기가 있는 특별한 시금치를 만든다.

13 이 식물들이 폭탄의 흔적을 흡수하면, 감지기가 빛난다.

14 제2차 세계대전에서의 당근

15 1940년, 영국 공군은 제2차 세계 대전에서 레이더 시스템을 사용해 독일군을 패배시켰다.

16 영국 정부는 이 기술을 비밀로 하기를 원했기 때문에, 신문에 기사를 하나 냈다.

17 그것은 영국 비행사들이 당근을 많이 먹어 야간 시력이 좋아졌다는 내용이었다.

18 모두가 그 이야기를 믿었고 전보다 훨씬 많은 당근을 먹기 시작했다.

19 우리는 정말 당근을 많이 먹어서 야간 시력을 높일 수 있을까?

20 실제로 그렇지는 않지만, 당근은 많은 비타민 A를 함유하는데, 그것은 정말로 우리 눈을 건강하게 유지해 준다.

21 미래에는, 당근이 실제로 전쟁에 이용될지도 모른다.

22 스코틀랜드의 연구원들은 당근을 매우 강하고 가벼운 물질로 바꾸는 방법을 발견했다.

23 그것은 심지어 전함을 만드는 데 사용될 수도 있다.

24 이 새로운 소재는 이미 스노보드와 자전거를 만드는 데 사용되었다.

25 토마토, 가장 무서운 채소

26 우리는 모두 토마토가 건강에 좋다는 것을 안다.

27 그러나, 1800년대까지 대부분의 미국인들은 토마토에 독성이 있다고 생각했다.

28 1820년에, Robert Johnson이라는 이름의 남자가 토마토가 먹기에 안전하다는 것을 증명하기를 원했다.

29 그래서, 그는 그를 지켜보는 많은 사람들 앞에서 한 바구니의 토마토를 먹었다.

30 그들은 모두 그가 죽을 것이라고 예상했으나 그에게는 아무 일도 일어나지 않았다.

31 그 이후로, 미국인들은 토마토를 먹는 것을 즐겼다.

32 우리는 더 이상 토마토를 두려워하지 않지만, 몇몇 곤충들은 여전히 그것을 무서워한다.

33 만약 곤충들이 방에 들어오지 않게 하고 싶다면, 으깬 토마토 한 그릇을 방구석에 놓아 두어라.

34 곤충들은 토마토 가까이 오지 않을 것이다.

본문 TEST Step 4-Step 5   p.60~63

1 Hidden Stories about Plants

2 Popeye and the Great Spinach

3 Popeye is a world-famous cartoon character.

4 He gets his super power by eating spinach.

5 When Popeye became popular in the 1930s in the United States, a lot of children began to eat spinach.

6 Crystal City in Texas, which is called the spinach capital of the world, even built a statue of Popeye.

7 Although eating spinach will not give us super powers, spinach does have a lot of nutrients.

8 It is actually considered one of the ten healthiest foods on the planet.

9 Spinach can be used in a surprising way.

10 When it absorbs water, spinach also absorbs many other things from the soil.

11 Some scientists have used this characteristic of spinach to find bombs hidden in the ground.

12 They make special spinach plants with sensors on their leaves.

13 When these plants soak up traces from bombs, the sensors light up.

14 Carrots in World War II

15 In 1940, the Royal Air Force defeated German fighters during World War II by using a radar system.

16 The British government wanted to keep this technology a secret, so it published an article in the newspaper.

17 It said that British pilots improved their night vision because they ate a lot of carrots.

18 Everybody believed the story and began to eat a lot more carrots than before.

19 Can we really improve night vision by eating lots of carrots?

20 Not really, but carrots contain a lot of vitamin A, which does keep our eyes healthy.

21 In the future, carrots may actually be used in wars.

22 Scottish researchers have discovered a way to turn carrots into a very strong and light material.

23 It can even be used to make battleships.

24 This new material has already been used to make snowboards and bicycles.

25 Tomatoes, the Scariest Vegetables

26 We all know that tomatoes are good for our health.

27 Up until the 1800s, however, most Americans thought that tomatoes were poisonous.

28 In 1820, a man named Robert Johnson wanted to prove that tomatoes were safe to eat.

29 So, he ate a basket of tomatoes in front of many people watching him.

30 They all expected him to die, but nothing happened to him.

31 Ever since then, Americans have enjoyed eating tomatoes.

32 We are no longer afraid of tomatoes, but some insects are still scared of them.

33 If you want to keep insects away from your room, place a bowl of crushed tomatoes in a corner of your room.

34 Insects will not come near the tomatoes.

구석구석지문 TEST Step 1 — p.64

Inventions from Plants

1. good way to produce
2. battery invented from, of using, characteristic of sunflowers
3. Like, faces, during the day, more electricity than other batteries

After You Read A Read and Match

1. Spinach
2. secret, super power
3. one of the ten healthiest foods
4. with, to find bombs hidden
5. Carrots
6. to make snowboards
7. into, light material
8. which keeps our eyes healthy
9. Tomatoes
10. keeping insects away
11. poisonous until

Write

1. are good for
2. keep your heart healthy, lower blood pressure
3. solve your skin problems
4. mixed with, makes, soft, clear
5. In addition, help, lose weight
6. stay full for a long time
7. help, stay healthy

---

3. • one of the ten healthiest foods on the planet
4. • used with sensors to find bombs hidden in the ground
5. 2. Carrots
6. • used to make snowboards and bicycles
7. • made into a very strong and light material
8. • containing a lot of vitamin A, which keeps our eyes healthy
9. 3. Tomatoes
10. • good for keeping insects away
11. • considered poisonous until the 1800s

Write

1. Potatoes are good for your health.
2. They keep your heart healthy because they lower blood pressure.
3. They also solve your skin problems.
4. Potato juice mixed with honey makes your skin soft and clear.
5. In addition, they help you lose weight.
6. If you eat potatoes, you will stay full for a long time.
7. Potatoes help you stay healthy in many ways.

구석구석지문 TEST Step 2 — p.65

Inventions from Plants

1. The Sunflower Battery is a good way to produce energy.
2. It is a battery invented from the idea of using the characteristic of sunflowers.
3. Like sunflowers, it faces the sun during the day, so it produces more electricity than other batteries.

After You Read A Read and Match

1. 1. Spinach
2. • the secret of Popeye's super power

단어 TEST Step 1   p.66

01 온실	02 수확하다	03 광고
04 전시회, 박람회	05 수중의, 물속에서	06 해양의, 바다의
07 전국적인	08 해외의	
09 홍보하다, 촉진하다		10 교량, 다리
11 지역 공동체	12 감동받은	13 유산
14 환경	15 해산물	16 몇몇의
17 생계를 책임지는 사람, 가장		18 여성의
19 화산의, 화산 작용에 의한		20 세계적으로
21 완성[완료]하다	22 호흡하다	23 파괴하다
24 폭포	25 좁은 길	
26 무형의, 만질 수 없는		27 해파리
28 누르다; 언론, 기자	29 지하의	30 적합한, 적절한
31 청중	32 과로하다	33 경로, 길
34 깨닫다, 인식하다	35 ~을 기원하다	36 우연히 ~하다
37 ~을 따라 걷다	38 두 서너 개의	39 ~에 들어가다
40 ~에 적절하다	41 강의하다, 연설하다	
42 조금, 약간	43 ~에 유익하다	

단어 TEST Step 2   p.67

01 waterfall	02 ad(=advertisement)	
03 path	04 overwork	05 bridge
06 trail	07 underground	08 worldwide
09 volcanic	10 greenhouse	11 destroy
12 exhibition	13 promote	14 complete
15 several	16 breadwinner	17 suitable
18 female	19 press	20 community
21 intangible	22 underwater	23 jellyfish
24 marine	25 harvest	26 audience
27 heritage	28 breathe	29 nationwide
30 overseas	31 realize	32 tightly
33 beat	34 good harvest	35 go on vacation
36 get into	37 happen to	38 walk along
39 be good for	40 keep -ing	41 cheer up
42 give (someone) a hand		
43 give a presentation		

단어 TEST Step 3   p.68

1 harvest, 수확하다   2 underground, 지하의

3 complete, 완성[완료]하다   4 beat, (북 등을 치는) 소리

5 waterfall, 폭포   6 suitable, 적합한   7 breathe, 호흡하다

8 community, 지역 공동체   9 heritage, 유산

10 intangible, 무형의, 만질 수 없는   11 overseas, 해외의

12 seafood, 해산물   13 destroy, 파괴하다   14 ad, 광고

15 bridge, 다리   16 breadwinner, 생계를 책임지는 사람, 가장

대화문 TEST Step 1   p.69~70

Listen & Speak 1 A-1

look at, bridge, ad, where the photo was taken / How do, know / went there with, last summer

Listen & Speak 1 A-2

Look over I wonder why, waiting in line / waiting to get into / famous / on / should try, then

Listen & Speak 2 A-1

I'd like to borrow / Here, are / explain how to use it / Press, what to do

Listen & Speak 2 A-2

Are, going somewhere / going to, walk along / Could you explain what that is / long hiking path around / enjoy your trip

Communicate A

I wonder where, coming from / over there, check it out / strong beat, traditional / called, a kind of community / Could you explain a little bit / traditionally, cheer up, wish for. good harvest / are dancing to, rhythm / part of, completes / Let's join / Why not

Progress Check 1

I wonder why there are so many cars / Lots of, going on vacation / why don't we, too

Progress Check 2

Excuse, copy machine / how to make double-sided copies / Press, double-sided copies, press

대화문 TEST Step 2   p.71~72

Listen & Speak 1 A-1

G: Wow, look at the bridge in this ad. I wonder where the photo was taken.

B: That's Gwangandaegyo in Busan.

G: How do you know that?

B: I went there with my family last summer.

Listen & Speak 1 A-2

B: Look over there. I wonder why there are so many people waiting in line.

G: They're waiting to get into the new bakery there.

B: Why? Is it famous?

G: Yes. It was on a TV program.

B: Really? We should try their bread then.

G: Sure.

Listen & Speak 2 A-1

W: Excuse me, I'd like to borrow an audio guide.

M: Here you are.

W: Could you explain how to use it?

M: Sure. Press this button, and it'll tell you what to do.

Listen & Speak 2 A-2

B: Are you going somewhere this summer?

G: I'm going to Jejudo to walk along the Jeju Olle Trail.

B: The Jeju Olle Trail? Could you explain what that is?

G: It's a long hiking path around Jejudo.

B: Oh, I see. I hope you enjoy your trip!

Communicate A

Jaden: Do you hear that? I wonder where that music is coming from.

Yuri: I think it's coming from over there. Do you want to go and check it out?

Jaden: Yes, I love that strong beat. Is it traditional Korean music?

Yuri: Yes, it's called nongak. It's a kind of community band music.

Jaden: Nongak? Could you explain a little bit more about it?

Yuri: It's traditionally used to cheer up farmers and wish for a good harvest.

Jaden: I see. Look! Some people are dancing to the rhythm.

Yuri: Yes, that's a big part of nongak. Dancing together completes the music.

Jaden: Let's join them.

Yuri: Sure. Why not?

Progress Check 1

W: Look over there. I wonder why there are so many cars on the road.

M: Lots of people are going on vacation this weekend.

W: Really? Then, why don't we go somewhere, too?

M: O.K.

Progress Check 2

B: Excuse me, I'd like to use a copy machine.

W: O.K. You can use this machine.

B: Could you explain how to make double-sided copies?

W: Sure. Press the button for double-sided copies, and then press the start button.

B: Thank you.

본문 TEST Step 1 p.73~74

01 Haenyeo, Female Divers

02 several, underwater, promoted, worldwide

03 female, harvest, without, breathing

04 made, Intangible, Heritage list

05 last, interviewed, experience, taking

06 become interested in taking

07 One day, happened to   08 was surprised to find

09 Until, seen, looked, tired

10 kept laughing, been, over

11 realized, should take   12 isn't it difficult to

13 At, why I wanted

14 looked pretty in, wetsuits

15 So, very special

16 show, culture to, world

17 opened up, then

18 make them look beautiful

19 tell us more about   20 so special about

21 can tell you, things

22 symbol, strong women

23 volcanic, suitable, farming, breadwinners

24 form, own, each other

25 example, more-experienced, less-experienced

26 stay, without, breathing, catch

27 good for, underwater environment

28 marine, time, destory, place

29 what, planning, do, future

30 attended, exhibition, talk, lives

31 finished, held, hand tightly

32 said to, so much

33 such a special person

34 crying with happiness

35 was deeply moved

36 never forget, moment, continue

37 more beautiful stories about

01 Female Divers
02 underwater photographer, has promoted, worldwide
03 female divers, without any breathing devices
04 made UNESCO's Intangible Cultural Heritage list
05 was interviewed, experience of taking picutres
06 become interested in taking
07 One day, happened to
08 was surprised to find, was enjoying
09 Until then, had only seen, looked very tired
10 kept laughing, for over five hours
11 realized, should take pictures
12 isn't it difficult to take pictures
13 At first, why I wanted
14 looked pretty in their wetsuits
15 very special   16 show, to
17 opened up, then
18 Of course, make them, beautiful
19 more about   20 so special
21 can tell you
22 symbol of strong women
23 which, is not suitable for, have become the breadwinners for
24 form, own communities, each other
25 more-experienced, less-experienced
26 because, without, breathing devices, can't catch
27 is good for, underwater environment
28 Catching, at one time in one place can destory
29 what, planning to do
30 attended, overseas exhibition, give a talk
31 held my hand tightly
32 so much
33 whole life, such a special person
34 crying with happiness
35 was deeply moved
36 can never forget, continue to take
37 more beautiful stories about them

1 해녀, 한국의 여성 잠수부
2 지난 몇 년 동안, 수중 사진작가 Zin Kim은 제주 해녀 문화를 전 세계에 홍보해 왔다.
3 해녀는 어떤 호흡 장치도 사용하지 않고 해산물을 채취하는 한국의 여성 잠수부들이다.
4 그들의 문화는 2016년에 유네스코 무형문화유산에 등재되었다.
5 지난주 그녀의 작업실에서, Zin Kim과 해녀의 사진을 찍는 그녀의 경험에 대해 인터뷰를 했다.
6 Q. 어떻게 해녀의 사진을 찍는 것에 관심을 가지게 되었나요?
7 어느 날, 저는 우연히 한 해녀의 사진을 찍게 되었어요.
8 저는 그녀가 자신의 일을 즐겁게 하는 것을 보고 놀랐습니다.
9 그때까지, 저는 흑백 사진 속의 아주 지친 모습의 해녀만 봐 왔죠.
10 하지만, 그녀는 다섯 시간이 넘도록 물속에 있은 후에도 계속 웃었어요.
11 저는 그때 해녀의 사진을 찍어야겠다고 깨달았어요.
12 Q. 작가님은 아름다운 해녀 사진들을 찍으시는데, 그들의 사진을 찍는 것이 어렵진 않으신가요?
13 처음에, 그들은 제가 왜 자신들의 사진을 찍으려고 하는지 이해하지 못했어요.
14 그들은 잠수복을 입은 자신들의 모습이 예뻐 보인다고 생각하지 않았으니까요.
15 그래서, 제가 그들에게 말했죠, "여러분들은 아주 특별해요.
16 저는 여러분의 문화를 세계에 알리고 싶어요."
17 그들은 그때 제게 마음을 열었어요.
18 물론, 저 또한 그들에게 제 사진 속에서 그들을 아름답게 보이도록 하겠다고 약속했지요.
19 Q. 해녀에 대해서 더 말씀해 주시겠어요?
20 그들은 무엇이 그렇게 특별한가요?
21 세 가지를 말씀 드릴게요.
22 첫 번째로, 해녀들은 강인한 여성의 상징이에요.
23 제주도는 화산섬이고, 이는 농사에 적합하지 않아서 많은 해녀들이 가족들의 생계비를 버는 가장이 되어 왔어요.
24 둘째로, 해녀들은 그들 자신의 공동체를 조직하고 서로 도와요.
25 예를 들어, 경험이 더 많은 해녀들이 경험이 적은 해녀들을 훈련시키지요.
26 세 번째로, 어떤 호흡 장치도 사용하지 않고 물속에 머물기 때문에, 해녀는 많은 해산물을 채취할 수가 없어요.
27 이것은 수중 환경에 좋은 것이지요.
28 한 번에 한 장소에서 너무 많은 해양생물을 채취하는 것은 바다를 파괴할 수 있으니까요.
29 Q. 마지막으로, 앞으로 계획하고 있는 것에 대해 말씀해 주세요.
30 예전에 두 명의 해녀들과 함께 그들의 삶에 대해 이야기하기 위해 해외에서 열리는 박람회에 참가한 적이 있어요.
31 제가 연설을 마쳤을 때, 해녀 중 한 분이 제 손을 꼭 잡았어요.
32 그분이 말했죠, "너무 고마워.
33 내 평생 내가 이렇게 특별한 사람이라는 걸 미처 알지 못했어."
34 그녀는 행복해서 울고 있었어요.
35 청중들 모두가 깊은 감동을 받았어요.
36 전 그 순간을 절대 잊을 수가 없기 때문에 해녀의 사진을 계속해서 찍을 거예요.
37 저는 그들에 대한 더 많은 아름다운 이야기들을 세계의 더 많은 사람들에게 알려 주고 싶어요.

1 Haenyeo, Female Divers of Korea

2 For the past several years, the underwater photographer Zin Kim has promoted the culture of Jeju haenyeo worldwide.

3 Haenyeo are Korean female divers who harvest seafood without any breathing devices.

4 Their culture made UNESCO's Intangible Cultural Heritage list in 2016.

5 At her studio last week, Zin Kim was interviewed about her experience of taking pictures of haenyeo.

6 Q. How did you become interested in taking photos of haenyeo?

7 One day, I happened to take pictures of a haenyeo.

8 I was surprised to find that she was enjoying her job.

9 Until then, I had only seen black-and-white photos of haenyeo who looked very tired.

10 However, she kept laughing even after she had been in the water for over five hours.

11 I realized then that I should take pictures of haenyeo.

12 Q. You take beautiful pictures of them, but isn't it difficult to take pictures of haenyeo?

13 At first, they didn't understand why I wanted to take their pictures.

14 They didn't think they looked pretty in their wetsuits.

15 So, I said to them, "You're very special.

16 I want to show your culture to the world."

17 They opened up to me then.

18 Of course, I also promised them that I would make them look beautiful in my pictures.

19 Q. Could you tell us more about haenyeo?

20 What's so special about them?

21 I can tell you three things.

22 First, haenyeo are a symbol of strong women.

23 Jejudo, which is a volcanic island, is not suitable for farming, so many haenyeo have become the breadwinners for their families.

24 Second, haenyeo form their own communities and help each other.

25 For example, more-experienced haenyeo train less-experienced haenyeo.

26 Third, because they stay in the water without any breathing devices, haenyeo can't catch a lot of seafood.

27 This is good for the underwater environment.

28 Catching too much marine life at one time in one place can destroy the ocean.

29 Q. Lastly, please tell us what you're planning to do in the future.

30 I once attended an overseas exhibition with a couple of haenyeo to give a talk about their lives.

31 When I finished my talk, one of the haenyeo held my hand tightly.

32 She said to me, "Thank you so much.

33 I've never known in my whole life that I was such a special person."

34 She was crying with happiness.

35 Everyone in the audience was deeply moved.

36 I can never forget that moment, so I'll continue to take pictures of haenyeo.

37 I want to tell more beautiful stories about them to many more people in the world.

Communicate – B Talk and Play

1. what these are
2. called songpyeon
3. explain more about
4. traditional Korean rice cakes

After You Read A

1. Photographer Who Loves
2. an underwater photographer, has promoted, worldwide
3. decided to take pictures, when she met, who was enjoying
4. It, easy taking, at first
5. However, that, their culture to the world, finally opened their minds
6. At an overseas exhibition, gave a talk
7. one of, was crying with happiness
8. would continue to take

Write

1. makes coffee drinks for a living
2. became a barista, had found out about his passion
3. His favorite part of, decorating coffee with, watching, enjoying
4. planning to open

Communicate – B Talk and Play

1. A: I wonder what these are.

2. B: They're called songpyeon.

3. A: Could you explain more about them?

4. B: They're traditional Korean rice cakes.

After You Read A

1. A Photographer Who Loves Haenyeo

2. Zin Kim, an underwater photographer, has promoted the culture of Jeju haenyeo worldwide.

3. She decided to take pictures of them when she met a haenyeo who was enjoying her job.

4. It was not easy taking their pictures at first.

5. However, when she told them that she wanted to show their culture to the world, the haenyeo finally opened their minds.

6. At an overseas exhibition, she gave a talk about the lives of haenyeo.

7. After her speech, one of the haenyeo was crying with happiness.

8. Zin Kim said that she would continue to take pictures of haenyeo.

Write

1. Kim Minho is a barista. He makes coffee drinks for a living.

2. He became a barista after he had found out about his passion for coffee.

3. His favorite part of his job is decorating coffee with hot milk and watching his customers enjoying it.

4. He is planning to open his own coffee shop.

MEMO

MEMO

적중 **1○○** + 특별부록

Plan B

우리학교
최신기출

미래 · 최연희 교과서를 배우는

학교 시험문제 분석 · 모음 · 해설집

전국단위 학교 시험문제 수집 및 분석
출제 빈도가 높은 문제 위주로 선별
문제 풀이에 필요한 상세한 해설

중3-1
영어

미래 · 최연희

◎ 선택형 문항의 답안은 컴퓨터용 수정 싸인펜을 사용하여 OMR 답안지에 바르게 표기하시오.
◎ 서술형 문제는 답을 답안지에 반드시 검정 볼펜으로 쓰시오.
◎ 총 26문항 100점 만점입니다. 문항별 배점은 각 문항에 표시되어 있습니다.

[경기 ○○중]

1. 다음 중 단어의 연결 관계가 나머지와 <u>다른</u> 하나는? (3점)

① love – lovely
② easy – easily
③ careful – carefully
④ complete – completely
⑤ immediate – immediately

[전북 ○○중]

2. 다음 대화의 흐름상, Anna가 밑줄 친 문장을 말한 의도로 가장 적절한 것은? (3점)

Suho: I'm planning to send some books to children in Africa. My aunt told me that they need books to read.
Anna: Good idea, Suho! Wait, aren't your books in Korean?
Suho: Oh, that's a problem.
Anna: Well, how about translating them into English?
Suho: Translating? That's a great idea, Anna.
Anna: <u>Do you want me to help you?</u>
Suho: Sure. If we run into any difficult expressions, let's ask our English teacher for help.
Anna: O.K. It's really great that we can help the children in Africa.

① 수호에게 도움을 제공하려고
② 수호를 생일 파티에 초대하려고
③ 자신이 생각한 방법을 제안하려고
④ 상대방의 의도를 물어보려고
⑤ 미래의 계획에 대해 질문하려고

[충북 ○○중]

3. Why do they want to collect signatures from students? (4점)

Bill: Sujin, can you help us?
Sujin: Sure. What can I do for you?
Bill: We're going to ask the school to make a parking space for bicycles.
Sujin: That's a great idea. Do you want me to help you collect signatures from students?
Bill: That would help us a lot. Thanks!

① To buy something for business
② To ask something of the school
③ To tell students about the school trip
④ To donate for helping people
⑤ To help people in danger

[강원 ○○중]

4. 주어진 말 다음에 이어질 대화의 순서로 가장 알맞은 것은? (4점)

A: What are you going to read for the book review homework?

(a) Oh, could you lend it to me?
(b) Good idea. I have the perfect book for you.
(c) I'm thinking of reading a book about young leaders.
(d) Sure. I'll bring it tomorrow.

① (a)-(b)-(c)-(d)
② (b)-(a)-(d)-(c)
③ (c)-(b)-(a)-(d)
④ (c)-(d)-(a)-(b)
⑤ (d)-(c)-(b)-(a)

5. 다음 대화의 밑줄 친 ⓐ~ⓔ 중에서 가리키는 대상이 나머지 넷과 다른 것은? (4점)

> Suho: Anna, do you have any children's books you don't read any longer?
>
> Anna: Sure. Why?
>
> Suho: I'm thinking of sending some books to children in Africa. My aunt told me that ⓐthey need books to read.
>
> Anna: Good idea, Suho! Wait, aren't your books in Korean?
>
> Suho: Oh, that's a problem.
>
> Anna: Well, how about translating ⓑthem into English?
>
> Suho: Translating? Oh, I see. African children can't read ⓒthem. If ⓓthey are translated into English, they can read ⓔthem. That's a great idea, Anna.
>
> Anna: O.K. It's really great that we can help the children in Africa.

① ⓐ ② ⓑ ③ ⓒ ④ ⓓ ⑤ ⓔ

6. 다음 대화를 한 뒤에 두 사람이 주말에 방문할 장소는? (3점)

> G: What are you doing this weekend?
>
> B: I'm thinking of doing some volunteer work at the child-care center.
>
> G: What would you do there?
>
> B: I would probably read some books to the children.
>
> G: That sounds interesting. Can I join you?
>
> B: Of course.

① bookstore   ② library

③ kindergarten   ④ child-care center

⑤ children's amusement park

7. 다음 대화 후에 두 사람이 할 일로 알맞은 것은? (4점)

> B: Sujin, can you help us?
>
> G: Sure. What can I do for you?
>
> B: We're going to ask the school to make a parking space for bicycles.
>
> G: That's a great idea. Do you want me to help you collect signatures from students?
>
> B: That would help us a lot. Thanks!

① 주차장 청소하기

② 함께 자전거 타기

③ 주차장 가는 길 안내하기

④ 학생들로부터 서명 받기

⑤ 자전거 타는 법 가르쳐 주기

8. 다음 중, 대화의 짝이 어색한 것은? (4점)

① A: What are you doing this weekend?

　B: I'm planning to do some volunteer work at a child-care center.

② A: What are you doing right now?

　B: I'm going to read a book about endangered animals next Monday.

③ A: I'm hungry. Is there anything to eat?

　B: Do you want me to make a sandwich?

④ A: Oh, we don't have any eggs for the sandwich.

　B: Let me go out and buy some eggs.

⑤ A: What is your plan for this vacation?

　B: I'm planning to review what we learned in English class.

[9~10] 다음 대화를 읽고 물음에 답하시오.

Suho: Anna, do you have any children's books you don't read any longer?
Anna: Sure. Why?
Suho: ⓐI'm thinking of sending some books to children in Africa. My aunt told me that they need books to read.
Anna: Good idea, Suho! Wait, aren't your books in Korean?
Suho: Oh, that's a problem.
Anna: Well, how about translating them into English?
Suho: Translating? That's a great idea, Anna.
Anna: Do you want me to help you?
Suho: Sure. If we run into any difficult expressions, let's ask our English teacher for help.
Anna: O.K. It's really great that we can help the children in Africa.

9. 위 대화의 밑줄 친 ⓐ와 전달하고자 하는 의미가 같은 것은? (4점)

① You'd better send some books
② I want you to send some books
③ It's too difficult to send some books
④ I'm considering sending some books
⑤ It would be a good idea to send some books

10. 위 대화로 알 수 있는 내용이 <u>아닌</u> 것은? (3점)

① Anna는 읽지 않는 어린이용 책이 좀 있다.
② Suho는 아프리카 아이들이 읽을 책을 보내려고 한다.
③ Suho의 이모가 아프리카 어린이들에게 학용품을 보내주라고 제안했다.
④ Suho와 Anna는 아프리카 아이들에게 보낼 책을 영어로 번역할 것이다.
⑤ Suho와 Anna는 어려운 표현이 나오면 영어 선생님께 도움을 청할 것이다.

11. 다음 중 어법상 <u>어색한</u> 것은? (4점)

① Give me what is in your hand.
② What I want for Christmas is a dress.
③ What you do today can change the world.
④ Is this the cap that you are looking for?
⑤ Thank you! This is exactly the present what I wanted.

12. 다음 중 빈칸에 'although'가 어울리는 것의 개수는? (4점)

• I went to hospital _____ I had a cold.
• She was sad _____ she lost her money.
• He missed the bus _____ he got up late.
• She passed the test _____ it was difficult.
• You should clean your room _____ you don't want to.

① 1개 ② 2개 ③ 3개 ④ 4개 ⑤ 5개

13. 다음 문장의 괄호 (A), (B), (C) 안에서 문맥에 맞는 접속사로 가장 적절한 것은? (4점)

• I didn't pass the exam (A)[because / although] I studied hard.
• It was cold, (B)[but / although] she did not wear a jacket.
• He is strong (C)[since / although] he is very old.

	(A)	(B)	(C)
①	because	but	since
②	because	although	although
③	although	but	although
④	although	although	although
⑤	although	although	since

[14~17] 다음 글을 읽고 물음에 답하시오.

(A) Four months later, our family drove to the Gulf of Mexico to deliver the things ⓐ _____ we collected and helped to save the animals. While we were working there, we learned something very useful. When we put mayonnaise into a turtle's throat, the turtle threw up. That way, we were able to get oil out of turtles.

(B) After we came home, we created an educational project about ⓑ_____ we could reduce plastic waste. In addition to this, our organization continues to do various projects to save animals. We started small, but we are making a big difference. ⓒ_____ you do today can change the world, so take that first step.

(C) A terrible oil spill occurred in the Gulf of Mexico. A lot of sea animals were completely covered with oil, and they were dying. So we started collecting animal rescue supplies from everyone in our neighborhood.

(D) On our last day, we met a marine life specialist. She said that plastic waste is more dangerous to sea animals than oil spills are. A lot of sea animals and sea birds die from eating plastic waste.   *I=Cater

14. 위 글에서 찾을 수 없는 단어의 영영풀이는? (4점)

① v. to make it smaller in size or amount, or less in degree

② n. all the people in a group or country who are of a similar age

③ a. relating to the sea or to the animals and plants that live in the sea

④ n. a person who has a particular skill or knows a lot about a particular subject

⑤ v. help someone or something to avoid harm or to escape from a dangerous or unpleasant situation

15. 위 글의 ⓐ~ⓒ에 들어갈 단어로 가장 적절하게 짝지어진 것은?   (4점)

	ⓐ	ⓑ	ⓒ
①	which	what	Why
②	which	how	What
③	that	how	Why
④	that	which	What
⑤	what	which	That

16. 위 글의 (A)~(D)를 글의 흐름에 맞게 배열한 것은?   (4점)

① (A)-(B)-(C)-(D)   ② (B)-(A)-(C)-(D)
③ (B)-(D)-(A)-(C)   ④ (C)-(A)-(D)-(B)
⑤ (D)-(B)-(C)-(A)

17. 위 글을 읽고 답할 수 <u>없는</u> 질문은?   (4점)

① When did a terrible oil spill occur?

② How could Carter get oil out of turtles?

③ What did Carter do after he came home?

④ Why did Carter's family go to the Gulf of Mexico?

⑤ Who did Carter meet on his last day?

18. 다음 빈칸에 공통으로 들어갈 알맞은 관계대명사를 쓰시오.   (5점)

• This is exactly _____ I wanted.
• Is this _____ you are looking for?

답: _____

[19~21] 다음 글을 읽고 물음에 답하시오.

When I was five, my little sister Olivia and I each adopted a cheetah. Did we (가)raise cheetahs at home? No, we donated to a charity (A)that ⓐprotect wild cheetahs in South Africa. Our parents told us (B)that if we did not protect them, we might not be able to see cheetahs in the near future.
We soon became interested in ⓑhelp other endangered animals. ⓒA little years later, with help from our parents, we created a non-profit organization to protect them. We wanted the next generation to ⓓbe able to see these animals, so we named our organization One More Generation. We studied endangered animals and ⓔeducate our friends about them.

19. 위 글의 밑줄 친 ⓐ~ⓔ 중, 어법상 옳은 것은? (3점)

① ⓐ   ② ⓑ   ③ ⓒ   ④ ⓓ   ⑤ ⓔ

20. 위 글의 (가)raise와 같은 의미로 쓰인 것은? (4점)

① The government is discussing raising taxes.
② Raise your voice so that I can hear you.
③ If you have any questions, just raise your hand.
④ We will need to raise more money next year.
⑤ I was born in Seoul and raised by my grandparents.

21. 위 글의 (A), (B)의 that과 쓰임이 같은 것을 다음 중에서 찾아 바르게 짝지은 것은? (4점)

㉠ She has two sons that are doctors.
㉡ They proved that he was right.
㉢ He promised that he would never be late.
㉣ I think that you can do it better.
㉤ Her gift was a toy car that could turn into a robot.

	(A)	(B)
①	㉠, ㉡	㉢, ㉣, ㉤
②	㉠, ㉤	㉡, ㉢, ㉣
③	㉡, ㉣	㉠, ㉣, ㉤
④	㉡, ㉢	㉠, ㉣, ㉤
⑤	㉢, ㉤	㉠, ㉡, ㉣

22. 다음 글의 내용과 일치하지 않는 것은? (4점)

One day, a terrible oil spill occurred in the Gulf of Mexico. A lot of sea animals were completely covered with oil, and they were dying. We had to do something. We started collecting animal rescue supplies such as pet carrying cages and rubber gloves from everyone in our neighborhood. Four months later, our family drove to the Gulf of Mexico to deliver what we collected and helped to save the animals. While we were working there, we learned something very useful. When we put mayonnaise into a turtle's throat, the turtle threw up. That way, we were able to get oil out of turtles. I never knew mayonnaise could be used to save animals!

① 멕시코만에서 기름이 유출되었다.
② 우리는 이웃들에게 동물 구조 물품들을 나눠 주었다.
③ 우리 가족은 멕시코만으로 가서 동물 구조를 도왔다.
④ 우리는 멕시코만에서 일하는 동안 유용한 것을 배웠다.
⑤ 우리는 마요네즈를 거북이 목구멍에 집어넣어 기름을 토하게 했다.

[23~25] 다음 글을 읽고 물음에 답하시오.

Then one day, a ⓐterrible oil spill occurred in the Gulf of Mexico. A lot of sea animals were completely covered with oil, and they were dying. We had to do something. We started collecting animal rescue supplies such as pet carrying cages and rubber gloves from everyone in our neighborhood.

Four months later, our family drove to the Gulf of Mexico to deliver (A)[that / what] we collected and helped to save the animals. While we were working there, we learned something very ⓑuseful. When we put mayonnaise into a turtle's throat, the turtle threw up. That way, we were ⓒable to get oil out of turtles. I never knew mayonnaise could (B)[use / be used] to save animals!

On our last day, we met a marine life specialist. She told us (C)[that / what] plastic waste is more dangerous to sea animals than oil spills are. A lot of sea animals and sea birds die from eating plastic waste.

After we came home, we created an educational project about how to ⓓincrease plastic waste. In addition to this, our organization continues to do various projects to save animals. Although we started small, we are making a ⓔbig difference. What you do today can change the world, so take that first step!

23. 위 글의 밑줄 친 ⓐ~ⓔ 중, 문맥상 적절하지 않은 것은? (4점)

① ⓐ ② ⓑ ③ ⓒ ④ ⓓ ⑤ ⓔ

24. 위 글의 괄호 (A), (B), (C) 안에서 어법적으로 올바른 것으로 짝지어진 것은? (4점)

	(A)	(B)	(C)
①	that	use	that
②	that	be used	that
③	what	be used	that
④	what	be used	what
⑤	what	use	what

25. 위 글의 내용과 일치하는 것은? (4점)

① 'I'의 동네에서 기름 유출 사고가 발생했다.
② 'we'는 멕시코 만에서 해양 생물 전문가를 만났다.
③ 'we'는 멕시코 만에서 동물 구조 물품들을 수집하였다.
④ 'I'는 마요네즈를 이용하여 거북이를 살리는 방법을 이웃들에게 가르쳐주었다.
⑤ 기름 유출은 플라스틱 폐기물보다 더 바다동물들에게 위험하다.

26. 다음 글의 제목으로 가장 알맞은 것은? (3점)

Asian black bears have a white V-shape on their chests. They mostly live in forests in Asia. They've become endangered because people hunt them for their body parts and destroy forests. We'll tell you what you can do for them. First, use less paper to protect forests. Second, you should not buy any Asian black bear products.

① Asian Black Bears
② Forests in Asia
③ Endangered Animals
④ People Who Hunt
⑤ Using Less Paper

◎ 선택형 문항의 답안은 컴퓨터용 수정 싸인펜을 사용하여 OMR 답안지에 바르게 표기하시오.
◎ 서술형 문제는 답을 답안지에 반드시 검정 볼펜으로 쓰시오.
◎ 총 28문항 100점 만점입니다. 문항별 배점은 각 문항에 표시되어 있습니다.

[전북 ○○중]

1. 다음 문장의 밑줄 친 어휘가 문장의 해석과 어울리지 <u>않는</u> 것은? (4점)

① He is facing a <u>serious</u> problem.
  → 그는 심각한 문제에 직면하고 있다.

② My grandmother knows many great <u>expressions.</u>
  → 우리 할머니는 많은 훌륭한 표현들을 알고 계신다.

③ Many fossils <u>proved</u> his theory.
  → 많은 화석이 그의 이론을 반박했다.

④ Don't give up hope of <u>rescue.</u>
  → 구조의 희망을 포기하지 마세요.

⑤ Lots of events will <u>occur</u> this year.
  → 올해 많은 일들이 일어날 것이다.

[대전 ○○중]

2. 다음 대화 후 'Jisoo'가 'Mike'를 돕기 위해 할 행동으로 가장 적절한 것은? (3점)

Mike: Jisoo, can you help us?
Jisoo: Sure. What can I do for you?
Mike: We're going to ask the school to make a parking space for bicycles.
Jisoo: That's a great idea. Do you want me to help you collect signatures from students?
Mike: That would help us a lot. Thanks!

① 자전거 빌려주기
② 자전거로 같이 등교하기
③ 학생들에게서 서명 모으기
④ 자전거 타는 법 알려주기
⑤ 학교에 자전거 주차 구역 만들기

[전북 ○○중]

3. 다음 대화에서 알 수 있는 것은? (2점)

B: What's your plan for this weekend?
G: I'm going to ride a bike.
B: Sounds good. Can I join you?
G: Sure. Let's meet in front of the park at ten.
B: O.K.

① 방학 계획
② 가입할 동아리
③ 약속 시간
④ 자전거 종류
⑤ 자전거의 안정성

[충북 ○○중]

4. 다음 대화의 밑줄 친 ⓐ~ⓓ 중, 어울리지 않는 대화의 의도는? (4점)

Suho: Anna, do you have any children's books you don't read any longer?
Anna: Sure. Why?
Suho: ⓐI'm thinking of sending some books to children in Africa. My aunt told me that they need books to read.
Anna: Good idea, Suho! Wait, aren't your books in Korean?
Suho: Oh, that's a problem.
Anna: ⓑWell, how about translating them into English?
Suho: Translating? ⓒThat's a great idea, Anna.
Anna: ⓓDo you want me to help you?
Suho: Sure. If we run into any difficult expressions. Let's ask our English teacher for help.

① 찬성하기
② 도움 제안하기
③ 의향 말하기
④ 사과하기
⑤ 제안하기

[5~6] 다음 대화를 읽고 물음에 답하시오.

Suho: Anna, do you have any children's books that you don't read any longer?

Anna: Sure. Why?

Suho: I'm thinking of (A)_____ some books to children in Africa. My aunt told me that they need books to read.

Anna: Good idea, Suho! Wait, aren't your books in Korean?

Suho: Oh, ⓐthat's a problem.

Anna: Well, how about (B)_____ them to English?

Suho: That's a great idea, Anna.

Anna: Do you want me to help you?

Suho: Sure. If we run into any difficult expressions, let's ask our English teacher for help.

Anna: O.K. It's really great that we can help the children in Africa.

5. 위 대화의 빈칸 (A), (B)에 어법상 적절한 것은? (4점)

	(A)	(B)
①	send	translate
②	sent	translating
③	sent	translated
④	sending	translate
⑤	sending	translating

6. 위 대화의 밑줄 친 ⓐ가 가리키는 것은? (4점)

① Anna에게 읽지 않은 책이 있는 것

② 아프리카로 책을 보내기가 어려운 것

③ Suho의 책이 한국어로 되어 있는 것

④ Anna와 Suho가 번역 경험이 없는 것

⑤ 아프리카의 아이들이 읽을 책이 부족한 것

7. 다음 대화에서 알 수 없는 것은? (3점)

Sangho: Jane, what are you doing this weekend?

Jane: I'm thinking of going for a bike ride.

Sangho: Sounds good. Can I join you?

Jane: Sure. Sangho, let's meet in front of the park at ten.

Sangho: O.K.

① 대화의 목적   ② 주말 계획

③ 약속 시간   ④ 약속 장소

⑤ 두 사람의 관계

8. 문맥상 빈칸에 들어갈 가장 적절한 말은? (4점)

G: _____?

B: I'm thinking of doing some volunteer work at the child-care center.

G: What would you do there?

B: I would probably read some books to the children.

G: That sounds interesting. Can I join you?

B: Of course.

① What did you do last weekend?

② What can I do for you?

③ What makes you think so?

④ How did you go to the child-care center?

⑤ What are you doing this weekend?

9. 밑줄 친 부분이 어법상 어색한 것은? (3점)

① I believe <u>what</u> you said.

② <u>What</u> I want to eat is pizza.

③ They were surprised at <u>what</u> they saw.

④ This is the book <u>what</u> I am looking for.

⑤ He knows <u>what</u> his mom wants for her birthday present.

[10~11] 다음 대화를 읽고 물음에 답하시오.

> Suho: Anna, do you have any children's books you don't read any longer?
> Anna: Sure. Why?
> Suho: I'm thinking of sending some books to children in Africa. My aunt told me that they need books to read.
> Anna: Good idea, Suho! Wait, aren't your books in Korean?
> Suho: Oh, that's a problem.
> Anna: Well, how about (A)_____ them into English?
> Suho: (A)_____? That's a great idea, Anna.
> Anna: Do you want me to help you?
> Suho: Sure. If we run into any difficult expressions, let's ask our English teacher for help.
> Anna: O.K. It's really great that we can help the children in Africa.

10. 위 대화의 빈칸 (A)에 공통으로 들어갈 말로 가장 알맞은 것은? (대·소문자 무시) (3점)

① transporting　　② translating
③ reading　　④ taking
⑤ editing

11. What are the speakers talking about? (4점)

① tips for choosing good children's books
② an easy way to read Korean books
③ plans to send books to children in Africa
④ writing some books for children
⑤ choosing interesting English books

12. 다음 대화 중 자연스럽지 않은 것은? (4점)

① A: What's your plan for this year?
　 B: I'm thinking of taking swimming lessons.
② A: What's your plan for this weekend?
　 B: I'm thinking of watching a movie.
③ A: My bike broke down.
　 B: Do you want me to fix it?
　 A: Yes, please.
④ A: I didn't bring an umbrella.
　 B: Do you want me to share your umbrella with you?
　 A: Yes, please.
⑤ A: Do you mind if I sit here?
　 B: No, not at all. Go ahead.

13. 다음 그림의 주인공의 계획을 묘사하기 위하여 빈칸을 완성하시오. 단, 동사 think를 활용할 것. (5점)

정답: I _____ _____ _____ reading books to children.

14. 빈칸에 들어갈 말로 가장 적절한 것은? (3점)

> Many young people are making the world a better place. For example, Carter and Olivia Ries have become leaders in saving animals. _____ they are only teenagers, they have actually made a difference in the world. How were they able to do that? Let's hear from Carter.

① If　　　② After　　　③ Unless
④ Although　　　⑤ Whenever

[15~16] 다음 글을 읽고 물음에 답하시오.

ⓐMany young people are making the world to a better place. For example, Carter and Olivia Ries have become leaders in saving animals. ⓑAlthough they are only teenagers, they have actually made a difference in the world. How were they able to do that? Let's hear from Carter.

When I was five, my little sister Olivia and I each adopted cheetah. Did we raise cheetahs at home? No, ⓒwe donated to a charity that protect wild cheetahs in South Africa. Our parents said that if we did not protect them, we might not be able to see cheetahs in the near future.

We soon became interested in helping other endangered animals. ⓓFew years later, we created a non-profit organization to protecting them. We wanted the next generation to be able to see these animals, ⓔso we named our organization for 'One More Generation'. We studied endangered animals and educated our friends about them.

15. 위 글의 ⓐ~ⓔ 중 어법상 옳은 것은? (4점)

① ⓐ ② ⓑ ③ ⓒ ④ ⓓ ⑤ ⓔ

16. 위 글의 내용과 일치하는 것은? (4점)

① Carter founded the organization to teach parents.

② Olivia's friends said that she should study endangered animals.

③ One More Generation protects wild animals in South Africa to earn money.

④ With the help of the charity, Carter and his sister raised two cheetahs at home.

⑤ Olivia and Carter hoped that the next generation could see the endangered animals.

[17~19] 다음 글을 읽고 물음에 답하시오.

Then one day, a terrible oil spill occurred in the Gulf of Mexico. A lot of sea animals were ⓐcompletely covered with oil, and they were dying. We had to do something. We started ⓑcollecting animal rescue supplies such as pet carrying cages and rubber gloves from everyone in our neighborhood. Four months later, our family drove to the Gulf of Mexico to deliver ⓒwhat we collected and helped ⓓto save the animals. While we were working there, _____.

When we put mayonnaise into a turtle's throat, the turtle threw up. That way, we were able to get oil out of turtles. I never knew mayonnaise could be used ⓔto saving animals!

17. 위 글의 ⓐ~ⓔ 중 어법상 어색한 것은? (4점)

① ⓐ ② ⓑ ③ ⓒ ④ ⓓ ⑤ ⓔ

18. 위 글의 내용과 일치하는 것은? (3점)

① 심각한 기름 유출이 멕시코 전역에서 발생했다.

② 우리는 농민들을 위한 물품을 모으기 시작했다.

③ 4주일 뒤, 우리는 구조 물품을 전달했다.

④ 우리는 해양 동물들을 구조하기 위해 자격증을 땄다.

⑤ 거북이 입에 마요네즈를 넣어 기름을 빼 주었다.

19. 문맥상 빈칸에 들어갈 가장 적절한 말은? (3점)

① we learned everything about saving animals

② we educated our friends about animals

③ we learned something helpful to sea animals

④ we learned how to make rescue supplies

⑤ we taught neighborhood how to save animals

[20~23] 다음 글을 읽고 물음에 답하시오.

Then one day, a (A)[terrible / terrific] oil spill occurred in the Gulf of Mexico. A lot of sea animals were completely covered with oil, and they were dying. We had to do something. We started collecting animal rescue supplies such as pet carrying cages and rubber gloves from everyone in our neighborhood. Four months later, our family drove to the Gulf of Mexico to deliver what we collected and helped to save the animals. While we were working there, we learned something very useful. When we put mayonnaise into a turtle's throat, the turtle threw up. That way, we were able to get oil out of turtles. I never knew mayonnaise could be used to save animals!

On our last day, we met a marine life specialist. She told us that plastic waste is (B)[more / less] dangerous to sea animals than oil spills are. A lot of sea animals and sea birds die from eating plastic waste. After we came home, we created an educational project about how to (C)[reduce / increase] plastic waste. In addition to this, our organization continues to do various projects to save animals. ⓐAlthough we started small, we are making a big difference. What you do today can change the world, so take that first step!

20. 위 글의 내용과 일치하는 것은?　　(3점)

① An oil spill is very dangerous to sea animals.
② The educational project was about the oil spill.
③ Carter sent the rescue supplies to the post office.
④ Carter's neighborhood didn't help him save animals.
⑤ Carter brought mayonnaise from home to help animals covered with oil.

21. 위 글의 괄호 (A), (B), (C) 안에서 가장 적절한 것은?　　(4점)

	(A)	(B)	(C)
①	terrific	more	increase
②	terrific	less	increase
③	terrible	more	increase
④	terrible	less	reduce
⑤	terrible	more	reduce

22. 위 글의 밑줄 친 ⓐ의 예시로서 가장 적절하지 않은 것은?　　(4점)

① 어떤 환경운동가의 1인 시위가 전 세계적인 환경 운동을 불러일으켰다.
② '나 하나쯤이야.' 라는 생각을 하고 '지구의 날'에 진행한 환경 보호 운동에 참여하지 않았다.
③ 한 젊은 간호사의 희생이 SNS를 통해 널리 퍼져 의료진들이 큰 용기와 힘을 얻을 수 있었다.
④ 학생들의 만세 운동이 전국적으로 퍼져 우리 민족이 적극적으로 독립운동을 펼치는 계기가 되었다.
⑤ 기름 유출로 피해를 입은 어민을 돕기 위한 한 명의 자원봉사자 덕분에 생태 환경이 금방 회복될 수 있었다.

23. 위 글을 읽고 배울 수 있는 점으로 가장 거리가 먼 것은?　　(3점)

① We should eat healthy foods.
② We should use less plastic products.
③ Even young people can change the world.
④ Small actions can create a huge change.
⑤ Plastic waste can kill a lot of sea animals.

[24~27] 다음 글을 읽고 물음에 답하시오.

(A)

Then one day, a terrible oil spill occurred in the Gulf of Mexico. A lot of sea animals were completely ⓐcovered with oil, and they were dying. We had to do something. We started collecting animals rescue supplies such as pet carrying cages and rubber gloves from everyone in our neighborhood.

(B)

In addition to this, we continue to do various projects to save animals. Although we started small, we are making a big difference. ⓑWhat you do today can change the world, so take that first step!

(C)

On our last day, we met a marine life specialist. She told us that plastic waste is ⓒdangerous to sea animals than oil spills are. A lot of sea animals and sea birds die from eating plastic waste. After we came home, we created an educational project about ⓓhow to reduce plastic waste.

(D)

Four months later, our family drove to the Gulf of Mexico to deliver the things that we collected and helped to save the animals. While we were working there, we learned something very useful. When we put mayonnaise into a turtle's throat, the turtle threw up. That way, we were able to get oil out of turtles. I never knew mayonnaise could be used ⓔto save animals!

24. 주어진 글 (A)에 이어질 내용을 순서에 맞게 배열한 것으로 가장 적절한 것은? (4점)

① (B)-(D)-(C)　　② (C)-(B)-(D)

③ (C)-(D)-(B)　　④ (D)-(B)-(C)

⑤ (D)-(C)-(B)

25. 밑줄 친 ⓐ~ⓔ 중에서 어법상 어색한 것은? (3점)

① ⓐ　② ⓑ　③ ⓒ　④ ⓓ　⑤ ⓔ

26. 위 글에 관한 내용으로 적절하지 않은 것은? (4점)

① 멕시코만의 기름 유출로 많은 해양 동물들이 죽어 갔다.

② 글쓴이는 해양 동물 구조를 위한 구조용품을 구매해서 구호기관에 보냈다.

③ 글쓴이는 동물 보호를 위해 많은 일을 하고 있다.

④ 글쓴이는 기름 유출보다 플라스틱 쓰레기가 해양 동물에게 더 위험하다고 들었다.

⑤ 마요네즈로 기름을 먹은 거북이를 구할 수 있었다.

27. 위 글의 요지로 가장 적절한 것은? (3점)

① Save wild animals.

② Protect the environment.

③ Don't spill oil into the oceans.

④ Our small activities can change our world.

⑤ Plastic can be the most dangerous thing to animals.

28. 다음 중 밑줄 친 부분의 쓰임이 어법상 어색한 것은? (4점)

① He gave me the cookies <u>that</u> he had made.

② Show me <u>what</u> is in your hand.

③ <u>Although</u> we started small, we are making a big difference.

④ This is <u>that</u> I am looking for.

⑤ <u>If</u> it rains tomorrow, I will stay at home.

◎ 선택형 문항의 답안은 컴퓨터용 수정 싸인펜을
 사용하여 OMR 답안지에 바르게 표기하시오.
◎ 서술형 문제는 답을 답안지에 반드시 검정
 볼펜으로 쓰시오.
◎ 총 27문항 100점 만점입니다. 문항별 배점
 은 각 문항에 표시되어 있습니다.

[전북 ○○중]

1. 다음 밑줄 친 어휘가 문장의 해석과 어울리지 <u>않는</u>
 것은? (4점)

① The smart girl answered the question
 <u>immediately.</u>
 → 그 영리한 소녀는 즉시 질문에 대답했다.

② It is cheap, and <u>moreover,</u> easy to use.
 → 그것은 싸고, 더욱이, 사용하기 쉽다.

③ I <u>bet</u> that she knows everything.
 → 나는 그녀가 모든 것을 다 안다고 장담한다.

④ The new culture successfully <u>took root</u> in
 Korea.
 → 새로운 문화는 한국에 성공적으로 뿌리를 내렸다.

⑤ He will <u>promise</u> to take us to the zoo.
 → 그는 우리를 동물원에 데려가겠다고 제안할 것이다.

[경북 ○○중]

2. 다음 중 짝지어진 단어의 관계가 나머지 넷과 <u>다른</u>
 하나는? (3점)

① actual : actually
② happy : happily
③ friend : friendly
④ complete : completely
⑤ careful : carefully

[대전 ○○중]

3. 다음 대화의 빈칸 (A)에 가장 적절한 것은? (3점)

Tom: Jane, is something wrong?
Jane: I have a stomachache.
Tom: Why don't you (A)_____?
Jane: O.K. I'll give it a try.

① wear a mask   ② eat more food
③ take a medicine   ④ study English hard
⑤ get up early in the morning

[경기 ○○중]

4. 다음 중 짝지어진 대화가 <u>어색한</u> 것은? (4점)

① A: Do you mind if I change the channel?
 B: Yes. You can change it. Go ahead.

② A: What makes you want to visit Iceland?
 B: I want to see the northern lights.

③ A: Do you want me to cook tteokbokki for
 you?
 B: That'd be great.

④ A: Is something wrong? You don't look
 good.
 B: I have a sore throat.

⑤ A: It's hard to lose weight. What do you
 think I should do?
 B: Why don't you exercise every day?

[양천구 ○○중]

5. 다음 ⓐ~ⓔ가 자연스러운 대화가 되도록 문장의
 순서를 나열한 것은? (4점)

ⓐ What made you come here?
ⓑ In that case, you should visit the Eiffel
 Tower.
ⓒ Is it your first time to visit France, Jaden?
ⓓ I'm really into French movies. I'm going
 to visit the places I saw in the movies.
ⓔ Yes, I've always wanted to come to Paris.

① ⓒ-ⓐ-ⓑ-ⓔ-ⓓ   ② ⓒ-ⓔ-ⓐ-ⓓ-ⓑ
③ ⓒ-ⓔ-ⓓ-ⓐ-ⓑ   ④ ⓓ-ⓑ-ⓐ-ⓔ-ⓒ
⑤ ⓓ-ⓔ-ⓐ-ⓒ-ⓑ

[6~8] 다음 대화를 읽고 물음에 답하시오.

Jaden: Hi, Yuri. What are you doing?

Yuri: Hi, Jaden. I'm reading a book on Norse myths. I'm really into them these days.

Jaden: (A)Why do you like them?

Yuri: The stories are very interesting, and there are lots of movies about Norse myths.

Jaden: Are they any good?

Yuri: Yes. There's actually a new movie about Thor, a famous god in Norse myths.

Jaden: Oh, I know him. He's my favorite online game character.

Yuri: In that case, we should go see the movie together.

Jaden: Do you mind if I borrow your book when you're finished? I want to read it before we see the movie.

Yuri: (B)_____. I'm sure you'll like this book, too.

6. 위 대화의 (A)와 의미가 같은 문장은?　　　(4점)

① What makes you like them?

② Why don't you like them?

③ When did you like them?

④ How come you don't like them?

⑤ How would you like them?

7. 위 대화의 (B)에 들어갈 말로 알맞지 <u>않은</u> 것은? (4점)

① No, not at all.

② Of course not.

③ Certainly not.

④ No, I don't mind.

⑤ Sorry, but you can't.

8. 위 대화의 내용과 일치하지 <u>않는</u> 것은?　　　(3점)

① Yuri is reading a book on Norse myths.

② Thor is Jaden's favorite online game character.

③ Jaden wants to borrow a book on Norse myths from Yuri.

④ Yuri thinks Jaden should read more about Thor.

⑤ Yuri is really interested in Norse myths these days.

9. 다음 대화의 주제로 가장 적절한 것은?　　　(4점)

Jaden: Hi, Yuri. What are you doing?

Yuri: Hi, Jaden. I'm reading a book on Norse myths. I'm really into them these days.

Jaden: What makes you like them so much?

Yuri: The stories are very interesting, and there are lots of movies about Norse myths.

Jaden: Are they any good?

Yuri: Yes, There's actually a new movie about Thor, a famous god in Norse myths.

Jaden: Oh, I know him. He's my favorite online game character.

Yuri: In that case we should go see the movies together.

Jaden: Do you mind if I borrow your book when you're finished? I want to read it before we see the movie.

Yuri: No, not at all. I'm sure you'll like this book, too.

① Books and movies about Norse myths

② Jaden's favorite books and movies

③ The reason Jaden likes Norse myths

④ Yuri's favorite online game character

⑤ Famous gods in Norse myths

10. 다음 대화에서 Jane이 4월을 좋아하는 이유는?

(3점)

> Jinho: April is the best month of the year.
> Jane: What makes you say so?
> Jinho: The weather is not cold, and flowers are blooming.
> Jane: I love April because my birthday is in April.
> Jinho: Really? We should throw you a party.

① 꽃이 많이 펴서
② 생일이 있어서
③ 공기가 상쾌해서
④ 날씨가 따뜻해서
⑤ 친구가 좋아해서

11. 다음 주어진 문장을 가장 적절하게 바꿔 쓴 것은?

(4점)

> • Sue lent me this novel, which I haven't read yet.

① Sue lent me this novel and I haven't read yet.
② Sue lent me this novel but I haven't read it yet.
③ Sue lent me this novel so I haven't read it yet.
④ Sue lent me this novel and it I haven't read yet.
⑤ Sue lent me this novel for it I haven't read yet.

12. 다음 중 밑줄 친 that의 쓰임이 나머지 넷과 다른 하나는?

(4점)

① It was at the cafeteria that I ate lunch.
② It is strange that he came to the party.
③ It is my dog that jumps on me at home.
④ It was yesterday that I had dinner with him.
⑤ It was a toy that Tom gave to his brother.

13. 다음 〈보기〉의 밑줄 친 부분과 쓰임이 같은 것은?

(3점)

> <보기>
> A: Sarah, what are you drawing?
> B: It's a white bear that I'm drawing now.

① It was Mike that called this morning.
② This is the car that he wants to buy.
③ It's important that we should keep the rules.
④ You will get to know that is very convenient.
⑤ Yena thought that her dad would be happy to hear the news.

14. 〈보기〉를 참고로 하여 주어진 조건에 맞게 다음 문장을 강조하는 문장으로 바꾸시오.

(6점)

> <보기>
> • Andy found his hat in the classroom last week.
> → [who] It was Andy who found his hat in the classroom last week.

> • Sally bought this cake at the market yesterday.

(A) → [who] _____
(B) → [which] _____
(C) → [when] _____

[15~16] 다음 글을 읽고 물음에 답하시오.

Loki knew only the sons of Ivaldi could make fine golden hair. He went to them and said, "I heard Brokk and his brother are the finest smiths. Is that true?"

"No, it is ⓐwe who are the finest smiths," the sons of Ivaldi replied.

"They're making three treasures for Odin, Thor, and Frey," said Loki. "Do you think you can make treasures better than ⓑtheirs?"

"Of course we can," ⓒthey answered.

"O.K., then you should also make three treasures for them", said Loki. "The gods will decide on the best treasure."

Loki also told them that one of the treasures had to be golden hair. ⓓThey went to work immediately.

Loki then went to see Brokk and his brother. "Ivaldi's sons are making three treasures for Odin, Thor, and Frey," said Loki. "I bet that you can never make treasures as fine as ⓔtheirs."

Brokk became angry and accepted the challenge. He and his brother produced three treasures of their own.

15. 위 글의 내용과 일치하는 문장은?　　(3점)

① Loki lied to the sons of Ivaldi.

② Loki believed that Brokk and his brother were better smiths.

③ The best treasure would be chosen by Loki.

④ Loki asked Brokk and his brother to make golden hair.

⑤ Brokk knew that Ivaldi's sons were making golden hair.

16. 위 글의 ⓐ~ⓔ 중, 가리키는 대상이 나머지 넷과 <u>다른</u> 대명사는?　　(4점)

① ⓐ　　② ⓑ　　③ ⓒ　　④ ⓓ　　⑤ ⓔ

[17~18] 다음 글을 읽고 물음에 답하시오.

Loki and Brokk went to see the three gods with all the treasures. Loki showed them the treasures from Ivaldi's sons. The first treasure was a spear which never missed its target. ⓐ<u>It was for Odin, and he had only one eye.</u> The second treasure was for Frey. ⓑ<u>It was a big ship that could turn into a piece of cloth.</u> The third treasure was for Thor. Loki showed Thor the flowing golden hair for his wife. Thor put the hair on his wife's head, and it took root and became real hair.

It was now Brokk's turn to show the gods his gifts. He gave a golden arm ring for Odin and a pig for Frey.

"My third treasure is for you, Thor," said Brokk, "This is the hammer Mjolnir, and you'll love it. ⓒ<u>It always comes back to you if you'll throw it.</u>"

It was an easy decision to choose the greatest treasure. ⓓ<u>What the three gods liked most was Mjolnir.</u> They thought the hammer would protect the gods from their enemies.

ⓔ<u>"It is Brokk that is the finest Smith,"</u> said Odin.

Brokk proved that Loki was wrong, and the three gods now had precious treasures.

17. 위 글의 ⓐ~ⓔ 중 어법상 <u>어색한</u> 것은?　　(3점)

① ⓐ　　② ⓑ　　③ ⓒ　　④ ⓓ　　⑤ ⓔ

18. 위 글을 읽고 답할 수 <u>없는</u> 질문은?　　(4점)

① What did Thor do with golden hair?

② Why did Odin have only one eye?

③ Who made a golden arm ring?

④ How many treasures did each god get?

⑤ Why did three gods like the hammer most?

[19~21] 다음 글을 읽고 물음에 답하시오.

Thor woke and knew immediately something was wrong. His wife's beautiful golden hair was gone. He knew only Loki could do such a terrible thing. Thor soon found Loki and he was drinking at home. "You'd better solve this problem, or you'll be sorry," Thor said angrily to Loki. Loki was scared. He promised that he would get golden hair for Thor's wife. Loki knew only the sons of Ivaldi could make fine golden hair. He went to them and said, "I heard Brokk and his brother are the finest smiths. Is that true?" "No, it is we that are the finest smiths," they replied. "ⓐ<u>They</u>'re making three treasures for Odin, Thor, and Frey," said Loki. "Do you think you can make treasures better than what ⓑ<u>they</u> made?" "Of course we can," they answered. "O.K., then you should also make three treasures for the three gods," said Loki. "ⓒ<u>They</u> will decide on the best treasure." Loki also (A)보물 중 하나는 금발 머리이어야 한다고 그들에게 말했다. They went to work immediately. Loki then went to see Brokk and his brother. "Ivaldi's sons are making three treasures for Odin, Thor, and Frey," said Loki. "I bet that you can never make treasures as fine as theirs." Brokk and his brother became angry, so ⓓ<u>they</u> said, "We will accept the challenge." ⓔ<u>They</u> started to produce treasures of their own.

19. ⓐ~ⓔ 중, 가리키는 대상이 <u>다른</u> 것은? (4점)

① ⓐ　　② ⓑ　　③ ⓒ　　④ ⓓ　　⑤ ⓔ

20. 위 글의 각 인물이 할 수 있는 말로 적절한 것은? (4점)

① Thor: "I woke and saw Loki cutting my wife's hair."

② Brokk: "My brother and I were already producing three treasures before Loki came to us."

③ Thor's wife: "Loki got the sons of Ivaldi to give three treasures to me."

④ Loki: "Only the sons of Ivaldi could help me to keep a promise I made with three gods."

⑤ The sons of Ivaldi: "We are certain that no one can make better treasures than us."

21. 위 글의 (A)를 바르게 영작한 것은? (3점)

① told that one of the treasures had to be golden hair them.

② told that them one of the treasure had to be golden hair.

③ told them that treasures of the one had to be golden hair.

④ told them that one of the treasures had to be golden hair.

⑤ told one of the treasures that had to be golden hair them.

22. 다음 글의 내용과 일치하지 <u>않는</u> 문장은? (4점)

Long ago, there were no kings in the southeastern part of Korea. One day, a strange voice was heard from Gujibong, which was a small hill. It said that a new country would be built here. When people were singing and dancing for their future king, a golden box came from the sky. They found six golden eggs in the box. Twelve days later, the six eggs turned into six boys. The boys became the kings of the six Gayas. It was King Kim Suro who was the strongest of them. His kingdom became the center of the six Gayas.

① 오래 전, 한국의 남서쪽에는 왕이 없었다.

② 사람들은 미래의 왕을 기다렸다.

③ 김수로는 알에서 태어났다.

④ 김수로와 다섯 소년은 여섯 가야의 왕이 되었다.

⑤ 김수로의 왕국이 여섯 가야 중에서 가장 강력했다.

[23~25] 다음 글을 읽고 물음에 답하시오.

Loki knew only the sons of Ivaldi could make fine golden hair. He went to them and said, "I heard Brokk and his brother are the finest smiths. Is that true?"

"No, (A)we are the finest smiths," the sons of Ivaldi replied.

"They're making three treasures for Odin, Thor, and Frey," said Loki. "Do you think you can make treasures better than theirs?"

"Of course we can," they answered.

ⓐ"O.K., then you should also make three treasures for them," said Loki. ⓑ"The gods will decide on the best treasure." ⓒThe people found six golden eggs in the box. ⓓLoki also told them that one of the treasures had to be golden hair. ⓔThey went to work immediately.

23. 위 글의 밑줄 친 (A)의 주어(We)를 강조하여 문장을 다시 쓰시오. (5점)

• We are the finest smiths.
→ _____ .

<조 건>
• It ~ that[who] ~ 구문을 사용할 것.

답: _____

24. 위 글의 내용과 같도록 밑줄 친 부분에 알맞은 것은? (3점)

• Loki asked the sons of Ivaldi to make _____ for Odin, Thor, and Frey.

① three pigs   ② three treasures
③ three rings   ④ three hammers
⑤ three books

25. 위 글의 ⓐ~ⓔ 중 내용상 어색한 문장은? (3점)

① ⓐ   ② ⓑ   ③ ⓒ   ④ ⓓ   ⑤ ⓔ

[26~27] 다음 글을 읽고 물음에 답하시오.

Odin, who is the highest god, gave up his eye for wisdom.

Thor is Odin's son and the strongest god of all.

Frey, who is the god of the harvest, controls the weather.

Loki is a god who plays tricks on others.

Thor woke and knew immediately something was wrong. His wife's beautiful golden hair was gone. He knew only Loki could do such a terrible thing. Thor soon found Loki, who was drinking at home.

"(A)네가 한 짓을 되돌려 놓는 것이 좋을 거야, or you'll be sorry," Thor said angrily to Loki.

Loki was scared. He promised that he would (B)_____ .

26. (A)의 우리말과 일치하도록 다음 괄호 안의 단어를 배열할 때 4번째 오는 단어는? (4점)

(better / did / you / you'd / undo / what)
→ _____
• 주어진 단어를 모두 한 번만 사용.

① better   ② did   ③ you'd
④ undo   ⑤ what

27. 위 글의 빈칸 (B)에 들어갈 말로 가장 적절한 것은? (3점)

① never drink at home
② get golden hair for Thor's wife
③ find who took the golden hair
④ focus on controlling the weather
⑤ ask the finest smith to make a hammer

3학년 영어 1학기 중간고사(2과) 2회

반		점수
이름		

문항수 : 선택형(26문항) 서술형(3문항) 20 . . .

[경기 ㅇㅇ중]

1. 다음 빈칸에 공통으로 들어갈 말로 가장 적절한 것은? (3점)

- 2022 FIFA World Cup will _____ place in Qatar.
- Would you _____ a picture of me and my brother?
- If you want to be a good student, you should _____ notes.

① do　　　② put　　　③ make
④ take　　　⑤ keep

[대전 ㅇㅇ중]

2. 다음 중 단어의 형태 변화가 적절히 연결된 것의 개수는? (3점)

- actual - actualy
- angry - angryly
- happy - happily
- careful - carefully
- immediate - immediatelly

① 1개　② 2개　③ 3개　④ 4개　⑤ 5개

[경북 ㅇㅇ중]

3. 다음 대화의 빈칸에 들어갈 표현으로 가장 알맞은 것은? (2점)

A: Do you mind if I open the window?
B: _____ I have a cold, and it's pretty windy today.

① No, I don't.
② I don't mind.
③ No, not at all.
④ Of course not.
⑤ Sorry, but you can't.

[양천구 ㅇㅇ중]

4. 다음 A와 B의 대화가 문맥상 가장 <u>어색한</u> 것은? (3점)

① A: What's the matter with you?
   B: I have a cold.
   A: How about drinking hot water? That will help you to get better.
② A: July is the worst month of the year.
   B: What makes you say so?
   A: It's too hot and humid.
③ A: Excuse me, is it all right if I take this chair?
   B: Sorry, but it's already taken.
   A: That would be great. I'll take it.
④ A: Oh, we don't have any eggs.
   B: Do you want me to go out and get some?
   A: Thanks. Can you get strawberry jam, too?
⑤ A: Do you have any books you don't read?
   B: Yes. Why?
   A: I'm considering sending books to the charity.

[전북 ㅇㅇ중]

5. 다음 대화에서 밑줄 친 A의 목적은? (4점)

A: Jane, <u>do you mind if I open the window?</u>
B: Sorry, but I have a cold, and it's pretty windy today.
A: O.K. No problem. Would you like some hot tea? It'd be good for your cold.
B: That would be great. Thanks.

① 능력 물어보기　　② 허락 요청하기
③ 친구 소개하기　　④ 물건 빌리기
⑤ 음식 주문하기

[6~7] 다음 대화를 읽고 물음에 답하시오.

Jaden: Hi, Yuri. What're you doing?

Yuri: Hi, Jaden. I'm reading a book on Norse myths. (A)I'm really into them these days.

Jaden: What makes you like them so much?

Yuri: The stories are very interesting, and there are lots of movies about Norse myths.

Jaden: (B)Are they any good?

Yuri: Yes. There's actually a new movie about Thor, a famous god in Norse myths.

Jaden: (C)Oh, I know him. He's my favorite online game character.

Yuri: (D)In that case, we should go see the movie together.

Jaden: Do you mind if I borrow your book when you're finished? I want to read it before we see the movie.

Yuri: (E)Of course. I'm sure you'll like this book, too.

6. 위 대화의 밑줄 친 (A)~(E) 중 전체 흐름상 어색한 문장은? (4점)

① (A) ② (B) ③ (C) ④ (D) ⑤ (E)

7. Why does Yuri like Norse myths? (3점)

① She is interested in a movie very much.

② She read many books about Norse myths last month.

③ She really enjoyed the TV programs about Norse myths.

④ She thinks the stories about Norse myths are so interesting.

⑤ There are lots of online game characters about Norse myths.

8. 다음 (A)~(C)를 자연스러운 대화가 되도록 가장 적절하게 배열한 것은? (2점)

A: Is it your first time to visit Korea, Mike?

(A) What made you come here?

(B) Yes, it is. I've always wanted to come to Seoul.

(C) I'm really into Korean TV shows. I'm going to go to the places I saw on TV.

① (A)-(C)-(B) ② (A)-(B)-(C) ③ (B)-(A)-(C)
④ (C)-(A)-(B) ⑤ (C)-(B)-(A)

9. 다음 대화를 읽고 주어진 질문에 적절한 답을 고른 것은? (4점)

W: Is it your first time to visit Korea, Mike?

M: Yes, it is. I've always wanted to come to Seoul.

W: What made you come here?

M: I'm really into Korean TV shows. I'm going to go to the places I saw on TV.

W: Have fun!

Q: Why did Mike come to Korea?
A: He came to Korea _____.

① to help his father

② to try Korean food

③ to visit his grandmother

④ to meet famous TV stars

⑤ to visit the places on TV shows

10. 다음 주어진 우리말과 같도록 괄호 안에서 한 단어를 고르시오. (3점)

• Brokk는 화가 나서 그 도전을 받아들였다.

→ Brokk became [angry / angrily] and accepted the challenge.

답: _____

11. Which is NOT true according to the following dialogue? (4점)

Jaden: Hi, Yuri. What're you doing?

Yuri: Hi, Jaden. I'm reading a book on Norse myths. I'm really into them these days.

Jaden: What makes you like them so much?

Yuri: The stories are very interesting, and there are lots of movies about Norse myths.

Jaden: Are they any good?

Yuri: Yes. There's actually a new movie about Thor, a famous god in Norse myths.

Jaden: Oh, I know him. He's my favorite online game character.

Yuri: In that case, we should go see the movie together.

Jaden: Can I borrow your book when you're finished? I want to read it before we see the movie.

Yuri: Of course. I'm sure you'll like this book, too.

① Yuri is very interested in Norse myths.

② Thor is Jaden's favorite online game character.

③ Yuri thinks that Jaden should read more about Thor.

④ Jaden wants to borrow a book on Norse myths from Yuri.

⑤ Yuri suggests going to see the new movie about Thor together.

12. 밑줄 친 ⓐ~ⓔ 중, 흐름상 어색한 것은? (4점)

B: April is the ⓐbest month of the year.

G: What makes you ⓑsay so?

B: Flowers are blooming, but I have to ⓒstay inside to study for my ⓓexams.

G: Oh, I know ⓔwhat you mean.

① ⓐ   ② ⓑ   ③ ⓒ   ④ ⓓ   ⑤ ⓔ

13. 다음 밑줄 친 부분 중 어법상 어색한 것은? (3점)

① I met Kathy, who lives in Seoul.

② I live in a city, that is not very big.

③ Thor soon found Loki, who was drinking at home.

④ I read *The Little Prince*, which is a world-famous novel.

⑤ The birthday party, which I was invited to, took place yesterday.

14. 다음 중 어법상 옳은 문장은? (4점)

① I had to stay up all night, which made me feel tired.

② This is the novel *The Sun*, that every student should read.

③ The film will be released next month, who stars Tom Cruise.

④ Jane Austen was an English novelist, which wrote four novels during her lifetime.

⑤ Hawaii, what consists of 8 major islands, is the most popular vacation spot in the world.

15. 다음 단어들을 괄호 안의 우리말에 해당하도록 어법에 맞게 모두 배열하였을 때 다섯 번째 오는 단어는? (4점)

that / Emily / me / mall / the / was yesterday / at / it / saw

→ _____.

(Emily가 어제 나를 본 곳은 바로 쇼핑몰에서였다.)

① me   ② saw   ③ mall

④ that   ⑤ Emily

[16~18] 다음 글을 읽고 물음에 답하시오.

The first treasure was for Odin ⓐwhom had only one eye. It was a spear that never missed its target. The second treasure was a big ship ⓑthat could turn into a piece of cloth. It was for Frey. The third treasure was for Thor. Loki showed Thor the flowing golden hair for his wife. Thor ⓒput the hair on his wife's head, and it took root and became real hair.

It was now Brokk's turn to ⓓshow the gods his gifts. He gave Odin a gold arm ring that produced eight more gold rings ⓔevery ninth night. Brokk then gave Frey a pig. It could pull his carriage (A)_____ (어느 말보다도 더 빨리).

16. 위 글의 밑줄 친 문장 중 문법적으로 어색한 문장은? (3점)

① ⓐ   ② ⓑ   ③ ⓒ   ④ ⓓ   ⑤ ⓔ

17. 위 글의 빈칸 (A)에 들어갈 말을 우리말 해석에 맞게 쓰시오. (5점)

정답: It could pull his carriage _____
_____ _____ _____.

18. 위 글에서 언급한 내용과 일치하지 <u>않는</u> 것은? (3점)

① 보물의 개수는 총 5개였다.
② 두 번째 선물은 Frey를 위한 것이었다.
③ 매끈한 금발머리는 토르 아내의 진짜 머리로 변했다.
④ Odin은 눈이 한쪽밖에 없었다.
⑤ 금팔찌는 아홉 번째 밤이 되면 사라진다.

[19~20] 다음 글을 읽고 물음에 답하시오.

Loki knew only the sons of Ivaldi could make fine golden hair. He went to them and said, "I heard Brokk and his brother ⓐare the finest smiths. Is that true?"

"No, it is we ㉠that are the finest smiths," the sons of Ivaldi replied.

"They're making three treasures for Odin, Thor, and Frey," said Loki. "Do you think you can make treasures better than theirs?"

"Of course we can," they answered. "O.K., then you should also make three treasures for them," said Loki. "The gods will ⓑdecide on the best treasure."

Loki also told them that ⓒone of the treasures had to be golden hair. They went to work immediately.

Loki then went to see Brokk and his brother. "Ivaldi's sons are making three treasures for Odin, Thor, and Frey," said Loki. "I bet that you can never make treasures ⓓas finest as theirs."

Brokk became angry and accepted the challenge. He and his brother produced three treasures ⓔof their own.

19. 밑줄 친 ㉠과 바꿔 쓸 수 있는 것은? (3점)

① which   ② where   ③ who
④ when   ⑤ what

20. ⓐ~ⓔ 중 <u>어색한</u> 것을 고르면? (3점)

① ⓐ   ② ⓑ   ③ ⓒ   ④ ⓓ   ⑤ ⓔ

21. 다음 문장의 밑줄 친 Eric을 강조하는 문장으로 다시 쓰시오. (5점)

• <u>Eric</u> broke the window.

정답: It _____.

- 22 -

[22~24] 다음 글을 읽고 물음에 답하시오.

Loki went to see the three gods with all the treasures. Brokk came along. Loki showed them the treasures from Ivaldi's sons. The first treasure was for Odin, who had only one eye. ⓐIt was a spear that never missed its target. The second treasure was a big ship that could turn into a piece of cloth. ⓑIt was for Frey. The third treasure was for Thor. Loki showed Thor the flowing golden hair for his wife. Thor put the hair on his wife's head, and ⓒit took root and became real hair.

It was now Brokk's turn to show the gods his gifts. He gave Odin a gold arm ring that produced eight more gold rings every ninth night. Brokk then gave Frey a pig. ⓓIt could pull his carriage faster than any horse. "My third treasure is for you, Thor," said Brokk. "This is the hammer Mjolnir, which you'll love. If you throw it, it'll always come back to you. (A)_____, nothing can ever break it."

ⓔIt was an easy decision to choose the greatest treasure. It was Mjolnir that the three gods liked most. They thought the hammer would protect the gods from their enemies.

"Brokk and his brother," said Odin, "are the better smiths."

Brokk proved that Loki was wrong, and the three gods now had precious treasures.

22. 위 글의 빈칸 (A)에 들어갈 말로 어색한 것은? (3점)

① For example   ② In addition

③ Besides   ④ Moreover

⑤ Furthermore

23. 위 글의 ⓐ~ⓔ의 'it'이 의미하는 것으로 어색한 것은? (3점)

① ⓐ: 첫 번째 보물   ② ⓑ: 큰 배

③ ⓒ: 금발머리   ④ ⓓ: 돼지

⑤ ⓔ: 망치

24. 위 글의 내용과 일치하지 않는 것은? (4점)

① Brokk가 Loki와 함께 신들에게 갔다.

② Ivaldi의 아들들이 만든 보물이 먼저 소개되었다.

③ Odin은 매일 밤마다 8개의 금팔찌를 더 만들어내는 팔찌를 받았다.

④ 신들은 망치를 이용하여 적들로부터 자신들을 보호할 수 있다고 생각했다.

⑤ Odin은 Brokk와 그의 남동생을 더 훌륭한 대장장이라고 말했다.

25. 다음 글의 내용과 일치하는 것은? (4점)

Long ago, there were no kings in the southeastern part of Korea. One day, a strange voice was heard from Gujibong, which was a small hill. It said that a new country would be built there. When people were singing and dancing for their future king, a golden box came from the sky. They found six golden eggs in the box. Twelve days later, the six eggs turned into six boys. The boys became the kings of the six Gayas. It was King Kim Suro who was the strongest of them. His kingdom became the center of the six Gayas.

① The southeastern part of Korea was a hill.

② People found six golden boxes on Gujibong.

③ There were six boys who had six golden eggs.

④ The strongest kingdom of Korea was called Gaya.

⑤ Kim Suro's kingdom was the center of the six Gayas.

[26~27] 다음 글을 읽고 물음에 답하시오.

Loki went to see the three gods with all the treasures. Brokk came along. Loki showed them the treasures from Ivaldi's sons. ⓐThe first treasure was for Odin, which had only one eye. It was a spear that never missed its target. The second treasure was a big ship that could turn into a piece of cloth. It was for Frey. The third treasure was for Thor. Loki showed Thor the flowing golden hair for his wife. Thor put the hair on his wife's head, and it took root and became real hair. ⓑIt was now Brokk's turn to showing the gods his gifts. He gave Odin a gold arm ring that produced eight more gold rings every ninth night. Brokk then gave Frey a pig. ⓒIt could pull his carriage fast than any horse. "My third treasure is for you, Thor," said Brokk. ⓓ"This is the hammer Mjolnir, who you'll love. If you throw it, it'll always come back to you. ⓔMoreover, nothing can ever break it." It was an easy decision to choose the greatest treasure. It was Mjolnir that the three gods liked most.

26. 위 글의 내용과 일치하지 않는 것은? (3점)

① Odin had only one eye.

② Brokk's third treasure was for Thor.

③ What the three gods liked most was a hammer.

④ A big ship could turn into a piece of cloth.

⑤ Ivaldi's sons made a spear, a big ship and a gold arm ring.

27. 위 글의 밑줄 친 부분 중, 어법상 올바른 것은? (3점)

① ⓐ   ② ⓑ   ③ ⓒ   ④ ⓓ   ⑤ ⓔ

28. 다음 글의 밑줄 친 ⓐ~ⓔ 중에서 가리키는 대상이 나머지 넷과 다른 것은? (4점)

Loki knew only the sons of Ivaldi could make fine golden hair. He went to ⓐthem and said, "I heard Brokk and his brother are the finest smiths. Is that true?"

"No, it is we who are the finest smiths," the sons of Ivaldi replied.

"ⓑThey're making three treasures for Odin, Thor, and Frey," said Loki. "Do you think you can make treasures better than theirs?"

"Of course we can," ⓒthey answered.

"O.K., then you should also make three treasures for them," said Loki. "The gods will decide on the best treasure."

Loki also told ⓓthem that one of the treasures had to be golden hair. ⓔThey went to work immediately.

① ⓐ   ② ⓑ   ③ ⓒ   ④ ⓓ   ⑤ ⓔ

29. 주어진 글 다음에 이어질 글의 순서로 가장 적절한 것은? (4점)

Thor woke and knew immediately something was wrong. His wife's beautiful golden hair was gone.

(A) Thor soon found Loki, and he was drinking at home.

(B) "You'd better undo what you did, or you'll be sorry," Thor said angrily to Loki.

(C) He promised that he would get golden hair for Thor's wife.

(D) Loki was scared.

(E) He knew only Loki could do such a terrible thing.

① (B)-(A)-(C)-(E)-(D)   ② (C)-(D)-(A)-(B)-(E)

③ (C)-(E)-(A)-(B)-(D)   ④ (E)-(D)-(A)-(B)-(C)

⑤ (E)-(A)-(B)-(D)-(C)

◎ 선택형 문항의 답안은 컴퓨터용 수정 싸인펜을 사용하여 OMR 답안지에 바르게 표기하시오.
◎ 서술형 문제는 답을 답안지에 반드시 검정 볼펜으로 쓰시오.
◎ 총 30문항 100점 만점입니다. 문항별 배점은 각 문항에 표시되어 있습니다.

[전북 ○○중]

1. 다음 중 해석이 <u>어색한</u> 것은?　　(3점)

① My mother works for the government.
　→ 나의 어머니는 정부를 위해 일하신다.
② It does not contain any information.
　→ 그것은 어떤 정보도 포함하지 않는다.
③ Paris is the capital of France.
　→ 파리는 프랑스의 수도이다.
④ Do you want to improve your English?
　→ 당신은 당신의 영어를 향상시키길 원합니까?
⑤ It is considered an important part of the country's culture.
　→ 그것은 그 나라 문화의 중요한 부분으로 추측된다.

[경북 ○○중]

2. 다음 연결된 단어의 관계가 나머지 넷과 <u>다른</u> 것은?　　(2점)

① art - artist
② invent - invention
③ direct - director
④ fight - fighter
⑤ interview - interviewer

[강원 ○○중]

3. 다음 〈보기〉의 예문에 공통으로 들어갈 단어를 쓰시오.　　(4점)

＜보기＞
(1) A child should learn to ＿＿＿＿＿ promises.
(2) This is very important. You should ＿＿＿＿＿ this in mind.
(3) When I was a child, I didn't ＿＿＿＿＿ a diary.

→ ＿＿＿＿＿＿

[양천구 ○○중]

4. 다음 (A)와 (B)의 대화에서 (가)에 공통으로 들어갈 말은?　　(2점)

(A)
B: Bomi, do you have some medicine?
G: Why? (가)＿＿＿＿＿＿＿＿＿＿＿＿＿
B: I feel sick. I went to bed too late last night.

(B)
B: (가)＿＿＿＿＿＿＿＿＿＿＿＿＿ You don't look so good.
G: I have a sore throat. It really hurts.

① Are you sure?
② Is something wrong?
③ What do you think I should do?
④ What do you advise me to do?
⑤ I think you should think about it.

[충북 ○○중]

5. 다음 대화의 밑줄 친 (A)의 우리말을 영어로 가장 바르게 옮긴 것은?　　(4점)

A: It's so hard to lose weight. (A)<u>너는 내가 무엇을 해야 한다고 생각하니?</u>
B: Well, why don't you walk your dog every day?
A: My dog would love it, but would it help me lose weight?
B: Sure. When you walk your dog, you're actually exercising, too.

① What do you think I should do?
② Do you think what should I do?
③ What do you think should I do?
④ Do you think what I should do?
⑤ Do you think what am I doing?

[6~8] 다음 대화를 읽고 물음에 답하시오.

Anna: Suho, is something wrong? You've very quiet today.
Suho: I'm just a bit tired. I slept very little last night.
Anna: Did you do something late last night?
Suho: Yes, I watched a movie on my phone until 2 a.m. That's (A)_____ I often do these days.
Anna: Oh, that's ⓐ_____ you have red eyes. You should go to bed before midnight for your health.
Suho: I think my eyes are getting worse. (B)_____ do you think I should do?
Anna: Try eating lots of carrots and tomatoes. They're rich in vitamin A, so they'll keep your eyes healthy.
Suho: I see. Thank you, Anna.

6. 위 대화의 빈칸 ⓐ에 들어갈 단어로 가장 적절한 것은? (4점)
① because   ② what   ③ where
④ why   ⑤ how

7. 위 대화의 (A)와 (B)에 공통으로 들어갈 단어를 쓰시오. (3점)
답: _____

8. 다음 대화에서 Susan의 조언은 무엇인가? (2점)

Susan: What's wrong? You look worried.
Tom: Well, I broke my mom's favorite plate. What do you think I should do?
Susan: Tell her the truth. She will understand.
Tom: I hope you're right.

① 열심히 공부해라.
② 엄마의 말씀을 잘 들어라.
③ 엄마에게 사실대로 말해라.
④ 그릇을 조심해서 다루어라.
⑤ 엄마에게 그릇을 선물해라.

9. 다음 중 주어진 상황에서 가장 적절한 조언을 제공한 대화는? (3점)
① A: I broke my leg.
   B: You should dry your hair.
② A: I cut my finger.
   B: You should put on a bandage.
③ A: I have a cough.
   B: Why don't you go to the dentist?
④ A: I have a fever.
   B: You should go to bed after midnight.
⑤ A: I have a toothache.
   B: Why don't you walk your dog every day?

10. 다음 ⓐ~ⓔ 중 대화의 흐름상 어색한 것은? (3점)

Anna: Suho, ⓐwhat's going on? You're very quiet today.
Suho: I'm just a bit tired.
Anna: ⓑWhat did you do yesterday?
Suho: I watched a movie on my phone for 3 hours until 2 a.m. That's what I often do these days.
Anna: Oh, that's why you have red eyes. ⓒYou should go to bed before midnight for your health.
Suho: I think my eyes are getting worse. ⓓDo you want me to help you?
Anna: Try eating lots of carrots and tomatoes. ⓔThey're rich in vitamin A, so they'll keep your eyes healthy.
Suho: I see. Thank you. Anna.

① ⓐ   ② ⓑ   ③ ⓒ   ④ ⓓ   ⑤ ⓔ

[11~12] 다음 대화를 읽고 물음에 답하시오.

Anna: Suho, is something wrong? You're very quiet today.
Suho: I'm just a bit tired. I slept very little last night. (A)
Anna: Did you do something late last night? (B)
Suho: Yes, I watched a movie on my phone until 2 a.m. That's what I often do these days.
Anna: Oh, that's why you have red eyes. You should go to bed before midnight for your health. (C)
Suho: I think my eyes are getting worse. (D)
Anna: Try eating lots of carrots and tomatoes. They're rich in vitamin A, so they'll keep your eyes healthy. (E)
Suho: I see. Thank you, Anna.

11. 위 대화의 (A)~(E) 중 다음 주어진 문장이 들어가기에 가장 적절한 곳은? (3점)

What do you think I should do?

① (A) ② (B) ③ (C) ④ (D) ⑤ (E)

12. 위 대화의 내용과 일치하지 않는 것은? (2점)
① Anna thinks that Suho is quiet today.
② Suho went to bed late last night.
③ Suho often watches movies on his phone these days.
④ Suho has red eyes because he cried a lot.
⑤ Anna tells Suho to eat carrots and tomatoes for his eye health.

13. 다음 밑줄 친 동사를 강조하여 문장을 다시 쓰시오.
(5점)

• I called you yesterday.

<조건>
• 문장 전체를 쓸 것

답: _____

14. 다음 밑줄 친 부분이 어법상 옳은 것은? (4점)
① Are you exciting for your new job?
② My exam results were a little disappointed.
③ The instructions on the box are very confusing.
④ What was the interested TV show you watched?
⑤ What music do you listen to if you feel depressing?

15. 다음 그림의 상황에 맞게 대화를 완성할 때, 빈칸 (a), (b)에 들어갈 말이 바르게 짝지어진 것은? (4점)

	(a)	(b)
①	does like soccer	did say that
②	do like soccer	do say that
③	do like soccer	did say that
④	does like soccer	does say that
⑤	did like soccer	did say that

[16~18] 다음 글을 읽고 물음에 답하시오.

In 1940, the Royal Air Force defeated German fighters during World War II by using a radar system. The British government wanted to keep this technology a secret, so it published an article in the newspaper. It said that British pilots improved their night vision because they ate a lot of carrots. Everybody believed the story and began eating a lot more carrots than before. Can we really improve night vision by eating lots of carrots? Not really, but carrots contain much vitamin A, which (A)keeps our eyes healthy. In the future, carrots (B)[be / wars / may / in / used]. Scottish researchers have discovered a way to turn carrots into a very strong and light material. It can even be used to make battleships. This new material has already been used to make snowboards and bicycles.

16. 위 글을 읽고 알 수 있는 내용은? (3점)
① 영국 공군은 레이더 시스템을 썼지만, 독일군에게 졌다.
② 영국 공군의 야간 시력은 당근 덕분에 높아졌다.
③ 당근에 함유된 비타민 A는 눈 건강에 도움을 준다.
④ 당근을 이용한 소재는 이미 전쟁에 사용되고 있다.
⑤ 당근을 이용한 소재는 스포츠에 사용될 것이다.

17. 위 글의 밑줄 친 문장 (A)를 〈조건〉에 맞게 변형하시오. (4점)

<조 건>
1. 강조의 'do'를 활용하여 아래의 해석에 맞게 영작할 것.
   "정말로 우리 눈을 건강하게 유지해 준다."
2. 대·소문자 및 철자에 유의할 것.

답: _____

18. 위 글의 (B)에서 괄호 안의 단어들을 재배열하여 〈조건〉에 맞게 문장을 완성하시오. (4점)

<조 건>
1. 아래의 해석에 맞게 재배열할 것.
   "전쟁에 이용될지도 모른다."
2. 대·소문자 및 철자에 유의할 것.

답: _____

[19~20] 다음 글을 읽고 물음에 답하시오.

Popeye and the Great Spinach
Popeye is a world-famous cartoon character. He gets his super power by eating spinach. When Popeye became popular in the 1930s in the United States, a lot of children began to eat spinach. Crystal City in Texas, which is called the spinach capital of the world, even built a statue of Popeye. Although eating spinach will not give us super powers, spinach does have a lot of nutrients. It is ⓐ considered one of the ten healthiest foods on the planet.

19. 위 글의 밑줄 친 ⓐ와 가장 의미가 비슷한 것은? (3점)
① hoped   ② wished   ③ wanted
④ thought   ⑤ imagined

20. 위 글의 내용과 일치하지 않는 것은? (4점)
① 시금치에는 10개의 영양소가 있다.
② 1930년대 미국에서 뽀빠이가 유명해졌다.
③ 뽀빠이 동상을 세운 도시가 Texas에 있다.
④ 시금치를 먹어도 초인적인 힘이 생기지 않는다.
⑤ 현재 뽀빠이는 세계적으로 유명한 만화 캐릭터이다.

[21~22] 다음 글을 읽고 물음에 답하시오.

In 1940, the Royal Air Force defeated German fighters during World War II by using a radar system. The British government wanted to keep this technology a secret, so it published an article in the newspaper. It said that British pilots improved their night vision because they ate a lot of carrots. Everybody believed the story and began to eat a lot more carrots than before. Can we really improve night vision by eating lots of carrots? Not really, but carrots contain a lot of vitamin A, which _____ keep our eyes healthy.
In the future, carrots may actually be used in wars. Scottish researchers have discovered a way to turn carrots into a very strong and light material. It can even be used to make battleships. This new material has already been used to make snowboards and bicycles.

21. 위 글의 빈칸에 들어갈 말로 가장 적절한 것은?

(3점)

① do   ② did   ③ does

④ done   ⑤ doing

22. 위 글의 내용과 일치하는 것을 <보기>에서 고른 것은?   (4점)

<보기>
a. 영국 정부는 레이더 기술을 비밀로 하고 싶어 했다.
b. 영국 조종사들은 당근을 많이 먹고 시력이 개선되었다.
c. 당근은 야간 시력을 높인다.
d. 당근은 비타민 A를 많이 함유하고 있다.
e. 당근으로 만든 소재가 스노보드와 자전거에 사용되었다.

① a, b, c   ② a, d, e   ③ b, c, d

④ b, d, e   ⑤ c, d, e

[23~24] 다음 글을 읽고 물음에 답하시오.

Tomatoes, the Scariest Vegetables

We all know that tomatoes are good for our health.

ⓐ In 1820, a man (A)[named / naming] Robert Johnson wanted to prove that tomatoes were safe to eat.

ⓑ Ever since then, Americans have enjoyed eating tomatoes.

ⓒ Up until the 1800s, however, most Americans thought that tomatoes were poisonous.

ⓓ They all expected him to die, but nothing happened to him.

ⓔ So, he ate a basket of tomatoes in front of many people (B)[watched / watching] him.

We are no longer afraid of tomatoes, but some insects are still scared of them. If you want to keep insects away from your room, place a bowl of (C)[crushed / crushing] tomatoes in a corner of your room. Insects will not come near the tomatoes.

23. 위 글의 문장 ⓐ~ⓔ를 순서대로 바르게 배열한 것은?   (3점)

① ⓐ-ⓑ-ⓒ-ⓓ-ⓔ   ② ⓐ-ⓓ-ⓒ-ⓔ-ⓑ

③ ⓒ-ⓐ-ⓑ-ⓔ-ⓓ   ④ ⓒ-ⓐ-ⓓ-ⓑ-ⓔ

⑤ ⓒ-ⓐ-ⓔ-ⓓ-ⓑ

24. 위 글의 괄호 (A), (B), (C) 안에서 어법에 맞는 표현으로 가장 적절한 것은?   (4점)

	(A)	(B)	(C)
①	named	watching	crushed
②	named	watched	crushed
③	named	watching	crushing
④	naming	watched	crushed
⑤	naming	watching	crushing

[25~28] 다음 글을 읽고 물음에 답하시오.

Popeye is a world-famous cartoon character. ⓐHe gets his super power by eating spinach. When Popeye became popular in the 1930s in the United States, a lot of children began to eat spinach. ⓑCrystal City in Texas, which is called the spinach capital of the world, even built a statue of Popeye. Although eating spinach will not give us super powers, spinach (A)does have a lot of nutrients. ⓒIt is actually considered one of the ten healthiest foods on the planet. Spinach can be used in a surprising way. ⓓWhen it absorbs water, spinach also absorbs many other things from the soil. ⓔThere are several ways to cook spinach. Some scientists have used this characteristic of spinach to find bombs hidden in the ground. They make special spinach plants with sensors on their leaves. When these plants soak up traces from bombs, the sensors light up.

25. 위 글의 제목으로 가장 적절한 것은? (4점)
① How to Cook Spinach
② The History of Popeye
③ Various Healthy Foods
④ Interesting Facts about Spinach
⑤ How to Find Bombs in the Ground

26. 위 글의 내용과 일치하는 것은? (3점)
① Spinach can't absorb water from the soil.
② There is a statue of Popeye in Crystal City.
③ If you eat spinach, you can have super powers.
④ Many people think spinach is not a healthy food.
⑤ Popeye found hidden bombs using spinach with sensors.

27. 위 글에서 전체 흐름과 관계없는 문장은? (3점)
① ⓐ　② ⓑ　③ ⓒ　④ ⓓ　⑤ ⓔ

28. 위 글의 (A)와 쓰임이 다른 하나는? (4점)
① I did call you yesterday.
② I do love playing tennis.
③ Emma did her homework.
④ Noah does want to help you.
⑤ My mom does know the answer.

[29~30] 다음 글을 읽고 물음에 답하시오.

We all know that tomatoes are good for our health. Up until the 1800s, however, most Americans thought that tomatoes were ⓐ_____. In 1820, a man ⓑ_____ Robert Johnson wanted to prove that tomatoes were safe to eat. So, he ate a basket of tomatoes in front of many people ⓒ_____ him. They all expected him to die, but nothing happened to him. Ever since then, Americans have enjoyed eating tomatoes.

29. 위 글의 흐름상, 빈칸 ⓐ에 들어갈 단어로 가장 알맞은 말은? (3점)
① healthy　② delicious　③ poisonous
④ safe　⑤ cheap

30. 위 글의 빈칸 ⓑ, ⓒ에 들어갈 말이 바르게 짝지어진 것은? (3점)
① naming – watched　② naming – watching
③ named – watched　④ named – watching
⑤ name – watch

3학년 영어 1학기 기말고사(3과) 2회

문항수 : 선택형(25문항) 서술형(1문항)   20 . . .

반		점수	
이름			

◎ 선택형 문항의 답안은 컴퓨터용 수정 싸인펜을 사용하여 OMR 답안지에 바르게 표기하시오.

◎ 서술형 문제는 답을 답안지에 반드시 검정 볼펜으로 쓰시오.

◎ 총 26문항 100점 만점입니다. 문항별 배점은 각 문항에 표시되어 있습니다.

[전북 ○○중]

1. 다음 문장의 빈칸에 공통으로 들어가기에 가장 적절한 단어는? (4점)

• I will _____ a diary in English every day.

• Don't tell her the truth. She can't _____ a secret.

• A child should learn to _____ promises.

① make   ② keep   ③ leave

④ fight   ⑤ interview

[전북 ○○중]

2. 다음 대화를 읽고, 빈칸에 들어갈 말로 가장 <u>어색한</u> 것은? (3점)

Anna: Suho, _____? You're very quiet today.

Suho: I'm just a bit tired. I slept very little last night.

① What should I do?   ② What's wrong?

③ Is something wrong?   ④ What's the matter?

⑤ What's the problem?

[전북 ○○중]

3. 다음 대화의 빈칸에 들어갈 말로 가장 알맞은 것은? (3점)

A: _____
B: I have a bad cold.
A: You should drink hot honey tea.

① What's that?

② What are you doing now?

③ Is something wrong?

④ What's your favorite drink?

⑤ What do you want to be in the future?

[충북 ○○중]

4. 다음 (A)~(D)를 자연스러운 대화가 되도록 가장 적절하게 배열한 것은? (4점)

(A) I have a sore throat. I think it's because of the fine dust these days.

(B) Is something wrong? You don't look so good.

(C) Really? I'll get a few plants right away.

(D) Put some plants in your room. They take bad air in and produce fresh air.

① (A)-(B)-(C)-(D)   ② (C)-(D)-(A)-(B)

③ (B)-(D)-(A)-(C)   ④ (A)-(B)-(D)-(C)

⑤ (B)-(A)-(D)-(C)

[전북 ○○중]

5. 다음 주어진 말에 이어질 대화의 순서로 가장 알맞은 것은? (4점)

Suho, is something wrong? You're very quiet today.

(A) Oh, that's why you have red eyes. You should go to bed before midnight for your health.

(B) I'm just a bit tired. I slept very little last night.

(C) Yes, I watched a movie on my phone until 2 a.m. That's what I often do these days.

(D) Did you do something late last night?

① (B)-(D)-(C)-(A)   ② (B)-(C)-(A)-(D)

③ (C)-(D)-(A)-(B)   ④ (C)-(B)-(D)-(A)

⑤ (A)-(C)-(B)-(D)

[6~7] 다음 대화를 읽고 물음에 답하시오.

> Anna: Suho, is something wrong? You're very quiet today.
>
> Suho: I'm just a bit tired. I slept very little last night.
>
> Anna: Did you do something late last night?
>
> Suho: Yes, I watched a movie on my phone until 2 a.m. That's what I often do these days.
>
> Anna: Oh, that's why you have red eyes. You should go to bed before midnight for your health.
>
> Suho: I think my eyes are getting worse. (A)_____
>
> Anna: Try eating lots of carrots and tomatoes. They're rich in vitamin A, so they'll keep your eyes healthy.
>
> Suho: I see. Thank you, Anna.

6. 위 대화의 빈칸 (A)에 들어갈 표현으로 <u>어색한</u> 것은? (3점)

① What can I do?

② What should I do?

③ Can you give me some advice?

④ What do you think I should do?

⑤ What do you think I want to do?

7. Which is TRUE according to the above dialogue? (4점)

① Suho watched a movie on TV last night.

② Anna thinks her eyes are getting worse.

③ Anna is asking for an advice about her bad habits.

④ Anna suggests that Suho should eat many carrots and tomatoes for his eyes.

⑤ It was unusual that Suho watched movie until 2 a.m.

8. 다음 대화를 읽고 주어진 질문에 적절한 답을 고른 것은? (4점)

> Boy: Bomi, do you have some medicine?
>
> Girl: Why? Is something wrong?
>
> Boy: I have a stomachache. I think I ate too much for lunch.
>
> Girl: Why don't you go for a walk?
>
> Boy: O.K. I'll give it a try.

> Q: What is wrong with the boy?
>
> A: _____

① He has a cold.

② He has a headache.

③ He has a backache.

④ He has a sore throat.

⑤ He has a stomachache.

9. 다음 대화의 빈칸에 들어갈 문장으로 가장 <u>어색한</u> 것은? (4점)

> B: _____ You don't look so good.
>
> G: I have a sore throat. I think it's because of the fine dust these days.
>
> B: Put some plants in your room. They take bad air in and produce fresh air.
>
> G: Really? I'll get a few plants right away.

① What's wrong?

② What's the matter?

③ Is something wrong?

④ What's the problem?

⑤ What do you think I should do?

[10~11] 다음 대화를 읽고 물음에 답하시오.

Anna: Suho, what's (A)_____? You're very quiet today.

Suho: I'm just a bit tired. I slept very little last night.

Anna: Did you do something late last night?

Suho: Yes, I watched a movie on my phone until 2 a.m. That's (B)_____ I often do these days.

Anna: Oh, that's why you have red eyes. ㉠_____

Suho: I think my eyes are getting worse. What do you think I should do?

Anna: Try (C)_____ lots of carrots and tomatoes. They're rich in vitamin A, so they'll (D)_____ your eyes healthy.

Suho: I see. Thank you, Anna.

10. 위 대화의 빈칸에 들어갈 말이 알맞게 연결된 것은? (4점)

	(A)	(B)	(C)	(D)
①	bothering	why	eating	keep
②	the matter	what	to eat	take
③	wrong	because	eating	take
④	wrong	what	eating	keep
⑤	the matter	because	to eat	keep

11. 빈칸 ㉠에 들어갈 말로 알맞지 <u>않은</u> 것은? (3점)

① You should go to bed earlier.

② You may go to bed earlier.

③ Why don't you go to bed earlier?

④ You'd better go to bed earlier.

⑤ How about going to bed earlier?

12. 다음 중 어법상 적절한 것은? (4점)

① We do watch TV yesterday.

② She does exercised every day.

③ I do hope he will get well soon.

④ He did studies English hard last night.

⑤ They does play soccer well in the game.

13. 다음 빈칸 (A)와 (B)에 들어갈 말로 가장 적절한 것은? (4점)

- Jake is the boy (A)_____ a big ball.
- Mary is erasing the scores (B)_____ on the board.

① throwing - written   ② thrown - writing

③ throwing - writing   ④ threw - written

⑤ thrown - written

14. 다음 중 A에서 B로 문장을 다시 쓴 것 중 어법상 <u>어색한</u> 것은? (2개) (단, A는 어법상 옳은 문장임.) (4점)

① A: The book which was published in Korea is now sold in the U.S.

→ B: The book published in Korea now being sold in the U.S.

② A: Could you bring me the books which are arranged in the cabinet?

→ B: Could you bring me the books arranged in the cabinet?

③ A: A boy who was born in a small town won the lottery.

→ B: A boy was born in a small town won the lottery.

④ A: The boy who is wearing glasses is Minjun.

→ B: The boy wearing glasses is Minjun.

⑤ A: Anyone who is responsible for this problem should be fired.

→ B: Anyone responsible for this problem should be fired.

[15~16] 다음 글을 읽고 물음에 답하시오.

Popeye gets his super power after eating spinach. When Popeye became popular in the 1930s in the United States, a lot of children began to eat spinach. Crystal City in Texas, which is called the spinach capital of the world, even built a statue of Popeye. Eating spinach cannot give us super powers, but spinach has a lot of nutrients. (A)_____ When it absorbs water, spinach also absorbs many other things from the soil. Some scientists have used this characteristic of spinach to find bombs hidden in the ground. They make special spinach plants with sensors on their leaves. When these plants soak up traces from bombs, the sensors light up.

15. 위 글의 (A)에 들어갈 가장 알맞은 말은? (4점)

① Spinach grows without water.
② There is a surprising way to use spinach.
③ The sensors of special spinach plants are on their roots.
④ Eating spinach is recommended by some doctors.
⑤ We should grow spinach to find hidden bombs.

16. 위 글과 관련된 설명 중 T(True)/F(False) 연결이 올바른 것은? (4점)

ⓐ	Popeye 덕분에 시금치의 값이 비싸졌다.
ⓑ	시금치를 먹으면 우리도 초인적인 힘이 생긴다.
ⓒ	텍사스 주의 크리스탈 시티는 시금치 재배를 처음 시작했다.
ⓓ	시금치는 땅속의 폭탄을 찾는 데 사용되기도 한다.

	ⓐ	ⓑ	ⓒ	ⓓ
①	T	T	F	F
②	T	F	T	F
③	F	T	F	T
④	F	F	T	F
⑤	F	F	F	T

[17~18] 다음 글을 읽고 물음에 답하시오.

Carrots in World War II

In 1940, the Royal Air Force defeated German fighters during World War II by using a radar system. The British government wanted to (A)_____ this technology a secret, so it published an article in the newspaper. ⓐIt said that British pilots improved their night vision because of they ate a lot of carrots. Everybody believed the story and ⓑbegan to eat a lot more carrots than before. Can we really improve night vision by eating lots of carrots? Not really, but carrots contain a lot of vitamin A, which does keep our eyes healthy.

In the future, ⓒcarrots may actually be used in wars. Scottish researchers have discovered a way to turn carrots into a very strong and light material. ⓓIt can even be used to make battleships. ⓔThis new material has already been used to make snowboards and bicycles.

17. 밑줄 친 부분 중, 어법상 어색한 것은? (3점)

① ⓐ   ② ⓑ   ③ ⓒ   ④ ⓓ   ⑤ ⓔ

18. 위 글의 빈칸 (A)에 들어갈 단어와 일치하지 않는 것은? (4점)

① Did you _____ any sugar in my coffee?
② She tries to _____ her promise to visit them.
③ She would _____ a diary when she was young.
④ They tend to _____ their money in the pocket.
⑤ Nowadays, I _____ wearing a mask every day.

[19~20] 다음 글을 읽고 물음에 답하시오.

Carrots in World War Ⅱ

In 1940, the Royal Air Force defeated German fighters during World War Ⅱ by using a radar system. The British government wanted to keep this technology a secret, so it published an article in the newspaper. It said that British pilots improved their night vision because they ate a lot of carrots. Everybody believed the story and began to eat a lot more carrots than before. Can we really improve night vision by eating lots of carrots? Not really, but carrots contain a lot of vitamin A, which does keep our eyes healthy.

In the future, carrots may actually be used in wars. Scottish researchers have discovered a way to turn carrots into a very strong and light material. It can even be used to make battleships. This new material has already been used to make snowboards and bicycles.

19. 위 글의 내용과 일치하는 것은? (4점)

① 영국 공군은 2차 세계 대전에서 독일군에게 패배했다.

② 당근을 먹는 것은 실제로 야간 시력 향상에 도움이 되었다.

③ 비타민 A는 눈을 건강하게 하는 데 별로 도움이 되지 않는다.

④ 당근을 이용한 물질을 실제로 전쟁에 사용하기는 힘들다.

⑤ 영국 정부가 낸 기사는 그들이 전쟁에서 사용한 기술을 숨기기 위한 것이었다.

20. 위 글을 읽고 다음 질문에 대한 알맞은 답을 세 개의 영어 단어로 쓰시오. (문장으로 쓰지 마시오.) (5점)

Q: What did the British government want to keep a secret?

→ _____

21. 다음 글을 읽고 답할 수 <u>없는</u> 질문은? (4점)

Popeye is a world-famous cartoon character. He gets his super power by eating spinach. When Popeye became popular in the 1930s in the United States, a lot of children began to eat spinach. Crystal City in Texas, which is called the spinach capital of the world, even built a statue of Popeye. Although eating spinach will not give us super powers, spinach does have a lot of nutrients. It is actually considered one of the ten healthiest foods on the planet.

① Who is Popeye?

② Where is the statue of Popeye?

③ What gives Popeye a super power?

④ What are the ten healthiest foods on the planet?

⑤ What happened when Popeye became popular in the 1930s in the United States?

22. 다음 글의 밑줄 친 ⓐ가 의미하는 바로 가장 적절한 것은? (4점)

Spinach can be used in a surprising way. When it absorbs water, spinach also absorbs many other things from the soil. Some scientists have used ⓐthis characteristic of spinach to find bombs hidden in the ground. They make special spinach plants with sensors on their leaves. When these plants soak up traces from bombs, the sensors light up.

① Spinach absorbs water.

② Spinach has sensors on its leaves.

③ Spinach soaks up lights from the Sun.

④ Spinach absorbs many things from the soil.

⑤ Spinach can be used to find bombs in the ground.

[23~24] 다음 글을 읽고 물음에 답하시오.

Popeye and the Great Spinach

Popeye is a world-famous cartoon character. He gets his super power by eating spinach. When Popeye became popular in the 1930s in the Unites States, a lot of children began to eat spinach. Crystal City in Texas, which is called the spinach capital of the world, even built a (A)_____ of Popeye. Although eating spinach will not give us super powers, spinach does have a lot of nutrients. It is actually considered one of the ten healthiest foods on the planet.

Spinach can be used in a surprising way. When it absorbs water, spinach also absorbs many other things from the soil. Some scientists have used this characteristic of spinach to find bombs (B)_____ in the ground. They make special spinach plants with sensors on their leaves. When these plants soak up traces from bombs, the sensors light up.

---

23. 위 글의 내용과 일치하지 <u>않는</u> 것은?　(4점)

① Popeye는 시금치를 먹음으로써 초인적인 힘을 얻는다.

② 텍사스의 크리스털 시티는 세계의 시금치 수도이다.

③ 시금치는 지구에서 가장 건강한 식품 10개 중 하나이다.

④ 시금치는 물을 흡수할 때, 흙 속의 다른 많은 것들도 빨아들인다.

⑤ 과학자들은 폭탄을 찾기 위해 뿌리에 감지기가 있는 특별한 시금치를 만든다.

24. 위 글에서 문맥상 (A), (B)에 들어갈 말로 가장 적절하게 짝지어진 것은?　(4점)

	(A)	(B)
①	shortage	to hide
②	stature	hiding
③	status	hide
④	statue	hidden
⑤	standard	hidden

[25~26] 다음 글을 읽고 물음에 답하시오.

Tomatoes, the Scariest Vegetables

We all know that tomatoes are good for our health. (A) Up until the 1800s, however, most Americans thought that tomatoes were poisonous. (B) In 1820, a man (a)[named / naming] Robert Johnson wanted to prove that tomatoes were safe to eat. (C) So, he ate a basket of tomatoes in front of many people (b)[watching / watched] him. (D) Ever since then, Americans have enjoyed eating tomatoes. (E)

We are no longer afraid of tomatoes, but some insects are still scared of them. If you want to keep insects away from your room, place a bowl of (c)[crushing / crushed] tomatoes in a corner of your room. Insects will not come near the tomatoes.

---

25. 위 글에서 어법상 (a), (b), (c)에 들어갈 말로 가장 적절하게 짝지어진 것은?　(4점)

	(a)	(b)	(c)
①	named	watched	crushing
②	named	watching	crushed
③	named	watched	crushed
④	naming	watching	crushed
⑤	naming	watched	crushing

26. 위 글의 흐름상 주어진 문장이 들어가기에 가장 적절한 곳은?　(4점)

They all expected him to die, but nothing happened to him.

① (A)　② (B)　③ (C)　④ (D)　⑤ (E)

문항수 : 선택형(26문항) 서술형(3문항)   20 . . .

◎ 선택형 문항의 답안은 컴퓨터용 수정 싸인펜을 사용하여 OMR 답안지에 바르게 표기하시오.

◎ 서술형 문제는 답을 답안지에 반드시 검정 볼펜으로 쓰시오.

◎ 총 29문항 100점 만점입니다. 문항별 배점은 각 문항에 표시되어 있습니다.

[전북 ○○중]

1. 다음 빈칸에 공통으로 들어갈 가장 알맞은 단어는? (3점)

- Can you _____ me a hand? I need some help.
- Let's talk about it tomorrow. I'll _____ you a call.

① make   ② give   ③ take
④ get   ⑤ have

[충북 ○○중]

2. 다음 밑줄 친 낱말이 어색한 것은? (3점)

① Deep breathing will consider you relax.

② The interviewer asked me about my future plans.

③ We learn many things from past mistakes.

④ The number of audience was more than a million.

⑤ She invited me to her photo exhibition.

[전북 ○○중]

3. 다음 대화의 빈칸에 가장 알맞은 표현은? (4점)

M: Do you hear that? _____
W: I think it's coming from over there. Do you want to go and check it out?
M: Yes, I love that strong beat. Is it traditional Korean music?
W: Yes, it's called nongak.

① How often do you play strong beats?

② Can you explain how to play that music?

③ I wonder where that music is coming from.

④ Are you going to wish for a good harvest?

⑤ Do you want to dance to the rhythm?

[경북 ○○중]

4. 다음 빈칸에 알맞은 말을 넣어 자연스러운 대화를 완성할 때, 들어갈 수 있는 표현을 아래 〈보기〉에서 모두 고른 것은? (3점)

A: Are you going somewhere this summer?
B: I'm going to Jejudo to walk along the Jeju Olle Trail.
A: The Jeju Olle Trail? _____
B: It's a long hiking path around Jejudo.
A: Oh, I see. I hope you enjoy your trip!

<보기>
ⓐ Could you explain what that is?
ⓑ How many times did you go there?
ⓒ Can you tell me more about it?
ⓓ I wonder where you go.
ⓔ Do you need more information about that?

① ⓐ   ② ⓐ, ⓒ
③ ⓐ, ⓒ, ⓔ   ④ ⓐ, ⓒ, ⓓ, ⓔ
⑤ ⓐ, ⓑ, ⓒ, ⓓ, ⓔ

[충북 ○○중]

5. 다음 대화의 우리말과 일치하도록 괄호 안의 단어를 사용하여 대화를 완성하시오. (3점)

A: Wow, look at the photo. Isn't it beautiful?
B: Yes. It's so wonderful. I wonder _____ _____. (the photo) (나는 네가 그 사진을 어디서 찍었는지 궁금해.)
A: That's Gwangandaegyo in Busan. I went there with my family last summer.

정답: I wonder _____.

[6~7] 다음 대화를 읽고 물음에 답하시오.

Jaden: Do you hear that? I wonder where that music is coming from.

Yuri: I think it's coming from over there. Do you want to go and check it out?

Jaden: Yes, I love that strong beat. Is it traditional Korean music?

Yuri: Yes, it's called *nongak*. It's a kind of community band music.

Jaden: *Nongak*? Could you explain a little bit more about it?

Yuri: It's traditionally used to cheer up farmers and wish for a good harvest.

Jaden: I see. Look! Some people are dancing to the rhythm.

Yuri: Yes, that's a big part of *nongak*. Dancing together completes the music.

Jaden: Let's join them.

Yuri: Sure. Why not?

6. 위 대화의 'nongak'에 대한 내용과 일치하지 않는 것은? (4점)

① It has a strong beat.

② People can't dance to it.

③ It is used to cheer up farmers.

④ People use it to wish a good harvest.

⑤ It is a kind of community band music.

7. 위 대화 후 'Jaden'과 'Yuri'의 행동으로 가장 적절한 것은? (3점)

① 농악을 배우러 간다.

② 농악 연주가에 대해 조사하러 간다.

③ 농악에 따라 춤추는 사람들과 합류한다.

④ 농악에 대해 음악 선생님에게 물어본다.

⑤ 농악 소리가 나는 곳이 어딘지 찾아본다.

8. 다음 대화에 대한 질문의 적절한 대답은? (3점)

B: Look over there. I wonder why there are so many people waiting in line.

G: They're waiting to get into the new bakery there.

B: Why? Is it famous?

G: Yes. It was on a TV program.

B: Really? We should try their bread then.

G: Sure.

Question: What are they going to do after the dialog?

→ They will _____.

① watch TV

② get in line

③ bake bread together

④ visit another bakery

⑤ speak to other people there

9. 다음 (A)~(D)를 자연스러운 대화가 되도록 바르게 배열한 것은? (3점)

(A) Sure. Press this button, and it'll tell you what to do.

(B) Here you are.

(C) Excuse me. I'd like to borrow an audio guide.

(D) Could you explain how to use it?

① (C)-(A)-(B)-(D)　　② (C)-(B)-(D)-(A)

③ (C)-(D)-(A)-(B)　　④ (D)-(A)-(C)-(B)

⑤ (D)-(B)-(A)-(C)

10. 다음 문장에서 어색한 부분을 찾아 바르게 고쳐 올바른 문장으로 쓰시오. (3점)

• Nobody knows why was Tom late.

→ Nobody knows _____.

답: _____

[11~12] 다음 대화를 읽고 물음에 답하시오.

Jaden: Do you hear that? (A)<u>나는 저 음악이 어디서 나오는지 궁금해.</u>

Yuri: I think it's coming from over there. Do you want to go and check it out?

Jaden: Yes, I love that strong beat. Is it traditional Korean music?

Yuri: Yes, it's called *nongak*. It's a kind of community band music.

Jaden: *Nongak*? Could you explain a little bit more about it?

Yuri: It's traditionally used to cheer up farmers and wish for a good harvest.

Jaden: I see. Look! Some people are dancing to the rhythm.

Yuri: Yes, that's a big part of *nongak*. Dancing together completes the music.

Jaden: Wow! I want to learn more about *nongak*.

11. 위 대화의 내용과 일치하는 것은? (3점)

① Jaden asks Yuri for more information about *nongak*.

② Yuri becomes interested in traditional Korean song.

③ *Nongak* is a community music used to pray for rain on the harvest day.

④ Dancing is not allowed while *nongak* band plays music.

⑤ Jaden and Yuri are going to enjoy the rhythm by dancing with the band.

12. 위 대화의 (A)를 〈보기〉의 단어를 모두 사용하여 하나의 문장으로 영작할 경우 5번째에 오는 단어는? (4점)

〈보기〉 coming / wonder / that / music / from / I / where / is

① music
② wonder
③ that
④ where
⑤ from

13. 다음 〈보기〉를 참고하여 주어진 두 문장을 연결하여 한 문장으로 고쳐 쓰시오. (어법이 어색한 경우 부분점수 없음.) (6점)

〈보기〉
• I wonder. + When will he come?
→ I wonder when he will come.

(A) Can you tell me? + What did you do?
(B) Nobody knows. + Why was she late?

(A) _____

(B) _____

14. 다음 중 어법상 어색한 문장은? (4점)

① I didn't understand why she wanted to take pictures of us.

② He asked me where I had eaten lunch.

③ They have visited the place many times before.

④ I have gone shopping at the market before I had dinner.

⑤ She was tired after she had played in the water for two hours.

15. 다음 빈칸 (A)에 들어갈 가장 적절한 것은? (3점)

• I wonder. + What did he buy yesterday?
→ I wonder (A)_____.

① what he buy yesterday
② what he bought yesterday
③ what did he buy yesterday
④ what he did bought yesterday
⑤ what did he bought yesterday

[16~17] 다음 글을 읽고 물음에 답하시오.

For the past several years, the underwater photographer Zin Kim has advertised the culture of Jeju haenyeo worldwide. ⓐHaenyeo are Korean female divers that harvests seafood without any breathing devices. Their culture made UNESCO's Intangible Cultural Heritage list in 2016. At her studio last week, ⓑZin Kim interviewed about her experience of taking pictures of haenyeo.

Q. *How did you become interested in taking photos of haenyeo?*
A. One day, I got a chance to take pictures of a haenyeo. ⓒI was surprised to find that she was enjoying her job. Until then, I had only seen black-and-white photos of haenyeo who looked very tired. However, ⓓshe had kept laughing even after she was in the water for over five hours. I realized then that I should take pictures of haenyeo.

Q. *Could you tell us more about haenyeo?*
A. Sure. Because they stay in the water without any breathing devices, haenyeo can't catch a lot of seafood. This is good for the underwater environment. ⓔIt can destroy the ocean catching too much marine life at one time in one place.

16. 위 글의 ⓐ~ⓔ 중 어법상 맞는 것은? (4점)
① ⓐ ② ⓑ ③ ⓒ ④ ⓓ ⑤ ⓔ

17. 위 글에서 답을 찾을 수 없는 질문은? (3점)
① What is the definition of haenyeo?
② Why does the way haenyeo work protect the ocean?
③ In which year was Jeju haenyeo's culture added to UNESCO's list?
④ What made Zin Kim interested in taking photos of haenyeo?

⑤ How do haenyeo keep catching seafood underwater without any breathing devices?

*definition: 정의, 뜻

[18~20] 다음 글을 읽고 물음에 답하시오.

(A) I'll tell you three things. First, haenyeo are a symbol of ⓐstrong women. (B) Jejudo, which is a volcanic island, is not ⓑsuitable for farming, so many haenyeo have become the breadwinners for their families. (C) Second, haenyeo ⓒform their own communities and help each other. For example, more-experienced haenyeo ⓓjoin less-experienced haenyeo. (D) Third, because they stay in the water without any breathing devices, haenyeo can't catch a lot of seafood. (E) Catching too much marine life at one time in one place can ⓔdestroy the ocean.

18. 위 글의 밑줄 친 ⓐ~ⓔ 중, 흐름상 낱말의 쓰임이 적절하지 않은 것은? (3점)
① ⓐ ② ⓑ ③ ⓒ ④ ⓓ ⑤ ⓔ

19. 위 글의 흐름으로 보아 (A)~(E) 중, 다음 문장이 들어가기에 가장 적절한 곳은? (4점)

This is good for the underwater environment.

① (A) ② (B) ③ (C) ④ (D) ⑤ (E)

20. 위 글은 어떤 질문에 대한 대답인가? (3점)
① What are you planning to do in the future?
② How long can haenyeo breathe underwater?
③ What's so special about haenyeo?
④ What has Zin Kim done for the past several years?
⑤ How can you protect marine life?

[21~23] 다음 글을 읽고 물음에 답하시오.

"Q: You take beautiful pictures of them, but isn't it (A)_____ to take pictures of haenyeo?"

At first, they didn't understand the reason that I wanted to take their pictures. They didn't think they looked pretty in their wetsuits. I said to them, "You are very special. I want to show your culture to the world." They opened up to me then. Of course, I also promised them that (a)내 사진 속에서 그들을 아름답게 보이도록 해주겠다고.

"Q: Could you tell us more about haenyeo? What's so special about them?"

I can tell you three things. First, haenyeo are a (B)_____ of strong women. Jejudo, which is a volcanic island, is not suitable for farming, so many haenyeo have become the breadwinners for their families. Second, haenyeo form their own communities and help each other. For example, more-experienced haenyeo train less-experienced haenyeo. Third, because they stay in the water without any breathing devices, haenyeo can't catch a lot of seafood. This is good for the underwater environment. Catching too much marine life at one time in one place can (C)_____ the ocean.

21. 위 글의 내용과 일치하는 것은? (3점)

① 해녀들은 잠수복을 입은 자신의 모습이 예뻐 보인다고 생각했다.
② 제주도는 농사짓기 좋은 섬이다.
③ 해녀들은 서로 가르쳐 주기보다는 스스로 훈련하는 경우가 많다.
④ 해녀들은 숨쉬기 위한 장치를 달고 물속에 머문다.
⑤ 한 장소에서 한 번에 많은 해양생물을 잡는 것은 환경에 좋지 않을 수 있다.

22. (a)를 영작한 것으로 옳은 것은? (3점)

① I would make them to look beautiful in my pictures.
② I would make them look beautiful in my pictures.
③ I would making them to look beautiful in my pictures.
④ I would be beautiful to look them in my pictures.
⑤ I would look beautiful to them in my pictures.

23. 위 글의 (A), (B), (C)에 들어갈 문맥상 알맞은 어휘로 짝지어진 것은? (3점)

	(A)	(B)	(C)
①	difficult	symbol	destroy
②	difficult	symptom	develop
③	different	symbol	destroy
④	different	symbol	develop
⑤	different	symptom	develop

24. 다음 글의 흐름으로 보아, 주어진 문장이 위치할 가장 적절한 곳은? (4점)

When I finished my talk, one of the haenyeo held my hand tightly.

(A) I once attended an overseas exhibition with a couple of haenyeo to give a talk about their lives. (B) She said to me, "Thank you so much. (C) I've never known in my life that I was such a special person." (D) She was crying with happiness. Everyone in the audience was deeply moved. (E)

① (A) ② (B) ③ (C) ④ (D) ⑤ (E)

[25~27] 다음 글을 읽고 물음에 답하시오.

Q: Could you tell us more about haenyeo? What's so special about them?

I can tell you three things. First, haenyeo are a symbol of strong women. Jejudo, which is a volcanic island, is not ⓐsuitable for farming, so many haenyeo have become the ⓑbreadwinners for their families. Second, haenyeo form their own communities and help each other.

For example, more-experienced haenyeo train ⓒless-experienced haenyeo. Third, because they stay in the water without any breathing devices, haenyeo can't catch a lot of seafood. This is ⓓgood for the underwater environment. Catching too much marine life at one time in one place can ⓔconserve ocean life.

Q. Lastly, please tell us what you're planning to do in the future.

I once (A)[attended / attended to] an overseas exhibition with a couple of haenyeo to give a talk about their lives. When I finished my talk, one of the haenyeo held my hand tightly. She said to me, "Thank you so much. I've never known in my whole life (가)that I was such a special person." She was crying with (B)[sadness / happiness]. Everyone in the audience (C)[were / was] deeply moved. I can never forget that moments, so I'll continue to take pictures of haenyeo. I want to tell more beautiful stories about them to many more people in the world.

25. 위 글에서 문맥상 (A), (B), (C)에 들어갈 말로 가장 적절하게 짝지어진 것은? (4점)

	(A)	(B)	(C)
①	attended	sadness	were
②	attended	happiness	was
③	attended to	happiness	was
④	attended to	sadness	were
⑤	attended to	sadness	was

26. 위 글의 밑줄 친 ⓐ~ⓔ 중 문맥상 낱말의 쓰임이 적절하지 않은 것은? (4점)

① ⓐ   ② ⓑ   ③ ⓒ   ④ ⓓ   ⑤ ⓔ

27. 위 글의 밑줄 친 (가)와 쓰임이 같은 것은? (3점)

① The book that is on the desk is mine.

② The dress that she is wearing is new.

③ He is the man that I met yesterday.

④ She thinks that he is a thief.

⑤ Have you found the keys that you lost?

[28~29] 다음 글을 읽고 질문에 답하시오.

For the past several years, the underwater photographer Zin Kim has promoted the culture of Jeju haenyeo worldwide. Haenyeo are Korean female divers who harvest seafood without any breathing devices. Their culture made UNESCO's _____ Cultural Heritage list in 2016. At her studio last week, Zin Kim was interviewed about her experience of taking pictures of haenyeo.

28. What has Zin Kim promoted for the past several years? (4점)

① 제주도의 해산물을 홍보해 왔다.

② 한국에 해녀 문화를 홍보해 왔다.

③ UNESCO의 장점에 대해 홍보해 왔다.

④ 전 세계에 해녀 문화를 홍보해 왔다.

⑤ 제주도의 해안 사진을 찍어 홍보해 왔다.

29. 위 글의 빈칸에 들어가기에 가장 적절한 단어는? (3점)

① Unimportant   ② Visible   ③ Touchable

④ Intangible   ⑤ Material

3학년 영어 1학기 기말고사(4과) 2회

문항수 : 선택형(25문항) 서술형(2문항) 20 . . .

반
이름

점수

◎ 선택형 문항의 답안은 컴퓨터용 수정 싸인펜을
　사용하여 OMR 답안지에 바르게 표기하시오.
◎ 서술형 문제는 답을 답안지에 반드시 검정
　볼펜으로 쓰시오.
◎ 총 27문항 100점 만점입니다. 문항별 배점
　은 각 문항에 표시되어 있습니다.

[전북 ○○중]

1. 다음 밑줄 친 부분을 **잘못** 해석한 것은?　　(3점)

One day, I happened to take pictures of a haenyeo. I was surprised to find that she was enjoying her job. Until then, I only have seen black-and-white photos of haenyeo who looked very tired. However, she kept laughing even after she had been in the water for over five hours. I realized then that I should take pictures of haenyeo.

① happened to: 우연히 ~했다
② was surprised to: ~해서 놀랐다
③ black-and-white: 흑백의
④ kept laughing: 계속 웃었다
⑤ realized: 실행했다

[전북 ○○중]

2. 상대방에게 도움을 청할 때 빈칸에 적합한 단어를
　각각 순서대로 쓰시오.　　(4점)

• Could you (A)_____ me a (B)_____?

답: (A)_____ (B)_____

[전북 ○○중]

3. 다음 (A)~(E)를 자연스러운 대화가 되도록 배열할
　때, 세 번째로 오는 것은?　　(4점)

(A) It's a long hiking path around Jejudo.
(B) I'm going to Jejudo to walk along the Jeju Olle Trail.
(C) Oh, I see. I hope you enjoy your trip!
(D) The Jeju Olle Trail? Could you explain what that is?
(E) Are you going somewhere this summer?

① (A)　② (B)　③ (C)　④ (D)　⑤ (E)

[경북 ○○중]

4. According to the following dialogue, which is NOT true about nongak?　　(4점)

Jaden: Do you hear that? I wonder where that music is coming from.
Yuri: I think it's coming from over there. Do you want to go and check it out?
Jaden: Yes, I love that strong beat. Is it traditional Korean music?
Yuri: Yes, it's called nongak. It's a kind of community band music.
Jaden: Nongak? Could you explain a little bit about it?
Yuri: It's traditionally used to cheer up farmers and wish for a good harvest.
Jaden: I see. Look! Some people are dancing to the rhythm.
Yuri: Yes, that's a big part of nongak. Dancing together completes the music.
Jaden: Let's join them.
Yuri: Sure. Why not?

① It has a strong beat.
② It's a traditional Korean music.
③ It's used to wish for a good harvest.
④ It's a sort of community band music.
⑤ It's music just for viewing and enjoying quietly.

[대전 ○○중]

5. 대화의 빈칸 (A)에 가장 적절한 것은?　　(3점)

Andy: Wow, look at the bridge in this ad. I wonder (A)_____ the photo was taken.
Robert: That's Gwangandaegyo in Busan. I went there with my family last summer.

① how　② when　③ what
④ where　⑤ which

[6~7] 다음 대화를 읽고 물음에 답하시오.

Jaden: Do you hear that? I wonder (A)_____ that music is coming from.
Yuri: I think it's coming from over there. Do you want to go and check it out?
Jaden: Yes, I love that strong beat. Is it traditional Korean music?
Yuri: Yes, it's called nongak. It's a kind of community band music.
Jaden: Nongak? Could you explain a little bit more about it?
Yuri: It's traditionally used to cheer up farmers and wish for a good harvest.
Jaden: I see. Look! Some people are dancing to the rhythm.
Yuri: Yes, that's a big part of nongak. Dancing together completes the music.
Jaden: Let's join them.
Yuri: Sure. Why not?

6. 위 대화의 빈칸 (A)에 들어갈 알맞은 것은?　(3점)

① where　　② when　　③ how

④ why　　⑤ what

7. 위 대화의 내용과 일치하는 것은?　(4점)

① 몇몇 사람들이 리듬에 맞춰 노래를 부르고 있다.
② Jaden은 농악에 관심이 없다.
③ 농악은 해녀들의 힘을 북돋운다.
④ 농악은 공동체 악단 음악의 한 종류이다.
⑤ 두 사람은 공연에 참여하고 싶어 하지 않는다.

8. 다음 (A)~(D)를 자연스러운 대화가 되도록 바르게 배열한 것은?　(4점)

(A) I agree. I wonder how we can promote that place worldwide.
(B) How about posting an article introducing the cultural heritage of Ikseon-dong on SNS with pictures?
(C) I think Ikseon-dong is a great place to experience Korean cultures.
(D) In that picture, people will know this place shows the harmony of the old and new cultures of Korea.

① (C)-(A)-(B)-(D)　　② (B)-(C)-(A)-(D)
③ (B)-(D)-(C)-(A)　　④ (A)-(C)-(B)-(D)
⑤ (C)-(D)-(A)-(B)

9. 다음 대화의 흐름상 빈칸에 들어갈 말로 가장 적절한 것은?　(3점)

A: Look over there. _____
B: They're waiting to get into the new bakery there.
A: Why? Is it famous?
B: Yes. It was on a TV program.
A: Really? We should try their bread then.
B: Sure.

① I wonder why there is a new store.
② I wonder what they ate for lunch.
③ I wonder why you look upset today.
④ I wonder why there is a boy riding a bicycle.
⑤ I wonder why there are so many people waiting in line.

10. 다음 우리말에 맞도록 주어진 단어들을 사용하여 올바른 문장으로 만드시오.　(5점)

why / understand / the boy / is / angry / his mom / doesn't (그 소년은 자신의 엄마가 왜 화가 나는지 이해하지 못한다.)

답: _____

[11~12] 다음 대화를 읽고 물음에 답하시오.

A: Do you hear that? I wonder where that music is coming from.
B: I think it's coming from over there. Do you want to go and check it out?
A: Yes, I love that strong beat. Is it traditional Korean music?
B: Yes, it's called nongak. It's a kind of community band music.
A: Nongak? Could you explain a little bit more about it?
B: It's traditionally used to cheer up farmers and wish for a good harvest.
A: I see. Look! Some people are dancing to the rhythm.
B: Yes, that's a big part of nongak. Dancing together completes the music.
A: ⓐ_____
B: Sure. Why not?

11. 위 대화로 알 수 있는 사실이 <u>아닌</u> 것은? (4점)

① A likes a strong beat music.
② B knows the traditional Korean music, nongak.
③ Chances are that A hears the nongak for the first time.
④ Nongak is used to cheer up farmers and wish for a good harvest.
⑤ A wants to know about nongak in detail and now he hears the explanation of nongak from the band.

12. 위 대화의 빈칸 ⓐ에 들어갈 말로 알맞지 <u>않은</u> 것은? (4점)

① Would you mind joining them?
② Why don't we join them?
③ How about joining them?
④ Shall we join them?
⑤ Let's join them.

13. 다음 중 어법상 올바른 것은? (4점)

① Peter had lost the key that I gave to him.
② My father has gone to China three times.
③ How long has she lived there when she got married?
④ Before John arrived at home, his family has already left.
⑤ Last weekend, Mina bought a new cell phone with the money she had saved.

14. 다음 주어진 문장을 어법상 적절하게 영어로 옮긴 것은? (3점)

• 내가 기차역에 도착했을 때 기차는 이미 떠났다.

① I had arrived at the station after the train left.
② The train had already left when I arrived at the station.
③ When the train left, I had already arrived at the station.
④ When I arrived at the station, the train has already left.
⑤ I arrived at the station before the train had already left.

15. 한 문장으로 바꿔 쓸 때 알맞은 것은? (3점)

• I wonder. + Why did she leave so early?

① I wonder why did she leave so early.
② I wonder why she leave so early.
③ I wonder why she left so early.
④ I wonder why she leaves so early.
⑤ I wonder why she did left so early.

[16~18] 다음 글을 읽고 물음에 답하시오.

For the past several years, the underwater photographer Zin Kim has promoted the culture of Jeju haenyeo worldwide. Haenyeo are Korean female divers who harvest seafood without any breathing devices. Their culture made UNESCO's Intangible Cultural Heritage list in 2016. At her studio last week, Zin Kim was interviewed about her experience of taking pictures of haenyeo.

Q. How did you become interested in taking photos of haenyeo?

One day, I happened to take pictures of a haenyeo. (A) I was surprised to find that she was enjoying her job. (B) Until then, I had only seen black-and-white photos of haenyeo who looked very tired. ⓐ_____, she kept laughing even after she had been in the water for over five hours. (C) I realized then that I should take pictures of haenyeo.

Q. You take beautiful pictures of them, but isn't it difficult to take pictures of haenyeo?

At first, they didn't understand why I wanted to take their pictures. (D) So, I said to them, "You're very special. I want to show your culture to the world." They opened up to me then. (E) Of course, I also promised them that I would make them look beautiful in my pictures.

16. 위 글을 읽고 답할 수 없는 질문은? (3점)

① What does Zin Kim do for a living?
② What did Zin Kim promise the haenyeo?
③ Why did Zin Kim become a photographer?
④ Why did Zin Kim want to take pictures of haenyeo?
⑤ What has Zin Kim promoted for the past several years?

17. 빈칸 ⓐ에 들어갈 말로 알맞은 것은? (4점)

① So   ② Finally   ③ Also
④ However   ⑤ Therefore

18. 위 글의 (A)~(E) 중 다음 문장이 들어가기에 가장 알맞은 곳은? (4점)

Because they didn't think they looked pretty in their wetsuits.

① (A)   ② (B)   ③ (C)   ④ (D)   ⑤ (E)

19. 다음 글의 괄호 (A), (B), (C) 안에서 문법상 적절한 표현끼리 짝지은 것은? (4점)

Q. Lastly, please tell us what you're planning to do in the future.

I once attended an overseas exhibition with a couple of haenyeo to give a talk about their lives. When I finished my talk, one of the haenyeo held my hand tightly. She said to me, "Thank you so much. I've never (A)[know / known] in my whole life that I was such a special person." She was crying with happiness.

Everyone in the audience (B)[was / were] deeply moved. I can never forget that moment, so I'll continue (C)[to take / take] pictures of haenyeo. I want to tell more beautiful stories about them to many more people in the world.

	(A)	(B)	(C)
①	known	was	take
②	know	was	take
③	known	was	to take
④	know	were	to take
⑤	known	were	to take

[20~22] 다음 글을 읽고 물음에 답하시오.

ⓐFor the past several years, the underwater photographer Zin Kim has promoted the culture of Jeju haenyeo worldwide. Haenyeo are Korean female divers who harvest seafood without any breathing devices. ⓑTheir culture made UNESCO's Intangible Cultural Heritage list in 2016. At her studio last week, Zin Kim was interviewed about her experience of taking pictures of haenyeo.

Q: ⓒ*How did you become interested in taking photos of haenyeo?*
ⓓOne day, I happened to taking pictures of a haenyeo. I was surprised (A)to find that she was enjoying her job. Until then, I had only seen black-and-white photos of haenyeo who looked very tired. However, ⓔshe kept laughing even after she had been in the water for over five hours. I realized then that I should take pictures of haenyeo.

Q: You take beautiful pictures of them, but isn't it difficult to take pictures of haenyeo?
At first, they didn't understand why I wanted to take their pictures. They didn't think they looked pretty in their wetsuits. So, I said to them, "You're very special. I want to show your culture to the world." They opened up to me then. Of course, I also promised them that I would make them look beautiful in my pictures.

20. 위 글의 내용과 일치하지 않는 것은? (4점)

① 해녀는 호흡 장치 없이 해산물을 채취한다.
② 해녀 문화는 2016년에 유네스코 무형문화유산에 등재되었다.
③ Zin Kim은 제주 해녀로 활동하고 있다.
④ 처음에 해녀들은 자신들의 잠수복 입은 모습이 예뻐 보이지 않는다고 생각했다.
⑤ 사진작가는 사진에서 해녀들의 모습이 아름답게 나오도록 노력할 것이다.

21. 위 글의 밑줄 친 ⓐ~ⓔ 중 어법상 어색한 문장은? (4점)

① ⓐ   ② ⓑ   ③ ⓒ   ④ ⓓ   ⑤ ⓔ

22. 위 글의 밑줄 친 (A)와 용법이 같은 것은? (3점)

① We continue to do various projects for saving animals.
② Isn't it difficult to take pictures of haenyeo?
③ I was very excited to meet my Korean fans again.
④ Do you have time to help me write my essay?
⑤ The meeting is to be held next Friday.

23. 다음 글의 흐름으로 보아 주어진 문장이 들어가기에 가장 적절한 곳은? (4점)

For example, more-experienced haenyeo train less-experienced haenyeo.

Q: Could you tell us more about haenyeo? What's so special about them?
I can tell you three things. (A) First, haenyeo are a symbol of strong women. Jejudo, which is a volcanic island, is not suitable for farming, so many haenyeo have become the breadwinners for their families. (B) Second, haenyeo form their own communities and help each other. (C) Third, because they stay in the water without any breathing devices, haenyeo can't catch a lot of seafood. (D) This is good for the underwater environment. (E) Catching too much marine life at one time in one place can destroy the ocean.

① (A)   ② (B)   ③ (C)   ④ (D)   ⑤ (E)

[24~25] 다음 글을 읽고 물음에 답하시오.

Q. (A)_____

I can tell you three things. First, haenyeo are a symbol of strong women. Jejudo, which is a volcanic island, is not suitable for farming, so many haenyeo have become the breadwinners for their families. Second, haenyeo form their own communities and help each other. For example, more-experienced haenyeo train less-experienced haenyeo. Third, because they stay in the water without any breathing devices, haenyeo can't catch a lot of seafood. This is good for the underwater environment. Catching too much marine life at one time in one place can destroy the ocean.

Q. *Lastly, please tell us what you're planning to do in the future.*

I once attended an overseas exhibition with a couple of haenyeo to give a talk about their lives. When I finished my talk, one of the haenyeo held my hand tightly. She said to me, "Thank you so much. I've never known in my whole life that I was such a special person." ⓐShe was crying with happiness. Everyone in the audience was deeply moved. I can never forget that moment, so I'll continue to take pictures of haenyeo. I want to tell more beautiful stories about them to many more people in the world.

24. 빈칸 (A)에 들어갈 가장 적절한 것은? (4점)

① What is special about haenyeo?

② What kind of seafood do you like?

③ How can you take pictures of haenyeo?

④ Why is Jejudo not suitable for farming?

⑤ Why can't haenyeo catch a lot of seafood?

25. ⓐ에 담겨 있는 감정으로 적절한 것은? (3점)

① 슬픔　　　② 후회　　　③ 안도

④ 걱정　　　⑤ 기쁨

[26~27] 다음 글을 읽고 물음에 답하시오.

Q. *How did you become interested in taking photos of haenyeo?*

One day, I happened to take pictures of a haenyeo. I was surprised to find that she was enjoying her job. Until then, I had only seen black-and-white photos of haenyeo who looked very tired. However, she kept laughing even after she had been in the water for over five hours. I realized then that (A)_____.

Q. *You take beautiful pictures of them, but isn't it difficult to take pictures of haenyeo?*

At first, they didn't understand why I wanted to take their pictures. They didn't think they looked pretty in their wetsuits. So, I said to them, "You're very special. I want to show your culture to the world." They opened up to me then. Of course, I also promised them that I would make them look beautiful in my pictures.

26. 위 글의 빈칸 (A)에 들어갈 말로 가장 적절한 것은? (4점)

① it is very hard for haenyeo to hold their breath

② I took only black-and-white photos

③ I should take pictures of haenyeo

④ they are interested in staying in the water

⑤ the ocean is in danger because of the plastic waste

27. 위 글의 내용과 일치하지 <u>않는</u> 것은? (4점)

① 처음에 해녀들은 작가를 이해하지 못했다.

② 해녀들은 잠수복을 입은 자신들의 모습이 예쁘지 않다고 생각했다.

③ 작가는 해녀의 문화를 세계에 알리고자 했다.

④ 해녀들은 작가의 말을 듣고 마음을 열었다.

⑤ 해녀들은 아름답게 보이도록 하겠다고 약속했다.

정답 및 해설

Lesson 1 (중간)

01 ①	**02** ①	**03** ②	**04** ③	**05** ①	**06** ④	**07** ④
08 ②	**09** ④	**10** ③	**11** ⑤	**12** ②	**13** ③	**14** ②
15 ②	**16** ④	**17** ①	**18** what		**19** ④	**20** ⑤
21 ②	**22** ②	**23** ④	**24** ③	**25** ②	**26** ①	

01 ①번은 '명사-형용사'의 관계이지만 나머지는 모두 '형용사-부사'의 관계이다.

02 '내가 너를 도와주기를 원하니?'라는 의미이므로 '①번 수호에게 도움을 제공하려고'가 적절하다.

03 Bill이 학교에 자전거용 주차 구역을 만들어 달라고 요청하려는데 그것을 위한 서명을 받는 것이다.

04 무엇을 읽으려는지 묻는 글에 이어 (c) 젊은 지도자에 관한 책을 읽으려 한다고 답하고 (b) 좋은 생각이라며 책을 갖고 있다고 하자 (a) 빌려줄 수 있는지 묻고 (d) 내일 가져오겠다고 답하는 순서가 적절하다.

05 ⓐ는 'children in Africa'를 가리키고, 나머지는 모두 '수호의 책들(books)'을 가리킨다.

06 'I'm thinking of doing some volunteer work at the child-care center.'라고 했다.

07 G의 'Do you want me to help you collect signatures from students?'라는 질문에 B가 'That would help us a lot.'라고 했으므로 '④번 학생들로부터 서명 받기'가 적절하다.

08 지금 하고 있는 것을 물었는데 '멸종 위기에 처한 동물에 관한 책을 읽을 예정'이라고 답하는 것은 어색하다.

09 'I'm thinking of ~'는 '의향'을 말하는 표현이며 'I'm considering ~'도 같은 의미로 쓸 수 있다.

10 'My aunt told me that they need books to read.'라고 했다.

11 'the present'라는 선행사가 있으므로 'what'이아니라 'that'이나 which가 되어야 한다.

12 순서대로 because, because, because, although, although가 적절하다.

13 (A), (C) 앞의 절과 뒤의 절의 내용이 대조되므로 although (B) although를 쓰면 '재킷을 입지 않았을지라도 추웠다'라는 이상한 말이 된다. but으로 역접으로 쓰는 것이 적절하다.

14 각각 ① reduce ③ marine ④ specialist ⑤ save이며, ②에 해당하는 단어(generation)는 없다.

15 ⓐ 선행사 'the things'가 있으므로 which나 that ⓑ 온전한 절이 이어지므로 how ⓒ do의 목적어와 can의 주어 역할을 할 수 있는 What이 적절하다.

16 (C) 멕시코만에서 석유 유출 사건이 발생하고 (A) 4개월 후에, 멕시코만으로 운전해 가서 동물들을 구하는 일을 돕고 (D) 마지막 날 해양 생물 전문가를 만나서 석유 유출보다 플라스틱 쓰레기가 해양 동물에게 더 위험하다는 것을 알게 되고 (B) 집으로 돌아와서 플라스틱 쓰레기를 줄일 수 있는 방법에 관한 교육 프로젝트를 만드는 순서가 적절하다.

17 석유 유출 사건이 언제 발생했는지는 알 수 없다.

18 what은 선행사를 포함하는 관계대명사로 문장에서 두 가지 역할(명사 두 개의 역할)을 한다.

19 ⓐ protects ⓑ helping ⓒ A few ⓔ educated

20 (가)와 ⑤: 기르다 ①, ②, ③: 올리다 ④: 모금하다

21 (A)와 ㉠, ㉤: 주격 관계대명사 (B)와 ㉡, ㉢, ㉣: 접속사

22 'We started collecting animal rescue supplies such as pet carrying cages and rubber gloves from everyone in our neighborhood.'라고 했다.

23 '플라스틱 쓰레기'를 '줄일' 수 있는 방법에 관한 교육 프로젝트'가 적절하므로 ⓓ의 increase를 reduce로 바꿔야 한다.

24 (A) deliver와 collected의 목적어로 쓰일 수 있는 what, (B) mayonnaise가 사용되는 것이므로 수동태 be used, (C) 이어지는 절이 완전하므로 접속사 that이 적절하다.

25 'On our last day, we met a marine life specialist.'라고 했다.

26 'Asian black bear'의 특징과 사는 곳, 현재의 문제점, 대책 등에 대해 기술한 내용이다.

Lesson 1 (중간)

01 ③	**02** ③	**03** ③	**04** ④	**05** ⑤	**06** ③	**07** ⑤
08 ⑤	**09** ④	**10** ②	**11** ③	**12** ④		
13 am thinking of		**14** ④	**15** ②	**16** ⑤	**17** ⑤	
18 ⑤	**19** ③	**20** ①	**21** ⑤	**22** ②	**23** ①	**24** ⑤
25 ③	**26** ②	**27** ④	**28** ④			

01 prove: 증명하다, 입증(立證)하다

02 'Do you want me to help you collect signatures from students?'라는 물음에 'That would help us a lot.'이라고 했으므로 '③번 학생들에게서 서명 모으기'가 적절하다.

03 'Let's meet in front of the park at ten.'이라고 했다.

04 각각 'ⓐ 의향 말하기', 'ⓑ 제안하기', 'ⓒ 찬성하기', 'ⓓ 도움 제안하기'이다.

05 (A) 전치사 of의 목적어로 동명사 sending이 적절하다. (B) 전치사 about의 목적어로 동명사 translating이 적절하다.

06 대화에서의 ⓐ의 that은 'Suho's books are in Korean(Suho의 책이 한국어로 된 것)'을 가리킨다.

07 '두 사람의 관계'에 대한 언급은 없다.

08 '~을 생각 중'이라는 '의향'을 말하고 있으므로 '계획'을 묻는 것이 적절하다.

09 'the book'이 선행사로 나와 있으므로 that[which]을 써야 한다.

10 한국어를 영어로 '번역(translate)'하는 것이다.

11 아프리카의 아이들에게 책을 보내는 것에 관해 대화를 나누고 있다.

12 'Do you want me to share my umbrella with you?'가 맞다.

13 'I'm thinking of ~'는 '계획이나 의향'을 말하는 표현이다.

14 서로 상반되는 내용이 뒤에 이어지고 '~이지만'으로 연결되므로 'Although'가 적절하다.

15 ⓐ to 삭제 ⓒ protect → protects ⓓ Few → A few, protecting → protect ⓔ for 삭제

16 'We wanted the next generation to be able to see these animals'라고 했다.

17 be used to ~ing: ~에 익숙하다, be used to부정사: ~하는 데 사용되다 saving을 save로 바꿔야 한다.

18 'When we put mayonnaise into a turtle's throat, the turtle threw up.'이라고 했다.

19 마요네즈를 거북이의 목구멍에 집어넣으면, 거북이가 토하는 것을 배웠으므로 ③번이 적절하다.

20 'A lot of sea animals were completely covered with oil, and they were dying.', 'plastic waste is more dangerous to sea animals than oil spills are.'라고 했다.

21 (A) terrific: 아주 좋은, 멋진 terrible: 끔찍한 (B) 뒤에서 '플라스틱 쓰레기를 줄일 수 있는 방법에 관한 교육 프로젝트를 만들었다.'고 했으므로 more, (C) '쓰레기를

'줄일 수' 있는 방법'이므로 reduce가 적절하다.

22 ②번은 '작은 것부터 시작했지만, 큰 변화를 만들어 내고 있는 것'이 아니다.

23 '건강한 음식을 먹어야 한다'는 것은 본문의 내용과 거리가 멀다.

24 석유 유출 사건이 일어나고 (D) 4개월 후 모았던 것들을 전달하고 돕기 위해서 멕시코만으로 가고 (C) 마지막 날 해양 생물 전문가를 만나서 석유 유출보다 플라스틱 쓰레기가 해양 동물에게 더 위험하다는 것을 알게 되고 (B)의 this가 (C)의 '플라스틱 쓰레기를 줄일 수 있는 방법에 관한 교육 프로젝트를 만든 것'이므로 (B)가 (C) 다음에 나온다.

25 뒤에 than이 나오므로 비교급으로 쓰는 것이 적절하다.

26 'We started collecting animals rescue supplies such as pet carrying cages and rubber gloves from everyone in our neighborhood.'라고 했다.

27 글의 마지막 문장(What you do today can change the world, so take that first step!)에 잘 나타나 있다.

28 is의 보어와 for의 목적어 역할을 할 수 있는 what이 적절하다.

Lesson 2 (중간) 〔1회〕

01 ⑤ **02** ③ **03** ③ **04** ① **05** ② **06** ① **07** ⑤
08 ④ **09** ① **10** ② **11** ② **12** ② **13** ①
14 (A) It was Sally who bought this cake at the market yesterday. (B) It was this cake which Sally bought at the market yesterday. (C) It was yesterday when Sally bought this cake at the market.
15 ① **16** ② **17** ③ **18** ② **19** ③ **20** ⑤ **21** ④
22 ① **23** It is we that[who] are the finest smiths.
24 ② **25** ③ **26** ⑤ **27** ②

01 promise: 약속하다, ~의 가망[희망]이 있다

02 ③번은 '명사 - 형용사'의 관계이지만, 나머지는 모두 '형용사 - 부사'의 관계이다.

03 배가 아프다고 했으므로 '약을 먹으라'는 말이 적절하다.

04 mind는 '꺼리다'라는 동사이므로 'Yes.'로 답한 다음에는 부정의 뜻이 어울린다.

05 ⓒ 프랑스 방문이 처음인지 묻자 ⓔ 그렇다며 오고 싶었다고 답하고 ⓐ 온 이유를 묻자 ⓓ 영화에서 본 곳들을 방문하려 한다고 답하고 ⓑ 에펠탑에 가라고 응수하는 순서이다.

06 왜 그것들을 좋아하니?(Why ~?) = 무엇이 그것들을 좋

아하게 만드니?(What makes ~) What makes ~? = Why ~?

07 동사 mind로 물었으므로 '부정'의 형식으로 답해야 '긍정'의 의미를 지닌다.

08 'In that case, we should go see the movie together.'라고 했다.

09 'Norse myths'의 책과 그 신화에 나오는 Thor에 관한 영화에 대해 말하고 있다.

10 'I love April because my birthday is in April.'이라고 했다.

11 계속적 용법의 관계대명사는 '접속사+대명사'로 바꿔 쓸 수 있다. 주어진 문장에서는 'but+it' 정도로 쓸 수 있다.

12 ②번은 진주어를 이끄는 접속사이고 나머지는 모두 강조 용법의 that이다.

13 <보기>와 ①: 강조 용법 ② 관계대명사 ③ 진주어를 이끄는 접속사 ④ 지시대명사 ⑤ 목적어절을 이끄는 접속사

14 (A) who로 사람인 Sally를, (B) which로 사물인 this cake을, (C) when으로 시간의 부사 yesterday를 강조한다.

15 Loki는 Brokk 형제에게 가기 전에 Ivaldi의 아들들에게 가서 Brokk 형제가 세 가지 보물을 만들고 있다고 거짓말했다.

16 ⓑ는 'Brokk and his brother'이고 나머지는 'sons of Ivaldi'이다.

17 조건절에서는 미래시제 대신에 현재시제를 쓴다.

18 왜 Odin의 눈이 한쪽밖에 없는지는 본 지문에는 나와 있지 않다.

19 ⓒ는 'three gods'이지만 나머지는 'Brokk and his brother'이다.

20 '"No, it is we that are the finest smiths," they replied.'라고 했다.

21 'tell+목적어+that절'로 쓰는 것이 적절하다.

22 남서쪽이 아니라 남동쪽이다.

23 It is와 that[who] 사이에 강조하고자 하는 것을 쓰고 나머지는 that[who] 다음에 쓴다.

24 세 가지 보물을 만들라고 요청했다.

25 세 가지 보물에 대한 이야기에서 ⓒ는 아무 관련이 없다.

26 영작하면 'You'd better undo what you did'이다.

27 '네가 한 짓을 되돌려 놓으라'는 말에 하는 약속이므로 ② 번이 적절하다.

Lesson 2 (중간) **2회**

01 ④	**02** ②	**03** ⑤	**04** ③	**05** ②	**06** ⑤	**07** ④
08 ③	**09** ⑤	**10** angry		**11** ③	**12** ①	**13** ②
14 ①	**15** ③	**16** ①	**17** faster than any horse			
18 ⑤	**19** ③	**20** ④				

21 (It) was Eric that[who] broke the window.

22 ①	**23** ⑤	**24** ③	**25** ⑤	**26** ⑤	**27** ⑤	**28** ②
29 ⑤						

01 take place: 개최되다[일어나다] take a picture: 사진을 찍다 take notes: 기록하다, 필기를 하다

02 • actually • angrily • immediately

03 감기에 걸렸다고 하는 것으로 보아 열지 말라고 했을 것이다. mind는 '꺼리다'라는 뜻임에 유의한다.

04 자리에 주인이 있다는데 자기가 차지하겠다는 것은 어색하다.

05 '내가 ~해도 괜찮을까?'라고 허락을 요청할 때 쓰는 표현이다.

06 'Do you mind if ~?'로 물었으므로 '허락'의 대답으로는 'Of course not.'이 되어야 한다.

07 'The stories are very interesting, and there are lots of movies about Norse myths.'라고 했다.

08 처음 한국에 왔는지 묻자 (B) 그렇다며 항상 오고 싶었다고 답하고 (A) 이유를 묻자 (C) 한국 TV 프로그램들을 정말 좋아한다고 답한다.

09 'I'm going to go to the places I saw on TV.'라고 했다.

10 동사 became의 보어로 형용사 angry가 적절하다.

11 Yuri가 Jaden이 Thor에 관한 책을 더 많이 읽어야 한다고 생각한다는 언급은 없다.

12 꽃이 피는데 시험 때문에 공부로 집안에만 있어야 해서 4월은 '최악의 달'이라고 하는 것이 어울린다.

13 관계대명사 that은 계속적 용법으로 쓰이지 않는다.

14 ② that → which ③ who → which ④ which → who ⑤ what → which

15 영작하면 'It was at the mall that Emily saw me yesterday.'이다.

16 주격 관계대명사가 필요하므로 whom이 아닌 who가 적절하다.

17 '~보다 더 빨리'를 비교급으로 나타내며 '어떤 ~라도'의 의미로 any를 쓰는 것에 주의한다.

18 'that produced eight more gold rings every ninth night'라고 했다.

19 'It ~ that ...' 강조 용법에서 강조하는 것이 사람으로 주격이므로 who로 바꿔 쓸 수 있다.

20 'as ~ as'로 비교할 때는 as 사이에 원급이 들어가야 한다.

21 It과 that[who] 사이에 Eric을 쓰고 과거이므로 was로 쓴다.

22 ①은 예를 들어 말할 때 쓰이지만 나머지는 모두 '추가'할 때 쓰인다.

23 ⓔ의 It은 '망치'가 아니라 '가주어'이다.

24 'He gave Odin a gold arm ring that produced eight more gold rings every ninth night.'라고 했다.

25 'It was King Kim Suro who was the strongest of them. His kingdom became the center of the six Gayas.'라고 했다.

26 'a gold arm ring'은 Brokk와 그의 남동생이 만든 것이다.

27 ① which → who ② showing → show
③ fast → faster ④ who → which

28 ⓑ는 'Brokk and his brother'이지만 나머지는 'sons of Ivaldi'이다.

29 (E)의 such a terrible thing이 주어진 글의 내용이므로 제일 먼저 나오고, (A) Thor가 Loki를 찾은 후 (B) 되돌려 놓으라고 말한다. (D) Loki가 겁이 나서 (C) 금발머리를 얻어 오겠다고 약속하는 순서가 적절하다.

Lesson 3 (기말)

01 ⑤	02 ②	03 keep		04 ②	05 ①	06 ④
07 what[What]			08 ③	09 ②	10 ④	11 ④
12 ④	13 I did call you yesterday.			14 ③	15 ③	
16 ③	17 does keep our eyes healthy					
18 may be used in wars				19 ④	20 ①	21 ③
22 ②	23 ⑤	24 ①	25 ④	26 ②	27 ⑤	28 ③
29 ③	30 ④					

01 consider: 고려하다, 여기다

02 모두 '동사 - 행위자'의 관계이지만 ②번은 '동사 - 명사'의 관계이다.

03 (1) keep a promise: 약속을 지키다
(2) keep ~ in mind: ~을 명심하다
(3) keep a diary: 일기를 쓰다

04 '무슨 문제 있니?'라는 뜻으로 상대방에게 안부를 묻는 'Is something wrong?'이 적절하다.

05 상대방에게 조언을 구할 때 쓰는 표현으로 think 동사가

06 that's why: 그것이 ~한 이유이다

07 (A) is의 보어와 do의 목적어 역할을 할 수 있는 what, (B) '내가 어떻게 해야 한다고 생각해?'라고 상대방에게 조언을 구할 때 쓰는 'What do you think I should do?'

08 'Tell her the truth.'라고 했다.

09 손가락을 베었다는 말에 붕대를 감으라고 조언한다.

10 '눈이 점점 나빠지는 것 같아.'라고 말 한 후에 '내가 도와주기를 원하니?'라고 묻는 것은 어색하다.

11 조언을 구할 때 쓰는 표현이므로 (D)가 가장 적절하다.

12 'I watched a movie on my phone until 2 a.m.'이라고 했다.

13 동사를 강조할 때는 'do/does/did'를 인칭과 시제에 맞게 쓴다.

14 주어가 감정을 느낄 때는 과거분사를 쓰고 주어가 감정을 일으킬 때는 현재분사를 쓴다.

15 (a) 주어가 I이고 현재이므로 do로 강조한다. (b) 주어가 she이고 과거이므로 did로 강조한다.

16 'carrots contain much vitamin A, which keeps our eyes healthy'라고 했다.

17 주어가 3인칭 단수이고 현재이므로 does를 이용한다.

18 조동사 may를 먼저 쓰고 'be used'를 쓴 후, 부사구 in wars를 쓴다.

19 'consider'는 '고려하다'라는 의미로 think가 가장 비슷하다. ⑤ imagine: 상상하다, 가정하다, 추측하다

20 'It is considered one of the ten healthiest foods on the planet'이라고 했다.

21 뒤에 동사원형 keep이 있고 선행사가 vitamin A로 단수이므로 does가 적절하다.

22 'Can we really improve night vision by eating lots of carrots?'에 'Not really'라고 하고 있다.

23 however로 첫 문장과 상반되는 ⓒ가 나오고 ⓐ Robert가 토마토가 안전하다는 것을 증명하려 함 ⓔ 그래서 사람들이 보는 데서 토마토를 먹음 ⓓ 아무 일도 일어나지 않음 ⓑ 그때 이래로 토마토를 먹음

24 (A) 이름이 붙여진 것으로 수동의 named (B) 사람들이 보고 있는 진행의 watching (C) 으깨진 수동의 의미로 crushed가 맞다.

25 시금치에 관한 다양한 흥미로운 사실들을 언급하고 있다.

26 'Crystal City in Texas. which is called the spinach capital of the world, even built a statue of Popeye.'라고 했다.

27 시금치의 놀라운 사용법을 말하는 내용에서 요리 방법을 언급하는 것은 어색하다.

28 ③번은 본동사로 쓰였고 (A)와 나머지는 '강조'로 쓰였다.

29 모든 사람이 Robert가 죽을 것으로 예상했다는 내용에서 ③번(poisonous: 유독한, 독성의)이 적절함을 알 수 있다.

30 ⓑ 이름이 붙여진 것이므로 수동의 의미를 갖는 named가 ⓒ 사람들이 보고 있는 것이므로 진행의 의미를 갖는 watching이 적절하다.

Lesson 3 (기말)

01 ②	**02** ①	**03** ③	**04** ⑤	**05** ①	**06** ⑤	**07** ④
08 ⑤	**09** ⑤	**10** ④	**11** ②	**12** ③	**13** ①	
14 ①, ③		**15** ②	**16** ⑤	**17** ①	**18** ①	**19** ⑤
20 a radar system			**21** ④	**22** ④	**23** ⑤	**24** ④
25 ②	**26** ④					

01 keep a diary: 일기를 쓰다 keep a secret: 비밀을 지키다 keep a promise: 약속을 지키다

02 ①번은 '조언'을 구하는 표현이지만 나머지는 '무슨 일이 있는지' 묻는 표현이다.

03 감기에 걸렸다는 답으로 보아 '무슨 문제가 있는지' 묻는 것이 적절하다.

04 (B) 무슨 일이 있는지 묻고 (A) 미세먼지 때문에 목이 아프다고 하자 (D) 방에 식물을 좀 놓으라고 하고 (C) 당장 식물을 몇 그루 가져오겠다는 순서이다.

05 무슨 일이 있는지 묻는 질문에 이어 (B) 조금 피곤하다고 답하고 (D) 어젯밤 뭘 했는지 묻자 (C) 새벽 2시까지 휴대폰으로 영화를 봤다고 답하자 (A) 그래서 눈이 충혈됐다며 건강을 위해 자정 전에는 잠자리에 들라는 충고로 이어진다.

06 ⑤번은 '내가 뭘 원한다고 생각하니?'라는 말로 대화와 아무 관계가 없지만 나머지는 '무엇을 해야 할지' '조언'을 구하는 말이다.

07 조언을 구하는 말에 'Try eating lots of carrots and tomatoes.'라고 했다.

08 'I have a stomachache.'라고 했다.

09 ⑤번은 '조언'을 구하는 표현이지만 나머지는 모두 '무슨 문제 있는지' 상대방에게 안부를 묻는 표현이다.

10 (A) what's wrong[the matter]?: 무슨 일이니? (B) is 의 보어와 do의 목적어 역할을 하는 what (C) try ~ing: 시험삼아 ~해 보다 (D) keep ~ healthy: ~을 건강하게

유지시키다

11 ②번은 '허락'하는 표현이지만 나머지는 '충고'하는 표현이다.

12 ① do → did ② exercised → exercise ④ studies → study ⑤ does → did 또는 do

13 '주격 관계대명사+be동사'가 생략된 형태로 (A) '능동'의 의미로 현재분사 (B) '수동'의 의미로 과거분사가 적절하다.

14 '주격 관계대명사+be동사'는 생략할 수 있다. ① now being → is now ③ was 삭제

15 시금치를 이용해 숨겨진 폭탄을 찾는 데에 사용한다는 내용이 나오므로 '사용하는 놀라운 방식'이 있다는 것이 적절하다.

16 ④의 내용은 사실이지만 나머지는 없거나 틀린 내용이다.

17 뒤에 절이 이어지므로 of를 뺀 because가 적절하다.

18 ①에는 keep이 어색하지만 (A)와 나머지는 keep이 적절하다.

19 'The British government wanted to keep this technology a secret, so it published an article in the newspaper.'라고 했다.

20 '영국 정부는 이 기술을 비밀로 하기를 원했기 때문에'에서 '이 기술'은 바로 'a radar system'이다.

21 시금치가 지구상에서 가장 건강한 식품 10개 중 하나로 여겨진다고 했지만 무엇이 그 10가지인지는 언급되지 않았다.

22 ⓐ는 앞 문장에서 언급한 'spinach also absorbs many other things from the soil'이다.

23 '뿌리'가 아닌 '잎'에 감지기가 있는 특별한 시금치를 만든다.

24 (A) stature: 키, 신장 status: 상태 statue: 상(像), 조상(彫像) (B) 땅에 숨겨진 '수동'의 의미이므로 과거분사가 적절하다.

25 (a) 이름이 붙여진 것으로 수동의 named (b) 사람들이 보고 있는 진행의 watching (c) 으깨진 수동의 의미로 crushed가 맞다.

26 They가 (D) 앞 문장의 many people이므로 (D)가 적절하다.

01 ② 02 ① 03 ③ 04 ②
05 where you took the photo 06 ② 07 ③ 08 ②
09 ② 10 why Tom was late 11 ① 12 ①
13 (A) Can you tell me what you did?
　　(B) Nobody knows why she was late.
14 ④ 15 ② 16 ③ 17 ⑤ 18 ④ 19 ⑤ 20 ③
21 ⑤ 22 ② 23 ① 24 ② 25 ② 26 ⑤ 27 ④
28 ④ 29 ④

01 give a hand: 돕다 give a call: 전화하다

02 consider는 '고려하다'라는 뜻으로 make 정도로 바꿔야 한다.

03 'I think it's coming from over there.'라는 답으로 보아 궁금한 것을 물을 때 쓰는 'I wonder ~.' 표현의 ③번이 적절하다.

04 'It's a long hiking path around Jejudo.'라고 설명하고 있으므로 '설명'을 요청하는 표현이 적절하다.

05 궁금하다는 표현의 'I wonder'가 이미 있으므로 의문사가 where로 시작하여 간접의문문의 어순(의문사+주어+동사)으로 쓴다.

06 'Some people are dancing to the rhythm.'이라고 했다.

07 Jaden이 'Let's join them.'이라고 하자 Yuri가 'Sure. Why not?'이라고 했다.

08 'We should try their bread then.'에 'Sure.'라고 했다.

09 (C) 음성 가이드를 대여하고 싶다는 말에 (B) 여기 있다고 하고 (D) 사용법 설명을 요청하자 (A) 설명해 주는 순서이다.

10 간접의문문은 '의문사+주어+동사'의 어순이다.

11 'Could you explain a little bit more about it?'이라고 했다.

12 영작하면 'I wonder where that music is coming from.'이다.

13 간접의문문은 '의문사+주어+동사'의 어순이다.

14 과거보다 앞선 시제이므로 과거완료로 쓰는 것이 적절하다. have gone → had gone

15 간접의문문은 '의문사+주어+동사'의 어순이다.

16 ⓐ harvests → harvest ⓑ interviewed → was interviewed ⓓ had kept → kept, was → had been ⓔ 전체 → Catching ~ place can destroy the ocean.

17 어떻게 해녀들이 어떤 호흡 장치도 없이 물속에서 계속 해산물을 채취하는지는 알 수 없다.

18 ⓓ는 join이 아니라 train 정도가 적절하다.

19 This가 (E) 앞 문장의 내용을 가리키므로 (E)가 적절하다.

20 해녀의 특별한 점에 대해 답하는 내용이다.

21 'Catching too much marine life at one time in one place can destroy the ocean.'이라고 했다.

22 사역동사 make 다음에 '목적어+동사원형'이 나오도록 쓴다.

23 (A) 해녀의 사진을 찍기 시작했을 때의 어려움을 토로하고 있다. (B) 해녀들이 가족들의 생계비를 버는 가장이 되어 왔다는 것으로 보아 강한 여성의 '상징'이 적절하다. (C) 한곳에서 한 번에 너무 많은 해산물을 채취하면 바다를 파괴할 수 있다.

24 (B) 다음의 She가 주어진 문장의 'one of the haenyeo'이므로 (B)가 적절하다.

25 (A) attend가 '참석하다'라는 뜻의 타동사로 쓰였다. (B) 앞에서 '특별한 사람'이라고 했으므로 happiness가 적절하다. (C) Everyone이 주어이므로 단수 was가 적절하다.

26 ⓔ의 conserve는 '보호하다'라는 뜻으로 destroy가 적절하다.

27 (가)와 ④는 접속사이고 나머지는 모두 관계대명사이다.

28 'Zin Kim has promoted the culture of Jeju haenyeo worldwide'라고 했다.

29 intangible: 만질 수 없는, 만져서 알 수 없는, 무형의

01 ⑤ 02 (A) give (B) hand 또는 (A) do (B) favor
03 ④ 04 ⑤ 05 ④ 06 ① 07 ④ 08 ① 09 ⑤
10 The boy doesn't understand why his mom is angry.
11 ⑤ 12 ① 13 ⑤ 14 ② 15 ③ 16 ③ 17 ④
18 ④ 19 ③ 20 ③ 21 ④ 22 ③ 23 ③ 24 ①
25 ⑤ 26 ③ 27 ⑤

01 realize: 깨닫다, 인식하다

02 give someone a hand: 도와주다 do someone a favor: 호의를 베풀다, 남의 부탁을 들어주다

03 순서대로 배열하면 (E)-(B)-(D)-(A)-(C)이다.

04 '보고 즐기기만을 위한 음악'이라는 내용은 잘못되었다.

05 'That's Gwangandaegyo in Busan.'이라는 답으로

보아 '장소'를 물었음을 알 수 있다.

06 'it's coming from over there'라는 답으로 보아 '장소'를 물었음을 알 수 있다.

07 'It's a kind of community band music.'이라고 했다.

08 (C) 익선동이 좋은 곳이라고 하자 (A) 동의하며 홍보 방법을 궁금해 하자 (B) SNS에 사진과 기사 게시를 제안하고 (D) 사진으로 사람들이 알게 될 것이라고 하는 순서가 적절하다.

09 'They're waiting ~'이라는 답으로 보아 ⑤번이 적절하다.

10 간접의문문의 어순, '의문사+주어+동사'에 주의한다.

11 'from the band'가 아니라 'from B'이다.

12 'mind'로 물으면 '부정'으로 답해야 '긍정'의 의미가 된다.

13 ① had lost → lost, gave → had given
② gone → been
③ has she lived → had she lived
④ has → had

14 내가 도착한 것보다 기차가 떠난 것이 앞서므로 '내가 도착한 것'은 '과거'로, '기차가 떠난 것'은 '과거완료'로 쓴다.

15 간접의문문은 '의문사+주어+동사'의 어순이다.

16 왜 Zin Kim이 사진작가가 되었는지는 알 수 없다.

17 앞의 내용과 상반되는 내용이 이어지므로 'However'가 적절하다.

18 Because로 (D) 앞 문장의 'why I wanted to take their pictures'에 대한 이유를 언급하므로 (D)가 적절하다.

19 (A) 완료시제이므로 과거분사 known이, (B) Everyone이 주어이므로 단수 was가, (C) continue의 목적어로 to take가 적절하다.

20 Zin Kim은 사진작가이다.

21 happen to+동사원형: 우연히 ~하다

22 (A)와 ③: 부사적 용법 ①, ②: 명사적 용법 ④, ⑤: 형용사적 용법

23 'For example'로 (C) 앞 문장의 예를 들고 있으므로 (C)가 적절하다.

24 대답으로 해녀의 특별한 점에 대해 언급하고 있다.

25 'with happiness'로 보아 '기쁨'이다.

26 '어떻게 해녀의 사진을 찍는 것에 관심을 갖게 되었는지'에 대한 답이므로 ③번이 적절하다.

27 사진작가가 해녀들이 아름답게 보이도록 하겠다고 약속했다.